Totemism and Exogamy, Vol. I
(in four volumes)

SIR JAMES GEORGE FRAZER

NEW YORK

Totemism and Exogamy, Vol. I (in four volumes)
Cover Copyright © 2009 by Cosimo, Inc.

Totemism and Exogamy, Vol. I (in four volumes) was originally published in 1910.

For information, address:
P.O. Box 416, Old Chelsea Station
New York, NY 10011

or visit our website at:
www.cosimobooks.com

Ordering Information:
Cosimo publications are available at online bookstores. They may also be purchased for educational, business or promotional use:
- *Bulk orders:* special discounts are available on bulk orders for reading groups, organizations, businesses, and others. For details contact Cosimo Special Sales at the address above or at info@cosimobooks.com.
- *Custom-label orders:* we can prepare selected books with your cover or logo of choice. For more information, please contact Cosimo at info@cosimobooks.com.

Cover Design by www.popshopstudio.com

ISBN: 978-1-60520-978-4

As I have already observed, it seems evident that rules of marriage and descent at once so complex and so regular cannot be the result of a train of accidents, but must have been deliberately devised in order to effect a definite purpose. That purpose appears to have been to prevent the marriage of parents with children, and it was effectually attained by arranging that children should always belong to a subclass into which neither their father nor their mother might marry. If that simple rule was observed, the marriage of parents with children was thenceforth impossible. Only we must remember that in speaking of fathers, mothers, and children in this connection we employ these terms of relationship not in our narrow sense of the words, but in the much wider classificatory sense which the Australian aborigines give to them, and in accordance with which every person has a whole group of "fathers" and a whole group of "mothers."

—from "Totemism in South-Eastern Australia"

TO

MY WIFE

TO WHOSE ENCOURAGEMENT AND INSPIRATION

I OWE MORE THAN I CAN TELL

I DEDICATE THIS BOOK

AS A MEMORIAL

OF LOVE AND GRATITUDE

PREFACE

THE man who more than any other deserves to rank as the discoverer of totemism and exogamy was the Scotchman John Ferguson McLennan. It was not that he was the first to notice the mere existence of the institutions in various races nor even that he added very much to our knowledge of them. But with the intuition of genius he perceived or divined the far-reaching influence which in different ways the two institutions have exercised on the history of society. The great service which he rendered to science was that he put the right questions; it was not that he answered them aright. He did indeed attempt, with some confidence, to explain the origin of exogamy, but his explanation is probably erroneous. On the origin of totemism he did not even speculate, or, if he did, he never published his speculations. To the last he appears to have regarded that problem as unsolved, if not insoluble.

While McLennan's discovery of exogamy attracted attention and excited discussion, his discovery of totemism made comparatively little stir, and outside of a small circle of experts it passed almost unnoticed in the general world of educated opinion. The very few writers who touched on the subject contributed little to its elucidation. For the most part they contented themselves with repeating a few familiar facts or adding a few fresh theories; they did not attempt a wide induction on the basis of a systematic collection and classification of the evidence. Accordingly, when in the year 1886 my revered friend William Robertson Smith, a disciple of McLennan's, invited me to write the article on totemism for the Ninth Edition of the *Encyclopædia Britannica*, which was then in course of publication under his editorship, I had to do nearly the whole work of collection and classification for myself with very little help from my predecessors. The article which embodied my researches having proved somewhat too long for its purpose, an abridgment of it only was inserted in the *Encyclopædia*; but through Robertson Smith's friendly mediation Messrs. A. & C. Black kindly consented to publish the original article, unabridged and unchanged, in the form of a small volume. The book comprised little more than a classified collection of facts, for when I wrote it I had as yet formed no theory either of totemism or of exogamy. However, the new evidence which it contained appears to have been welcome to students of primitive man; for since the appearance of the volume in 1887 totemism has received a large, perhaps exorbitant, share of their attention; the literature of the subject, which was extremely scanty before, has swollen enormously in volume; and, better than all, there has been a large accession of facts observed and recorded among living totemic tribes by competent scientific investigators. As the little book has long been out of print and is still, I am told, in demand, I decided to reprint it; and it now occupies the first place in these volumes. The errors which subsequent research has revealed in it are generally not very serious. Such as they are, the reader will find them corrected in the Notes appended to the last volume, in which I have also been careful to retrench the boundaries of totemism wherever, in the first ardour of exploration, I had pushed them too far. I beg the reader, therefore, to read the "Notes and Corrections" throughout in connection with my original treatise.

Having decided to reprint *Totemism* I resolved to add

to it by way of supplement some essays which in the meantime I had written on the subject. The main purpose of these essays, which appeared in *The Fortnightly Review* for the years 1899 and 1905, was to direct attention to the great importance of the discoveries of Messrs. Spencer and Gillen in Central Australia and to point out the necessity of revising and remodelling our old ideas of totemism and exogamy in the light of the new evidence. My judgment as to the need of that revision has never wavered since, but it is only after many years of study that I have come to see how thoroughgoing that revision must be if our conceptions are to square with the facts. Holding this view I felt that to reprint *Totemism* without noticing discoveries which had, in my opinion, revolutionised the whole aspect of the subject, would be unpardonable; hence my decision to add the essays in question as an appendix to the reprint. They now occupy the second place in this work. Like the original *Totemism* they are republished without any change except the addition of a marginal summary. Such corrections and modifications of them as subsequent reflection and increased knowledge have suggested will be found in the Notes appended to the last volume.

This was all that at first I proposed to do; for my intention had long been to defer writing a larger treatise on totemism until the whole totemic harvest should have been reaped and garnered; and moreover at the time, a little more than two years ago, I was deeply engaged in other work which I was unwilling to interrupt. To-day the totemic harvest still stands white to the sickle in many fields, but it may be left for others hereafter to see the sheaves brought home. My sun is westering, and the lengthening shadows remind me to work while it is day. Be that as it may, having begun with a notice of the new Australian evidence I thought I could hardly pass over in silence the additions which had been made to our knowledge of totemism in other parts of the world, and thus insensibly, step by step, I was led into writing the Ethnographical Survey of Totemism which now forms the great bulk of this book. Its aim is to provide students with what may be called a digest or corpus of totemism and exogamy, so far as the two institutions are found in conjunction. I have taken pains to compile it from the best sources, both published and unpublished, so far as these were accessible, to the rigid exclusion of all such as appeared to me to be of dubious or less than dubious authority. The facts are arranged in ethnographical order, tribe by tribe, and an attempt has been made to take account of the physical environment as well as of the general social conditions of the principal tribes which are passed in review. In this way I have sought to mitigate the disadvantages incidental to the study of any institution viewed abstractedly and apart from the rest of the social organism with which it is vitally connected. Such abstract views are indeed indispensable, being imposed by the limitations of the human mind, but they are apt to throw the object out of focus, to exaggerate some of its features, and to diminish unduly others which may be of equal or even greater importance. These dangers cannot be wholly avoided, but they may be lessened by making our study as concrete as is compatible with the necessary degree of abstraction. This accordingly I have attempted to do in writing the Survey.

My account of the facts would be very much more imperfect than it is, had it not been for the liberal assistance which I have received from experts, who have freely imparted to me of their knowledge, generously permitting me in many cases to make use of unpublished information. Amongst those to whom I am indebted for help of various kinds I desire particularly to thank: for Australia, Professor Baldwin Spencer and the late Dr. A. W. Howitt; for New Guinea, Dr. C. G. Seligmann; for Melanesia and Polynesia, the Rev. George Brown, D.D., and especially Dr. W. H. R. Rivers; for India, Mr. J. D. Anderson, Mr. W. Crooke, Colonel P. R. T. Gurdon, Sir Herbert Risley, and Mr. Edgar Thurston; for Africa, the Hon. K. R. Dundas, Mr. C. W. Hobley, Mr. A. C. Hollis, Mr. T. A. Joyce, the Rev. H. E. Maddox, Mr. H. R. Palmer, the Rev. John Roscoe, and Mr. N. W. Thomas. My gratitude above all is due to my valued friend the Rev. John Roscoe, formerly of the Church Missionary Society, for the great generosity with which he has placed all the stores of his unrivalled knowledge of Central African tribes, especially of the Baganda, unreservedly at my disposal for the purposes of this work. If my account of Central African totemism contains not a little that is new and instructive, it is to him chiefly that I owe it. For America, I desire to return my grateful thanks to the authorities of the Bureau of American Ethnology, the Smithsonian Institution, the American Museum of Natural History at New York, and the Field Columbian Museum at Chicago, who have liberally supplied me with many valuable publications which have been of the greatest assistance to me in my work. Nor would I omit to mention my gallant correspondent, the late Captain J. G. Bourke, of the United States Cavalry, who in the intervals of his arduous professional duties devoted much time to studying and describing with the pen the Indians whom he had fought with the sword.

My primary subject is totemism, and I have treated of exogamy for the most part only so far as it occurs in conjunction with totemism; for the two institutions not only differ but overlap, each of them being sometimes found without the other. Tribes which are exogamous without being totemic do not properly fall within the scope of the book; but I have noticed a few of them, such as the Todas in India and the Masai in Africa, either on the ground of their association with totemic tribes or because their social system presents some features of special interest. However,

I must request the reader to bear constantly in mind that the two institutions of totemism and exogamy are fundamentally distinct in origin and nature, though they have accidentally crossed and blended in many tribes. The distinction was for the first time placed in a clear light by the epoch-making researches of Spencer and Gillen in Central Australia, which proved that the exogamous class is a totally different social organisation from the totemic clan and not, as we had previously inclined to suppose, a mere extension of it. Still more recently the same sharp line between totemism and exogamy has been detected by Dr. W. H. R. Rivers in the Banks' Islands, where the natives have pure totemism and pure exogamy, existing side by side, without the one institution exercising the least influence upon the other. That example should finally set at rest the doubt whether exogamy is or is not a necessary feature of true totemism. If the reader will only remember that the two things, though often conjoined, are really distinct and independent, he will escape many perplexities and much confusion of thought in tracing the history of their relations to each other in the following pages.

Inseparably connected with exogamy is the classificatory system of relationship, and accordingly I have treated it as an integral part of my subject. The discovery of that remarkable system, which is now known to obtain throughout a large part of the human race, was the work of the great American ethnologist L. H. Morgan alone. In spite of its apparent complexity the system originated very simply. A community was bisected into two exogamous and intermarrying groups, and all the men and women were classified according to the generation and the group to which they belonged. The principle of the classification was marriageability, not blood. The crucial question was not, Whom am I descended from? but, Whom may I marry? Each class no doubt included blood relations, but they were placed in it not on the ground of their consanguineous but of their social relationship to each other as possible or impossible husbands and wives. When the custom of group marriage had been replaced by individual marriage, the classificatory terms of relationship continued in use, but as the old group rights fell into abeyance the terms which once expressed them came more and more to designate ties of blood and affinity in our sense of the words. Hence in most races of the world the classificatory system of relationship now survives only as a social fossil testifying to a former condition of exogamy and group marriage which has long passed away.

Having completed the survey of totemism, exogamy, and the classificatory system of relationship I have endeavoured in the last volume to mark the place which the institutions occupy in the history of society, to discuss some theories of their origin, and to state those which I believe to be true or probable. That my conclusions on these difficult questions are final, I am not so foolish as to pretend. I have changed my views repeatedly, and I am resolved to change them again with every change of the evidence, for like a chameleon the candid enquirer should shift his colours with the shifting colours of the ground he treads. All I can say is that the conclusions here formulated are those which I have at present reached after a careful consideration of all the facts known to me. I have not discussed the vexed question of totemism in classical and Oriental antiquity. With the evidence at our disposal the problem hardly admits of a definite solution, and in any case an adequate discussion of it would require a treatise to itself.

In estimating the part played by totemism in history I have throughout essayed, wherever the occasion offered, to reduce within reasonable limits the extravagant pretensions which have sometimes been put forward on behalf of the institution, as if it had been a factor of primary importance in the religious and economic development of mankind. As a matter of fact the influence which it is supposed to have exercised on economic progress appears to be little more than a shadowy conjecture; and though its influence on religion has been real, it has been greatly exaggerated. By comparison with some other factors, such as the worship of nature and the worship of the dead, the importance of totemism in religious evolution is altogether subordinate. Its main interest for us lies in 'the glimpse which it affords into the working of the childlike mind of the savage; it is as it were a window opened up into a distant past.

Exogamy is also a product of savagery, but it has few or none of the quaint superstitions which lend a certain picturesque charm to totemism. It is, so to say, a stern Puritanical institution. In its rigid logic, its complex rules, its elaborate terminology, its labyrinthine systems of relationship, it presents an aspect somewhat hard and repellant, a formality almost mathematical in its precision, which the most consummate literary art could hardly mollify or embellish. Yet its interest for the student of history is much deeper than that of its gayer and more frivolous sister. For whereas totemism, if it ever existed among the ancestors of the civilised races, has vanished without leaving a trace among their descendants, exogamy has bequeathed to civilisation the momentous legacy of the prohibited degrees of marriage.

However the two institutions may have survived into higher planes of culture, both of them have their roots in savagery, and the intrinsic interest of their study is enhanced by the circumstances of the age in which we live. Our contemporaries of this and the rising generation appear to be hardly aware that we are witnessing the last act of a long drama, a tragedy and a comedy in one, which is being silently played, with no fanfare of trumpets or roll of drums, before our eyes on the stage of history. Whatever becomes of the savages, the curtain must soon descend on savagery for ever. Of late the pace of civilisation has so quickened, its expansion has become so beyond example rapid, that many savage races, who only a hundred years ago still led their old life unknown and undisturbed in the depth of virgin forests or in remote islands of the sea, are now being rudely hustled out of existence or transformed into a pathetic burlesque of their conquerors. With their disappearance or transformation an element of quaintness, of picturesqueness, of variety will be gone from the world. Society will probably be happier on the whole, but it will be soberer in tone, greyer and more uniform in colouring. And as savagery recedes further and further into the past, it will become more and more an object of curiosity and wonder to generations parted from it by an impassable and ever-widening gulf of time. Its darker side will be forgotten, its brighter side will be remembered. Its cruelties, its hardships, its miseries will be slurred over; memory will dwell with delight on whatever was good and beautiful, or may seem to have been good and beautiful, in the long-vanished life of the wilderness. Time, the magician, will cast his unfailing spell over these remote ages. An atmosphere of romance will gather round them, like the blue haze which softens into tender beauty the harsher features of a distant landscape. So the patriarchal age is invested for us with a perennial charm in the enchanting narratives of Genesis and the Odyssey, narratives which breathe the freshness of a summer morning and glister as with dewdrops in the first beams of the rising sun of history.

It is thus that by some strange witchery, some freak of the fairy imagination, who plays us so many tricks, man perpetually conjures up for himself the mirage of a Golden Age in the far past or the far future, dreaming of a bliss that never was and may never be. So far as the past is concerned, it is the sad duty of anthropology to break that dream, to dispel that mirage, to paint savagery in its true colours. I have attempted to do so in this book. I have extenuated nothing, I have softened nothing, and I hope I have exaggerated nothing. As a plain record of a curious form of society which must soon be numbered with the past, the book may continue to possess an interest even when, with the progress of knowledge, its errors shall have been corrected and its theories perhaps superseded by others which make a nearer approach to truth. For though I have never hesitated either to frame theories which seemed to fit the facts or to throw them away when they ceased to do so, my aim in this and my other writings has not been to blow bubble hypotheses which glitter for a moment and are gone; it has been by a wide collection and an exact classification of facts to lay a broad and solid foundation for the inductive study of primitive man.

J. G. FRAZER.

CAMBRIDGE,
27th February 1910.

CONTENTS

PREFACE . . . . Pp. vii-xvi

TOTEMISM.   Reprinted from the First Edition, Edinburgh, 1887
Pp. 1-87

Totem defined, 3 ; etymology of the word, 3 ; totem distinguished from fetish, 4 ; kinds of totem—clan totem, sex totem, individual totem, 4 ; religious and social sides of totemism, 4 *sq.*

I. *Clan Totems*, 4-47, 53-76.

Religious Side of Totemism. Descent from totem, 5-8 ; marks of respect for totem, 8-13 ; cross totems, cross-split totems, 14 ; totem animal kept in captivity, 14 *sq.* ; dead totem mourned and buried, 15 *sq.* ; totem not spoken of directly, 16 ; supposed ill effects of ill-treating the totem, 16-18 ; Samoan mode of appeasing offended totem, 18 ; Australian food taboos, 18 *sq.* ; diminished respect for totem, 19 *sq.* ; totem expected to help his people, 20 ; tests of kinship with sacred animals, 20 *sq.* ; some judicial ordeals and oaths perhaps derived from totemism, 21 *sq.* ; totem cures, 22 ; totem omens, 22 *sq.* ; compulsion applied to totem, 23 *sq.* ; inanimate totems, 24 *sq.* ; artificial totems, 25 ; assimilation of men to their totems by dressing in the skins, etc., of their totems, 25 *sq.* ; by dressing hair in imitation of totems, 26 *sq.* ; by knocking out or filing teeth, 27 ; by nose-sticks, 27 *sq.* ; by tattooing, 28 *sq.* ; by painting, 29 ; totem carved or painted on huts, canoes, grave-posts, etc., 29-31 ; birth ceremonies, 31 *sq.* ; marriage ceremonies, 32-34 ; death and burial ceremonies, 34-36 ; initiation ceremonies at puberty, 36-45 ; social side of these ceremonies, 36-38 ; dances at initiation, 37-39 ; other animal dances, 39 *sq.* ; religious or magical side of initiation ceremonies, 40-45 ; food taboos imposed at initiation, 40-42 ; admission to life of clan by blood-smearing, etc., 42 *sq.* ; initiatory ceremony of resurrection and new birth, 43 *sq.* ; ceremonial killing of sacred animals, 44 *sq.* ; sacred dancing associations in North America, 46 *sq.*

II. *Sex Totems*, 47 *sq.*

III. *Individual Totems*, 49-52.

Individual totems in Australia, 49 ; individual totems in America, 50 ; sacrifices to individual totems, 50 *sq.* ; modes of acquiring individual totems, 51 *sq.* ; the *tamaniu* in the Banks' Islands, 52.

Social Side of Totemism. Blood feud, 53 *sq.* ; exogamy, 54-65 ; phratries, 55-62 ; phratries in America, 55-60 ; origin of phratries and of split totems, 57-60 ; phratries in Australia, 60-62 ; equivalence of tribal subdivisions throughout Australia, 63 *sq.* ; Australian traditions as to the origin of these tribal subdivisions, 64 sq. ; rules of descent, 65-73 ; female and male descent in Australia, America, Africa, and India, 65-68 ; indirect female and male descent in Australian subphratries, 68 sq. ; sons reported to take totem from father, daughters from mother, 69 sq. ; transition from female to male descent, transference of children, or of wife and children, to husband's clan, 71-73 ; couvade, 72 sq. ; cannibalism, 73-75 ; arrangement of totem clans in camp, village, and graveyard, 75 sq.

IV. *Subphratric and Phratric Totems*, 76-78.

V. *Subtotems*, 78-80.

Subtotems, clan totems, subphratric and phratric totems, how related to each other, 81 ; transformation of totems into anthropomorphic gods with animal attributes, 81-83 ; transformation of totem clans into local clans, 83 ; relaxation of the rule of exogamy, 83 sq.
Geographical diffusion of totemism, 84-87 ; origin of totemism, 87 ; influence of totemism on animals and plants, 87 ; literature of totemism, 87.

THE ORIGIN OF TOTEMISM. Reprinted from the *Fortnightly Review*, April and May 1899 . . . . . Pp. 89-138

THE BEGINNINGS OF RELIGION AND TOTEMISM AMONG THE AUSTRALIAN ABORIGINES. Reprinted from the *Fortnightly Review*, July and September 1905 . . . Pp. 139-172

The beginnings of religion, 141-153 ; the beginnings of totemism, 154-172.

AN ETHNOGRAPHICAL SURVEY OF TOTEMISM . . Pp. 173-579

CHAPTER I.—TOTEMISM IN CENTRAL AUSTRALIA Pp. 175-313

§ 1. The Social Line of Demarcation in Central Australia, pp. 175 sq.

§ 2. Totemism in the Urabunna Tribe, pp. 176-186.

§ 3. Totemism in the Arunta and North-Central Tribes, pp. 186-256.

§ 4. Exogamous Classes in the Arunta Nation and Northern Tribes, pp. 256-271.

§ 5. On the Exogamous Organisation of Australian Tribes, pp. 271-288.

§ 6. The Classificatory System of Relationship in the Central and Northern Tribes, pp. 289-313.

CHAPTER II.—TOTEMISM IN SOUTH-EASTERN AUSTRALIA
Pp. 314-514

§ 1. Physical Geography of South-Eastern Australia in Relation to Aboriginal Society, pp. 314-339.

§ 2. Tribes with two Classes (Kararu and Matteri) and Female Descent, pp. 339-380.

§ 3. Tribes with two Classes (Mukwara and Kilpara) and Female Descent, pp. 380-392.

§ 4. Tribes with two Classes (Eagle-hawk and Crow) and Female Descent, pp. 392-395.

§ 5. Tribes with four Subclasses and Female Descent, pp. 395-434.

§ 6. Tribes with two Classes and Male Descent, pp. 434-441.

§ 7. Tribes with four Subclasses and Male Descent, pp. 441-451.

§ 8. Tribes with Anomalous Class Systems and Female Descent, pp. 451-472.

§ 9. Tribes with Anomalous Class Systems and Male Descent, pp. 472-493.

§ 10. Tribes with neither Exogamous Classes nor Totem Clans, pp. 493-507.

§ 11. Equivalence of the Exogamous Classes, pp. 507-514.

CHAPTER III.—TOTEMISM IN NORTH-EAST AUSTRALIA
Pp. 515-545

CHAPTER IV.—TOTEMISM IN WEST AUSTRALIA . Pp. 546-579

§ 1. Totemism in South-West Australia, pp. 546-567.

§ 2. Totemism in North-West Australia, pp. 567-579.

TOTEMISM

Reprinted from the First Edition, Edinburgh 1887

TOTEMISM

A TOTEM is a class of material objects which a savage regards with superstitious respect, believing that there exists between him and every member of the class an intimate and altogether special relation. The name is derived from an Ojibway (Chippeway) word *totem*, the correct spelling of which is somewhat uncertain. It was first introduced into literature, so far as appears, by J. Long, an Indian interpreter of last century, who spelt it *totam*.[1] The form *toodaim* is given by the Rev. Peter Jones, himself an Ojibway;[2] *dodaim* by Warren[3] and (as an alternative pronunciation to totem) by Morgan;[4] and *ododam* by Francis Assikinack, an Ottawa Indian.[5] According to the abbé Thavenet[6] the word is properly *ote*, in the sense of "family or tribe," possessive *otem*, and with the personal pronoun *nind otem* "my tribe," *kit otem* "thy tribe." In English the spelling *totem* (Keating, James, Schoolcraft,[7] etc.) has become established by custom. The connection between a man and his totem is mutually beneficent; the totem protects the man, and the man shows his respect for the totem in various ways, by not killing it if it be an

<small>Totem defined.</small>

<small>Connection between a man and his totem.</small>

---

[1] *Voyages and Travels of an Indian Interpreter*, p. 86, London, 1791.
[2] *History of the Ojebway Indians*, London, 1861, p. 138.
[3] "History of the Ojibways," in *Collections of the Minnesota Historical Society*, vol. v. (St. Paul, Minn., 1885) p. 34.
[4] *Ancient Society*, p. 165.
[5] See *Academy*, 27th Sept. 1884, p. 203.
[6] In J. A. Cuoq's *Lexique de la langue Algonquine* (Montreal, 1886), p. 312. Thavenet admits that the Indians use *ote* in the sense of "mark" (limited apparently to a family mark), but argues that the word must mean family or tribe.
[7] *Expedition to Itasca Lake*, New York, 1834, p. 146, etc. Petitot spells it *todem* in his *Monographie des Dènè-Dindjié*, p. 40; but he writes *otémisme* in his *Traditions Indiennes du Canada Nord-ouest*, p. 446.

animal, and not cutting or gathering it if it be a plant. As distinguished from a fetich, a totem is never an isolated individual, but always a class of objects, generally a species of animals or of plants, more rarely a class of inanimate natural objects, very rarely a class of artificial objects.

<small>Three kinds of totem: the clan totem, the sex totem, the individual totem.</small>

Considered in relation to men, totems are of at least three kinds:—(1) the clan totem, common to a whole clan, and passing by inheritance from generation to generation; (2) the sex totem, common either to all the males or to all the females of a tribe, to the exclusion in either case of the other sex; (3) the individual totem, belonging to a single individual and not passing to his descendants. Other kinds of totems exist and will be noticed, but they may perhaps be regarded as varieties of the clan totem. The latter is by far the most important of all; and where we speak of totems or totemism without qualification, the reference is always to the clan totem.

<small>The clan totem.</small>

The Clan Totem.—The clan totem is reverenced by a body of men and women who call themselves by the name of the totem, believe themselves to be of one blood, descendants of a common ancestor, and are bound together by common obligations to each other and by a common faith in the totem.

<small>Totemism both a religious and a social system.</small>

Totemism is thus both a religious and a social system. In its religious aspect it consists of the relations of mutual respect and protection between a man and his totem; in its social aspect it consists of the relations of the clansmen to each other and to men of other clans. In the later history of totemism these two sides, the religious and the social, tend to part company; the social system sometimes survives the religious; and, on the other hand, religion sometimes bears traces of totemism in countries where the social system based on totemism has disappeared. How in the origin of totemism these two sides were related to each other it is, in our ignorance of that origin, impossible to say with certainty. But on the whole the evidence points strongly to the conclusion that the two sides were originally inseparable; that, in other words, the farther we go back, the more we should find that the clansman regards himself and his totem as beings of the same species, and the less he distinguishes between conduct towards his totem and towards his fellow-clansmen. For the sake of exposition, however, it is convenient to separate the two. We begin with the religious side.

Totemism as a Religion, or the Relation between a Man and his Totem.—The members of a totem clan call themselves by the name of their totem, and commonly believe themselves to be actually descended from it.

Totemism as a religion.

Thus the Turtle clan of the Iroquois are descended from a fat turtle, which, burdened by the weight of its shell in walking, contrived by great exertions to throw it off, and thereafter gradually developed into a man.[1] The Bear and Wolf clans of the Iroquois are descended from bears and wolves respectively.[2] The Cray-Fish clan of the Choctaws were originally cray-fish and lived underground, coming up occasionally through the mud to the surface. Once a party of Choctaws smoked them out, and, treating them kindly, taught them the Choctaw language, taught them to walk on two legs, made them cut off their toe nails and pluck the hair from their bodies, after which they adopted them into the tribe. But the rest of their kindred, the cray-fish, are still living underground.[3] The Carp clan of the Outaouaks are descended from the eggs of a carp which had been deposited by the fish on the banks of a stream and warmed by the sun.[4] The Ojibways are descended from a dog.[5] The Crane clan of the Ojibways are descended from a pair of cranes, which after long wanderings settled on the rapids at the outlet of Lake Superior, where they were transformed by the great spirit into a man and woman.[6] The Black Shoulder clan (a Buffalo clan) of the Omahas were originally buffaloes and dwelt under the surface of the water.[7] The Osages are descended from a male snail and a female beaver. The snail burst his shell, developed arms, feet, and legs, and

Belief in the descent of people from their totems.

---

[1] *Second Annual Report of the Bureau of Ethnology*, Washington, 1883, p. 77.
[2] Timothy Dwight, *Travels in New England and New York* (London, 1823), iv. p. 184.
[3] Catlin, *North American Indians*, ii. p. 128.
[4] *Lettres Édifiantes et Curieuses*, Paris, 1781, vi. p. 171.
[5] A. Mackenzie, *Voyages through* the Continent of North America, p. cxviii; Bancroft, *Native Races of the Pacific States*, i. 118. So with the Kaniagmuts, Dall, *Alaska and its Resources*, p. 404 sq.
[6] Morgan, *Anc. Soc.*, p. 180.
[7] *Third Ann. Rep. of Bur. of Ethnol.*, Washington, 1884, pp. 229, 231. Another Buffalo clan among the Omahas has a similar legend (*ib.* p. 233).

6   TOTEMISM

Belief in the descent of people from their totems.

became a fine tall man; afterwards he married the beaver maid.¹ The clans of the Iowas are descended from the animals from which they take their names, namely, eagle, pigeon, wolf, bear, elk, beaver, buffalo, and snake.² The Moquis say that long ago the Great Mother brought from the west nine clans in the form of deer, sand, water, bears, hares, tobacco-plants, and reed-grass. She planted them on the spots where their villages now stand and transformed them into men, who built the present pueblos, and from whom the present clans are descended.³ The Californian Indians, in whose mythology the coyote or prairie-wolf is a leading personage, are descended from coyotes. At first they walked on all fours; then they began to have some members of the human body, one finger, one toe, one eye, etc., then two fingers, two toes, etc., and so on till they became perfect human beings. The loss of their tails, which they still deplore, was produced by the habit of sitting upright.⁴ The Lenape or Delawares were descended from their totem animals, the wolf, the turtle, and the turkey; but they gave precedence to the Turtle clan, because it was descended, not from a common turtle, but from the great original tortoise which bears the world on its back and was the first of living beings.⁵ The Haidas of Queen Charlotte Islands believe that long ago the raven, who is the chief figure in the mythology of the north-west coast of America, took a cockle from the beach and married it; the cockle gave birth to a female child whom the raven took to wife, and from their union the Indians were produced.⁶ The

---

¹ Schoolcraft, *The American Indians*, p. 95 *sq.*; Lewis and Clarke, *Travels to the Source of the Missouri River*, 8vo, London, 1815, i. p. 12.
² Schoolcraft, *Indian Tribes*, iii. 268 *sq.*
³ Schoolcraft, *Ind. Tri.*, iv. 86. With the Great Mother Mr. Morgan compares the female deity worshipped by the Shawnees under the title of "Our Grandmother" (*Anc. Soc.*, p. 179 *n.*).
⁴ Schoolcraft, *op. cit.*, iv. 224 *sq.*, *cf.* v. 217; Boscana, in A. Robinson's *Life in California*, p. 298. Mr. Stephen Powers, perhaps the best living authority on the Californian Indians, finds no totems among them (*Tribes of California*, p. 5). See, however, pp. 147, 199 of his work for some traces of totemism.
⁵ Brinton, *The Lenape and their Legends*, p. 39.
⁶ *Geological Survey of Canada, Report of Progress for 1878-79*, p. 149B *sq.*; F. Poole, *Queen Charlotte Islands*, p. 136; *Ausland*, 6th October 1884, p. 796. Among the neighbouring Thlinkets the raven (Jĕshl) is rather a creator than an ancestor. See Holmberg, "Ethnographische Skizzen ueber die Voelker des russischen Amerika,"

Kutchin trace the origin of their clans to the time when all beasts, birds, and fish were people; the beasts were one clan, the birds another, and the fish another.¹ The Arawaks in Guiana assert that their clans are descended from the eponymous animal, bird, or plant.² Some of the aboriginal tribes of Peru (not the Inca race) were descended from eagles, others from condors.³ Some of the clans of Western Australia are descended from ducks, swans, and other water fowl.⁴ The Geawe-gal tribe in New South Wales believe that each man is akin to his totem in an unexplained way.⁵ The Santals in Bengal, one of whose totems is the wild goose, trace their origin to the eggs of a wild goose.⁶ In Senegambia each family or clan is descended from an animal (hippopotamus, crocodile, scorpion, etc.) with which it counts kindred.⁷ The inhabitants of Funafuti or Ellice Island in the South Pacific believe that the place was first inhabited by the porcupine fish, whose offspring became men and women.⁸ The Kalang, who have claims to be considered the aborigines of Java, are descended from a princess and a chief who had been transformed into a dog.⁹ Some of the inhabitants of the islands Ambon, Uliase, Keisar (Makisar), and Wetar, and the Aaru and Babar archipelagoes, are descended from trees, pigs, eels, crocodiles, sharks, serpents, dogs, turtles, etc.¹⁰

Somewhat different are the myths in which a human ancestress is said to have given birth to an animal of the totem species. Thus the Snake clan among the Moquis *Descent of totem animals from women.*

in *Acta Soc. Sc. Fennicae*, Helsingfors, iv. (1856) p. 292 *sq.*; Baer and Helmersen, *Beitr. zur Kenntn. des russ. Reiches*, i. p. 104. So with the wolf in North-West America; it made men and women out of two sticks (Baer and Helmersen, *op. cit.* i. 93). In Thlinket mythology the ancestor of the Wolf clan is said never to appear in wolf form (Holmberg, *op. cit.*, p. 293).
¹ Dall, *Alaska*, p. 197.
² Im Thurn, *Among the Indians of Guiana*, p. 184.
³ Garcilasso de la Vega, *Royal Commentaries of the Incas*, pt. i. bk. i. chs. 9, 18.

⁴ Sir George Grey, *Vocabulary of the Dialects of South-Western Australia*, pp. 29, 61, 63, 66, 71.
⁵ Fison and Howitt, *Kamilaroi and Kurnai*, p. 280.
⁶ Dalton, *Descriptive Ethnology of Bengal*, p. 209; *Asiat. Quart. Rev.*, July 1886, p. 76.
⁷ *Revue d'Ethnographie*, iii. p. 396, v. p. 81.
⁸ Turner, *Samoa*, p. 281.
⁹ Raffles, *History of Java*, ed. 1817, i. p. 328.
¹⁰ J. G. F. Riedel, *De sluik- en kroesharige Rassen tusschen Selebes en Papua* (The Hague, 1886), pp. 32, 253, 334, 414, 432.

8   TOTEMISM

Other myths explanatory of totemism.

of Arizona are descended from a woman who gave birth to snakes.¹ The Bakalai in Western Equatorial Africa believe that their women once gave birth to the totem animals; one woman brought forth a calf, others a crocodile, hippopotamus, monkey, boa, and wild pig.² In Samoa the prawn or cray-fish was the totem of one clan, because an infant of the clan had been changed at birth into a number of prawns or cray-fish.³ In some myths the actual descent from the totem seems to have been rationalised away. Thus the Red Maize clan among the Omahas say that the first man of the clan emerged from the water with an ear of red maize in his hand.⁴ A subclan of the Omahas say that the reason why they do not eat buffalo tongues and heads is that one of their chief men, while praying to the sun, once saw the ghost of a buffalo, visible from the flank up, rising out of a spring.⁵ Two clans of Western Australia, who are named after a small species of opossum and a little fish, think that they are so called because they used to live chiefly on these creatures.⁶ Some families in the islands Leti, Moa, and Lakor reverence the shark, and refuse to eat its flesh, because a shark once helped one of their ancestors at sea.⁷ The Ainos of Japan say that their first ancestor was suckled by a bear, and that is why they are so hairy.⁸

Respect shown to totems: totem animals not killed nor eaten.

Believing himself to be descended from, and therefore akin to, his totem, the savage naturally treats it with respect. If it is an animal he will not, as a rule, kill or eat it. In the Mount Gambier tribe (South Australia) "a man does not kill or use as food any of the animals of the same subdivision with himself, excepting when hunger compels; and then they express sorrow for having to eat their *wingong* (friends) or *tumanang* (their flesh). When using the last word they touch their breasts, to indicate the close relationship, meaning almost a part of themselves. To illustrate: —One day one of the blacks killed a crow. Three or four

---

¹ Bourke, *Snake Dance of the Moquis of Arizona*, p. 177.
² Du Chaillu, *Explorations and Adventures in Equatorial Africa*, p. 308.
³ Turner, *op. cit.*, p. 77.
⁴ E. James, *Expedition from Pittsburgh to the Rocky Mountains*, London, 1823, ii. p. 48 *sq.*; *Third Ann. Rep. of Bur. of Ethnol.*, p. 231.
⁵ *Third Report*, p. 231.
⁶ Grey, *Vocabulary*, 4, 95.
⁷ Riedel, *op. cit.*, p. 376 *sq.*
⁸ Reclus, *Nouv. Géogr. Univ.*, vii. p. 755.

days afterwards a Boortwa (crow) named Larry died. He had been ailing for some days, but the killing of his *wingong* hastened his death."[1] Here the identification of the man with his totem is carried very far; it is of the same flesh with him, and to injure any one of the species is physically to injure the man whose totem it is. Mr. Taplin was reproached by some of the Narrinyeri (South Australia) for shooting a wild dog; he had thereby hurt their *ngaitye* (totem).[2] The tribes about the Gulf of Carpentaria greatly reverence their totems; if any one were to kill the totem animal in presence of the man whose totem it was, the latter would say, "What for you kill that fellow? that my father!" or "That brother belonging to me you have killed; why did you do it?"[3] Again, among some Australian tribes "each young lad is strictly forbidden to eat of that animal or bird which belongs to his respective class, for it is his brother."[4] Sir George Grey says of the Western Australian tribes that a man will never kill an animal of his *kobong* (totem) species if he finds it asleep; "indeed, he always kills it reluctantly, and never without affording it a chance to escape. This arises from the family belief that some one individual of the species is their nearest friend, to kill whom would be a great crime, and to be carefully avoided."[5] Amongst the Indians of British Columbia a man will never kill his totem animal; if he sees another do it, he will hide his face for shame, and afterwards demand compensation for the act. Whenever one of these Indians exhibits his totem badge (as by painting it on his forehead), all persons of the same totem are bound to do honour to it by casting property before it.[6] The Osages, who, as we have seen, believe themselves descended from a female beaver, abstained from hunting the beaver, "because in killing that animal they killed a brother of the Osages."[7] The Ojibways (Chippeways) do not kill, hunt, or eat their totems. An Ojibway

---

[1] Stewart, in Fison and Howitt, *Kamilaroi and Kurnai*, p. 169.
[2] *Native Tribes of South Australia*, p. 64.
[3] *Jour. Anthrop. Inst.*, xiii. p. 300.
[4] *Ib.*, p. 303.
[5] Grey, *Journals of Two Expeditions of Discovery in North-West and Western Australia*, ii. p. 228.
[6] R. C. Mayne, *British Columbia*, p. 258.
[7] Lewis and Clark, i. p. 12.

Totem animals not killed nor eaten. who had unwittingly killed his totem (a bear) described how, on his way home after the accident, he was attacked by a large bear, who asked him why he had killed his totem. The man explained, apologised, and was dismissed with a caution.[1] Being descended from a dog, the Ojibways will not eat dog's flesh, and at one time ceased to employ dogs to draw their sledges.[2] Some of the Indians of Pennsylvania would not kill the rattlesnake, because they said it was their grandfather, and gave them notice of danger by its rattle. They also abstained from eating rabbits and ground-hogs, because "they did not know but that they might be related to them."[3] The Damaras in South Africa are divided into totem clans, called "eandas"; and according to the clan to which they belong they refuse to partake, *e.g.*, of an ox marked with black, white, or red spots, or of a sheep without horns, or of draught oxen. Some of them will not even touch vessels in which such food has been cooked, and avoid even the smoke of the fire which has been used to cook it.[4] The negroes of Senegambia do not eat their totems.[5] The Mundas (or Mundaris) and Oraons in Bengal, who are divided into exogamous totem clans, will not kill or eat the totem animals which give their names to the clans.[6] A remarkable feature of some of these Oraon totems is, that they are not whole animals, but parts of animals, as the head of a tortoise, the stomach of a pig. In such cases (which are not confined to Bengal) it is of course not the whole animal, but only the special part which the clansmen are forbidden to eat. Such totems may be distinguished as *split totems*. The Jagannáthi Kumhár in Bengal abstain from killing or injuring the totems of their respective clans

---

[1] J. Long, *op. cit.*, p. 87.

[2] A. Mackenzie, *loc. cit.*; Bancroft, i. 118. The dog does not appear in the list of Ojibway totems given by Morgan (*A. S.*, p. 166) and P. Jones (*Hist. of Ojebway Indians*, p. 138).

[3] J. Heckewelder, "Account of the History, Manners, and Customs of the Indian Nations who once inhabited Pennsylvania and the neighbouring States," in *Trans. Amer. Philos. Soc.*, Philadelphia, 1819, i. p. 245. This, combined with the mention of the ground-hog in the myths of their origin, points, as Heckewelder observes, to a ground-hog tribe or clan (*ib.*, p. 244).

[4] C. J. Andersson, *Lake Ngami*, p. 222 *sq*.

[5] *Revue d'Ethnographie*, iii. p. 396.

[6] Dalton, in *Trans. Ethnolog. Soc.*, New Series, vi. p. 36; *id.*, *Ethnol. of Bengal*, pp. 189, 254; *As. Quart. Rev.*, July 1886, p. 76. Among the Munda totems are the eel and tortoise; among the Oraons the hawk, crow, heron, eel, kerketar bird, tiger, monkey, and the leaves of the *Ficus Indicus*.

TOTEMISM

(namely tiger, snake, weasel, cow, frog, sparrow, tortoise), and they bow to their totems when they meet them.[1] The Badris, also in Bengal, may not eat of their totem, the heron.[2] The inhabitants of Ambon Uliase, Keisar (Makisar), Wetar, and the Aaru and Babar archipelagoes may not eat the pigs, crocodiles, sharks, serpents, dogs, turtles, eels, etc., from which they are respectively descended.[3]

When the totem is a plant the rules are such as these. A native of Western Australia, whose totem is a vegetable, "may not gather it under certain circumstances and at a particular period of the year."[4] The Oraon clan, whose totem is the leaf of the *Ficus Indicus*, will not eat from the leaves of that tree (the leaves are used as plates).[5] Another Oraon clan, whose totem is the Kujrar tree, will not eat the oil of that tree, nor sit in its shade.[6] The Red Maize clan of the Omahas will not eat red maize.[7] Those of the people of Ambon and Uliase who are descended from trees may not use these trees for firewood.[8] *Respect shown to totem plants.*

The rules not to kill or eat the totem are not the only taboos; the clansmen are often forbidden to touch the totem or any part of it, and sometimes they may not even look at it. *Other totem taboos.*

Amongst the Omaha taboos are the following. (1) The Elk clan neither eat the flesh nor touch any part of the male elk, and they do not eat the male deer.[9] (2) A subclan of the Black Shoulder (Buffalo) clan may not eat buffalo tongues nor touch a buffalo head (split totem).[10] (3) The Hanga clan is divided into two subclans, one of which may not eat buffalo sides, geese, swans, nor cranes, but they may eat buffalo tongues; the other may not eat buffalo tongues but may eat buffalo sides (split totems).[11] (4) Another subclan may not touch the hide of a black bear nor eat its flesh.[12] (5) The Eagle subclan, curiously enough, *Omaha taboos.*

---

[1] *As. Quart. Rev.*, July 1886, p. 79.
[2] Dalton, *Ethnol. of Bengal*, p. 327.
[3] Riedel, *op. cit.*, pp. 61, 253, 341, 414, 432.
[4] Grey, *Journals*, ii. 228 sq.
[5] Dalton, *Ethn. of Bengal*, p. 254; *As. Quart. Rev.*, July 1886, p. 76.
[6] Dalton, *op. cit.*, 254; *id.*, in *Trans. Ethnol. Soc.*, vi. p. 36; *As. Quart. Rev.*, loc. cit.
[7] E. James, *Expedition from Pittsburgh to the Rocky Mountains*, ii. p. 48; *Third Rep. Bur. Ethnol.*, p. 231.
[8] Riedel, *op. cit.*, p. 61.
[9] James, *op. cit.*, ii. 47; *Third Rep.*, 225.
[10] *Third Rep.*, 231.
[11] *Ib.*, 235.
[12] *Ib.*, 237.

Totem taboos among the Omahas.

may not touch a buffalo head.[1] (6) A Turtle subclan may not eat a turtle, but they may touch or carry one.[2] (7) Another clan may not touch verdigris.[3] (8) The Buffalo-Tail clan may not eat a calf while it is red, but they may do so when it turns black; they may not touch a buffalo head; they may not eat the meat on the lowest rib, because the head of the calf before birth touches the mother near that rib.[4] (9) The Deer-Head clan may not touch the skin of any animal of the deer family, nor wear moccasins of deer skin, nor use the fat of the deer for hair-oil; but they may eat the flesh of deer.[5] (10) A subclan of the Deer-Head clan had a special taboo, being forbidden to touch verdigris, charcoal, and the skin of a wild cat. According to others, the whole Deer-Head clan was forbidden to touch charcoal.[6] (11) Another clan does not eat a buffalo calf.[7] (12) Another clan does not touch worms, snakes, toads, frogs, nor any other kind of reptiles; hence they are sometimes called Reptile People.[8]

Totem taboos in India.

Of the totem clans in Bengal it is said that they "are prohibited from killing, eating, cutting, burning, carrying, using, etc.," the totem.[9] The Keriahs in India not only do not eat the sheep, but will not even use a woollen rug.[10] Similarly in ancient Egypt (a nest of totems) the sheep was reverenced and eaten by no one except the people of Wolf town (Lycopolis), and woollen garments were not allowed to be carried into temples.[11] Some of the Bengal totem taboos are peculiar. The Tirki clan of the Oraons, whose totem is young mice, will not look at animals whose eyes are not yet open, and their own offspring are never shown

---

[1] *Third Rep.*, 239. There seems to be a cross connection between the Eagles and the Buffaloes among the Omahas; for a subclan of the Buffalo clan (the Black Shoulder clan) had a series of eagle birth-names in addition to the buffalo birth-names common to the whole clan (*ib.*, 231 *sq.*).
[2] *Ib.*, 240. James (*op. cit.*, ii. 49) says they "do not touch turtles or tortoises."
[3] James, *loc. cit.*; *Third Rep.*, 241.
[4] James, *loc. cit.*; *Third Rep.*, 244.
[5] James, *loc. cit.*; *Third Rep.*, 245.
[6] *Third Rep.*, 245 *sq.* Verdigris was thought to symbolise the blue sky.
[7] *Third Rep.*, 248.
[8] James, ii. 50; *Third Rep.*, 248.
[9] *As. Quart. Rev.*, July 1886, p. 75.
[10] V. Ball, *Jungle Life in India*, p. 89.
[11] Herod., ii. 42, 81; Plut. *Is. et Os.*, §§ 4, 72. Again the sheep was worshipped in Samos (Aelian, *N. A.* xii. 40; Clem. Alex., *Protrept.*, 39); and Pythagoras, a native of Samos, forbade his followers to wear or be buried in woollen garments (Herod., ii. 81; Apuleius, *De Magia*, 56).

till they are wide awake.¹ Another Oraon clan objects to water in which an elephant has bathed.² A Mahili clan will not allow their daughters to enter their houses after marriage; a Kurmi clan will not wear shell ornaments; another will not wear silk; another give children their first rice naked.³

The Bechuanas in South Africa, who have a well-developed totem system, may not eat nor clothe themselves in the skin of the totem animal.⁴ They even avoid, at least in some cases, to look at the totem. Thus to a man of the Bakuena (Bakwain) or Crocodile clan, it is "hateful and unlucky" to meet or gaze on a crocodile; the sight is thought to cause inflammation of the eyes. So when a Crocodile clansman happens to go near a crocodile he spits on the ground as a preventive charm, and says, "There is sin." Yet they call the crocodile their father, celebrate it in their festivals, swear by it, and make an incision resembling the mouth of a crocodile in the ears of their cattle as a mark to distinguish them from others.⁵ The puti (a kind of antelope) is the totem of the Bamangwats, another Bechuana clan; and to look on it was a great calamity to the hunter or to women going to the gardens.⁶ The common goat is the sacred animal (totem?) of the Madenassana Bushmen; yet "to look upon it would be to render the man for the time impure, as well as to cause him undefined uneasiness." ⁷

Totem taboos in Africa.

A Samoan clan had for its totem the butterfly. The insect was supposed to have three mouths; hence the Butterfly men were forbidden "to drink from a cocoa-nut shell water-bottle which had all the eyes or openings perforated. Only one or at the most two apertures for drinking were allowed. A third would be a mockery, and bring down the wrath of his butterflyship." ⁸

Totem taboos in Samoa.

---

¹ Dalton, in *Tr. Ethnol. Soc.*, vi. 36. For the totem, *id.*, *Ethnol. of Bengal*, p. 254; *As. Quart. Rev.*, 76. The reason of the taboo is perhaps a fear of contracting blindness. Some North American Indians will not allow their children to touch the mole, believing that its blindness is infectious (J. Adair, *History of the American Indians*, p. 133).
² *Tr. Ethnol. Soc.*, vi. 36.

³ *As. Quart. Rev.*, July 1886, p. 77.
⁴ Casalis, *The Basutos*, p. 211.
⁵ Livingstone, *Missionary Travels and Researches in South Africa*, p. 255; John Mackenzie, *Ten Years North of the Orange River*, p. 135 *n.*; Casalis, *The Basutos*, p. 211.
⁶ J. Mackenzie, *op. cit.*, 391 *sq.*; cf. *Jour. Anthrop. Inst.*, xvi. p. 84.
⁷ J. Mackenzie, *op. cit.*, 135.
⁸ Turner, *Samoa*, p. 76.

Cross totems, i.e. totems which comprise several distinct species.

Cross Totems.—Another Samoan clan had for its totem the ends of leaves and of other things. These ends were considered sacred, and not to be handled or used in any way. It is said to have been no small trouble to the clansmen in daily life to cut off the ends of all the taro, bread-fruit, and cocoa-nut leaves required for cooking. Ends of yams, bananas, fish, etc., were also carefully laid aside and regarded as being as unfit for food as if they had been poison.[1] This is an example of what may be called a cross totem, *i.e.* a totem which is neither a whole animal or plant, nor a part of one particular species of animal or plant, but is a particular part of all (or of a number of species of) animals or plants. Other examples of cross totems are the ear of any animal (totem of a Mahili clan in Bengal);[2] the eyes of fish (totem of a Samoan clan);[3] bone (totem of the Sauks and Foxes in North America);[4] and blood (totem of the Blackfeet Indians).[5] More exactly, such totems should be called cross-split totems; while the name cross totem should be reserved for a totem which, overstepping the limits of a single natural species, includes under itself several species. Examples of such cross totems are the small bird totem of the Omahas, the reptile totem of the Omahas,[6] and the big tree totem of the Sauks and Foxes.[7]

Totem animals fed or kept in captivity.

Sometimes the totem animal is fed or even kept alive in captivity. A Samoan clan whose totem was the eel used to present the first fruits of the taro plantations to the eels;[8] another Samoan clan fed the cray-fish because it was their totem.[9] The Delawares sacrificed to hares; to Indian corn they offered bear's flesh, but to deer and bears Indian corn; to fishes they offered small pieces of bread in the shape of fishes.[10] Amongst the Narrinyeri in South Australia men of the Snake clan sometimes catch snakes, pull out their teeth or sew up their mouths, and keep them as pets.[11] In a Pigeon clan of Samoa a pigeon was carefully kept and

---

[1] Turner, *Samoa*, 70.
[2] *As. Quart. Rev.*, July 1886, p. 77.
[3] Turner, *op. cit.*, p. 74.
[4] Morgan, *A. S.*, p. 170.
[5] *Ib.*, p. 171.
[6] *Third Rep.*, 238, 248.
[7] Morgan, *A. S.*, 170.
[8] Turner, *op. cit.*, p. 71.
[9] *Ib.*, p. 77.
[10] Loskiel, *History of the Mission of the United Brethren in North America*, i. p. 40; De Schweinitz, *Life of Zeisberger*, p. 95 *sq.*
[11] *Native Tribes of South Australia*, p. 63.

fed.¹ Amongst the Kalang in Java, whose totem is the red dog, each family as a rule keeps one of these animals, which they will on no account allow to be struck or ill-used by any one.² Eagles are kept in cages and fed in some of the Moqui villages, and the eagle is a Moqui totem.³ The Ainos in Japan keep eagles, crows, owls, and bears in cages, and show a superstitious reverence for them; the young bear cubs are suckled by the women.⁴

The dead totem is mourned for and buried like a dead clansman. In Samoa, if a man of the Owl totem found a dead owl by the road-side, he would sit down and weep over it and beat his forehead with stones till the blood flowed. The bird would then be wrapped up and buried with as much ceremony as if it had been a human being. "This, however, was not the death of the god. He was supposed to be yet alive, and incarnate in all the owls in existence."⁵ The generalisation here implied is characteristic of totemism; it is not merely an individual but the species that is reverenced. The Wanika in Eastern Africa look on the hyæna as one of their ancestors, and the death of a hyæna is mourned by the whole people; the mourning for a chief is said to be as nothing compared to the mourning for a hyæna.⁶ A tribe of Southern Arabia used to bury a dead gazelle wherever they found one, and the whole tribe mourned for it seven days.⁷ The lobster was generally considered sacred by the Greeks, and not eaten; if the people of Seriphos (an island in the Aegean) caught a lobster in their nets they put it back into the sea; if they found a dead one, they buried it and mourned over it as over one of themselves.⁸ At Athens any man who killed a wolf had to

<small>Dead totem animals mourned and buried.</small>

---

¹ Turner, *op. cit.*, p. 64.
² Raffles, *Hist. of Java*, i. p. 328, ed. 1817.
³ Bourke, *Snake Dance of the Moquis of Arizona*, pp. 252, 336.
⁴ *J. A. I.*, ii. 252, 254; *id.*, iii. 239; Rein, *Japan*, i. 446 *sq.*; Siebold, *Ethnol. Stud. ueber die Ainos*, p. 26; Scheube, *Der Baerencultus und die Baerenfest der Ainos*, p. 44 *sq.* Young bears are similarly brought up (though not suckled) by the Giljaks, a people on the lower Amoor, who are perhaps akin to the Ainos (Scheube, *Die Ainos*, p. 17; *Revue d'Ethnographie*, ii. p. 307 *sq.*).
⁵ Turner, *op. cit.*, p. 21, *cf.* 26, 60 *sq.*
⁶ Charles New, *Life, Wanderings, and Labours in Eastern Africa*, p. 122.
⁷ Robertson Smith, *Kinship and Marriage in Early Arabia*, p. 195.
⁸ Aelian, *N. A.*, xiii. 26. The solemn burial of a sardine by a river-side is a ceremony observed in Spain on Ash Wednesday (*Folk-Lore Record*, iv. 184 *sq.*).

bury it by subscription.¹ A Californian tribe which reverenced the buzzard held an annual festival at which the chief ceremony was the killing of a buzzard without losing a drop of its blood. It was then skinned, the feathers were preserved to make a sacred dress for the medicine-man, and the body was buried in holy ground amid the lamentations of the old women, who mourned as for the loss of a relative or friend.²

Totem animals not spoken of by their proper names.

As some totem clans avoid looking at their totem, so others are careful not to speak of it by its proper name, but use descriptive epithets instead. The three totems of the Delawares—the wolf, turtle, and turkey—were referred to respectively as "round foot," "crawler," and "not chewing," the last referring to the bird's habit of swallowing its food; and the clans called themselves, not Wolves, Turtles, and Turkeys, but "Round Feet," "Crawlers," and "Those who do not chew."³ The Bear clan of the Ottawas called themselves not Bears but Big Feet.⁴ The object of these circumlocutions is probably to give no offence to the worshipful animal, just as Swedish herd girls are careful not to call the wolf and the bear by their proper names, fearing that if they heard themselves so called the beasts would attack the cattle. Hence the herd girls call the wolf "the silent one," "grey legs," "golden tooth"; and the bear "the old man," "great father," "twelve men's strength," "golden feet," etc.⁵ Similarly the Kamtchatkans never speak of the bear and wolf by their proper names, believing that these animals understand human speech.⁶ Bushmen think it very unlucky to refer to the lion by name.⁷

Supposed ill effects of ill-treating the totem.

The penalties supposed to be incurred by acting disrespectfully to the totem are various. The Bakalai think that if a man were to eat his totem the women of his clan would miscarry and give birth to animals of the totem kind,

---

¹ ἀγείρει αὐτῷ τὰ πρὸς τὴν ταφήν. Schol. on Apollonius Rhodius, ii. 124.
² Boscana, in Alfred Robinson's *Life in California*, p. 291 *sq.*; Bancroft, *Native Races of the Pacific States*, iii. p. 168.
³ Brinton, *The Lenape and their Legends*, p. 39; Morgan, *A. S.*, p. 171; Heckewelder, p. 247.

⁴ *Acad.*, 27th Sept. 1884, p. 203, quoting from the *Canadian Journal* (Toronto), No. 14, March 1858.
⁵ L. Lloyd, *Peasant Life in Sweden*, p. 251.
⁶ Steller, *Beschr. von dem Lande Kamtschatka*, p. 276.
⁷ J. Mackenzie, *Ten Years North of the Orange River*, p. 151.

TOTEMISM

or die of an awful disease.¹ The Elk clan among the Omahas believe that if any clansman were to touch any part of the male elk, or eat its flesh or the flesh of the male deer, he would break out in boils and white spots in different parts of the body.² The Red Maize subclan of the Omahas believe that, if they were to eat of the red maize, they would have running sores all round their mouth.³ And in general the Omahas believe that to eat of the totem, even in ignorance, would cause sickness, not only to the eater, but also to his wife and children.⁴ White hair is regarded by them as a token that the person has broken a totem taboo, *e.g.* that a man of the Reptile clan has touched or smelt a snake.⁵ The inhabitants of Wetar think that leprosy and madness are the result of eating the totem.⁶ The worshippers of the Syrian goddess, whose creed was saturated with totemism, believed that if they ate a sprat or an anchovy their whole bodies would break out in ulcers, their legs would waste away, and their liver melt, or that their belly and legs would swell up.⁷ The Egyptians, one of whose totems seems to have been the pig, thought that if a man drank pig's milk his body would break out in a scab.⁸ The Bosch negroes of Guiana think that if they ate the *capiaï* (an animal like a pig) it would give them leprosy.⁹ The Singhie tribe of Dyaks, whose totem seems to be the deer (they will not eat its flesh nor allow it to be carried into their houses or cooked at their fires; the grown men will not even touch it), believe that if any man were to eat deer's flesh he would go mad; a man who ran about the forest naked, imitating the noises and habits of a deer, was thought to have eaten venison.¹⁰

The Samoans thought it death to injure or eat their totems. The totem was supposed to take up his abode in the sinner's body, and there to gender the very thing which he had eaten till it caused his death.¹¹ Thus if

In Samoa death the consequence of injuring the totem.

---

¹ Du Chaillu, *Equat. Afr.*, p. 309.
² *Third Rep.*, 225.
³ *Ib.*, 231.
⁴ James, *Expedition to the Rocky Mountains*, ii. p. 50.
⁵ *Third Rep.*, 275.
⁶ Riedel, *op. cit.*, p. 452.

⁷ Plutarch, *De Superst.*, 10; Selden, *De dis Syris*, p. 269 *sq.*, Leipsic, 1668.
⁸ Plutarch, *Isis et Os.*, 8.
⁹ J. Crevaux, *Voyages dans l'Amérique du Sud*, p. 59.
¹⁰ Low, *Sarawak*, p. 265 *sq.*, 306.
¹¹ Turner, *Samoa*, p. 17 *sq.*

18 TOTEMISM

In Samoa death the consequence of injuring the totem.

a Turtle man ate of a turtle he grew very ill, and the voice of the turtle was heard in his inside saying, "He ate me; I am killing him."[1] If a Prickly Sea-Urchin man consumed one of these shell-fish, a prickly sea-urchin grew in his body and killed him.[2] Pig's heart and octopus were equally fatal to the eater who had these for his totem.[3] If a Mullet man ate a mullet he squinted.[4] If a Cockle man picked up a cockle and carried it away from the shore, it appeared on some part of his person; if he actually ate it, it grew on his nose.[5] If a man whose totem was the ends of banana leaves used one of them as a cap, baldness was the result.[6] If a Butterfly man caught a butterfly, it struck him dead.[7] The Wild Pigeon clan might not use as plates the reddish-seared breadfruit leaves "under a penalty of being seized with rheumatic swellings, or an eruption all over the body called tangosusu, and resembling chicken-pox."[8] If a Domestic Fowl man ate of that bird, delirium and death were the consequence.[9]

Samoan mode of appeasing an offended totem.

In such cases, however, the Samoans had a mode of appeasing the angry totem. The offender himself or one of his clan was wrapped in leaves and laid in an unheated oven, as if he were about to be baked. Thus if amongst the Cuttle-Fish clan a visitor had caught a cuttle-fish and cooked it, or if a Cuttle-Fish man had been present at the eating of a cuttle-fish, the Cuttle-Fish clan met and chose a man or woman who went through the pretence of being baked. Otherwise a cuttle-fish would grow in the stomach of some of the clan and be their death.[10] So with the stinging ray fish and the mullet. But if a member of the clan of which these two fish were the joint totem tasted either of them, then, in addition to the baking, he had to drink a cup of rancid oil dregs, probably as a purgative.[11] This pretence of cooking a clansman seems to have been especially obligatory when the totem had been cooked in the oven. To have afterwards used the oven without going through this form of expiation would have been fatal to the family.[12]

In Australia, also, the punishment for eating the totem

[1] Turner, *Samoa*, p. 50.
[2] *Ib.*, 51.
[3] *Ib.*, 72.
[4] *Ib.*, 61, 75.
[5] *Ib.*, 40.
[6] *Ib.*, 76.
[7] *Ib.*, 76.
[8] *Ib.*, 70.
[9] *Ib.*, 37.
[10] *Ib.*, 31 *sq.*
[11] *Ib.*, 38, *cf.* 72.
[12] *Ib.*, 59, *cf.* 58, 69 *sq.*, 72.

appears to have been sickness or death.¹ But it is not merely the totem which is tabooed to the Australians; they have, besides, a very elaborate code of food prohibitions, which vary chiefly with age, being on the whole strictest and most extensive at puberty, and gradually relaxing with advancing years. Thus young men are forbidden to eat the emu; if they ate it, it is thought that they would be afflicted with sores all over their bodies.² The restrictions on women till they are past the age of child-bearing seem to be more numerous than those on men. Children are not restricted at all, nor are old men and old women.³ These restrictions are removed by an old man smearing the person's face with the fat of the forbidden animal.⁴ *[Food taboos in Australia.]*

In some tribes the respect for the totem has lessened or disappeared. Thus the Narrinyeri in South Australia do not kill their totem unless it is an animal which is good for food, when they have no objection to eating it.⁵ Mr. Eyre never observed any reluctance on the part of the natives of South Australia to kill their totems.⁶ Some natives of New South Wales, though they will not themselves kill their totem, have no objection to any one else killing it and they will then eat it.⁷ The Dieri in South Australia pay no particular respect to their totems, and they eat them.⁸ A Samoan of the Turtle clan, though he would not himself eat a turtle, would help a neighbour to cut up and cook one; but in doing so he kept a bandage over his mouth lest an embryo turtle should slip down his throat, grow up, and kill him.⁹ *[Respect for totem lessened or lost.]*

A Bechuana will kill his totem if it be a hurtful animal, e.g. a lion, but not without apologising to the animal; and the slayer must go through a form of purification for the sacrilege.¹⁰ Similarly in North America, if an Outaouak of the Bear clan killed a bear, he made the beast a feast of its *[Apologies for killing totem.]*

---

¹ *J. A. I.*, xiii. p. 192.
² T. L. Mitchell, *Three Expeditions into the Interior of Eastern Australia*, ii. p. 341.
³ See especially Eyre, *Journals of Expeditions of Discovery into Central Australia*, ii. 293 *sq.*; but see below, p. 41 *sq.*
⁴ *J. A. I.*, xiii. 456, xiv. 316.
⁵ *Native Tribes of South Australia*, p. 63.
⁶ Eyre, *Jour.*, ii. 328.
⁷ *J. A. I.*, xiv. 350.
⁸ Mr. Samuel Gason of Beltana, South Australia, in a letter to the present writer. See *J. A. I.*, xvii.
⁹ Turner, *op. cit.*, p. 67 *sq.*
¹⁰ Casalis, *The Basutos*, p. 211.

own flesh and harangued it, apologising for the necessity he was under of killing it, alleging that his children were hungry, etc.[1] Some but not all of the Moqui clans abstain from eating their totems.[2] The tribes about Alabama and Georgia had no respect for their totems, and would kill them when they got the chance.[3] The Omahas do not worship their totems.[4]

<small>Totem expected to help his people.</small>
The relation between a man and his totem is one of mutual help and protection. If the man respects and cares for the totem, he expects that the totem will do the same by him. ⟨In Senegambia the totems, when they are dangerous animals, will not hurt their clansmen; *e.g.* men of the Scorpion clan affirm that scorpions (of a very deadly kind) will run over their bodies without biting them.[5] A similar immunity from snakes was claimed by a Snake clan (Ophiogenes) in Cyprus.[6] Another Snake clan (Ophiogenes) in Asia Minor, believing that they were descended from snakes, and that snakes were their kinsmen, submitted to a practical test the claims of any man amongst them whom they suspected of being no true clansman. They made a snake bite him; if he survived, he was a true clansman; if he died, he was not.[7]⟩

<small>Tests of kinship with sacred animal.</small>
Similar is the test of a medicine-man among the Moxos of Peru. One of their totems is the tiger (jaguar); and a candidate for the rank of medicine-man must prove his kinship to the tiger by being bitten by that animal and surviving the bite.[8] The Psylli, a Snake clan in Africa, had a similar test of kinship; they exposed their new-born children to snakes, and if the snakes left them unharmed or only bit without killing them, the children were legitimate; otherwise they were bastards.[9] In Senegambia, at the

---

[1] *Lett. Édif.*, vi. p. 171.
[2] Morgan, *A. S.*, p. 180, *cf. id.*, 86.
[3] Adair, *Hist. Amer. Indians*, p. 16.
[4] Dorsey, in *American Antiquarian*, v. 274.
[5] *Revue d'Ethnographie*, iii. p. 396.
[6] Pliny, *N. H.*, xxviii. 30.
[7] Varro in Priscian x. 32, vol. i. p. 524, ed. Keil. For the snake descent of the clan see Strabo, xiii. 1, 14; Aelian, *N. A.*, xii. 39.

[8] "Relation de la Mission des Moxes dans le Perou," printed in Fr. Coreal's *Voyages aux Indes Occidentales*, iii. p. 249, and in *Lett. Édif.*, viii. p. 89.
[9] Varro, *loc. cit.*; Pliny, *N. H.*, vii. § 14. Pliny has got it wrong end on. He says that if the snakes did *not* leave the children they were bastards. We may safely correct his statement by Varro's.

present day, a python is expected to visit every child of the Python clan within eight days after birth; a Mandingo of this clan has been known to say that if his children were not so visited, he would kill them.¹ The Malagasy custom of placing a new-born child at the entrance to a cattle-pen, and then driving the cattle over it to see whether they would trample on it or not, was perhaps originally a kinship test.² Another birth test of kinship with the sacred animal (though of a different kind) is that used to discover the new Dhurma Raja in Assam. He is supposed to be an incarnation of the deity; and when he dies the child that refuses its mother's milk and prefers that of a cow is the new Dhurma Raja.³ This points to a cow totem.

Other totem clans regard a man who has been bitten by the totem, even though he survives, as disowned by the totem, and therefore they expel him from the clan. Among the Crocodile clan of the Bechuanas, if a man has been bitten by a crocodile, or merely had water splashed over him by a crocodile's tail, he is expelled the clan.⁴ Some judicial ordeals may have originated in totem tests of kinship. Thus, in Travancore, there was a judicial ordeal by snake-bite; the accused thrust his hand into a mantle in which a cobra was wrapped up; if it bit him, he was guilty; if not, he was innocent.⁵ That we have here a relic of totemism appears not only from the worship of snakes in the district, but also from the fact that, if a dead cobra was found by the people, it was burned with the same ceremonies as the body of a man of high caste.⁶ Oaths were originally ordeals, and some of them are of totem origin. The Crocodile clan of the Bechuanas swear by the crocodile; the Santals (or Sonthals), a totem tribe of Bengal, are said to adore the tiger (which probably means that the tiger is one of their

Some judicial ordeals and oaths perhaps derived from totemism.

---

¹ *Revue d'Ethnographie*, iii. p. 397.
² Ellis, *Hist. of Madagascar*, i. p. 157. According to Mr. Sibree, this was only done with children born in the month Alakaosy (*Folk-Lore Rec.*, ii. 35 *sq.*).
³ Robinson, *Descriptive Account of Assam*, p. 342 *sq.*

⁴ Livingstone, *South Africa*, p. 255.
⁵ J. Canter Visscher, *Letters from Malabar*, p. 69. For an ordeal by crocodiles in Madagascar (where the crocodile is much reverenced) see *Folk-Lore Rec.*, ii. p. 35, *cf.* p. 21.
⁶ Visscher, *op. cit.*, p. 162. For ordeal by snake-bite *cf. Asiatick Researches*, i. p. 391.

totems), and to swear on a tiger's skin is their most solemn oath.¹

Benefits conferred by the totem on his people.

But it is not enough that the totem should merely abstain from injuring, he must positively benefit the men who put their faith in him. The Snake clan (Ophiogenes) of Asia Minor believed that if they were bitten by an adder they had only to put a snake to the wound and their totem would suck out the poison and soothe away the inflammation and the pain.² Hence Omaha medicine-men, in curing the sick, imitate the action and voice of their (individual) totem.³ Members of the Serpent clan in Senegambia profess to heal by their touch persons who have been bitten by serpents.⁴ A similar profession was made in antiquity by Snake clans in Africa, Cyprus, and Italy.⁵ The Small Bird subclan of the Omahas, though ordinarily they are forbidden to eat small birds, in sickness may eat prairie chickens.⁶ The Samoan clan whose totem was the ends of leaves and of other things, though in ordinary life they might not use them, were allowed and even required to fan a sick clansman with the ends of cocoa-nut leaflets.⁷ Members of the Sea-Weed clan in Samoa, when they went to fight at sea, took with them some sea-weed, which they threw into the sea to hinder the flight of the enemy; if the enemy tried to pick it up it sank, but rose again when any of the Sea-Weed clan paddled up to it.⁸ This resembles the common incident in folk tales of magic obstacles thrown out by fugitives to stay pursuit.

Totem gives omens to his people.

Again, the totem gives his clansmen important information by means of omens. In the Coast Murring tribe of New South Wales each man's totem warned him of coming danger; if his totem was a kangaroo, a kangaroo would warn him against his foes.⁹ The Kurnai in Victoria reverence

---

¹ Dalton, *Eth. of Ben.*, p. 214. For the Sonthal (Santal) totems see *As. Quart. Rev.*, July 1886, p. 76. For other oaths bearing strong impress of a totem origin (swearing on a bear's skin, a lizard's skin, earth of an ant hill, etc.) see Dalton, *op. cit.*, pp. 38, 158, 294.
² Strabo, xiii. 1, 14. In Madagascar a god of healing was also, like Aescula-pius, a god of serpents; his attendants carried living serpents in their hands (*Folk-Lore Rec.*, ii. 20).
³ James, *Expedition to the Rocky Mountains*, i. p. 247.
⁴ *Revue d'Ethnographie*, iii. p. 396.
⁵ Pliny, *N. H.*, xxviii. 30.
⁶ *Third Rep.*, 238.
⁷ Turner, *Samoa*, 70. ⁸ *Ib.*, p. 71.
⁹ *J. A. I.*, xiii. 195 *n.*, xvi. 46.

the crow as one of their ancestors, and think that it watches over them and answers their questions by cawing.[1] The Samoan totems gave omens to their clansmen. Thus, if an owl flew before the Owl clan, as they marched to war, it was a signal to go on; but if it flew across their path, or backwards, it was a sign to retreat.[2] Some kept a tame owl on purpose to give omens in war.[3] The appearance of the totem in or about the house was by some clans regarded as an omen of death; the totem had come to fetch his kinsman. This was the case with land-crabs and eels.[4]

When the conduct of the totem is not all that his clansmen could desire, they have various ways of putting pressure on him. In harvest time, when the birds eat the corn, the Small Bird clan of the Omahas take some corn which they chew and spit over the field. This is thought to keep the birds from the crops.[5] If worms infest the corn the Reptile clan of the Omahas catch some of them and pound them up with some grains of corn which have been heated. They make a soup of the mixture and eat it, believing that the corn will not be infested again, at least for that year.[6] During a fog the men of the Turtle subclan of the Omahas used to draw the figure of a turtle on the ground with its face to the south. On the head, tail, middle of the back, and on each leg were placed small pieces of a red breech-cloth with some tobacco. This was thought to make the fog disappear.[7] Another Omaha clan, who are

Compulsion applied to totem.

[1] *J. A. I.*, xv. p. 415.
[2] Turner, *Samoa*, 21, 24, 60.
[3] *Ib.*, 25 *sq.* Other omens were drawn from the rainbow (*ib.*, 21, 35), shooting star (21), species of fish (27), clouds (27), cuttle-fish (29), herons (35), a creeper-bird (38), lizards (44, 47), a species of bird (48), kingfishers (48, 54), dogs (49), bats (51), shark's teeth (55), lightning (59 *sq.*), rail bird (61, 65), the bird called porphyris Samoensis (64), eels (66), and centipedes (69).
[4] Turner, *ib.*, 66, 72.
[5] *Third Report*, p. 238 *sq.* The idea perhaps is that the birds eat in the persons of their clansmen, and give tangible evidence that they have eaten their fill. But *cf.* Riedel, *op. cit.*, p. 327.

[6] *Third Rep.*, 248. With this custom compare a Syrian superstition. When caterpillars invaded a vineyard or field the virgins were gathered and one of the caterpillars was taken and a girl made its mother. Then they bewailed and buried it. Thereafter they conducted the "mother" to the place where the caterpillars were, consoling her, in order that all the caterpillars might leave the garden (Lagarde, *Reliquiæ juris Ecclesiastici Antiquissimæ*, p. 135). *Cf. Zeitschrift für Ethnologie*, xv. p. 93; *The People of Turkey*, by a Consul's daughter and wife, ii. p. 247.
[7] *Third Rep.*, 240.

described as Wind people, "flap their blankets to start a breeze which will drive off the mosquitoes."[1]

Inanimate objects as totems.
It is more difficult to realise the relation between a man and his totem when that totem is an inanimate object. But such totems are rare.

In Australia we find: thunder (Encounter Bay tribe, S. Australia) (*Nat. Tr. S. Aust.*, 186), rain (Dieri, S. Australia) (*J. A. I.*, xii. 33 *n.*), the star *a* Aquilae or Fomalhaut (Mukjarawaint, W. Victoria) (*id.*, xii. 33 *n.*, xiii. 193 *n.*), hot wind and sun (Wotjoballuk, N.W. Victoria) (*id.*, xvi. 31 *n.*; *Report of the Smithsonian Institution for 1883*, p. 818), honey (Kamilaroi, N.S. Wales) (*J. A. I.*, xii. 500), and clear water (Kuin-Murbura, Queensland) (*id.*, xiii. 344). Floodwater and lightning are names of what Messrs. Fison and Howitt call the two primary classes of the Kiabara tribe in Queensland (*id.*, xiii. 336). As we shall see, they probably are or were totems. In America we find ice (Punka totem) (Morgan, *A. S.*, 155), thunder (Omaha, Kaw, Winnebago, Potawattamie, Sauk and Foxes) (*ib.*, 155, 156, 157, 167, 170), earth (Kaw) (*ib.*, 156), water (Minnitaree, Miami, Moqui) (*ib.*, 159, 168; Bourke, *Snake Dance of the Moquis of Arizona*, 50, 117, 335), wind (Creek) (Morgan, *op. cit.*, 161; Adair, *Hist. Amer. Indians*, p. 15; Gatschet, *Migration Legend of the Creek Indians*, i. p. 155), salt (Creek) (Morgan, *loc. cit.*; Gatschet, *op. cit.*, i. 156), sun (Miami, Moqui) (Morgan, *op. cit.*, 168; Bourke, *op. cit.*, 50, 117, 335 *sq.*), snow (Miami) (Morgan, *loc. cit.*; *cf.* below, p. 36), bone (Sauk and Foxes) (*ib.*, 170), sea (Sauk and Foxes) (*ib.*, 170), sand (Moqui) (*ib.*, 179; Bourke, *op. cit.*, 335), and rain (Moqui) (Morgan, *op. cit.*, 179). In Africa sun and rain are Damara totems (Andersson, *Lake Ngami*, p. 221). In India one of the constellations is a Santal (Sonthal) totem (*As. Quart. Rev.*, July 1886, p. 76); and the foam of the river is an Oraon totem and not to be eaten by the clansmen (Dalton in *Tr. Ethnol. Soc.*, N. S., vi. 36). In Samoa we have the rainbow, shooting star, cloud, moon, and lightning (Turner, *Samoa*, 21, 27, 35, 53, 59, 67).

In a few cases colours are totems: thus red is an Omaha totem (Morgan, *A. S.*, p. 155), red paint and blue

[1] *Third Rep.*, 241.

are Cherokee totems (*ib.*, 164), and vermilion is the name of a subdivision of the Delawares (*ib.*, 172; however, the nature of these subdivisions of the three Delaware clans is not clear). This perhaps explains the aversion which some tribes exhibit for certain colours. Thus red was forbidden in one district of Mangaia (in the South Pacific) because it was thought offensive to the gods (Gill, *Myths and Songs of the South Pacific*, p. 29). Light yellow is a detestable colour to a Hervey islander (*ib.*, 227). The Yezidis abominate blue (Layard, *Nineveh*, i. p. 300).

It is remarkable how small a part is played in totemism by the heavenly bodies. In the lists of totems before us, the sun occurs once in Australia, once in Africa, and several times in America (besides Morgan and Bourke as above, *cf.* M'Lennan in *Fortn. Rev.*, October 1869, p. 413). The sun was the special divinity of the chiefs of the Natchez, but that it was a totem is not certain; *cf.* Lafitau, *Mœurs des Sauvages Ameriquains*, i. 168; Charlevoix, *Hist. de la Nouvelle France*, vi. 177 *sq.*; *Lett. Édif.*, vii. 9 *sq.*; Chateaubriand, *Voyage en Amerique*, 227 *sq.*, ed. 12mo, Michel Lévy; C. C. Jones, *Antiquities of the Southern Indians*, p. 23); but a star or constellation appears only twice, and the moon appears, with a doubtful exception in America (S. Hearne, *Journey from Prince of Wales Fort in Hudson's Bay to the Northern Ocean*, p. 148; it may have been an individual totem), only in Samoa.

The heavenly bodies as totems.

With regard to artificial totems, we are told generally that Bengal totems include artificial objects (*As. Quart. Rev.*, July 1886, p. 75), and net is given as a Kurmi totem (*ib.*, 77). In America, tent is a totem of the Kaws (Morgan, *A. S.*, 156); ball of the Onondaga Iroquois (*ib.*, 91);[1] good knife of the Mandans (*ib.*, 158); and knife, lodge, and bonnet of the Minnitarees (*ib.*, 159). Schoolcraft gives cord as a Huron (Wyandot) totem, but it is not included in Morgan and Powell's lists of Huron totems (Schoolcraft, *Ind. Tr.*, iv. 204; Morgan, *op. cit.*, 153; *First Rep. Bur. Ethnol.*, p. 59).

Artificial objects as totems.

In order, apparently, to put himself more fully under

---

[1] But according to Mr. Beauchamp (*American Antiquarian*, viii. p. 85) no such totem existed, and the mention of it is due to a misunderstanding.

26   TOTEMISM

Assimilation of men to their totems.
the protection of the totem, the clansman is in the habit of assimilating himself to the totem by dressing in the skin or other part of the totem animal, arranging his hair and mutilating his body so as to resemble the totem, and representing the totem on his body by cicatrices, tattooing, or paint. The mental state thus revealed is illustrated by the belief held by many North American Indians that they have each an animal (bison, calf, tortoise, frog, bird, etc.) in their bodies.[1]

Dressing in the skin or feathers of the totem.
In going to battle the Minnitarees dress in wolf skins; the skin with the tail attached hangs down the back, the man's head is inserted in a hole in the skin, and the wolf's head hangs down on his breast.[2] Lewis and Clarke saw a Teton Indian wearing two or three raven skins fixed to the back of the girdle, with the tails sticking out behind; on his head he wore a raven skin split into two parts and tied so as to let the beak project from the forehead.[3] Amongst the Thlinkets on solemn occasions, such as dances, memorial festivals, and burials, individuals often appear disguised in the full form of their totem animals; and, as a rule, each clansman carries at least an easily recognisable part of his totem with him.[4] Condor clans in Peru, who believed themselves descended from the condor, adorned themselves with the feathers of the bird.[5]

The hair dressed in imitation of the totem.
The Iowa clans have each a distinguishing mode of dressing the hair, e.g. the Buffalo clan wear two locks of hair in imitation of horns. These modes of dressing the hair, however, are confined to male children, who, as soon as they are grown, shave off all the hair except the scalp-lock, with a fringe of hair surrounding it.[6] Amongst the Omahas, the smaller boys of the Black Shoulder (Buffalo) clan wear two locks of hair in imitation of horns.[7] The Hanga clan of the Omahas (also a Buffalo clan) wear a crest of hair about two

---

[1] Maximilian, Prinz zu Wied, *Reise in das innere Nord-Amerika*, ii. pp. 190, 270.
[2] *Ib.*, ii. 224. The Minnitarees regard the wolf as especially strong "medicine" (*ib.*). This is the spirit, if not the letter, of totemism.
[3] Lewis and Clarke, *Travels to the Source of the Missouri River*, i. p. 123, London, 1815.
[4] Holmberg, in *Acta Soc. Scient. Fennicæ*, iv. 293 *sq.*, 328; Petroff, *Report on the Population, Industries, and Resources of Alaska*, p. 166.
[5] J. G. Müller, *Gesch. d. americanischen Urreligionen*, p. 327.
[6] Schoolcraft, *Ind. Tr.*, iii. 269.
[7] *Third Rep.*, 229.

inches long, standing erect and extending from ear to ear; this is in imitation of the back of a buffalo.¹ The Small Bird clan of the Omahas "leave a little hair in front, over the forehead, for a bill, and some at the back of the head, for the bird's tail, with much over each ear for the wings."² The Turtle subclan of the Omahas "cut off all the hair from a boy's head, except six locks; two are left on each side, one over the forehead, and one hanging down the back in imitation of the legs, head, and tail of a turtle."³ Amongst the Manganja in Eastern Africa "one trains his locks till they take the admired form of the buffalo's horns; others prefer to let their hair hang in a thick coil down their backs, like that animal's tail."⁴

The practice of knocking out the upper front teeth at puberty, which prevails in Australia and elsewhere, is, or was once, probably an imitation of the totem. The Batoka in Africa who adopt this practice say that they do so in order to be like oxen, while those who retain their teeth are like zebras.⁵ The Manganja chip their teeth to resemble those of the cat or crocodile.⁶ It is remarkable that among some Australian tribes who knock out one or two of the upper front teeth of boys, the most prized ornaments of the women are the two upper front teeth of the kangaroo or wallaby; those are tied together at the roots so as to form a V, and are worn in a necklace or hung amongst the hair.⁷ In other cases it is the boys' teeth which the women wear round their necks.⁸ *Teeth knocked out or chipped, perhaps in imitation of the totem.*

The bone, reed, or stick which some Australian tribes thrust through their nose may be also an imitation of the totem. It is not worn constantly, but is inserted when danger is apprehended; which perhaps means that the man then seeks most to assimilate himself to his totem when he *Nose-stick perhaps an imitation of the totem.*

---

¹ *Third Rep.*, 235.
² *Ib.*, 238.   ³ *Ib.*, 240.
⁴ Livingstone, *Zambesi*, p. 114. But it does not appear whether this people have totems or not.
⁵ Livingstone, *South Africa*, p. 532.
⁶ *Id.*, *Zambesi*, p. 115. On the general custom of filing the teeth among savages see *Zeitschrift für Ethnologie*, xiv. p. 213 *sq.*

⁷ *Tr. Ethnol. Soc.*, New Series, i. p. 287 *sq.*; *Jour. and Proc. R. Soc. N.S. Wales*, xvii. (1883) p. 26; *cf.* G. F. Angas, *Savage Life and Scenes in Austr. and New Zeal.*, i. pp. 92, 98; Eyre, *Jour.*, ii. p. 342.
⁸ Collins, *Account of the English Colony of N.S. Wales*, London, 1798, p. 581.

most needs the totem's protection.[1] Kurnai medicine-men could only communicate with the ghosts when they had these bones in their noses.[2]

<small>Totems tattooed on the bodies of the people.</small> The Haidas of Queen Charlotte Islands are universally tattooed, the design being in all cases the totem, executed in a conventional style. When several families of different totems live together in the same large house, a Haida chief will have all their totems tattooed on his person.[3] The Iroquois tattooed their totems on their persons.[4] Mr. E. James, a high authority on the North American Indians, denies that it was a universal—from which we infer that it was a common—practice with them to have their totems tattooed on their persons.[5] Mackenzie says that the Ojibways (Chippeways) are tattooed on their cheeks or forehead "to distinguish the tribe to which they belong."[6] The Assinibois (Assiniboëls) tattooed figures of serpents, birds, etc. (probably their totems) on their persons.[7] Tribes in South America are especially distinguished by their tattoo marks, but whether these are totem marks is not said.[8] The same applies to the natives of Yule Island,[9] Eskimos of Alaska,[10] and Manganjas in Africa.[11] In one of the Hervey Islands (South Pacific) the tattooing was an imitation of the stripes on two different species of fish, probably totems.[12] The Australians do not tattoo but raise cicatrices; in some tribes these cicatrices are arranged in patterns which serve as the tribal badges, consisting of lines,

---

[1] T. L. Mitchell, *Three Expeditions into the Interior of New South Wales*, ii. p. 339.
[2] Fison and Howitt, *Kamilaroi and Kurnai*, p. 253.
[3] *Geolog. Surv. of Canada, Rep. for 1878-79*, pp. 108B, 135B; *Smithsonian Contrib. to Knowl.*, vol. xxi. No. 267, p. 3 *sq.*; *Nature*, 20th January 1887, p. 285; *Fourth Annual Report of the Bureau of Ethnology*, Washington, 1886, p. 67 *sq.* How different the conventional representation in tattooing may be from the true, we learn from the Hindu tattoo marks (conventionally supposed to represent ducks, geese, peacocks, etc.) depicted by Major-General A. Cunningham in his work, *The Stûpa of Bharut*, plate lii.
[4] E. de Schweinitz, *Life and Times of David Zeisberger*, p. 78.
[5] James, in *Narrative of the Captivity and Adventures of John Tanner*, p. 315.
[6] A. Mackenzie, *Voyages through the Continent of North America*, p. cxx.
[7] *Lettr. Édif.*, vi. 32.
[8] Martius, *Zur Ethnographie America's zumal Brasiliens*, p. 55.
[9] D'Albertis, *New Guinea*, i. p. 419.
[10] Bancroft, *Native Races of the Pacific States*, i. 48.
[11] Livingstone, *Last Journals*, i. p. 110, *cf.* p. 125.
[12] Gill, *Myths and Songs of the S. Pacific*, p. 95.

TOTEMISM

dots, circles, semicircles, etc.¹ According to one authority, these Australian tribal badges are sometimes representations of the totem.² For the cases in which the women alone tattoo see the note below.³

Again, the totem is sometimes painted on the person of the clansman. This, as we have seen (p. 9), is sometimes done by the Indians of British Columbia. Among the Hurons (Wyandots) each clan has a distinctive mode of painting the face, and, at least in the case of the chiefs at installation, this painting represents the totem.⁴ Among the Moquis the representatives of the clans at foot-races, dances, etc., have each a conventional representation of his totem blazoned on breast or back.⁵ A Pawnee, whose totem was a buffalo head, is depicted by Catlin with a buffalo's head clearly painted on his face and breast.⁶ *[Totems painted on the bodies of the people.]*

The clansman also affixes his totem mark as a signature to treaties and other documents,⁷ and paints or carves it on his weapons, hut, canoe, etc. *[Totems painted or carved on weapons, huts, canoes, etc.]*

Thus the natives of the upper Darling carve their totems on their shields.⁸ The Indians who accompanied Samuel

---

¹ Brough Smyth, *Aborigines of Victoria*, i. pp. xli *sq.*, 295, ii. 313; Eyre, *Journ.*, ii. 333, 335; Ridley, *Kamilaroi*, p. 140; *Journ. and Proceed. R. Soc. N.S. Wales*, 1882, p. 201.

² Mr. Chatfield, in Fison and Howitt, *Kamilaroi and Kurnai*, p. 66 *n.* On tattooing in connection with totemism see Haberlandt, in *Mittheil. der anthrop. Gesell. in Wien*, xv. (1885) p. [53] *sq.*

³ Among most of the Californian tribes, the Ainos of Japan, the Chukchi in Siberia, and many of the aborigines of India, it is the women alone who are tattooed. See S. Powers, *Tribes of California*, p. 109; Siebold, *Ethnol. Stud. ueber die Ainos*, p. 15; Scheube, *Die Ainos*, p. 6; Nordenskiöld, *Voyage of the Vega*, p. 296, popular edition; Dalton, *Ethnol. of Bengal*, pp. 114, 157, 161, 219, 251. (Among the Nagas of Upper Assam the men tattoo. Dalton, *op. cit.*, p. 39 *sq.*) Old pioneers in California are of opinion that the reason why the women alone tattoo is that in case they are taken captive they may be recognised by their own people when opportunity serves. This idea, Mr. Powers says, is borne out by the fact that "the California Indians are rent into such infinitesimal divisions, any one of which may be arrayed in deadly feud against another at any moment, that the slight differences in their dialects would not suffice to distinguish the captive squaws" (Powers, *Tr. of Calif.*, p. 109). There may therefore be a grain of truth in the explanation of tattooing given by the Khyen women in Bengal; they say that it was meant to conceal their beauty, for which they were apt to be carried off by neighbouring tribes (*Asiatick Researches*, xvi. p. 268; Dalton, *op. cit.*, p. 114).

⁴ *First Rep.*, pp. 62, 64.
⁵ Bourke, *Snake Dance*, p. 229.
⁶ Catlin, *N. Amer. Ind.*, ii. plate 140.
⁷ Heckewelder, *Indian Nations*, p. 247.
⁸ Brough Smyth, *Aborigines of Victoria*, i. pp. xlii, 284.

Totems painted or carved on weapons, huts, canoes, etc.

Hearne on his journey from Hudson's Bay to the Pacific painted their totems (sun, moon, and diverse birds and beasts of prey) on their shields before going into battle.[1] Some Indian tribes going to war carry standards, consisting of representations of their totems drawn on pieces of bark, which are elevated on poles.[2] Among the Thlinkets shields, helmets, canoes, blankets, household furniture, and houses are all marked with the totem, painted or carved. In single combats between chosen champions of different Thlinket clans, each wears a helmet representing his totem.[3] In front of the houses of the chiefs and leading men of the Haidas are erected posts carved with the totems of the inmates. As the houses sometimes contain several families of different totems, the post often exhibits a number of totems, carved one above the other.[4] Or these carvings one above the other represent the paternal totems in the female line, which, descent being in the female line, necessarily change from generation to generation.[5] The coast Indians of British Columbia carve their totems on the beams which support the roofs of their lodges, paint them over the entrance, and paint or carve them on their paddles and canoes.[6] The Pawnees mark their huts and even articles of apparel with their totems.[7] The Delawares (Lenape) painted their totems on their houses. The Turtle clan painted a whole turtle; but the Turkey clan painted only a foot of a turkey; and the Wolf clan only one foot of a wolf, though they sometimes added an outline of the whole animal.[8] In the Ottawa villages the different clans had separate wards, at the gates of which were posts bearing the figure of the clan totem or

---

[1] S. Hearne, *Journey to the Northern Ocean*, p. 148 *sq.* These, however, may have been individual totems. Some of the Indians had many such figures on their shields.

[2] Chateaubriand, *Voy. en. Amér.*, pp. 194, 199, 224; Charlevoix, *Hist. de la Nouv. Fr.*, v. p. 329.

[3] Holmberg, in *Acta Soc. Sc. Fennicae*, iv. 294, 323; Aurel Krause, *Die Tlinkit-Indianer*, p. 130 *sq.*; Petroff, *Report on Alaska*, pp. 166, 170.

[4] *Smithsonian Contrib. to Knowl.*, xxi. No. 267, p. 3 *sq.*; *Geol. Surv. of Canada, Rep. for 1878-79*, p. 148B; *Ausland*, October 6, 1884, p. 794; *id.*, 7 September 1885, p. 701. Totemposts, 50 to 100 feet high, in front of nearly every Thlinket house (Petroff, *Report on Alaska*, p. 165; Krause, *l.c.*; Sheldon Jackson, *Alaska*, p. 78).

[5] *American Antiquarian*, ii. p. 110; Sheldon Jackson, *Alaska*, p. 81.

[6] Mayne, *Brit. Columb.*, p. 257 *sq.*

[7] *Magazine of American History*, iv. p. 260.

[8] Heckewelder, *op. cit.*, p. 247; Brinton, *The Lenape and their Legends*, pp. 39 *sq.*, 68 *sq.*

of parts of it.¹ The Omaha clans paint their totems on their tents.² Amongst the Iroquois the totem sign over each wigwam consisted, at least in some cases, of the skin of the totem animal, as of a beaver, a deer, a bear.³ Sometimes the skin is stuffed and stuck on a pole before the door.⁴ Lastly, the totem is painted or carved on the clansman's tomb or grave-post, the figure being sometimes reversed to denote death. It is always the Indian's totem name, not his personal name, which is thus recorded.⁵ Sometimes the stuffed skin of the totem is hung over the grave, or is placed at the dead man's side.⁶

The identification of a man with his totem appears further to have been the object of various ceremonies observed at birth, marriage, death, and other occasions.

Birth Ceremonies.—On the fifth day after birth a child of the Deer-Head clan of the Omahas is painted with red spots on its back, in imitation of a fawn, and red stripes are painted on the child's arms and chest. All the Deer-Head men present at the ceremony make red spots on their chests.⁷ When a South Slavonian woman has given birth to a child, an old woman runs out of the house and calls out, "A she-wolf has littered a he-wolf," and the child is drawn through a wolfskin, as if to simulate actual birth from a wolf. Further, a piece of the eye and heart of a wolf are sewed into the child's shirt, or hung round its neck; and if several children of the family have died before, it is called Wolf. The reason assigned for some of these customs is, that the witches who devour children will not attack a wolf.⁸ In other words, the human child is disguised as a wolf to cheat its supernatural foes. The same desire for protection against supernatural danger may be the motive of similar totemic customs, if not of totemism in general. The legend of the birth of Zamolxis

Totemic birth ceremonies.

---

¹ *Acad.*, Sept. 27, 1884, p. 203.
² *Third Rep.*, 229, 240, 248.
³ *Second Rep.*, p. 78.
⁴ R. I. Dodge, *Our Wild Indians* (Hartford, Conn., 1882), p. 225.
⁵ Schoolcraft, *Ind. Tr.*, i. p. 356 *sq.*, ii. 49, v. 73; A. Mackenzie, *Voyages*, etc., pp. xcix, 316; J. Dunn, *Hist. of the Oregon Territory*, p. 94; Mayne, *Br. Columb.*, pp. 258, 271; A. Krause, *Die Tlinkit-Indianer*, p. 230; *American Antiquarian*, ii. p. 112. It has been conjectured that the animal-shaped mounds in the Mississippi valley (chiefly in the State of Wisconsin) are representations of totems (*American Antiquarian*, iii. p. 7 *sq.*; vi. pp. 8, 326 *sq.*).
⁶ Dodge, *op. cit.*, pp. 158, 225.
⁷ *Third Rep.*, p. 245 *sq.*
⁸ Krauss, *Sitte und Brauch der Südslaven*, p. 541 *sq.*

(it is said that he was so called because a bearskin was thrown over him at birth[1]) points to a custom of wrapping infants at birth in a bearskin, and this again perhaps to a bear totem. The belief of the Getae that their dead went to Zamolxis would thus be the totemic view that the dead clansman is changed into his totem. When a Hindu child's horoscope portends misfortune or crime, he is born again from a cow, thus: being dressed in scarlet and tied on a new sieve, he is passed between the hind legs of a cow forward through the fore legs to the mouth and again in the reverse direction, to simulate birth; the ordinary birth ceremonies (aspersion, etc.) are then gone through, and the father smells his son as a cow smells her calf.[2] In India grown persons also may be born again by passing through a golden cow in simulation of birth; this is done when, *e.g.*, they have polluted themselves by contact with unbelievers.[3]

Totemic marriage ceremonies.

Marriage Ceremonies.—Among the Kalang of Java, whose totem is the red dog, bride and bridegroom before marriage are rubbed with the ashes of a red dog's bones.[4] Among the Transylvanian gypsies, bride and bridegroom are rubbed with a weasel skin.[5] The sacred goatskin (*aegis*) which the priestess of Athene took to newly married women may have been used for this purpose.[6] At Rome bride and bridegroom sat down on the skin of the sheep which had been sacrificed on the occasion.[7] An Italian bride smeared the doorposts of her new home with wolf's fat.[8] It is difficult to separate from totemism the custom observed by totem clans in Bengal of marrying the bride and bridegroom to trees before they are married to each other. The bride touches with red lead (a common

---

[1] Porphyry, *Vit. Pythag.*, 14. On the etymology of Zamolxis and the possible identity of —olxis with the Greek ἄρκτος, Latin *ursus*, "a bear," see V. Hehn, *Kulturpflanzen und Hausthiere*, p. 450.

[2] *Jour. Asiat. Soc. Beng.*, liii. (1884) pt. i. p. 101.

[3] *Asiatick Researches*, vi. p. 535 *sq.*; Liebrecht, *Gervasius von Tilbury*, p. 171; *id.*, *Zur Volkskunde*, p. 397. For an Ojibway birth ceremony *cf.* P. Jones, *Hist. of Ojebway Indians*, p. 160, *cf.* p. 138.

[4] Raffles, *Hist. of Java*, i. 328. On rubbing with ashes as a religious ceremony *cf.* Spencer, *De legibus Hebraeorum ritualibus*, vol. ii. Diss. iii. Lib. iii. cap. 1.

[5] *Original-Mittheil. aus der ethnolog. Abtheil. der Königl. Museen zu Berlin*, i. p. 156.

[6] Suidas, *s.v.* αἰγίς.

[7] Servius on Virgil, *Aen.*, iv. 374; Festus, *s.v. In pelle*.

[8] Pliny, *Nat. Hist.*, xxviii. 142.

marriage ceremony) a mahwá tree, clasps it in her arms, and is tied to it. The bridegroom goes through a like ceremony with a mango tree.[1]

Traces of marriage to trees are preserved in Servia. The bride is led to an apple-tree (apples often appear in South Slavonian marriage customs) under which stands a pitcher full of water. Money is thrown into the pitcher; the bride's veil is taken from her and fastened to the tree; she upsets the pitcher of water with her foot; and a dance three times round the tree concludes the ceremony.[2] Tree marriage appears very distinctly in the Greek festival of the Daedala, at which an oak-tree, selected by special divination, was cut down, dressed as a bride, and conveyed, like a bride, in solemn procession on a waggon with a bridesmaid beside it. The mythical origin of the festival was a mock marriage of Zeus to an oak.[3] The identification with a tree, implied in these marriage ceremonies, is illustrated by a Ricara custom. Ricara Indians used to make a hole in the skin of their neck, pass a string through it, and tie the other end to the trunk of an oak-tree; by remaining tied in this fashion for some time, they thought they became strong and brave like the tree.[4]

Marriage to trees.

The idea of substitution or disguise, which seems to be at the root of these marriage (as of the birth) ceremonies, appears in some Hindu marriages. Thus when a man has lost several wives in succession, he must marry a bird with all ceremony before another family will give him their

Marriage to birds, plants, earthen vessels, etc.

---

[1] Dalton, *Ethn. of Bengal*, p. 194 (Mundas), p. 319 (Kurmis). Among the Mundas both bride and bridegroom are sometimes married to mango trees. For Kurmi totems see *As. Quart. Rev.*, July 1886, p. 77.

[2] Krauss, *Südsl.*, p. 450. With regard to upsetting the pitcher, it is to be noted that water is an important element in marriage ceremonies, *e.g.* among the same Mundas who are married to trees, a pitcher of water is poured over both bride and bridegroom (Dalton, *op. cit.*, 194). Two cabbages, one from the garden of the bride and another from that of the bridegroom, play a very important part in rural weddings in Lorraine (George Sand, *La Mare au Diable*, Appendix v.; *Folk-Lore Rec.*, iii. p. 271 *sq.*).

[3] Pausanias, ix. 3; Eusebius, *Praep. Evang.*, iii. 1 and 2. The oak was especially associated with Zeus. See Bötticher, *Der Baumkultus der Hellenen*, p. 408 *sq.* The oak of Zeus (like a totem) gave omens to its worshippers; and the ceremony of making rain by means of an oak branch (Paus., viii. 38) is remarkably like ceremonies observed for the purpose of making rain by the sacred Buffalo society among the Omahas (*Third Rep.*, p. 347) and by a set of worshippers in totem-ridden Samoa (Turner, *Samoa*, p. 45).

[4] Lewis and Clarke, i. p. 155, 8vo, 1815.

daughter to wife.¹ Or wishing to marry a third wife, whether his other wives are alive or not, he must first formally wed a plant of a particular kind.² When the planets threaten any one with misfortune in marriage, he or she is married to an earthen vessel.³ Dancing girls of Goa are married to daggers before they may exercise their profession.⁴ Courtesans born of courtesans are married to flowering plants, which are planted in the house for the purpose; they water and tend the plants, and observe mourning for them when they die.⁵

Some cases of marriage of human beings to inanimate objects seem to be unconnected with totemism.⁶ A totemic marriage ceremony of a different kind is that observed by a Tiger clan of the Gonds, in which two men imitate tigers by tearing to pieces a living kid with their teeth.⁷

Death Ceremonies.—In death, too, the clansman seeks to become one with his totem. Amongst some totem clans it is an article of faith that as the clan sprang from the totem, so each clansman at death reassumes the totem form. Thus the Moquis, believing that the ancestors of the clans were

[Marginal note: Totemic death ceremonies.]

---

¹ *Indian Antiquary*, x. p. 333.
² *Ind. Antiq.*, iv. p. 5; *Jour. Asiat. Soc. Bengal*, liii. pt. i. p. 99 *sq.*
³ *J. A. S. Beng.*, liii. i. p. 100.
⁴ *Ind. Antiq.*, xiii. p. 168 *sq.*
⁵ *Ind. Antiq.*, ix. p. 77. We are reminded of the Gardens of Adonis. See W. Mannhardt, *Antike Wald- und Feldkulte*, p. 279 *sq.*
⁶ Thus in Java the man who taps a palm for palm wine goes through a form of marriage with the tree before he begins to tap it (Wilken, in *De Indische Gids*, June 1884, p. 963, *cf.* 962). The Hurons annually married their fishing nets, with great ceremony, to two young girls (*Relations des Jésuites*, 1636, p. 109; *ib.*, 1639, p. 95; Charlevoix, *Hist. de la Nouv. Fr.*, v. p. 225; Chateaubriand, *Voy. en Amer.*, p. 140 *sq.*; Parkman, *Jesuites of North America*, p. lxix.). The old Egyptian custom, in time of drought, of dressing a woman as a bride and throwing her into the Nile is the subject of Ebers's novel *Nilbraut*, noticed in the *Athenæum*, July 2, 1887, p. 12.

The custom seems to be the foundation of legends like those of Andromeda and Hesione. For a Norse Andromeda see Asbjörnsen og Moe, *Norske Folke-Eventyr* (First Series), No. 24 (Dasent's *Tales from the Norse*, p. 125 *sq.*). The custom shadowed forth in these legends may be only another form of the Egyptian customs referred to by Pindar (in Strabo, xvii. 1, 19—the full passage is omitted in some MSS. and editions; *cf.* Aelian, *Nat. An.*, vii. 19; Herodotus, ii. 46; Plutarch, *Brut. Rat. Uti*, 5; Clemens Alex., *Protr.*, 32; and of which a trace appears in Italy (Ovid, *Fast.*, ii. 441). This would bring us round to totemism. It is therefore notable that the Andromeda story occurs in Senegambia, where totemism exists. See Bérenger-Feraud, *Contes populaires de la Senegambia*, p. 185 *sq.* The Mandan custom (Catlin, *O-Kee-pa*, Fol. reserv. ii.) is hardly parallel, though Liebrecht (*Zur Volkskunde*, p. 395) seems to think so.
⁷ Dalton, *op. cit.*, p. 280.

respectively rattlesnakes, deer, bears, sand, water, tobacco, etc., think that at death each man, according to his clan, is changed into a rattlesnake, a deer, etc.[1] Amongst the Black Shoulder (Buffalo) clan of the Omahas a dying clansman was wrapped in a buffalo robe with the hair out, his face was painted with the clan mark, and his friends addressed him thus: "You are going to the animals (the buffaloes). You are going to rejoin your ancestors. You are going, or your four souls are going, to the four winds. Be strong."[2] Amongst the Hanga clan, another Buffalo clan of the Omahas, the ceremony was similar, and the dying man was thus addressed: "You came hither from the animals, and you are going back thither. Do not face this way again. When you go, continue walking."[3]

Members of the Elk clan among the Omahas, though in life they may not touch any part of a male elk nor taste of a male deer, are buried in moccasins of deer skin.[4] Egyptian queens were sometimes buried in cow-shaped sarcophaguses.[5] Among the Australian Wotjoballuk, men of the Hot-Wind totem are buried with the head in the direction from which the hot wind blows, and men of the Sun totem are buried with their heads towards the sunrise.[6] Among the Marias, a Gond clan whose name is thought to be derived from Mara, "a tree," the corpse of an adult male is fastened by cords to a mahwa tree in an erect position and then burned.[7] On the anniversary of the death of their kinsmen, the Nataranes in Paraguay carried dead ostriches in procession as representatives of the deceased, probably

Totemic burial ceremonies.

---

[1] Schoolcraft, *Ind. Tr.*, iv. 86.
[2] *Third Rep.*, p. 229. As to the "four souls," many savages are much more liberally provided with souls than civilised men. See *Rel. des Jés.*, 1636, p. 133; Maximilian, Prinz zu Wied, *Nord-Amerika*, ii. 206; Charlevoix, *Hist. de la Nouv. Fr.*, vi. p. 75; Laborde, "Rel. de l'origine, etc., des Caraibes," p. 15, in *Recueil de divers Voyages faits en Afrique et en l'Amerique* (Paris, 1684); Washington Matthews, *The Hidatsa Indians*, p. 50; Macpherson, *Memorials of Service in India*, p. 91 *sq.*; Schoolcraft, *Am.*

Ind., pp. 127, 204; *id.*, *Ind. Tr.*, iv. 70; *Arctic Papers for the Expedition of 1875*, p. 275; Williams, *Fiji*, i. p. 241; Wilken, "Het animisme bij de volken van den indischen archipel," in *Ind. Gids*, June 1884, p. 929 *sq.*; *id.*, *Ueber das Haaropfer*, p. 75 *n.*
[3] *Third Rep.*, p. 233.
[4] *Ib.*, 225.
[5] Lepsius, *Chronologie der Aegypter*, p. 309 *n.*; *cf.* Herodotus, ii. 129; Stephanus Byzant. *s.v.* Βούσιρις.
[6] *J. A. I.*, xvi. p. 31 *n.*
[7] Dalton, *Ethn. of Beng.*, pp. 278, 283.

because the ostrich was the clan totem.¹ Men of the Snow totem among the Pouteoüatmi, contrary to the general custom of the tribe, were burned instead of buried, the belief being that, as snow comes from on high, so the bodies of men of the Snow totem should not be poked away underground, but suffered to rejoin their Snow kindred in the upper air. Once when a man of the Snow totem had been buried underground, the winter was so long and the snow fell so deep that nobody ever thought to see spring any more. Then they bethought them of digging up the corpse and burning it; and lo, the snow stopped falling and spring came with a burst.²

Ceremonies at puberty. *Ceremonies at Puberty.*—The attainment of puberty is celebrated by savages with ceremonies, some of which seem to be directly connected with totemism. The Australian rites of initiation at puberty include the raising of those scars on the persons of the clansmen and clanswomen which serve as tribal badges or actually depict the totem. They also include those mutilations of the person by knocking out teeth, etc., which we have seen reason to suppose are meant to assimilate the man to his totem. When we remember that the fundamental rules of totem society are rules regulating marriage, or rather sexual intercourse, and that these rules are based on distinctions of totem, persons of the same totem being forbidden, under pain of death, to have connection with each other, the propriety of imprinting these marks on the persons of the clansmen and of inculcating these rules on their minds at the very moment when transgression of these all-important rules first becomes possible, is immediately apparent; and the necessity for such marks will further appear when we consider the minute subdivision of savage tribes into local groups, which, at once united and divided by an elaborate code of sexual permissions and prohibitions, are at the same time disjoined by a difference of dialect or even of language, such as, in the absence of some visible symbolism, must have rendered all these permissions and prohibitions inoperative. On this view, a chief object of these initiation ceremonies was to

---

¹ Charlevoix, *Hist. du Paraguay*, i. p. 462.

² *Rel. des Jés.*, 1667, p. 19; *Lettr. Édif.*, vi. 169 *sq*.

teach the youths with whom they might or might not have connection, and to put them in possession of a visible language, consisting of personal marks and (as we shall see immediately) gestures, by means of which they might be able to communicate their totems to, and to ascertain the totems of, strangers whose language they did not understand. So far, the consideration of these ceremonies would fall naturally under the section dealing with the social side of totemism. But as the rules which it is an object of these ceremonies to inculcate are probably deductions from that fundamental and as yet unexplained connection between a man and his totem, which constitutes the religion of totemism, they may fairly be considered here.

That lessons in conduct, especially towards the other sex, form part of these initiatory rites is certain. The youth is charged "to restrict himself to the class (totem division) which his name confines him to.... The secrets of the tribe are imparted to him at this time. These instructions are repeated every evening while the *Bora* ceremony lasts, and form the principal part of it."[1] To supply the youth with a gesture language for the purpose already indicated may be the intention of the totem dances or pantomimes which form part of the initiatory rites. *Lessons in conduct imparted at initiation.*

E.g., at one stage of these rites in Australia a number of men appear on the scene howling and running on all fours in imitation of the dingo or native Australian dog; at last the leader jumps up, clasps his hands, and shouts the totem name "wild dog."[2] The Coast Murring tribe in New South Wales had an initiatory ceremony at which the totem name "brown snake" was shouted, and a medicine-man produced a live brown snake out of his mouth.[3] The totem clans of the Bechuanas have each its special dance or pantomime, and when they wish to ascertain a stranger's *Animal dances or pantomimes at initiation.*

---

[1] *J. A. I.*, xiii. 296, *cf.* 450.
[2] *J. A. I.*, xiii. 450.
[3] *Ib.*, xvi. p. 43. At the initiatory rites of the Phrygian god Sabazius, a snake (or a golden image of one) was drawn through the novice's robe. Arnobius, *Adv. Nat.*, v. 21 ; Firmicus Maternus, *De errore profan. relig.*, 10 ; Clem. Alex., *Protrept.*, § 16. *Cf.* Demosth., p. 313 (*De Corona*, § 260) ; Strab., x. 3, 18. See Foucart, *Des Associations religieuses chez les Grecs*, p. 66 *sq.*

clan, they ask him "What do you dance?"[1] We find elsewhere that dancing has been used as a means of sexual selection. Thus among the Tshimsians, one of the totem tribes on the north-west coast of North America, one of the ceremonies observed by a girl at puberty is a formal dance before all the people.[2] Amongst the Kasias in Bengal, amongst whom husband and wife are always of different clans, Kasia maidens dance at the new moon in March; the young men do not dance but only look on, and many matches are made at these times.[3] On the 15th day of the month Abh the damsels of Jerusalem, clad in white, used to go out and dance in the vineyards, saying, "Look this way, young man, and choose a wife. Look not to the face but rather to the family."[4] Attic maidens between the ages of five and ten had to pretend to be bears; they were called bears, and they imitated the action of bears. No man would marry a girl who had not thus "been a bear."[5]

Animal dances intended to give the novice power over the animals.

The totem dances at initiation are to be distinguished from those animal dances, also practised at initiation, the object of which appears to be to give the novice power over the animals represented. Thus an initiatory ceremony in New South Wales is to present to the novices the effigy of a kangaroo made of grass. "By thus presenting to them the dead kangaroo, it was indicated that the power was about to be imparted to them of killing that animal." The men then tied tails of grass to their girdles and hopped about in imitation of kangaroos, while two others followed

---

[1] Livingstone, *South Africa*, p. 13; J. Mackenzie, *Ten Years North of the Orange River*, p. 391, cf. p. 135 n.; *J. A. I.*, xvi. p. 83.

[2] *Geol. Surv. of Canada, Report for 1878-79*, p. 131B; for the Tshimsian totems, *ib.*, 134B.

[3] *Tr. Eth. Soc.*, New Series, vii. 309; for Kasia exogamy, Dalton, *Ethn. of Beng.*, p. 56.

[4] Mishna, *Taanith*, iv. 8 (Surenhus., ii. p. 385).

[5] Schol. on Aristophanes, *Lysist.* 645; Harpocration, s.v. ἀρκτεῦσαι; Suidas, s.v. ἀρκτεῦσαι and ἄρκτος ἢ βραυρωνίοις; Bekker's *Anecd. Gr.*, p. 206, 4; *ib.* 444, 30. This sacred dance or pantomime was a dedication of the damsels to either the Brauronian or Munychian Artemis; and legend said that a tame bear had been kept in her sanctuary. The Arcadian Artemis, as K. O. Müller says (*Dorier*,[2] i. p. 376), appears to be identical with Callisto; and Callisto was the ancestress of the Arcadians (= Bear people, from ἄρκος, another form of ἄρκτος), was herself turned into a bear, and was represented seated on a bearskin (Paus., x. 31, 10). For an African example see Dapper, *Description de l'Afrique* (Amsterdam, 1686), p. 249.

them with spears and pretended to wound them.¹ An imitation of a wallaby hunt forms another Australian initiatory ceremony.² These hunting dances, or rather pantomimes, at initiation are therefore closely similar to those pantomimes which savage hunters perform before going to the chase, believing that through a sort of sympathetic magic the game will be caught like the actors in the mimic hunt. Thus, before the Koossa Caffres go out hunting one of them takes a handful of grass in his mouth and crawls about on all fours to represent the game, while the rest raise the hunting cry and rush at him with their spears till he falls apparently dead.³ Negroes of Western Equatorial Africa, before setting out to hunt the gorilla, act a gorilla hunt, in which the man who plays the gorilla pretends to be killed.⁴

Before hunting the bear the Dacotas act a bear pantomime, in which a medicine-man dresses entirely in the skin of a bear, and others wear masques consisting of the skin of the bear's head, and all of them imitate bears.⁵ When buffaloes are scarce, the Mandans dance wearing the skins of buffaloes' heads with the horns on their heads.⁶ "Each hunt," says Chateaubriand, "has its dance, which consists in the imitation of the movements, habits, and cries of the animal to be hunted; they climb like a bear, build like a beaver, galop about like a buffalo, leap like a roe, and yelp like a fox."⁷ The Indians of San Juan Capistrano acted similar hunting pantomimes before the stuffed skin of a coyote or of a mountain cat before they set out for the chase.⁸ The ancient Greeks had similar dances for the purpose of catching beasts and birds. Thus a man wearing a headdress or necklace in imitation of a species of owl

Animal dances or pantomimes before hunting.

---

¹ Collins, *Account of the English Colony of New South Wales*, London, 1798, pp. 569, 571; Angas, *Savage Life and Scenes in Australia and New Zealand*, ii. p. 219.
² *J. A. I.*, xiii. p. 449.
³ Lichtenstein, *Travels in S. Afr.*, i. p. 269.
⁴ W. W. Reade, *Savage Africa*, p. 194 *sq.*
⁵ Catlin, *Amer. Indians*, i. p. 245. *Cf.* Schoolcraft, *Ind. Tr.*, iv. 60; the Dacotas "pretend to charm some kinds of animals by mimicking them, and sometimes succeed in killing game in this way."
⁶ Catlin, *op. cit.*, i. 127. *Cf.* Maximilian, Prinz zu Wied, *Nord-Amerika*, ii. p. 263 *sq.*
⁷ Chateaubriand, *Voy. en Amér.*, p. 142 *sq.*
⁸ Bancroft, *Nat. Races of the Pac. St.*, iii. p. 167.

mimicked the bird and was supposed thus to catch it.[1] Such pantomimes, acted in presence of the animal, may be entirely rational, as in the common cases where the savage disguises himself in the animal's skin and is thus enabled either to act as a decoy to the herd[2] or to approach and kill the animal.[3] But these pantomimes, when they are acted before the hunt takes place, are of course purely magical.[4]

Magical ceremonies at initiation.

But in these rites of initiation the religious aspect of totemism is also prominent. In some of the dances this is certainly the case. Thus at their initiatory rites the Yuin tribe in New South Wales mould figures of the totems in earth and dance before them, and a medicine-man brings up out of his inside the "magic" appropriate to the totem before which he stands: before the figure of the porcupine he brings up a stuff like chalk, before the kangaroo a stuff like glass, etc.[5] Again, it is at initiation that the youth is solemnly forbidden to eat of certain foods; but as the list of foods prohibited to youths at puberty both in Australia and America extends far beyond the simple totem, it would seem that we are here in contact with those unknown general ideas of the savage, whereof totemism is only a special product. Thus the Narrinyeri youth at initiation are forbidden to eat twenty different kinds of game, besides any food belonging to women. If they eat of these forbidden foods it is thought they will grow ugly.[6] In the

Food taboos imposed at initiation.

---

[1] Julius Pollux, iv. 103; Aelian, *N. A.*, xv. 28; Athenaeus, 391ab, 629f.

[2] Schoolcraft, *Ind. Tr.*, iv. 93.

[3] *E.g. American Naturalist*, iv. 136 sq.; *American Antiquarian*, viii. 328. Iroquois hunters wore skeleton frameworks of wood over which they threw the skin of whatever animal they wished to imitate. *J. A. I.*, xiv. p. 246.

[4] For other examples of animal dances or pantomimes (some of them apparently merely recreations) see Schoolcraft, *Ind. Tr.*, v. p. 277; Catlin, *Amer. Ind.*, ii. 126, 248; Maximilian, Prinz zu Wied, *Nord-Amerika*, ii. p. 246; S. Powers, *Tr. of Calif.*, p. 199 sq.; Bancroft, *Nat. Races of the Pac. St.*, i. p. 706; *Rep. of Internat. Polar Exped. to Point Barrow, Alaska*, p. 41 sq.; E. James, *Exped. to the Rocky Mountains*, ii. 58; *American Antiquarian*, vii. p. 211; A. R. Wallace, *Travels on the Amazon and Rio Negro*, p. 296 sq.; *Revue d'Ethnographie*, vi. (1887) p. 54; Dalton, *Ethn. of Beng.*, p. 155 sq.; Pallas, *Reise durch verschiedene Theile des russischen Reichs*, iii. p. 64 sq.; Andersson, *Lake Ngami*, p. 230; *Original-Mittheil. aus der ethnolog. Abth. der Königl. Museen zu Berlin*, i. pp. 179 sq., 184; Eyre, *Journals*, ii. p. 233.

[5] *Journ. and Proc. R. Soc. N.S. Wales*, 1882, p. 206.

[6] *Nat. Tribes of S. Austral.*, p. 17.

Mycoolon tribe, near the Gulf of Carpentaria, the youth at initiation is forbidden to eat of eaglehawk and its young, native companion and its young, some snakes, turtles, anteaters, and emu eggs.[1] In New South Wales the young men at initiation are forbidden to kill and eat (1) "any animal that burrows in the ground, for it recalls to mind the foot-holes[2] where the tooth was knocked out, *e.g.* the wombat; (2) such creatures as have very prominent teeth, for these recall the tooth itself; (3) any animal that climbs to the tree tops, for they are then near to Daramŭlŭn,[3] *e.g.* the native bear; (4) any bird that swims, for it recalls the final washing; (5) nor, above all, the emu, for this is Ngalalbal, the wife of Daramŭlŭn, and at the same time 'the woman'; for the novice during his probation is not permitted even so much as to look at a woman or to speak to one; and even, for some time after, he must cover his mouth with his rug when one is present." These rules are relaxed by degrees by an old man giving the youth a portion of the forbidden animal or rubbing him with its fat.[4] The Kurnai youth is not allowed to eat the female of any animal, nor the emu, nor the porcupine. He becomes free by having the fat of the animal smeared on his face.[5] On the other hand, it is said that "initiation confers many privileges on the youths, as they are now allowed to eat many articles of food which were previously forbidden to them."[6] Thus in New South Wales before initiation a boy may eat only the females of the animals which he catches; but after initiation (which, however, may not be complete for several years) he may eat whatever he finds.[7] About the lower Murray boys before initiation are forbidden to eat emu, wild turkey, swan, geese, black duck, and the eggs of these birds; if they infringed this rule, "their hair would become prematurely grey, and the

---

[1] *J. A. I.*, xiii. p. 295.

[2] Amongst these tribes the novice is placed with his feet in a pair of holes preparatory to the knocking out of the tooth (*J. A. I.*, xiii. p. 446 *sq.*; *ib.*, xiv. p. 359; *Journ. and Proc. R. Soc. N.S. Wales*, 1883, p. 26).

[3] *I.e.* the mythical being who is supposed to have instituted these ceremonies (*J. A. I.*, xiii. 442, 446).

[4] *J. A. I.*, xiii. p. 455 *sq.*

[5] *Ib.*, xiv. p. 316.

[6] *Ib.*, 360. So with the Uaupés on the Amazon (A. R. Wallace, *Travels on the Amazon and Rio Negro*, p. 496).

[7] *Journ. and Proc. R. Soc. N.S. Wales*, 1882, p. 208.

muscles of their limbs would waste away and shrink up."[1] The Dieri think that if a native grows grey or has much hair on his breast in youth, it has been caused by his eating iguana in childhood.[2] In North America the Creek youths at puberty were forbidden for twelve months to eat of young bucks, turkey-cocks, fowls, peas, and salt.[3] The Andamanese abstain from various kinds of food, including turtle, honey, and pork, for a year or several years before puberty; and amongst the ceremonies by which they are made free of these foods is the smearing of their bodies by the chief with honey and the melted fat of turtle and pork.[4]

Initiatory ceremonies intended to admit the novices to the life of the clan.

These ceremonies seem also to be meant to admit the youth into the life of the clan, and hence of the totem. The latter appears to be the meaning of a Carib ceremony, in which the father of the youth took a live bird of prey, of a particular species, and beat his son with it till the bird was dead and its head crushed, thus transferring the life and spirit of the martial bird to the future warrior. Further, he scarified his son all over, rubbed the juices of the bird into the wounds, and gave him the bird's heart to eat.[5] Amongst some Australian tribes the youth at initiation is smeared with blood drawn from the arms either of aged men or of all the men present, and he even receives the blood to drink. Amongst some tribes on the Darling this tribal blood is his only food for two days.[6] The meaning

---

[1] *Journ. and Proc. R. Soc. N.S. Wales*, 1883, p. 27.
[2] *Native Tribes of S. Australia*, p. 279.
[3] Gatschet, *Migration Legend of the Creek Indians*, i. p. 185. For superstitious abstinence from salt cf. Adair, *Hist. Amer. Indians*, pp. 59, 115, 125, 166; Acosta, *Hist. of the Indies*, v. 17; Schoolcraft, *Ind. Tr.*, v. p. 268; Du Tertre, *Histoire generale des Antilles*, vol. ii. (Paris, 1667) p. 371; Bancroft, *Nat. Races of the Pac. St.*, i. p. 520 n.; Sievers, *Reise in der Sierra Nevada de Santa Marta*, p. 94; C. Bock, *Headhunters of Borneo*, pp. 218, 223; Plutarch, *Qu. Conviv.*, viii. 8, 2; *id.*, *Is. et Osir.*, 5; A. R. Wallace, *Travels on the Amazon and Rio Negro*, p. 502; *Asiatick Researches*, vii. p. 307; Duff Macdonald, *Africana*, i. pp. 110, 170; Grierson, *Bihar Peasant Life*, p. 405. For an African example of the prohibition of different foods at successive periods of life see Dapper, *Description de l'Afrique*, p. 336.
[4] E. H. Man, *Aboriginal Inhabitants of the Andaman Islands*, p. 62 sq.
[5] Rochefort, *Hist. nat. et mor. des Iles Antilles* (Rotterdam, 1666), p. 556; Du Tertre, *Histoire generale des Antilles*, vol. ii. p. 377.
[6] *J. A. I.*, xiii. 128, 295; G. F. Angas, *Savage Life and Scenes in Austr. and New Zeal.*, i. 115; *Nat. Tribes of S. Austr.*, 162 sq., 227, 232, 234, 270; Brough Smyth, i. 67 sq.; Fison and Howitt, 286. The Australians also draw blood from themselves and give it to their sick relations to drink (*J. A. I.*, xiii. 132 sq.). So

TOTEMISM

of this smearing with blood seems put beyond a doubt by the following custom. Among the Gonds, a non-Aryan race of Central India, the rajas, by intermarriage with Hindus, have lost much of their pure Gond blood, and are half Hindus; hence one of the ceremonies at their installation is "the touching of their foreheads with a drop of blood drawn from the body of a pure aborigine of the tribe they belong to."[1] Further, the Australians seek to convey to the novices the powers and dignity of manhood by means of certain magic passes, while the youths receive the spiritual gift with corresponding gestures.[2] Among some tribes the youths at initiation sleep on the graves of their ancestors, in order to absorb their virtues.[3] It is, however, a very notable fact that the initiation of an Australian youth is said to be conducted, not by men of the same totem, but by men of that portion of the tribe into which he may marry.[4] In some of the Victorian tribes no person related to the youth by blood can interfere or assist in his initiation.[5] Whether this is true of all tribes and of all the rites at initiation does not appear.[6]

Connected with totemism is also the Australian ceremony at initiation of pretending to recall a dead man to life by the utterance of his totem name. An old man lies down in a grave and is covered up lightly with earth; but *Initiatory ceremonies of resurrection and new birth.*

---

do the Hare Indians in America (Petitot, *Monographie des Dènè-Dindjié*, p. 60; *id.*, *Traditions Indiennes du Canada Nord-ouest*, p. 269). Amongst the Guamos on the Orinoco the chief was bound to draw blood from his body wherewith to anoint the stomach of a sick clansman. If sickness was at all prevalent he was thus reduced to great emaciation (Gumilla, *Hist. de l'Orenoque*, i. p. 261). The Chinese sometimes cut pieces out of their flesh and give them to their sick parents to eat (Dennys, *Folk-Lore of China*, p. 68 *sq.*). Amongst some of the Caribs a new-born child was smeared with its father's blood (Rochefort, *op. cit.*, p. 552). In all these cases the idea is that the life of the clan or family is in the blood, and may be transferred with the blood from one member of it to another. For another way of communicating the common life of the clan to a sick member of it, see *Jour. and Proc. R. Soc. N.S. Wales*, 1883, p. 32.

[1] J. Forsyth, *Highlands of Central India*, p. 137.
[2] *J. A. I.*, xiii. 451.
[3] *Jour. and Proc. R. Soc. N.S. Wales*, 1882, p. 172.
[4] Howitt, in *J. A. I.*, xiii. 458.
[5] Dawson, *Australian Aborigines*, p. 30.
[6] We should certainly expect it not to be true of the blood-smearing. And this ceremony appears not to be practised by the tribes referred to by Howitt and Dawson, *ll.cc.* The plucking out of the hair of the pubis (see below) is performed by men of a different tribe (Eyre, *Journals*, ii. p. 337).

at the mention of his totem name he starts up to life.¹ Sometimes it is believed that the youth himself is killed by a being called Thuremlui, who cuts him up, restores him to life, and knocks out a tooth.² Here the idea seems to be that of a second birth, or the beginning of a new life for the novice; hence he receives a new name at the time when he is circumcised, or the tooth knocked out, or the blood of the kin poured on him.³ Amongst the Indians of Virginia and the Quojas in Africa, the youths after initiation pretended to forget the whole of their former lives (parents, language, customs, etc.) and had to learn everything over again like new-born babes.⁴ A Wolf clan in Texas used to dress up in wolf skins and run about on all fours, howling and mimicking wolves; at last they scratched up a living clansman, who had been buried on purpose, and, putting a bow and arrows in his hands, bade him do as the wolves do—rob, kill, and murder.⁵ This may have been an initiatory ceremony, revealing to the novice in pantomime the double origin of the clan—from wolves and from the ground. For it is a common belief with totem clans that they issued originally from the ground.⁶

Ceremonial killing of sacred animals. Connected with this mimic death and revival of a clansman appears to be the real death and supposed revival of the totem itself. We have seen that some Californian Indians killed the buzzard, and then buried and mourned over it like a clansman. But it was believed that, as often as the bird was killed, it was made alive again. Much the same idea appears in a Zuni ceremony described by an eye-witness, Mr. Cushing. He tells how a procession of fifty

---

¹ *J. A. I.*, xiii. 453 *sq.*
² *Ib.*, xiv. 358.
³ Angas, i. 115; Brough Smyth, i. 75 *n.*; *J. A. I.*, xiv. 357, 359; *Nat. Tr. of S. Austr.*, pp. 232, 269. Hence, too, the plucking of the hair from the pubis or incipient beard of the youth at initiation. See Eyre, *Journals*, ii. pp. 337 *sq.*, 340; *Native Tribes of S. Australia*, p. 188.
⁴ R. Beverley, *History of Virginia* (London, 1722), p. 177 *sq.*; Dapper, *Description de l'Afrique*, p. 268. On initiation regarded as a new birth see Kulischer, in *Zeitschrift für Ethnologie*, xv. p. 194 *sq.*
⁵ Schoolcraft, *Ind. Tr.*, v. 683.
⁶ Lewis and Clarke, i. 190, ed. 1815; Dwight, *Travels in New England and New York*, iv. p. 185; *Third Rep.*, p. 237; Maximilian, Prinz zu Wied, *Nord-Amerika*, ii. 160; C. C. Jones, *Antiquities of the Southern Indians*, p. 4 *sq.* The Californian Indians think that their coyote ancestors were moulded directly from the soil (S. Powers, *Tribes of California*, pp. 5, 147).

men set off for the spirit-land, or (as the Zunis call it) "the home of our others," and returned after four days, each man bearing a basket full of living, squirming turtles, One turtle was brought to the house where Mr. Cushing was staying, and it was welcomed with divine honours. It was addressed as, "Ah! my poor dear lost child or parent, my sister or brother to have been! Who knows which? May be my own great great grandfather or mother?" Nevertheless, next day it was killed and its flesh and bones deposited in the river, that it might "return once more to eternal life among its comrades in the dark waters of the lake of the dead." The idea that the turtle was dead was repudiated with passionate sorrow; it had only, they said, "changed houses and gone to live for ever in the home of 'our lost others.'"[1] The meaning of such ceremonies is not clear. Perhaps, as has been suggested,[2] they are piacular sacrifices, in which the god dies for his people. This is borne out by the curses with which the Egyptians loaded the head of the slain bull.[3] Such solemn sacrifices of the totem are not to be confused with the mere killing of the animal for food, even when the killing is accompanied by apologies and tokens of sorrow. Whatever their meaning, they appear not to be found among the rudest totem tribes, but only amongst peoples like the Zuni and Egyptians, who, retaining totemism, have yet reached a certain level of culture. The idea of the immortality of the individual totem, which is brought out in these ceremonies, appears to be an extension of the idea of the immortality of the species, which is, perhaps, of the essence of totemism, and is prominent, *e.g.*, in Samoa. Hence it is not necessary to suppose that the similar festivals, which, with mingled lamentation and joy, celebrate the annual death and revival of vegetation,[4] are directly borrowed from totemism; both may spring independently from the observation of the mortality of the individual and the immortality of the species.

---

[1] Mr. Cushing, in *Century Magazine*, May 1883.
[2] See *Encyclopaedia Britannica*, article "Sacrifice," vol. xxi. p. 137.
[3] Herod., ii. 39.
[4] See *Ency. Brit.*, ninth ed., article "Thesmophoria."

46 TOTEMISM

Sacred dancing associations in North America.

Closely connected with totemism, though crossing the regular lines of totem kinship, are the sacred dancing bands or associations, which figure largely in the social life of many North American tribes. These bands for the most part bear animal names, and possess characteristic dances, also badges which the members wear in dancing, and which often, though not always, consist of some parts (skin, claws, etc.) of the animals from which the bands take their name. As distinguished from totem clans, these bands consist not of kinsmen, but of members who have purchased the privilege of admission, and who in each society are generally all about the same age, boys belonging to one band, youths to another, and so on through the different stages of life. In some tribes both sexes belong to all the bands; in others there are separate bands for the sexes. Some of the bands are entrusted with certain police functions, such as maintaining order in the camp, on the march, in hunting, etc.[1] Such associations probably originate in a feeling that the protection of the totem is not by itself sufficient; feeling this, men seek an additional protection. Hence some of these bands have "medicines" with which they rub their bodies before going into battle, believing that this makes them invulnerable.[2] However, in the Snake Band of the Moquis we have an instance of a kinship group expanding by natural growth into a religious association,[3] and this is probably not an isolated case. The "clans" which Mr. Philander Prescott described as existing among the Dacotas in 1847[4] appear to have been religious associations rather than totem clans. These Dacota "clans" were constituted by the use of the same roots for "medicine"; each "clan" had its special "medicine," and there were constant feuds between them owing to the belief that each "clan" employed its magic "medicine" to injure men of other "clans." Each "clan" had some sacred animal (bear, wolf, buffalo, etc.), or part of an animal (head, tail, liver, wing, etc.), which they venerated through life, and might not eat nor (if it was a

---

[1] See Maximilian, Prinz zu Wied, *Nord-Amerika*, i. 401, 440 sq., 576-579, ii. 138-146, 217-219, 240 sq.; *Third Rep.*, pp. 342-355, cf. *Second Rep.*, p. 16.

[2] *Third Report*, 349, 351.

[3] Bourke, *Snake Dance*, p. 180 sq.

[4] In Schoolcraft's *Ind. Tr.*, ii. 171, 175.

whole animal) kill; nor might they step on or over it.¹ Violation of these rules was thought to bring trouble on the offender. All this is totemic; but the mode of admission to the "clans" (namely, through the great medicine dance) seems appropriate rather to associations.

At this point a few words may be added on two subordinate kinds of totems which have been already referred to.

Sex Totems.—In Australia (but, so far as is known at present, nowhere else) each of the sexes has, at least in some tribes, its special sacred animal, whose name each individual of the sex bears, regarding the animal as his or her brother or sister respectively, not killing it nor suffering the opposite sex to kill it. These sacred animals therefore answer strictly to the definition of totems. Thus amongst the Kurnai all the men were called Yeerung (Emu-Wren) and all the women Djeetgun (Superb Warbler). The birds called Yeerung were the "brothers" of the men, and the birds called Djeetgun were the women's "sisters." If the men killed an emu-wren they were attacked by the women, if the women killed a superb warbler they were assailed by the men. Yeerung and Djeetgun were the mythical ancestors of the Kurnai.² The Kulin tribe in Victoria, in addition to sixteen clan totems, has two pairs of sex totems; one pair (the emu-wren and superb warbler) is identical with the Kurnai pair; the other pair is the bat (male totem) and the small night-jar (female totem). The latter pair extends to the extreme north-western confines of Victoria as the "man's brother" and the "woman's sister."³ Amongst the Coast Murring tribe, as among the Kurnai and Kulin, the emu-wren is the "man's brother," but the "woman's sister" is the tree creeper.⁴ Among the Mūkjarawaint in Western Victoria, who have regular clan totems (white cockatoo, black cockatoo, iguana, crow, eaglehawk, etc.), all the men have, besides, the bat for their totem, and all the women have the small night-jar

[marginal note: Sex totems in Australia.]

---

¹ Stepping over a person or thing is not, to the primitive mind, merely disrespectful; it is supposed to exercise an injurious influence on the person or thing stepped over.

² Fison and Howitt, 194, 201 *sq.*, 215, 235.

³ *J. A. I.*, xv. p. 416, *cf.* xii. p. 507.

⁴ *Id.*, xv. 416.

48   TOTEMISM

Sex totems in Australia.

for theirs.¹ The Ta-ta-thi group of tribes in New South Wales, in addition to regular clan totems, has a pair of sex totems, the bat for men and a small owl for women; men and women address each other as Owls and Bats; and there is a fight if a woman kills a bat or a man kills a small owl.² Of some Victorian tribes it is said that "the common bat belongs to the men, who protect it against injury, even to the half killing of their wives for its sake. The fern owl, or large goatsucker, belongs to the women, and although a bird of evil omen, creating terror at night by its cry, it is jealously protected by them. If a man kills one, they are as much enraged as if it was one of their children, and will strike him with their long poles."³ At Gunbower Creek on the lower Murray the natives called the bat "brother belonging to blackfellow," and would never kill one; they said that if a bat were killed, one of their women would be sure to die.⁴ Among the Port Lincoln tribe, South Australia, the male and female of a small lizard seem to be the male and female totems respectively; at least either sex is said to have a mortal hatred of the opposite sex of these little animals, the men always destroying the female and the women the male. They have a myth that the lizard divided the sexes in the human species.⁵

Sex totems quite distinct from clan totems.

Clearly these sex totems are not to be confounded with clan totems. To see in them, as Messrs. Fison and Howitt do or did, merely clan totems in a state of transition from female to male kinship is to confound sex with kinship. Even if such a view could have been held so long as sex totems were only known to exist among the Kurnai, who have no clan totems left, it must have fallen to the ground when sex totems were found coexisting with clan totems, and that either with female or male (uterine or agnatic) descent. The sex totem seems to be still more sacred than the clan totem; for men who do not object to other people killing their clan totem will fiercely defend their sex totem against any attempt of the opposite sex to injure it.⁶

¹ *J. A. I.*, xii. 45.
² *Id.*, xiv. 350.
³ Dawson, *Australian Aborigines*, p. 52.
⁴ *Trans. Philosoph. Soc. N.S. Wales*, 1862-1865, p. 359 *sq.*
⁵ Angas, *op. cit.*, i. 109; *Nat. Tr. of S. Austr.*, p. 241.
⁶ *J. A. I.*, xiv. p. 350.

Individual Totems.—It is not only the clans and the sexes that have totems; individuals also have their own special totems, *i.e.* classes of objects (generally species of animals), which they regard as related to themselves by those ties of mutual respect and protection which are characteristic of totemism. This relationship, however, in the case of the individual totem, begins and ends with the individual man, and is not, like the clan totem, transmitted by inheritance. The evidence for the existence of individual totems in Australia, though conclusive, is very scanty. In North America it is abundant.

In Australia we hear of a medicine-man whose clan totem through his mother was kangaroo, but whose "secret" (*i.e.* individual) totem was the tiger-snake. Snakes of that species, therefore, would not hurt him.[1] An Australian seems usually to get his individual totem by dreaming that he has been transformed into an animal of the species. Thus a man who had dreamed several times that he had become a lace-lizard was supposed to have acquired power over lace-lizards, and he kept a tame one, which was thought to give him supernatural knowledge and to act as his emissary for mischief. Hence he was known as Bunjil Bataluk (Old Lizard).[2] Another man dreamed three times he was a kangaroo; hence he became one of the kangaroo kindred, and might not eat any part of a kangaroo on which there was blood; he might not even carry home one on which there was blood. He might eat cooked kangaroo; but if he were to eat the meat with the blood on it, the spirits would no longer take him up aloft.[3]

Individual totems.

Individual totems in Australia.

[1] *J. A. I.*, xvi. p. 50.
[2] *Ib.*, 34.
[3] *Ib.*, 45. The aversion, in certain cases, of savages to blood seems to be an important factor in their customs. The North American Indians, "through a strong principle of religion, abstain in the strictest manner from eating the blood of any animal" (Adair, *Hist. Amer. Ind.*, p. 134). They "commonly pull their new-killed venison (before they dress it) several times through the smoke and flame of the fire, both by the way of a sacrifice and to consume the blood, life, or animal spirits of the beast, which it would be a most horrid abomination to eat" (*ib.*, p. 117). Many of the Slave, Hare, and Dogrib Indians will not taste the blood of game; hunters of the two former tribes collect the blood in the paunch of the animal and bury it in the snow at some distance from the flesh (Petitot, *Monographie des Dènè-Dindjié*, p. 76). Men have a specia objection to see the blood of wom at least at certain times; they say if they were to see it they would n able to fight against their enemies would be killed (Mrs. James S

Individual totems in America.

In America the individual totem is usually the first animal of which a youth dreams during the long and generally solitary fasts which American Indians observe at puberty. He kills the animal or bird of which he dreams, and henceforward wears its skin or feathers, or some part of them, as an amulet, especially on the war-path and in hunting.[1] A man may even (though this seems exceptional) acquire several totems in this way; thus an Ottawa medicine-man had for his individual totems the tortoise, swan, woodpecker, and crow, because he had dreamed of them all in his fast at puberty.[2] The respect paid to the individual totem varies in different tribes. Among the Slave, Hare, and Dogrib Indians a man may not eat, skin, nor if possible kill his individual totem, which in these tribes is said to be always a carnivorous animal. Each man carries with him a picture of his totem (bought of a trader); when he is unsuccessful in the chase, he pulls out the picture, smokes to it, and makes it a speech.[3]

Sacrifices to individual totems.

The sacrifices made to the individual totem are sometimes very heavy; a Mandan has been known to turn loose the whole of his horses and abandon them for ever as a sacrifice to his "medicine" or individual totem.[4] The sacrifices at the fasts at puberty sometimes consist of finger joints.[5] The Mosquito Indians in Central America, after dreaming of the beast or bird, sealed their compact with it by drawing blood from various parts of their body.[6] The Innuits of Alaska (who are not Indians, but belong to the Eskimo family and

---

The Booandik Tribe, p. 5). Hence, although bleeding is a common Australian cure for men, women are not allowed to be bled (Angas, i. p. 111). This aversion is perhaps the explanation of that seclusion of women at puberty, child-birth, etc., which has assumed different forms in many parts of the world.

[1] Catlin, *N. Amer. Indians*, i. p. 36 *sq.*; Schoolcraft, *Ind. Tr.*, v. p. 196; *id.*, *Amer. Ind.*, p. 213; *Lettr. Édif.*, vi. 173; Washington Matthews, *Hidatsa Indians*, p. 50; Sproat, *Scenes and Studies of Savage Life*, p. 173 *sq.*; Bancroft, i. 283 *sq.*; *id.*, iii. 156; Mayne, *Brit. Columb.*, p. 302; P.

Jones, *Hist. Ojebway Indians*, p. 87 *sq.*; Loskiel, i. 40; *Tr. Ethnol. Soc.*, New Series, iv. 281, 295 *sq.*; Petitot, *Monographie des Dènè-Dindjié*, p. 36; *Collect. Minnes. Hist. Soc.*, v. p. 65; *American Antiquarian*, ii. p. 10; Parkman, *Jesuits in North America*, p. lxx *sq.*

[2] Schoolcraft, *Am. Ind.*, p. 210.

[3] *Annual Report of the Smithsonian Institution for 1866*, p. 307; *cf.* Petitot, *l.c.*

[4] Lewis and Clarke, i. p. 189 *sq.*, 8vo ed., 1815.

[5] Maximilian, Prinz zu Wied, *Nord-Amerika*, ii. p. 166.

[6] Bancroft, i. p. 740 *sq.*

have no clan totems) do not scruple to eat their guardian animals, and, if unsuccessful, they change their patron. Innuit women have no such guardian animals.¹ The Indians of Canada also changed their okki or manitoo (individual totem) if they had reason to be dissatisfied with it; amongst them, women had also their okkis or manitoos, but did not pay so much heed to them as did the men. They tattooed their individual totems on their persons.² Amongst the Indians of San Juan Capistrano, a figure of the individual totem, which was acquired as usual by fasting, was moulded in a paste made of crushed herbs on the right arm of the novice. Fire was then set to it, and thus the figure of the totem was burned into the flesh.³ Sometimes the individual totem is not acquired by the individual himself at puberty, but is fixed for him independently of his will at birth. Thus among the tribes of the Isthmus of Tehuantepec, when a woman was about to be confined, the relations assembled in the hut and drew on the floor figures of different animals, rubbing each one out as soon as it was finished. This went on till the child was born, and the figure that then remained sketched on the ground was the child's *tona* or totem. When he grew older the child procured his totem animal and took care of it, believing that his life was bound up with the animal's, and that when it died he too must die.⁴ Similarly in Samoa, at child-birth the help of several "gods" was invoked in succession, and the one who happened to be addressed at the moment of the birth was the infant's totem. These "gods" were dogs, eels, sharks, lizards, etc. A Samoan had no objection to eat another man's "god"; but to eat his own would have been death or injury to him.⁵ Amongst the Quiches in Central America, the sorcerer gives the infant the name of an animal, which becomes the child's guardian spirit for life.⁶ In all such cases there is the possibility of the totem being ancestral; it may be that of the mother or father.

Various modes of acquiring individual totems.

¹ Dall, *Alaska*, p. 145.
² Charlevoix, *Hist. de la Nouv. Fr.*, vi. 67 *sq*. The word *okki* is Huron; *manitoo* is Algonkin (*ib.*; Sagard, *Le grand Voyage du pays des Hurons*, p. 231).
³ Boscana, in A. Robinson's *Life in California*, pp. 270 *sq.*, 273; Bancroft, i. 414, iii. 167 *sq*.
⁴ Bancroft, i. 661.
⁵ Turner, *Samoa*, 17.
⁶ Bancroft, i. 703.

In one Central American tribe the son of a chief was free to choose whether he would accept the ancestral totem or adopt a new one; but a son who did not adopt his father's totem was always hateful to his father during his life.[1] Sometimes the okkis or manitoos acquired by dreams are not totems but fetiches, being not classes of objects but individual objects, such as a particular tree, rock, knife, pipe, etc.[2] When the okkis or manitoos are, as sometimes happens, not acquired by a special preparation like fasting, but picked up at hazard, they have no longer any resemblance to totems, but are fetiches pure and simple.[3] The Andamanese appear to have individual totems, for every man and woman is prohibited all through life from eating some one (or more) fish or animal; generally the forbidden food is one which the mother thought disagreed with the child; but if no food disagreed with him, the person is free to choose what animal he will avoid.[4] Some of the people of Mota, Banks Islands, have a kind of individual totem called *tamaniu*. It is some object, generally an animal, as a lizard or snake, but sometimes a stone, with which the person imagines that his life is bound up; if it dies or is broken or lost, he will die. Fancy dictates the choice of a *tamaniu*; or it may be found "by drinking an infusion of certain herbs and heaping together the dregs. Whatever living thing is first seen in or upon the heap is the *tamaniu*. It is watched but not fed or worshipped." It is thought to come at call.[5] But as the *tamaniu* seems to be an individual object, it is a fetich rather than a totem.

The tamaniu, a kind of individual totem in the Banks Islands.

Other kinds of totems. Besides the clan totem, sex totem, and individual totem, there are (as has been indicated) some other kinds or varieties of totems; but the consideration of them had better be deferred until the social organisation based on totemism has been described.

---

[1] Bancroft, i. 753.
[2] Lafitau, *Mœurs des Sauvages Ameriquains*, i. 370 *sq.*; Charlevoix, *Hist. de la Nouv. Fr.*, vi. 68; Kohl, *Kitchi Gami*, i. 85 *sq.*
[3] *Rel. des Jés.*, 1648, p. 74 *sq.*
[4] E. H. Man, *Aboriginal Inhabitants of the Andaman Islands*, p. 134.

[5] The Rev. R. H. Codrington, in *Trans. and Proc. Roy. Soc. of Victoria*, xvi. p. 136. The Banks Islanders are divided into two exogamous intermarrying divisions with descent in the female line (*ib.*, p. 119 *sq.*), but these divisions seem not to possess totems.

Social Aspect of Totemism, or the relation of the men of a totem to each other and to men of other totems. *Social aspect of Totemism.*

(1) All the members of a totem clan regard each other as kinsmen or brothers and sisters, and are bound to help and protect each other.[1] The totem bond is stronger than the bond of blood or family in the modern sense. This is expressly stated of the clans of Western Australia and of North-western America,[2] and is probably true of all societies where totemism exists in full force. Hence in totem tribes every local group, being necessarily composed (owing to exogamy) of members of at least two totem clans, is liable to be dissolved at any moment into its totem elements by the outbreak of a blood feud, in which husband and wife must always (if the feud is between their clans) be arrayed on opposite sides, and in which the children will be arrayed against either their father or their mother, according as descent is traced through the mother, or through the father.[3] In blood feud the whole clan of the aggressor is responsible for his deed, and the whole clan of the aggrieved is entitled to satisfaction.[4] Nowhere perhaps is this solidarity carried further than among the Goajiros in Colombia, South America. The Goajiros are divided into some twenty to thirty totem clans, with descent in the female line; and amongst them, if a man happens to cut himself with his own knife, to fall off his horse, or to injure himself in any way, his family on the mother's side immediately demand payment as blood-money from him. "Being of their blood, he is not allowed to spill it without paying for it." His father's family also demands compensation, but not so much.[5]

The totem clan is a body of kinsmen bound together by the obligation of the blood feud.

---

[1] James, in *Narrative of the Captivity and Adventures of John Tanner*, p. 313; P. Jones, *Hist. Ojebway Indians*, p. 138; *Geol. Surv. of Canada, Rep. for 1878-79*, p. 134B; H. Hale, *The Iroquois Book of Rites*, p. 52; A. Hodgson, *Letters from North America*, i. p. 246; Morgan, *League of the Iroquois*, p. 81 sq.

[2] Grey, *Journ.*, ii. 231; *Report of the Smithsonian Inst. for 1866*, p. 315; Petroff, *Rep. on Alaska*, p. 165. Other authorities speak to the superiority of the totem bond over the tribal bond (Morgan, *League of the Iroquois*, p. 82; Mayne, *Brit. Columb.*, p. 257; *American Antiquarian*, ii. p. 109).

[3] Grey, *Journals*, ii. 230, 238 sq.; *Smithsonian Rep.*, loc. cit.

[4] Fison and Howitt, 156 sq., 216 sq. Sometimes the two clans meet and settle it by single combat between picked champions (*Journ. and Proc. R. Soc. N.S. Wales*, 1882, p. 226).

[5] Simons, in *Proc. R. Geogr. Soc.*, Nov. 1885, p. 789 sq. Simons's information is repeated by W. Sievers, in his *Reise in der Sierra Nevada de Santa Marta* (Leipsic, 1887), p. 255 sq.

To kill a fellow-clansman is a heinous offence. In Mangaia "such a blow was regarded as falling upon the god [totem] himself; the literal sense of 'ta atua' [to kill a member of the same totem clan] being god-striking or god-killing."[1]

Exogamy of the totem clan: persons of the same totem may not marry each other.

(2) *Exogamy.*—Persons of the same totem may not marry or have sexual intercourse with each other. The Navajos believe that if they married within the clan "their bones would dry up and they would die."[2] But the penalty for infringing this fundamental law is not merely natural; the clan steps in and punishes the offenders. In Australia the regular penalty for sexual intercourse with a person of a forbidden clan is death. It matters not whether the woman be of the same local group or has been captured in war from another tribe; a man of the wrong clan who uses her as his wife is hunted down and killed by his clansmen, and so is the woman; though in some cases, if they succeed in eluding capture for a certain time, the offence may be condoned. In the Ta-ta-thi tribe, New South Wales, in the rare cases which occur, the man is killed but the woman is only beaten or speared, or both, till she is nearly dead; the reason given for not actually killing her being that she was probably coerced. Even in casual amours the clan prohibitions are strictly observed; any violations of these prohibitions "are regarded with the utmost abhorrence and are punished by death."[3] Sometimes the punishment stops short at a severe beating or spearing. Amongst some of the Victorian tribes, "should any sign of affection and courtship be observed between those of 'one flesh,' the brothers or male relatives of the woman beat her severely; the man is brought before the chief, and accused of an intention to fall into the same flesh, and is severely reprimanded by the tribe. If he persists and runs away with the object of his affections, they beat and 'cut his head all over,' and if the woman was a consenting party she is half killed."[4] An important

---

[1] Gill, *Myths and Songs of the South Pacific*, p. 38.
[2] Bourke, *Snake Dance of the Moquis of Arizona*, p. 279.
[3] Howitt, in *Rep. of the Smithsonian Inst. for 1883*, p. 804; Fison and Howitt, pp. 64-67, 289, 344 *sq.*; *J. A. I.*, xiv. p. 351 *sq.*
[4] Dawson, *Austr. Abor.*, p. 28.

exception to these rules, if it is correctly reported, is that of the Port Lincoln tribe, which is divided into two clans Mattiri and Karraru, and it is said that though persons of the same clan never marry, yet "they do not seem to consider less virtuous connections between parties of the same class [clan] incestuous."[1] Another exception, which also rests on the testimony of a single witness, is found among the Kunandaburi tribe.[2] Again, of the tribes on the lower Murray, lower Darling, etc., it is said that though the slightest blood relationship is with them a bar to marriage, yet in their sexual intercourse they are perfectly free, and incest of every grade continually occurs.[3]

In America the Algonkins consider it highly criminal for a man to marry a woman of the same totem as himself, and they tell of cases where men, for breaking this rule, have been put to death by their nearest relations.[4] Amongst the Ojibways also death is said to have been formerly the penalty.[5] Amongst the Loucheux and Tinneh the penalty is merely ridicule. "The man is said to have married his sister, even though she may be from another tribe and there be not the slightest connection by blood between the two."[6] *Exogamy of the totem clan in America.*

In some tribes the marriage prohibition only extends to a man's own totem clan; he may marry a woman of any totem but his own. This is the case with the Haidas of the Queen Charlotte Islands,[7] and, so far as appears, the Narrinyeri in South Australia,[8] and the Western Australian tribes described by Sir George Grey.[9] Oftener, however, the prohibition includes several clans, in none of which is a man allowed to marry. For such an exogamous group of clans within the tribe it is convenient to have a name; we shall therefore call it a phratry (L. H. Morgan), defining it as an exogamous division intermediate between the tribe *Often the marriage prohibition extends to several totem clans: such an exogamous group of clans may be called a phratry.*

---

[1] *Nat. Tr. of S. Australia*, p. 222.
[2] Howitt, in *Ann. Rep. of the Smithsonian Inst. for 1883*, p. 804.
[3] *Journ. and Proc. R. Soc. N.S. Wales*, 1883, p. 24; *Transactions of the Royal Society of Victoria*, vi. p. 16.
[4] James, in Tanner's *Narr.*, p. 313.
[5] *Collect. Minnesota Histor. Soc.*, v. p. 42.
[6] *Ann. Rep. Smithson. Inst. for 1866*, p. 315.
[7] *Geol. Surv. of Canada, Rep. for 1878-79*, p. 134B.
[8] *Nat. Tr. of S. Austr.*, p. 12; *J. A. I.*, xii. p. 46.
[9] Grey, *Journ.*, ii. p. 226.

and the clan. The evidence goes to show that in many cases it was originally a totem clan which has undergone subdivision.

<small>Exogamous phratries in America.</small>

Examples.—The Creek Indians are at present divided into about twenty clans (Bear, Deer, Panther, Wild-Cat, Skunk, Racoon, Wolf, Fox, Beaver, Toad, Mole, Maize, Wind, etc.), and some clans have become extinct. These clans are (or were) exogamous; a Bear might not marry a Bear, etc. But further, a Panther was prohibited from marrying not only a Panther but also a Wild-Cat. Therefore the Panther and Wild-Cat clans together form a phratry. Similarly a Toad might not marry a member of the extinct clan Tchu-Kotalgi; therefore the Toad and Tchu-Kotalgi clans formed another phratry. Other of the Creek clans may have been included in these or other phratries; but the memory of such arrangements, if they existed, has perished.[1] The Moquis of Arizona are divided into at least twenty-three totem clans, which are grouped in ten phratries; two of the phratries include three clans, the rest comprise two, and one clan (Blue-Seed-Grass) stands by itself.[2] The Choctaws were divided into two phratries, each of which included four clans; marriage was prohibited between members of the same phratry, but members of either phratry could marry into any clan of the other.[3] The Chickasas are divided into two phratries—(1) the Panther phratry, which includes four clans, namely, the Wild-Cat, Bird, Fish, and Deer; and (2) the Spanish phratry, which includes eight clans, namely, Racoon, Spanish, Royal, Hush-ko-ni, Squirrel, Alligator, Wolf, and Blackbird.[4] The Seneca tribe of the Iroquois was divided into two phratries, each including four clans, the Bear, Wolf, Beaver, and Turtle clans forming one phratry, and the Deer, Snipe, Heron, and Hawk clans forming the other. Originally, as among the Choctaws, marriage was prohibited within the phratry but was permitted with any of the clans of the other phratry; the prohibition, however, has now broken down, and a Seneca may marry a woman of any clan but his own. Hence phratries, in our sense, no longer exist

---

[1] Gatschet, *Migration Legend of the Creek Indians*, p. 154 sq.
[2] Bourke, *Snake Dance*, p. 336.
[3] *Archæologia Americana, Trans. and Collect. Americ. Antiq. Soc.*, vol. ii. p. 109; Morgan, *A. S.*, pp. 99, 162.
[4] Morgan, *A. S.*, pp. 99, 163.

among the Senecas, though the organisation survives for certain religious and social purposes.¹ The Cayuga tribe of Iroquois had also two phratries and eight clans, but one phratry included five clans (Bear, Wolf, Turtle, Snipe, Eel) and the other included three (Deer, Beaver, Hawk).² The Onondaga-Iroquois have also eight clans, unequally distributed into two phratries, the Wolf, Turtle, Snipe, Beaver, and Ball forming one phratry, and the Deer, Eel, and Bear clans forming the other.³ Amongst the Tuscarora-Iroquois the Bear, Beaver, Great Turtle, and Eel clans form one phratry; and the Grey Wolf, Yellow Wolf, Little Turtle, and Snipe form the other.⁴ The Wyandots (Hurons) are divided into four phratries, the Bear, Deer, and Striped Turtle forming the first; the Highland Turtle, Black Turtle, and Smooth Large Turtle the second; Hawk, Beaver, and Wolf the third; and Sea Snake and Porcupine the fourth.⁵

The phratries of the Thlinkets and the Mohegans deserve especial attention, because each phratry bears a name which is also the name of one of the clans included in it. The Thlinkets are divided as follows :—Raven phratry, with clans Raven, Frog, Goose, Sea-Lion, Owl, Salmon; Wolf phratry, with clans Wolf, Bear, Eagle, Whale, Shark, Auk. Members of the Raven phratry must marry members of the Wolf phratry, and *vice versa*.⁶ Considering the prominent parts played in Thlinket mythology by the ancestors of the two phratries, and considering that the names of the phratries are also names of clans, it seems probable that the Raven and Wolf were the two original clans of the Thlinkets, which afterwards by subdivision became phratries. This was the opinion of the Russian missionary Veniaminof, the best early authority on the tribe.⁷ Still more clearly do the Mohegan phratries appear to have been formed by subdivision from clans. They are as follows:⁸—Wolf phratry, with clans Wolf, Bear, Dog, Opossum; Turtle phratry, with clans Little Turtle, Mud Turtle, Great Turtle, Yellow Eel; Turkey

Phratries sometimes apparently formed by the subdivision of totem clans.

---

¹ Morgan, *op. cit.*, pp. 90, 94 *sq.*
² Morgan, *op. cit.*, p. 91.
³ Morgan, *op. cit.*, p. 91 *sq.*
⁴ Morgan, *op. cit.*, p. 93.
⁵ *First Rep.*, p. 60.
⁶ A. Krause, *Die Tlinkit-Indianer*, 112, 220; Holmberg, *op. cit.*, 293, 313; Pinart, in *Bull. Soc. Anthrop. Paris*, 7th Nov. 1872, p. 792 *sq.*; Petroff, *Rep. on Alaska*, p. 165 *sq.*
⁷ Petroff, *op. cit.*, p. 166.
⁸ Morgan, *op. cit.*, p. 174.

phratry, with clans Turkey, Crane, Chicken. Here we are almost forced to conclude that the Turtle phratry was originally a Turtle clan which subdivided into a number of clans, each of which took the name of a particular kind of turtle, while the Yellow Eel clan may have been a later subdivision. Thus we get a probable explanation of the origin of split totems; they seem to have arisen by the segmentation of a single original clan, which had a whole animal for its totem, into a number of clans, each of which took the name either of a part of the original animal or of a subspecies of it. We may conjecture that this was the origin of the Grey Wolf and the Yellow Wolf, and the Great Turtle and the Little Turtle clans of the Tuscarora-Iroquois (see above, p. 57); the Black Eagle and the White Eagle, and the Deer and Deer-Tail clans of the Kaws;[1] and of the Highland Turtle (striped), Highland Turtle (black), Mud Turtle, and Smooth Large Turtle clans of the Wyandots (Hurons).[2] This conclusion, so far as concerns the Hurons, is strengthened by the part played in Huron (and Iroquois) mythology by the turtle, which is said to have received on its back the first woman as she fell from the sky, and to have formed and supported the earth by the accretion of soil on its back.[3]

Explanation of the origin of split totems.

Personal names derived from the totem of the clan.

This explanation of the origin of split totems is confirmed by the custom of calling each member of a clan by a name which has some reference to the common totem of the clan. Thus among the birth-names[4] of boys in the Elk clan of the Omahas the following used to be given to sons in order of

---

[1] Morgan, *op. cit.*, p. 156.
[2] *First Rep.*, p. 59.
[3] *Rel. des Jés.*, 1636, p. 101; Lafitau, *Mœurs des Sauvages Ameriquains*, i. p. 94; Charlevoix, *Hist. de la Nouv. Fr.*, vi. p. 147; T. Dwight, *Travels in New England and New York*, iv. p. 180 *sq.* Precedence was given to the Turtle clan among the Iroquois (the kindred of the Hurons) (T. Dwight, *op. cit.*, iv. p. 185; Zeisberger, in H. Hale, *The Iroquois Book of Rites*, p. 54 *n.*), the Delawares (Brinton, *The Lenape and their Legends*, p. 39; De Schweinitz, *Life of Zeisberger*, p. 79), and the Algonkins (Leland, *Algonquin Legends of New England*, p. 51 *n.*); and Heckewelder (*op. cit.*, p. 81) states generally that the Turtle clan always takes the lead in the government of an Indian tribe. In the Delaware mythology the turtle plays the same part as in the Huron mythology (see above, p. 6).

[4] "Two classes of names were in use, one adapted to childhood and the other to adult life, which were exchanged at the proper period in the same formal manner; one being taken away, to use their expression, and the other bestowed in its place" (Morgan, *A. S.*, p. 79).

their birth—Soft Horn, Yellow Horn, Branching Horn, etc. Amongst the men's names in the same clan are Elk, Standing Elk, White Elk, Big Elk, Dark Breast (of an elk), Stumpy Tail (of an elk), etc. Amongst the women's names in the same clan are Female Elk, Tail Female, etc.[1] Amongst the names of men in the Black Shoulder (Buffalo) clan of the Omahas are Black Tongue (of a buffalo), He that walks last in the herd, Thick Shoulder (of a buffalo), etc.[2] And so with the names of individual members of other clans.[3] The same custom of naming clansmen after some part or attribute of the clan totem prevails also among the Encounter Bay tribe in South Australia; a clan totem of that tribe is the pelican, and a clansman may be called, *e.g.*, Pouch of a Pelican.[4] Clearly split totems might readily arise from single families separating from the clan and expanding into new clans, while they retained as clan names the names of their individual founders, as White Elk, Pouch of a Pelican. Hence such split totems as Bear's Liver,[5] Head of a Tortoise, Stomach of a Pig (see above, p. 10); such taboos as those of the subclans of the Omaha Black Shoulder clan (see above, p. 11); and such subclans as the sections of the Omaha Turtle subclan, namely, Big Turtle, Turtle that does not flee, Red-Breasted Turtle, and Spotted Turtle with red eyes.[6] Finally, Warren actually states that the numerous Bear clan of the Ojibways was formerly subdivided into subclans, each of which took for its totem some part of the Bear's body (head, foot, ribs, etc.), but that these have now merged into two, the common Bear and the Grizzly Bear.[7] The subdivision of the Turtle (Tortoise) clan, which on this hypothesis has taken place among the Tuscarora-Iroquois, is nascent among the Onondaga-Iroquois, for among them "the name of this clan is Hahnowa, which is the general word for tortoise; but the clan is divided into two septs or subdivisions, the Hanyatengona, or Great Tortoise, and the

---

[1] *Third Rep.*, p. 227 *sq.*
[2] *Ib.*, 232.
[3] *Ib.*, 236, 237, 238, 239, 240, 241, 243, 244, 245, 246, 247, 248, 250; Morgan, *A. S.*, p. 169 *n.*
[4] *Nat. Tr. of S. Austr.*, p. 187.
[5] P. Jones, *Hist. Ojebway Ind.*, p. 138.
[6] *Third Rep.*, p. 240 *sq.*
[7] *Collections of the Minnesota Historical Society*, v. p. 49.

60   TOTEMISM

Nikahnowaksa, or Little Tortoise, which together are held to constitute but one clan."[1]

<small>Fusion of totem clans.</small>

On the other hand, fusion of clans is known to have taken place, as among the Haidas, where the Black Bear and Fin-Whale clans have united;[2] and the same thing has happened to some extent among the Omahas and Osages.[3] We may also suspect fusion of clans wherever apparently disconnected taboos are observed by the same clan, as, *e.g.*, the prohibition to touch verdigris, charcoal, and the skin of a cat (*supra*, p. 12). Fusion of clans would also explain those totem badges which are said to be composed of parts of different animals joined together.[4]

<small>Phratries in Australia.</small>

In Australia the phratries are still more important than in America. Messrs. Howitt and Fison, who have done so much to advance our knowledge of the social system of the Australian aborigines, have given to these exogamous divisions the name of classes; but the term is objectionable, because it fails to convey (1) that these divisions are kinship divisions, and (2) that they are intermediate divisions; whereas the Greek term phratry conveys both these meanings, and is therefore appropriate.

<small>In Australia the phratries are often subdivided into subphratries.</small>

We have seen examples of Australian tribes in which members of any clan are free to marry members of any clan but their own; but such tribes appear to be exceptional. Often an Australian tribe is divided into two (exogamous) phratries, each of which includes under it a number of totem clans; and oftener still there are subphratries interposed between the phratry and the clans, each phratry including two subphratries, and the subphratries including totem clans. We will take examples of the former and simpler organisation first.

<small>Examples of Australian tribes divided into two phratries with totem clans.</small>

The Turra tribe in Yorke Peninsula, South Australia, is divided into two phratries, Wiltū (Eaglehawk) and Mūlta (Seal). The Eaglehawk phratry includes ten totem clans (Wombat, Wallaby, Kangaroo, Iguana, Wombat-Snake, Bandicoot, Black Bandicoot, Crow, Rock-Wallaby, and

---

[1] H. Hale, *The Iroquois Book of Rites*, p. 53 *sq*.
[2] *Geol. Surv. of Canada, Rep. for 1878-79*, p. 134B.
[3] *Third Rep.*, p. 235; *American Naturalist*, xviii. p. 114.
[4] *Acad.*, 27th Sept. 1884, p. 203.

Emu); and the Seal phratry includes six (Wild Goose, Butterfish, Mullet, Schnapper, Shark, and Salmon). The phratries are of course exogamous, but (as with the Choctaws, Mohegan, and, so far as appears, all the American phratries) any clan of the one phratry may intermarry with any clan of the other phratry.[1] Again, the Wotjoballuk tribe in North-western Victoria is divided into two phratries (Krokitch and Gamutch), each of which includes three totem clans; the rule of intermarriage is the same as before.[2] The Ngarego and Theddora tribes in New South Wales are divided into two phratries, Merūng (Eaglehawk) and Yŭkembrūk (Crow); and each phratry includes eight totem clans.[3]

In Australia, as in America, we have an instance of a tribe with its clans arranged in phratries, but with an odd clan unattached to a phratry. This occurs in Western Victoria, where there are five totem clans thus arranged:

First phratry . . { (1) Long-Billed Cockatoo clan.
                    { (2) Pelican clan.
Second phratry . . { (3) Banksian Cockatoo clan.
                    { (4) Boa Snake clan.
                     (5) Quail clan.

Here clans 1 and 2 may marry 3, 4, 5; 3 and 4 may marry 1, 2, 5; 5 may marry 1, 2, 3, 4.[4]

But the typical Australian tribe is divided into two exogamous phratries; each of these phratries is subdivided into two subphratries; and these subphratries are subdivided into an indefinite number of totem clans. The phratries being exogamous, it follows that their subdivisions (the subphratries and clans) are so also. The well-known Kamilaroi tribe in New South Wales will serve as an example. Its subdivisions are as follows:[5]—

The typical Australian clan is divided into two phratries, four sub-phratries, and an indefinite number of totem clans.

---

[1] Fison and Howitt, p. 285.
[2] Howitt, in *Rep. of the Smithson. Inst. for 1883*, p. 818.
[3] *J. A. I.*, xiii. p. 437 *n*.
[4] Dawson, *Austr. Abor.*, p. 26 *sq*.
[5] *J. A. I.*, xii. 500.

[TABLE.

Phratries.	Subphratries.	Totem Clans.
Dilbi.	{ Muri.[1] Kubi.	{ Kangaroo, Opossum, Bandicoot, Padimelon, Iguana, Black Duck, Eaglehawk, Scrub Turkey, Yellow-Fish, Honey-Fish, Bream.
Kupathin.	{ Ipai. Kumbo.	{ Emu, Carpet-Snake, Black Snake, Red Kangaroo, Honey, Walleroo, Frog, Cod-Fish.

The freedom of marriage much restricted in a typical Australian tribe.

In such tribes the freedom of marriage is still more curtailed. A subphratry is not free to marry into either subphratry of the other phratry; each subphratry is restricted in its choice of partners to one subphratry of the other phratry; Muri can only marry Kumbo, and *vice versa*; Kubi can only marry Ipai, and *vice versa*. Hence (supposing the tribe to be equally distributed between the phratries and subphratries), whereas under the two phratry and clan system a man is free to choose a wife from half the women of the tribe, under the phratry, subphratry, and clan system he is restricted in his choice to one quarter of the women.

The Kiabara tribe, south of Maryborough in Queensland, will furnish another example:[2]—

Phratries.	Subphratries.	Totem Clans.
Dilcbi (Flood-Water).	{ Baring (Turtle). Turowine (Bat).	} ?
Cubatine (Lightning).	{ Bulcoin (Carpet-Snake). Bundah (Native Cat).	} ?

Here Baring marries Bundah, and Turowine marries Bulcoin, and *vice versa*.

[1] The names of the subphratries here given are the names of the male members of each. There is a corresponding female form for each, formed by the addition of *tha* to the masculine. Thus Muri — Matha (contracted for Muritha), Kubi — Kubitha, Ipai — Ipatha, Kumbo — Butha (contracted for Kumbatha) (Fison and Howitt, p. 37 *n.*). In a tribe of Western Victoria the feminine termination is *heear* (Dawson, *Austr. Abor.*, p. 26); in a Queensland tribe it is *an* (Fison and Howitt, p. 33); in some tribes it is *un* or *gun* (Ridley, in Brough Smyth, ii. p. 288). The tribe at Wide Bay, Queensland, appears to have five subphratries, with male and female names (Ridley, *loc. cit.*). In some tribes the male and female names of the subphratries are distinct words (see *J. A. I.*, xiii. pp. 300, 343, 345). In describing the rules of marriage and descent these feminine forms or names are for simplicity's sake omitted.

[2] *J. A. I.*, xiii. 336, 341.

A remarkable feature of the Australian social organisation is that divisions of one tribe have their recognised equivalents in other tribes, whose languages, including the names for the tribal divisions, are quite different. A native who travelled far and wide through Australia stated that "he was furnished with temporary wives by the various tribes with whom he sojourned in his travels; that his right to these women was recognised as a matter of course; and that he could always ascertain whether they belonged to the division into which he could legally marry, 'though the places were 1000 miles apart, and the languages quite different.'"[1] Again, it is said that "in cases of distant tribes it can be shown that the class divisions correspond with each other, as for instance in the classes of the Flinders river and Mitchell river tribes; and these tribes are separated by 400 miles of country, and by many intervening tribes. But for all that, class corresponds to class in fact and in meaning and in privileges, although the name may be quite different and the totems of each dissimilar."[2] Particular information, however, as to the equivalent divisions is very scanty.[3] Hence it often happens that husband and wife speak different languages and continue to do so after marriage, neither of them ever thinking of changing his or her dialect for that of the other.[4] Indeed, in some tribes of Western Victoria a man is actually forbidden to marry a wife who speaks the same dialect as himself; and during the preliminary visit which each pays to the tribe of the other neither is permitted to speak the language of the tribe whom he or she is visiting.[5] This systematic correspondence

The divisions of Australian tribes have their recognised equivalents in other tribes.

---

[1] Fison and Howitt, p. 53 sq.; cf. Brough Smyth, i. p. 91.
[2] *J. A. I.*, xiii. p. 300.
[3] For a few particulars see Fison and Howitt, 38, 40; Brough Smyth, ii. 288; *J. A. I.*, xiii. 304, 306, 346, xiv. 348 sq., 351.
[4] *Nat. Tr. of S. Austr.*, p. 249.
[5] Dawson, *Austr. Abor.*, 27, 30 sq.; cf. Fison and Howitt, p. 276. The custom observed in some places of imposing silence on women for a long time after marriage may possibly be a relic of the custom of marrying women of a different tongue (cf. Haxthausen, *Transkaukasia*, i. 200 sq.; *ib.*, ii. 23; Krauss, *Südsl.*, p. 450; Hahn, *Albanes. Stud.*, i. 147). Hence too perhaps the folk-lore incident of the silent bride (cf. Grimm, *Kinder und Hausmährchen*, No. 3; Crane, *Popular Italian Tales*, p. 54 sq.). In a modern Greek folk-tale which presents some points of resemblance to the legend of Peleus and Thetis the silent bride is a Nereid; hence Schmidt conjectures with great probability that the expression of Sophocles, quoted by the scholiast on Pindar, *Nem.* iv. 60 (ἀφθόγγους γάμους), means that Thetis

between the intermarrying divisions of distinct and distant tribes, with the rights which it conveys to the members of these divisions, points to sexual communism on a scale to which there is perhaps no parallel elsewhere, certainly not in North America, where marriage is always within the tribe, though outside the clan.[1] But even in Australia a man is always bound to marry within a certain kinship group; that group may extend across the whole of Australia, but nevertheless it is exactly limited and defined. If endogamy is used in the sense of prohibition to marry outside of a certain kinship group, whether that group be exclusive of, inclusive of, or identical with the man's own group, then marriage among the totem societies of Australia, America, and India is both exogamous and endogamous; a man is forbidden to marry either within his own clan or outside of a certain kinship group.[2]

Australian traditions as to the origin of these tribal divisions.

Native Australian traditions as to the origin of these various tribal divisions, though small credit can be given to them, deserve to be mentioned. The Dieri tribe has a legend that mankind married promiscuously till Muramura (Good Spirit) ordered that the tribe should be divided into branches which were to be called after objects animate and inanimate (dogs, mice, emus, iguanas, rain, etc.), the members of each division being forbidden to intermarry.[3] The tribes of Western Victoria, whose totems are long-billed cockatoo, pelican, banksian cockatoo, boa snake, and quail, say that their progenitor was a long-billed cockatoo who had a

was silent during her married life (B. Schmidt, *Volksleben der Neugriechen*, p. 116). Amongst the Caribs the language of the men differed to some extent from that of the women (see Rochefort, *Hist. des Iles Antilles*, p. 350; La Borde, "Relation de l'origine, etc., des Caraibes," in *Rec. de divers voyages faits en Afr. et en l'Amer.*, Paris, 1684, pp. 4, 39; Humboldt, *Reise in die Aequinoctial-Gegenden des Neuen Continents*, iv. 204 *sq.* (Hauff's German trans.); Im Thurn, *Among the Indians of Guiana*, 186; Lucien de Rosny, *Les Iles Antilles*, 23, 261). So amongst the Mbayas in Paraguay (Azara, *Voyages dans l'Amérique Méridionale*, ii. p. 106). In the Booandik tribe, South Australia, persons connected by marriage talk to each other in a low whining voice and use words different from those in common use (Mrs. James Smith, *The Booandik Tribe*, p. 5).

[1] *First Rep.*, p. 63. Between North-American tribes "there were no intermarriages, no social intercourse, no intermingling of any kind, except that of mortal strife" (Dodge, *Our Wild Indians*, p. 45).
[2] Cf. *First Rep.*, loc. cit.; *As. Quart. Rev.*, July 1886, p. 89 *sq.*
[3] *Nat. Tr. of S. Austr.*, p. 260 *sq.*

banksian cockatoo to wife; their children, taking their clan from their mother, were Banksian Cockatoos; but, being forbidden by the laws of consanguinity to marry with each other, they had to introduce "fresh flesh," which could only be done by marriage with strangers; so they got wives from a distance, and hence the introduction of the pelican, snake, and quail totems.[1]

(3) *Rules of Descent.*—In a large majority of the totem tribes at present known to us in Australia and North America descent is in the female line, *i.e.* the children belong to the totem clan of their mother, not to that of their father. In Australia the proportion of tribes with female to those with male descent is as four to one; in America it is between three and two to one. The table which follows is a very rough one. For instance, the Western Australians, given as one tribe, no doubt include many; and it is possible that the Western Victorian tribes given on Dawson's authority may include some tribes mentioned separately by other authorities.

Table of Male and Female Descent.

AUSTRALIA.—*Female Descent.*— 1, West Australians (Grey, *Journ.*, ii. 226; Brough Smyth, ii. 267); 2 and 3, Ngarego and Theddora (*J. A. I.*, xiii. 437); 4, Wakelbura (*J. A. I.*, xii. 43); 5, Kunandaburi (*ib.*); 6, Mukjarawaint (*ib.*); 7, Yerrunthully (*J. A. I.*, xiii. 339, 342); 8, Koogo-Bathy (*ib.*, 339, 343); 9, Kombinegherry (*ib.*, 340, 343); 10, Wonghibon (*id.*, xiv. 348, 350); 11, Barknji (*ib.*, 349, 350); 12, Ta-ta-thi (*ib.*); 13, Keramin (*ib.*); 14, Wiraijuri (*id.*, xiii. 436); 15, Wolgal (*ib.*, 437); 16, Wotjoballuk (*Smithson. Rep. for 1883*, p. 818); 16-26, Western Victorian tribes, ten in number (Dawson, *Aust. Ab.*, 1 *sq.*, 26); 27, Wa-imbio (Fison and Howitt, 291; Brough Smyth, i. 86); 28, Port Lincoln tribe (*Nat. Tr. of S. Aust.*, 222); 29, Kamilaroi (Fison and Howitt, 43, 68); 30, Mount Gambier tribe (*ib.*, 34); 31, Darling River tribe (*ib.*); 32, Mackay tribe, Queensland (*ib.*).

[1] Dawson, *Austr. Abor.*, p. 27.

66   TOTEMISM

<small>Male descent of the totem in Australia.</small> *Male Descent.* — 1, Turra (Fison and Howitt, 285; *J. A. I.*, xii. 44); 2, Narrinyeri (*J. A. I.*, xii. 44, 508; *Nat. Tr. of S. Aust.*, p. 12); 3, Kulin (*J. A. I.*, xii. 44, 507); 4, Aldolinga (*J. A. I.*, xii. 506); 5, Wolgal (*ib.*); 6, Ikula— partly male (*J. A. I.*, xii. 509); 7, Kiabara (*J. A. I.*, xiii. 336, 341); 8, Mycoolon (*J. A. I.*, xiii. 339, 343); a large tribe or group of tribes (no names given) to the south of the Gulf of Carpentaria (*J. A. I.*, xii. 504). The Gournditch-Mara have male descent, but among them the rule of exogamy has disappeared (Fison and Howitt, p. 275 *sq.*).

With regard to the Kurnai in Victoria, after all the explanations of Messrs. Fison and Howitt, it remains uncertain whether descent in that tribe is female or male. The existence of sex totems among them (which Messrs. Fison and Howitt took as evidence that descent was "male as to boys, female as to girls") proves nothing. The tribe is organised in local districts, and apparently a man may take a wife neither from his father's nor his mother's district (Fison and Howitt, p. 226 *sq.*). How deceitful inferences from local prohibitions may be appears from Dawson's account of the Western Victorian tribes. Among these tribes a man may not marry into his father's tribe (which seems to be a local division). From this one might infer that descent was male. But in addition to these local exogamous divisions, there are among these tribes totem clans, and children belong to their mother's clan and may not marry into it. Therefore in these tribes descent is after all female (Dawson *Aust. Abor.*, p. 26).

<small>Female descent of the totem in America.</small> AMERICA.—*Female Descent.*—1, Thlinkets (A. Krause, *Die Tlinket-Ind.*, p. 231 *sq.*); 2, British Columbians (Mayne, *Br. Columb.*, 258); 3, Haidas (*Geol. Surv. of Canada, Rep. for 1878-79*, p. 134B); 4, Loucheux (*Smithson. Rep. for 1866*, p. 315); 5, Kutchin (Dall, *Alaska*, p. 197); 6, Iroquois (Morgan, *League of the Iroquois*, 83; *id., A. S.*, 64); 7, Wyandots or Hurons (*First Report*, 60; Morgan, *A. S.*, 153); 8, Bella Coola Indians, British Columbia (*Original-Mittheil.*, etc., i. p. 186); 9-17, Creeks, Seminoles, Hitchetes, Yoochees, Alabamas, Coosatees, Natchez (Gatschet, *Migration Legend of the Creek Indians*, p. 153; Morgan, *A. S.*, 160 *sq.*; *Archæologia Americana*, ii. p. 109); 18, 19,

TOTEMISM

Choctaws, Cherokees (*Archæol. Amer., loc. cit.*; Morgan, *op. cit.*, 162, 164); 20, Lenape or Delawares (Morgan, *op. cit.*, 166, 172); 21, 22, Otoes and Missouris (Morgan, *op. cit.*, 156); 23, Mandans (Morgan, *op. cit.*, 158); 24, Minnitarees (*ib.*, 159); 25, Upsarokas or Crows (*ib.*, 159); 26, Chickasas (*ib.*, 163); 27, Menominees (*ib.*, 170); 28, Munsees (*ib.*, 173); 29, Mohegans (*ib.*, 174); 30, Pequots (*ib.*); 31, Narragansetts (*ib.*); 32, Moquis (Bourke, *Snake Dance*, p. 230); 33, Goajiros (*Proc. Roy. Geogr. Soc.*, December 1885, p. 790); 34, Arawaks (Brett, *Ind. Tr. of Guiana*, 98; Im Thurn, *Among the Indians of Guiana*, p. 185).

Male Descent.—1, Omahas (*Third Rep.*, 225; Morgan, *op. cit.*, 155); 2, Punkas (Morgan, *loc. cit.*); 3, Iowas (Morgan, 156); 4, Kaws (*ib.*); 5, Winnebagoes (*id.*, 157); 6, Ojibways (*id.*, 166; *Collect. Minnesota Histor. Soc.*, v. p. 42); 7, Pottawatamies (Morgan, *op. cit.*, 167); 8, Miamis (*id.*, 168); 9, Shawnees (*id.*, 169); 10, Sauks and Foxes (*id.*, 170); 11, Blood Blackfeet (*id.*, 171); 12, Piegan Blackfeet (*ib.*); 13, Abenakis (*id.*, 175). {Male descent of the totem in America.}

As to the totem tribes of Africa, descent among the Damaras is in the female line,[1] and there are traces of female kin among the Bechuanas.[2] Among the Bakalai property descends in the male line, but this is not a conclusive proof that descent is so reckoned;[3] all the clans in the neighbourbood of the Bakalai have female descent both for blood and property.[4] In Bengal, where there is a considerable body of totem tribes, Mr. Risley says that after careful search he and his coadjutors have found no tribe with female descent, and only a single trace of it in one.[5] Colonel Dalton, however, states that the Kasias in Bengal are divided into exogamous tribes with descent in the female line; and with regard to this people he mentions, on the {Rules as to descent of the totem in Africa and India.}

---

[1] Andersson, *Lake Ngami*, p. 221.
[2] Casalis, *The Basutos*, p. 179 *sq.*
[3] Because property may descend in the male, while kinship is traced in the female line, as with the natives of Western Australia (Grey, *Journals*, ii. 230, 232 *sq.*) and some Victorian tribes (Dawson, *Austral. Aborigines*, 7, 26). In Mota, Banks Islands, where kinship is traced in the female line, landed property descends in the female line (*i.e.* to sister's children), but personal property in the male line (*i.e.* to sons); but the practice is for the sons to redeem the land with the personal property. See the Rev. R. H. Codrington, in *Trans. and Proc. Roy. Soc. of Victoria*, xvi. p. 119 *sq.*
[4] Du Chaillu, *Journey to Ashango Land*, 429; *id., Equat. Afr.*, 308 *sq.*
[5] *As. Quart. Rev.*, July 1886, p. 94.

authority of Colonel Yule, that "some individuals have a superstitious objection to particular kinds of food, and will not allow such to be brought into their houses. Is not this superstition," asks Colonel Dalton very properly, "connected with their tribal divisions as amongst the Oraons of Chota Nagpur and the Bechuanas of Africa, who cannot eat the animal after which their tribe is named?" At least if this is not totemism, it is uncommonly like it.[1] In the exogamous clans or "motherhoods" of the Garos in Bengal descent is also in the female line, and some of the Garo legends point to totemism.[2] It is remarkable either that these examples should have been overlooked by Mr. Risley and his coadjutors or that both these tribes should have exchanged female for male kinship within the fourteen[3] years which elapsed between the publication of Colonel Dalton's work and Mr. Risley's paper. With regard to the other undoubtedly totem tribes of Bengal (Oraons, etc.), we may take it on Mr. Risley's authority that descent is in the male line.

<small>Indirect male and female descent in typical Australian tribes.</small>

In the Australian tribal organisation of two phratries, four subphratries, and totem clans, there occurs a peculiar form of descent of which no plausible explanation has yet been offered. It seems that in all tribes thus organised the children are born into the subphratry neither of their father nor of their mother, and that descent in such cases is either female or male, according as the subphratry into which the children are born is the companion subphratry of their mother's or of their father's subphratry. In the former case we have what may be called indirect female descent; in the latter, indirect male descent. But it is only in the subphratry that descent is thus indirect. In the totem clan it is always direct; the child belongs to the clan either of its mother or of its father. Thus in the typical Australian organisation, descent, whether female or male, is direct in the phratry, indirect in the subphratry, and direct in the clan. To take examples, the following is the scheme of descent, so far as the phratries and subphratries are concerned, in the Kamilaroi.

[1] Dalton, *Ethnol. of Beng.*, p. 56 *sq.*
[2] Dalton, *op. cit.*, 60, 63.
[3] Or seven years, if we accept the statements in the *Indian Antiquary*, viii. (1879) p. 205; but these may be borrowed from Colonel Dalton.

Phratries.		Male.	Marries	Children are	Indirect female descent.
Dilbi	{	Muri. Kubi.	Kumbo. Ipai.	Ipai. Kumbo.	
Kupathin	{	Ipai. Kumbo.	Kubi. Muri.	Muri. Kubi.	

This is an example of indirect female descent, because the children belong to the companion subphratry of their mother, not to the companion subphratry of their father. But in the totems the female descent is direct; *e.g.* if the father is Muri-Kangaroo and the mother is Kumbo-Emu, the children will be Ipai-Emu; if the mother is Kumbo-Bandicoot the children will be Ipai-Bandicoot.[1]

The following is the scheme of descent in the Kiabara tribe [2]:— *Indirect male descent.*

Phratries.		Male.	Marries	Children are
Dilebi	{	Baring Turowine.	Bundah. Bulcoin.	Turowine. Baring.
Cubatine	{	Bulcoin. Bundah.	Turowine. Baring.	Bundah. Bulcoin.

This is an example of indirect male descent, because the children belong to the companion subphratry of their father, not to the companion subphratry of their mother. We have no information as to the totems, but on the analogy of indirect female descent we should expect them to be taken from the father. This at any rate is true of a large tribe or group of tribes to the south of the Gulf of Carpentaria; their rules of marriage and descent, so far as concerns the subphratries, are like those of the Kiabara, and the totems (which at the lower Leichhardt river are the names of fish) are inherited from father to son.[3]

In some Australian tribes sons take their totem from their father and daughters from their mother. Thus the Dieri in South Australia are divided into two phratries, each of which includes under it sixteen totem clans *Father's totem transmitted to sons, mother's totem to daughters.*

[1] Fison and Howitt, p. 37 *sq.*; *J. A. I.*, xiii. 335, 341, 344.
[2] *J. A. I.*, xiii. 336, 341.
[3] *J. A. I.*, xii. 504. Mr. Howitt, to whom we are indebted for this information, omits to give the names of the tribe and its subdivisions.

Descent of father's totem to sons, and of mother's totem to daughters. (Caterpillar, Mullet, Dog, Rat, Kangaroo, Frog, Crow, etc.);[1] and if a Dog man marries a Rat woman, the sons of this marriage are Dogs and the daughters are Rats.[2] The Ikula (Morning Star) tribe, at the head of the Great Australian Bight, has, with certain exceptions, the same rule of descent.[3] The tribe includes four totem clans, namely, Būdera (Root), Kura (Native Dog), Būdū (Digger), and Wenŭng (Wombat). The rules of marriage and descent are as follows :—

Male.	Marries	Children are
(m.)[4] Budera	(f.) Kura or (f.) Wenŭng	(m.) Budera ; (f.) Kura. (m.) and (f.) Budera.
(m.) Kura	(f.) Budera or (f.) Būdū	(m.) Kura ; (f.) Budera. (m.) and (f.) Kura.
(m.) Būdū	(f.) Wenŭng.	(m.) Būdū ; (f.) Wenŭng.
(m.) Wenŭng	(f.) Būdū	(m.) Wenŭng ; (f.) Būdū.

Here, in all cases except two, the son takes his totem from his father, the daughter from her mother. The exceptions are where Budera (m.) marries Wenung (f.), and where Kura (m.) marries Budu (f.); in both which cases the children, whether sons or daughters, take their father's totem. This, combined with the fact that no male of Budu or Wenung is allowed to marry a female of Budera or Kura, points, as Mr. Howitt says, to a superiority of Budera and Kura over Budu and Wenung.

It is obvious that the totems of the Dieri and Ikula are not sex totems. A sex totem is confined to members of one sex; whereas all the totems of the Dieri and Ikula are common to both men and women. It is of these totems (and not of sex totems) that it may be said in the words of Messrs. Fison and Howitt, that descent is " male as to boys, female as to girls." [5]

[1] *J. A. I.*, xii. 500.
[2] Letter of Mr. S. Gason to the present writer. [3] *J. A. I.*, xii. 509.
[4] m. = male ; f. = female.
[5] *J. A. I.*, xii. 45. The opposite rule of descent (sons belong to the mother's, daughters to the father's family) is observed in the islands of Leti, Moa, and Lakor (Riedel, *op. cit.*, pp. 384, 392).

Besides the tribes whose line of descent is definitely fixed in the female or male line, or, as with the Dieri and Ikula, half-way between the two, there are a number of tribes which are wavering between female and male descent; amongst whom, in other words, a child may be entered in either his mother's or his father's clan. After the researches of Bachofen, M'Lennan, and Morgan, we may be sure that such a wavering marks a transition from female to male descent, and not conversely. Among the Haidas, children regularly belong to the totem clan of their mother; but in very exceptional cases, when the clan of the father is reduced in numbers, the newly born child may be given to the father's sister to suckle. It is then spoken of as belonging to the paternal aunt, and is counted to its father's clan.[1] Amongst the Delawares descent is regularly in the female line; but it is possible to transfer a child to its father's clan by giving it one of the names which are appropriated to the father's clan.[2] A similar practice prevails with the Shawnees, except that with them male descent is the rule and transference to the mother's clan (or any other clan) by naming is the exception.[3] In the Hervey Islands, South Pacific, the parents settled beforehand whether the child should belong to the father's or mother's clan. The father usually had the preference, but sometimes, when the father's clan was one which was bound to furnish human victims from its ranks, the mother had it adopted into her clan by having the name of her totem pronounced over it.[4] In Samoa at the birth of a child the father's totem was usually prayed to first; but if the birth was tedious, the mother's totem was invoked; and whichever happened to be invoked at the moment of birth was the child's totem for life.[5]

Tribes wavering between female and male descent.

These modes of effecting the change of kin touched only the children; others affected the children through the mother; they were transferred to their father's clan by the previous transference of the mother. This, as M'Lennan

Transference of children from mother's to father's clan.

---

[1] *Geol. Surv. of Canada, Rep. for 1878-79*, p. 134B.
[2] Morgan, *A. S.*, p. 172 *sq.*
[3] *Ib.*, 169.
[4] Gill, *Myths and Songs of the South Pacific*, p. 36.
[5] Turner, *Samoa*, p. 78 *sq.* The child might thus be transferred to a clan which was that neither of his father nor of his mother (see above, p. 51).

TOTEMISM

Transference of children from mother's to father's clan.

has observed, was perhaps the intention and doubtless must have been the effect of the custom in Guinea of dedicating one wife to the husband's Bossum or god.[1] The transference of the wife to the husband's clan seems to have been the intention of smearing bride and bridegroom with each other's blood.[2] Amongst some of the totem clans of Bengal the bride is transferred to the husband's clan by ceremoniously eating or drinking with him.[3] Another mode is to purchase the woman and her offspring. Amongst the Banyai on the Zambesi, if the husband gives nothing, the children of the marriage belong to the wife's family; but if he gives so many cattle to his wife's parents the children are his.[4] In the Watubela Islands between New Guinea and Celebes a man may either pay for his wife before marriage, or he may, without paying, live as her husband in her parents' house, working for her and her parents. In the former case the children belong to him; in the latter they belong to his wife's family, but he may acquire them subsequently by paying the price.[5] So in Sumatra.[6] Similarly in some Californian tribes, the husband must live with his wife's family and work for them till he has paid the full price for her and her children; the children of a wife who has not been paid for are regarded as bastards, and treated with contempt.[7]

The couvade or custom in accordance with which the

---

[1] M'Lennan, *Patriarchal Theory*, 235 *sq.*; Bosman's "Guinea," in Pinkerton's *Voyages and Travels*, xvi. 420.

[2] Dalton, *Eth. of Beng.*, p. 220. In some parts of New Guinea bride and bridegroom draw blood from each other's foreheads (S. Müller, *Reizen en Onderzoekingen in den Indischen Archipel*, i. p. 105). In Bengal the ceremony appears to have usually degenerated into smearing each other with red lead (Dalton, *op. cit.*, 160, 194, 216, 253, 319). The blood of animals, when used for this purpose, as by the Dyaks, may be a substitute for that of the bride and bridegroom; possibly it may be the blood of the totem (Perelaer, *Ethnogr. Beschrijv. der Dajaks*, p. 52; *Tijdschrift v. Indische Taal- Land- en Volkenkunde*, xxv. (1879) p. 116; *Ausland*, 16th June 1884, p. 469; *Journals of James Brooke, Rajah of Sarawak*, i. p. 204; Carl Bock, *Head-Hunters of Borneo*, p. 222).

[3] Dalton, *op. cit.*, 193, 216; *cf.* Lewin, *Wild Races of South-Eastern India*, 177 *sq.*

[4] Livingstone, *Travels in S. Afr.*, 622 *sq.*; *cf.* M'Lennan, *Patriarchal Theory*, 324 *sq.*

[5] Riedel, *De sluik- en kroesharige rassen tusschen Papua en Selebes*, 205 *sq.*

[6] Marsden, *Hist. of Sumatra*, 257 *sq.*; Schreiber, *Die Battas in ihrem Verhältniss zu den Malaien von Sumatra*, p. 34; Junghuhn, *Die Battaländer auf Sumatra*, ii. 131 *sq.*

[7] Bancroft, *Native Races of the Pacific States*, i. 350.

TOTEMISM 73

husband takes to his bed and is treated as an invalid when his wife has given birth to a child, is perhaps a fiction intended to transfer to the father those rights over the children which, under the previous system of mother-kin, had been enjoyed by the mother alone.[1] The same may possibly be the intention of the apparently widespread custom of men dressing as women and women as men at marriage. Thus in the Greek island of Cos the bridegroom was attired as a woman when he received his bride.[2] In Central Africa a Masai man dresses as a girl for a month after marriage.[3] Argive brides wore false beards when they slept with their husbands.[4] The Alsatian custom of men dressing as women and women as men at the vintage festival is clearly part of an old marriage ceremony.[5] But perhaps all these mummeries are to be otherwise explained.

The couvade and certain marriage customs may have been intended to transfer the children to their father's clan.

Lastly, the transference of the child to the father's clan may be the object of a ceremony observed by the Todas in Southern India. When the wife has gone seven months with her first child she retires with her husband to the forest, where, at the foot of a tree, she receives from her husband a bow and arrows. She asks him, "What is the name of your bow?" each clan apparently having a different name for its bow. The question and answer are repeated three times. She then deposits the bow and arrows at the foot of the tree. The pair remain on the spot all night, eating a meal in the evening and another in the morning before they return home.[6]

Custom observed by the Todas in the seventh month of pregnancy.

As a rule, perhaps, members of the same totem clan do not eat each other. To this, however, there are large exceptions. The Kurnai and Maneroo observe the rule, eating their slain enemies but not their slain friends.[7] But tribes

Rules of cannibalism among totem clans.

---

[1] This is the view of Bachofen, *Mutterrecht*, 255 sq.; Giraud-Teulon, *Les origines du mariage et de la famille*, 138 sq.; Post, *Die Anfänge des Staats- und Rechtslebens*, 18; and (with some limitations) Zmigrodzki, *Die Mutter bei den Völkern des arischen Stammes*, 270.
[2] Plutarch, *Qu. Gr.*, 58.
[3] J. Thomson, *Through Masai Land*, 442.
[4] Plutarch, *De mul. virt.*, 4.

[5] Mannhardt, *Der Baumkultus*, 314. For forms of marriage as means of communicating fertility to the fields cf. ib., 480 sq.; id., *Mythol. Forsch.*, 340; Wilken, in *De Indische Gids*, June 1884, pp. 958, 962.
[6] Marshall, *Travels among the Todas*, 214 sq. The Todas have male descent for themselves, but retain female descent for their sacred cattle (ib., 132).
[7] Fison and Howitt, 214, 218, 223 sq.

Rules of cannibalism among totem clans.

about the Gulf of Carpentaria after a battle eat their slain friends but not their enemies; and amongst them children, when they die, are eaten.[1] Some Victorian tribes kill their new-born children, eat them, and give them to their elder children to eat, believing that the latter will thus possess the strength of the babes in addition to their own.[2] In some parts of New South Wales it was the custom for the first-born child of every woman to be eaten by the tribe as part of a religious ceremony.[3] The eating of aged relations[4] is intelligible on the principle that "the life is not allowed to go out of the family." Some of the Victorian tribes, who ate their relations but not their enemies nor members of a different tribe, asserted that they did so, not to gratify their appetites, but only as a symbol of respect and regret for the dead. They only ate the bodies of relations who had died by violence.[5] The Dieri have exact rules according to which they partake of the flesh of dead relations; the mother eats of her children and the children eat of their mother; but the father does not eat of his offspring, nor the offspring of their father.[6] This custom points to the time when the Dieri had female kinship, when therefore the father, as a member of a different tribe, had no right to partake of his child. The eating of dead relations is parallel to the custom of smearing the person with the juices which exude from their decaying corpses.[7] The object of these and similar ceremonies (see above, p. 42 *sq.*) is to keep the life, regarded as incarnate in the body and blood of the kinsmen, within the circle of the kin. Hence in some tribes at circumcision boys are laid on a platform, formed by the living bodies of the tribesmen,[8] and when the tooth is knocked out they are seated on the shoulders of men on whose breast the blood flows and is not wiped away.[9] The blood of the

---

[1] *J. A. I.*, xiii. 283.
[2] *Trans. Ethn. Soc.*, New Series, i. 289.
[3] Brough Smyth, ii. 311.
[4] For examples see *Journals of James Brooke, Rajah of Sarawak*, i. p. 209; Garcilasso de la Vega, *Royal Commentaries of the Incas*, I. i. 12; Riedel, *op. cit.*, p. 267; Herodotus, iv. 26; Mela, II. i. 9.

[5] Dawson, *Austr. Abor.*, 67.
[6] *Nat. Tr. of S. Australia*, p. 274.
[7] Fison and Howitt, 243 *sq.*; Riedel, *op. cit.*, p. 308.
[8] *Nat. Tr. of S. Austr.*, 230; Brough Smyth, i. 75 *n.*; Eyre, *Journals*, ii. p. 335.
[9] Collins, *Account of the English Colony of N.S.W.*, London, 1798, p. 580.

TOTEMISM

tribe is not allowed to be spilt on the ground, but is received on the bodies of tribesmen. Bleeding is a native Australian cure for headache, etc.; but in performing the operation they are very careful not to spill any of the blood on the ground, but sprinkle it on each other.[1] Similarly when bleeding is done as a means of producing rain, the blood is made to flow on men, not on the ground.[2] Another form of transferring the blood, *i.e.* the life of the kin, is seen in an Australian funeral ceremony; the relations gash themselves over the corpse till it and the grave are covered with their blood; this is said to strengthen the dead man and enable him to rise in another country.[3] Among some South American tribes the bones of deceased relations are ground into powder, mixed with a liquid, and so swallowed.[4]

When a North American tribe is on the march, the members of each totem clan camp together, and the clans are arranged in a fixed order in camp, the whole tribe being arranged in a great circle or in several concentric circles.[5] When the tribe lives in settled villages or towns, each clan has its separate ward.[6] The clans of the Osages are divided into war clans and peace clans; when they are out on the buffalo hunt, they camp on opposite sides of the tribal circle; and the peace clans are not allowed to take animal life of any kind; they must therefore live on vegetables unless they can obtain meat in exchange for vegetables from the war clans.[7] Members of the same clan are buried together and apart from those of other clans; hence the remains of husband and wife, belonging as they do to separate clans, do not rest together.[8] It is remarkable that

Totem clans grouped together in camp, village, and graveyard.

---

[1] Angas, *Savage Life and Scenes in Australia and New Zealand*, i. 110 *sq.*
[2] *Nat. Tr. of S. Aust.*, 277.
[3] Brough Smyth, ii. 274; Grey, *Journ.*, ii. 332; *J. A. I.*, xiii. 134 *sq.*
[4] J. G. Müller, *Gesch. der Amerik. Urreligionen*, 289 *sq.*; A. R. Wallace, *Travels on the Amazon and Rio Negro*, p. 498. Artemisia drank the ashes of Mausolus (Aulus Gellius, x. 18; Valerius Maximus, iv. 6, 5). On the question of American cannibalism *cf.* Müller, *op. cit.*, p. 144 *sq.*; R. I. Dodge, *Hunting Grounds of the Great West*, p. 420.
[5] *First Rep.*, 64; *Third Rep.*, 219 *sq.*; *American Naturalist*, xviii. p. 113 *sq.*
[6] Gatschet, *Migration Legend of the Creek Indians*, 154; Bourke, *Snake Dance*, 229; *Acad.*, 27th Sept. 1884, p. 203.
[7] The Rev. J. Owen Dorsey, in *American Naturalist*, xviii. p. 113.
[8] Adair, *Hist. Amer. Ind.* 183 *sq.*; Morgan, *A. S.*, 83 *sq.*; Brinton, *The Lenâpé and their Legends*, 54; *id.*, *Myths of the New World*, 87 *n.*; A. Hodgson, *Letters from North America*, i. p. 259; Dalton, *Eth. of Beng.*, 56; *cf.* Robertson Smith, *Kinship and Marriage in Early Arabia*, 315 *sq.*

76 TOTEMISM

among the Thlinkets the body must always be carried to the funeral pyre and burned by men of another totem,[1] and the presents distributed on these occasions by the representatives of the deceased must always be made to men of a different clan.[2]

Evidence for the existence of phratric totems.

Here we must revert to the religious side of totemism, in order to consider some facts which have emerged from the study of its social aspect. We have seen that some phratries, both in America and Australia, bear the names of animals;[3] and in the case of the Thlinkets and Mohegans we have seen reason to believe that the animals which give their names to the phratries were once clan totems. The same seems to hold of the names of the Australian phratries, Eaglehawk, Crow, and Seal, or at least of the two former. For Eaglehawk and Crow are clan totems in other tribes, and are, besides, important figures in Australian mythology. Eaglehawk and Crow, as names of phratries, "extended over a large part of Victoria and over the greater part of the extreme west of New South Wales."[4] They are clan totems of the Dieri in South Australia,[5] the Mukjarawaint in Western Victoria,[6] and the Ta-ta-thi and the Keramin tribes in New South Wales.[7] The eaglehawk is besides a clan totem of the Kamilaroi in New South Wales,[8] the Mycoolon in Queensland,[9] the Barinji in New South Wales,[10] and the Kūinmŭrbŭra in Queensland.[11] The crow is further a clan totem of the Turra tribe,[12] and the Mount Gambier tribe in South Australia,[13] the Kunandaburi in Queensland,[14] and of the Wonghibon in New South Wales.[15] Among the Dieri the eaglehawk was supposed to inflict a penalty for violating a rule in connection with the knocking

---

[1] Holmberg, op. cit., 324.
[2] Krause, Die Tlinkit-Indianer, 223.
[3] As among the Chickasas, Thlinkets, and Mohegans in America; and the Turra, Ngarego, and Theddora tribes in Australia (see above, pp. 56-58, 60 sq.). The subphratries of the Kiabara also bear animal names. See above, p. 62.
[4] J. A. I., xiii. 437, n. 1; Fison and Howitt, 322.
[5] J. A. I., xii. 500; id., xiii. 338.
[6] Id., xii. 45.
[7] Id., xiv. 349.
[8] Id., xii. 500, xiii. 335.
[9] Id., xiii. 303, 339.
[10] Id., xiv. 348.
[11] Id., xiii. 336, 344.
[12] Id., xii. 45.
[13] Fison and Howitt, 168.
[14] J. A. I., xii. 45, xiii. 338.
[15] Id., xiv. 348.

out the teeth at initiation.¹ Among the Kurnai the eaglehawk is greatly reverenced; his plumes and talons were used in necromancy; and he figures in their stories in company with the little owl.² The Kurnai also reverence the crow as one of their ancestors,³ and consult it as a bird of omen.⁴ According to a Victorian myth, the crow and the eaglehawk were the progenitors, or among the progenitors, of the human race, and now shine as stars in the sky.⁵ According to another Victorian myth the eagle and the crow were the creators of the world, and divided the Murray blacks into two classes (clans or phratries), the Eaglehawk and Crow.⁶

Further, there are traces in Australia of the splitting of totems. Thus in the Ta-ta-thi tribe in New South Wales there are two Eaglehawk clans, namely, the Light Brown Eaglehawk and the Brown Coloured Eaglehawk, one in each of the two phratries.⁷ Amongst the Kamilaroi there is a Kangaroo clan and a Red Kangaroo clan, one in each of the two phratries.⁸ In the Kūnandabŭri tribe in Queensland there are totem clans—Brown Snake, Speckled Brown Snake, Carpet-Snake, also Rat, Kangaroo Rat, and Bush Rat.⁹ In the Mūkjarawaint in Western Victoria there are White Cockatoo and Black Cockatoo, also Buff-coloured Snake and Black Snake;¹⁰ in other Victorian tribes there are the Long-Billed Cockatoo and the Banksian Cockatoo;¹¹ in the Wakelbŭra in Queensland there are Large Bee and Small Bee in different phratries;¹² in the Mycoolon there are Whistling Duck and Black Duck.¹³

<small>Traces of the splitting of totems in Australia.</small>

From all this we should infer that the objects from which the Australian phratries take their names were once totems. But there seems to be direct evidence that both the phratries and subphratries actually retain, at least in some tribes, their totems. Thus the Port Mackay tribe in Queensland is divided into two phratries, Yungaru and Wutaru, with subphratries Gurgela, Burbia, Wungo, and

<small>Phratric and subphratric totems in Australia.</small>

---

¹ *Nat. Tr. of S. Austr.*, 267.
² Fison and Howitt, 323.
³ *J. A. I.*, xv. 415.
⁴ *Id.*, xvi. 46.
⁵ Brough Smyth, i. 431.
⁶ *Id.*, i. 423 *sq.*
⁷ *J. A. I.*, xiv. 349.
⁸ *Id.*, xii. 500.
⁹ *J. A. I.*, xii. 45.   ¹⁰ *Ib.*
¹¹ Dawson, *Austr. Abor.*, p. 26.
¹² *J. A. I.*, xiii. 337.
¹³ *Ib.*, 339.

Phratric and subphratric totems in Australia.

Kubera; and the Yungaru phratry has for its totem the alligator, and Wutaru the kangaroo;[1] while the subphratries have for their totems the emu (or the carpet snake), iguana, opossum, and kangaroo (or scrub turkey).[2] As the subphratries of this tribe are said to be equivalent to the subphratries of the Kamilaroi, it seems to follow that the subphratries[3] of the Kamilaroi (Muri, Kubi, Ipai, and Kumbo) have or once had totems also. Hence it appears that in tribes organised in phratries, subphratries, and clans, each man has three totems—his phratry totem, his subphratry totem, and his clan totem. If we add a sex totem and an individual totem, each man in the typical Australian tribe has five distinct kinds of totems. What degree of allegiance he owes to his subphratry totem and phratry totem respectively we are not told; indeed, the very existence of such totems, as distinct from clan totems, appears to have been generally overlooked. But we may suppose that the totem bond diminishes in strength in proportion to its extension; that therefore the clan totem is the primary tie, of which the subphratry and phratry totems are successively weakened repetitions.

Subtotems, i.e. natural objects classed under the totem and sharing the respect due to it.

In these totems superposed on totems may perhaps be discerned a rudimentary classification of natural objects under heads which bear a certain resemblance to genera, species, etc. This classification is by some Australian tribes extended so as to include the whole of nature. Thus the Port Mackay tribe in Queensland (see above, p. 77 *sq.*) divides all nature between the phratries; the wind belongs to one phratry and the rain to another; the sun is Wutaru and the moon is Yungaru; the stars, trees, and plants are also divided between the phratries.[4] As the totem of Wutaru

---

[1] Fison and Howitt, 38 *sq.*, 40. The Rockhampton tribe (Queensland) has the same phratries, but its subphratries are different (*J. A. I.*, xiii. 336).

[2] Fison and Howitt, p. 41. The totems of the phratries and subphratries are given by different authorities, who write the native names of the subphratries differently. But they seem to be speaking of the same tribe; at least Mr. Fison understands them so.

[3] The names of the Kamilaroi phratries, Dilbi and Kupathin, are clearly identical with Dilebi and Cubatine, the names of the Kiabara phratries (see above, p. 62), and the latter mean Flood-water and Lightning. Are these phratric totems both of the Kamilaroi and Kiabara?

[4] Brough Smyth, i. 91; Fison and Howitt, 168; *cf. J. A. I.*, xiii. 300.

is kangaroo and of Yungaru alligator, this is equivalent to making the sun a kangaroo and the moon an alligator.

The Mount Gambier tribe in South Australia is divided into two phratries (Kumi and Kroki), which again are subdivided into totem clans. Everything in nature belongs to a totem clan, thus [1]:— *Subtotems in the Mount Gambier tribe.*

Phratries.	Totem Clans.	Includes
Kumi.	1. Mūla = Fish-Hawk.	Smoke, honeysuckle, trees, etc.
	2. Parangal = Pelican.	Dogs, blackwood trees, fire, frost (fem.)
	3. Wā = Crow.	Rain, thunder, lightning, winter, hail, clouds, etc.
	4. Wīla = Black Cockatoo.	Stars, moon, etc.
	5. Karato = A harmless Snake.	Fish, stringybark trees, seals, eels, etc.
Kroki.	1. Wērio = Tea-Tree.	Ducks, wallabies, owls, crayfish, etc.
	2. Mūrna = An edible Root.	Bustards, quails, dolvich (a small kangaroo).
	3. Karáal = Black crestless Cockatoo.	Kangaroo, sheoak trees, summer, sun, autumn (fem.), wind (fem.)

With reference to this classification Mr. D. S. Stewart, the authority for it, says, " I have tried in vain to find some reason for the arrangement. I asked, ' To what division does a bullock belong?' After a pause came the answer, ' It eats grass: it is Boortwerio.' I then said, ' A cray-fish does not eat grass; why is it Boortwerio?' Then came the standing reason for all puzzling questions: 'That is what our fathers said it was.'"[2] Mr. Stewart's description of the respect paid by a tribesman to the animals of the same "subdivision" as himself has been already quoted (see above, p. 8 *sq.*); it seems to imply that a man is debarred from killing not only his clan totem (when that is an animal) but also all the animals which are classed under his clan. The natural objects thus classed under and sharing the respect due to the totem may be conveniently called, as Mr. Howitt proposes,[3] subtotems. Again, the Wakelbura tribe (Elgin Downs, Queensland) is divided into two phratries (Mallera and Wuthera), four subphratries (Kurgila, Banbe, Wungo, and Obu), and totem clans. Everything in nature is classed *Subtotems of the Wakelbura tribe.*

---

[1] Fison and Howitt, *loc. cit.*
[2] Fison and Howitt, 169.
[3] In *Smithson. Rep. for 1883*, p. 818.

80   TOTEMISM

Subtotems of the Wakelbura tribe.

under its phratry and subphratry. Thus the broad-leaved box-tree is of the Mallera phratry and the Banbe subphratry, and so is the dingo or native dog. When a man of this tribe dies his corpse must be covered with the boughs of a tree which belongs to the same phratry and subphratry as himself; thus if he is Mallera-Banbe he is covered with boughs of the broad-leaved box-tree, for it also is Mallera-Banbe.[1] So in summoning an assembly the message stick carried by the messenger must be of the same tribal division as the sender and the bearer of the message.[2] Of a group of tribes in N.S. Wales it is said that everything in nature is divided among the tribesmen, some claiming the trees, others the plains, others the sky, stars, wind, rain, and so forth.[3] Again, the Wotjoballuk tribe in North-western Victoria has a system of subtotems, thus[4]:—

Subtotems of the Wotjoballuk tribe.

Phratries.	Totem Clans.	Subtotems.
Krokitch.	1. Hot Wind. 2. White crestless Cockatoo. 3. Belonging to the Sun.	Each totem has subordinate to it a number of objects, animal or vegetable, *e.g.* kangaroo, red gum-tree, etc.
Gamutch.	4. Deaf Adder. 5. Black Cockatoo. 6. Pelican.	Do.

Of the subtotems in this tribe Mr. Howitt says, "They appear to me to be totems in a state of development. Hot wind has at least five of them, white cockatoo has seventeen, and so on for the others. That these subtotems are now in process of gaining a sort of independence may be shown by the following instance: a man who is Krokitch-Wartwut (hot wind) claimed to own all the five subtotems of hot wind (three snakes and two birds), yet of these there was one which he specially claimed as 'belonging' to him, namely, Moiwuk (carpet-snake). Thus his totem, hot wind, seems to have been in process of subdivision into minor totems, and this man's division might have become hot wind carpet-snake had not civilisation rudely stopped the process by almost extinguishing the tribe."

[1] *J. A. I.*, xiii. 191, 337.
[2] *Ib.*, 438 *n*.
[3] *J. A. I.*, xiv. 350.
[4] *Smithson. Rep.*, *loc. cit.*

Combining this important evidence as to the growth of totems with the evidence already noticed of the process by which clans tend to become phratries, we get a view of the growth, maturity, and decay of totems. As subtotems they are growing; as clan totems they are grown; as subphratric and phratric totems they are in successive stages of decay. As fast as one totem attains its full development, and then, beaten out thinner and thinner, melts into the vast reservoir of nature from which it sprang, it is followed at equal intervals by another and another; till all things in nature are seen to be, as it were, in motion, and after a period of mustering and marshalling to fall into their places in the grand totem march.[1] *(Growth, maturity, and decay of totems.)*

When, through the change of female to male kinship, and the settlement of a tribe in fixed abodes, society has ceased to present the appearance of a constantly shifting kaleidoscope of clans, and has shaken down into a certain stability and permanence of form, it might be expected that with the longer memory which accompanies an advance in culture the totems which have been generalised into the divinities of larger groups should no longer pass into oblivion, but should retain an elevated rank in the religious hierarchy, with the totems of the subordinate tribal divisions grouped under them either as subordinate divinities or as different manifestations of the general tribal gods. This appears to have been the state of totemism in Polynesia, where geographical conditions favoured an isolation and hence a permanence of the local groups such as was scarcely attainable by savages on the open plains of Australia or the prairies and savannahs of America.[2] Hence in Polynesia we find a considerable approximation to a totem Olympus. In Samoa there were general village gods as well as gods of particular families; and the same deity is incarnate in the form of different animals. One god, for example, is *(Under the influence of social changes the totems tend to pass into human gods with animal symbols.)*

---

[1] In America, as in Australia, the totems seem always to have been in a state of flux. Mr. Beauchamp has shown this for the Iroquois (*American Antiquarian*, viii. 82 *sq.*).

[2] Mr. Horatio Hale says that the American totem clans "were not permanent, but were constantly under- going changes, forming, dividing, coalescing, vanishing" (H. Hale, *The Iroquois Book of Rites*, p. 51). On the rapid disintegration of North American tribes whenever external pressure is removed see Dodge, *Our Wild Indians*, p. 45 *sq.*

Transformation of totems into human gods with animal symbols.

incarnate in the lizard, the owl, and the centipede;[1] another in the bat, domestic fowl, pigeon, and prickly sea urchin;[2] another in the bat, the sea-eel, the cuttle-fish, the mullet, and the turtle;[3] another in the owl and the mullet;[4] another in the bird *Porphyris Samoensis*, the pigeon, the rail-bird, and the eel;[5] another in the turtle, sea-eel, octopus, and garden lizard.[6] It seems a fair conjecture that such multiform deities are tribal or phratric totems, with the totems of the tribal or phratric subdivisions tacked on as incarnations. As the attribution of human qualities to the totem is of the essence of totemism, it is plain that a deity generalised from or including under him a number of distinct animals and plants must, as his animal and vegetable attributes contradict and cancel each other, tend more and more to throw them off and to retain only those human qualities which to the savage apprehension are the common element of all the totems whereof he is the composite product. In short, the tribal totem tends to pass into an anthropomorphic god. And as he rises more and more into human form, so the subordinate totems sink from the dignity of incarnations into the humbler character of favourites and clients; until, at a later age, the links which bound them to the god having wholly faded from memory, a generation of mythologists arises who seek to patch up the broken chain by the cheap method of symbolism. But symbolism is only the decorous though transparent veil which a refined age loves to throw over its own ignorance of the past.

Tendency to create a deity presiding over the totem species.

Apart from the social changes which have favoured the passage of totemism into a higher form of faith, we can detect in the totemic philosophy itself some advances towards the formation of a deity distinct from and superior to all the individuals of the totem species. Thus some North American Indians think that each species of animal has an elder brother, who is the origin of all the animals of the species, and is besides marvellously great and powerful. The elder brothers of birds are in the sky; the elder brothers of animals are in the waters.[7] The Patagonians,

---

[1] Turner, *Samoa*, 46 sq.
[2] *Ib.*, 51.
[3] *Ib.*, 56 sq.
[4] *Ib.*, 60 sq.
[5] *Ib.*, 64 sq.
[6] *Ib.*, 72.
[7] *Rel. des Jés.*, 1634, 13; cf. *Lettr. Édif.*, vi. 334; Charlevoix, *Hist. de la Nouv. Fr.*, v. 443; vi. 78.

who are divided into clans of the Tiger, Lion, Guanoco, Ostrich, and so on, think that these clans have each its appropriate deity living in vast caverns underground, with whom the souls of dead clansmen go to dwell.[1] The Peruvians thought that "of all the beasts of the earth, there is one alone in heaven like unto them, that which hath care of their procreation and increase."[2] In all such views the strict totemic standpoint is abandoned. Pure totemism is democratic; it is a religion of equality and fraternity; one individual of the totem species is as good as another. When, therefore, one individual of the totem species is, as elder brother, guardian spirit, or what not, raised to a position of superiority over all the rest, totemism is practically given up, and religion, like society, is advancing to the monarchical stage.

While totemism as a religion tends to pass into the worship first of animal gods and next of anthropomorphic gods with animal attributes, totem clans tend, under the same social conditions, to pass into local clans. Amongst the Kurnai, shut in between the mountains and the sea, phratries and clans have been replaced by exogamous local groups, which generally take their names from the districts, but in some cases from men of note.[3] The Coast Murring tribe in New South Wales has also substituted exogamous local groups for kinship divisions; but, though their totems are decadent and anomalous, they still keep a dying grip on the people, for a man cannot marry a woman of the permitted locality if she is of the same totem as himself.[4]

Totem clans tend to pass into local clans.

The totem clans of the Bechuanas have made some progress towards becoming local groups; for the clans as a rule keep together in their own districts, which are known accordingly as "the dwelling of the men of the chamois," "the abode of the men of the monkey," etc.[5] In America, if we cannot detect the substitution of local for kindred groups, we can at least see a step towards it in that relaxation of the rule of exogamy which has been observed in widely separated tribes. For example, among the Omahas,

Relaxation of the rule of exogamy.

---

[1] T. Falkner, *Description of Patagonia* (Hereford, 1774), p. 114.
[2] Acosta, *History of the Indies*, ii. p. 305 (Hakluyt Society).
[3] Fison and Howitt, 224 *sq.*
[4] *J. A. I.*, xiii. 437.
[5] Casalis, *The Basutos*, p. 212.

84   TOTEMISM

who have male descent, a man may marry a woman of the same totem as himself provided she be of another tribe.[1]

Distribution of totemism in Australia and America.

Geographical Diffusion of Totemism. — In Australia totemism is almost universal.[2] In North America it may be roughly said to prevail, or have prevailed, among all the tribes east of the Rocky Mountains,[3] and among all the Indian (but not the Eskimo) tribes on the north-west coast as far south as the United States frontier. On the other hand, highly competent authorities have failed to find it among the tribes of Western Washington, North-western Oregon, and California.[4] In Panama it exists apparently among the Guaymies: each tribe, family, and individual has a guardian animal, the most prevalent being a kind of parrot.[5] In South America totemism is found among the Goajiros on the borders of Colombia and Venezuela,[6] the Arawaks in Guiana,[7] the Bosch negroes also in Guiana,[8] and the Patagonians.[9] Finding it at such distant points of the continent, we should expect it to be widely prevalent; but with our meagre knowledge of the South American Indians this is merely conjecture. The aborigines of Peru

---

[1] *Third Rep.*, 257. For general statements of the relaxation of exogamy see Baer and Helmersen, *Beitr. z. Kenntn. des russischen Reiches*, i. 104; P. Jones, *Hist. Ojebway Indians*, 138; *Collect. Minnesota Hist. Soc.*, v. p. 42; *Smithson Rep. for 1866*, 315; Dall, *Alaska*, 196 *sq.*; Im Thurn, *Among the Indians of Guiana*, 175. The Dacotas (Sioux) seem to have lost the totem system since 1767 (see Morgan, *A. S.*, 154; J. Carver, *Travels*, 255 *sq.*, London, 1781; Keating, *Expedition to the Source of the Missouri River*, ii. 157; James, in Tanner's *Narrative*, 313 *sq.*; *Collect. Minnes. Hist. Soc.*, v. p. 43). In Australia, though the exogamy of the clan seems to remain intact, the exogamy of the subphratry is relaxed in the case (apparently exceptional) of the Kamilaroi permission to marry a half-sister on the father's side (see Fison and Howitt, p. 42 *sq.*).

[2] Perhaps the only known exceptions are the Kurnai in eastern, and the Gournditch-mora in Western Victoria.

For the latter see Fison and Howitt, p. 275. Of the aborigines on the lower Murray it is said that "they are not divided into clans, castes, or grades, but live on a footing of perfect equality" (Beveridge, in *Trans. Roy. Soc. Victoria*, vi. p. 21). But probably this does not exclude the existence of totem clans.

[3] Gatschet, *Migration Legend of the Creek Indians*, 153; H. Hale, *The Iroquois Book of Rites*, p. 51.

[4] George Gibbs, in *Contrib. to N. American Ethnol.*, i. 184; S. Powers, *Tr. of Calif.*, 5.

[5] A. Pinart, in *Revue d'Ethnographie*, vi. p. 36.

[6] Simons, in *Proc. R. Geog. Soc.*, Dec. 1885, pp. 786, 796.

[7] Brett, *Ind. Tribes of Guiana*, 98; Im Thurn, *Among the Indians of Guiana*, 175 *sq.*

[8] Crevaux, *Voyages dans l'Amérique du Sud*, p. 59. One clan has the red ape for its totem, others the turtle, crocodile, etc.

[9] Falkner, *Descr. of Patagonia*, 114.

and the Salivas on the Orinoco believed in the descent of their tribes from animals, plants, and natural objects, such as the sun and earth;[1] but this, though a presumption, is not a proof of totemism.

In Africa we have seen that totemism prevails in Senegambia, among the Bakalai on the equator, and among the Damaras and Bechuanas in Southern Africa.[2] There are traces of totemism elsewhere in Africa. In Ashantee different animals are worshipped in different districts, which points to totemism.[3] In Eastern Africa the Gallas are divided into two exogamous sections and have certain forbidden foods.[4] In Abyssinia certain districts or families will not eat of certain animals or parts of animals.[5] The territory of the Hovas in Madagascar is divided and subdivided into districts, the names of the subdivisions referring "rather to clans and divisions of people than to place." One of these names is "the powerful bird," *i.e.* either the eagle or the vulture. The same clan is found occupying separate districts.[6] One Madagascar tribe regard a species of lemur as "an embodiment of the spirit of their ancestors, and therefore they look with horror upon killing them."[7] Other Malagasy tribes and families refrain from eating pigs and goats;[8] others will not eat certain vegetables nor even allow them to be carried into their houses.[9] The only occasion when the Sakalava tribe in Madagascar kill a bull is at the circumcision of a child, who is placed on the bull's back during the customary invocation.[10]

In Bengal, as we have seen, there are numerous totem tribes among the non-Aryan races. In Siberia the Yakuts are divided into totem clans; the clansmen will not kill

Distribution of totemism in Africa.

Distribution of totemism in Asia.

---

[1] Garcilasso de la Vega, *Royal Commentaries of the Incas*, pt. i. bk. i. chs. 9, 10, 11, 18; Gumilla, *Hist. de l'Orenoque*, i. 175 *sq.*
[2] *Revue d'Ethnographie*, iii. 396 *sq.*, v. 81; Du Chaillu, *Équat. Afr.*, 308 *sq.*; *id., Journey to Ashango Land*, 427, 429; C. J. Andersson, *Lake Ngami*, 221 *sq.*; Livingstone, *Trav. in S. Africa*, 13; Casalis, *The Basutos*, 211; J. Mackenzie, *Ten Years North of the Orange River*, 393; *J. A. I.*, xvi. 83 *sq.*
[3] Bowdich, *Mission to Ashantee*, ed. 1873, p. 216.
[4] Charles New, *Life, Wanderings, and Labours in Eastern Africa*, 272, 274.
[5] Mansfield Parkyns, *Life in Abyssinia*, 293; *Tr. Ethnol. Soc.*, New Series, vi. 292.
[6] Ellis, *Hist. of Madagascar*, i. 87.
[7] *Folk-Lore Record*, ii. 22.
[8] *Ib.*
[9] *Ib.*, 30.
[10] *Id.*, iv. 45.

86   TOTEMISM

their totems (the swan, goose, raven, etc.);[1] and the clans are exogamous.[2] The Altaians, also in Siberia, are divided into twenty-four clans, which, though interfused with each other, retain strongly the clan feeling; the clans are exogamous; each has its own patron divinity and religious ceremonies; and the only two names of clans of these and kindred tribes of which the meanings are given are names **Totemism** of animals.[3] There are traces of totemism in China.[4] In **in Poly-** Polynesia it existed, as we have seen, in Samoa. In **nesia,** **Melanesia,** Melanesia it appears in Fiji,[5] the New Hebrides,[6] and **the East** the Solomon Islands.[7] Amongst the Dyaks there are **Indies, etc.** traces of totemism in the prohibition of the flesh of certain animals to certain tribes, respect for certain plants, etc.[8] It exists in the islands of Ambon, Uliase, Leti, Moa, Lakor, Keisar (Makisar), Wetar, and the Aaru and Babar archipelagoes.[9] In the Philippine Islands there are traces of it in the reverence for certain animals, the belief that the souls of ancestors dwell in trees, etc.[10]

Totemism With regard to ancient nations, totemism may be re**among the** garded as certain for the Egyptians, and highly probable **civilised** **races of** for the Semites,[11] Greeks, and Latins. If proved for one **antiquity.** Aryan people, it might be regarded as proved for all; since totemism could scarcely have been developed by any one Aryan branch after the dispersion, and there is no evidence or probability that it ever was borrowed. Professor Sayce

[1] Strahlenberg, *Description of the North and Eastern Parts of Europe and Asia, but more particularly of Russia, Siberia, and Great Tartary*, London, 1738, p. 383.

[2] Middendorf, *Siber. Reise*, p. 72, quoted by Lubbock, *Origin of Civilisation*, p. 135. The present writer has been unable to find the passage of Middendorf referred to.

[3] W. Radloff, *Aus Sibirien*, i. 216, 258. The Ostiaks, also in Siberia, are divided into exogamous clans, and they reverence the bear (Castren, *Vorlesungen ueber die Altaischen Völker*, 107, 115, 117). This, however, by no means amounts to a proof of totemism.

[4] Morgan, *A. S.*, p. 364 *sq.* One of the aboriginal tribes of China worships the image of a dog (Gray, *China*, ii. 306).

[5] Williams, *Fiji and the Fijians*, ed. 1860, i. 219 *sq.*

[6] Turner, *Samoa*, 334.

[7] Fison and Howitt, p. 37 *n.*

[8] Low, *Sarawak*, 265 *sq.*, 272-274, 306; *Journal of the Indian Archipelago*, iii. p. 590; St. John, *Life in the Forests of the Far East*, i. 186 *sq.*, 203; *cf.* Wilken, in *Ind. Gids*, June 1884, p. 988 *sq.*; *Ausland*, 16th June 1884, p. 470.

[9] Riedel, *De sluik- en kroesharige rassen tusschen Papua en Selebes*, pp. 32, 61, 253, 334, 341, 376 *sq.*, 414, 432.

[10] Blumentritt, *Der Ahnencultus und die religiösen Anschauungen der Malaien des Philippinen Archipel*, 159 *sq.*

[11] See W. Robertson Smith, *Kinship and Marriage in Early Arabia.*

finds totemism among the ancient Babylonians, but his evidence is not conclusive.[1]

Origin of Totemism.—No satisfactory explanation of the origin of totemism has yet been given. Mr. Herbert Spencer finds the origin of totemism in a "misinterpretation of nicknames": savages first named themselves after natural objects; and then, confusing these objects with their ancestors of the same names, reverenced them as they already reverenced their ancestors.[2] The objection to this view is that it attributes to verbal misunderstandings far more influence than, in spite of the so-called comparative mythology, they ever seem to have exercised. Sir John Lubbock also thinks that totemism arose from the habit of naming persons and families after animals; but in dropping the intermediate links of ancestor-worship and verbal misunderstanding, he has stripped the theory of all that lent it even an air of plausibility.[3] *{Spencer's theory that totemism originated in a misinterpretation of nicknames.}*

Lastly, it may be observed that, considering the far-reaching effects produced on the fauna and flora of a district by the preservation or extinction of a single species of animals or plants, it appears probable that the tendency of totemism to preserve certain species of plants and animals must have largely influenced the organic life of the countries where it has prevailed. But this question, with the kindred question of the bearing of totemism on the original domestication of animals and plants, is beyond the scope of the present article. *{Effects of totemism on the fauna and flora of a country.}*

Literature.—Apart from the original authorities which have been referred to, the literature on totemism is very scanty. The importance of totemism for the early history of society was first recognised by Mr. J. F. M'Lennan, in papers published in the *Fortnightly Review* (October and November 1869, February 1870). The subject has since been treated of by E. B. Tylor, *Early History of Mankind*, p. 284 *sq.*; Sir John Lubbock, *Origin of Civilisation*, 260 *sq.*; A. Lang, *Custom and Myth*, p. 260, etc.; E. Clodd, *Myths and Dreams*, p. 99 *sq.*; W. Robertson Smith, *Kinship and Marriage in Early Arabia*. See also *Encyclopædia Britannica*, 9th ed., article "Sacrifice," vol. xxi. p. 135.

---

[1] A. H. Sayce, *The Religion of the Ancient Babylonians* (Hibbert Lectures, 1887), p. 279 *sq.*

[2] Spencer, *Principles of Sociology*, i. 367.

[3] Lubbock, *Origin of Civilisation*, p. 260.

THE ORIGIN OF TOTEMISM

*Reprinted from the Fortnightly Review,
April and May 1899*

THE ORIGIN OF TOTEMISM

I

NEARLY thirty years have passed since, in the pages of the *Fortnightly Review*, the late J. F. M'Lennan drew the attention of students to Totemism as a system which, in his opinion, had deeply influenced the religious and social history of mankind.[1] His brilliant disciple, my lamented friend the late W. Robertson Smith, took up the subject, and, carrying out the investigation on the lines laid down by his predecessor, essayed to show that Totemism lay at the root of Semitic religion, and hence of the faith which is now embraced by the most civilised nations of the earth. Of late years the theory has been pushed still further by Mr. F. B. Jevons, who finds in this rude scheme of society and superstition the germs out of which not only all religion but all material progress have been evolved in the course of ages. *[side note: Totemism and theories concerning it.]*

It is fortunate that while theories on this subject have accumulated, facts have also accumulated, though perhaps not in an equal proportion. The two regions of the world in which the Totemic system is known to have prevailed most extensively are North America and Australia, and both of them, within the last three decades, have yielded a harvest, not inconsiderable in amount, to the anthropological reaper. In North America the enlightened efforts of the United States Government, setting an example which, alas, no other Government has had the wisdom to follow, have *[side note: Totemism in North America and Australia.]*

---

[1] J. F. M'Lennan, "The Worship of Animals and Plants," *Fortnightly Review*, Oct. and Nov. 1869, Feb. 1870.

92   THE ORIGIN OF TOTEMISM

been directed towards gleaning all that still remains to be learned of the ancient manners and customs of the aboriginal race, who are now rapidly disappearing or being absorbed by their conquerors. On the north-west coast of the same continent, where the disintegrating influence of European civilisation has penetrated more slowly, and where, consequently, the fabric of native society has held longer together, inquiries instituted by the British Association have also borne good fruit. In Australia the harvest is still abundant, but the labourers are few. Yet the study of the aborigines of this continent is of incalculable importance for the history of man, since in their archaic forms of society and modes of thought we seem to touch the farthest past, the most rudimentary stage of human life now open to observation on the globe. It is the honourable distinction of two men, Mr. A. W. Howitt and Mr. Lorimer Fison, to have perceived the immense value of the Australian facts, and to have laboured untiringly to collect and explain them. To their influence and example it is due in large measure that we now possess a considerable body of information on the remarkable social organisation of the Australian tribes, and not the least of their claims to be gratefully remembered by posterity will be the stimulus they gave to the inquiries of Messrs. Spencer and Gillen, whose great work on the natives of Central Australia has lately been published.[1] In this work we possess for the first time a full and authentic account of thoroughly primitive savages living in the totem stage, and practically unaffected by European influence. Its importance as a document of human history can, therefore, hardly be over-estimated. A little consideration will enable the reader to realise this more clearly.

The work of Spencer and Gillen on the natives of Central Australia.

The backwardness of the Australian savages an effect of their isolation.

Among the great land masses or continents of the world Australia is at once the smallest and the most isolated, and hence its plants and animals are in general of a less developed and more archaic type than those of the other continents. For the same reason aboriginal man has

[1] *The Native Tribes of Central Australia.* By Baldwin Spencer, M.A., some time Fellow of Lincoln College, Oxford, Professor of Biology in the University of Melbourne; and F. J. Gillen, Special Magistrate and Sub-Protector of the Aborigines, Alice Springs, South Australia. London: Macmillan & Co. 1899.

THE ORIGIN OF TOTEMISM 93

remained on the whole, down to the present day, in a more primitive state in Australia than elsewhere. In the struggle for existence progress depends mainly on competition: the more numerous the competitors the fiercer is the struggle, and the more rapid, consequently, is evolution. The comparatively small area of Australia, combined with its physical features—notably the arid and desert nature of a large part of the country—has always restricted population, and by restricting population has retarded progress. This holds true above all of the central region, which is not only cut off from the outer world by its position, but is also isolated by natural barriers from the rest of the continent. Here, then, in the secluded heart of the most secluded continent the scientific inquirer might reasonably expect to find the savage in his very lowest depths, to detect humanity in the chrysalis stage, to mark the first blind gropings of our race after freedom and light.

The reader who turns to *The Native Tribes of Central Australia* with such hopes and expectations will not, I venture to predict, be disappointed. Here he will find a full description of what is perhaps the most extraordinary set of customs and beliefs ever put on record. To illustrate the gulf which divides these savages from ourselves it must here suffice to mention two facts. In the first place, although they suffer much from cold at night under the frosty stars of the clear Australian heaven, the idea of using as garments the warm furs of the wild animals which they kill and eat has never entered into their minds. They huddle, naked and shivering, about little fires, into which, when they drop off to sleep, they are apt to roll and scorch themselves. In the second place, they have no notion that mankind is propagated by the union of the sexes; indeed, when the idea is suggested to them they steadfastly reject it. Their own theory to account for the continuation of the species is sufficiently remarkable. They suppose that in certain far-off times, to which they give the name of "Alcheringa," their ancestors roamed about in bands, each band consisting of members of the same totem group. Where they died their spirits went into the ground and formed, as it were, spiritual store-houses, the external mark of which is some

[marginal note: The primitiveness of the Central Australians illustrated by two facts, their lack of all clothing and their belief that mankind is not propagated by the union of the sexes.]

natural feature, generally a stone or tree. Such spots are scattered all over the country, and the ancestral spirits who haunt them are ever waiting for a favourable opportunity to be born again into the world. When one of them sees his chance he pounces out on a passing girl or woman and enters into her. Then she conceives, and in due time gives birth to a child, who is firmly believed to be a reincarnation of the spirit that darted into the mother from the rock or tree. It matters not whether a woman be young or old, a matron or a maid, all are alike liable to be thus impregnated by the spirits, although it has been shrewdly observed by the natives that the spirits on the whole exhibit a preference for such women as are young and fat. Accordingly, when a plump damsel, who shrinks from the burden of maternity, is obliged to pass one of the spots where the disembodied spirits are supposed to lurk, she disguises herself as a withered old hag and hobbles past, bent up double, leaning on a stick, wrinkling her smooth young face, and mumbling in a cracked and wheezy voice, "Don't come to me, I am an old woman." Thus, in the opinion of these savages, every conception is what we are wont to call an immaculate conception, being brought about by the entrance into the mother of a spirit apart from any contact with the other sex. Students of folk-lore have long been familiar with notions of this sort occurring in the stories of the birth of miraculous personages,[1] but this is the first case on record of a tribe who believe in immaculate conception as the sole cause of the birth of every human being who comes into the world. A people so ignorant of the most elementary of natural processes may well rank at the very bottom of the savage scale.

Great importance of the record of these tribes for the early history of mankind.
Thus it will be obvious that a complete and accurate record of the thoughts and habits of a people so low down in the scale of humanity must possess the highest scientific interest; for it is now generally admitted that all the civilised races of mankind have at some time passed through the stage of savagery, and that on a close scrutiny the seeds of most of the institutions on which we pride ourselves may

[1] Many examples are collected by Mr. E. S. Hartland, in his learned work, *The Legend of Perseus.*

be discovered, still partially or wholly undeveloped, in the customs of the rudest tribes. A record of this sort has been given to the world by the devoted labours of Messrs. Spencer and Gillen, who have thereby earned the gratitude, not of this generation only, but of all future generations who shall henceforth interest themselves in tracing the slow evolution of civilisation out of savagery. It is no exaggeration to say that, among the documents which students of the early history of man will in future be bound to consult, there can, from the nature of the case, be few or none of more capital importance than *The Native Tribes of Central Australia.* For in a few years the simple savages who, at the end of the nineteenth century still think the thoughts and retain the habits of primeval man, will have perished, or be so changed that all their old-world ways will be gone irretrievably. Everywhere the savages are dying out, and as they go they take with them page after page of the most ancient history of our race. The study of savage man may be compared to the Sibyl, who, as she threw away leaf after leaf, still demanded the same price for the ever diminishing number that remained. Our chances of preserving for future generations a record of these tribes—the beaten and dying runners in life's race—are lessening year by year, enhancing rather than diminishing, as they drop away, the value of the few trustworthy records we have secured. For there is this difference between the Sibyl of Cumæ and the Sibyl of anthropology: the revelation promised by the former was not lost for ever with the fluttering leaves—the future will in time reveal itself to the future; but who shall read in ages to come the vanished record of the past?

I will illustrate by a single example the way in which the customs and beliefs of these Central Australian savages may throw light on the growth of a great institution. The institution which I shall select is great enough, for it is the Roman Empire. We have all read in our schooldays of the device to which Romulus is said to have resorted for the purpose of peopling the city that was destined to become the mistress of the ancient world. On the slope of the Capitoline Hill, then buried deep in the shady horror of a dark and tangled wood, he established a sanctuary of

Illustration of the light thrown by the customs of the Central Australians on the growth of institutions.

96 THE ORIGIN OF TOTEMISM

Origin of Rome in an asylum for outlaws.

some god or spirit unknown, and proclaimed that all who resorted thither, whether bond or free, should be safe, and should receive lands and citizenship. Lured by these promises, a multitude of broken men—slaves escaping from their masters, debtors who had outrun the bailiffs, murderers with the avengers of blood hot on their tracks—flocked from all the country round to the new town on the Tiber, and a motley population of wretches, ruffians, and desperadoes soon gathered within the massive walls and became the terror of their neighbours.[1] This tradition has not received from historians the attention it deserves. There are good grounds for believing that many cities have sprung up in nearly the same way as Rome is said to have done, not so much through the arbitrary decree of a founder as through the existence of an immemorial sanctuary, within which outlawed and desperate men have found safety and taken up their abode. I propose to show that the germ of such an institution exists, or has existed, in many savage communities, and that the full-grown institution still flourishes in various parts of the world.

Asylums in Central Australia, New Guinea, and America.

To begin with the lowest savages, the natives of Central Australia have certain sacred spots—generally caves in the heart of their wild and lonely hills—which may be regarded as the first rudiment of a city or house of refuge. Here are kept the mysterious sticks and stones (*churinga*) with which the spirits not only of all their dead ancestors but also of all the living members of the tribe are intimately associated. Everything in such spots and their immediate neighbourhood is sacred; nothing must be done to disturb the spirits. No plant may be pulled there, no branch broken. The very animals that run thither are safe from the hunter; no native would dare to spear a kangaroo or wallaby on the holy ground. Within its limits men, too, are safe from their pursuers; so long as they do not pass the bounds they may not be touched.[2] In some parts of New Guinea the *dubu* or temple serves as an asylum. A man who is pursued by

---

[1] Dionysius Halicarnasensis, *Antiquit. Rom.*, i. 15; Livy, i. 8; Strabo, v. 230, ed. Casaubon; Plutarch, *Romulus*, 9.

[2] Spencer and Gillen, *The Native Tribes of Central Australia*, p. 134 *sq.*

his enemy and takes refuge in it is perfectly safe. If any one tried to smite him in the temple it is believed that his arms and legs would shrivel up, and that he could do nothing but wish for death.[1] Similarly, among the rude Indians of California, described by the Spanish missionary, Father Boscana, every temple enjoyed the right of asylum. Criminals who had once reached a temple (*vanquech*) were secure, not only within but also outside the precinct; they might thenceforth go abroad without fear of molestation; the mere entrance into the sacred place had purged their guilt.[2] The Ojibways are said to have had sanctuaries in which every murderer might seek refuge, it being universally believed that no vengeance might be taken on him there. The German traveller, J. G. Kohl, heard that the murderer of a Governor of the Hudson's Bay Company was actually living at the time securely in one of these asylums.[3]

Among more advanced peoples it seems that the tombs, or other places believed to be haunted by the spirits of dead chiefs or kings, are especially apt to develop into asylums. Thus in the monarchical States of the Gallas, in Eastern Africa, homicides enjoy a legal right of asylum if they have succeeded in taking refuge in a hut near the burial-place of the King, which is not far from the King's house.[4] Similarly, among the Barotse of Southern Africa, the tombs of the Kings, in number about seventy-five, are sanctuaries or places of refuge; and so, too, are the residences of the Queen and the Prime Minister.[5] Among the Ovambo of South-western Africa the village of a great chief is abandoned at his death; only the members of a certain family remain to prevent it from falling into utter decay. Condemned criminals who contrive to escape to one of these deserted villages are safe, at least for a time; for even the chief himself may not pursue a fugitive into the sacred place.[6] In Upolu, one of the Samoan islands, a certain

Asylums in Africa and Samoa.

---

[1] J. Chalmers and W. Wyatt Gill, *Work and Adventure in New Guinea*, p. 186.
[2] Boscana, in [A. Robinson's] *Life in California*, p. 262. New York, 1846.
[3] J. G. Kohl, *Kitschi-Gami*, ii. p. 67. Bremen, 1859.
[4] Ph. Paulitschke, *Ethnographie Nordost-Afrikas: Die Geistige Cultur der Danâkil, Galla und Somâl*, p. 157. Berlin, 1896.
[5] L. Decle, *Three Years in Savage Africa*, p. 75. London, 1898.
[6] H. Schinz, *Deutsch-Südwest-Afrika*, p. 312.

god, Vave, had his abode in an old tree, which served as an asylum for murderers and other offenders who had incurred the penalty of death. " If that tree was reached by the criminal, he was safe, and the avenger of blood could pursue no farther, but wait investigation and trial. It is said that the King of a division of Upolu, called Atua, once lived at that spot. After he died the house fell into decay, but the tree was fixed on as representing the departed King, and out of respect for his memory it was made the substitute of a living and Royal protector. It was called *o le asi pulu tangata*, ' the asi tree, the refuge of men.' This reminds me of what I once heard from a native of another island. He said that at one time they had been ten years without a King, and so anxious were they to have some protecting substitute that they fixed upon a large O'a tree (*Bischoffia Javanica*), and made it the representative of a King, and an asylum for the thief or the homicide when pursued by the injured in hot haste for vengeance."[1]

Asylum in Borneo.

In Koetei, a district of Borneo, criminals guilty of capital offences who can take refuge in the Sultan's *dalam* may not be slain there, but they lose their freedom for ever, and their children also become slaves. Such refugees, male and female, generally intermarry, and serve the Sultan as domestics, retainers, soldiers, police-agents, and so on. They are a curse to the country. Being drawn, for the most part, from the scum of the population, and always going about armed, they terrify peaceable folk by their brutal and insolent behaviour.[2]

How asylums may grow into cities.

This last example is instructive. It shows how outlaws or refugees may grow into an important and dangerous element of the population. All that is needed to produce this effect is, besides immunity, a rule that the descendants of outcasts shall themselves be outcasts. Where this rule prevails, and the outlaws are segregated in towns or villages of their own, it is obvious that we have a state of matters very like that which is said to have obtained at Rome in its earliest days. Now such a condition of things actually

[1] G. Turner, *Samoa*, pp. 64 *sq*.
[2] S. W. Tromp, "Uit de Salasila van Koetei," *Bijdragen tot de taal- land-en volkenkunde van Nederlandsch Indië*, xxxvii. p. 84 *sq*. 1888.

exists at present among the secluded and barbarous tribes of the Siah Posh Kafirs, who inhabit the savage glens and highlands of the Hindu Kush. Amongst them every manslayer is obliged to quit his home and take up his abode in one or other of certain villages or "cities of refuge," as Sir George Robertson calls them. And it is not merely the slayer himself who is thus banished: his sons, if they are not grown up at the time of the homicide, generally become outcasts too, and so do his daughters' husbands and their descendants. The result is that there are whole villages peopled mainly by manslayers or their offspring.[1] It is well known that the Hebrews had cities of refuge, within which a manslayer might not be touched by the avenger of blood.[2] A similar institution existed among the more advanced aboriginal tribes of North America, and has been described by a writer of last century, who laboured under the impression that in the Redskins he had discovered the long lost Ten Tribes of Israel. This luminous idea does not, however, impair the value of his testimony, of which we have independent confirmation. He says: "Each of these Indian nations have either a house or a town of refuge, which is a sure asylum to protect a manslayer or the unfortunate captive if they can once enter into it. The Cheerake, though now exceedingly corrupt, still observe the law so inviolably as to allow their beloved town the privilege of protecting a wilful murderer; but they seldom allow him to return home afterwards in safety—they will revenge blood for blood, unless in some very particular case." "Formerly," says the same writer, "when one of the Cheerake murdered an English trader, he immediately ran off for the town of refuge; but as soon as he got in view of it the inhabitants discovered him by the close pursuit of the shrill war whoo-whoop, and, for fear of irritating the English, they instantly answered the war-cry, ran to arms, intercepted, and drove him off into Tennase River (where he escaped, though mortally wounded), lest he should have entered the reputed holy ground and thus it had been stained with the blood of their friend, or he had obtained sanctuary

[1] Sir G. S. Robertson, *The Kafirs of the Hindu Kush*, p. 440 *sq.*, London, 1896.   [2] *Numbers*, xxxv. 6-34.

THE ORIGIN OF TOTEMISM

to the danger of the community."[1] Among the Creek Indians the cities of refuge were called the White Towns, while the towns which afforded no asylum were known as the Red or War Towns.[2]

Sanctuaries developing into cities of refuge in West Africa.   A link is wanting to connect these cities of refuge in America, Palestine, and the Hindu Kush, with the less developed forms of asylum which we have met with among various tribes of savages. For none of these cities is reported to have grown up gradually through the drifting of the waifs and strays of society towards a rock of refuge, such as a tomb or other holy place offers in the troubled sea of barbarism. This missing link appears to be supplied in Western Africa. Here, in the regions of the French Congo and Calabar, are sanctuaries in which evildoers of all kinds —for example, thieves, sorcerers, and women who have been guilty of the inexpiable offence of giving birth to twins —seek, and find, safety. These sanctuaries cover considerable tracts of ground, being large enough to contain a whole village with its lands. Whoever can make good his escape to one of them is absolutely secure. But the society, as might be expected, is rather numerous than select; its great charm lies more in a general easiness and freedom of manners than in any natural delicacy or studied refinement. A man of Miss Kingsley's acquaintance, who had been obliged to betake himself for a time to one of these communities, found the society so intolerable that he preferred to quit it at all hazards.[3]

Many cities may have originated in this way.   With these facts before us, we may fairly conjecture that not a few towns in ancient and modern times may have arisen through the gradual accretion of the dregs and outcasts of society about some spot of peculiar holiness. The view that Rome originated in this manner is supported by tradition, and is, perhaps, not belied by anything in the ancient or modern history of the city; certainly it accords well with the belief of the ancients themselves that the Romans were a mixed race. Thus, to go back to the point

---

[1] J. Adair, *History of the American Indians*, p. 158. London, 1775.

[2] H. Schoolcraft, *Indian Tribes of the United States*, v. p. 279.

[3] Miss Mary H. Kingsley, *Travels in West Africa*, p. 466. London, 1897. In the text I have embodied some additional details, which Miss Kingsley was kind enough to give me in conversation.

from which we started, the sacred caves of the rude savages in the wilds of Australia may not unreasonably be regarded as representing in germ an institution out of which a great city, perhaps even a great empire, might, under more favourable circumstances, have been developed.

But it is time to turn to my more immediate subject. In this paper I desire to call attention to some of the novel features of Central Australian Totemism, as they are disclosed to us by the researches of Messrs. Spencer and Gillen, and further to consider how far the new facts may require us to modify or recast our old views of Totemism in general. It may be well to begin by reminding the reader that a totem is a class of natural phenomena or material objects—most commonly a species of animals or plants—between which and himself the savage believes that a certain intimate relation exists. The exact nature of the relation is not easy to ascertain; various explanations of it have been suggested, but none has as yet won general acceptance. Whatever it may be, it generally leads the savage to abstain from killing or eating his totem, if his totem happens to be a species of animals or plants. Further, the group of persons who are knit to any particular totem by this mysterious tie commonly bear the name of the totem, believe themselves to be of one blood, and strictly refuse to sanction the marriage or cohabitation of members of the group with each other. This prohibition to marry within the group is now generally called by the name of Exogamy. Thus, Totemism has commonly been treated as a primitive system both of religion and of society. As a system of religion it embraces the mystic union of the savage with his totem; as a system of society it comprises the relations in which men and women of the same totem stand to each other and to the members of other totemic groups. And corresponding to these two sides of the system are two rough-and-ready tests or canons of Totemism: first, the rule that a man may not kill or eat his totem animal or plant; and second, the rule that he may not marry or cohabit with a woman of the same totem. Whether the two sides—the religious and the social—have always co-existed or are essentially independent, is a

Novel features of Central Australian Totemism.

Old canons of Totemism, the prohibitions to kill or eat the totem animal or plant and to marry a woman of the same totem.

question which has been variously answered. Some writers —for example, Sir John Lubbock and Mr. Herbert Spencer —have held that Totemism began as a system of society only, and that the superstitious regard for the totem developed later, through a simple process of misunderstanding. Others, including J. F. M'Lennan and Robertson Smith, were of opinion that the religious reverence for the totem is original, and must, at least, have preceded the introduction of Exogamy.

Discrepancy between the traditions and the practice of the Central Australians in regard to Totemism. Now, when we consider the totemic system of the Central Australian tribes, as it is described by Messrs. Spencer and Gillen, one of the things that strikes us most is the extraordinary discrepancy between their traditions and their practice. If their traditions may be trusted, their ancestors certainly did not observe the totemic rules which are now practised by their descendants. Let us take what I have called the canons of Totemism and see how they apply to the present practice of these natives, and to what is represented as having been the practice of their forefathers in days gone by.

First, though the natives at present do not generally kill or eat their totems, it seems that their ancestors did so regularly. First, the rule that a man may not kill or eat his totem animal or plant. Roughly speaking, this rule is fairly well observed, with certain remarkable exceptions, by the Central Australians at present. "A man will only eat very sparingly of his totem, and even if he does eat a little of it, which is allowable to him, he is careful, in the case, for example, of an Emu man, not to eat the best part, such as the fat."[1] In a note on this passage the authors add : "The people of the Emu totem very rarely eat the eggs, unless very hungry and short of food, in which case they would eat, but not too abundantly. If an Emu man found a nest of eggs, and was very hungry, he might cook one, but he would take the remainder into camp and distribute them. If he were not very hungry all the eggs would be distributed. The flesh of the bird may be eaten sparingly, but only a very little of the fat ; the eggs and fat are more *ekirinja*, or taboo, than the meat. The same principle holds good through all the totems ; a Carpet-snake man will eat sparingly of a poor snake, but he will scarcely touch the

[1] *The Native Tribes of Central Australia,* p. 202.

reptile if it be fat." Elsewhere, Messrs. Spencer and Gillen observe that "at the present day the totemic animal or plant, as the case may be, is almost, but not quite, taboo, or, as the Arunta people call it, *ekirinja*, to the members of the totem."[1] Yet the traditions of these same natives represent their ancestors as possessing and freely exercising the right to kill and eat their totem animals and plants, "as if this were, indeed, a functional necessity."[2]

Second, the rule that a man may not marry or cohabit with a woman of the same totem. At the present day this rule is strictly observed by a group of Central Australian tribes, of which the Urabunna may be taken as typical. It is not observed at all by another group of tribes, of which the Arunta may be regarded as representative. Among these latter tribes the totemic system has no effect on marriage and descent; a man may marry a woman of the same totem or he may not, and his children may belong either to his or to his wife's totem, or to neither, or some to one and some to the other. Very different was the state of things in the past, if we may trust tradition, the evidence of which "seems to point back to a time when a man always married a woman of his own totem. The reference to men and women of one totem always living together in groups would appear to be too frequent and explicit to admit of any other satisfactory explanation. We never meet [in tradition] with an instance of a man living with a woman who was not of his own totem."[3] {Though some of the Central Australians now strictly observe the rule of exogamy, it appears that their ancestors on the contrary always married women of the same totem as themselves.}

Thus the Central Australian tribes have clear and positive traditions of a time when they regularly killed and ate their totem, and always married women of the same totem as themselves. Such traditions, it is plain, fly straight in the face of all our old notions of Totemism. Are we, therefore, at liberty to reject them as baseless? Certainly not. Their very discordance with the practice of the natives at the present day is the best guarantee that they contain a substantial element of truth. They could not have been invented to explain customs which they contradict. Every theory of Central Australian Totemism must reckon with {The very fact that these traditions contradict the present practice of the people is the best proof of their genuineness.}

[1] *The Native Tribes of Central Australia*, p. 206.
[2] *Op. cit.*, p. 209.
[3] *Op. cit.*, p. 419.

them; none can be satisfactory which does not show how the gulf between the present and past totemic system of the natives can be bridged.

Bearing this in mind, let us look at the existing system more closely. First, we must note that while the totems of these tribes are generally animals or plants, they are not exclusively so: we hear of totems of the wind, the sun, the evening star, fire, water, cloud, and so on; "in fact there is scarcely an object, animate or inanimate, to be found in the country occupied by the natives which does not give its name to some totemic group of individuals."[1] Next, let us observe that each totem group performs certain sacred ceremonies called *Intichiuma*, the object of which, whenever the totem happens to be an animal or plant, is to ensure the multiplication of the animals or plants of that species. These ceremonies, to which the natives seem to attach more importance than to any others,[2] are generally held at what may be called the approach of the Australian spring. "The *Intichiuma* are closely associated with the breeding of the animals and the flowering of the plants with which each totem is respectively identified, and as the object of the ceremony is to increase the number of the totemic animal or plant, it is most naturally held at a certain season. In Central Australia the seasons are limited, so far as the breeding of animals and the flowering of plants is concerned, to two—a dry one of uncertain and often great length, and a rainy one of short duration and often of irregular occurrence. The latter is followed by an increase in animal life and an exuberance of plant growth which, almost suddenly, transforms what may have been a sterile waste into a land rich in various forms of animals, none of which have been seen for, it may be, many months before, and gay with the blossoms of endless flowering plants. In the case of many of the totems it is just when there is promise of the approach of a good season that it is customary to hold the ceremony."[3]

The analogy of these ceremonies to the spring and midsummer festivals of our European peasantry, as the latter have been interpreted by W. Mannhardt, is obvious. To

Each totem group performs ceremonies called Intichiuma for the multiplication of the totem animal or plant.

---

[1] *The Native Tribes of Central Australia*, p. 112.
[2] *Op. cit.*, p. 167.
[3] *Op. cit.*, p. 169 *sq.*

THE ORIGIN OF TOTEMISM

dwell on the analogy would be out of place here. I shall have an opportunity elsewhere of pointing the moral which is to be drawn from it. Here I will only ask the reader to observe that, like their European analogues these Australian ceremonies are in their essence magical rather than religious. The distinction between religion and magic may be said to be that while the former is an attempt to propitiate or conciliate the higher powers, the latter is an attempt to compel or coerce them. Thus, while religion assumes that the great controlling powers of the world are so far akin to man as to be liable, like him, to be moved by human prayers and entreaties, magic makes no such assumption. To the magician it is a matter of indifference whether the cosmic powers are conscious or unconscious, spiritual or material, for in either case he imagines that he can force them by his enchantments and spells to do his bidding. Now as the *Intichiuma* ceremonies are supposed to produce their effect directly and necessarily, and " their performance is not associated in the native mind with the idea of appealing to the assistance of any supernatural being,"[1] it is plain that they are magical in their nature, rather than religious. A brief notice of some of them will set this in a clear light.

The Intichiuma ceremonies are magical rather than religious.

In order to ensure a plentiful supply of a certain grub known as the witchetty grub, which is a favourite article of diet with the natives, and only appears for a short time after rain, the men of the Witchetty Grub totem repair to a shallow cave in a ravine, where lies a large block of quartzite, surrounded by some small rounded stones. The large block represents the full-grown grubs; the small stones stand for the eggs. On reaching the cave the head man of the totem group begins to sing, while he taps the large block with a wooden trough, such as is used for scooping the earth out of burrows. All the other men at the same time tap it with twigs of a particular gum-tree, chanting the while. The burden of their song is an invitation to the insect to go and lay eggs. Next the leader takes up one of the smaller stones, representing an egg, and strikes each man in the stomach with it, saying, "You have eaten much food," after

Ceremonies performed by Witchetty Grub men for the multiplication of witchetty grubs.

[1] *The Native Tribes of Central Australia*, p. 170.

which he butts at the man's stomach with his forehead. When this ceremony is over, they all descend from the cave into the bed of the ravine, and stop under a rock, at which a great leader of the Witchetty Grub totem in the far past is said to have cooked, pulverised, and eaten the grub. The head man of the party strikes this rock with his trough, while the older men again chant invitations to the animal to come from all directions and lay eggs. Ceremonies of the same sort are performed at ten different places. When the round has been completed the party returns home. Here, at some distance from the main camp, a long narrow structure of boughs has meanwhile been got ready; it is designed to represent the chrysalis from which the full-grown insect emerges. Into this structure the men, every one with the sacred design of the totem painted in red ochre and pipeclay on his body, enter and sing of the grub in the various stages of its development. After chanting thus for a while, they shuffle out of the mock chrysalis one by one with a gliding motion, singing all the time about the emergence of the real insect out of the real chrysalis, of which their own performance is clearly an imitation. The whole of these ceremonies, from beginning to end, must be performed by the men fasting; not until the whole is over are the performers allowed to eat and drink.

Ceremonies performed by Emu men for the multiplication of emus.

When men of the Emu totem desire to multiply emus they set about it as follows. Several of the men open veins in their arms and allow the blood to stream on the ground, till a patch about three yards square is saturated with it. When the blood is dry it forms a hard surface, on which the men of the totem paint in white, red, yellow and black a design intended to represent various parts of the emu, such as the fat, of which the natives are very fond, the eggs in various stages of development, the intestines, and the feathers. Further, several men of the totem, acting the part of ancestors of the Emu clan, dress themselves up to resemble emus and imitate the movements and aimless gazing about of the bird; on their heads are fastened sacred sticks (*churinga*), about four feet long, and tipped with emu feathers, to represent the long neck and small head of the emu.

Again, when men of the Hakea Flower totem wish to produce a plentiful supply of the flower they go to a certain stone which stands in a shallow pit beside an ancient hakea tree. The stone is supposed to represent a mass of hakea flowers, and the tree to mark the spot where an ancestress of the clan passed into the ground long ago. The men sit down in the pit round about the stone and chant songs, inviting the tree to flower much, and the blossoms to be full of honey. Then one of them opens a vein in his arm, and lets the blood spurt all over the stone; this is meant to imitate the preparation of a favourite beverage made by steeping the flower in water. *[margin: Ceremonies performed by Hakea Flowermen for the multiplication of hakea flowers.]*

Again, there is a sort of manna which the natives use as food, and which forms the totem of one of their clans. It is produced by the mulga tree (*Acacia aneura*). When the members of the totem clan desire to ensure an abundant crop of this manna they resort to a certain great boulder of grey rock, which is oddly marked with black and white seams. This boulder is thought to represent a mass of the manna, and the same significance is attributed to some smaller stones which lie on the top of it. The ceremony begins by the digging up of a sacred bull-roarer (*churinga*), which is buried in the ground at the foot of the great boulder. It, too, stands for a mass of manna. Then the head man climbs to the top of the boulder and rubs it with the bull-roarer, after which he takes the smaller stones and rubs them, too, on the great boulder. Meanwhile, the other men, sitting around, chant an invitation to the dust produced by the rubbing of the stones to go out and generate a plentiful supply of manna on the mulga trees. Finally, with twigs of the mulga, the leader sweeps away the dust which has gathered on the surface of the stone; his intention, thereby, is to cause the dust to settle on the trees, and so produce manna. *[margin: Ceremonies performed by Manna men for the multiplication of manna.]*

The last of the *Intichiuma* ceremonies which I shall cite is the one performed by men of the Kangaroo totem, to ensure the multiplication of kangaroos. For this purpose they proceed to the foot of a hill on the slope of which, some twenty feet above the plain, two blocks of stone project, one above the other. One of these stones is supposed *[margin: Ceremonies performed by Kangaroo men for the multiplication of kangaroos,]* to represent a male kangaroo, and the other a female kangaroo. The head man of the totem clan and another man, who stands to the former in the relation of mother's uncle, whether blood or tribal, climb up the hill and rub these two blocks with a stone, one of them rubbing the one block and the other the other. Lower down the hill is a rocky ledge, supposed to be haunted by the spirits of multitudes of kangaroos which died here long ago. This ledge is next painted with alternate vertical stripes of red and white to indicate the red fur and white bones of a kangaroo. When the painting is done, some young men go up, seat themselves on the ledge, and opening veins in their arms, allow the blood to spurtle over the edge of the rock on which they are seated. The object of this ceremony, according to the natives, is to drive the spirits of the kangaroos out of the rock in all directions, and so to ensure the multiplication of the animals. While the young men are thus bleeding themselves on the top of the ledge the others sit down below, watching them and singing songs in reference to the increase in the number of kangaroos which is expected to follow from this performance.

These ceremonies for the multiplication of animals and plants are intended to increase the supply of food for the tribe.

Without entering into more details, I may say that ceremonies of the same general character as the preceding appear to be practised by members of all the other clans or groups who have animals or plants for their totems. The object of all such ceremonies, avowedly, is to increase the number of the totem animal or plant, and this object the natives sincerely believe that they attain by these means. Thus we see that each totem clan imagines itself possessed of a direct control over the animal or plant whose name it bears, and this control it exercises for the purpose of multiplying the number of its totem plant or animal. But the question at once suggests itself, Why should they trouble themselves to multiply animals or plants which, by their rules, they are almost wholly debarred from eating? For it is to be remembered that the totem animal or plant is almost, though not quite, tabooed to men and women of the totem. The answer to this question can only be that, though the members of each totem group do not benefit, or hardly benefit at all, by multiplying their totem animal or

THE ORIGIN OF TOTEMISM

plant, the members of all the other totem groups do benefit by it, since their food supply is believed to be increased thereby. In other words, the *Intichiuma* ceremonies are performed by each totem group, not on its own behoof, but on behoof of all the others, the general effect of all the ceremonies being supposed to be an increase of the total supply of food available for the whole tribe, which, it is needful to bear in mind, includes a large number of totem clans. The system is, in fact, one of co-operative magic—each group works its spells for the good of all the rest and benefits in its turn through the enchantments practised by the others.

The conclusion that ceremonies for the multiplication of certain plants and animals, all of which are used as food by some members of the tribe, can have no other aim than that of increasing the food supply of the tribe as a whole may seem so obvious as to need no argument in its support. Yet the view of Totemism which it implies is so novel and so totally opposed to all our previous notions on the subject that it is desirable to put it beyond the reach of doubt. For the view is neither more nor less than this: that one at least of the functions of a totem clan is to provide a plentiful supply of its own totem animal or plant to be used as food by the other members of the tribe. That this is, indeed, the intention of the *Intichiuma* ceremonies among the Central Australian tribes is clearly brought out by the following facts. *Hence it appears that one function of a totem clan is to provide a supply of its totem animal or plant for the consumption of the rest of the tribe.*

When the ceremony for the multiplication of the witchetty grubs has been performed, and the grub becomes plentiful and fully grown, the Witchetty Grub men, women, and children go out daily and collect large supplies of the grub, which they bring into camp and cook, so that it becomes dry and brittle; and in this state they store it away in wooden troughs and pieces of bark. At the same time, the others, who do not belong to the Witchetty Grub totem, are also out gathering the grub, but they must bring all that they find into the camp; for this food must on no account be eaten like other food out in the bush, or the men of the totem would be angry and the grub would disappear. The supply of grubs lasts only a very short time, and when *The Witchetty Grub people collect and cook large quantities of witchetty grubs for people who do not belong to the Witchetty Grub totem.*

they grow less plentiful the store of cooked grubs is taken to the men's camp, where, acting under the instructions of the head man of the Witchetty Grub totem, all the men assemble. Those who do not belong to the totem then place their stores before those who do, and the head man thereupon takes one of the troughs and, with the help of other men of the totem, grinds up the dried grubs between stones. Next he and the same men all help themselves to a little of the food and eat it, after which he hands back what remains to the other people. Then he takes a trough from his own store, and after he has ground up the contents he and the men of the totem once more eat a little; lastly, they pass the bulk of what remains to those who do not belong to the Witchetty Grub totem. After this ceremony, the Witchetty Grub men and women may eat very sparingly of the grub. They are not absolutely forbidden to eat it, but they must do so only to a small extent, for if they were to eat too much the power of successfully performing the *Intichiuma* ceremony would depart from them, and there would be very few grubs. On the other hand, it is just as important for them, and especially for the head man, to eat a little of the totemic animal, since to eat none would have the same disastrous effect as to eat too much.

Ceremony performed by Kangaroo men before the rest of the people may eat kangaroos.

Similarly, when the ceremony for increasing the number of kangaroos has been performed, the younger men go out hunting kangaroos and bring back the animals which they have killed to the older men, who have stayed in the camp. Here the old men of the Kangaroo totem eat a little of the kangaroo and anoint the bodies of those who took part in the ceremony with its fat, after which the meat is distributed to all the men assembled. When this has been done, the Kangaroo men may eat sparingly of kangaroos; but there are certain choice parts of the animal, such as the tail, which no Kangaroo man or woman must on any account touch.

Ceremony performed by men of the Irriakura totem before the irriakura bulb may be eaten.

Again, there is a certain bulb of a Cyperaceous plant which the natives call *irriakura*. When the men of the Irriakura totem have performed their ceremony for multiplying the bulb, they do not eat of it for some time afterwards. Then persons who do not belong to the totem bring in a quantity of the bulb to the camp and hand it over to the head man and other men of the Irriakura totem. These latter rub some of the tubers between their hands, thus getting rid of the husks, and then, putting the tubers in their mouths, blow them out again in all directions. After this the Irriakura people may eat sparingly of the bulbs.

After the magic rite for multiplying bandicoots has been performed by men of the Bandicoot totem the animal is not eaten until it becomes plentiful. When this is so, men who do not belong to the Bandicoot totem go out in search of a bandicoot, and when they have caught it they bring it into the camp and there put some of the animal's fat into the mouths of the Bandicoot men; moreover, they rub the fat over their own bodies. After this the Bandicoot men may eat a little of the animal. *Ceremony performed by Bandicoot men before bandicoots may be eaten.*

Once more, when the *Intichiuma* ceremony for increasing the supply of the *idnimita* grub has been performed, and the grub (which is that of a large longicorn beetle) has become plentiful, the men who do not belong to the Idnimita totem collect the insects and bring them into the camp. There they lay their store before the men of the totem, who eat some of the smaller grubs and hand back the rest to the men who do not belong to the totem. When this has been done the men of the Idnimita totem may eat sparingly of the grub. *Ceremony performed by men of the Idnimita totem before the idnimita grub may be eaten.*

Thus we see that, after the ceremonies for the multiplication of the various totemic animals and plants have been observed, these animals and plants are killed or gathered and eaten, sparingly by the men who have the particular animal or plant for their totem, but freely by the rest. There can, therefore, be no doubt that the intention of the *Intichiuma* ceremonies, so far as the totems are edible animals or plants, is to ensure a plentiful supply of food for the tribe. In other words, the performance of one of these solemn rites by men who have an animal for their totem is merely a means to enable the other members of the tribe to kill and eat that animal. Indeed, the men of the totem will even, as we saw in the case of the Witchetty Grub men, kill and cook their totem in large quantities for the benefit of the rest of the community. The same readiness on the part of a man to aid others in catching and killing *Thus the intention of the Intichiuma ceremonies is to ensure a plentiful supply of food for the tribe.*

his own totem came out in the case of a Euro man who made and charmed a magic implement (*churinga*) for the express purpose of thereby enabling a Plum-tree man to catch and kill euros (a kind of kangaroo).[1]

<small>The ceremonies seem to show that the men of a totem are supposed not only to control the numbers of their totem animal or plant, but also to have the first right to eat it.</small>

This explanation of the *Intichiuma* rites is the one given by Messrs. Spencer and Gillen, whose arguments and conclusion I have merely stated in a slightly different form. No other explanation of the ceremonies seems to me to be possible. But further, as the authors acutely point out, the facts which we have passed in review appear to indicate that the men of any particular totem are supposed not only to control the numbers of their totem animal or plant, but also to have a first right to eat it. This appears from the custom of bringing in the first supply of the animal or plant into camp, and laying it before the men of the totem, who are permitted, and indeed required, to eat of it before any one else is allowed to do so. The same idea comes out very clearly in some of the native traditions. Thus they say that once on a time a Hakea Flower woman was changed into a Bandicoot woman by another woman of the latter totem, and that after the transformation she ate bandicoots, that is, her totem animal. Again, it is said that a Euro man once started out in pursuit of a kangaroo which he was anxious to kill and eat, but that to enable himself to do so he first of all changed himself into a Kangaroo man. These traditions point to a time when, if you wished to eat bandicoot you had to belong to the Bandicoot totem; and if you wished to kill and eat kangaroos, you had to belong to the Kangaroo totem; in short, they seem to carry us back to a time when among these tribes a man's special function in life was to kill and eat his totem animal. At the present day this old system, if it was indeed such, has been greatly modified. As a rule, a man no longer kills and eats his totem animal, and the aid which he gives his fellow-tribesmen in filling their stomachs with it, though it is regarded as very important, is still only indirect.

Hitherto we have considered only the *Intichiuma* ceremonies which deal with animal and vegetable totems. But, as we have seen, the totems of the Central Australian

---

[1] *The Native Tribes of Central Australia*, p. 203.

THE ORIGIN OF TOTEMISM

tribes comprise almost every natural object known to the native, and each totem clan or group has its own *Intichiuma* ceremony. The ceremony performed by the men of the Water totem has for its end the making of rain; it is held especially at the season when rain may be expected to fall, but may also be held whenever there has been a long drought and water is scarce. Like the other *Intichiuma* rites, those of the Water totem are purely magical in their nature. A man decorated with white down struts slowly up and down a trench, causing his body and legs to quiver in an extraordinary way, and when he is done some young fellows, who have been lying down in a shelter of branches, jump up and rush out screaming in imitation of the spur-winged plover. As to the *Intichiuma* ceremonies of the other inanimate totems, such as wind, fire, sun, cloud, and so on, we have unfortunately no information; but, arguing by analogy, we may surmise that just as it is the business of Kangaroo men to make kangaroos, of Hakea Flower men to make Hakea flowers, and of Water men to make rain, so it is the business of Wind men to make wind, of Fire men to make fire, of Sun men to make sunshine, and similarly with the rest. In short, Totemism among the Central Australian tribes appears, if we may judge from the *Intichiuma* ceremonies, to be an organised system of magic intended to procure for savage man a plentiful supply of all the natural objects whereof he stands in need.

<small>Ceremonies performed by Water men for the purpose of making rain.</small>

<small>Thus in Central Australia, Totemism seems to be an organised system of magic intended to procure a supply of necessaries.</small>

The thought naturally presents itself to us: Have we not in these *Intichiuma* ceremonies the key to the original meaning and purpose of Totemism among the Central Australian tribes, perhaps even of Totemism in general? The suggestion is not made by Messrs. Spencer and Gillen in *The Native Tribes of Central Australia*, but it occurred to me in reading the proofs of their book last September, and in a letter written in that month I communicated it to Professor Spencer. From his reply I learned, without surprise, that he had been coming independently to a similar conclusion. To quote from his letter, which is dated Melbourne, October 20, 1898:—

<small>Perhaps the *Intichiuma* ceremonies give the key to the original meaning of Totemism among the Central Australians, possibly even of Totemism in general.</small>

"In thinking over the totem question I have been coming more and more to the conclusion that the religious aspect

VOL. I   I

114 THE ORIGIN OF TOTEMISM

View of Professor Baldwin Spencer.

of the totem is the more ancient, and that the now existing social aspect has been tacked on at a later period, and, so far as our central tribes are concerned, your theory that each group of people was originally charged with the duty of securing the multiplication of the particular object the name of which it bears appears to me to fit in admirably with the facts. In many of the central tribes (Arunta, Ilpirra, Warramunga, etc.) the religious aspect is developed almost to the exclusion of the social, while in others (Dieri, Urabunna, etc.) the social is more strongly developed, but

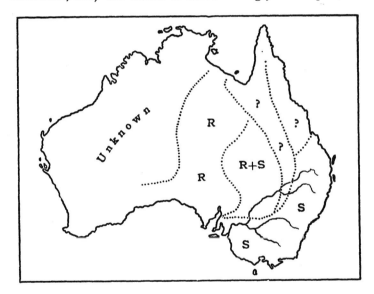

at the same time the presence of *Intichiuma* ceremonies indicates the existence of a religious aspect which is, moreover, identical in nature with that of the Arunta, etc., system. A rough map of Australia is, perhaps, rather instructive in connection with this. The dotted outline with R indicates the area occupied by tribes amongst whom the religious aspect is predominant. R + S indicates that the tribes have the same religious aspect associated with the totem, but that the social (as indicated by the totems regulating marriage) is also well developed; while S indicates that the social aspect is the predominant one. It is also worth noting that over the large area in the centre, where conditions of life are more precarious in the matter of food and water supply, the religious aspect predominates, whilst it is least marked in the area which is well wooded and watered and where the food supply is more constant. This serves to indicate, so far as Australia is concerned, a relationship between food supply and the development of the religious aspect of the totemic system at the present day."

On this I will only remark that if the *Intichiuma* ceremonies do really give the clue to Totemism, the aspect of the totemic system, which we have hitherto been accustomed to describe as religious, deserves rather to be called magical, and in this change of designation I believe that Professor Baldwin Spencer is now disposed to acquiesce. His own views as to the probable origin of Totemism will be found stated in a forthcoming number of the *Journal of the Anthropological Institute*. In the main they accord with those which I was led to adopt from a consideration of the same facts. The merit of the discovery, if it should prove to be such, clearly belongs to the writers who have laboriously collected the facts, and presented them in such a masterly form that any one may see for himself the conclusion to which they point.

[Sidenote: On this theory the aspect of Totemism which has been described as religious should rather be called magical.]

II

Thus Totemism seems to be an organised and co-operative system of magic for the benefit of the whole community.

THE general explanation of Totemism to which the *Intichiuma* ceremonies seem to point is that it is primarily an organised and co-operative system of magic designed to secure for the members of the community, on the one hand, a plentiful supply of all the commodities of which they stand in need, and, on the other hand, immunity from all the perils and dangers to which man is exposed in his struggle with nature. Each totem group, on this theory, was charged with the superintendence and control of some department of nature from which it took its name, and with which it sought, as far as possible, to identify itself. If the things which composed the department assigned to a particular group were beneficial to man, as in the case of edible animals and plants, it was the duty of the group to foster and multiply them; if, on the other hand, they were either noxious by nature, or might, under certain circumstances, become so, as in the case of ravenous beasts, poisonous serpents, rain, wind, snow, and so on, then it was the duty of the group to repress and counteract these harmful tendencies, to remedy any mischief they might have wrought, and perhaps to turn them as efficient engines of destruction against foes. This latter side of totemic magic, which may perhaps be described as the negative or remedial side, hardly appears in our accounts of Central Australian Totemism; but we shall meet with examples of it elsewhere.

In favour of this hypothetical explanation of Totemism I would urge that it is simple and natural, and in entire conformity with both the practical needs and the modes of thought of savage man. Nothing can be more natural than that man should wish to eat when he is hungry, to drink

THE ORIGIN OF TOTEMISM

when he is thirsty, to have fire to warm him when he is cold, and fresh breezes to cool him when he is hot; and to the savage nothing seems simpler than to procure for himself these and all other necessaries and comforts by magic art. We need not, therefore, wonder that in very ancient times communities of men should have organised themselves more or less deliberately for the purpose of attaining objects so natural by means that seemed to them so simple and easy. The first necessity of savage, as of civilised, man is food, and with this it accords that wherever Totemism exists the majority of the totems are invariably animals or plants—in other words, things which men can eat. The great significance of this fact has hitherto been concealed from us by the prohibition so commonly laid on members of a totem clan to eat their totem animal or plant. But the discovery of the *Intichiuma* ceremonies among the Central Australian tribes proves that in keeping our eye on the prohibition to eat the totem we have hitherto been looking at only one side of the medal, and that the less important of the two. For these ceremonies show—what no one had previously dreamed of—that the very man who himself abstains in general from eating his totem will, nevertheless, do all in his power to enable other people to eat it; nay, that his very business and function in life is to procure for his fellow-tribesmen a supply of the animal or plant from which he takes his name, and to which he stands in so intimate a relation. With the new facts before us, we may safely conjecture that whatever the origin of the prohibition observed by each clan to eat its totem, that prohibition is essentially subordinate, and probably ancillary to the great end of enabling the community as a whole to eat of it—in other words, of contributing to the common food supply.

This explanation of Totemism is simple, natural, and conformable to the modes of thought of savages.

Viewed in this light, Totemism is a thoroughly practical system designed to meet the everyday wants of the ordinary man in a clear and straightforward way. There is nothing vague or mystical about it, nothing of that metaphysical haze which some writers love to conjure up over the humble beginnings of human speculation, but which is utterly foreign to the simple, sensuous, and concrete modes of thought of the savage. Yet for all its simplicity and direct-

On this hypothesis Totemism is a practical system designed to control nature for the benefit of man; religion has no place in it.

ness we cannot but feel that there is something impressive, and almost grandiose, in the comprehensiveness, the completeness, the vaulting ambition of this scheme, the creation of a crude and barbarous philosophy. All nature has been mapped out into departments; all men have been distributed into corresponding groups; and to each group of men has been assigned, with astounding audacity, the duty of controlling some one department of nature for the common good. Religion, it will be observed, has no place in the scheme. Man is still alone with nature, and fancies he can sway it at his will. Later on, when he discovers his mistake, he will bethink himself of gods, and beg them to pull for him the strings that hang beyond his reach.

This way of regarding Totemism agrees with the traditions as well as the practice of the Central Australians. A further recommendation of this way of regarding Totemism is that it falls in with the traditions as well as with the practice of the Central Australian tribes. We have seen that, according to these traditions, people began by regularly eating their totems, and marrying women of the same totem group as themselves. To the ordinary view of Totemism, which treats as fundamental the prohibitions to eat the totem animal or plant, and to marry a woman of the same totem group, these traditions present almost insuperable difficulties; the adherents of that view have, indeed, little choice but to reject the traditions as baseless, although strong grounds exist, as I have pointed out, for holding them to be authentic. But if we accept the theory that Totemism is merely an organised system of magic intended to secure a supply, primarily of food, and secondarily of everything else that a savage wants, the difficulties vanish. For, on this hypothesis, why should not a man partake of the food which he is at so much pains to provide? And why should he not marry a woman whose function in life is the same as his own? Nay, we may go a step farther, and say that, according to a fundamental principle of Totemism, there are good reasons why he should do both of these things. That principle, to which I would now direct the reader's attention, is the identification of a man with his totem.

Principle of the identification of a man with his totem.

Among the Central Australians, we are told, "the totem of any man is regarded, just as it is elsewhere, as the same thing as himself."[1] Thus a Kangaroo man, discussing the matter with Messrs. Spencer and Gillen, pointed to a photograph of himself which had just been taken, and remarked: "That one is just the same as me; so is a kangaroo." This incapacity to distinguish between a man and a beast, difficult as it is for us to realise, is common enough, even among savages who have not the totemic system. A Bushman, questioned by a missionary, "could not state any difference between a man and a brute—he did not know but a buffalo might shoot with bows and arrows as well as a man, if it had them."[2] When the Russians first landed on one of the Alaskan Islands the natives took them for cuttle-fish, "on account of the buttons on their clothes."[3] The Bororos, a tribe of Brazilian Indians, calmly maintain that they are birds of a gorgeous red plumage, which live in their native forests. It is not merely that they will be changed into these birds at their death, but they actually are identical with them in their life, and they treat the birds accordingly, as they would their fellow-tribesmen, keeping them in captivity, refusing to eat their flesh, and mourning for them when they die. However, they kill the wild birds for their feathers, and, though they will not kill, they pluck the tame ones to adorn their own naked brown bodies with the brilliant plumage of their feathered brethren.[4] Now, it is by identifying himself with his totem that the Central Australian native produces the effects he aims at. If he desires to multiply grubs, he pretends to be a grub himself, emerging from the chrysalis state; if his wish is to ensure a plentiful supply of emus, he dresses himself up as an emu, and mimicks the bird; for by thus converting himself into a grub, or an emu, he thinks he can move the other grubs and emus to comply with his wishes.

But it is not merely by disguising himself as an animal and copying its habits that the Central Australian savage seeks to identify himself with his totem. All over the

---

[1] *The Native Tribes of Central Australia*, p. 202, *cf.* p. 168.
[2] J. Campbell, *Travels in South Africa, being a Narrative of a Second Journey in that Country*, ii. p. 34.
[3] I. Petroff, *Report on the Population, Industries, and Resources of Alaska*, p. 145.
[4] K. von den Steinen, *Unter den Naturvölkern Zentral-Brasiliens*, pp. 352, 512.

In order to identify himself with his totem animal the Central Australian eats of it.

world primitive man believes that by absorbing the flesh and blood of an animal he acquires the qualities of the creature, and so far identifies himself with it. Examples of the belief are too well known to be cited. The same idea forms the basis of the familiar blood-covenant practised by so many races: two men make themselves akin by each transfusing into the veins of the other. a little of his own blood. From this point of view it is quite natural that the savage, desirous of uniting himself as closely as possible with his totem, should partake of its flesh and blood. And we have seen that according to the Central Australian traditions men did commonly eat their totems in days of old. In those early times the Kangaroo people may have lived chiefly on kangaroos, strengthening their kangaroo nature by constantly absorbing the flesh of the animal whose name they took and whose habits they copied. The Opossum men may have justified their name by consuming more opossum meat than anybody else; and so with the members of the other totem clans. With this it would agree that two clans of Western Australia, who are named after a small species of opossum and a little fish, believe themselves to be so called because they used to live chiefly on these creatures.[1]

This ceremonial eating of the totem animal is a sort of totem sacrament.

Even at the present day in Central Australia, though men are in general nearly forbidden to partake of their totem animal or plant, they are still bound occasionally to eat a little of it as a solemn ceremony, because it is believed that otherwise they could not successfully perform the *Intichiuma* ceremonies, and that the supply of the plant or animal would consequently fail. Clearly they think that, in order to multiply the members of their totem, they must identify themselves with it by taking into their bodies the flesh and blood of the animal or the fibre of the plant. Here, then, in the heart of Australia, among the most primitive savages known to us, we find the actual observance of that totem sacrament which Robertson Smith, with the intuition of genius, divined years ago,[2] but of which positive examples have hitherto been wanting.

[1] Sir George Grey, *Vocabulary of the Dialects of South-Western Australia*, pp. 4, 95.

[2] *Religion of the Semites*, p. 276 sq. Edinburgh, 1889.

The reason why men should in course of time deny themselves the food on which they had formerly subsisted, and which they continued to provide for the use of others, is not obvious. We may conjecture that the change came about through an attempt to carry out more consistently than before that identification of a man with his totem, which seems to be of the essence of the system. Men may have remarked that animals as a rule, and plants universally, do not feed upon their own kind; and hence a certain inconsistency may have been perceived in the conduct of Grub men who lived on grubs, of Grass-seed men who ate grass-seed, and so with the other animal and vegetable totems. It might be argued that men who behaved so unlike the real animals and plants could not be true Grubs, Emus, Grass-seeds, and so on, and therefore could not effectively perform the all-important ceremonies for multiplying the beasts, birds, and vegetables on which the tribe depended for its subsistence. Further, a wish to conciliate and entice the creatures which it was desired to catch for food may have helped to establish the taboo on killing and eating the totem. This wish is widely prevalent among savages, and manifests itself in many quaint observances, which the hunter and his friends are bound to comply with for the sake of alluring the game, and making death appear to them as painless and even attractive as may be. Among tribes which have the totemic system this need of adopting a conciliatory attitude towards any particular sort of animal would naturally be felt chiefly by that part of the community whose special business it was to breed and kill the animal in question; in other words, it would be felt chiefly by the group or clan which had the particular species of animal for its totem. For it is to be remembered that in early times the members of a clan appear to have been by profession the hunters or butchers as well as the breeders of their totem animal; this comes out in the legend of the Euro man who turned himself into a Kangaroo man in order to kill a kangaroo, and a trace of the same custom appears in the case of the other Euro man, at the present day, who made and charmed a magical instrument for the very purpose of enabling a Plum-tree man to catch euro

The prohibition to eat the totem may have arisen partly from an observation that plants and animals do not as a rule feed upon their own kind, and partly from a wish to conciliate and entice the creatures which were to be caught for food.

Now, if it came to be generally thought that a Kangaroo man, for example, would be more likely to entice kangaroos to their fate if he were, so to say, personally known to them as one who had no selfish ends to gain by cultivating their acquaintance, public opinion would gradually impress on the Kangaroo men the duty of abstaining in the interest of the majority from the slaughter and consumption of kangaroos, and they would be urged to confine themselves to their more important function of securing by magical means a plentiful supply of the animal for their fellows. If this explanation is right, the common practice of sparing the totem animal originated in anything but a superstitious reverence for the creature as a superior being endowed with marvellous attributes; it was more analogous to the blandishments which a shepherd or herdsman will lavish on a sheep or a bullock for the purpose of catching the animal and handing it over to the butcher. Nor need we suppose that in abdicating their ancient right of eating kangaroo-flesh the men of the Kangaroo totem were either coerced by their fellows or animated by a noble impulse of disinterested devotion to the common weal. A similar self-denying ordinance would be simultaneously imposed by common consent on all the other clans which had animals or plants for their totem; and thus each clan, in renouncing a single kind of food for the benefit of the community, would calculate on receiving in return a more abundant supply of all the rest, not so much because there would be fewer mouths to feed with each kind of viand, as because the abstinence practised by the several clans was expected to add to the efficacy of their charms for multiplying and attracting the game. For we must bear in mind that under the totemic system the various clans or stocks do not live isolated from each other, but are shuffled up together within a narrow area, and exert their magic powers for the common good.

This answer to the question why men gave up the right of eating their totems is put forward with diffidence. The problem is difficult, and I am far from feeling confident that the solution here suggested is the true one. So far as the explanation rests on a supposed desire to conciliate the totem it is open to the objection, raised by my friend Professor Baldwin Spencer, in the letter to which I have referred, that the Central Australian natives at the present day seem to show no other trace of an attempt to conciliate or appease the game which they kill and eat. I have no wish to disguise or extenuate the force of the objection. Indeed, I had myself, nearly ten years ago, remarked on this absence of the conciliation of game among the Australian aborigines, whom in that respect I contrasted with the North American Indians.[1] Yet it is not easy to see how, without introducing the idea of conciliation in some form, we are to explain the attitude of the savage towards his totem animal.

However, the Central Australians do not as a rule attempt to conciliate the game which they kill and eat.

On the new theory of Totemism it is thus quite easy to understand why men should have begun by regularly eating their totem animal or plant, as in fact they seem to have done, if the Central Australian traditions can be trusted. The real difficulty, indeed, is to explain how they ever came to give up the habit. Similarly the theory suggests a very simple reason why men should have begun by marrying women of their own totem group in preference to any others, as they are represented doing in the Central Australian legends. On the principle of the identification of the members of a clan with their totem, what can be more natural than that an Emu man should wed an Emu woman and an Opossum man should marry an Opossum woman, just as an emu cock mates with an emu hen and a male opossum pairs with a female opossum? Now this, which may be described as the natural system of Totemism, is just the one which appears from their traditions to have prevailed among the Central Australian tribes before the introduction of Exogamy.[2] Whatever the origin of Exogamy, there is the clearest traditional testimony that among the Central Australians it was an innovation imposed on an existing system of totem clans who previously knew nothing of such

On the new theory of Totemism it is easy to understand both why men originally ate their totem animal or plant, and why they married women of the same totem, since animals mate with their own kind.

---

[1] "The aborigines of Australia have Totemism in the most primitive form known to us, but, so far as I am aware, there is no evidence that they attempt, like the North American Indians, to conciliate the animals which they kill and eat. The means which the Australians adopt to secure a plentiful supply of game appear to be based, not on conciliation, but on sympathetic magic."—*The Golden Bough*, ii. p. 133 *sq.*   [2] See above, p. 103.

a rule.[1] This accords perfectly with the present hypothesis that the natural and original system of Totemism was one in which men and women of the same totem regularly cohabited with each other. Further, it is supported by the striking fact that among a large group of the Central Australian tribes the law of Exogamy is not now, and apparently never has been, applied to the totem clans.[2]

<small>The Central Australians seem to have identified themselves with their totems, first, by eating them, and, second, by certain magical instruments called *churinga* and *nurtunjas*.</small>

The principle of the identification of a man with his totem may be looked at from the two points of view according, as we think mainly of identifying the man, let us say, with an animal, or of identifying the animal with the man. In the former case we have, so to say, a man who is transformed into an animal, in the latter case we have an animal which is changed into a man. Now the Central Australian natives appear to have taken measures to ensure this double transformation. By transfusing the life of their totem animals into their own bodies, the men and women of each clan converted themselves, as far as they could, into animals; and by transfusing their own human life into the bodies of animals they converted the animals, as far as it lay in their power, into men and women. The first of these transferences of life was effected by eating the flesh and blood of the animals; the second appears to have been effected by means of certain magical instruments called *churinga* and *nurtunjas*.

The *churinga* are slabs of stone or wood carved, for the most part, with devices relating to the totem; in shape they generally resemble the well-known instrument called a bullroarer, which is employed by savages in many parts of the world in the performance of their most solemn rites and deepest mysteries. Among the Central Australian tribes

---

[1] *The Native Tribes of Central Australia*, p. 420.

[2] This remarkable exception to the rule that totem clans, when they fall within the sphere of our observation, are generally exogamous, appears to be susceptible of a very simple explanation in accordance with the hypothesis here put forward. Briefly stated, the explanation is this: that the object of Exogamy was to prevent the marriage, primarily of brothers with sisters, and secondarily, of parents with children; and that in consequence of the peculiar rules regulating the descent of the totems in these tribes an application of the principle of Exogamy to their totem clans could not have prevented such marriages, and was, therefore, never attempted. This I hope to explain fully at some future time in dealing with the origin of Exogamy. (See below, pp. 165 *sq.*)

every man, woman, and child has one of these mysterious implements specially associated with him or her from birth to death; those of each group are kept together hidden away in a small cave or crevice in some secluded spot among the hills, and the entrance to the cave is carefully blocked up with stones arranged so naturally as not to arouse the suspicion of a chance wayfarer that here lie concealed the most sacred possessions of the tribe. The loss of these deeply-prized sticks and stones is the most terrible evil that can befall a group of people; natives who found their cave robbed of its precious contents have been known to remain in camp for a fortnight, weeping and lamenting over the loss, and plastering themselves with pipeclay, the emblem of mourning for the dead. Further, it is believed that in the far-off times of the Alcheringa their ancestors also had each his own *churinga*, which he carried with him in his wanderings about the country, and dropped on the ground where he died. On this belief Messrs. Spencer and Gillen remark :—" We meet in tradition with unmistakable traces of the idea that the churinga is the dwelling-place of the spirit of the Alcheringa ancestors. In one special group of Achilpa men, for example, the latter are reported to have carried about a sacred pole or nurtunja with them during their wanderings. When they came to a camping-place and went out hunting the nurtunja was erected, and upon this the men used to hang their churinga when they went out from camp, and upon their return they took them down again and carried them about. In these churinga they kept, so says the tradition, their spirit part."[1] Further, the same writers observe : " We have evidently in the churinga belief a modification of the idea which finds expression in the folk-lore of so many peoples, and according to which primitive man, regarding his soul as a concrete object, imagines that he can place it in some secure spot apart, if needs be, from his body, and thus, if the latter be in any way destroyed, the spirit part of him still persists unharmed."[2] At the present day, as the authors point out, this ancient belief has been modified among the tribes of Central Australia. The loss or injury of the *churinga* is

The *churinga* are sacred sticks and stones with which the souls of all members of the tribe are closely associated.

[1] *The Native Tribes of Central Australia*, p. 138.   [2] *Op. cit.*, p. 137.

THE ORIGIN OF TOTEMISM

indeed a thing to be deeply deplored, and the man who suffers such a mishap fears vaguely that some evil thing will befall him in consequence of it; but he does not apprehend that the loss, or even the destruction of the sacred stick or stone, must necessarily entail his death. In short, the natives no longer regard the *churinga* as the abode of their spirits laid up for safety in the secret cave, like the soul of the ogre or warlock in the children's story, hidden far, far away in some fairy bird or beast at the world's end. Even to the naked savage of the Australian wilderness the time for such beliefs has gone by. Yet they are nearer far to him than to us, for he ascribes them, not as we do to imaginary beings, to the giants and monsters of nursery tales, but to his own real forefathers, whose figures can yet be discerned, faint and dim, in the distance as they recede down the long road that leads to fairyland.

The *nurtunjas* are sacred poles which represent the totems.

The second of the implements by means of which the Central Australian appears, like the giant or ogre in the story, to have formerly transferred his spirit to some beast or bird or thing is the magic pole or *nurtunja*.[1] This is an instrument which still plays a great part in the sacred ceremonies of the natives. It takes many forms, but in every case it stands for the totem with which the particular ceremony is concerned. Thus, if the ceremony relates to the Wild Cat totem, the *nurtunja* will represent a wild cat; if it relates to the Sun totem, the *nurtunja* will represent the sun; and so on. Hence, when we hear that in the remote days of the Alcheringa the men of the Achilpa, or Wild Cat totem, before they went out hunting, hung up their *churinga*, in which they kept their spirits, on a *nurtunja*, which necessarily represented a wild cat, we can hardly avoid the inference that in doing so they believed themselves to be placing their spirits in their totem animals, the wild cats. That they permanently kept their spirits in the animals is not suggested by the legend; on the contrary, as they are said to have hung up the *churinga* on the *nurtunja* when they went out hunting, and to have taken them down again when they came

By means of the *churinga* and *nurtunjas* the Central Australians seem to have tried to transfer their spirits temporarily to their totems.

---

[1] An equivalent, though differently shaped, instrument is known among the Southern Arunta as a *waninga*. See *The Native Tribes of Central Australia*, pp. 306-309.

back, the natural inference seems to be that they only deposited their spirits temporarily in the animals for a definite purpose and withdrew them again when the occasion was over. Now, the occasion mentioned in the legend is the chase, and as in the days of the Alcheringa, to which the legend refers, people seem to have subsisted mainly on their totem animal or plant, we may conjecture that when the Wild Cat men went out hunting the game they sought above all were wild cats. If this was so, the previous transference of their spirits to the animals, effected by hanging up the sticks or stones, in which they kept their spirits, on a pole which represented a wild cat, can hardly have had any other intention than that of compelling the creatures to come to the hunters and be quietly knocked on the head. "If we can only put ourselves or a good part of ourselves," so these primitive huntsmen may have argued, "into yon wild cats which are now scurrying from us, we shall very soon make them, whether they like it or not, walk straight up to us, and so we shall kill them quite comfortably and make a meal of them. And, of course, in doing so we shall get back the vital part of ourselves which we temporarily transferred to the animals." On the other hand, if the game which the Wild Cat men went out to hunt were not wild cats, the motive of the hunters in depositing their spirits in the *nurtunja*, and hence in their totem, the wild cats, must have been different. It may have been done simply for safety, lest during the hunt any accident should befall them; for clearly, in the absence of their spirits, which they had taken the precaution of leaving elsewhere before they started, nothing that might happen to their mere empty carcases could have any serious consequences. Whichever of these explanations be adopted, the tradition points clearly to a custom of depositing a man's spirit, for longer or shorter periods, in the body of his totem animal. Vestiges of the same custom are also preserved in the practice, which the natives still keep up, of hanging their *churinga* upon *nurtunjas* in certain solemn ceremonies concerned with the totems.[1] The practice is identical with that ascribed to the Wild Cat men in the legend, and its original meaning is probably the

[1] *The Native Tribes of Central Australia*, pp. 253, 284, 312 *sq.*

same. For example, before the novices undergo the painful operation of subincision they are made to embrace a sacred pole (*nurtunja*) to which some *churinga* are often, though not invariably, attached. The effect of thus embracing the pole is thought to be that the lads will not feel the griding knife. Perhaps their ancestors, who invented this primitive pain-killer, held that by extracting the spirits of the novices from their bodies and transferring them for a time to the pole, or to the totem which it represented, they rendered the bodies of the youth inert and numb. To effect this salutary purpose it may originally have been deemed needful in every case to attach to the pole the *churinga* or receptacles in which the lads kept their spirits; but with the decay of old ideas about the *churinga* it is no longer considered indispensable to fasten any *churinga* at all to the pole, and a simple embrace bestowed on the latter by the novice now passes occasionally for a sufficient anæsthetic.

<small>This temporary transference of the soul to the totem seems to have been intended primarily to enable the man to control the totem for the common good, though secondarily it may have been intended to deposit the soul in a safe place.</small>

Some time ago I suggested that the transference of a man's spirit or soul for safety to some external object constituted the essence of Totemism, that in fact a totem is no more than a sort of strong box, in which a savage keeps his soul. The evidence for the former practice of such a soul-transference among the Central Australians has now been put before the reader. That it is slight and scanty I fully admit. Such as it is, when considered along with the *Intichiuma* ceremonies and other indications, it seems to show that the purpose of the transference was not so much to deposit the man's life in a secure place as to enable him to control the totem for his own and the common good. When the totem was an animal this control was directed to multiplying the species and compelling the members of it to come and be killed for food. When the totem was the sun the savage would hope, by placing a vital part of himself in the luminary, to direct its course and secure a due supply of light and heat for himself and his fellows. And so, *mutatis mutandis*, with the other totems. But it is quite possible that the other motive—the natural desire of frail man to put all that is mortal of him beyond the reach of chance and change—may also have operated. That it really did so is strongly suggested both by the rigorous precautions taken to conceal the precious objects with which the spirits of the tribesmen are so closely associated, and by the bitter grief and vague alarm excited by their loss.

If the intention of transfusing a portion of a man's life into an animal was in part at least to exercise a sort of mesmeric attraction over the creature, and thereby to catch and kill it, the apparent inconsistency in the conduct of the hunter, who first endows a beast with his own spirit, and then kills and devours it, need cause no difficulty, for, in consuming the flesh and blood, he recovers all of himself that he put into the animal. The case, however, is somewhat different when the animal which contains his life is killed and eaten by somebody else. If I deposit my soul in a hare, and my brother John shoots that hare, roasts, and swallows it, what becomes of my soul? Am I not thereby put in the parlous state of being left without a soul? To meet this obvious danger it is necessary that John should know the state of my soul, and that, knowing it, he should, whenever he shoots a hare, take steps to extract and restore to me my soul before he cooks and dines upon the animal. This, we may conjecture, is in part the intention of a Central Australian rite which has been already described. We have seen that after the *Intichiuma* ceremony the first supply of the totem animal which is brought into the camp is solemnly laid before the men of the totem, who eat a little of it and then pass on the remainder to the others to be consumed by them. By thus partaking first of their totem animal the men of the totem may be supposed not merely to absorb its qualities sacramentally but also to recover that portion of their own spirit which they had temporarily deposited in the animal. In this connection the ceremonies observed by a Brazilian tribe in killing some sorts of game and fish are instructive. The Bororos believe that the souls of their medicine-men transmigrate at death into the bodies of certain kinds of large and succulent animals and fish, which are reckoned the greatest dainties, such, for instance, as the tapir, the cayman, the large *jahu* fish, and a sort of shad. Whenever one of these creatures is killed a ceremony has to be performed over it by a medicine-man before its flesh can be eaten, the purpose of the ceremony being to make sure

When a man deposits his soul in an animal, and a friend kills the animal, the friend must take steps to restore the soul to its proper owner.

that the animal cannot be restored to life. Cowering down on the ground, the wizard blows and spits upon the carcase, claps it, and shrieks and spits into its open mouth. Nay more, he is bound to be present at the actual killing of the animal. If, for example, a *jahu* fish or a shad were caught in a net when no medicine-man was by, the fish would be set free again. The Indians think that any one who ate fish, flesh, or fowl over which the needful ceremony had not been performed would soon die.[1] The analogy between the Brazilian and the Australian practice is, if I am right, very close. Both peoples believe that the bodies of certain animals are tenanted by the souls of men belonging to their tribe; both use these animals as food; and both perform certain ceremonies over the dead animals for the purpose of disengaging the souls of their friends from the carcases of the beasts before they proceed to convey the latter into their own bellies. The only essential difference between them is that in the Brazilian case the souls so disengaged are the souls of the dead, while in the Australian case they are the souls of the living.[2]

We have still to ask whether magical ceremonies like the Intichiuma are performed by totem clans in other parts of the world.

We have still to inquire how far the explanation of Totemism suggested by the new Australian facts is confirmed by similar facts observed among totemic peoples in other parts of the world. I may remind the reader that the explanation, based on the *Intichiuma* ceremonies, is that the totem clans are essentially bands of magicians charged with the duty of controlling and directing the various departments of nature for the good of man. A crucial question, therefore, is, Are analogous ceremonies performed by totem groups in other parts of the world? and in general are totem clans elsewhere than in Australia credited with the power of exercising control over the totem? Before adducing some evidence of the existence of such beliefs and practices in various parts of the world, I would ask the reader to remember that,

---

[1] K. von den Steinen, *Unter den Naturvölkern Zentral-Brasiliens*, pp. 492 *sq.*, 512.

[2] The remarkable ceremonies observed by some of the Torres Straits Islanders before they will eat of the turtles which they have caught may, perhaps, be explained in the same way. Among some of the islanders the turtle is a totem. See A. C. Haddon, "The Secular and Ceremonial Dances of Torres Straits," *Internationales Archiv für Ethnographie*, vi. (1893) p. 150 *sq.*

THE ORIGIN OF TOTEMISM

although the *Intichiuma* ceremonies have probably been practised from time immemorial in the centre of Australia, they were never observed by Europeans until quite lately; nay, that one of the authors, to whom we are indebted for their discovery, lived (as I understand) on intimate terms with the natives for many years without getting the least inkling that any such solemn ceremonies were going on around him. With his experience before us we may surmise that similar rites practised by other totem tribes have escaped the notice of Europeans elsewhere, and that the scantiness of the evidence for their existence is due not so much to the rarity of the ceremonies themselves as to the ignorance or carelessness of observers. With this caution I proceed to give the few notices I have thus far collected of customs and beliefs analogous to those revealed in the *Intichiuma* ceremonies of the Central Australians.

In one of the Torres Straits Islands members of the Dog clan were believed to understand the habits of dogs, and to be able to exercise special control over them.[1] In one of the New Hebrides, when a man wished to catch octopus he used to take one of the members of the Octopus family with him; the latter stood on the beach and called out, "So-and-so wants octopus," and then plenty of octopuses would come and be caught.[2] On a cloudy morning the Sun clan of the Bechuanas were wont to make the sun shine out through the clouds; the chief kindled a new fire in his dwelling, and every one of his subjects carried a light from it to his own hut.[3] The intention of the ceremony clearly was, by means of sympathetic magic, to blow up into a brighter blaze the smouldering fire of the sun. In the Murray Islands, Torres Straits, it is the duty of the Sun clan to imitate the rising and setting of the sun,[4] probably to ensure the punctual performance of his daily duties by the orb of day. Among the Omahas of North America the Small Bird clan performs a magic ceremony to keep small

In point of fact magical ceremonies for the control of the totem have been performed by totem clans in Torres Straits, Africa, and America.

---

[1] A. C. Haddon, in *Journal of the Anthropological Institute*, xix. pp. 325, 393. 1890.
[2] R. C. Codrington, *The Melanesians*, p. 26.
[3] Arbouset et Daumas, *Voyage d'Exploration au Nord-est de la Colonie du Cap de Bonne Espérance*, p. 350 sq. Paris, 1842.
[4] A. E. Hunt, in *Journal of the Anthropological Institute*, xxviii. p. 6.

birds from the corn; the Reptile clan performs a similar ceremony to protect the crops from worms; and the Wind clan think they can start a breeze by flapping their blankets.[1] The same Wind clan practises a magic rite to stop a blizzard. They paint one of their boys red, and he rolls over and over in the snow, reddening it for some distance all around him. This stops the blizzard,[2] the notion apparently being that the white snow will not fall when it knows that it will be thus reddened and defiled. In another North American tribe the Hare clan seems to have been credited with the power of stopping a heavy and long-continued fall of snow; at least, this seems a natural inference from a passage in one of the letters of the early Jesuit missionaries. The writer tells a story to explain why the body of a certain old man, who had just died, was burned instead of being buried, though interment was the regular mode of disposing of the dead in the tribe. "They regard it as certain," says he, "that the father of this old man was a hare, which walks on the snow in winter, and that thus the snow, the hare, and the old man are of the same village, that is to say, are kinsmen. They add that the hare said to his wife that he would not suffer his children to remain under ground—it was not suitable to their rank, seeing they were kinsmen of the snow, whose country is high up in the sky; and that if ever his children were put in the ground after their death he would pray to the snow, his kinsman, to punish mankind for their fault by falling so thick and so long that there would be spring no more." In confirmation of this story the Indians told the missionary that three years ago the brother of this same old man died at the beginning of winter, and that as he was buried instead of burned the snow fell so heavily and the winter was so long that they began to fear they would never see spring again. However, they bethought themselves of digging up the body of the kinsman of the snow and burning it; and no sooner had they done so than, sure

---

[1] J. Owen Dorsey, in *Third Annual Report of the Bureau of Ethnology*, pp. 238 sq., 241, 248. Washington, 1884.

[2] J. Owen Dorsey, in *Eleventh Annual Report of the Bureau of Ethnology*, p. 410 sq. Washington, 1894.

enough, the snow ceased to fall, and spring came with a burst.[1] Apparently, the men whose bodies had thus to be burnt belonged to the Hare clan, and yet were deemed so closely akin to the snow that to burn their bodies was equivalent to melting the snow itself. We may conjecture that the same men were believed in their lifetime to be able to stop a snowfall by their charms and spells.

Some of these examples explain the attitude of a totem clan towards its totem when the totem is or may, under certain circumstances, become of a noxious and maleficent nature. In such cases it is the function of the clan, not, of course, to multiply the numbers of the totem or increase its virulence, but, on the contrary, to disarm, counteract, and keep within due bounds its dangerous influence. Hence, members of the Snake clan in Senegambia profess to heal by their touch persons who have been bitten by serpents ;[2] and the same profession was made by Serpent clans in antiquity.[3] Similarly, in Central Australia, members of the Fly totem claim to cure, by the touch of a magic implement (*churinga*), eyes which are swollen and inflamed with fly-bites.[4] And, on analogy, we may conjecture that certain Arab families, who believed their blood to be a remedy for hydrophobia,[5] were descended from men of a Dog totem. *When the totem is noxious, the magical ceremonies are intended not to multiply it but to counteract its dangerous influence.*

Further, when the case of the Indian, who was a kinsman of the snow as well as of hares, is considered in the light of the preceding discussion, we arrive at a simple explanation of a peculiar feature of Australian Totemism which has hitherto baffled inquirers. In many Australian tribes the members of a totem clan believe themselves to stand in a very intimate relation, not merely to their own totem, but to a number of other natural objects or phenomena ; and this relation seems to amount to a claim of ownership, the natives affirming that the things belong to them.[6] It has been proposed by Mr. Howitt to designate *Besides their totems, many Australian clans have sub-totems, that is, other natural objects which they claim to own.*

---

[1] *Relations des Jésuites* (1667), p. 19 (of the Canadian reprint). Compare *Lettres édifiantes et curieuses*, vi. pp. 169-171.
[2] *Revue d'Ethnographie*, iii. p. 396.
[3] Strabo, xiii. p. 588 (ed. Casaubon); Pliny, *Nat. Hist.*, xxviii. 30.
[4] *The Native Tribes of Central Australia*, p. 546.
[5] W. Robertson Smith, *Religion of the Semites*, p. 369. New edition, 1894.
[6] A. W. Howitt, in *Journal of the Anthropological Institute*, xviii. p. 61.

these things as sub-totems or pseudo-totems; they might also be called multiplex totems. To take instances of them, we are told that in some tribes of New South Wales "everything in the universe is divided among the different members of the tribe; some claim the trees, others the plains, others the sky, stars, wind, rain, and so forth."[1] Another writer, speaking of a tribe in Queensland, says: "Everything in nature, according to them, is divided between the classes. The wind belongs to one, and the rain to the other. The sun is Wutaroo, and the moon is Yungaroo. The stars are divided between them; and if a star is pointed out they will tell you to which division it belongs."[2] Among the Wakelbura and kindred tribes of Northern Queensland we are told that everything, animate and inanimate, belongs to one or other of the two exogamous classes into which the tribes are divided. A wizard in performing his incantations may use only things which belong to his own class. The stage on which a corpse is set must be made of the wood of a tree which is of the same class as the deceased, and similar rules hold in other matters.[3] In the Mount Gambier tribe of South Australia, which includes ten totem clans, the men of the Black Cockatoo totem claim to stand in this peculiar relation towards the moon, the stars, etc.; men of the Fish-Hawk totem claim honeysuckle, smoke, etc.; men of the Pelican totem claim dogs, blackwood trees, fire, frost, etc.; men of the Crow totem claim thunder, lightning, rain, hail, winter, clouds, etc.; men of a Snake totem claim fish, seals, eels, stringy-bark trees, etc.; men of the Tea-tree totem claim ducks, wallabies, owls, crayfish, opossum, etc.; men of the black, crestless Cockatoo claim kangaroos, sheoak trees, sun, wind, summer and autumn. A man will not, if he can help it, either kill or eat any of the animals which he thus regards as peculiarly his own; if he is compelled by hunger to do so, he expresses his sorrow at having to eat his "friends," or his "flesh," by touching his breast as a sign of

---

[1] A. L. P. Cameron, in *Journal of the Anthropological Institute*, xiv. p. 350.

[2] G. F. Bridgman, in Fison and Howitt's *Kamilaroi and Kurnai*, p. 168. Compare *id.*, in Brough Smyth's *Aborigines of Victoria*, i. p. 91.

[3] J. C. Muirhead, cited by Mr. Howitt, in *Journal of the Anthropological Institute*, xviii. p. 61, note. Compare *id.*, in E. M. Curr's *Australian Race*, iii. p. 27 *sq.*

THE ORIGIN OF TOTEMISM

relationship.[1] In the Wotjoballuk tribe of North-western Victoria men of the Hot Wind totem looked upon as their own three different kinds of snakes and two kinds of birds; the men of the White Cockatoo totem asserted a right to no less than seventeen different species of plants and animals; and claims of the same sort were advanced by the members of the other totem clans, namely, the Black Cockatoo clan, the Sun clan, the Deaf Adder clan, and the Pelican clan.[2]

Now, on the hypothesis that each totem clan is a band of magicians, whose function it is to control certain natural phenomena for the common good, we can easily see that, where the totem clans were not numerous, it might be found necessary to entrust several departments of nature to each clan. Thus, to take the case of the Wotjoballuk tribe, which we have just been considering, it seems to have included no more than six totem clans, four of which were concerned with species of birds or beasts (pelican, adder, black and white cockatoo), one with the sun, and one with the wind. Clearly, if each of these six clans were to give its attention exclusively to its particular totem, whole departments of nature, including multitudinous species of animals and plants, would be uncared for, and the consequences to the tribe might be disastrous. What would become of kangaroos, opossums, and wallabies if it was nobody's business to multiply them? How could gumtrees be reasonably expected to flourish, and plum-trees to bear fruit, if they were suffered to droop and dwine in the cold shade of indifference and neglect? The thing was not to be thought of. There was nothing for it but that the members of each clan should buckle to and, after discharging their primary duty to their totem, should devote their superfluous energies to the laudable task of keeping a few more of the great processes of nature a-going. Again, take the ten clans of the Mount Gambier tribe, with their totems— fish-hawk, pelican, crow, two sorts of black cockatoo, a harmless snake, the tea-tree, and an edible root (the totems of two clans are unknown). Consider how far even fish-

On the present hypothesis sub-totems are departments of nature which a totem clan undertakes to regulate for the common good.

---

[1] D. S. Stewart, in Fison and Howitt's *Kamilaroi and Kurnai*, p. 168 *sq.*; *id.*, in E. M. Curr's *Australian Race*, iii. p. 461 *sq.*

[2] A. W. Howitt, in *Report of the Smithsonian Institute for 1883*, p. 818.

hawks, pelicans, crows, black cockatoos, etc., are from exhausting the sum total of the universe, and you will readily perceive why Crow men, in addition to looking after crows, had to take charge of thunder, lightning, rain, hail, etc.; why Black Cockatoo men, not content with exercising a due supervision over black cockatoos, had to extend the sphere of their operations to the sun, the wind, the summer, the autumn, and so on. In short, the fewer the clans the more numerous necessarily were the magical functions to be discharged by each, if the great cosmic movement was still to go on.

<small>The many animals which Queensland clans are forbidden to eat may be nothing but sub-totems.</small>

We can now hazard a conjecture as to the meaning of the numerous prohibitions imposed on each of the clans in the Queensland tribes, whose social system has been so patiently observed and recorded by Mr. W. E. Roth.[1] Among these tribes the members of each exogamous class are forbidden to eat, not merely one, but several, and sometimes many different kinds of animals. The exogamous classes are four in number, and the lists of foods prohibited to each class, though constant throughout each tribe, are found to vary from tribe to tribe. In one district, for example, the class called Koopooroo are not allowed to eat iguana, whistler duck, black duck, "blue-fellow" crane, yellow dingo, and small yellow fish "with-one-bone-in-him"; another class, called Woongko, have to avoid scrub-turkey, eagle-hawk, bandicoot, brown snake, black dingo, and white duck; a third class have to do without kangaroo, carpet-snake, teal, white-bellied brown-headed duck, various kinds of diver birds, "trumpeter" fish, and a kind of black bream; while members of the fourth class, called Bunburi, dare not eat emu, yellow snake, galah parrot, and a certain species of hawk. They firmly believe that if any one were to eat a forbidden food he would fall sick and probably die, and that the food could never satisfy his hunger. Should the delinquent be caught in the act by his fellow tribesmen, he would in all probability be put to death.[2] With the evidence as to

---

[1] W. E. Roth, *Ethnological Studies among the North-west-central Queensland Aborigines* (Brisbane and London, 1897); id., *Notes on Social and Individual Nomenclature among certain North Queensland Aborigines*, read before the Royal Society of Queensland, Nov. 13, 1897.

[2] W. E. Roth, *Ethnological Studies*, etc., p. 57 *sq.*

the *Intichiuma* ceremonies of the Central Australians before us, we may surmise that the animals which are thus tabooed to the various intermarrying classes of these Queensland tribes are neither more nor less than what I have proposed to call multiplex totems, and that the members of each of these classes are, or have at some time been, bound to perform ceremonies of the same sort as the *Intichiuma* for the multiplication of all the kinds of animals which they are forbidden to eat. The surmise is confirmed by the circumstance that, though the members of each class are forbidden to eat the animals in question, they are not forbidden to kill them. In other words, they are at liberty to provide their fellows with the food of which they may not themselves partake. This entirely agrees with the view of Totemism here suggested, that it is a co-operative system designed to procure for the community a supply, primarily of food, and secondarily of all the other necessaries of life. It is interesting to observe that Mr. Roth, to whom we are indebted for our knowledge of the social system of these Queensland tribes, has been led by a different chain of reasoning to the conclusion that "the whole class system has been devised by a process of natural selection, to regulate the proper distribution of the total quantity of food available."[1] But under a superficial appearance of agreement his conclusion differs fundamentally from the one which we have reached. For while he supposes that the rules of abstinence imposed on each class had no other object than that of leaving more food for the remaining mouths of the tribe, the conclusion to which we have been led by a consideration mainly of the *Intichiuma* ceremonies is, that such rules of abstinence originated rather in a belief that by observing them the members of each group or class would possess, in a higher degree than before, those magical powers for the multiplication and enticing of the game to which the tribe, as a whole, trusted for its supply of food.[2]

Mr. Roth's theory of the origin of these prohibitions.

---

[1] *Notes on Social and Individual Nomenclature among certain North Queensland Aborigines* (read before the Royal Society of Queensland, Dec. 11, 1897), p. 10.

[2] The Battas of Sumatra seem also to have multiplex totems. They are divided into exogamous clans called *margas*, one of which has for its totems the ape and the goat; another has the tiger, the panther, and beasts of that sort; while a third has the wild turtle,

The introduction of such an elaborate social system, based on co-operation, may have been effected by the influence of a few able men.

It may be asked how an elaborate social organisation, based on the mutual co-operation of many separate groups, and aiming at nothing less than a systematic control of the whole of nature, can possibly have sprung up among savages so rude as the Australians. The answer seems to be that the system may have begun in a humble way by the union of a few neighbouring groups under the influence of some able men, and may have gradually spread to more distant groups, extending its scope and perfecting its organisation as more and more groups fell in with the scheme. That such a thing may have happened appears to result from the observations of Messrs. Spencer and Gillen. They remark that, "after carefully watching the natives during the performance of their ceremonies, and endeavouring as best we could to enter into their feelings, to think as they did, and to become, for the time being, one of themselves, we came to the conclusion that if one or two of the most powerful men settled upon the advisability of introducing some change, even an important one, it would be quite possible for this to be agreed upon and carried out."[1]

It might be premature to say that the admirable researches and discoveries of Messrs. Spencer and Gillen have finally solved the problem of Totemism; but at least they seem to point to a solution more complete and satisfactory than any that has hitherto been offered.

and other kinds of pigeons. See J. B. Neumann, "Het Pane en Bila-stroomgebied op het eiland Sumatra," *Tijdschrift van het Nederlandsch Aardrijkskundig Genootschap*, Tweede Serie, Deel iv., Afdeeling: Meer uitgebreide artikelen, No. 1, p. 8 *sq.* Amsterdam, 1887.

[1] *The Native Tribes of Central Australia*, p. 12.

THE BEGINNINGS OF RELIGION AND TOTEMISM AMONG THE AUSTRALIAN ABORIGINES

Reprinted from the Fortnightly Review, July and September 1905

THE BEGINNINGS OF RELIGION AND TOTEMISM AMONG THE AUSTRALIAN ABORIGINES

I

THE BEGINNINGS OF RELIGION

THE theory that in the history of mankind religion has been preceded by magic is confirmed inductively by the observation that among the aborigines of Australia, the rudest savages as to whom we possess accurate information, magic is universally practised, whereas religion in the sense of a propitiation or conciliation of the higher powers seems to be nearly unknown. Roughly speaking, all men in Australia are magicians, but not one is a priest; everybody fancies he can influence his fellows or the course of nature by sympathetic magic, but nobody dreams of propitiating gods by prayer and sacrifice. "It may be truly affirmed," says a recent writer on the Australians, "that there was not a solitary native who did not believe as firmly in the power of sorcery as in his own existence; and while anybody could practise it to a limited extent, there were in every community a few men who excelled in pretension to skill in the art. The titles of these magicians varied with the community, but by unanimous consent the whites have called them 'doctors,' and they correspond to the medicine-men and rain-makers of other barbarous nations. The power of the doctor is only circumscribed by the range of his fancy. He communes with spirits, takes aërial flights at

<small>Among the Australian aborigines magic is universally practised, but religion, in the sense of a propitiation of the higher power, seems to be nearly unknown</small>

pleasure, kills or cures, is invulnerable and invisible at will, and controls the elements."[1] Speaking of the Australian aborigines, Dr. A. W. Howitt observes: "The belief in magic in its various forms, in dreams, omens, and warnings, is so universal, and mingles so intimately with the daily life of the aborigines, that no one, not even those who practise deceit themselves, doubts the power of other medicine-men, or that if men fail to effect their magical purposes the failure is due to error in the practice, or to the superior skill or power of some adverse practitioner."[2] On the same subject Mr. E. M. Curr wrote: "In connection with the manners and customs of our aboriginal race a great motor power is the belief in sorcery or witchcraft. In the everyday life of the Black, a pressure originating in this source may be said to be always at work. As it seems to me, no writer has given this fact quite its due weight, and yet it is impossible to appreciate correctly the manners and customs of our tribes until the more salient features in connection with their ideas about sorcery have been mastered. The groundwork of sorcery amongst the Blacks is the belief that several things of importance can be effected by means of charms and incantations. The tribes differ somewhat in details and ceremonies, but there is no doubt that the system is the same throughout."[3]

Yet among these savages there are beliefs and practices which might have developed into a regular religion.

Yet though religion, in the sense in which I use that word, seems to be nearly unknown among the Australian aborigines, some of them nevertheless hold beliefs and observe practices which might have grown into a regular religion, if their development had not been cut short by European intervention. Thus in the south-eastern parts of the continent, where the conditions of life in respect of climate, water, and food are more favourable than elsewhere,

---

[1] J. Mathew, *Eaglehawk and Crow*, p. 142. Similarly among the Fuegians, another of the lowest races of mankind, almost every old man is a magician, who is supposed to have the power of life and death, and to be able to control the weather. But the members of the French scientific expedition to Cape Horn could detect nothing worthy the name of religion among these savages. See *Mission Scientifique du Cap Horn*, vii. "Anthropologie, Ethnographie," par P. Hyades et J. Deniker (Paris, 1891), pp. 253-257.

[2] A. W. Howitt, *Native Tribes of South-East Australia*, p. 356.

[3] E. M. Curr, *The Australian Race*, i. 45.

THE BEGINNINGS OF RELIGION

some rudiments of religion appear in a regard for the comfort of departed friends. For example, certain Victorian tribes are said to have kindled fires near the bodies of their dead in order to warm the ghost, but "the recent custom of providing food for it is derided by the intelligent old aborigines as 'white fellow's gammon.'"[1] Among the Dieri, if the deceased was a person of importance, food is placed for many days at the grave, and in winter a fire is lighted in order that the ghost may warm himself at it.[2] Some of the natives of Western Australia keep up a fire for this purpose on the grave for more than a month. But they expect the dead to return to life, for they detach the nails from the thumb and forefinger of the deceased and deposit them in a small hole beside the grave, in order that they may know him again when he comes back to the world.[3]

Thus some tribes show a certain regard for the comfort of the departed, which might easily grow into a worship of the dead.

Again, the natives of the Herbert river, in North-east Queensland, often put food and water in the grave, and they deposit with the dead his weapons, ornaments, and indeed everything he used in life. On the other hand, they generally break his legs to prevent him from wandering at night, and for the same purpose they cut gashes in his stomach, shoulders, and lungs, and fill the gashes with stones.[4] The Turribul tribe placed their dead in trees. If the deceased was a man, they left a spear and a club near him that his spirit might kill game for its sustenance in the future state; but if the deceased was a woman, they laid a yam stick near her body in order that she might dig for roots.[5] Among the Jupagalk, a person in great pain would call on some dead friend to come and help him—that is, to visit him in a dream, and teach him some song whereby he might avert the evil magic that was hurting him.[6] Customs like these, it is plain, might easily develop into a worship of the dead.

---

[1] J. Dawson, *Australian Aborigines*, p. 50 *sq.*
[2] Mr. O. Siebert, in A. W. Howitt's *Native Tribes of South-East Australia*, p. 448.
[3] R. Salvado, *Mémoires historiques sur l'Australie* (Paris, 1854), p. 261; *Missions Catholiques*, x. (1878) p. 247. For more instances of lighting fires for this purpose, see Dr. A. W. Howitt, *Native Tribes of South-East Australia*, pp. 452, 455, 470.
[4] A. W. Howitt, *op. cit.*, p. 474.
[5] A. W. Howitt, *op. cit.*, p. 470.
[6] A. W. Howitt, *op. cit.*, p. 435.

Again, some Australians invoke their totems, which might easily grow into a worship of the totems.

Further, the Queensland aborigines on the Tully river and Proserpine river are wont to call on their totems by name before they fall asleep, and they believe that they derive certain benefits from so doing. For example, if their totem is an animal, it will warn the man who thus invokes it of the approach of other animals, and so forth, during his sleep; or, if it is itself a dangerous creature, such as a crocodile or a snake, it will not bite or sting the man without serving him with due notice of its intention to injure him. Again, if his totem is thunder or rain, the man who fails to invoke it will lose his power of making thunder or rain at will.[1] Such beliefs and practices, it is clear, might grow into a regular propitiation or worship of the totems.

Among the Warramunga a fabulous water-snake, which is one of their totems, seems to be in process of developing into a god.

Again, the Warramunga of Central Australia believe in the existence of a gigantic but wholly fabulous water-snake called Wollunqua, the totem and ancestor of one of their clans. His home is in a rocky gorge which runs into the heart of the Murchison Ranges. In this secluded spot there is a picturesque pool of deep water with a sandy margin on the south and a little precipice of red rock curving round the northern edge. Over these red rocks after rain the water tumbles in a cascade into the pool below, and the rocks are hollowed out below so that they beetle over the water, forming a long shallow cave, from the roof of which roots of trees, that have forced their way down through clefts, hang pendulous. According to the natives, the Wollunqua lives in the water of the pool, and the pendulous roots are his whiskers. They have a tradition that he once came out of the pool and destroyed some men and women, but was at last obliged to retreat under a shower of stones. To prevent him from repeating his ravages they perform ceremonies by which they seem to think that they can at once propitiate and coerce him. Thus they make a long mound of wet sand and draw wavy bands on it to represent the water-snake. Round this at night they sing and dance by the light of fires until the earliest streak of dawn glimmers in the east. Then they attack the mound fiercely with their weapons and soon demolish it. If shortly afterwards they

[1] W. E. Roth, *North Queensland Ethnography*, Bulletin No. 5 (Brisbane, 1903), § 74, p. 20 *sq.*

THE BEGINNINGS OF RELIGION 145

hear thunder rumbling in the distance, they declare that it is the voice of the water-snake saying that he is pleased with what they have done and that he will send rain. But if the remains of the ruined mound are left uncovered, he growls, and his growl is a peal of thunder. When they hear it they hasten to cover the ruins with branches, lest the snake should come and eat them up. On the other hand, the savage destruction of the mound seems to imply that they can to some extent control the beast by force. The Wollunqua differs from all other known Australian totems in that he is a purely mythical being. He is not the only snake totem of the Warramunga, but he is the most important, and, more than that, he apparently occupies in the native mind the position of a dominant totem.[1] In short, he seems to be a totem on the high road to become a god.

Again, in the south-eastern parts of Australia "a belief exists in an anthropomorphic supernatural being, who lives in the sky, and who is supposed to have some kind of influence on the morals of the natives. . . . This supernatural being, by whatever name he is known, is represented as having at one time dwelt on the earth, but afterwards to have ascended to a land beyond the sky, where he still remains, observing mankind. As Daramulun, he is said to be able 'to go anywhere and do anything.' He can be invisible; but when he makes himself visible, it is in the form of an old man of the Australian race. He is evidently everlasting, for he has existed from the beginning of things, and he still lives. But in being so he is merely in that state in which, these aborigines believe, every one would be, if not prematurely killed by evil magic. . . . In this being, though supernatural, there is no trace of a divine nature. All that can be said of him is that he is imagined as the ideal of those qualities which are, according to their standard, virtues worthy of being imitated. Such would be a man who is skilful in the use of weapons of offence and defence, all-powerful in magic, but generous and liberal to his people, who does no injury or violence to any one, yet treats with severity any breaches of custom or morality. Such is,

In South-eastern Australia there is said to be a belief in a supernatural but anthropomorphic being, a sort of ideal headman, who lives in the sky.

[1] Spencer and Gillen, *Northern Tribes of Central Australia*, chap. vii., and p. 495 *sq.*

according to my knowledge of the Australian tribes, their ideal of a headman, and naturally it is that of Biamban, the master, in the sky-country. Such a being, from Bunjil to Baiame, is *Mami-ngata*, that is, 'our father'; in other words, the All-father of the tribes. . . . Although it cannot be alleged that these aborigines have consciously any form of religion, it may be said that their beliefs are such that, under favourable conditions, they might have developed into an actual religion, based on the worship of Mungan-ngaua, or Baiame. There is not any worship of Daramulun; but the dances round the figure of clay and the invocating of his name by the medicine-men certainly might have led up to it. If such a change as a recognised religion had ever become possible, I feel that it would have been brought about by those men who are the depositaries of the tribal beliefs, and by whom in the past, as I think, all the advances in the organisation of their society have been effected. If such a momentous change to the practice of a religion had ever occurred, those men would have readily passed from being medicine-men to the office of priests."[1]

<small>But no such belief is found among the Central Australians, though they have invented moral bogies to frighten women and children.</small>

On the other hand, "the Central Australian natives, and this is true of the tribes extending from Lake Eyre in the south to the far north, and eastwards across to the Gulf of Carpentaria, have no idea whatever of the existence of any supreme being who is pleased if they follow a certain line of what we call moral conduct, and displeased if they do not do so. They have not the vaguest idea of a personal individual other than an actual living member of the tribe who approves or disapproves of their conduct, so far as anything like what we call morality is concerned. . . . It must not, however, be imagined that the Central Australian native has nothing in the nature of a moral code. As a matter of fact he has a very strict one, and during the initiation ceremonies the youth is told that there are certain things which he must do and certain others which he must not do, but he quite understands that any punishment for the infringement of these rules of conduct, which are thus laid down for him, will come from the older men, and not

---

[1] A. W. Howitt, *The Native Tribes of South-East Australia*, pp. 500, 506 *sqq.*

THE BEGINNINGS OF RELIGION 147

at all from any supreme being, of whom he hears nothing whatever. In fact, he then learns that the spirit creature, whom up to that time, as a boy, he has regarded as all-powerful, is merely a myth, and that such a being does not really exist, and is only an invention of the men to frighten the women and children."[1] The aborigines of Central Australia are not the only people who have invented bugbears for the moral edification of youth. The Ona Indians of Tierra del Fuego pretend that the natural features of their country, such as the woods and rocks, the white mists and running waters, are haunted by spirits of various sorts, "bogies in which they themselves do not believe, but which are a strong moral aid in dealing with refractory wives and wilful children." To impress this salutary belief on the feminine and youthful mind the men act the part of the spirits, disguised in appropriate costumes. Thus the spirit of the beech forests is represented by a man clad in moss and the bark of trees; the spirit of the lichen-grown rocks is played by an actor who is painted slate-colour, with daubs of red and yellow clay; the spirit of clouds and mist is dressed all in white, with a very long head partly made up of twigs, which are covered with skin and painted. Till they are initiated into these mysteries at the age of fourteen or so, the boys firmly believe in the bogies, and no wonder, inasmuch as they have been chased and scared by them. When the time of their initiation draws near, the lads are seriously exhorted by their elders. They must be keen hunters, and quick to avenge the spilt blood of their family. They must be careful of their own bodies, despising greed, and, above all, letting no woman share their inmost thoughts. At a series of nocturnal meetings they then learn the true nature of the "moral aid" by which their green unknowing youth has been trained in the way it should go. They are in fact introduced to the bogies, who turn out to be members of their own family. Any boy or man who betrays the secret is quietly put to death; and the same fate overtakes any woman who is suspected of knowing more than is good for her.[2]

Such moral bogies also flourish among the Ona Indians of Tierra del Fuego.

---

[1] Spencer and Gillen, *Northern Tribes of Central Australia*, p. 491 *sq.*
[2] W. S. Barclay, "The Land of Magellanes, with some Account of the Ona and other Indians," *The Geographical Journal*, xxiii. (1904) p. 74 *sq.*

148 THE BEGINNINGS OF RELIGION

According to Spencer and Gillen there is no high ethical religion among the Australian savages.

In regard to the precepts inculcated on Central Australian boys at initiation, Messrs. Spencer and Gillen think it " most probable that they have originated in the first instance in association with the purely selfish desire of the older men to keep all the best things for themselves, and in no case whatever are they supposed to have the sanction of a superior being."[1] "As to the 'discovery' of a high ethical religion amongst the lowest savages there is not, I am convinced, any such thing in Australia. The great difficulty is that we have had statements made on the authority of men like Gason. The latter was a police-trooper, I believe, who was perfectly honest, but at the same time perfectly incapable of dealing with matters such as these. In the days when the evidence of Baiame and Daramulun was collected the importance of securing minute and detailed information was really not realised, nor was it imagined that there were men without any so-called religious ideas; and as I have endeavoured to point out in one of our chapters, it is the easiest thing possible to be misled by what a native tells you in regard to such a point as this."[2]

Gason's mistake in thinking that the Mura-mura of the Dieri was a Good Spirit or Deity.

As an example of the mistakes into which it is possible to fall on this subject, we may take Mr. S. Gason's statement that the Mura-mura of the Dieri is a Good Spirit or Deity,[3] whereas further inquiries have ascertained that the Mura-muras, male and female, young and old, are nothing more than the legendary predecessors or prototypes of the Dieri, who roamed over the country, resembling the present natives in their customs and mode of life, though they excelled them in their magical powers and the wonderful feats they performed.[4] Yet Mr. Gason was an honest man, and he enjoyed the best opportunities for making himself acquainted

[1] Spencer and Gillen, *Northern Tribes*, p. 504.

[2] Prof. Baldwin Spencer, in a letter to me dated 19th August 1902. In quoting from my friend's letter I have struck out four words in accordance with a wish expressed by him in another letter of 18th March 1904. The omission does not affect the sense of the passage.

[3] *Native Tribes of South Australia* (Adelaide, 1879), p. 260.

[4] A. W. Howitt, *Native Tribes of South-East Australia*, pp. 475-482, 644 *sqq.*, 779 *sqq.*; *id.*, "Legends of the Dieri and Kindred Tribes of Central Australia," *Journal of the Anthropological Institute*, xxxiv. (1904) pp. 100-129; Miss E. B. Howitt, in *Folklore*, xiii. (1902) pp. 403-417. Dr. Howitt's informant is the Rev. Otto Siebert, a German missionary to the aborigines at Killalpanina, on the Cooper river, in Central Australia.

THE BEGINNINGS OF RELIGION

with the beliefs of the Dieri, for he lived among them on terms of intimacy for years, and he took a special interest in their customs and ideas, bequeathing to us accounts of them which, in spite of some grave mistakes, contain much that is valuable.[1] His error as to the supposed "Good Spirit" of the Dieri only shows how easy it is even for an honest inquirer, with the best intentions and the amplest means of ascertaining the facts, to misinterpret savage ideas in accordance with his own religious creed. Precisely the same mistake which Mr. Gason made as to the Mura-muras of the Dieri, other people have made as to the Balimo of the Basutos in South Africa. On this subject an experienced missionary writes: "The Basutos, like the Caffres in general, had no religious ideas before they came into contact with the whites. It has been asked whether they knew at least the name of God. Their idea of the divinity must have been very confused, if I may judge by the heathen whom I have associated with for thirteen years. It is the missionaries, I believe, who have employed in the singular the name of God, *Molimo*, 'He who is on high,' for in the language *molimo* would mean 'ancestor,' and was not used except in the plural *Balimo* ('the ancestors'). However it may be with their vague knowledge of the name of God, it is certain that they had no worship, no prayer for the Supreme Being. No ruins of a temple have been found, no vestige of a sacrifice to God, no word designating a priest dedicated to His service. All that was found sixty or seventy years ago, when the first whites arrived in Basutoland, is to be found there to-day among the heathen; that is, the sacrifices to

A similar mistake has been made as to the Balimo of the Basutos.

---

[1] "The Manners and Customs of the Dieyerie Tribe of Australian Aborigines," in *Native Tribes of South Australia*, pp. 253-307; "Of the tribes Dieyerie, Auminie, Yandrawontha, Yarawuarka, Pilladapa," *Journal of the Anthropological Institute*, xxiv. (1895) pp. 167-176. Compare A. W. Howitt, "The Dieri and other Kindred Tribes of Central Australia," *Journal of the Anthropological Institute*, xx. (1891) pp. 30-104. Another grave blunder of Mr. Gason's, concerning the fundamental question of the descent of the totems (*murdus*), was corrected by Dr. A. W. Howitt many years ago. See *Journal of the Anthropological Institute*, xvii. (1888) pp. 185 *sq.*; *id.*, xix. (1890) p. 90. Further, "Gason supplied the information that only certain of the men were subincised, and that only those who were purposely left alone could beget children.... It is absolute nonsense, and makes me regard Gason as very unreliable, especially when taken in connection with his Mura-mura" (Prof. Baldwin Spencer, in a letter to me dated 18th March 1904).

the ancestors."[1] Similarly, Dr. G. M'Call Theal, the learned historian of South Africa, writes of the Bantus in general, of whom the Basutos are a branch: "No man of this race, upon being told of the existence of a single supreme God, ever denies the assertion, and among many of the tribes there is even a name for such a being, as, for instance, the word Umkulunkulu, the Great Great One, used by the Hlubis and others. From this it has been assumed by some investigators that the Bantu are really monotheists, and that the spirits of their ancestors are regarded merely as mediators or intercessors. But such a conclusion is incorrect. The Great Great One was once a man, they all assert, and before our conception of a deity became known to them, he was the most powerful of the ancient chiefs, to whom tradition assigned supernatural knowledge and skill."[2]

The accounts which savages give of their religious beliefs are often deliberately fabricated by them to deceive or please the white man.

Again, there is reason to believe that the accounts which savages give of their religious beliefs are often deliberately fabricated by them in order to deceive the white man. This source of error, though it is not limited to the religious sphere, applies especially to it, since the uncivilised, like the civilised, man is, in general, loth to reveal his most sacred beliefs to any chance inquirer. To win his confidence and elicit his inmost thoughts, it is necessary for the investigator either to have known him intimately for a long time, or to give evidence that he himself has already been initiated into mysteries of the same sort. But the deception practised by the savage sometimes springs from a different motive. In his amiable anxiety to oblige a stranger, he will often tell him whatever he imagines that the inquirer would like to hear, without the least regard to the truth. Thus it is a custom with the Bantu "not to dispute with honoured guests, but to profess agreement with whatever is stated. This is regarded by those people as politeness, and it is carried to such an absurd extent that it is often difficult to obtain correct information from them. Thus if one asks a man, is it far to such a place? politeness requires him to reply it is

---

[1] Father Porte, "Les reminiscences d'un missionaire du Basutoland," *Missions Catholiques*, xxviii. (1896) p. 370. Compare E. S. Hartland, in *Folklore*, xii. (1901) p. 24 *sqq.*

[2] G. M'Call Theal, *Records of South-Eastern Africa*, vii. (1901) p. 401.

far, though it may be close by. The questioner, by using the word far, is supposed to be under the impression that it is at a distance, and it would be rudeness to correct him. They express their thanks for whatever is told them, whether the intelligence is pleasing or not, and whether they believe it or not. Then, too, no one of them ever denies the existence of a Supreme Being, but admits it without hesitation as soon as he is told of it, though he may not once have thought of the subject before."[1]

In regard to the Australian aborigines, it appears that this source of error has also vitiated some of the accounts which have been given of their religious notions. "Many persons try to persuade themselves that they can detect the existence amongst these natives of a true religion and a knowledge of a Supreme Being, but they forget that these Blacks are extremely shrewd, so that when they perceive the object of the conversation, they readily adapt all that they have been taught on this subject to their replies. I have always found that the rigmarole stories which many of them have told me, and which are supposed to represent their religious belief, were founded upon the teachings of missionaries and others."[2] "I am strongly of opinion that those who have written to show that the Blacks had some knowledge of God, practised prayer, and believed in places of reward and punishment beyond the grave, have been imposed upon, and that until they had learnt something of Christianity from missionaries and others the Blacks had no beliefs and practices of the sort. Having heard the missionaries, however, they were not slow to invent what I may call kindred statements with aboriginal accessories, with a view to please and surprise the Whites."[3] In pursuing his researches in this subject, Dr. A. W. Howitt was on at least one occasion surprised, though not pleased, with "kindred statements" of this sort. Wishing to learn the native belief as to Brewin, a spirit whom the Kurnai dread, he questioned two of the most intelligent men, one of whom

This source of error seems to have vitiated some of the accounts which have been given of the religious notions of the Australian savages.

---

[1] G. M'Call Theal, *op. cit.* vii. 497.
[2] J. F. Mann, "Notes on the Aborigines of Australia," *Proceedings of the Geographical Society of Australasia,* i. (1885) p. 40.
[3] E. M. Curr, *The Australian Race,* i. 45.

THE BEGINNINGS OF RELIGION

was a member of the Church of England. After consulting together for a few minutes, one of them said, "We think that he is Jesus Christ." When this answer proved unsatisfactory, they laid their heads together again, and after mature deliberation declared that he must be the devil.[1] The anecdote is instructive, because it illustrates the readiness with which the natives adapt their answers to the supposed taste of the inquirer, and the little dependence that can consequently be placed on their statements as to this subject.

Incredulity of Baldwin Spencer as to alleged Australian beliefs in a Supreme Being.

Now it is to be observed that the reports of moral Supreme Beings among the Australian aborigines come chiefly from Victoria and New South Wales, that is, the parts of the continent where the natives have been longest under the influence of the white man. If we could deduct from these reports the elements of error and fraud, we should probably find that the residue would be small indeed; and we might acquiesce in the opinion of Professor Baldwin Spencer: "I do not think that there is really any direct evidence of any Australian native belief in a 'supreme being' in our sense of the term."[2]

However, some tribes believe in spiritual beings who can make or mar them.

But though the natives of Central Australia appear to be equally destitute of ancestor worship,[3] and of a belief in a Supreme Being, the guardian of morality, some of the tribes on the Gulf of Carpentaria have a notion of spiritual beings who can help or injure them. The Binbinga, Mara, and Anula tribes believe that the sky is inhabited by two unfriendly beings who are always anxious to come down and kill people, but are prevented from doing so by a friendly spirit who lives in the woods. When an Anula man falls ill, his friends sing to the friendly spirit in the woods to come and make him well.[4] Such beliefs and such a practice might in time develop into a regular propitiation of these spirits, that is, they might grow into a religion.

Thus, if the Australian aborigines had been left to themselves, they might have evolved a native religion along

---

[1] Fison and Howitt, *Kamilaroi and Kurnai*, p. 255.

[2] Letter to me dated 15th April 1903.

[3] Spencer and Gillen, *Northern Tribes*, p. 494.

[4] Spencer and Gillen, *op. cit.*, p. 501 *sq.*

THE BEGINNINGS OF RELIGION

several more or less independent lines. Their regard for the comfort of departed friends might have given rise to a worship of the dead, provided always that the theory of reincarnation, which prevails among the central tribes and is obviously incompatible with a deification of the ancestral spirits,[1] had been exchanged for a belief that these spirits, instead of returning to earth and being born again in the flesh, dwell for ever in some happy land, whence, though unseen by mortal or at least vulgar eyes, they watch over their children and aid them in their time of need. Again, totemism might have led to a cult of the totem animal or plant, as indeed seems to be happening to the Wollunqua or mythical water-snake of the Warramunga. Further, a belief in friendly or hostile spirits, neither ancestral nor totemic, who live on earth or in the sky, and can help or harm mankind, is not far from a religion of nature. Finally, if the abstract idea of a powerful headman, kind to his own people and terrible to their foes, had blended with a belief in the immortality of the dead, it might easily have culminated in the worship of a tribal or national god. And these various lines of development might have co-existed in the same tribe, leading up to a complex religion in which a cult of the totems should have been combined with a worship of other natural powers, and a general propitiation of the dead should have gone hand-in-hand with the special worship of a tribal or national god, who had grown out of an ideal or legendary headman. Such a complex religion would conform to the general rule that fully developed religions are compounded of many different elements, which spring from diverse roots.

Thus if the Australian aborigines had been left to themselves they might have developed a native religion along several independent lines.

[1] Spencer and Gillen, *op. cit.*, p. 494.

II

THE BEGINNINGS OF TOTEMISM

The same regions of Australia which exhibit the rudiments of religion exhibit also an advance towards a higher form of social life. That advance is marked by the substitution of individual for group marriage, and of paternal for maternal descent of the totem.

IT is significant that the rudiments of a native religion in Australia, so far as they are known to us, make their appearance for the most part either in the south-eastern districts or on the northern coast, but are, on the whole, conspicuously absent from the centre,[1] while on the contrary magical ceremonies for the multiplication of the totems attain their highest vogue among the central tribes, and gradually diminish in number and importance as we approach the sea, till on the Gulf of Carpentaria they have almost disappeared.[2] Now it can hardly be an accidental coincidence that, as Dr. Howitt has well pointed out,[3] the same regions in which the germs of religion begin to appear have also made some progress towards a higher form of social and family life. That progress in Australia is marked by two great steps: individual marriage has been substituted for group marriage,[4] and paternal descent of the totem has prevailed over maternal descent, as well as over an even older mode of transmitting the totem which still survives among the Arunta and Kaitish.

---

[1] The Warramunga respect for the Wollunqua water-snake and the Dieri custom of leaving food for the dead are exceptions.

[2] Spencer and Gillen, *Northern Tribes*, pp. 14 *sq.*, 23, 311 *sq.*, 315-319.

[3] A. W. Howitt, *Native Tribes of South-East Australia*, p. 500.

[4] A. W. Howitt, "Further Notes on the Australian Class System," *Journal of the Anthropological Institute*, xviii. (1889) p. 66 *sqq.*; *id.*, "The Dieri and other Kindred Tribes of Central Australia," xx. (1891) p. 98 *sqq.*; *id.*, *Native Tribes of South-East Australia*, chap. v.; Spencer and Gillen, *Native Tribes of Central Australia*, p. 92 *sqq.* The evidence marshalled by these writers appears to me to render it practically certain that in Australia individual marriage has everywhere been preceded by group marriage, and that again by a still wider sexual communism.

THE BEGINNINGS OF TOTEMISM

In regard to the first of these changes, whereas group marriage exists to this day as an institution among several of the central tribes, such as the Dieri and Urabunna,[1] it has disappeared from all the other tribes known to us, only leaving traces of itself in the classificatory system of relationship, and in the licence accorded to the sexes on certain occasions, especially at marriage. In regard to the second change, the inheritance of the totem in the paternal line is fixed and invariable among the tribes on the coast of the Gulf of Carpentaria, but as we pass inland from them we find that it gradually grows rarer and rarer, until among the Arunta and Kaitish tribes, in the very heart of the continent, it totally disappears, and is replaced by an entirely different mode of determining the totem.[2] For in these tribes a person derives his totem neither from his father nor from his mother, but from the place where his mother first became aware that she was with child. Scattered all over the country are what Messrs. Spencer and Gillen call local totem centres, that is, spots where the souls of the dead are supposed to live awaiting reincarnation, each of these spots being haunted by the spirits of people of one totem only; and wherever a pregnant woman first feels the child in her womb, she thinks that a spirit of the nearest totem centre has entered into her, and accordingly the child will be of that local totem, whatever it may be, without any regard to the totem either of the father or of the mother.[3]

This mode of determining the totem has all the

(marginal notes: Group marriage and a peculiar mode of determining the totem still exist among some of the central tribes, but have disappeared from all the others. Among the central tribes a person takes his totem neither from his father nor his mother, but from the place where his mother first felt she was with child.)

---

[1] A. W. Howitt, "The Dieri and other Kindred Tribes of Central Australia," *Journal of the Anthropological Institute*, xx. (1891) p. 53 *sqq.*; Spencer and Gillen, *Native Tribes of Central Australia*, p. 55 *sqq.* On this subject Dr. A. W. Howitt writes to me: "When I wrote the paper quoted from I did not know of the *pirrauru* [group marriage] practice in other tribes. It exists in all the Lake Eyre tribes, and I am satisfied that it also extended to the Parnkalla at Port Lincoln, to the Kurnandaburi at Mount Howitt, and the Wakelbura in East Queensland." For the detailed evidence see Dr. Howitt's book, *Native Tribes of South-East Australia*, p. 175 *sqq.*

[2] Spencer and Gillen, *Northern Tribes of Central Australia*, pp. 144, 163 *sqq.*, 169 *sqq.*, 174-176. The descent of the totem must be carefully distinguished from the descent of the exogamous class, which is invariably in the paternal line among all these central and north-central tribes, except the Dieri and Urabunna, among whom the descent both of the totem and of the class is in the maternal line.

[3] Spencer and Gillen, *Native Tribes of Central Australia*, p. 123 *sqq.*

156 THE BEGINNINGS OF TOTEMISM

This mode of determining the totem appears to be very ancient, since it ignores paternity altogether: it may be called conceptional or local, as distinguished from hereditary totemism.

appearance of extreme antiquity. For it ignores altogether the intercourse of the sexes as the cause of offspring, and further, it ignores the tie of blood on the maternal as well as the paternal side, substituting for it a purely local bond, since the members of a totem stock are merely those who gave the first sign of life in the womb at one or other of certain definite spots. This form of totemism, which may be called conceptional or local to distinguish it from hereditary totemism,[1] may with great probability be regarded as the most primitive known to exist at the present day, since it seems to date from a time when blood relationship was not yet recognised, and when even the idea of paternity had not yet presented itself to the savage mind. Moreover, it is hardly possible that this peculiar form of local totemism, with its implied ignorance of such a thing as paternity at all, could be derived from hereditary totemism, whereas it is easy to understand how hereditary totemism, either in the paternal or in the maternal line, could be derived from it. Indeed, among the Umbaia and Gnanji tribes we can see at the present day how the change from local to hereditary totemism has been effected. These tribes, like the Arunta and Kaitish, believe that conception is caused by the entrance into a woman of a spirit who has lived in its disembodied state, along with other spirits of the same totem, at any one of a number of totem centres scattered over the country; but, unlike the Arunta and Kaitish, they almost always assign the father's totem to the child, even though the infant may have given the first sign of life at a place haunted by spirits of a different totem. For example, the wife of a snake man may first feel her womb quickened at a tree haunted by spirits of goshawk people; yet the child will not be a goshawk but a snake, like its father. The theory by which the Umbaia and Gnanji reconcile these apparently incon-

But conceptional could easily pass into hereditary totemism, either in the paternal or the maternal line.

---

[1] But this peculiar form of local totemism must not be confused with another form of totemism, in which hereditary totem clans inhabit each its own separate district of country or quarter of a village; for this latter species of totemism, which combines the local with the hereditary principle, seems to be a very late development. See above, p. 83; A. C. Haddon, *Head-hunters*, pp. 132, 171; *Reports of the Cambridge Anthropological Expedition to Torres Straits*, v. (Cambridge, 1904) pp. 159, 172 *sqq.*, 188 *sqq.*

sistent beliefs is that a spirit of the husband's totem follows the wife and enters into her wherever an opportunity offers, whereas spirits of other totems would not think of doing so. In the example supposed, a snake spirit is thought to have followed up the wife of the snake man and entered into her at the tree haunted by goshawk spirits, while the goshawk spirits would refuse to trespass, so to say, on a snake preserve by quartering themselves in the wife of a snake man.[1] This theory clearly marks a transition from local to hereditary totemism in the paternal line. And precisely the same theory could, *mutatis mutandis*, be employed to effect a change from local to hereditary totemism in the maternal line; it would only be necessary to suppose that a pregnant woman is always followed by a spirit of her own totem, which sooner or later effects a lodgment in her body. For example, a pregnant woman of the bee totem would always be followed by a bee spirit, which would enter into her wherever and whenever she felt her womb quickened, and so the child would be born of her own bee totem. Thus the local form of totemism which obtains among the Arunta and Kaitish tribes is older than the hereditary form, which is the ordinary type of totemism in Australia and elsewhere, first, because it rests on far more archaic conceptions of society and of life, and, secondly, because both the hereditary kinds of totemism, the paternal and the maternal, can be derived from it, whereas it can hardly be derived from either of them.[2]

I have said that the form of totemism which prevails in the most central tribes of Australia, particularly the Arunta and Kaitish, is probably the most primitive known to exist at the present day. Perhaps we may go a step further, and say that it is but one remove from the original pattern, the absolutely primitive type of totemism. The theory on which it is based denies implicitly, and the natives themselves deny explicitly,[3] that children are the fruit of the commerce of

Conceptional totemism among the Central Australians seems to be only one remove from absolutely primitive totemism,

[1] Spencer and Gillen, *Northern Tribes of Central Australia*, pp. 169 *sq.*, 176.
[2] I may remark in passing that the irregularity or total absence of paternal descent of the totems among tribes who have strict paternal descent of the exogamous classes is one proof amongst others that these classes are of more recent origin than totemism; in other words, that totemism is older than exogamy.
[3] Spencer and Gillen, *Native Tribes of Central Australia*, pp. 124 *sq.*, 265.

158   THE BEGINNINGS OF TOTEMISM

which was apparently a theory to account for pregnancy and childbirth at a time when their true cause was unknown.

the sexes. So astounding an ignorance of natural causation cannot but date from a past immeasurably remote. Yet that ignorance, strange as it seems to us, may be explained easily enough from the habits and modes of thought of savage man. In the first place, the interval which elapses between the act of impregnation and the first symptoms of pregnancy is sufficient to prevent him from perceiving the connection between the two. In the second place, the custom, common among savage tribes, of allowing unrestricted licence of intercourse between the sexes under puberty has familiarised him with sexual unions that are necessarily sterile; from which he may not unnaturally conclude that the intercourse of the sexes has nothing to do with the birth of offspring.[1] Hence he is driven to account for pregnancy and child-birth in some other way. The theory which the Central Australians have adopted on the subject is one which commends itself to the primitive mind as simple and obvious. Nothing is commoner among savages all the world over than a belief that a person may be possessed by a spirit, which has entered into him, thereby disturbing his organism and creating an abnormal state of body or mind, such as sickness or lunacy. Now, when a woman is observed to be pregnant, the savage infers, with perfect truth, that something has entered into her. What is it? and how did it make its way into her womb? These are questions which he cannot but put to himself as soon as he thinks about the matter. For the reasons given above, it does not occur to him to connect the first symptoms of pregnancy with a sexual act, which preceded them by a considerable interval. He thinks that the child enters into the woman at the time when she first feels it stirring in her womb, which, of course, does not happen until long after the real moment of conception. Naturally enough, when she is first aware of the mysterious movement within her, the mother fancies that something has that very moment passed into her body, and it is equally natural that in her attempt to ascertain what the thing is she should fix upon

---

[1] This latter consideration has already been indicated by Mr. W. E. Roth (*North Queensland Ethnography*, *Bulletin No.* 5, Brisbane, 1903, § 83, p. 23).

some object that happened to be near her and to engage her attention at the critical moment. Thus if she chanced at the time to be watching a kangaroo, or collecting grass-seed for food, or bathing in water, or sitting under a gum-tree, she might imagine that the spirit of a kangaroo, of grass-seed, of water, or of a gum-tree had passed into her, and accordingly, that when her child was born, it was really a kangaroo, a grass-seed, water, or a gum-tree, though to the bodily eye it presented the outward form of a human being. Amongst the objects on which her fancy might pitch as the cause of her pregnancy we may suppose that the last food she had eaten would often be one. If she had recently partaken of emu flesh or yams she might suppose that the emu or yam, which she had unquestionably taken into her body, had, so to say, struck root and grown up in her. This last, as perhaps the most natural, might be the commonest explanation of pregnancy; and if that was so, we can understand why, among the Central Australian tribes, if not among totemic tribes all over the world, the great majority of totems are edible objects, whether animals or plants.[1]

Now, too, we can fully comprehend why people should identify themselves, as totemic tribes commonly do with their totems, to such an extent as to regard the man and his totem as practically indistinguishable. A man of the emu totem, for example, might say, "An emu entered into my mother at such and such a place and time; it grew up in her, and came forth from her. I am that emu, therefore I am an emu man. I am practically the same as the bird, though to you, perhaps, I may not look like it." And so with all the other totems. On such a view it is perfectly natural that a man, deeming himself one of his totem species, should regard it with respect and affection, and that he should imagine himself possessed of a power, such as men of other totems do not possess, to increase or diminish it, according to circumstances, for the good of

On this view of totemism we can understand why men should identify themselves with their totem, and should imagine themselves possessed of special power over it.

---

[1] As to the Central Australian totems, see Spencer and Gillen, *Northern Tribes of Central Australia*, Appendix B, pp. 767-773. Amongst the two hundred and one sorts of totems here enumerated, no less than a hundred and sixty-nine or a hundred and seventy are eaten.

himself and his fellows. Thus the practice of *Intichiuma*, that is, magical ceremonies performed by men of a totem for its increase or diminution, would be a natural development of the original germ or stock of totemism.[1]

If the germ of totemism was a primitive theory of conception, which may have occurred independently to men in many parts of the world, we can understand the wide diffusion and other characteristic features of totemism.

That germ or stock, if my conjecture is right, is, in its essence, nothing more or less than an early theory of conception, which presented itself to savage man at a time when he was still ignorant of the true cause of the propagation of the species. This theory of conception is, on the principles of savage thought, so simple and obvious that it may well have occurred to men independently in many parts of the world. Thus we could understand the wide prevalence of totemism among distant races without being forced to suppose that they had borrowed it from each other. Further, the hypothesis accounts for one of the most characteristic features of totemism, namely, the intermingling in the same community of men and women of many different totem stocks. For each person's totem would be determined by what may be called an accident, that is, by the place where his mother happened to be, the occupation in which she was engaged, or the last food she had eaten at the time when she first felt the child in her womb ; and such accidents (and with them the totems) would vary considerably in individual cases, though the range of variation would necessarily be limited by the number of objects open to the observation, or conceivable by the imagination, of the tribe. These objects would be chiefly the natural features of the district, and the kinds of food on which the community subsisted ; but they might quite well include artificial and even purely imaginary objects, such as boomerangs and mythical beasts. Even a totem like Laughing Boys, which

[1] When some years ago these *Intichiuma* ceremonies were first discovered on a great scale among the Central Australians, I was so struck by the importance of the discovery that I was inclined to see in these ceremonies the ultimate origin of totemism ; and the discoverers themselves, Messrs. Spencer and Gillen, were disposed to take the same view. See Baldwin Spencer, F. J. Gillen, and J. G. Frazer, in *Journal of the Anthropological Institute*, xxviii. (1899) pp. 275-286 ; and above, pp. 113 *sqq*. Further reflection has led me to the conclusion that magical ceremonies for the increase or diminution of the totems are likely to be a later, though still very early, outgrowth of totemism rather than its original root. At the present time these magical ceremonies seem to constitute the main function of totemism in Central Australia. But this does not prove that they have done so from the beginning.

we find among the Arunta, is perfectly intelligible on the present theory. In fact, of all the things which the savage perceives or imagines, there is none which he might not thus convert into a totem, since there is none which might not chance to impress itself on the mind of the mother, waking or dreaming, at the critical season.

If we may hypothetically assume, as the first stage in the evolution of totemism, a system like the foregoing, based on a primitive theory of conception the whole history of totemism becomes intelligible. For in the first place, the existing system of totemism among the Arunta and Kaitish, which combines the principle of conception with that of locality, could be derived from this hypothetical system in the simplest and easiest manner, as I shall point out immediately. And in the second place, the existing system of the Arunta and Kaitish could, in its turn, readily pass into hereditary totemism of the ordinary type, as, in fact, it appears to be doing in the Umbaia and Gnanji tribes of Central Australia at present.[1] Thus what may be called conceptional totemism pure and simple furnishes an intelligible starting-point for the evolution of totemism in general. In it, after years of sounding, our plummets seem to touch bottom at last.

On this hypothesis the whole history of totemism becomes intelligible.

I have said that a primitive system of purely conceptional totemism could easily give rise to the existing system of the Arunta and Kaitish, which appears to be but one remove distant from it. Among the Arunta and Kaitish the choice of the totem is not left absolutely to chance or to the imagination of the mother. The whole country is parcelled out into totem districts, each with its centre, where the disembodied spirits of the totems are supposed to linger, awaiting reincarnation; and the child's totem is determined by the particular totem centre to which its mother happened to be nearest when she felt her womb quickened; one of the local spirits is supposed to have entered into her. Thus the wide range of accidents which, under a system of conceptional totemism pure and simple, might settle the totem of the individual, is, under the existing system, restricted to the accident of place; and in virtue of this restriction an original

Hypothetical passage of a primitive system of purely conceptional totemism into the local variety of it which is actually found in Central Australia.

[1] See above, pp. 156 *sq.*

system of purely conceptional totemism has, while it retains the conceptional principle, developed into a species of local totemism. How the restriction in question has been brought about can only be a matter of conjecture. But it is not difficult to imagine that when several women had, one after the other, felt the first premonitions of maternity at the same spot and under the same circumstances, the place would come to be regarded as haunted by spirits of a particular sort; and so the whole country might in time be dotted over with totem centres and distributed into totem districts. Any striking natural feature of the landscape, such as a conspicuous tree, a curiously-shaped rock, or a pool of clear water, would be likely to impress itself on the mind of women at such times, and so to lend a certain uniformity to their fancies.

The hypothesis does not account for the exogamy of the totem stocks, because exogamy forms no part of true totemism; it was a social reform introduced at a later time, when the community composed of totem stocks was bisected into two or afterwards four exogamous divisions, in order to prevent

Thus the hypothesis that totemism is, in its origin, a savage theory of conception seems to furnish a simple and adequate explanation of the facts. But there is one feature of totemism, as that system commonly meets us, which the hypothesis does not account for, namely, the exogamy of the totem stocks; in other words, the rule that a man may not marry nor have connection with a woman of the same totem as himself. That rule is, indeed, quite inexplicable on the view that men and women regard themselves as identical with their totem animals; for as these animals mate with their kind, why should not men and women of the same totem do so too, seeing that they are only slightly-disguised forms of their totem animals? But the truth is, exogamy forms no part of true totemism. It is a great social reform of a much later date, which, in many communities, has accidentally modified the totemic system, while in others it has left that system entirely unaffected. Native Australian traditions represent, doubtless with truth, exogamy as an innovation imported into a community already composed of totem stocks;[1] and these traditions are amply

---

[1] Spencer and Gillen, *Native Tribes of Central Australia*, pp. 392 sq., 418-422; id., *Northern Tribes of Central Australia*, pp. 429, 438 sq.; A. W. Howitt, *Native Tribes of South-East Australia*, pp. 480-482. As Dr. Howitt here points out, the tradition which represents the totemic system of the Dieri as introduced for the purpose of regulating marriage appears to be merely one of Mr. Gason's blunders.

confirmed by a study of the social organisation of the Australian tribes, which proves, as Messrs. Howitt, Spencer, and Gillen have rightly perceived, that the primary exogamous unit was not the totem stock, but the moiety of the whole tribe. Each tribe was, in fact, divided into two halves, all the children of the same mother being assigned to the same half, and the men of each half were obliged to take their wives from the other half. At a later time each of these halves was, in some tribes, again subdivided into two, and the men and women in each of the four quarters thus constituted were forced to take their wives or husbands from a particular one, and only one, of the remaining three quarters; while it was arranged that the children should belong neither to their mother's nor to their father's quarter, but to one of the remaining two quarters. The effect of the division of the tribe into two exogamous halves, with all the children of the same mother ranged on the same side, is obviously to prevent the marriage of brothers with sisters. The effect of the division of the tribe into four exogamous quarters, coupled with the rules that every person may marry only into one quarter, and that the children must belong to a quarter which is neither that of their father nor that of their mother, is to prevent the marriage of parents with children.[1] Now, since these successive bisections of the tribe into two, four, or even eight exogamous divisions, with an increasingly complicated rule of descent, have every appearance of being artificial, we may fairly infer that the effect they actually produce is the effect they were intended to produce; in other words, that they were deliberately devised and adopted as a means of preventing the marriage, at first, of brothers with sisters, and, at a later time, of parents with children.

The intermarriage, first, of brothers with sisters, and next of parents with children.

That this was so I regard as practically certain. But the question why early man in Australia, and, apparently,

[1] This observation, the truth of which can easily be demonstrated in a tabular form, was communicated by me to my friend Dr. A. W. Howitt, who did me the honour to mention it with approval in his book. See his *Native Tribes of South-East Australia*, pp. 284-286. The conclusion here stated was briefly indicated in my paper, "The Origin of Totemism," *Fortnightly Review*, May 1899, p. 841, note 2 [above, p. 124, note ²]. Nearly the same observation was afterwards made independently by Mr. E. Crawley in his book, *The Mystic Rose* (London, 1902), pp. 469-472.

The antipathy of early man to incest can hardly have been based on grounds which we should regard as moral;

in many other parts of the world, objected to these unions, and took elaborate precautions to prevent them, is difficult to answer, except in a vague and general way. We should probably err if we imagined that this far-reaching innovation or reform was introduced from any such moral antipathy to incest, as most, though by no means all, races have manifested within historical times. That antipathy is rather the fruit than the seed of the prohibition of incest. It is the slowly accumulated effect of a prohibition which has been transmitted through successive generations from time immemorial. To suppose that the law of incest originated in any instinctive horror of the act would be to invert the relation of cause and effect, and to commit the commonest of all blunders in investigating early society, that of interpreting it in the light of our modern feelings and habits, and so using the late products of evolution to account for its primordial germs; in short, it would be to explain the beginning by the end, instead of the end by the beginning.

nor can it have originated in a belief that incest is injurious to the offspring.

Further, the original ground of objection to incestuous unions certainly cannot have been any notion that they were injurious to the offspring, and that for two reasons. In the first place, it is a moot question among men of science at the present day whether the closest interbreeding has, in itself, when the parents are perfectly healthy, any such harmful effect.[1] However that question may be finally decided, we cannot suppose that the rudest savages perceived ages ago what, with all the resources of accurate observation and long-continued experiments in breeding animals, modern science has not yet conclusively established. But in the second place, not only is it impossible that the savage can have detected so very dubious an effect, but it is impossible that he can even have imagined it. For if, down to the present day, the Central Australians, who practise strict exogamy, do not believe that children are the result of the intercourse of the sexes, their still ruder forefathers certainly

---

[1] See Ch. Darwin, *Variation of Animals and Plants under Domestication*[2] (London, 1875), ii. chap. xvii. pp. 92-126; A. H. Huth, *The Marriage of Near Kin*[2] (London, 1887); G. A. Wilken, "Die Ehe zwischen Blutsverwandten," *Globus*, lix. (1891) pp. 8-12, 20-24, 35-38.

cannot have introduced exogamy at a more or less remote period for the purpose of remedying the action of a cause, the existence of which they denied.

But if the prohibition of incestuous unions was based neither on what we might call a moral instinct, nor on a fear of any evil, real or imaginary, which they were supposed to entail on the offspring, the only alternative open to us seems to be to infer that these unions were forbidden because they were believed to be injurious to the persons who engaged in them, even when they were both in perfect health. Such a belief, I apprehend, is entirely groundless, and can only have arisen in some mistaken notion of cause and effect; in short, in a superstition. What that superstition precisely was, in other words, what exact harm was supposed to be done by incest to the persons immediately concerned, I am unable to guess. Thus the ultimate origin of exogamy, and with it of the law of incest—since exogamy was devised to prevent incest—remains a problem nearly as dark as ever. All that seems fairly probable is that both of them originated in a savage superstition, to which we have lost the clue. To say this is not to prejudice the question of the effect for good or ill which these institutions have had on the race; for the question of the working of any institution is wholly distinct from that of its historical origin. Just as a bad practice may be adopted from a good motive, so, on the other hand, an excellent custom may be instituted for a reason utterly false and absurd.

Apparently the prohibition of incest must have been founded on a superstition that incestuous unions are injurious to those who engage in them.

I have said that the introduction of exogamy affected the totemic system of some tribes, but not that of others. This I will now explain. Where totemism had become hereditary, that is, where every person received his totem either from his father or from his mother, the introduction of exogamy naturally resulted in making the totem stocks exogamous. For when the tribe was split up into two intermarrying moieties the hereditary totem stocks would be distributed between the moieties, the whole of each stock being placed in one or other of the moieties, and not divided between the two. From this it would follow that as each moiety was exogamous, so necessarily were all the totem stocks of which it was composed. The exogamy of the hereditary

The introduction of exogamy affected the totemic system only of those tribes among whom totemism had become hereditary; it could not affect the system among tribes who retained

totem stocks was thus a direct, though accidental, consequence of the exogamy of the two moieties. On the other hand, where the old conceptional, as opposed to the newer hereditary, type of totemism survived, as we see it, in a slightly modified form, among the Arunta and Kaitish tribes, the introduction of exogamy would have no effect on the totem stocks as such; that is, it would not make them exogamous. The reason is simple. Exogamy was introduced, as I have pointed out, at first to prevent the marriage of brothers with sisters, and afterwards to prevent the marriage of parents with children. But under a system like that of the Arunta, where, in virtue of the accidents which determine the totem of each individual, brother and sister may be of different totems, and the totem of the child may differ from that both of the father and of the mother, it is obvious that to make the totem stocks exogamous would not necessarily effect the purpose for which the rule of exogamy was devised; for even with strict exogamy of the totem stocks it would still be open to a brother to marry a sister, and to a parent to marry a child, in all the cases—and they would probably be the majority of cases—in which the totem of the brother differed from that of the sister, and the totem of the parent differed from that of the child. When we find, therefore, that the rule of exogamy is not applied to the totem stocks in the very cases where, if it were applied, it would be powerless to prevent the marriage of brothers with sisters, and of parents with children, we can hardly help regarding this omission to apply the rule in these circumstances as a strong additional proof that exogamy was devised expressly for the purpose of preventing such marriages. Further, it appears to demonstrate that the machinery by which exogamy was introduced and worked was not the organisation of the community in totem stocks, but its bisection, single or repeated, into two, four, or eight exogamous divisions, or classes and sub-classes, as they may, with Dr. A. W. Howitt, be conveniently designated. For we have to remember that though, for the reason I have given, the Arunta and the Kaitish do not apply the principle of exogamy to their totem stocks, they fully recognise and act on the principle, the whole community being divided into eight exogamous classes, a division which is quite distinct from, and probably far later than, the distribution of the community into totem stocks.

Finally, I have to point out that, if the present theory of the development of totemism is correct, the common assumption that inheritance of the totem through the mother always preceded inheritance of it through the father need not hold good. If the transition from the conceptional to the hereditary form of totemism was effected in the manner in which it seems to be actually taking place at present among the Central Australian tribes, it is clear that the change could be made just as readily to paternal as to maternal descent. For it would be quite as easy to suppose that a spirit of the husband's totem had entered into his wife as that a spirit of her own totem had done so: the former supposition would give paternal descent of the totem, the latter would give maternal descent. Only we have to bear in mind that the notion of paternity among these tribes is a totally different thing from what it is with us. Denying, as they do explicitly, that the child is begotten by the father, they can only regard him as the consort, and, in a sense, the owner of the mother, and therefore, as the owner of her progeny, just as a man who owns a cow owns also the calf she brings forth. In short, it seems probable that a man's children were viewed as his property long before they were recognised as his offspring.

Since conceptional totemism can pass as readily into hereditary totemism in the male as in the female line, it follows that paternal descent of the totem need not have been preceded by maternal descent of it; both lines of descent may have sprung independently from the conceptional system. The primitive notion of paternity was probably that of ownership.

From the foregoing discussion it follows that, judged either by the type of social organisation or by the relation of magic to religion, the central tribes of Australia are the more backward, and the coastal tribes the more progressive. To put it otherwise, in aboriginal Australia social and religious progress has spread or is spreading from the sea inland, and not in the reverse direction.

Thus, the central tribes of Australia are more backward than the coastal tribes.

This conclusion is no more than might have been anticipated on general grounds without any knowledge of the particular facts. For the interior of a country is naturally less open to foreign influence than its coasts, and is therefore more tenacious of old ways. But quite apart

This conclusion might have been anticipated on general grounds

from the from any foreign influence, which before the coming of Europeans seems hardly to have affected the Australian race, there is a special cause why the coastal tribes of Australia should take the first steps towards civilisation, and that is the greater abundance of water and food in their country as compared with the parched and barren table-lands of the interior.[1] Central Australia lies in the desert zone of the southern hemisphere, and has no high mountains to condense the vapours from the surrounding ocean. The most extensive tract of fertile and well-watered country is on the east and south-east, where a fine range of mountains approaches, in the colony of Victoria, the limits of perpetual snow.[2] And in the north, on the shores of the Gulf of Carpentaria, a heavier rainfall produces a more abundant vegetation and a more plentiful supply of food than can be found in the arid wilderness of the interior. Thus, even among the rude savages of Australia, we can detect the operation of those natural laws which have ordained that elsewhere all the great civilisations of the world should arise in well-watered and fertile lands within the atmospheric influence of the sea. An abundant supply of good food stimulates progress in more ways than one. By leaving men with leisure on their hands it affords them greater opportunities for observation and thought than are enjoyed by people whose whole energies are absorbed in an arduous struggle for a bare subsistence; and by improving the physical stamina of the race it strengthens and sharpens the intellectual faculties which, in the long run, are always depressed and impaired by a poor and meagre diet. Thus, if in Australia the tide of progress, slow but perceptible, has set from the sea towards the interior, it has probably been in large measure under the impulse of a more plentiful supply of food, which in its turn is due

Marginal notes: from the seclusion of the central tribes and the desert nature of their country; for observation teaches us that civilisation arises in fertile countries, not in deserts, abundance of food being essential to an advance in culture.

---

[1] This cause has been assigned by Dr. Howitt for the social advance, and by Messrs. Spencer and Gillen for the decrease of *Intichiuma* magic, on the coast. See A. W. Howitt, "Further Notes on the Australian Class Systems," *Journal of the Anthropological Institute*, xviii. (1889) p. 33 *sq.*; *id.*, *Native Tribes of South-East Australia*, p. 154 *sq.*; Spencer and Gillen, *Northern Tribes of Central Australia*, pp. 173, 311, 318.

[2] A. R. Wallace, *The Geographical Distribution of Animals* (London, 1876), i. 387 *sq.* Mr. Wallace here states that the Victorian mountains actually reach the limit of perpetual snow. But this, as Prof. Baldwin Spencer tells me, is a mistake.

to the heavier rainfall on the coast and the neighbouring regions.

But it is not merely by starving the vital energies and hence cramping the intelligence of the race that the physical character and climate of Central Australia have retarded progress and favoured the survival of a faith in magic after that faith had begun to waver in more fertile districts. A little reflection will probably convince us that the more variable the course of nature throughout the year, the more persistent probably will be man's efforts to regulate it for his benefit, and the firmer will be his faith in his power to do so. In other words, the more marked the changes of the seasons, the greater will tend to be the prevalence of magic and the belief in its efficacy, though naturally that tendency may be counteracted by other causes. On the other hand, where nature is bounteous and her course is uniform or varies but little from year's end to year's end, man will neither need nor desire to alter it by magic or otherwise to suit his convenience. For he makes magic, just as he prays and sacrifices, in order to obtain what he has not got; if he already possesses all he wants, why should he exert himself? It is in times of need and distress rather than of abundance and prosperity that man betakes himself to the practice both of magic and of religion. Hence in some tropical regions of eternal summer, where moisture, warmth, and sunshine never fail, where the trees are always green and fruits always hang from the boughs, where the waters perpetually swarm with fish and the forests teem with an exuberance of animal life, ceremonies for the making of rain and sunshine and for the multiplication of edible beasts and plants are for the most part absent or inconspicuous. For example, we hear little or nothing of them, so far as I remember, among the Indians of the luxuriant forests of Brazil. Far otherwise is it with countries where a brief summer alternates with a chilly spring, a fickle autumn, and a long and rigorous winter. Here of necessity man is put to all his shifts to snatch from a churlish nature boons that are at once evanescent and precarious. Here, accordingly, that branch of magic which aims at procuring the necessaries of life may be expected to

[marginal notes: The physical character and climate of Central Australia have favoured the survival of magic in another way; for magic tends to prevail in porportion to the range of variations of the seasons, these annual changes serving to confirm man's belief that he can bring them about by magical arts.]

flourish most. To put it generally, the practice of magic for the control of nature will be found on the whole to increase with the variability and to decrease with the uniformity of the course of nature throughout the year. Hence the increase will tend to become more and more conspicuous as we recede from the equator, where the annual changes of natural conditions are much less marked than elsewhere.[1] This general rule is no doubt subject to many exceptions which depend on local varieties of climate. Where the contrast between a wet and a dry season is sharply marked, as in the track of the monsoons, magic may well be invoked to secure the advantages or remedy the inconveniences of heavy rain or drought. But, on the whole, this department of magic, if not checked by civilisation or other causes, would naturally attain its highest vogue in the temperate and polar zones rather than in the equatorial regions; while, on the other hand, the branch of magical art which deals directly with mankind, aiming for example at the cure or infliction of disease, tends for obvious reasons to be diffused equally over the globe without distinction of latitude or climate. And the same causes which impel men to practise magic for the control of nature confirm their belief in its efficacy; for the very changes which the magician seeks to bring about by his spells are silently wrought by the operation of natural law, and thus the apparent success of his efforts greatly strengthens the wizard's confidence in his imaginary powers.

In Central Australia the changes of the seasons are so sudden and violent that even Europeans have compared them to the effect of magic; it is no wonder therefore

Nowhere, apparently, in the world are the alternations of the seasons so sudden and the contrasts between them so violent, nowhere, accordingly, is the seeming success of magic more conspicuous than in the deserts of Central Australia. The wonderful change which passes over the face of nature after the first rains of the season has been compared even by European observers to the effect of magic; what marvel, then, that the savage should mistake it for such in very truth? It is difficult, we are told, to realise the contrast between the steppes of Australia in the dry and in the rainy season. In the dry season the landscape

[1] On the uniformity, nay, monotony of nature in the equatorial regions, see A. R. Wallace, *Tropical Nature* (London, 1878), p. 1 *sqq.*

THE BEGINNINGS OF TOTEMISM

presents a scene of desolation. The sun shines down hotly on stony plains or yellow sandy ground, on which grow wiry shrubs and small tussocks of grass, not set closely together, as in moister lands, but straggling separately, so that in any patch the number of plants can be counted. The sharp, thin shadows of the wiry scrub fall on the yellow ground, which betrays no sign of animal life save for the little ant-hills, thousands of whose inmates are seen rushing about in apparently hopeless confusion, or piling leaves and seeds in regular order around the entrance to their burrows. A desert oak, as it is called, or an acacia tree, may here and there afford a scanty shade, but for weeks together there are no clouds to hide the brightness of the sun by day or of the stars by night. All this is changed when heavy rains have fallen and torrents rush down the lately dry beds of the rivers, sweeping along uprooted trees and great masses of tangled wrack on their impetuous current, and flooding far and wide the flat lands on either bank. Then what has been for months an arid wilderness is suddenly changed into a vast sheet of water. Soon, however, the rain ceases to fall and the flood subsides rapidly. For a few days the streams run, then dry up, and only the deeper holes here and there retain the water. The sun once more shines down hotly, and in the damp ground seeds which have lain dormant for months sprout and, as if by magic, the desert becomes covered with luxuriant herbage, and gay with the blossoms of endless flowering plants. Birds, frogs, lizards, and insects of all sorts may be seen and heard where lately everything was parched and silent. Plants and animals alike make the most of the brief time in which they can grow and multiply; the struggle for existence is all the keener because it is so short. If a young plant can strike its roots deep enough to reach the cool soil below the heated surface, it may live; if not, it must perish. If a young animal grows fast enough to be able to burrow while the banks of the water-hole in which it lives are still damp, it, too, stands a chance of surviving. Now it is just when there is promise of a good season that the natives of these regions are wont especially to perform their magical ceremonies for the multiplication of the plants and animals

that the Central Australian savage should believe them to be so in earnest.

which they use as food.[1] Can we wonder that the accomplishment of their wishes, which so soon follows, should appear to them a conclusive proof of the efficacy of their incantations? Nature herself seems to conspire to foster the delusion.

[1] Spencer and Gillen, *Native Tribes of Central Australia*, pp. 4, 170. I have reproduced the graphic description of these writers almost verbally.

AN ETHNOGRAPHICAL SURVEY
OF TOTEMISM

CHAPTER I

TOTEMISM IN CENTRAL AUSTRALIA

§ 1. *The Social Line of Demarcation in Central Australia*

SINCE the first edition of *Totemism* was published in 1887 a new era in the study of the subject has been opened by the researches of Messrs. Baldwin Spencer and F. J. Gillen among the tribes of Central and North-Central Australia. Through their labours we possess for the first time a detailed and accurate account of Totemism as it exists in full bloom among tribes which have hardly been affected by European influence. There is no other such record in the literature of the subject, and its importance for an insight into the true nature of Totemism can scarcely be over-estimated. Accordingly I shall begin this ethnographical survey of Totemism with the tribes of Central and Northern Australia, basing my account of their totemic system on the two great works of Messrs. Spencer and Gillen.[1] Some of the results of their enquiries have already been noticed in this book,[2] but here it may be convenient to give, even at the cost of certain repetitions, a general view of the facts which these two careful and trustworthy observers have brought to light.

<small>The researches of Spencer and Gillen in Central and Northern Australia.</small>

In regard to the totemic and social system of Central Australia there is a very sharp line of demarcation between the true central and the southern-central tribes which come into contact with each other a little to the north-west of Lake

<small>Division between the true central and southern-central tribes.</small>

---

[1] Baldwin Spencer and F. J. Gillen, *The Native Tribes of Central Australia* (London, 1899); id., *The Northern Tribes of Central Australia* (London, 1904). For the sake of brevity these two works will be cited as *Native Tribes* and *Northern Tribes* respectively.

[2] Above, pp. 91 *sqq.*, 154 *sqq.*

Eyre, and it looks as if this were the meeting-place of two sets of tribes which had migrated southwards, following roughly parallel lines, one stream of tribes having traversed the centre of the continent and the other having pursued a more easterly course till it turned westward and joined the other stream at Lake Eyre. In the southern-central tribes, of which the Urabunna may be taken as a type, descent both of the totem and of the exogamous class is reckoned in the maternal line. In the true central tribes, of which the Arunta may be taken as a type, descent of the exogamous class is reckoned in the paternal line, and the totem is derived neither from the father nor from the mother, though as we pass from the centre northwards we find the totem tending more and more to be taken from the father, until among the tribes on the Gulf of Carpentaria the descent of the totem is as strictly paternal as is the descent of the exogamous class.[1] We begin our survey with the southern-central tribes, of which the Urabunna are typical.

§ 2. *Totemism in the Urabunna Tribe*

The Urabunna tribe divided into two exogamous classes and a number of totem clans.

The whole tribe of the Urabunna is divided up into two exogamous intermarrying moieties (classes or phratries), which are respectively called Matthurie and Kirarawa, and the members of these two moieties (classes or phratries) are again subdivided into a series of totemic groups or clans, for which the native name is *thunthunie*. A Matthurie man must marry a Kirarawa woman; and more than that, a man of one totem must marry a woman of another totem, certain totems being confined to one or other of the two exogamous moieties or classes. Thus a dingo man or woman marries a water-hen woman or man; a cicada marries a crow; an emu marries a rat; a wild turkey marries a cloud; a swan marries a pelican; and a wild duck marries a carpet-snake. The tribal organisation may be shown in the following table, in which only a limited number of totems are indicated.

[1] *Native Tribes*, pp. 113-115; *Northern Tribes*, pp. 143 *sq.*

TOTEMISM IN THE URABUNNA TRIBE

Class (phratry).	Totem.
Matthurie.	Wild duck (*Inyarrie*). Cicada (*Wutnimmera*). Dingo (*Matla*). Emu (*Warraguti*). Wild turkey (*Kalathurra*). Black swan (*Guti*), etc.
Kirarawa.	Cloud (*Kurara*). Carpet snake (*Wabma*). Lace lizard (*Capirie*). Pelican (*Urantha*). Water-hen (*Kutnichilli*). Crow (*Wakala*), etc.[1]

Descent is reckoned through the mother both as regards class (phratry) and totem, so that if the mother, for example, is of the Kirarawa class and of the water-hen totem, then all her children will be Kirarawa Water-hens. Hence marriage and descent in the Urabunna tribe can be represented by the following diagram, in which the letter *f* signifies the female and the letter *m* the male.

In the Urabunna tribe descent is in both of the class and of the totem is in the female line, children taking both class and totem from their mother, not from their father.

<pre>
                m. Dingo Matthurie
                      marries
                 f. Water-hen Kirarawa
              ┌─────────────┴─────────────┐
    m. Water-hen Kirarawa   f. Water-hen Kirarawa
         marries   marries
    f. Dingo Matthurie   m. Dingo Matthurie
           │   │
    m. or f. Dingo Matthurie   m. or f. Water-hen Kirarawa.[2]
</pre>

These are not the only restrictions to marriage. A man may not marry a woman of the proper totem unless she is a daughter of his mother's *elder* brother or (what comes to the same thing) of his father's *elder* sister, where the terms "father" and "mother," "brother" and "sister" are used in the classificatory sense to denote group relationships, a man giving the name of "father" to all the men whom his

Further, a man may only marry the daughters of his mother's elder brothers or of his father's elder sisters, these terms of relationship being used in the classificatory sense.

---

[1] *Native Tribes*, pp. 59 *sq.*, 114; *Northern Tribes*, pp. 70 *sq.*, 144. On this organisation of the Urabunna it is observed by Messrs. Spencer and Gillen that "the most difficult point to determine is exactly what totems intermarry. Whilst the intermarriage of the totems now described is correct so far as it goes, further investigation may reveal the fact that, for example, a man of the crow totem may marry women of other totems besides the cicada" (*Native Tribes*, p. 60 note).

[2] *Native Tribes*, pp. 60 *sq.*; *Northern Tribes*, p. 71.

mother might have lawfully married, the name of "mother" to all the women whom his father might have lawfully married, and the names of "brothers" and "sisters" to the offspring of all such men and women, whether they are related to him by blood in our sense of the term or not.[1] It follows that in the Urabunna tribe a man may not marry a woman of the right totem if she is a daughter of his mother's *younger* brother or (what comes to the same thing) of his father's *younger* sister. Thus a man's wife must always belong to the senior side of the clan, so far as he is concerned; and a woman's husband must always belong to the junior side of the clan, so far as she is concerned. All the women of a totemic clan into which a man may marry stand to him in one of the four following relationships: (1) *nowillie*, or father's sisters; (2) *biaka*, children or brother's children; (3) *apillia*, daughters of his mother's younger brothers or (what comes to the same thing) of his father's younger sisters; (4) *nupa*, the daughters of his mother's elder brothers or (what comes to the same thing) of his father's elder sisters, where again the terms "father," "mother," "brother," "sister" are used in the classificatory sense. Women in the first of these relationships (*nowillie*) belong to an older generation; women in the second of these relationships (*biaka*) belong to a younger generation; women in the third and fourth relationship (*apillia* and *nupa*) belong to a man's own generation, but even among them he may marry only women who stand to him in the fourth relationship (*nupa*). The term *nupa* is reciprocal, being mutually applied to each other by marriageable men and women; in other words, a man calls a woman whom he may marry *nupa*, and she calls him *nupa* also. But whereas a man's *nupa* is always on the senior side of the clan in reference to him, a woman's *nupa* is always on the junior side of the clan in reference to her. Thus if we were to draw up a genealogical tree in the Urabunna tribe, placing the elder members on the left side and the younger members on the right side, then every woman's *nupa* would lie to the right, and every man's *nupa* would lie to the left side of her or his position in the genealogical tree.

---

[1] As to the Classificatory System of Relationship, see below, pp. 286 *sqq.*

A simple genealogical tree will illustrate this marriage *Genealogical tree to illustrate the Urabunna marriage.* rule. In the following table the Kirarawa man numbered 8 may only marry a woman who stands to him in the relationship of the one numbered 7. She is his *nupa* and he is hers; whereas the woman numbered 9 is his *apillia*, and he may not have any marital relations with her.

1. Matthurie, *f.*	2. Matthurie, *m.*	3. Matthurie, *f.*
4. Kirarawa, *m.*	5. Kirarawa, *f.*	6. Kirarawa, *m.*
7. Matthurie, *f.*	8. Kirarawa, *m.*	9. Matthurie, *f.*
	7. Matthurie, *f.*	

In this table it will be observed that the wife (Matthurie 7) of the man Kirarawa 8 is the daughter both of his mother's elder brother (Kirarawa 4) and of his father's elder sister (Matthurie 1). This is not an accident; in the Urabunna system a man's wife is always the daughter both of his mother's elder brother and of his father's elder sister, since under that system his mother's elder brother is the proper husband of his father's elder sister.[1]

This sharp distinction in respect of marriageability between the children of elder and younger brothers and sisters occurs not only in tribes like the Urabunna which count descent in the female line, but also in tribes like the Arunta, which reckon descent of the classes and subclasses in the male line.[2] The origin of the rule which obliged a man to marry a woman on the senior side of the appropriate family and forbade him to marry a woman on the junior side, is no doubt to be sought in the nature of the classificatory system of relationship, though the precise reason for it is still obscure. A pregnant hint as to the way in which the distinction may have originated in a social system based on group marriage and the classificatory system of relationship has been given by Dr. Rivers. "In such a state of society," he says, "I suppose that the status of a child would change when he becomes an adult, and that with this change of status there would be associated a change in the relationship in which he would stand to the members of the different groups. The

Dr. Rivers' explanation of the distinction in respect of marriageability between the children of elder and younger brothers and sisters.

---

[1] *Native Tribes*, pp. 61-65; *Northern Tribes*, pp. 71 *sq.*   [2] *Native Tribes*, p. 65.

great difficulty in the acceptance of my scheme is to see how the relationships set up by these age-groups developed into those regulated by generations such as we find among most people of low culture at the present time. I cannot here attempt to follow out such a development in any detail, but I think it is possible to see the general lines on which one almost universal feature of the classificatory system may have evolved, viz. the distinction between elder and younger, especially frequent in the case of brothers and sisters. A man would probably tend to distinguish with some definiteness those who became adults earlier than himself from those who came later to this rank; he would tend to distinguish sharply between those who helped in his initiatory ceremonies and those to whom he was himself one of the initiators, and this distinction between seniors and juniors would probably be carried over into the system of relationships which gradually developed as the group-relations developed into more individual relations between men and women, and as the society became organized into generations in the place of status- or age-groups." [1]

Men perhaps forbidden to marry women who were initiated after them.
To make this hint of Dr. Rivers explicit I would point out that if after a lad had passed through the initiatory ceremonies at puberty and thereby became a full-grown man, it was deemed essential at once to provide him with a wife, this could only be done by taking her from among those women who had attained to puberty and had been initiated either simultaneously with him or before him; his wife obviously could not be drawn from those girls who were not marriageable because they had not yet reached puberty and had not yet been initiated. Hence might easily arise a rule that no man should marry a woman who had been initiated after him; and this, when society became organised in generations instead of in age-groups, might easily in time be replaced by the rule that a man might only choose a wife from the senior branch of the group or clan into which he was entitled to marry.

It will be observed that under the Urabunna system a

---

[1] W. H. R. Rivers, "On the Origin of the Classificatory System of Relationships," in *Anthropological Essays presented to Edward Burnett Tylor* (Oxford, 1907), pp. 320 *sq*.

man's proper wife is always one of those whom we should call his first cousins, being the daughter of his mother's brother or of his father's sister. On the other hand he is strictly forbidden to marry certain other first cousins, namely the daughter of his mother's sister and the daughter of his father's brother; and the reason why both these first cousins are prohibited to him is that they belong to the same exogamous class as himself and are therefore barred from him by the fundamental law which forbids a man to marry a woman of his own exogamous class. For example, if he is a Kirarawa, then, descent being in the maternal line, his mother, his mother's sister, and his mother's sister's daughter, his first cousin, must all be Kirarawa; hence he may not marry that particular first cousin, his mother's sister's daughter. Again, if he is a Kirarawa, his father and his father's brother will be Matthurie, but his father's brother's daughter, his first cousin, descent being in the female line, will be Kirarawa; hence again he may not marry that particular first cousin, his father's brother's daughter. This distinction between marriageable and non-marriageable cousins is observed, as we shall see, by many totemic peoples. The general rule is that cousins who are the children of a brother and a sister respectively may marry each other or are even expected as a matter of custom to do so; while cousins who are the children either of two sisters or of two brothers are strictly forbidden to marry each other, their union being barred by the fact that such cousins always belong to the same exogamous group, whether descent is reckoned in the maternal or in the paternal line. *Marriageable and non-marriageable cousins.*

The account which the Urabunna give of the origin of their totems is as follows. In those remote and mythical times which they call *ularaka* and which the Arunta call *alcheringa*, there existed at first a comparatively small number of individuals who were half-human and half-animal or half-plant. How they arose is more than the Urabunna can say. Anyhow they are the exact equivalents of the *alcheringa* ancestors of the Arunta, about whom we shall hear presently. These semi-human creatures were endowed with far greater powers than any living men or women now possess. They could walk about either on the earth or *Urabunna account of the origin of their totems.*

beneath it and could fly through the air. They were the ancestors of the various totemic clans. Thus a large carpet-snake gave rise to the carpet-snake clan; two jew-lizards gave rise to the jew-lizard clan; one or two rain creatures did the same for the rain clan; and so on.[1]

These old semi-human ancestors wandered about all over the country now occupied by the Urabunna, performing sacred ceremonies, and when they did so they deposited in the ground or in some natural feature such as a rock or a water-pool, which arose to mark the spot, a number of spirit individuals called *mai-aurli*. After a time some of these became changed into men and women, who formed the first series of totem clans. For example, some of the *mai-aurli* left behind by the carpet-snake ancestor changed into carpet-snake men and women; some of those left behind by the lizards changed into lizard men and women; and so on through the other totemic clans. Since the time long ago when the totemic clans were thus instituted, these spirit individuals or *mai-aurli* have been continually undergoing reincarnation, and their embodiments in the flesh are Urabunna men and women.[2]

The places where the spirit-children or *mai-aurli* were left behind by the animal or semi-human ancestors are called *paltinta* by the Urabunna, and the corresponding places are called *oknanikilla* by the Arunta. Some of these places in the Urabunna territory are inhabited by spirits of one particular totem only, others are inhabited by the spirits of two or more different totems. Thus close to a spot where Messrs. Spencer and Gillen encamped there is a large group of granite boulders, which arose to mark the place where in the far-off times the ancestors of the pigeon clan danced and played about. Of these boulders one represents an old male and another a female ancestor. The rocks are supposed to be inhabited only by pigeon spirits which emanated from the bodies of the two ancestors. On the other hand, a quarter of a mile away from these granite rocks there is a pool inhabited by spirits which were left there by emu, rain, and a grub ancestor. Sometimes there seems to be a special bond of relationship

[1] *Northern Tribes*, pp. 145 *sq.* [2] *Ibid.* p. 146.

between the totemic clans whose spirits congregate at the same place. For example, there is a pool of water haunted by spirits of people who all belong to the mosquito, the blow-fly, the march-fly, or the sand-fly totem. Whenever a person dies, his or her spirit goes back to the place where it was left long ago by the totemic ancestor in the days of old (the *ularaka* or *alcheringa*). The spirits of pigeon people, for example, go back into the rocks where the pigeon ancestors performed ceremonies and deposited the spirit children of the pigeon clan. The spirits of mosquito people go back into the pool where the mosquito ancestors performed ceremonies and left behind them the spirit children of the mosquito clan, and so forth.[1]

A curious feature of the reincarnation theory of the Urabunna is this: they think that at each successive reincarnation the new-born child changes its sex, its class or phratry (moiety, as Messrs. Spencer and Gillen call it), and its totem. Thus, for instance, if a Kirarawa man of the emu totem dies, his spirit goes back to the place where it was left by the emu ancestor in the olden (*alcheringa*) days. There it remains for some time, but sooner or later it is born again as a girl from the body of a Matthurie woman, who, of necessity, belongs to another totem; and thus at each reincarnation the individual changes his or her class (phratry), sex, and totem. They think that if the spirit of a Kirarawa man were reincarnated in a Kirarawa woman, it would either be born prematurely and die or would cause the death of the mother. Premature births and accidents at child-birth are always attributed by the Urabunna to the entrance of a child-spirit into the body of a wrong woman. In the course of ages any single individual can thus, by a series of rebirths, run through the whole gamut of the totems, alternating from side to side (from Kirarawa to Matthurie) of the tribe, but alway returning at death to its original home.[2]

A child changes its sex, class and totem at each reincarnation.

Just as in the Arunta and other central tribes so in the Urabunna, the members of the totem clans are supposed to be responsible for the production of the totem animal or plant from which the clan takes its name, and for this

Magical ceremonies performed by the Urabunna for the multiplication of their totems.

[1] *Northern Tribes*, pp. 146 *sq.* [2] *Ibid.* pp. 148 *sq.*

purpose they perform magical ceremonies which they call *pitjinta*. These ceremonies correspond exactly in nature and intention to the *intichiuma* ceremonies of the Arunta.[1]

Ceremony to make rain.
For example, there is a local centre of the rain totem at a water-hole called Tjantjiwanperta, close to Mount Kingston, and here the headman of the rain clan performs ceremonies for the production of rain. While he is engaged in this solemn function he wears a head-dress of hair-string completely coated over with white down, which covers his shoulders and chest. A tuft of cockatoo feathers forms a crest to the head-dress, and bunches of eagle-hawk feathers hang down from his girdle. The costume is perhaps intended to mimick the clouds. Holding a spear-thrower in his hand the rain-maker squats on the ground, while two men strike the earth with stones and chant a charm. Then the performer rises to a stooping position, striking out and moving the spear-thrower backwards and forwards, quivering his body and turning his head from side to side. At intervals he lifts his body and gazes into the sky in imitation of certain cloud men, who according to tradition used to ascend into the sky and make the clouds from which the rain came down.[2]

Ceremony to multiply snakes.
Again, the headman of a snake clan performs a ceremony for the multiplication of snakes by piercing the skin of his arms with sharp bones, his body being streaked with lines of red and yellow ochre, and his head adorned with a sort of banner. When the bones employed in this rite are not in use, they are wrapped in hair cut from the head of a snake man. After the ceremony, when the snakes have become plentiful, men who do not belong to the snake clan go out and catch some of the reptiles and bring them to the headman of the snake clan. A younger tribal brother who does not belong to the clan presents him with some fat taken from one of the snakes. He rubs his arms with the fat and says, "You eat—all of you." They think that if men of other clans were to eat snakes without thus obtaining permission from the headman of the snake clan, he would warn them that by and by they would see no more snakes.[3]

---

[1] *Northern Tribes*, pp. 149, 283 *sq.* 214 *sqq.* As to the *intichiuma* ceremonies, see above, pp. 104 *sqq.*, and below, pp.
[2] *Northern Tribes*, pp. 284-286.
[3] *Ibid.* pp. 286 *sq.*

TOTEMISM IN THE URABUNNA TRIBE

Similarly in the Wonkgongaru tribe, which has the same social organisation as the Urabunna, the headman of the fish clan makes fish by going into a pool and piercing his scrotum and the skin round the navel with little pointed bones, till his blood reddens the water, which is supposed to produce fish. Again, in order to produce a crop of lice a man of the louse clan takes mud from a sandbank and rubs it on two trees, one of them an ordinary louse tree and the other a crab louse tree. After that he throws the mud about in all directions and the vermin swarm out in consequence. Similarly a man of the jew lizard clan can make lizards plentiful very simply by knocking chips off the face of a certain rock and throwing them about. The rock, which may be seen on a hill called Coppertop, is supposed to represent an old jew lizard standing up and throwing boomerangs. On the hill there grows a tree, the rough bark of which is thought to be or to resemble the skin of the lizard. The Wonkgongaru natives have no jew lizard man among them, so when they wish to increase the supply of these reptiles they invoke the aid of the jew lizard man of the Urabunna tribe, who obligingly goes to the lizard tree, strips off some of the bark, and sends it to the Wonkgongaru men. They burn the bark in their own country, and by that means ensure a supply of the animal.[1]

Ceremonies to multiply fish, lice, and lizards.

In the Urabunna tribe, as in most Australian tribes, every person is strictly forbidden to eat his or her totem animal or plant, but there is no objection to his killing the animal and handing it over to be eaten by men of other totems.[2] Indeed, as we have just seen, the headman of a totem clan performs magical ceremonies for the very purpose of multiplying his totem animal or plant in order that it

Among the Urabunna a man may not eat his totem, but he may kill his totem animal and hand it over to be eaten by men of other totems.

---

[1] *Northern Tribes*, pp. 287 *sq*. In regard to the magical production of lice it is to be remembered that these vermin are regularly eaten by many savages.

[2] *Native Tribes*, p. 467 ; *Northern Tribes*, p. 149. In the former passage Messrs. Spencer and Gillen add : "For example, an emu man or woman must not in any way injure an emu, nor must he partake of its flesh even when he has not killed it himself."

The rule not to injure the totem animal would naturally include the prohibition to kill it. Yet in their later work (*Northern Tribes, l.c.*) the writers tell us that among the Urabunna there is no objection to a man's killing his totem. We may accept the latter statement as the more correct of the two, since it was written after the authors had paid a special visit to the Urabunna tribe.

186   TOTEMISM IN CENTRAL AUSTRALIA   CHAP.

may be eaten by men of other clans. In this respect the Urabunna are in agreement with the rest of the central tribes, whatever differences in social organisation there may be between them. "The fundamental idea, common to all of the tribes, is that men of any totemic group are responsible for the maintenance of the supply of the animal or plant which gives its name to the group, and that the one object of increasing the number of the totemic animal or plant is simply that of increasing the general food-supply. If I am a kangaroo man, then I provide kangaroo flesh for emu men, and in return I expect them to provide me with a supply of emu flesh and eggs, and so on right through all of the totems. At the present day this is actually the belief of the Central Australian savage. Further still, no man must do anything which will impair his power to cause the increase of his totem."[1]

§ 3. *Totemism in the Arunta and North-Central Tribes*[2]

Differences of totemic and social organisation between the Arunta and the Urabunna.

The totemic and social organisation of the Arunta and kindred tribes is sharply distinguished from that of the Urabunna in the following respects:—

[1] *Northern Tribes*, p. 327.
[2] Messrs. Spencer and Gillen (*Northern Tribes*, pp. 75 *sq.*) divide the central and north-central tribes of Australia into five groups or nations, the tribes in each group or nation being more or less akin to each other and distinct from the rest in social organisation and customs. Each nation may be named after the principal or most typical tribe which it includes. The five nations distinguished by Messrs. Spencer and Gillen are as follows: (1) The DIERI nation (including the Dieri and Urabunna tribes, etc., in the basin of Lake Eyre); (2) The ARUNTA nation (including the Arunta, Ilpirra, Iliaura, Unmatjera, and Kaitish tribes); (3) The WARRAMUNGA nation (including the Warramunga, Worgaia, Tjingilli, Umbaia, Bingongina, Walpari, Wulmala, and Gnanji tribes); (4) The BINBINGA nation (including the Binbinga, Allaua, and probably other tribes on the west side of the Gulf of Carpentaria); (5) The MARA nation (including the Mara, Anula, and probably other tribes on the western coast of the Gulf of Carpentaria).

Since the following account of Arunta totemism was written I have received a volume of Arunta myths, traditions, and folk-tales collected by the Rev. C. Strehlow of the German Lutheran Mission at Hermannsburg in South Australia (*Mythen, Sagen und Märchen des Aranda Stammes in Zentral Australien, gesammelt von Carl Strehlow, bearbeitet von Moritz Freiherrn von Leonhardi*, Frankfurt am Main, 1907). As to the work of the Mission to which Mr. Strehlow belongs, Professor Baldwin Spencer writes to me as follows (letter dated Melbourne, 10th March 1908): "For at least twenty years the Lutheran Missions have been teaching the natives that *altjira* means 'god,' and that all their sacred ceremonies, in fact even their ordinary corroborees,

(1) Whereas among the Urabunna the totems are hereditary, children always inheriting the totem of their mother, among the Arunta and kindred tribes the totems are not hereditary, but are determined for each individual by the particular place at which his or her mother first felt her womb quickened.

Arunta totems are not hereditary.

(2) Whereas in the Urabunna the totems regulate marriage, a man being always forbidden to marry women of his own totem and of certain other totems, in the Arunta and kindred tribes the totems have no influence whatever on marriage, a man being free to marry a woman of his own or any other totem, provided that she belongs to the class and subclass (phratry and subphratry) into which he is bound to marry.

and do not regulate marriage.

(3) Whereas the Urabunna are divided into two exogamous sections (classes or phratries), the Arunta and kindred tribes are divided into eight exogamous sections (classes and subclasses, or phratries and subphratries), though in some places only four of these sections bear special names.

The Arunta are divided into eight exogamous classes

(4) Whereas in the Urabunna tribe the descent of the classes or phratries is in the maternal line, the children taking their class or phratry from their mother, in the Arunta and kindred tribes the descent of the classes or phratries is in the paternal line, the children taking their class or phratry from their father.[1]

with descent in the paternal line.

are wicked things. They have prohibited any being performed on the Mission station, and have endeavoured in every way to put a stop to them and to prevent the natives from attending them, and certainly they have never seen one performed. Under these conditions it is not altogether surprising that when S. questions the natives he discovers that *altjira* means god, and gets very doubtful information in regard to all sacred or secret matters. It would be a strange thing if the natives were to talk to him freely and truthfully on these matters. . . . Not only have the missionaries for years past sternly rebuked the members of their flock (whose presence in church and school is an indispensable condition to a participation in the distribution of flour, tobacco, etc.) for any inclination towards the heathen and devilish beliefs and practices of their parents, but they have actually attempted to break these down to the extent *of marrying individuals of wrong groups.* It is rather late for any one of them, however well he may know the language, to attempt an investigation into sacred beliefs and customs." In these circumstances it seems to me that the sources from which Mr. Strehlow has drawn his accounts are deeply tainted; and as it would be impossible for me, who have no first-hand knowledge of these tribes, to filter the native liquid clear of its alien sediment, I shall abstain from making use of Mr. Strehlow's information.

[1] *Native Tribes*, pp. 59 *sq.*, 70 *sqq.*, 113 *sqq.*; *Northern Tribes*, pp. 70 *sq.*, 74 *sq.*, 143 *sq.*, 150 *sq.*

Apparent confusion of totems among the Arunta.

The effect of the first two of these rules is at first sight to produce great confusion in the totemic system of the Arunta. For in the first place "no one totem is confined to the members of a particular class or subclass; in the second place the child's totem will sometimes be found to be the same as that of the father, sometimes the same as that of the mother, and not infrequently it will be different from that of either parent; and in the third place there is no definite relationship between the totem of the father and mother, such as exists in the Urabunna and many other Australian tribes—in fact perhaps in the majority of the latter. You may, for example, examine at first a family in which the father is a witchetty grub and the mother a wild cat, and you may find, supposing there be two children, that they are both witchetty grubs. In the next family examined perhaps both parents will be witchetty grubs, and of two children one may belong to the same totem, and the other may be an emu; another family will show the father to be, say, an emu, the mother a plum-tree, and of their children one may be a witchetty grub, another a lizard, and so on, the totem names being apparently mixed up in the greatest confusion possible."[1]

This apparent confusion is reduced to order by the Arunta theory, that the spirits of the dead congregate at certain spots, which may be described as local totem centres, the spirits of each totemic clan keeping together and not mixing with the spirits of other clans.

The Arunta theory, which reduces this seeming confusion to order, is as follows. In the remote *alcheringa* times there lived ancestors "who, in the native mind, are so intimately associated with the animals or plants the name of which they bear that an *alcheringa* man of, say, the kangaroo totem may sometimes be spoken of either as a man-kangaroo or as a kangaroo-man. The identity of the human individual is often sunk in that of the animal or plant from which he is supposed to have originated."[2] These semi-human ancestors, endowed with powers which are not possessed by their living descendants, roamed about the same country which is still inhabited by the tribe, and in their wanderings they gave rise to many of the most marked features of the landscape, such as the gaps and gorges which cleave the Macdonnell Ranges. Each troop or band of these semi-mythical folk consisted of members of one particular totem clan, whether the totem was the wild cat, the witchetty

[1] *Native Tribes*, p. 115.   [2] *Ibid.* p. 119.

grub, the kangaroo, the frog, the Hakea flower, or what not. And every man and woman of the band carried about with him or her one or more of the sacred stones which the Arunta call *churinga*, each of which is intimately associated with the spirit part of some individual man or woman. Either where they originated and stayed or else where, during their wanderings, they camped for a time, there were formed what the natives call *oknanikilla*, which we may describe as local totem centres. At each of these spots, which are all well known to the old men, who hand the knowledge down from generation to generation, a certain number of the *alcheringa* ancestors went into the ground, each of them carrying his sacred stone (*churinga*) with him. His body died, but some natural feature, such as a rock or tree, arose to mark the spot, while his spirit part remained in the *churinga*. At the same time many of the *churinga* which they carried with them, and each one of which was associated with a spirit individual, were placed in the ground, and in every such case a natural feature of the landscape was formed to mark the spot. Thus the whole country is now dotted over with *oknanikilla* or local totem centres, at each of which are deposited a number of sacred stones or *churinga*, with spirit individuals associated with them. Each local totem centre (*oknanikilla*) is tenanted by the spirits of one totem only. One spot, for example, is haunted by spirits of the wild cat totem; another by spirits of the emu totem; another by spirits of the frog totem; and so on through all the totems. The totemic districts, as we may call them, which surround these totemic centres vary from a few square yards to many square miles. The whole country of the Arunta, Kaitish, and Ilpirra tribes can be mapped out into a large number of such areas of various sizes.[1]

This idea of spirit individuals associated with *churinga* and resident at certain definite spots lies at the root of the present totemic system of the Arunta and kindred tribes. For the natives believe that every living member of the tribe is the reincarnation of one of these spirits. Each of these disembodied spirits takes up its abode in some natural object, such as a tree or rock, at its own local totem centre; *From these spots the disembodied spirits of the dead pass into women and are born again as children,*

[1] *Native Tribes*, pp. 119-123, 126.

and this abode of the spirit is called its *nanja*. From time to time, when a woman approaches one of these haunted spots, a spirit passes from it into her body, and in due time is born as a child. The totem of the child thus born is necessarily that of the local totem centre at which the mother first felt her womb quickened; for according to the native belief the child is nothing but a reincarnation of one of the spirits which haunted the spot. Thus, if a woman first becomes aware that she is with child near a place haunted by spirits of the emu totem, then her child will be of the emu totem; if she felt the first premonitions of maternity at a spot haunted by spirits of the kangaroo totem, then her child will be of the kangaroo totem; and so forth.[1]

[sidenote: who take their totem from the local totem centre near which their mother first felt her womb quickened.]

"We may take the following as a typical example of how each man and woman gains a totem name. Close to Alice Springs is a large and important witchetty grub totem centre or *oknanikilla*. Here there were deposited in the *alcheringa* a large number of *churinga* carried by witchetty grub men and women. A large number of prominent rocks and boulders and certain ancient gum-trees along the sides of a picturesque gap in the ranges, are the *nanja* trees and rocks of these spirits, which, so long as they remain in spirit form, they usually frequent. If a woman conceives a child after having been near to this gap, it is one of these spirit individuals which has entered her body, and therefore, quite irrespective of what the mother's or father's totem may chance to be, that child, when born, must of necessity be of the witchetty grub totem; it is, in fact, nothing else but the reincarnation of one of these witchetty grub people of the *alcheringa*. Suppose, for example, to take a particular and actual instance, an emu woman from another locality comes to Alice Springs, and whilst there becomes aware that she has conceived a child, and then returns to her own locality before the child is born, that child, though it may be born in an emu locality, is an *Udnirringita* or witchetty grub. It must be, the natives say, because it entered the mother at Alice Springs, where there are only witchetty grub spirit

[sidenote: Examples of this theory of conception.]

[1] *Native Tribes*, pp. 123 *sq.*; *Northern Tribes*, p 150.

individuals. Had it entered her body within the limits of her own emu locality, it would as inevitably have been an emu. To take another example, quite recently the lubra or wife of a witchetty grub man, she belonging to the same totem, conceived a child while on a visit to a neighbouring *Quatcha* or water locality, which lies away to the east of Alice Springs, that child's totem is water; or, again, an Alice Springs woman, when asked by us as to why her child was a witchetty grub (in this instance belonging to the same totem as both of its parents), told us that one day she was taking a drink of water near to the gap in the Ranges where the [witchetty grub] spirits dwell when suddenly she heard a child's voice crying out, '*Mia, mia!*'—the native term for relationship which includes that of mother. Not being anxious to have a child, she ran away as fast as she could, but to no purpose; she was fat and well favoured, and such women the spirit children prefer; one of them had gone inside her, and of course it was born a witchetty grub." [1]

This theory of conception as a reincarnation of the dead is universally held by all the Central Australian tribes which have been investigated by Messrs. Spencer and Gillen; every man, woman, and child is supposed by them to be a reimbodiment of an ancestral spirit. "In the whole of this wide area, the belief that every living member of the tribe is the reincarnation of a spirit ancestor is universal. This belief is just as firmly held by the Urabunna people, who count descent in the female line, as it is by the Arunta and Warramunga, who count descent in the male line." [2] "The natives, one and all in these tribes, believe that the child is the direct result of the entrance into the mother of an ancestral spirit individual. They have no idea of procreation as being directly associated with sexual intercourse, and firmly believe that children can be born without this taking place. There are, for example, in the

The theory of conception as a reincarnation of the dead is universally held by all Central Australian tribes.

---

[1] *Native Tribes*, pp. 124 *sq.* The writers add that "spirit children are also supposed to be especially fond of travelling in whirlwinds, and, on seeing one of these, which are very frequent at certain times of the year, approaching her, a woman will at once run away."

[2] *Northern Tribes*, p. xi.; compare *id.* pp. 145, 606. Among the tribes which hold this belief are mentioned the Binbinga and Anula, two northern tribes on or near the coast of the Gulf of Carpentaria (*op. cit.* p. 145).

Arunta country certain stones which are supposed to be charged with spirit children who can, by magic, be made to enter the bodies of women, or will do so of their own accord."[1]

Stone where the spirits of dead plum-tree people congregate, waiting to be born again.

Such stones go by the name of *erathipa*, which means "child." There is one of them, for example, about fifteen miles to the south-south-east of Alice Springs. It is a rounded stone projecting from the ground to a height of about three feet among mulga scrub. The spirits which haunt it are of the plum-tree totem. On one side of the stone there is a round hole through which the spirits of dead plum-tree people look out for women who may chance to pass near; and it is firmly believed that if a woman visits the stone she will conceive a plum-tree child. Should a young woman who does not wish to become a mother be obliged to pass near the stone, she will carefully disguise her youth, distorting her face and hobbling along on a crutch. She will bend double like an old hag, and mimicking the cracked voice of age she will say, "Don't come to me, I am an old woman." Not only may women become pregnant by visiting the stone, but it is believed that, by performing a very simple ceremony, a malicious man may cause women and even children to conceive. All that he has to do is to go to the stone by himself and, having cleared a space of ground about it, to rub the stone with his hands and mutter these words, "Plenty of young women, you look and go quickly."[2]

Trees where the spirits of dead black snake people gather.

Again, to take another example, the ancestor of the black snake totem in the Warramunga tribe is said to have wandered over the country performing ceremonies, making creeks and hills, and leaving all along his tracks many spirits of black snake children, which now

---

[1] *Northern Tribes*, pp. 330 *sq.* In their earlier work, before they had extended their researches from the centre of Australia to the Gulf of Carpentaria, Messrs. Spencer and Gillen expressed themselves as follows on this subject: "We have amongst the Arunta, Luritcha, and Ilpirra tribes, and probably also amongst others such as the Warramunga, the idea firmly held that the child is not the direct result of intercourse, that it may come without this, which merely, as it were, prepares the mother for the reception and birth also of an already-formed spirit child who inhabits one of the local totem centres. Time after time we have questioned them on this point, and always received the reply that the child was not the direct result of intercourse" (*Native Tribes*, p. 265).

[2] *Native Tribes*, pp. 335-338.

dwell in the rocks around the pools and in the gum-trees which border a creek. No Warramunga woman at the present day would dare to strike one of these trees with an axe, because she is firmly convinced that to do so would release one of the black snake spirits who would immediately dart into her body. They imagine that the spirit is very minute—about the size of a small grain of sand—and that it enters the woman through the navel and grows within her into a child.[1]

Each spirit individual, as we saw, is supposed to be closely bound up with his sacred stone or *churinga*, which he carried with him when he wandered about his ancestral home (the *oknanikilla*) or rested on the *nanja* tree or stone which he is believed especially to frequent. The natives think that when a spirit child enters a woman to be born, he drops his sacred stone (*churinga*). When the child is born, the mother tells the father the position of the tree or rock near which she supposes the child to have entered her, and he with one or two of the older men goes to the spot and searches for the dropped *churinga*. This precious object is usually, but not always, thought to be a stone marked with a device peculiar to the totem of the spirit child, and therefore of the newly born infant. If it cannot be found, the men cut a wooden one out of the hard wood tree which is nearest to the *nanja* tree or stone, that is, to the tree or stone where the spirit of the new-born child dwelt before its reincarnation. Having cut the wooden *churinga* they carve on it some device peculiar to the totem. Ever afterwards the *nanja* tree or stone of the spirit is the *nanja* of the child, and the *churinga* thus found or made is its *churinga nanja*. A definite relation is supposed to exist between every person and his *nanja* tree or stone. Every animal on the tree is tabooed (*ekerinja*) to him; for instance, if an opossum climbs up it or a bird alights on it, the animal or the bird is sacred and must on no account be molested. A native has been known earnestly to beg a white man not to cut down a particular tree because it was his *nanja* tree, and he feared that if it were felled some evil would befall him.[2]

Every spirit has its churinga (birth-stick or birth-stone) and its nanja tree or stone, where it lives in its disembodied state.

[1] *Northern Tribes*, pp. 162, 330 *sq.*
[2] *Native Tribes*, pp. 132 *sq.* As to the *churinga*, see above, pp. 124-126.

The ertna-tulunga, or secret store-house in which the churinga (the sacred birth-stones or birth-sticks) are kept.

In each local totem centre (*oknanikilla*) there is a spot which the natives call the *ertnatulunga*. This is a sacred storehouse, usually a small cave or crevice in some lonely spot among the rugged hills. The entrance is carefully blocked up with stones arranged so naturally as to let no chance passer-by suspect that here lie concealed the most sacred possessions of the tribe. These treasures consist of the sacred stones or sticks (*churinga*), one of which was always found here whenever one of the local totem spirits entered into a woman to be born. Often the precious sticks or stones are carefully tied up in bundles. Every member of the tribe, man, woman, and child, has his or her birth-stone or birth-stick (*churinga nanja*) in one or other of these secret storehouses. The spot at which a child was born and brought up, and at which it will probably spend the greater part of its life, has nothing whatever to do with determining the resting-place of his birth-stone (*churinga nanja*). That necessarily goes to the storehouse of the local totem centre from which his spirit came, that is to the spot where the *churinga* and their accompanying spirits were deposited by the mythical ancestors in the far-off times of the *alcheringa*. For example, a witchetty grub woman, who lives at Alice Springs, conceived a child at an emu locality twelve miles away to the north. She gave birth to the child at her own home, and the child lives there, but its *churinga nanja* was found as usual at the place of conception, and it is now deposited there in the sacred storehouse of the emu clan.[1] Each sacred storehouse is under the charge of the local headman (*alatunja*); indeed, his most important function is to take care of the hallowed spot.[2]

Sanctity of the store-houses in which the birth-stones and birth-sticks (churinga) are preserved.

Though women as well as men have their birth-stones or birth-sticks in these sacred storehouses (*ertnatulunga*), the women are never allowed to see them; indeed only the very old women know of the existence of these mysterious objects. Into the mysteries of the sacred storehouse and its contents no woman dare pry at risk of death.[3] The

---

[1] *Native Tribes*, pp. 133 sq.
[2] *Ibid.* p. 11.
[3] "Near to this storehouse, which is called an *ertnatulunga*, no woman, child, or uninitiated man dares venture on pain of death" (*Native Tribes*, p. 11).

general position, though not the exact spot, of this primitive sanctuary is known to the women, who must go long distances in order to avoid approaching it. For example, a deep ravine some miles long is the only pass through the mountains which lie to the south of Alice Springs, and in the side of the ravine is one of the storehouses. Till the white men came, no woman was ever allowed to traverse the pass; if she wished to cross the mountains, she had laboriously to climb the steep slopes at some distance from the ravine and then to pick her way down on the other side. The immediate neighbourhood of any one of the sacred storehouses is a kind of haven of refuge for wild animals; for once they come near it, they are safe; no pursuer would dare to spear a hunted kangaroo, emu, wallaby, or any other creature which had run, by instinct or by chance, to the holy ground. Even the plants which grow there are never touched or interfered with in any way. The sanctity of such spots will be better understood when it is remembered that they house the birth-stones not only of all the living but also of all the deceased members of the tribe, and that with these birth-stones the spirits of all the people, whether alive or dead, are believed to be closely bound up. Thus the sacred storehouses in the recesses of the solitary hills are in a sense temples or synagogues in which from time to time the living meet to hold solemn communion with the dead. The loss of the birth-stones or birth-sticks, which are thus associated with the spirits of the whole community, is the most serious calamity that can befall a tribe. Robbed of these spiritual treasures the men have been known to weep and wail for a fortnight, plastering themselves with white clay as if they were mourning for the dead.[1]

Before a man is allowed to see one of these sanctuaries he must not only have passed through the ceremonies of circumcision and subincision, but must also have shown himself capable of self-restraint and worthy of being admitted to the tribal mysteries. If he be light and frivolous, a babbler like a woman, many years may elapse before the great secret is revealed to him. When he is at last deemed ripe for the honour, a time is appointed for his initiation by the headman

Introduction of young men to these sanctuaries and revelation to them of their sacred names.

[1] *Native Tribes*, pp. 134-136.

of the local group to which he belongs, and he is escorted by the older men to the hallowed spot. There he is shown the sacred sticks and stones; one by one they are examined carefully and reverently, while the old men tell him to whom among the dead or the living they belong. While the revelation is proceeding the men sing in a low voice of the olden times (the *alcheringa*), and at its close the man is told his secret name (*aritna churinga*) and warned that he must never allow any one, except the men of his own group, to hear it uttered. Such secret names are given soon after birth to every member of the tribe. The headman of the particular group in whose sacred storehouse an infant's birth-stone (*churinga nanja*) is deposited, consults with the older men of the group and bestows the name on the child. It may be either a new name or the name of some famous man or woman of the olden time (*alcheringa*), of whom the child is thought to be a reincarnation. This secret name is never uttered except on the most solemn occasions, when the birth-stones or birth-sticks (*churinga*) are being examined, and it is known only to the fully initiated men of the local totem group. To mention it in the hearing of women or of men of another group would be a sort of sacrilege. The native believes that a stranger who knew his secret name would be able to work him ill by magic. After his mystic name has been revealed to him for the first time at the sacred storehouse (*ertnatulunga*), the man is painted on the face and body with the particular device of his totem. This is done by the headman and the older men, who stand to the novice in relationship of tribal or actual father. In one of the local groups of the witchetty grub clan the totemic pattern so painted consists of parallel stripes of pink and red copied from a sacred painting which has existed time out of mind on the smooth face of a rock in the Emily Gap, the totem centre of the Witchetty Grubs. On his return from the holy ground the novice wears the painted device on his body till it wears off with time and weather.[1]

[1] *Native Tribes*, pp. 138-140. On the subject of sacred names and their connection with the theory of reincarna- tion Professor Baldwin Spencer writes to me as follows (10th March 1908): "This is one of their most sacred beliefs, and

The beliefs and practices of the Unmatjera and Kaitish tribes in regard to the sacred birth-stones are similar to those of the Arunta. In the Unmatjera tribe the names both for the things themselves (*churinga*) and for the sacred storehouses (*ertnatulunga*) in which they are kept are the same; but in the Kaitish tribe both names are different. In both tribes the sacred storehouse is under the charge of the headman of the local totem group, and in the Kaitish tribe, as in the Arunta, the immediate neighbourhood of the storehouses is sacred ground, and nothing may be destroyed there, because it is haunted by the spirits associated with the *churinga*. When a Kaitish man wishes a woman to conceive, he will take a *churinga* and carry it to a spot where there is a special stone called *kwerka-punga* or "child-stone." This stone he rubs with the *churinga*, at the same time asking a child spirit (*kurinah*) to go straight into the woman.[1] In the Unmatjera and Kaitish tribes, just as in the Arunta, every person has his or her secret or *churinga* name; sometimes the name is that of the *alcheringa* ancestor of whom he or she is supposed to be the reincarnation.[2]

The *churinga*, which play so important a part in the customs and beliefs of the Arunta and kindred tribes, are always under the charge of the headman of the local totem group and cannot be touched without his consent.[3] They are rounded, oval, or elongate flattened stones and slabs of wood, varying in length from three or four inches to over five feet. In shape, at least among the Arunta, they are usually oval or tapering at either end into a more or less

The beliefs and practices of the Unmatjera and Kaitish tribes in regard to the sacred birth-stones and storehouses are like those of the Arunta.

Description of the *churinga*.

the one about which they are most secretive. Every individual is a reincarnation of a previously existing individual, or his spirit is one of those carried about in the *alcheringa* by the old ancestors (associated with their stores of *churinga*). The most difficult thing to learn is the 'sacred' name of any individual: this they never mention except in a very subdued tone, and only in the presence of really elder men. I remember that when I had been amongst them only a short time—though I had been watching their sacred ceremonies —Gillen asked an old man something about one of these 'sacred names'—he just shut up like an oyster. I saw that there was something the matter, and casually moved away, when he told Gillen what the latter wanted to know, only in a whisper. As a matter of fact the men have as their secret names those of ancestors mentioned in their myths simply because they are supposed to be their reincarnations, and, further still, the *churinga* of those ancestors are their *churinga*."

[1] *Northern Tribes*, pp. 269-271. As to the "child-stones" of the Arunta, see above, pp. 191 *sq*.
[2] *Northern Tribes*, p. 273.
[3] *Native Tribes*, p. 154.

rounded point. But a few old wooden *churinga*, belonging to two lizard totems, have been found in the shape of a curved boomerang. The stone *churinga* are always flat on both sides: the wooden ones have usually one side flat and the other slightly concave. A certain number of the smaller wooden *churinga* have a hole pierced through them at one end, to which is attached a string made of hair. Such *churinga* are used as bull-roarers at certain ceremonies, being whirled rapidly round at the end of the string so as to make a humming or booming noise. A certain number of the stone *churinga* are similarly bored, but they are never used as bull-roarers nor indeed, at the present day, for any purpose which would require them to be thus bored.[1]

Patterns incised on the *churinga*.

By far the most of the Arunta *churinga*, whether made of wood or stone, have patterns incised upon them with the teeth of an opossum. These patterns represent, or at all events have reference to, the totems; but in all cases the design is purely conventional and never attempts to reproduce the true form of the particular object it stands for. The most important feature is almost always indicated by a series of concentric circles or by spiral lines, while tracks of men and animals seem to be represented by dots arranged in circular or straight lines. Individual men and women appear to be uniformly symbolised by semi-circular lines and may be said generally to be regarded as subordinate to the animal or plant in the design, which is represented by complete circles or spirals. But the same pattern will stand for, say, a tree on one *churinga*, a frog on another, a kangaroo on another, and so on. Hence it is difficult or impossible to obtain a true interpretation of the design on any particular *churinga* except from one of the old men of the totemic group to whom it belongs, for it is only the old men who continually see and examine the *churinga* of their group. Time after time these elders visit the sacred storehouse, take out the *churinga*, rub them with powdered red ochre, and explain to the younger men the meaning of the patterns on them. Thus the knowledge of the ancestors to whom the *churinga* belonged, and of the designs incised on them, is handed down from generation to generation.[2] Hence

[1] *Native Tribes*, pp. 128, 143.   [2] *Ibid.* pp. 143-145, 151.

TOTEMISM OF THE ARUNTA, ETC.

these carved sticks and stones deposited in secret places of the desolate Australian mountains are a rude kind of historical records: they represent in germ the inscribed monuments of classical antiquity and the national archives of modern Europe.

The exact contents of a sacred storehouse (*ertnatulunga*) naturally vary from group to group; in most of them perhaps the wooden *churinga* are more numerous than the stone ones.[1] Amongst the *churinga* in each storehouse are usually a certain number of larger ones made by *alcheringa* men, or by famous men of old who lived since the *alcheringa*, for the special purpose of being used at totemic ceremonies. These are spoken of as *churinga*, but they differ from the majority in not having a spirit associated with them. Besides these the storehouse will sometimes contain other kinds of *churinga* which represent various objects such as, for example, implements carried by *alcheringa* ancestors or the eggs of the witchetty grub. This last kind of *churinga* consists of small rounded stones and stands for the eggs with which the bodies of the Witchetty Grub people, both men and women, were supposed to be filled in the days of the *alcheringa*. These people laid the eggs at places where they camped, especially at the Emily Gap, a short but narrow gorge hemmed in by precipitous rocks of red quartzite. To this day the disembodied spirits of Witchetty Grub people carry some of these stone eggs about with them, and when one of them enters into a woman and is born again as a child he lays a few of the eggs at the foot of the tree which he haunted before his reincarnation, and they may be found there after his rebirth. The older Witchetty Grub men usually carry some of these eggs about with them; and when a Witchetty Grub man lies dying, if he has no eggs of his own a few are always brought from the sacred storehouse and placed under his head, that he may depart in peace. It is the last sacrament, the *Nunc dimittis*. After his death the eggs are buried with him. Of the origin and meaning of this custom the natives can or will give no explanation.[2] It may perhaps be intended to

Various kinds of churinga.

---

[1] *Native Tribes*, p. 140.
[2] *Ibid.* pp. 142 *sq.*, 156 *sq.*, 424 *sq.*, 427 *sq.*

secure the spiritual resurrection of the dead man in his ancestral form of a witchetty grub.

Sacredness of the churinga and their connection with the totems.

So sacred are the *churinga* that they may not be seen by women or uninitiated men under pain of death or very severe punishment, such as blinding with a firestick. Indeed the word *churinga* means something sacred or secret, and is used not only as a substantive to denote a concrete object but also as an adjective to connote its quality of sacredness, as when the natives speak of a man's *churinga* name, that is, his sacred or secret name.¹ One and all of the *churinga* are connected with the totems,² and among the Arunta and other tribes in the very centre of the Australian continent they figure prominently in the sacred totemic ceremonies which none but initiated men may witness. Indeed in the Arunta tribe, when a series of sacred ceremonies is about to be performed, the first thing to be done is for one or two of the old men to go to the sacred storehouse and bring thence a large number of *churinga*. These they place on a special platform built on the ceremonial ground, and the spot is regarded as sacred so long as the *churinga* remain there.³

The sanctity of the churinga is greatest among the central tribes and diminishes as we go northwards to the sea.

It is a significant fact that the sanctity of the *churinga* is greatest and their use most frequent among the tribes in the very heart of Australia, and that the reverence for the implement and the frequency of its employment both diminish as we pass northwards from the centre to the sea. As Messrs. Spencer and Gillen put it : "The very central part of the continent occupied by the Arunta, Ilpirra, Iliaura, and Unmatjera tribes may be described as the home of the *churinga* and of the beliefs which cluster round this sacred object. In all of the tribes with which we are acquainted we meet with *churinga* or their equivalents, but it is in the central area only that we find them intimately associated with the spirit parts of the different individual members, and carefully treasured up and hidden away from view in the *ertnatulunga* or sacred storehouses of the various local totemic groups."⁴ On the other hand in the more northerly

---

¹ *Native Tribes*, pp. 128-132, 648 ; *Northern Tribes*, pp. 258 *sq*. On very rare occasions the *churinga* may be seen by women and uninitiated men, but then only at a distance and indistinctly (*Native Tribes*, pp. 130, 132).
² *Native Tribes*, p. 130.
³ *Northern Tribes*, p. 178.
⁴ *Ibid.* p. 257.

tribes of the Warramunga, Wulmalla, Walpari, Tjingilli, Umbaia, and Gnanji the *churinga* are indeed intimately associated with the totems, but they are practically not used in the sacred totemic ceremonies, nor is there any idea of the association of spirit individuals with them. Still further to the north, on or near the shores of the Gulf of Carpentaria, in the Binbinga, Anula, and Mara tribes the *churinga* are very few in number; there is not the intimate connection between them and the totems which exists in the other tribes, nor are spirit individuals supposed to be associated with them. "The only conclusion which it seems possible to arrive at is that in the more northern tribes the *churinga* represent the surviving relics of a time when the beliefs amongst these tribes were similar to those which now exist in the Arunta."[1]

Some of the ceremonies observed by these tribes on the occasion of a death seem to be designed to facilitate the return of the liberated spirit to its old home, the *nanja* spot, where it will tarry with its spiritual comrades of the same totem till its time shall come to be again born of a woman. With this intention the Arunta, who bury their dead doubled up in the ground and raise a low mound over the grave, regularly leave a depression on one side of the mound to allow the spirit easy egress from the narrow house. The depression is always made on that side of the mound which looks towards the place where the dead man or woman camped in the olden time. But until the ceremonies of mourning have been accomplished, the soul of the departed is thought to spend part of its time in the grave watching over its near relatives, and part of its time away with its spiritual double at its old home. So the depression in the mound allows the spirit to flit freely to and fro between the grave and its home all the days of mourning.[2] *Burial customs designed apparently to allow the soul of the dead to return to its old home (the nanja spot), where it tarries in the intervals between its incarnations.*

In the Unmatjera, Kaitish, Warramunga, Tjingilli, and other tribes to the north of the Macdonnell Ranges the bodies of the dead are usually left for some time on a platform in the branches of trees; afterwards the bones, now stript of flesh, are taken down and buried in the earth.[3] When this final *Tree-burial in some tribes.*

---

[1] *Northern Tribes*, p. 281.
[2] *Native Tribes*, p. 497; *Northern Tribes*, p. 506.
[3] *Northern Tribes*, pp. 506 *sqq.*

202 TOTEMISM IN CENTRAL AUSTRALIA CHAP.

Ceremony performed by the Warramunga over an arm-bone of the dead.

burial takes place, the Warramunga perform a curious ceremony with one of the arm-bones, which is not buried with the rest. It is very carefully wrapt up in bark, wound about with fur-strings, and a tuft of feathers is added; if the deceased was a man, the feathers are those of an owl, but if the deceased was a woman, the feathers are those of an emu. The final rite performed over the arm-bone always takes place towards the close of a long series of totemic ceremonies, in connection with which certain designs, emblematic of some totem, are drawn upon the ground. In the two rites of this sort witnessed by Messrs. Spencer and Gillen these drawings referred to snake totems of the tribal moiety to which the dead person belonged; in one of the two rites the totem was that of the deceased, but it need not be so. A small pit was dug beside the totemic design on the ground, and a few yards off a shallow trench, some fifteen feet long, was cut in the soil. Over this trench ten men, their bodies elaborately decorated with totemic designs in red, white, and yellow, stood straddle-legged, and the women crept in single file through the trench on hands and feet under the legs of the men. The last of the women carried the arm-bone, and as she emerged from the trench it was snatched from her and at once carried across to a man who stood ready with a stone axe uplifted beside the little pit. With one blow of the axe he smashed the bone and thrust it hastily out of sight into the pit beside the totemic emblem of the deceased. Then he closed the opening with a large flat stone to indicate that the days of mourning were over, and that their departed sister (for in this case she was a woman) had been gathered to her totem. When once this ceremony of breaking the bone and burying it beside the totemic design has been performed, the spirit of the dead, which is no larger than a grain of sand, returns to the place where it camped in ancient days, there to dwell with the spirits of other men and women of its totem until such time as it undergoes reincarnation.[1]

Burial ceremony among the Binbinga.

The close association between a man and his totem comes out very clearly also in the burial rites observed by the Binbinga tribe. On such occasions the natives assemble

[1] *Northern Tribes*, pp. 168 *sq.*, 537-542.

from various districts, and ceremonies relating to the ancestor of the totemic clan of which the deceased was a member are performed under the superintendence of the dead person's father. Finally, a hollow log is brought on to the ceremonial ground, decorated with some design characteristic of the totem, and in this the bones are deposited. Then the totemic coffin with the bones is placed in the boughs of a tree beside a pool, where the beautiful blue water-lilies grow, the coffin being so fixed that, if possible, it overhangs the water. There it is left untouched, and there it may remain for years, till the log with its totemic design rots and falls with a splash among the blue lilies, or is swept far away by some rising flood and buried deep in the ooze and sludge of the river. So the dead man in the coffin is gathered to his totem.[1]

The great majority of the sacred ceremonies which may not be witnessed by women and children are connected with the totems and refer to episodes in the lives of totemic ancestors. Ceremonies of this sort are celebrated by all the central and north-central tribes of Australia studied by Messrs. Spencer and Gillen, and probably at one time or another they have been celebrated by all other Australian tribes,[2] though in these, unhappily, they have seldom been observed and described. It is astonishing, we are told, how large a part of a native's life is occupied with these ceremonies. The older he grows, the greater is the share he takes in them, until finally they absorb most of his thoughts. The rites which seem so trivial to us are most serious matters to him. For they have all to do with the great forefathers of the tribe, and he is firmly convinced that at death his spirit will join theirs in the old home and remain there in communion with them till the time comes for him to be born again into the world.[3]

Importance of the totemic ceremonies in the eyes of the natives.

---

[1] *Northern Tribes*, pp. 173 *sq.*, 552-554. As to the blue water-lilies, which deck the surface of the pools in countless thousands, see *ib.* p. 9. The flowers are eaten by the natives, who think that the bones of the dead promote the growth of the lilies (*ib.* p. 546). The natives of North Queensland eat the seeds of the splendid pink water-lily and the seeds, seed-stalks, and large rough tubers of the blue water-lily. See E. Palmer, "On Plants used by the Natives of North Queensland, Flinders and Mitchell Rivers," *Journal and Proceedings of the Royal Society of New South Wales*, xvii. (Sydney, 1884) p. 101; *id.*, in *Journal of the Anthropological Institute*, xiii. (1884) p. 315.

[2] *Northern Tribes*, pp. 177, 224.

[3] *Ibid.* pp. 33 *sq.*, 177.

Often these ceremonies last for two or three months together, during the whole of which time one or more ceremonies will be performed daily. They are often, though by no means always, associated with the rites of initiation through which lads have to pass at puberty, and in regard to their general features there is a remarkable similarity between those of all the central and northern tribes. In the Arunta tribe, when a lad is circumcised or subincised, he is always shown a few of these ceremonies for the first time. At a later time he goes through the elaborate rites of the Engwura, when natives congregate from various places and a very large number of ceremonies are performed. The Engwura rites which Messrs. Spencer and Gillen witnessed began in the middle of September and lasted with hardly a break till the middle of January. During that time there was a constant succession of ceremonies, from one to five or six ceremonies being usually performed daily.[1]

In these solemn ceremonies the novice sees with awe and wonder the ancestors of the tribe personated as they are supposed to have been and to have acted in life. The actors are disguised in quaint costumes which for the most part represent those totemic animals or plants, of which the ancestors are believed to have been the direct transformations or descendants. A stranger who witnessed these little plays or pantomimes for the first time might easily imagine that they mimicked nothing but the uncouth gambols of animals, the growth of plants, and so forth. But to the native these dramas are fraught with a far deeper significance, since they set forth the doings of his semi-animal or semi-plant forefathers, whose immortal spirits still haunt the rocks, the trees, the gay flowers, the solitary pools, the wild gorges of his native land, or are incarnate in himself and in all the living members of the tribe. It is thus that the past history, or what he believes to be the past history, of his people is stamped upon every young man's imagination and memory for life. He does not read it in books: he sees it acted before his eyes.[2] Nor are these dramas purely historical, that is, intended to preserve and hand down from generation to generation the traditions of the past. They are also magical,

[1] *Northern Tribes*, pp. 177 *sq.*   [2] *Native Tribes*, pp. 227-230.

being believed, at least by the Warramunga, to contribute directly to the maintenance of the food supply; for among the central tribes every totemic clan is held responsible for the maintenance of the material object which is its totem,[1] and every clan has to perform magical ceremonies to multiply that object, generally an edible animal or plant, for the good of the community. Thus not merely the memory of the past but the present and future existence of the people is thought to turn on the proper performance of the totemic rites. No wonder that the natives take them seriously.

The magical ceremonies which aim directly and simply at the multiplication of the totems have already been touched upon and we shall recur to them presently.[2] Here we are concerned with those ceremonies which on the surface appear to be purely historical and dramatic, although amongst the Warramunga, and perhaps other tribes, they have also a practical significance. For the most part these historical or perhaps rather miracle plays are short and simple, lasting only a few minutes, though the preparation for them may have occupied hours; for the decoration of the actors is often elaborate. A few examples will illustrate their nature.

The bulbs of the *Cyperus rotundus* are a favourite food of the Arunta and form the totem of a clan who call themselves Irriakura after the native name of the bulb (*irriakura*). A ceremony of this totem was witnessed by Messrs. Spencer and Gillen at a place called Soda Creek. One man only was decorated for the performance, but the design was very quaint and striking. A ring of grass-stalks measuring about two feet across was made and covered with white down. The shoulders, stomach and arms of the performer were striped with broad bands of a light pearl colour, made by rubbing on some blue grey wad, and each band was edged with white down. His hair was done up into a head-dress, and all the front of it as well as the whole of his face was covered with down. Then the ring was put over his head and slanting forwards rested on his shoulders. A great

Arunta ceremony of a bulb (*irriakura*) totem.

---

[1] *Northern Tribes*, p. 197.
[2] As to the *intichiuma* or magical ceremonies for the multiplication of the totems, see above, pp. 104-115, and below, pp. 214 *sqq*.

many little bunches, not less than a hundred, of the red-barred tail feathers of the black cockatoo had been prepared, half of them tipped with white and half with red down, and these were stuck into the ring so as to radiate outwards all round it, while many more were inserted in his head-dress and beard. The dark chocolate hue of the man's skin, the black and red feathers, the pearly-grey bands on his body, the pink and white down, together with the light yellow sand on which he sat, made up a gay and not inharmonious blend of colours. Thus arrayed the actor sat down in front of a dozen bunches of cockatoo tail feathers, decorated with down, which were arranged in a row on the sand. Then swaying slightly from side to side he scooped the bunches up, one after the other, with his hands, pausing now and then to look about him as if he heard a sound that startled him but could not tell what it was. The tufts of feathers represented the growing *irriakura* bulbs, which the performer was supposed to be gathering. Meantime the other men sat to one side watching the performance and singing about the dead man whom the actor was personating. When the last tuft of feathers had been grubbed up, the ceremony came to an end. Then the ring of grass-stalks was taken off the performer's head and put in turn on the heads of all the other men of the bulb totem who were present. The tradition which the little drama set forth ran thus. In the far off days of the *alcheringa* a man of the bulb totem was eating these bulbs, when he heard the ring-necked parrots, which are the mates of the bulb men, scream out to warn him that a mob of strange men was coming that way. So he dropped the bulbs and hurried off. However, the strangers were also of the bulb totem and they left two of their number on the spot, whose reincarnations are still living, at least they were living a few years ago. Then the Bulb men went on to the other side of the Jay River, and there they founded a local centre (*oknanikilla*) of the bulb totem, from which a number of Bulb people have sprung.[1]

In this ceremony it is interesting to note that a man of the bulb totem is represented gathering the bulbs, and that

[1] *Native Tribes*, pp. 318-320.

in the corresponding tradition the man whom the actor personated is said to have eaten the bulbs, his totem. Similarly in an Arunta ceremony of the plum-tree totem Plum-tree men are represented knocking down plums from a tree and eating them;[1] in another Arunta ceremony of the fish totem a Fish man is seen not only mimicking the movements of a fish but also pretending to catch it;[2] in a ceremony of the *chankuna*-berry totem a man of the totem is represented eating his totem berries which he plucks from his beard;[3] and in Warramunga ceremonies of the ant totem men make believe to search for and gather ants because two ancestresses of the ant clan are said to have fed on ants all day long when they were not performing ceremonies. In these ceremonies of the ant totem the upper part of the performer's body, together with his face and a sort of helmet which he wears, is often covered with a dense mass of little specks of red down, which stand for the living ants.[4] All such ceremonies point clearly to a time in the past history of the tribe when, contrary to the present practice, people were allowed to partake freely of their totem animals and plants.[5]

In the totemic ceremonies men are often representing their totems, which is contrary to the present practice of the tribes.

As another example of these totemic dramas we may take an Arunta ceremony of the white bat totem, which was performed at midnight by the flickering light of a camp fire. Eleven men took part in it. Ten of them, decorated with pipe-clay and red and white down, stood in a row, being joined together by a rope made of human hair and ornamented with pink and white down which passed through the girdle of each man. Four of them had *churinga* on their heads and were supposed to represent certain gum-trees, the roots of which were indicated by the rope. The other six men in the row stood for bats perched on the trees. The eleventh man was free of the rope and his decoration differed from that of the rest; for he had a long band of charcoal, edged with red down, on each side of his body. He danced up and down in front of the others, stooping and

Arunta ceremony of the white bat totem.

---

[1] *Native Tribes*, p. 320, with fig. 51, p. 293.
[2] *Ibid.* pp. 316 *sq*.
[3] *Ibid.* p. 208.
[4] *Northern Tribes*, pp. 199-202, with fig. 65, p. 209.
[5] *Native Tribes*, p. 320, compare pp. 207-210.

making a shrill whistling sound like that emitted by a small bat as it flits to and fro. At the same time the roped men moved in unison first to the right and then to the left, presenting with the dancer in front of them a curious spectacle in the fitful light of the fire.[1]

<small>Arunta ceremony of the frog totem.</small>

Another illustration of these totemic ceremonies may be drawn from the ritual of the Frog clan among the Arunta. At Imanda, which is known to white men as the Bad Crossing on the Hugh River, there is an important centre of the frog totem. The following ceremony of that totem was witnessed by Messrs. Spencer and Gillen. The performer came from the neighbourhood of Imanda and, though he did not himself belong to the frog totem, had inherited many frog ceremonies from his father. During the performance he wore on his head a sort of flat helmet completely covered with concentric circles of alternate pink and white down. These represented the roots of a particular gum-tree at Imanda. The whole of his back and chest down to his waist was one mass of white spots, each of them encircled by white down. These spots were of various sizes and stood for frogs of various ages. On the inner sides of the performer's thighs were white lines representing the legs of fully-grown frogs. On his head he wore a large frog *churinga*, five feet long, decorated with bands of down and tipped with a bunch of owl feathers. All around the base of this were arranged tufts of black eagle-hawk feathers, each fastened to a stick, so that they radiated from the head-dress. Many strings of opossum fur, covered with pink and white down and decked at one end with tufts of the black and white tail tips of the rabbit-kangaroo, hung down from the head as a sort of veil hiding the face, which was itself enveloped in a mass of down. The *churinga* represented a celebrated tree at Imanda and the pendant strings were its roots. When all was ready a shallow pit about three feet across was scooped out in the sand, and in this the performer squatted with a short stick in his hands. Except for the hands holding the stick, there was little to show that the elaborate and towering structure, with its gay decorations, concealed from view a man. Slightly swaying

[1] *Native Tribes*, pp. 352, 354.

his body from side to side, the performer dug up the sand with his stick, while two old men, swinging bull-roarers, drove the novices who were being initiated towards him. Round and round him they raced with loud shouts, the old men with the bull-roarers driving them in upon him as close as possible. This lasted for about three minutes and the ceremony then came to an end.[1]

Another little drama exhibited to an Arunta novice at initiation illustrated a tradition that a wild Dog man had attacked and been killed by a Kangaroo man. One man, decorated with a sacred object emblematic of a kangaroo, stood with his legs wide apart moving his head from side to side and mimicking the cry of the kangaroo. Another man, who acted a dog, barked at the pretended kangaroo and ran between his legs. But when he repeated this manœuvre, the Kangaroo man caught him, shook him, and made believe to bump his head against the ground, at which the pretended dog howled with pain. When at last the dog was supposed to be killed by the kangaroo, the man who played the dog ran along on all fours to where the novice sat and laid himself down on the top of him; after which the old kangaroo man came hopping along and got on the top of both of them, so that the lad had to bear the weight of the two men for about two minutes. When the performers got up, the novice, still lying down, was instructed by the old men in the meaning of the ceremony which he had just seen and felt.[2] *Arunta ceremony of the dog and kangaroo totems.*

Again, another Arunta ceremony of the *unchalka* grub totem was performed by a man whose body was decorated with lines of white and red down in imitation of the *unchalka* bush on which the grub lives first of all; and a shield was ornamented with concentric circles of down representative of the *udniringa* bush on which the adult insect lays its eggs. This emblematic shield was laid on the ground, and the performer, kneeling before it, alternately bent his body double and lifted it up, quivering his extended arms, which represented the wings of the insect. Every now and then he stooped forward, swaying up and down and from side to side over the shield, in imitation of the insect hovering over *Arunta ceremonies of grub and emu totems.*

[1] *Native Tribes*, pp. 341-344.   [2] *Ibid.* pp. 224-226.

the bushes where it lays its eggs.[1] Similarly, in an Arunta ceremony of the witchetty grub totem, a performer who personated a celebrated Witchetty Grub ancestor wriggled his body to represent the fluttering of the insect when it first sloughs off its chrysalis case and attempts to fly.[2] Again, in an Arunta ceremony of the emu totem the actor wears a tall head-dress tipped with emu feathers to look like the long neck and head of an emu, while he stalks backwards and forwards in the aimless fashion of the bird.[3]

Arunta ceremony of the eagle-hawk totem.

Again, we may describe an Arunta ceremony of the eagle-hawk totem which was witnessed by Messrs. Spencer and Gillen. The drama, which represented two eagle-hawks quarrelling for a piece of meat, was cleverly acted by two men. Their hair was bunched up and they wore conical crowns of cassia twigs. Human blood, which is very commonly used in these ceremonies to make the down adhere to the skin of the performer or to the decorated object, was smeared over the front part of the head-dress and across the body in the form of a broad band round the waist and a band over each shoulder, the two bands uniting back and front. Each band was about six inches wide, and each, when the decoration was complete, was a solid mass of pink down edged with a line of white. Into the hair girdle behind was fixed a large bunch of the black feathers of the eagle-hawk, and into the top of each man's head-dress were fastened three *churinga*. Each of these *churinga* was about three feet long, tipped with a tuft of eagle-hawk feathers and adorned with close rows of down coloured alternately red and white. They made a very heavy head-dress. In his mouth one of the actors carried a small cylindrical mass of grass tied up with hair-string and covered with lines of down. Thus equipped, the two performers squatted opposite to each other on the ground. They acted two eagle-hawks quarrelling for a piece of flesh, which was represented by the downy mass in one man's mouth. First they waved their arms up and down to mimic the flapping of the eagle-hawks' wings; then they jumped up and with bodies bent and arms flapping

---

[1] *Northern Tribes*, pp. 179 *sq.*, with fig. 45, p. 181.
[2] *Ibid.* p. 180.
[3] *Native Tribes*, pp. 358 *sq.*, with fig. 73, p. 343.

they circled round and round each other, as if each were afraid of coming to grips. At last they grappled and fought, butting at each other with their heads for the possession of the meat. This went on for some time till two men stepped out from among the audience and relieved the performers of the weight of the *churinga*, which must have placed a considerable strain on their heads and necks in the great heat of the summer afternoon. Thus lightened, the two actors began once more prowling round and round each other, flapping their arms, jumping up and falling back, just like eagle-hawks fighting, until finally they again closed, and the assailant, seizing the piece of meat with his teeth, wrenched it from the other's mouth. The acting in this ceremony was particularly good, the movements of the birds being admirably represented.[1]

As the great majority of Central Australian totems consist of animals and plants,[2] it is natural that in the totemic ceremonies the actors should generally personate animals or plants or the semi-human ancestors who are supposed to have been in one way or other developed out of them. But there are some totems which are neither plants nor animals, and these also have their appropriate ceremonies. For example, in an Arunta ceremony of the sun totem a performer carried a small disc made of grass-stalks and covered with down, of which the alternate red and white lines represented the sun's rays;[3] and in a ceremony of the water totem of the same tribe there figured an elaborate structure like a screen or banner, on which clouds, rain, thunder and lightning were represented by strings, plain or coloured, and by patches and bands of white down; while red feathers and blood-smeared chips of wood on the performers' heads stood for the masses of dirty brown froth which often float on the top of waters in flood.[4]

In the totemic ceremonies the actors generally personate animals or plants, but sometimes inanimate objects are represented.

---

[1] *Native Tribes*, pp. 294-297.
[2] See below, p. 253.
[3] *Northern Tribes*, p. 182.
[4] *Native Tribes*, pp. 306-308. The totemic emblem described in the text is called a *waninga*. Its structure varies, but commonly it consists of a long spear with one, two, or three cross-bars lashed to it and connected with each other by strings made of human hair or fur. Sometimes the vertical support is only a stick little more than a foot long. The implement may stand for any totem. For example, in a ceremony of the rat totem, witnessed by Messrs. Spencer and Gillen, the *waninga* represented the body of a rat, the main part was supposed to be

Among the Arunta each totemic ceremony belongs to an individual, who has either inherited it or received it from the ancestral spirits.

Each totem has its own special ceremonies, and in the Arunta tribe each ceremony may be regarded as the property of an individual man, who has either inherited it from its previous owner, such as a father or elder brother, or received it as a gift directly from the *iruntarinia* or disembodied spirits of his forefathers.[1] For some men are credited with the faculty of seeing and conversing with these spirits, and such a man will sometimes tell his fellows that the spirits have revealed to him a ceremony and made him a present of it. These announcements perhaps sometimes originate in dreams, for what a savage sees in a dream is just as real to him as what he sees in his waking hours. The thoughts of the natives are at times so much taken up with the performance of sacred ceremonies that it is quite natural they should dream of them and take the visionary images of sleep for revelations of those spirits with whom their own spirit has been communing during the lethargy of the body. Or men of a more original and ingenious turn of mind than the rest, and such the Australian magicians generally are, may have simply invented some of the ceremonies and then palmed them off as inspirations of the higher powers upon their credulous fellows.[2] Whether inherited or invented, a totemic ceremony need not necessarily be either owned or performed by a man of the particular totem to which it refers. And the owner of a ceremony may, and frequently does, invite some one else to perform it, the invitation being looked upon as a compliment.[3] For example, a man of the snake totem may own a ceremony of the fish totem and may perform it himself;[4] or a Grass-seed man may possess a grass-seed ceremony and invite an Emu man and a Witchetty Grub man to perform it.[5] But if a man has received a ceremony

---

the trunk of the animal, the point was the tail, the handle the head, and the cross-bars the limbs. The use of the *waninga* extends south from the Arunta to the sea at Port Lincoln. In the northern part of the Arunta territory the place of the *waninga* is taken by a sacred pole called a *nurtunja*, which also represents the particular totem with which any given ceremony is concerned. See *Native Tribes*, pp. 231 *sq.*, 306-309, 627-629, 653.

[1] *Native Tribes*, p. 278. As to the *iruntarinia*, see *ib.* pp. 512 *sqq.*

[2] *Ibid.* p. 278; *Northern Tribes*, pp. 450 *sq.*

[3] *Native Tribes*, p. 279.

[4] *Ibid.* pp. 316 *sq.*

[5] *Ibid.* p. 311.

as a revelation from a spirit and hands it over as a gift to another man, that man must be of the totem with which the ceremony is concerned. For instance, a celebrated medicine-man, who was a Witchetty Grub, received from a spirit the revelation of an eagle-hawk ceremony, and instead of keeping it for himself he generously passed it on to his own father, who was an Eagle-hawk.[1] Again, the totem of the novice has no influence on the nature of the ceremonies which are performed for him at initiation: these ceremonies may be of any totem.[2]

In regard to these totemic ceremonies, or sacred dramas as we may call them, the practice of the Warramunga differs in some respects from that of the Arunta. Thus whereas among the Arunta each separate ceremony is the property of a particular individual, who alone has the right of performing it or of requesting some one else to do so, among the Warramunga the ceremonies are each and all of them the property, not of an individual, but of the whole totemic group, and they are under the charge of the headman of the group. They are not strictly his property, but he acts in a vague sort of way as the representative of the totemic group or clan. Even he, however, cannot enact them of his own initiative; he can only perform them or have them performed at the request of members of that half of the tribe to which he himself does not belong. Further, whereas among the Arunta the totemic ceremonies are performed in no definite order, and without any reference to those which have preceded or will follow, among the Warramunga on the other hand all of the ceremonies connected with a given totem are performed in a regular sequence. The history of every ancestor is well known, and if, say, he arose at a spot A and walked on successively to spots B, C, D, E, F, and so forth, halting at them and performing ceremonies, as these first ancestors always did, then whenever his descendants perform these ceremonies at the present day, it is incumbent on them to begin at the beginning and go steadily through the series. To a Warramunga the performance of ceremony F without the previous performance in regular order of A, B, C, D, and E would

The totemic ceremonies of the Warramunga differ in some respects from those of the Arunta; for they belong to the whole totemic clan, not to individuals, they are performed in definite series, and they are supposed magically to increase the supply of the totems.

[1] *Native Tribes*, p. 294.   [2] *Ibid.* p. 226.

seem a very strange proceeding, whilst in the Arunta tribe one or all of them would be performed in any order. Lastly, whereas the Arunta distinguish these commemorative or dramatic ceremonies from those magical ceremonies (*intichiuma*) which are intended to multiply the totems, in the Warramunga tribe the commemorative or dramatic ceremonies are intimately associated with, and are performed at certain times as, *intichiuma* ceremonies, in other words as magical rites for the multiplication of the totems.[1]

<small>Essential features of the *intichiuma* ceremonies among the Arunta.</small>

The magical rites for the multiplication of the totems which are performed by the Arunta and Urabunna have already been described.[2] In the Arunta tribe the essential features of these rites (*intichiuma*) are as follows:—

(1) The men of each totem perform a definite ceremony, the sole object of which is to ensure the continuance and increase of the totemic animal, plant, or whatever it may be.

(2) Except on these special occasions, the members of a totem clan eat only very sparingly of their totemic animal or plant. A very strict man will not eat of it even sparingly.

(3) But the headman (*alatunja*), who presides over and conducts the *intichiuma* ceremony, is obliged by custom to eat a little of his totemic animal or plant, otherwise it is thought that he could not perform the ceremony with success.

(4) After the men of the totem have eaten a little of their totemic animal or plant at the *intichiuma* ceremony, they hand on the rest to the men of other totems and give them leave to eat it freely.

(5) Only men of the totem and of the right moiety (class or phratry) of the tribe are allowed, except in very rare cases, to share in the ceremony of *intichiuma*.[3]

<small>Kaitish ceremonies to promote the growth of grass-seed.</small>

In the Kaitish tribe, to the north of the Arunta, the magical ceremonies for the multiplication of the totems are called *ilkitnainga*, not *intichiuma*; but just as among the Arunta they are conducted by the headman (*ulqua*) of the

---

[1] *Northern Tribes*, pp. 192, 193.
[2] The *intichiuma* of the Arunta tribe are described and discussed by Messrs. Spencer and Gillen in their *Native Tribes of Central Australia*, pp. 167-211. See above, pp. 104-120. As to the *intichiuma* of the Urabunna, see above, pp. 183-185.
[3] *Northern Tribes*, p. 291.

totem. The ceremony for the propagation of grass-seed is as follows. When the headman of the grass-seed totem decides that it is time to perform the rite, he goes to the sacred storehouse, clears the ground all about it, and taking out the *churinga* greases them well, chanting certain traditionary words of which the meaning is forgotten. Then he takes two of the *churinga*, smears them with red ochre, and decorates them with lines and dots of down, of which the dots represent the grass-seed. After that he rubs the *churinga* together so that the dust flies off in all directions. Then he replaces them in the sacred storehouse (*ertnatulunga*) and returns quietly to his camp. Next day he goes to the ground where sacred ceremonies are performed, and there he is decorated by the men who belong to the other moiety of the tribe. Then in the presence of all the men he performs a ceremony which refers to an incident in the ancient history of the grass-seed clan.[1] In the Arunta tribe no such historical drama forms any part of the magical ceremonies for the multiplication of the totems, nor among the Arunta is the headman decorated by members of the other moiety of the tribe; indeed with the Arunta it is a general rule that men of the other moiety may not come near the place where the ceremony is being prepared. This Kaitish ceremony is therefore an intermediate stage between the practice of the Arunta and that of the Warramunga. For among the Warramunga the ceremonies for the multiplication of the totems consist for the most part simply of dramatic representations of scenes in the life of the totemic ancestors, and among them these ceremonies may only be performed at the invitation of men of the other moiety of the tribe.[2] After the headman of the grass-seed totem has acted his little historical drama about his Grass-seed ancestors, he walks about for days in the scrub "singing" the grass-seed, that is, enchanting it in the literal sense of the word, and carrying one of the *churinga* with him. At night he hides the *churinga* in the bush and, returning to the camp, sleeps on one side of the fire, while his wife sleeps on the other; for so long as he is performing these sacred

[1] *Northern Tribes*, pp. 291 *sq.*   [2] *Ibid.* pp. 292, 297, 298.

ceremonies to make the grass-seed grow, he may not come at his wife. During the whole of that time he is supposed to be so full of magical power derived from the *churinga*, that were he to have intercourse with his wife, the grass-seed would be spoiled and his own body would swell up when he tasted of it.[1]

<small>Further Kaitish ceremonies to make grass-seed grow.</small>

When the seed begins to sprout, the headman still goes on chanting and enchanting it to make it grow more till at length, when it is fully grown, he brings his *churinga* hidden in bark to his camp. Then he and his wife go out and gather a store of the grass-seed and bring it to the camp, where his wife grinds it up with stones. The man himself takes some to the men's private camp (*ungunja*) and grinds it there, and while he does so, the men of one of the four subclasses (subphratries) in the other moiety of the tribe catch the grass-seed in their hands as it falls from the edge of the grinding-stone. One of these men puts a little of the seed in the Grass-seed man's mouth and he blows it away in all directions, which is supposed to make the grass grow plentifully everywhere. After this he leaves the seed with the men of the other moiety of the tribe, saying: "You eat the grass-seed in plenty; it is very good and grows in my country." The only men who are allowed to be present are the men of three out of the four subclasses in the other moiety of the tribe; the men of the fourth of these subclasses are excluded. Any old men of the Grass-seed man's own subclass who happen to be in camp will accompany the headman, but they may not receive any of the seed. When he returns to his ordinary camp, he gives some of the seed to his wife, bidding her to eat of it and to tell the other women to eat of it also, unless they belong to the grass-seed totem. Thereupon the woman makes four cakes out of the grass-seed, and at sundown her husband returns to the men's private camp with three cakes, and gives three of them to the men of three out of the four subclasses in the other moiety of the tribe, but the fourth cake he tells his wife to give to the men of the fourth subclass. A woman of his own moiety, but not of his own subclass, then gives him some seed which he takes to his

---

[1] *Northern Tribes*, p. 293.

own camp and hands over to his wife to make into another cake. Of this he eats a little and gives the rest to the men who are his tribal fathers, saying, "I am glad to give you this." These men belong to his own moiety of the tribe, but the grass-seed is not tabooed to them unless they are of the grass-seed totem. Then he tells his wife to instruct the women of all classes to go out and gather the seed in plenty. He himself sits down quietly at his own camp and watches the women as they return with the seed, all of which they carry to the men of the other moiety of the tribe except a little which his own wife and other women of her subclass bring in to him. After a time the men of the other moiety of the tribe again come to the headman of the grass-seed totem bringing a little seed with them, but leaving the greater part of it in their own camp. He eats what they bring, and gives them in exchange the supply which the women brought him, and then he tells the men that all is now over, and that they may eat grass-seed freely. He himself and the other Grass-seed men eat of it only sparingly. If a man of any totemic clan eats too much of his own totem, he will be, as the natives say, "boned," that is, killed by means of a charmed bone by men who belong to the other moiety of the tribe, because by partaking too freely of his totem he loses the power of magically multiplying it for the public benefit.[1]

In these magical ceremonies for the growth of grass-seed a particularly interesting feature is the scattering of the seed in all directions by the headman of the grass-seed totem,[2] because such a procedure might really have the intended effect of propagating the seed, and if the natives observed, as they might very well, the success of the ceremony, they might in time come to sow the seed without the accompaniment of those chants or spells to which at first they ascribed a great part of the efficacy of the rite. In other words, a purely rational agriculture might spring by a natural course of development directly out of what was in origin a purely magical ceremony. May not this, or something like it, have

Out of these magical ceremonies for the growth of grass-seed a rational agriculture might in time be developed.

---

[1] *Northern Tribes*, pp. 293 *sq.* The wife of the Grass-seed man is not of the grass-seed totem, and she necessarily belongs to the other moiety of the tribe.
[2] Compare the Arunta mode of multiplying manna (above, p. 107).

been in more advanced communities the real origin of agriculture?

<small>Kaitish ceremony for the making of rain.</small>

When rain is wanted, the headman of the water totem in the Kaitish tribe makes it as follows. Accompanied by the old men of the totem he repairs to a sacred totemic storehouse (*ertnatulunga*) of the Water clan, where in the olden time two aged men sat down and drew water from their whiskers. These whiskers are now represented by stones, out of which the rainbow arose. First of all the headman of the water totem paints these stones with red ochre, and then close to them he paints on the ground a curved band to represent a rainbow. Also he paints one or more rainbows on his own body and another on a shield, which he also decorates with zigzag lines of white pipe-clay in imitation of lightning. While he sings incantations over the stones he pours water from a vessel on them and on himself. Then he returns to camp, carrying with him the shield, which may not be seen by men of the other moiety of the tribe; for were they to see it the rain would not fall. They think that the rainbow is a son of the rain, and that with filial solicitude he is always trying to prevent his father from falling down. Hence when the shield with its scutcheon of lightning and rainbow has been brought back to the camp, it is carefully hidden away until rain enough has fallen, after which the shield is brought forth and the device of the rainbow is rubbed out. Meanwhile the headman of the water totem keeps a vessel full of water beside him in the camp, and from time to time he scatters bits of white down, which stand for clouds, in various directions to make the rain descend. At the same time the Water men who went with him to the sacred storehouse go away and camp by themselves; for neither they nor the headman of the water totem may have any intercourse with women while the rain is brewing. So when the leader returns to his camp from the hallowed spot, his wife arranges to be absent, and when she comes back at a later time he mimics the call of the plover, a cry which in these parts is always associated with the rainy season. As yet, however, the head Water man may not even speak to his wife, and early next morning he returns to the sacred storehouse of the water totem and covers up the stones with bushes. After another silent night in his own camp he and the other men and women go out in different directions, the women in search of vegetable food and honey ants, and the men in quest of game. When the two parties meet on their return to camp they all raise the cry of the plover. Then the leader's mouth is touched with some of the food which has been brought in, and so the ban of silence is removed. If rain soon follows, it is attributed to the efficacy of the ceremony; if it does not, it only means that some more powerful magician has held it up.[1]

These ceremonies for the making of rain are clearly based on the principle of imitative or homœopathic magic. The pouring of water on the rainbow stones, the painting of rainbows and lightning, the scattering of white down to represent clouds, the imitation of the cry of the plover, are all so many transparent examples of this logical fallacy, and unlike the parallel ceremonies for the multiplication of grass-seed they offer no hope of ever developing into really efficacious means of producing the desired end. Magical rites may be compared to shots discharged at random in the dark, some of which by accident hit the mark. If the gunner learns to distinguish between his hits and his misses, he will concentrate his hitherto scattered fire in the right direction and accomplish his purpose. If he fails to make the distinction, he will continue his random discharges with as little result as before. A scientific farmer is an artilleryman of the former sort; an Australian headman of the grass-seed totem is an artilleryman of the latter sort. It is the distinction between magic and science, between savagery and civilisation. *The rain-making ceremonies are based on the principle of imitative magic.*

Another example of unscientific farming is furnished by the magical ceremonies which the headman of the yam totem in the Worgaia tribe performs for the purpose of making yams grow. He first of all takes a *churinga* wrapt in bark and leaves it on the ground at a spot where yams grow. Then he is decorated by men of the other moiety of the tribe and performs ceremonies of the yam totem. After that the men ask him to go about in the bush and "sing" or enchant the yams, as they wish them to grow. He does *Worgaia ceremony to make yams grow.*

[1] *Northern Tribes*, pp. 294-296.

this every day for about two weeks, going about and chanting with his *churinga* under his arm. At last, when he sees the plants growing well, he tells the men of the other moiety to go out and gather some. They do so, and leaving the main supply in their own camps bring a few of the yams to the headman of the yam totem with a request that he will make the yams grow big and sweet. He bites a small one and throws the bits in all directions, which, like the scattering of the grass-seed, is supposed to produce the desired effect. After that he eats no more of his totem the yam, nor may his children touch it, whatever their totems may be. Finally, he says to the men of the other moiety of the tribe, "I have made plenty of yams for you to eat. Go and get them and eat them, and you make plenty of sugar-bags for me to eat." When he is a very old man he will be allowed to eat yams if they are given to him by a man of the other moiety.[1] In this ceremony the request of the Yam man that the other men should make honeycomb for him to eat, in return for the yams which he makes for them, clearly illustrates the co-operative aspect of these magical ceremonies: men of any totem multiply it for the good of their fellows who belong to other totems, but at the same time they expect the men thus benefited to return the benefit in kind. The whole system is based, not on a philanthropic impulse, but on a cool though erroneous calculation of economic interest.[2]

Warramunga ceremonies for the multiplication of the totems consist for the most part in dramatic scenes representing the history of the totemic ancestor.

In the Warramunga tribe, whose territory lies immediately to the north of that of the Kaitish and to the west of that of the Worgaia, the magical ceremonies for the multiplication of the totems consist for the most part, as we have seen, simply in the performance of a series of scenes representing dramatically the ancient history of the totemic ancestor. For in this tribe each totemic clan usually traces itself up to one great ancestor, who arose in some particular spot and walked across the country, making on his journey various natural features, such as creeks, plains, mountains,

---

[1] *Northern Tribes*, pp. 296 *sq*. "Sugar-bags" is a name for the honeycomb of a species of bee which builds in trees. This honeycomb (*kulpu*) is eaten by the natives and is a totem in several tribes. See *Northern Tribes*, p. 772.

[2] See above, pp. 108 *sq*.

and pools, and leaving behind him spirit individuals who have since been reincarnated. The *intichiuma* or, as the Warramunga call it, the *thalamminta*, that is, the magical ceremony for the multiplication of the totem, consists in tracking the journeys of the totemic ancestor and repeating, one after the other, ceremonies commemorative of the spots where he left the spirit children behind him.[1] Hence ceremonies of this sort in the Warramunga tribe occupy a considerable amount of time. For example, some sets of totemic ceremonies which were witnessed by Messrs. Spencer and Gillen began on July 26 and were not yet finished on September 18: in the interval more than eighty of them had been performed.[2]

The Warramunga tribe is divided into two exogamous moieties (classes or phratries), which are called Uluuru and Kingilli respectively. All the totems are divided up between these moieties, and though the members of a totem clan perform their own ceremonies, or ask some one else of the same moiety to perform them or to assist in the performance, they may not do so of their own initiative: they must be requested to perform the ceremony by a member of the other moiety of the tribe. Thus the Uluuru men only perform their ceremonies when they are invited to do so by the Kingilli; nay, more than that, no Uluuru men, except the actual performers, may be present on the ground during the preparations for the ceremony. Everything used in the ceremony, such as the down, the blood, and all the materials used in the decorations, must be provided and made up for the Uluuru performers by the Kingilli men, to whom the Uluuru afterwards make presents. In exactly the same way the Uluuru men take charge of the Kingilli ceremonies and receive presents from the Kingilli performers.[3] This responsibility of the one moiety of the tribe for the totemic ceremonies performed by the other moiety may be based on the idea that, as the members of a totem clan multiply their totem not for their own good but for the good of the rest of the community, the expenses of the ceremonies ought, in

Among the Warramunga the members of a totemic clan may only perform their ceremonies at the request of the men of the other moiety of the tribe, who provide all the decorations for the ceremonies and receive presents from the performers.

---

[1] These spots are called *mungai* by the Warramunga and *oknanikilla* by the Arunta. See above, pp. 189 *sqq.*

[2] *Northern Tribes*, pp. 297, 298 *sq.*

[3] *Ibid.* p. 298.

fairness, to be borne by the persons whom they are intended to benefit, and not by the performers who reap no personal profit from them.

Warramunga ceremonies for the multiplication of black snakes.

As an illustration of the historical dramas which the Warramunga act for the purpose of multiplying their totemic animals and plants we may take the ceremonies of the black snake totem. The black snake, Thalaualla, arose first at a rocky water-hole called Tjinqurokora in the bed of Tennant Creek. This water-hole is now a sacred spot, at which no men of the black snake totem and no women at all may drink.[1] As the black snake belongs to the Uluuru moiety of the tribe, whenever it is desired to increase the number of these snakes, which are used as food, the Kingilli men must ask the Uluuru men to perform their ceremonies. These ceremonies were witnessed by Messrs. Spencer and Gillen.[2] The first ceremony represented the snake at the water-hole. It was acted by two men, each of whom had a curved black band, edged with masses of white down, to represent the black snake. When the little scene was over, the other men stroked the drawing of the snake on the backs of the performers, an action which is supposed to please the snake. Tradition says that, after coming up out of the earth, the snake made Tennant Creek and then travelled on to the Macdouall Range, which he also created. As he went along he performed sacred ceremonies (*thuthu*) just like those which the natives still perform, and wherever he did so he left spirit children behind him. At such times and places he always shook himself, so that the spirit children emanated from his body. Hence at these spots the natives who perform the ceremonies shake themselves in like manner, so that the white down with which their bodies are decorated flies off in all directions. This, for example, they do at a place called Lantalantalki, at the foot of the Macdouall Range. From this place, where there are some small rock-holes, the black snake travelled on to another water-hole called Orpa. In the ceremony here performed the two actors had each a small red disc of down on the stomach

---

[1] *Northern Tribes*, p. 299. For a more exact account of the rules observed as to drinking at this sacred pool, see below, p. 235.

[2] *Ibid.* pp. 300, 770.

and back to indicate the water-hole, and a curved red band to represent the snake. From Orpa the snake travelled up towards the source of the creek, performing sacred ceremonies and leaving spirit children behind him at Pittimulla. In the second of two ceremonies connected with this spot a special drawing was made upon the ground. A small space a few feet square was smoothed down, its surface damped, and coated with red ochre. A curved branching line, about three inches wide, was first of all outlined in white dots on the red ochre, and then all the rest of the space was filled in with similar dots. The red line thus left curving about on the white background represented the creek and its branches.[1]

Finally, when the old snake had finished making the Macdouall Ranges and the creeks running out from them as far as Mount Cleland on the east, he returned to his original home, the water-hole at Tjinqurokora, and the remaining ceremonies had to do with incidents which happened there. In the olden time some women of the yam totem arose not far from the black snake's water-hole at Tjinqurokora. He thought that they wished to watch him at his mystic rites, so he bade them begone. They went away, dropping yams as they went, mainly in Worgaia country. The yams which the women thus left behind them turned into stones; and it is over one of these stones that the Worgaia man sings his magic song when he goes out into the bush to make the yams grow. On that occasion the stone is decorated with

More Warramunga ceremonies for the multiplication of black snakes.

---

[1] *Northern Tribes*, pp. 300-302. For the ground-drawings made at the black snake ceremonies, see *ib.* pp. 741-743, figures 313, 314, 315. These ground-drawings of the Warramunga are a very interesting feature of the ceremonies designed to multiply the totems. The drawings seen by Messrs. Spencer and Gillen were painted in red or black on a hard crust of yellow or red ochre, and covered a space of from seven to eighteen feet in length. The bands and circles which formed the main feature of the design were traced by the leading man with his finger, and the background was patiently filled in by younger men with close-set dots of pipe-clay, while they continually sang of the journeys of the totemic ancestor. The patterns were a curious mixture of purely conventional and, to a certain extent, imitative designs. See *Northern Tribes*, pp. 737 *sqq.* As to a similar ground-drawing of the emu totem in the Arunta tribe, see above, p. 106. M. Salomon Reinach has made the interesting suggestion that the prehistoric paintings of animals found in caves of South-Western France may in like manner have been intended to multiply by magic the game on which the cave-men subsisted. He observes that all the animals so depicted are edible, not beasts of prey. See his *Cultes, Mythes et Religions*, i. (Paris, 1905) pp. 125-136.

red ochre, and a long dark line down the middle represents the roots of the yam. The last three ceremonies of the black snake totem all referred to these Yam women, and the decorations of the men consisted merely of red lines and ovals or circles, the ovals representing the yams and the lines the strings with which the women used to tie them up. In the last ceremony eight men took part, all of them representing the Yam women. On the ground a design was painted which, by means of concentric circles and connecting lines, was supposed to portray the women sitting down, tired out, with their legs drawn up, after they had been sent away by the black snake. Four of the men wore head-dresses with pendants, the head-dresses representing yams and the pendants representing the witchetty grubs on which the women fed. During the same night the men all assembled at the ceremonial ground, painted with black, and sang about the walking of the black snake and the Yam women. This ended the series of dramatic ceremonies for the multiplication of black snakes. The old original black snake is said to have perished in single combat with a white snake. He went down into the ground at the water-hole of Tjinqurokora, from which he had first emerged; and his adversary the white snake went down into another water-hole close by.[1]

Warramunga rules as to the eating of black snakes.

When the black snake ceremonies have been performed, and the marching of the black snake ancestor has been sung, it is supposed that black snakes will multiply in numbers. But there is no ceremony, as among the Arunta and Kaitish in similar cases, of bringing in the snakes to men of the snake totem. It is the men of the snake totem who are supposed to cause the increase of the reptile, but they can only do so at the request of men of the other moiety (class or phratry) of the tribe. It is these men of the other moiety of the tribe who make all the preparations for the ceremony, and who alone benefit by it. The men of the snake totem are absolutely forbidden to eat snakes under any circumstances, except when they are grown very old, and then in the Warramunga tribe restrictions as to food are practically removed, save that any special food must be given

[1] *Northern Tribes*, pp. 302-308.

by some one who has not got that food for his totem. Apart from this exceptional case it is believed that were the men of a totemic clan to eat of their totem animal it would cause their death, and at the same time prevent the animal from multiplying. Nor is the prohibition to eat snakes confined to men of the snake totem; it applies also to every member of the particular subclass or subphratry (to wit Thapanunga) to which the snake totem belongs; and it extends further to every member of another subclass or subphratry (the Thapungarti) in the same moiety (the Uluuru) of the tribe. Men of the other two subclasses or subphratries (namely the Tjunguri and the Tjapeltjeri) of the same moiety (the Uluuru) may eat the snake if it be given them by men of the other moiety (the Kingilli); and the men of the latter moiety (Kingilli) may eat snakes freely at any time. There is, however, no restriction as to killing snakes. The reptiles may be killed by all Uluuru men, even by men of the snake totem; but whenever any of these men do kill a snake they must hand it over to the men of the Kingilli moiety.[1]

The principle that men multiply their totemic animals and plants for the benefit of other people, but not for their own, may be called the self-denying ordinance of Central Australian totemism. It is illustrated by the words spoken by Warramunga headmen after they have performed their ceremonies for the increase of their totems. Thus when the headman of the ant totem has performed his ceremonies for the multiplication of ants, and these insects, which are not eaten as food, have begun to increase, he tells the others to go and gather the ants which he has made for them, but they do not bring any to him. Again, when the headman of the carpet-snake totem has performed his ceremonies for the increase of carpet-snakes, and the reptiles appear, men of the other moiety of the tribe bring him one of the carpet-snakes and say to him, "Do you want to eat this?" But he replies, "No, I have made it for you. If I were to eat it, then it might go away. All of you go and eat it." Again, when a man of the honey totem has performed ceremonies for the increase of honey, some of the honey is brought to him, but he refuses to eat it, and tells the others

Self-denying ordinance of Central Australian totemism: men multiply their totems for the benefit of others, not for their own.

[1] *Northern Tribes*, p. 308.

that he has made it for them, and that they may go out and gather and eat it. They believe that to eat of their own totem would cause their death and prevent the animal from multiplying.¹

Warramunga ceremony for the multiplication of white cockatoos.

Though the ceremonies performed by the Warramunga for the increase of their totems are for the most part historical dramas rather than magical rites in the strict sense of the word, yet the purely magical element crops up occasionally in them. Thus men of the white cockatoo totem perform ceremonies of the usual dramatic sort for the multiplication of white cockatoos, which are eaten. But in addition they perform another, which is believed to increase the birds to a wonderful extent. Messrs. Spencer and Gillen were privileged to see but especially to hear the miracle. It consisted simply in an imitation of the harsh cry of the cockatoo, which the old headman of the white cockatoo totem, aided and abetted by his son, kept up with exasperating monotony the whole night long. The performance began at ten o'clock one evening, and lasted till after sunrise next morning. Holding in his hands a conventional representation of the bird, the old man screeched like a cockatoo till he could screech no more, whereupon his son took up his parable and continued the screech till his aged parent, like a giant refreshed, was able to resume his excruciating labours. This went on without a break for between eight and nine hours, and it is not surprising to learn that when the sun had risen on the two performers after a night made truly hideous by their exertions, there was hardly a squeak left in them.²

Warramunga ceremony for the multiplication of euros.

Another magical ceremony observed by the Warramunga for the multiplication of game is as follows. There is a species of kangaroo called a euro (*Macropus robustus*) which is eaten by the natives, and is a totem in several tribes. Near the water-hole in which the great mythical water-snake Wollunqua is supposed to live³ may be seen a number of round water-worn stones of various sizes from which euros are thought to emanate, because a wild dog caught and killed a euro here in days of old. The larger stones

¹ *Northern Tribes*, pp. 308 *sq.* ² *Ibid.* pp. 309 *sq.*
³ See above, pp. 144 *sq.*

represent male euros, the smaller represent female euros, and the smallest stand for the young of the animal. They are carefully hidden under little heaps of rocky debris, but old men who pass by, whatever their totem may be, will take the stones out, renew the red ochre with which they are covered, and rub them well. This proceeding is believed to increase the number of euros which emanate from the stones.[1] In this case the power of magically increasing euros is not limited to Euro men but is exercised by old men of any totem. The extension seems to show that totemism, regarded as a system of magical functions distributed between strictly limited departments, is breaking down among the Warramunga and merging into a more centralised or tribal system, which ignores the old departmental limits of the totem clans. So too in the matter of the prohibition to eat the totemic animal, the extension of that taboo beyond the limits of the totem clan[2] points in like manner to a decay of totemism proper; and as the new and extended limits assigned to these food prohibitions coincide with the exogamous subdivisions of the tribe, it looks as if the old organisation in totem clans, whose main function among the central tribes at the present day is to regulate the food supply, were being gradually superseded even for economic purposes by the newer organisation in classes and subclasses, which was originally instituted purely for the purpose of regulating marriage.[3]

This decay of totemism as an organised system of magic is more and more marked the further we proceed from the centre of Australia northwards in the direction of the sea. The Tjingilli and Umbaia tribes, immediately to the north of the Warramunga, perform ceremonies like those of their southern neighbours for the multiplication of their totemic animals and plants; that is to say, the ceremonies consist in the performance of a long series of dramatic scenes representing incidents in the life of their totemic ancestors. Messrs. Spencer and Gillen do not describe these scenes, but in regard to a ceremony of rain-making among the Tjingilli they mention the significant fact that it may be performed

Totemism as an organised system of magic seems to decay as we proceed from the centre of Australia towards the sea.

---

[1] *Northern Tribes*, p. 310.
[2] See above, p. 225.
[3] See above, pp. 162 *sq.*, and below, pp. 256 *sqq.*

only by men of one moiety (class or phratry of the tribe).[1] In other words, the ceremony for the making of rain, which among the strictly central tribes is only performed by men of the rain or water totem,[2] may be performed among the Tjingilli by all the men of one half of the tribe, and therefore by men of many totems. Here also, accordingly, it appears that the totemic organisation is breaking down under the weight of the social or exogamous organisation.

Among the tribes on the coast of the Gulf of Carpentaria ceremonies for the multiplication of the totems have almost disappeared.

When we leave the interior of Australia and pass to the tribes who inhabit the comparatively well-watered and wooded shores of the Gulf of Carpentaria, we find that magical ceremonies for the multiplication of the totems have nearly, though not quite, disappeared. These tribes do indeed, like their inland brethren, perform dramatic ceremonies commemorative of the traditional history of their remote ancestors, but none of these ceremonies are intended, as among the Kaitish, Warramunga, and Tjingilli, to increase the food supply by multiplying the totemic animals and plants. Further, there is not, as among the central tribes any obligation on the headman of a totem to perform ceremonies for the increase of his totemic animal or plant; for the natives here are sufficiently enlightened to recognise that the increase will take place without the intervention of their magic.[3] Still they may, if they choose, resort to magic for the purpose of assisting nature in the great process of reproduction.

Mara ceremony for the increase of honey.

For example, the men of the Mara tribe can increase the supply of honey, which is one of their totems, by the following simple means. On the banks of the Barramunda Creek, near the Limmen River, there is a big heavy stone, which is believed to represent a large honeycomb carried about by the old ancestor of the honey totem, and left by him on the spot where he finally went down into the ground. The men who form that half of the tribe to which the honey totem belongs can increase the supply of bees, and therefore of honey, by scraping the big stone and blowing the powder about in all directions; for this powder is supposed to turn into bees.[4] Here again it is to be observed that the ceremony for the increase of the totem need not be

---

[1] *Northern Tribes*, p. 311.
[2] See above, pp. 113, 184, 218 *sq.*
[3] *Northern Tribes*, pp. 311 *sq.*
[4] *Ibid.* p. 312.

performed by men of the totem; it may be performed by any men of that half of the tribe to which the totem belongs. Here also, therefore, the totemic organisation is being superseded by the social or exogamous organisation.

In the Anula tribe the sea-fish called dugong is a favourite article of food. Near the mouth of the Limmen River some white stones, which can be seen at low tide, represent dugongs of the olden time. Numbers of dugongs are believed to emanate from these stones without any help of the natives; but Dugong men can, if they please, facilitate the process by singing magical songs and throwing sticks at the rocks.[1] Again, in days of old a crocodile is said to have roamed about the country, making what is now called Batten Creek, and also various water-holes, in which he deposited crocodile spirits. Finally, he went down into the ground, at a place called Wankilli, where there is a large pool with a stone in the middle of it. Crocodiles still issue from that stone; and if Crocodile men wish to make them come out in larger numbers, they can do so by singing or enchanting the rock and throwing sticks of mangrove at it.[2] Two species of crocodiles are found in the northern parts of Central Australia. Both species are eaten by the natives, who accordingly have a sufficient motive for multiplying these dangerous reptiles.[3] While these Anula ceremonies for the multiplication of the totems are performed by men of the totem (Dugong men and Crocodile men respectively), we meet in this coastal tribe with clear evidence that the supersession of the totem clans by the exogamous classes or phratries is here also in progress. For the Anula have a tradition that a snake named Bobbi-bobbi founded local centres occupied by spirit individuals of exogamous classes, whose totems are not mentioned. This is the only case known to Messrs. Spencer and Gillen in which a local centre is haunted by spirits of exogamous classes, instead of by spirits of totem clans.[4]

Anula ceremonies for the increase of dugongs and crocodiles.

Thus whereas among the central tribes members of a totem clan are obliged to multiply their totems for the benefit of the rest of the community, there is no such

The decay of totemic magic on the coast as

[1] *Northern Tribes*, p. 313.
[2] *Ibid.* p. 313.
[3] *Ibid.* p. 770.
[4] *Ibid.* p. 437.

obligation laid on the totemic clans of the coastal tribes. Among the latter tribes there are only traces of those magical ceremonies which are universally prevalent among the former. In other words, totemic magic for the multiplication of totems flourishes in the centre of Australia and is decadent on the sea coast. The difference, as Messrs. Spencer and Gillen justly observe, is no doubt to be attributed to the difference in climate between the two regions, the more regular rainfall of the coast ensuring a more regular supply of food, and thereby superseding the supposed necessity of increasing it by magic.[1]

compared to the centre of Australia is an effect of the more regular rainfall and more assured supply of food.

The custom with regard to eating or not eating the totemic animal and plant similarly changes as we pass from Central Australia northward to the sea. In the Arunta tribe, at the heart of the continent, a man will only eat very sparingly of his totem, and even if he does eat a little of it, which he may do, he is careful not to eat the best part of it. For example, men of the emu totem very seldom eat the eggs of the bird. But if an Emu man is very hungry and finds a nest of emu eggs, he may cook one, but he will take the rest into camp and distribute them. If he were not very hungry, he would give all the eggs away. He may eat sparingly of the flesh of the emu, but only a very little of the fat; for the fat and the eggs are more tabooed than the flesh to him. The same holds good for all the totems; for instance, a Carpet-snake man will eat sparingly of a thin snake, but will scarcely touch a fat one.[2] Similarly Witchetty Grub men and women may eat only a very little of witchetty grubs; for it is believed that if they ate too much the power of performing magical ceremonies for the multiplication of the grubs would depart from them, and there would be very few grubs.[3] But, on the other hand, it is positively incumbent on the men, especially on the headman of the clan, to eat a little of the totemic animal, for to eat none would have the same effect as to eat too much; that is to say, if the men of a totem did not eat a little of it, they would lose the power of multiplying their totem, and the animal or plant would consequently be

The custom with regard to eating the totemic animal also changes as we pass from Central Australia to the sea. Among the Arunta people may eat a little of their totems; indeed they are obliged to do so, as otherwise it is thought that they would lose their power of magically multiplying their totems.

---

[1] *Northern Tribes*, pp. 173, 318. See above, pp. 167 *sqq.*
[2] *Native Tribes*, p. 202.
[3] *Ibid.* p. 204.

scarce.¹ We have seen how in the Arunta tribe, after the men of a totem have performed the *intichiuma* ceremonies for multiplying the totemic animal or plant, they have solemnly to partake of a little of it, which is ceremonially brought to them by men of other totems.² The custom seems to be a formal acknowledgment by the rest of the tribe that the totemic animal or plant properly belongs to the men of the totem, though these men have almost abnegated in favour of their fellows the right to eat the particular animal or plant.

In the Unmatjera and Kaitish tribes, to the north of the Arunta, this public acknowledgment of the proprietary rights possessed by a totem clan in its totemic animal, plant, or thing is still more conspicuous and more frequent; for it is not made only after the performance of *intichiuma* ceremonies for the multiplication of the totems, but on every occasion of daily life when a man wishes to eat or drink the totem of somebody else. In all such cases he is bound, wherever it is practicable, to obtain the permission of the men of the totem before he consumes the animal or plant or whatever the object may be to which they have in strictness an exclusive right. For example, if an Emu man comes into the district of a Grass-seed clan, he will gather some of the seed and take it to the headman of the Grass-seed clan, saying, "I have been getting grass-seed in your country." The Grass-seed man will reply, "That is right; you eat it." They think that if an Emu man were to eat grass-seed without the leave of the Grass-seed men, he would be very ill and probably die.³ When any animal is killed by a man whose totem it is not, it is first brought into the camp and cooked, and then, if any man of that totem happens to be in camp, it is taken to him by the men of the other moiety of the tribe, and he eats a little of it. After that, but not before, the animal may be eaten by the men of other totems.⁴ The same restriction applies to the use even of water. If a stranger who is not of the water totem comes to Anira, the central spot of the water totem in the Kaitish tribe, he must ask leave of the headman of

In the Unmatjera and Kaitish tribes people may not eat or drink other people's totems without their leave.

---

¹ *Native Tribes*, p. 204.
² See above, pp. 109-111, where the descriptions are based on *Native Tribes*, pp. 203-206.
³ *Northern Tribes*, pp. 159, 323.
⁴ *Ibid.* pp. 159 *sq.*, 324.

the Water clan before he may drink. The headman tells the men of the other moiety to give the stranger water. Were permission not thus obtained, the natives say that the headman of the water totem would kill the transgressor by means of a magic bone.[1]

But Kaitish people rarely partake of their own totems, except ceremonially at the intichiuma rites; for it is thought that otherwise they would lose the power of magically multiplying them.

But while Kaitish men of any totem are thus publicly acknowledged by the rest of the tribe to possess the exclusive right to that particular totem, they rarely avail themselves of that privilege of eating or drinking it which they freely grant to others. Under normal conditions a Kaitish man does not eat his totem except ceremonially at the time of the *intichiuma* rites, when the headman of the totem is bound to eat a little of it. Were he to partake too freely of his totem, the men of the other moiety of the tribe would kill him by means of a magic bone, because such conduct would, they believe, incapacitate him for performing the *intichiuma* ceremonies successfully, and so the rest of the community would consequently suffer through the diminution of the totemic animal or plant, and hence of the food supply.[2] Even in regard to such an absolute necessity of life as water, though the men of the water totem cannot, of course, deny themselves it altogether, they are subject to certain irksome restrictions in the use of it. If a man of the water totem be quite alone, he may draw it and drink it without offence; but if he be in the company of men belonging to other totems, he may not obtain it for himself, but must receive it from a member of the other moiety of the tribe. As a general rule, when a man of the water totem is in camp, he receives water from a man of the same subclass from which he, the Water man, takes his wife, in other words he receives water from one who is his tribal brother-in-law (*umbirna*). But if no man of that subclass happens to be in camp, the Water man may be provided with water by any member of the other moiety of the tribe.[3] To take another illustration of these self-denying ordinances of totemism among the Kaitish, if an Emu man be out hunting by himself in the scrub and sees an

---

[1] *Northern Tribes*, p. 326.
[2] *Ibid.* p. 323.
[3] *Ibid.* pp. 160, 325 *sq.* According to the latter passage he receives water from his tribal father-in-law (*ikuntera*).

emu, he will not touch it. But if he be in the company of men of other totems, he is free to kill the bird, but he must hand over its dead body to the other men.[1]

In the Unmatjera tribe, whose territory lies immediately to the north of the Arunta and immediately to the south of the Kaitish, the restrictions as to eating the totem are fundamentally similar to those of the Arunta. At the *intichiuma* ceremonies for the multiplication of the totem, a little of the totemic animal or plant is eaten by the members of the clan; and the remainder, which has been brought to the headman, is handed over by him to men who belong to the other half of the tribe. The Unmatjera believe that if a man were to eat his own totemic animal or plant, except during the performance of the *intichiuma* ceremonies, he would swell up and die. In this tribe, as in the Kaitish, whenever a man of the water totem is in the company of other men, he may not help himself to water, but must receive it from some one who has not got water for his totem.[2]

In the Unmatjera tribe also people as a rule only eat of their totems at the intichiuma ceremonies for multiplying them.

While thus among the really central tribes, the Arunta, Unmatjera, and Kaitish, men are not absolutely forbidden, nay, are on certain solemn occasions obliged, to eat of their totemic animal or plant, the prohibition to partake of it is absolute among all the more northern tribes from the Kaitish to the sea. In other words, among these northern tribes the totemic animal or plant is strictly tabooed to members of the totem clan; they may not even eat it ceremonially at rites observed for the purpose of multiplying the totem.[3] Nay further, in some of these tribes a man is debarred, either absolutely or in certain circumstances, from eating the totems of his father, his mother, and his father's father, whenever these totems differ from his own. In these tribes, say Messrs. Spencer and Gillen, the relationship between a man and his totem in regard to eating it is very simple, but at the same time very strict.

But in the northern tribes the prohibition to partake of the totem is absolute; and in some of the tribes a man is further debarred from eating the totems of his father, his mother, and his father's father, whenever these totems differ from his own.

---

[1] *Northern Tribes*, p. 160.
[2] *Ibid.* p. 324.
[3] *Ibid.* p. 326. To this rule water is doubtless an exception. In many Australian tribes old men enjoy an exemption from many restrictions in regard to food which are imposed on younger men. But it does not appear that this exemption extends to their totems. See *Native Tribes*, pp. 168, 468, 471; *Northern Tribes*, pp. 609-613; G. Taplin, "The Narrinyeri," *Native Tribes of South Australia*, p. 16.

He may neither kill nor eat it, and the same prohibition applies to the totem of his father and the totem of his father's father, whenever these totems, one or both of them, differ from his own. As a rule a man's totem is identical with that of his father and his father's father in these northern tribes, because with them the totem is generally hereditary in the male line. But if the totems should all differ, then a man is forbidden to kill and eat three different totems, to wit his own, his father's, and his father's father's. With regard to the relationship between a man and his mother's totem there is some difference of usage between the tribes. In the Worgaia tribe, at all events in the western section of it, the mother's totem is strictly tabooed and may not be eaten; but in the Walpari and Warramunga tribes a man may eat of his mother's totem, provided it be given him by a member of that half of the tribe to which the particular totem belongs. For instance, in the Walpari tribe if a Curlew man is the son of a Honey woman, he may eat honeycomb on condition that it is given him by a member of that moiety (the Kingilli) with which the honey totem is associated. Similar restrictions apply to the maternal totem when it happens not to be an edible object. Thus when the mother of a Walpari man has fire for her totem, then her son must obtain a fire-stick, when he wants one, from a member of that half of the tribe to which the fire totem belongs. Again, in the Warramunga tribe, if a Wild Cat man has an Emu mother, he will not kill the bird and will only eat it if it be given him by a member of the other moiety of the tribe to which the emu totem is reckoned. Similarly if a Warramunga man has a mother of the water totem, he ought in strictness to have water given him by a man of the other half of the tribe to which the water totem belongs; but if he happens to be alone and thirsty, the rigidity of the rule is relaxed so far as to allow him to get the water for himself.[1]

The black snake totem of the Warramunga may serve

[1] *Northern Tribes*, pp. 166 *sq*. In regard to a man's own totem Messrs. Spencer and Gillen elsewhere observe that "a Warramunga man, for example, will not hesitate, under certain conditions, to kill his totem animal, but he hands it over to men who do not belong to the same totemic group, and will not think of eating it himself" (*Northern Tribes*, p. 327).

as an illustration of these rules. That totem belongs to the Uluuru moiety of the tribe and to the subclasses Thapanunga and Thapungarti of that moiety. As we have seen,[1] it has its centre at the water-hole called Tjinqurokora on the Tennant Creek. Black Snake men and women, and those whose fathers or fathers' fathers were Black Snakes, may not eat the reptile at all. Any person whose mother was a Black Snake may only eat it if it be given to him or her by Uluuru men, that is, by men of the moiety who claim the black snake among their totems. The men of the other two subclasses of the Uluuru moiety, namely, the Tjunguri and Tjapeltjeri men, and those men of the Thapanunga and Thapungarti subclasses who do not belong to the black snake totem, may eat a black snake only if it be given to them by Kingilli men, that is, by the men of the other moiety of the tribe, who may eat it freely at all times.[2] No woman may go anywhere near the sacred pool to draw water: all initiated men may go there, but Black Snake men may not drink at the spot: all Uluuru men who are not Black Snakes may drink of the water only if it be given them by Kingilli men: finally, the Kingilli men, that is, the men of the tribal moiety to which the black snake totem does not belong, may drink freely of the water of the holy pool where the old original black snake was born and died.[3]

Thus it appears that in the Warramunga tribe the totemic prohibitions with regard to eating are much more extensive and numerous than among the more central tribes. For, in the first place, the prohibition to eat the totem is

[1] See above, p. 222.

[2] *Northern Tribes*, p. 167. The two moieties or classes (phratries) and the eight subclasses (subphratries) of the Warramunga tribe are as follows:—

Class.	Subclasses.	Class.	Subclasses.
Uluuru	Thapanunga Tjunguri Tjapeltjeri Thapungarti	Kingilli	Tjupila Thungalla Thakomara Tjambin

See below, pp. 265 *sq.*

[3] *Northern Tribes*, p. 167. As to the mythical history of the Black Snake ancestor, see above, pp. 222 *sqq.*

not confined to members of the totem clan, but is conditionally extended to all members of that moiety of the tribe in which the particular totem clan is included, for no member of that moiety may eat of the totem, even though it is not his own, unless it is given him by a man of the other moiety. As the same rule applies to every totem, it follows that all the totems of his own half of the tribe are tabooed to every man unless he receives them as a gift from men of the other half. In the second place, a man is prohibited from eating not only his own totem, but also the totems of his father and his father's father whenever these differ from his own, and, further, he is forbidden to eat his mother's totem unless it be given him by a member of his mother's tribal moiety. In the third place, not only are all these totems tabooed either absolutely or conditionally to every man and woman, but, further, the sacred birth-place or death-place of any one of these totems may also be tabooed to him or her. In short, in the Warramunga and kindred tribes, men and women live immeshed in a network of totemic taboos which must considerably restrict their eating, and from most of which the Arunta and other central tribes are entirely free. Totemism has apparently either tightened its hold on the northern tribes or relaxed it on the central tribes. Which of these two things has happened, we shall inquire presently. Meantime I will only again ask the reader to observe the significant fact, to which I have already called his attention,[1] that in these tribes the totemic prohibitions have been in a large measure extended beyond the limits of the totemic clans and now embrace those much wider kinship groups which we call classes or phratries, subclasses or subphratries. Here, therefore, the newer organisation of the tribe in exogamous divisions (classes or phratries) seems to be superseding the older organisation in totem clans.[2]

Among the Mara and Anula, two tribes situated on the coast of the Gulf of Carpentaria, a man may not eat his totem, and he only eats very sparingly the totem of his

---

[1] See above, pp. 225, 227.
[2] For evidence that the classes or phratries are newer than the totem clans, see above, pp. 162 sq., and below, pp. 251 sq., 351 sq.

mother. For example, a Fish-hawk man whose mother is a Shark will not eat fish-hawks at all and only very small sharks. This last exception to the general taboo is very common among these tribes. A man will usually not eat of the full-grown animals which are the totems of his mother's clan, but he has no objection to eat the half-grown animals, and sometimes he will eat just a little of an adult one.[1]

In the Mara and Anula tribes a man will not eat his own totem, and will eat his mother's totem only very sparingly.

[1] *Northern Tribes*, p. 173. In these two tribes, the Mara and the Anula, the totems are distributed as follows among the exogamous subclasses or subphratries (see *Northern Tribes*, p. 172):—

THE MARA TRIBE

Subclasses (Subphratries).	Totems.
Murungun	Eagle-hawk, yellow snake, hill kangaroo, large crocodile, parrot, galah, stone, salt water.
Mumbali	Whirlwind, a poisonous snake, white hawk, crow, opossum, salt-water mullet, stingaree.
Purdal	Blue-headed snake, big kangaroo, crane, wallaby, little fish-hawk, dingo, barramunda (a fresh-water fish), rain, sand-hill snake, little crocodile.
Kuial	Emu, turkey, goanna, white cockatoo, grasshopper, water snake, kite, jabiru, groper, turtle.

THE ANULA TRIBE

Subclasses (Subphratries).	Totems.
Awukaria	Dugong, two salt-water turtles, called respectively *murulanka* and *thuriutu*, a snake called *gnurwa*, native companion, euro, ground sugar-bag [honeycomb], large eagle-hawk, pearl oyster, small crocodile, small shark.
Roumburia	Large shark, snake called *napintipinti*, large crane, small crane, dollar bird, curlew, stingaree, mullet, whirlwind, opossum.
Wialia	Fish called *runutji*, sugar-bag [honeycomb], cold weather, wild fowl called *talulthalpuna*, emu, and a hawk called *mularakaka*.
Urtalia	A fish-hawk called *tjutjutju*, a snake called *rapupuna*, lightning, water-snake called *arrikarika*, barramunda, a fresh-water fish called *wurr-wurr*, and three salt-water fishes, called respectively *amukarra*, *warranunga*, *oaria*, and two turtles called *undiniuka* and *gnoalia*.

We have seen that the prohibitions to eat the totemic animals and plants are both more stringent and more extensive among the northern and coastal tribes than among the tribes of the centre, in which men are allowed to eat a little of their totem, nay, are even at certain times compelled as a public duty to do so. Which of these two usages is the older? in other words, which of them is more in harmony with ancient custom? the usage which absolutely forbids a man to eat his totem, or that which allows and even compels him to do so? If we can trust the traditions of the natives, the answer is not doubtful. The custom which allows and compels a man to partake of his totem is certainly older than that which taboos it to him entirely. For the native traditions relating to the remote *alcheringa* times constantly speak of men and women eating their totems freely and habitually as if it were the most natural thing in the world for them to do so. Such traditions cannot have been invented to explain the modern practice, for they flatly contradict it. We seem, therefore, driven to conclude that these traditions, carefully handed down from generation to generation, and stamped on the memory by being represented dramatically to the eyes of all initiated men, do faithfully preserve a recollection of a time when the ancestors of the present natives freely and habitually partook of their totems, whenever the animal or the plant was in season and accessible to them.[1] A few examples will illustrate these traditions.

The Arunta tell how a party of Wild Cat met some men of the plum-tree totem, and how the Wild Cat men were changed into Plum-tree men, and thereafter went on eating plums. Again, they say that a Bandicoot woman started out with a Hakea Flower woman and turned her companion into a Bandicoot woman like herself by performing a sacred ceremony and painting the Hakea Flower woman with down used in the bandicoot ceremony. After her transformation the new Bandicoot woman went on feeding on

---

[1] On this subject see the judicious remarks of Messrs. Spencer and Gillen, *Native Tribes*, pp. 207-210; *Northern Tribes*, pp. 320 *sq.* With the conclusion which these eminent authorities draw from their observations I am entirely at one.

bandicoots. Again, an Arunta man of the euro totem is said to have pursued a euro which carried fire in its body. He came up with it, killed it, and cooking the carcase with fire taken from its inside he ate it. Another Euro man started out in pursuit of a kangaroo which he was anxious to kill and eat, but in order to do so he first of all changed himself into a Kangaroo man. Arunta traditions also tell of a Fish man who was seen fishing in a pool for the fish on which he subsisted; of a Beetle Grub (*idnimita*) man who fed on beetle grubs; of a Plum-tree woman who was out gathering plums when a man came and stole a valuable implement which she had left in camp; and, lastly, of an Opossum man who on his nocturnal wanderings carried the moon about with him as a lantern to help him to catch opossums.[1]

In the Kaitish tribe similar traditions are current. For example, it is said that an Emu man found some Emu men eating emu and said, "Why do you not give me some emu?" They were angry, and killed him, and broke his back, and Central Mount Stuart arose to mark the spot where he perished. Again, we are told that some women of an edible bulb totem walked about digging up and eating their totemic bulbs, which indeed formed their staple food. The husks which they threw away made a heap, and the heap is now represented by a hill called Pulina.[2] Again, it is said that a young Rabbit Kangaroo (*atnunga*) man met an old Rabbit Kangaroo man, who being too infirm to hunt for himself gave the young Rabbit Kangaroo man a rabbit kangaroo *churinga* and told him to go and hunt for rabbit kangaroos all day, and dig them out of their burrows with the *churinga*. The young man did so, and brought the dead rabbit kangaroos to the old Rabbit Kangaroo man, who cooked and ate them. Lastly, we hear of a Grass-seed man who, after wandering about the country, sat down and spent all his time gathering and eating grass-seed.[3]

Again, the Unmatjera tell of a Wild Dog man who used to feed on wild dogs,[4] and of a celebrated Beetle Grub

Kaitish traditions of people eating their totems.

Unmatjera traditions of people eating their totems.

---

[1] *Native Tribes*, pp. 208 *sq.*; *Northern Tribes*, p. 321.
[2] *Northern Tribes*, pp. 321, 394 *sq.*
[3] *Ibid.* pp. 321 *sq.*
[4] *Ibid.* p. 405.

(*idnimita*) man, who habitually dug up beetle grubs with a nose-bone and ate them. Indeed there was little else for him to eat, for in those days we are told that there was nothing at all in the country but beetle grubs and a little bird called *thippathippa*. So the Beetle Grub man used to think within himself, "What shall I eat to-day? I have got no brother or son to collect beetle grubs for me: I will gather them for myself. If I do not eat beetle grubs I shall die." Spurred by this painful reflection he would rush out and collect the grubs and devour them. One day he observed to another Beetle Grub man, "I have been eating beetle grubs." At that up jumped another old Beetle Grub man and said, "I have been eating beetle grubs also; if I eat them always they might all die." Nevertheless the other old Beetle Grub man continued to perform ceremonies for the multiplication of the grubs, and then when the grubs swarmed out he would go and gather them himself or send a man to gather them for him. But one day when he had been out in pursuit of his daily bread, or, to be more precise, of his daily beetle grubs, boils appeared on his legs. Undeterred by this ominous symptom he went and gathered more grubs, and then he grew so ill that he could not walk, and had to lie down in his camp all that day. The hand of death was on him. He wasted visibly away, his throat closed up, and before the morning broke next day he burst open and died.[1]

The last of these traditions hints at doubts as to the propriety of a man's eating his own totem.

In this last narrative, though a Beetle Grub man is represented as subsisting on beetle grubs, it seems clear that the narrator had serious misgivings as to the propriety of such conduct. The statement that in those days there was nothing at all in the country except beetle grubs and *thippathippa* birds, is a manifest attempt to excuse a Beetle Grub man for eating beetle grubs by making out that he had really no choice in the matter. Beetle grubs or nothing, that was the alternative he had to face, and naturally he decided for beetle grubs. Further, the observation of the other old Beetle Grub man, "If I eat beetle grubs always, they might all die," shows that he also felt twinges of conscience in the matter; and the miserable end of the Beetle Grub man who

[1] *Northern Tribes*, pp. 324 *sq.*

ate beetle grubs might serve as an awful warning of what will happen to people who persist in devouring their totems even after boils have burst out on their legs.[1]

A very similar tale is told by the Kaitish of a Beetle Grub (*idnimita*) man who used to perform magical rites and chant spells for the multiplication of the grubs, and then, when he saw them rising out of the ground, he would gather, cook, and eat them. Yet he is said to have reflected, "Suppose I eat more grubs, then perhaps they might all die," and again, "Suppose I go on eating too much, they might be frightened and go away to another country."[2] Such reflections appear to be put in the mouth of the speaker by men of a later age, who had ceased to eat their totems freely, though they preserved a tradition of a contrary practice among their forefathers. The reason, too, alleged for the ancestor's hesitation to eat much of his totem is highly instructive. It is a fear that were he to eat too many grubs the other grubs would be frightened and go away to another country, so that all his charms and spells for the multiplication of the insect would be fruitless. Such a reason is perfectly in keeping with savage modes of thought, and may very well, as I have already indicated,[3] be the very reason which has led so many Australian tribes to abandon what appears to have been the original practice of freely eating their totems. If that is so, the motive at the bottom of totem taboos observed by men of the totem is nothing more or less than an attempt to conciliate the game which are killed and eaten. That attempt, as I have shown elsewhere,[4] is very commonly made by savage hunters and fishers who habitually kill and eat the animals and the fish which they flatter and appease. The only difference between the two cases is that whereas ordinary hunters and fishers themselves partake of their bag, the totemic magician

There are indications in tradition that the motive for abandoning the old custom of eating the totem was a desire to conciliate the totem animal and so to ensure a supply of it.

---

[1] Messrs. Spencer and Gillen observe (*Northern Tribes*, p. 325) that, "so far as we could ascertain, the old man's miserable ending had nothing to do with the fact that he ate *idnimita* [beetle grubs]." But taken along with other features of the tale the moral seems too pointed to be missed. It should be observed that the breaking out of sores on the body and other forms of skin disease are penalties often supposed to be incurred by those who eat their totems or other sacred food. See above, p. 17.

[2] *Northern Tribes*, pp. 322 sq.

[3] See above, pp. 121-123.

[4] *The Golden Bough*,[2] ii. 387 sqq.

does not: he contents himself with providing the rest of the community with his totemic animal or plant, and expects his fellows in return to provide him with theirs.

Thus in regard to eating their totems the central tribes have remained truer than the northern tribes to the primitive practice.

Thus the traditions of the Arunta, the Kaitish, and the Unmatjera point clearly to a time when their ancestors habitually ate of their totems whenever they had a chance of doing so; and among the very same tribes these traditions are reflected in those totemic ceremonies in which to this day men solemnly partake of their totems not only without the least indication that such conduct is blameworthy, but with the avowed intention of thereby ensuring the supply of food.[1] We may fairly, therefore, conclude that the ancient custom among all these tribes was for every man regularly to eat his totem animal or plant whenever he could, and that in so far as the central tribes have partially preserved that custom and the northern tribes have abandoned it entirely, to that extent the central tribes have remained truer than the northern tribes to the primitive practice.

The rules of marriage and descent of the totem also change as we pass from the centre northwards; for whereas among the central tribes men and women of the same totem are free to marry each other, and the totems are not hereditary, among the northern tribes men and women of the same

Thus we have seen that in several respects the totemic beliefs and customs of the tribes under consideration change as we pass northward from the centre to the sea. The use of *churinga* and their association with the totems,[2] the practice of magical ceremonies for the multiplication of the totems,[3] and the old freedom of eating the totemic animals and plants, all these things dwindle away or disappear entirely as we recede from the central to the coastal tribes. A great change also takes place in the customs with regard to marriage and the descent of the totems. Among the central tribes of the Arunta nation, as we saw, the totemic system has nothing to do with marriage, since a man is free to marry a woman of his own or any other totem; and further, the totem descends neither in the paternal nor in the maternal line, but is determined purely by the accident of the place where the mother happened first to feel the child in her womb.[4] All this changes gradually as we pass from the Arunta nation northward till among the coastal tribes we find that a man never marries a woman of his own

---

[1] See above, pp. 109-111, 120, 217, 220, 230 sq.
[2] See above, pp. 200 sq.
[3] See above, pp. 228-230.
[4] See above, pp. 187 sqq.

totem, and that a child invariably inherits the totem of its father.[1] In this last respect it can hardly be disputed that the central tribes have preserved the more primitive beliefs and customs, and that the gradual transition from a purely fortuitous determination of the totem to a strict inheritance of it in the paternal line marks a social and intellectual advance in culture. To imagine that the change had taken place in the opposite direction, in other words, that tribes which had once derived their totems invariably from their fathers afterwards abandoned the hereditary principle in favour of one which left the determination of their totems to the sick fancies of pregnant women—this would be a theory too preposterous to be worthy of serious attention.

totem are forbidden to marry each other, and the totems are strictly hereditary in the paternal line.

In this very interesting and important transition from promiscuous marriages between the totem clans and fortuitous determination of the totems to strict exogamy of the totem clans and strict heredity of the totems in the paternal line the principal stages are in brief as follows:—"In the Arunta, as a general rule, the great majority of the members of any one totemic group belong to one moiety of the tribe, but this is by no means universal, and in different totemic groups certain of the ancestors are supposed to have belonged to one moiety and others to the other, with the result that of course their living descendants also follow their example. In this respect the Unmatjera, Ilpirra, and Iliaura are in accord with the Arunta, but amongst the Kaitish the totems are more strictly divided between the two moieties, though the division is not so absolute as it is amongst the Urabunna in the south and the tribes further north, such as the Warramunga. As the totems are thus distributed it follows that in the Kaitish tribe a man does not usually marry a woman of the same totem as himself, but, provided she be of the right class, she is not actually forbidden to him as a wife because of this identity of totem as she would be in the Warramunga tribe. Two families will serve as an example of what takes place in this matter in the Kaitish. In the first the father was a Kangaroo man and his wife Emu; their children were a Grass-seed son and daughter and a Wild Cat son. In the second the father was Rain, the

Stages in the transition from promiscuous marriage and fortuitous determination of the totems to strict exogamy of the totem clans and strict heredity of the totems in the paternal line.

[1] *Northern Tribes*, pp. 151 *sq.*, 163 *sq.*, 165 *sq.*, 169-173, 175 *sq.*

mother Emu; there were two Rain sons and one Yam daughter. It will be seen from this that, as in the Arunta, the descent of the totem follows neither in the paternal nor in the maternal line."[1] Thus among the Kaitish, one of the two most northerly tribes of the Arunta nation, we may detect the first stage in the transition from promiscuous marriage and fortuitous descent of the totems to strict exogamy of the totem clans and strict heredity of the totems in the paternal line. For among the Kaitish "we find the totems divided to a large extent between the two moieties of the tribe, so that it is a very rare thing for a man to marry a woman of the same totem as himself; but there is very little indication of paternal descent so far as the totem is concerned. It may follow either that of the father or that of the mother, but there is no necessity, any more than there is in the Arunta, for it to follow either."[2]

Further to the north, "in the Warramunga, Wulmala, Walpari, Tjingilli, and Umbaia tribes the division of the totems between the two moieties is complete, and, with very few exceptions indeed, the children follow the father. They always pass into a totemic group belonging to the father's moiety, and a man may not marry a woman of his own totem."[3]

Still further to the north, in the Gnanji tribe, the totemic beliefs are fundamentally the same.[4] Among the Gnanji and the Umbaia "the totems are strictly divided up between the two moieties of the tribe. It therefore follows that a woman of the same totem as himself is forbidden as wife to a man of that totem. With only the very rarest exceptions the children follow the father."[5] Lastly, when we pass yet further to the north and reach the Binbinga, Mara, and Anula tribes, of which the two latter inhabit the coast, we find that "the totems are strictly divided up between the moieties or classes, so that a man is forbidden to marry a woman of his own totem. The totems of the children very strictly follow that of the father."[6]

---

[1] *Northern Tribes*, pp. 151 sq. By "totemic group" the writers mean what I call a totemic clan.

[2] *Ibid.* p. 175.

[3] *Ibid.* p. 175, compare pp. 163-166. Of the tribes here mentioned a single one (the Wulmala) lies to the west of the Kaitish; all the others lie to the north.

[4] *Northern Tribes*, p. 176.

[5] *Ibid.* p. 169.

[6] *Ibid.* p. 176, compare pp. 170-173.

It may naturally be asked, How is this strict descent of the totem in the paternal line among these northern tribes and in the maternal line among the Urabunna[1] consistent with the theory held by all these tribes that every individual is the reincarnation of an ancestral spirit which entered into the woman at the moment she first felt her womb quickened and not at all at the moment when she was really impregnated by her husband?[2] On this theory of conception the simplest and probably most primitive view seems to be that of the Arunta and other strictly central tribes that the child takes its totem neither from its father nor from its mother, but from the particular totemic spirit which darted into her at the first inward premonition of maternity, and that whatever the totem of that spirit was, such must of necessity be the totem of the child, without any regard to the totem either of the father or of the mother. How then can this theory be maintained along with strict paternal or maternal descent of the totem? These savages have found an ingenious and theoretically quite consistent and logical explanation of this seeming discrepancy. They say it is true that the child is not the offspring of its father, but simply the reincarnation of an ancestral spirit, but that at the same time only a spirit of the right totem will enter into the mother, and as among the Urabunna the right totem is the mother's, and among the northern tribes it is the father's, it follows quite naturally and necessarily that among the Urabunna the child is always of the same totem as its mother, and that among the northern tribes it is always of the same totem as its father. The disembodied spirit is believed to choose deliberately the woman into whom it will enter and to refuse as a matter of principle to enter into a woman of the wrong totem.[3] Thus "the Gnanji belief is that certain of the spirit individuals belonging to a man's totem follow him about if he travels into a part of the country not associated with his own totem. For example, we were speaking amongst others to a Snake man, close by the side of two water-holes in Gnanji country, one of which was

[1] See above, p. 177. [2] See above, pp. 188 *sqq.*
[3] *Northern Tribes*, pp. 148, 174 *sq.*

associated with, and had been made in, the *alcheringa* by a goshawk and the other by a bee. Certain trees and stones on their banks are supposed to be full of bee and goshawk spirits. The snake belongs to one moiety of the tribe and the bee and goshawk to the other, and the natives told us that the Snake man's wife could not possibly conceive a bee or goshawk child there, because no such spirit would think of going inside the wife of a Snake man. If she were to conceive a child at that spot it would simply mean that a snake spirit had followed the father up from his own place and had gone inside the woman. It is, they say, possible—but the cases in which it occurs are very rare—for a child not to belong to its father's totem, but in such instances it always belongs to one which is associated with his own moiety of the tribe."[1]

In the Warramunga tribe the heredity of the totem is made easier by the local distribution of the two exogamous moieties of the tribe, each with its totem clans, into two separate districts, a northern and a southern, the Kingilli moiety occupying the northern district and the Uluuru moiety the southern district.

Thus the disembodied totemic spirit in choosing a woman from whom to be born again, seldom makes a mistake as to her totem clan, never as to her exogamous moiety (class or phratry); it is always born in the right half of the tribe, though occasionally in the wrong clan. The moiety or half of the tribe is, so to say, a larger target for the spirit to hit than the totemic clan, which is always merely a part, and often only a small part, of the moiety. We need scarcely wonder, therefore, that the spirit in projecting itself into a woman should sometimes miss the smaller mark but never the larger. And its entrance into the right moiety, if not into the right clan, is greatly facilitated in the Warramunga nation or group of tribes by a convenient local arrangement of the moieties and clans. For in each of these tribes the two exogamous moieties occupy separate territories, the Uluuru moiety inhabitating the southern territory, and the Kingilli moiety inhabiting the northern territory, with a more or less sharply marked boundary-line dividing them. And the totemic clans in like manner are locally divided between the two districts, all the clans that belong to the Uluuru moiety being found in the Uluuru district, and all the clans that belong to the Kingilli moiety being found in the Kingilli district. From this geographical distribution of

[1] *Northern Tribes*, pp. 169 *sq*.

the moieties it follows that in any camp within the southern area of the tribe, apart from visitors, all the males will be Uluuru men, who have been born in this part of the country, and their wives will be Kingilli women who were born and lived till puberty in the northern area. The daughters of these Uluuru men and Kingilli women will be Uluuru, since in all these tribes the children belong to the moiety of their father; and when these Uluuru girls are grown up they will quit the land of their birth and take up their permanent home in the north country with their Kingilli husbands. Conversely in any camp of the northern territory all the men are Kingilli who have been born in this part of the country, and their wives are Uluuru women who were born and bred in the south; and the daughters will be Kingilli girls, who at marriage will quit the land of their birth and go away to live with their Uluuru husbands in the south. In this way all the men of the tribe are stationary from birth to death in their native land; and all the women are migratory, spending their early years in their native land and all their later years from marriage onwards in the foreign land of their husbands.[1] If children belonged to the moiety of their mother instead of to that of the father, in other words, if the exogamous divisions descended in the maternal line instead of in the paternal, the foregoing conditions would just be reversed. The women would be stationary all their lives in their native land, and the men would be migratory, living up to the date of their marriage in the land of their birth and ever afterwards in the land of their wives.

It is obvious that this local separation of the exogamous groups, by simplifying the distinction between them, must greatly help the natives to observe correctly their somewhat complex marriage laws. For if we take as an illustration the simplest marriage organisation of an Australian tribe, to wit, the bisection into two exogamous moieties (classes or phratries), and suppose that these two moieties occupy separate territories with a clearly marked boundary-line between them, then every grown man on one side of that line will know that every grown woman on the same side

This local separation of the exogamous groups must help the natives to observe their complex marriage laws, and we may suppose that the

[1] *Northern Tribes*, pp. 28-30.

separation of the line may be his wife. The possibility of confusion and mistake is almost completely avoided, since every adult female whom an adult male may not marry is separated from him and lives in a different country. And this holds good whether children belong to the moiety of their father or to that of their mother, in other words, whether descent is in the male or in the female line. With the arrival of puberty the separation between the persons who may not marry is carried out by sending away either the mature girls or the mature boys, according as descent is paternal or maternal, to the other district, there to find their proper husbands or wives as the case may be. Thus the temptation to break the stringent rule of exogamy, which forbids men and women of the same moiety to marry each other, is to a great extent removed. We may conjecture that when exogamy was first introduced in its simplest form as a bisection of the whole community into two exogamous moieties,[1] the working of the new rule was made easy by segregating the two moieties locally from each other, in order to secure that the men and women who were forbidden to each other should not normally meet. We need not suppose that from the outset the whole country of the tribe was parcelled out into two great areas, of which one was assigned to one half of the tribe, and the other to the other half, as is now done in the Warramunga nation. It would be enough that every local group should split into two sections, each of which should have its own camping and hunting grounds. A trace of this probably older practice seems to survive in the Arunta custom, according to which people of the same exogamous moiety always camp together and apart from the people of the other moiety, the two camps being regularly separated by some natural feature, such as a creek.[2]

separation was made when exogamy was first introduced.

With a segregation of the exogamous groups descent may be traced just as easily in

It is clear that such a segregation of the two exogamous moieties in separate districts would lend itself with equal ease to paternal or to maternal descent of the moiety. If paternal descent were adopted, the men would only have to remain stationary and treat as members of their own moiety all the children born on their side of the boundary-

[1] See above, pp. 162 sq.   [2] *Native Tribes*, pp. 31 sq., 70, 276 sq.

line, of whom all the girls at puberty would cross the line and find husbands on the other side. On the contrary, if maternal descent were adopted, all the women would remain stationary and treat as members of their own moiety all the children to whom they gave birth, of whom all the boys at puberty would cross the line and find wives on the other side. In this way, even if group marriage prevailed, that is, even if all the men of each moiety had free access to all the women of the other moiety, the group fatherhood of all the children would be just as certain as the group motherhood. It would be quite as easy to trace group relationship in the male as in the female line. Hence if, as is probable, the present marital customs of the Australian tribes have been everywhere preceded by group marriage, there is no reason why the practice of transmitting the exogamous prohibitions in the paternal line should not be quite as ancient as the other practice of transmitting them in the maternal line. When any tribe first divided itself into two exogamous and locally separate groups, it could choose for itself with perfect freedom whether the children should belong to the group of the fathers or to the group of the mothers, even although individual fatherhood might be unknown and individual motherhood forgotten.[1] The kinship terms under such a social system would be expressive of group relations, like the terms of the classificatory system of relationship, which in all probability sprang from just such a system of group marriage. But to that point we shall return later on.

the paternal as in the maternal line; hence if we start from group marriage we need not suppose that maternal descent is more primitive than paternal.

Now to revert to the totems. In the Warramunga nation the totemic groups with their local totem centres are sharply divided up between the two geographical areas into which the territory of each tribe is parcelled out. One set of totems is confined to the northern or Kingilli area, and the other set is confined to the southern or Uluuru area.

Further, the exogamy of the totem clans seems to be a direct consequence of their local segregation in separate areas.

---

[1] That with group marriage descent is reckoned just as easily in the paternal as in the maternal line has already been pointed out by Messrs. Spencer and Gillen. See their *Native Tribes*, p. 36 note[1]. As to the possibility of forgetting individual motherhood with a system of group marriage, see Dr. W. H. R. Rivers, "On the Origin of the Classificatory System of Relationships," in *Anthropological Essays presented to Edward Burnett Tylor* (Oxford, 1907), pp. 316-318.

The traditional explanation of this territorial division is that the ancestors of the one set of totems limited their wanderings almost exclusively to the north country, while the ancestors of the other set roamed the south country alone.[1] Whatever may be the origin of this local segregation of the two sets of totems in the Warramunga nation, it is clear that the separation must have materially co-operated to ensure that a child's totem should always belong to its father's tribal moiety, since the child's mother would, under the system described above, always after marriage reside in the territory of her husband's moiety, and could therefore, under normal conditions, only be impregnated by the totemic spirits who had their abode in that territory. We can thus easily understand why the irregular descent of the totems among the tribes of the Arunta nation should be suddenly exchanged for an almost perfectly regular paternal descent of the totems in the adjoining Warramunga nation. The local segregation of the totems in two separate territories supplies the key to the seeming mystery. And the same segregation of the totems equally explains the change from the promiscuous totemic marriages of the Arunta to the exogamous totemic marriages of the Warramunga. Among the Arunta, as we have seen,[2] the totems have no influence whatever on marriage. A man may marry a woman of his own or of another totem just as he pleases, whereas among the Warramunga, as among all the other northern tribes down to the sea, a man never marries a woman of his own totem.[3] The reason for the latter practice appears to be simply that, since in these tribes a man has always to take a wife from another local district (namely, the territory of the other tribal moiety) in which his own totem is not found at all, it is impossible that his wife should be of the same totem as himself. The exogamy of the totemic clans is thus a direct consequence of their local segregation in two separate areas. Whereas among the Arunta, among whom the local segregation of the two moieties is far less fully carried out,[4] it is always possible that a man's wife, though she must always

[1] *Northern Tribes*, pp. 28 sq.
[2] Above, p. 187.
[3] Above, pp. 243, 244.
[4] *Northern Tribes*, pp. 27 sq.; *Native Tribes*, p. 120.

be of the other tribal moiety, may yet be of his own totem clan.

In regard to these totemic marriage customs, as in regard to the descent of the totem and the practice of eating it or abstaining from it, we may ask which is the more primitive? the custom of the central tribes, which allows a man to marry a woman of his own totem? or the custom of the northern tribes, which strictly forbids him to do so? Again, as in regard to the practice of eating the totem, the voice of tradition is altogether in favour of the view that the custom of the central tribes is the more primitive. On this subject Messrs. Spencer and Gillen observe with regard to the Arunta traditions: "One thing appears to be quite clear, and that is, that we see in these early traditions no trace whatever of a time when the totems regulated marriage in the way now characteristic of many of the Australian tribes. There is not a solitary fact which indicates that a man of one totem must marry a woman of another; on the contrary we meet constantly, and only, with groups of men and women of the same totem living together; and, in these early traditions, it appears to be the normal condition for a man to have as wife a woman of the same totem as himself. At the same time there is nothing to show definitely that marital relations were prohibited between individuals of different totems, though, in regard to this, it must be remembered that the instances recorded in the traditions, in which intercourse took place between men and women of different totems, are all concerned with the men of special groups, such as the Achilpa [Wild Cat totem]; further still, it may be pointed out that these were powerful groups who are represented as marching across country, imposing certain rites and ceremonies upon other people with whom they come in contact. The intercourse of the Achilpa [Wild Cat] men with women of other totems may possibly have been simply a right, forcibly exercised by what may be regarded as a conquering group, and may have been subject to no restrictions of any kind. As to the people with whom the Achilpa [Wild Cat people] came into contact, and whom they found settled upon the land, the one most striking and at the same time most interesting fact is,

The custom of the central tribes, which allows a man to marry a woman of his own totem, seems to be more primitive than the custom of the northern tribes, which forbids him to do so; for the native traditions point back to a time when men regularly, if not always, married women of their own totems.

as just stated, that a man was free to marry a woman of his own totem (as he is at the present day), and further still we may even say that the evidence seems to point back to a time when a man always married a woman of his own totem. The references to men and women of one totem always living together in groups would appear to be too frequent and explicit to admit of any other satisfactory explanation. We never meet with an instance of a man living with a woman who was not of his own totem[1] as we surely might expect to do if the form of the traditions were simply due to their having grown up amongst a people with the present organisation of the Arunta tribe. It is only, during these early times, when we come into contact with a group of men marching across strange country that we meet, as we might expect to do, with evidence of men having intercourse with women other than those of their own totem."[2]

Thus the totemic customs of the central tribes are more primitive than those of the northern tribes. With regard to the nature and number of the Central Australian totems we do not possess a complete list of them, but they seem to include almost every material object.

Thus in respect of marriage with a woman of the same totem, as well as in respect of the determination of the totem, and the practice of eating the totemic animal or plant, the central tribes appear to have retained more primitive usages than the northern tribes.

With regard to the nature and number of the totems, they seem to be only limited by the knowledge or imagination of the natives. Messrs. Spencer and Gillen give a long list of those totems with which they personally came in contact, but they expressly warn us that it is far from complete, since to make out a full catalogue would necessitate a residence of years among the various tribes. As to the number and geographical distribution of the totems they observe: "Speaking generally, it may be said that almost every material object gives its name to some totemic group. If an animal, such as a kangaroo or emu, is widely distributed, then we find totemic groups of the same name widely distributed. There is naturally no such thing as a pearl oyster or a dugong totemic group in Central Australia,

---

[1] "That is in connection with those groups with whom the various wandering parties came in contact. The members of all wandering parties appear to have had intercourse more or less freely with women of other totems."

[2] *Native Tribes*, pp. 419 *sq.*

nor is there a porcupine-grass resin group on the shores of the Gulf of Carpentaria. At the same time there is nothing which would really give colour to the theory that the natives of any one district feed exclusively upon any one animal or plant. No native tribe, or group of tribes, for example, feeds exclusively, or even principally, upon kangaroos, emus, grass-seed, acacia-seed, dugongs, crocodiles, lilies, witchetty grubs, or pearl oysters. Every tribe, and every local group of a tribe, utilises as food, and apparently always has done so, every edible thing which grows in its district. The Anula people on the coast of the Gulf of Carpentaria feed upon the kangaroo just in the same way as the Arunta do, but at the same time are not able to feed upon the *munyeru* seed, for the simple reason that it does not grow in their country, and the Arunta are not able to feed upon crocodiles and dugongs, because they do not exist in the central area. In accordance with this distribution of animals and plants, we find a corresponding distribution of totemic groups." [1]

The list of totems which Messrs. Spencer and Gillen themselves met with comprises thirty-one different kinds of mammals, forty-six different kinds of birds, thirty different kinds of snakes (of which one, the *Wollunqua*, is mythical [2]), two different kinds of crocodiles, eighteen different kinds of lizards, three different kinds of turtles, one kind of frog, eight different kinds of fish, twenty-four different kinds of insects (including the honeycomb of two different kinds of bees), one kind of mollusc (the pearl oyster), twenty-two different kinds of plants, sixteen different kinds of inanimate objects, and two different kinds of human beings (Laughing Boys and Full-grown Men). Altogether, Messrs. Spencer and Gillen met with two hundred and four different sorts of totems, of which all but sixteen were animals and plants; and of these one hundred and eighty-eight kinds of plants and animals (among which I reckon the two kinds of human beings) one hundred and fifty-six kinds are eaten.[3] This large preponderance of edible objects in the totems is remarkable. I have already suggested an explanation of it.[4]

In a list of two hundred and four totems given by Spencer and Gillen no less than a hundred and fifty-six are edible animals and plants.

---

[1] *Northern Tribes*, pp. 767 sq.
[2] See above, pp. 144 sq.
[3] *Northern Tribes*, pp. 768-773.
[4] Above, p. 159, where in the note I have inadvertently overstated the number of edible totems.

The inanimate totems are as follows: boomerang, cold weather, darkness, fire, hailstone, lightning, the moon, red ochre, resin, salt water, the Evening Star, stone, the sun, water, whirlwind, and wind. Thus among the totems noticed by Messrs. Spencer and Gillen there is only one artificial object (boomerang). Of these inanimate totems the most widely spread is water, for it gives a name to totemic clans in all of the tribes. Next to water in popularity among inanimate objects come fire and the Evening Star, each of which was found in three tribes. The sun, the moon, stone, and whirlwind were found as totems only in two tribes each; and all the other inanimate objects only in one.[1]

In the Arunta tribe the members of some totem clans have also certain birds as their mates. In the Arunta tribe the members of some totem clans have, in addition to their totems, sundry birds which they regard as their mates. Thus there are certain birds which abound at the season when the witchetty grub is plentiful and are very rarely seen at other times. The natives call them *chantunga* and the Witchetty Grub people consider them as their mates. They think that the birds sing joyously when the witchetty grub is in season, and that they hop about the bushes all day long watching with delight the insect laying its eggs. The Witchetty Grub men will not eat the bird; for they say it would make their heart, or rather their stomach, ache to do so, and they explain their relation to the creature by alleging that in days of old some of the fully-grown witchetty grubs were transformed into the birds.[2]

Similarly men of the kangaroo totem have as mates certain grass parrots (called *atnalchulpira*) which are always hovering about kangaroos in the dry country. The natives think that these parrots bring water to the animals, and that in the olden time they stood in the relation of father's sisters (*uwinna*) to the Kangaroo men. Other little birds which may often be seen playing about on the backs of kangaroos are also mates of the Kangaroo men, who call them *kartwungawunga* and say that the birds are descended from certain ancient Kangaroo men who used always to kill and eat kangaroos, and were finally turned into these fowls.[3]

[1] *Northern Tribes*, p. 773. [2] *Native Tribes*, pp. 447 *sq.*
[3] *Ibid.* p. 448.

The men of the euro totem have also two sets of bird mates. One of them is the rock pigeon, which is supposed to bring water to the euros in the dry and thirsty mountains of this desert land. The natives say that in the days of old these rock pigeons were the fathers' sisters of the Euro men, and brought them water, just as their descendants still do to the euro animals. The other mate of the Euro men is the painted finch (*Emblema picta*), a beautifully coloured little bird, which in the far-off time was a Euro man. These Euro men used to devour so much euro that their bodies quite dripped with the blood of the beasts; and that is the reason why the painted finch is splashed with red.[1]

The Honey-ant people have also two bird mates. One of them is a little bird called *alatipa*, which like the honey-ant itself (*Camponotus inflatus*) only haunts the scrub country, where the mulga bushes grow. The other bird mate is a small "magpie," which the natives call *alpirtaka*. It also frequents the mulga scrub. Both birds were once Honey-ant people.[2]

The people of the water totem have water-fowl for their mates: the Emu people have for their mate the little striated wren (*Amytis striata*), which they call *lirra-lirra*; and two Big Lizard clans (the Echunpa and the Urliwatchera) have two smaller lizards (*Varanus punctatus* and *Varanus gouldii*) for their mates respectively.[3]

All these bird or lizard mates are held in affectionate regard by their human companions of the corresponding totems, though the Witchetty Grub people appear to be alone in refusing to eat their feathered comrades, who hop about and sing so merrily at sight of the witchetty grub laying its eggs. Men of some totems, such as the Wild Cat, the Hakea flower, and the Crow people, seem to have no bird mates of this kind at all.[4]

Besides those birds which are regarded as mates of various existing totem clans, others are thought to represent men of extinct totems. Thus certain little scarlet-breasted birds (*Ephthianura tricolor*) were men of old who painted themselves with red ochre till at last they changed into the

Some birds are thought to represent men sent of extinct totems.

[1] *Native Tribes*, p. 448.
[2] *Ibid.* p. 448.
[3] *Ibid.* pp. 448 *sq.*
[4] *Ibid.* p. 449.

red-fronted birds. Again, the Princess Alexandra parakeet has an odd habit of completely disappearing out of a district for years together and then suddenly reappearing in large numbers. The natives say that a wandering group of Lizard men once met with a group of men who had the Princess Alexandra parakeet for their totem, and that somehow they all changed into the birds. This happened at Simpson's Gap in the Macdonnell Ranges, since when the parakeets have lived far underground and only come up from time to time near their old camping-ground to look for grass-seed.[1]

Associated with the Lizard people is a small bird called *thippathippa*, which hovers about lizards so much that it often guides the natives to the animals.[2] These birds were once men of that totem who came and danced round the Lizard men when they were performing ceremonies. That is why at the great *Engwura* ceremonies they are sometimes still represented by two men who dance around a Lizard man.[3]

§ 4. *Exogamous Classes in the Arunta Nation and Northern Tribes*

The promiscuous marriage of the totem clans, which prevails among the central tribes, is replaced by strict exogamy among the coastal tribes.

We have seen that among the Arunta and other central tribes the totems have no influence on marriage, a man being free to marry a woman of his own or any other totem, but that as we pass northward from the Arunta to the Gulf of Carpentaria it becomes rarer and rarer for a man to marry a woman of his own totem, until, finally, among the coastal tribes such marriages appear never to occur. In other words, the totem clans are strictly exogamous on the coast, but not at all exogamous in the centre, while in the intermediate region between the coast and the centre, the totem clans are in what seems to be a transitional state between strict exogamy on the one side and unrestricted freedom of marriage on the other. Further, we have seen reason to believe that unrestricted freedom of marriage between the totem clans is the older phase of social evolution, which has gradually been replaced by a

[1] *Native Tribes*, p. 449.   [2] *Ibid.* p. 449.
[3] *Ibid.* p. 449.

more and more strict rule of exogamy the further we advance from the central to the coastal tribes.[1]

But though the Arunta and kindred tribes in the centre do not apply the rule of exogamy to their totem clans, they do apply it strictly to other subdivisions of the tribe, namely to the classes and subclasses. As these exogamous subdivisions of the tribe are not totemic, a notice of them in a work dealing with totemism might seem to be impertinent, and so indeed it would be, if our survey of totemism were limited to the system of the Arunta nation. But in point of fact exogamous subdivisions (classes and subclasses) of the same sort exist among the more northerly tribes, and have there carried with them as a direct consequence the exogamy of the totem clans. Hence among these northerly tribes totemism and exogamy, which in origin were probably quite distinct from each other, have become inseparably intertangled, so that it is not possible to consider the one adequately without the other. And since the same association of totemism with exogamy meets us almost universally everywhere else, in other words, since totem clans appear to be exogamous almost everywhere except in Central Australia, it follows that no view of totemism can be complete which does not take account also of exogamy. In Central Australia we are in a peculiarly favourable position for studying these two ancient institutions both in themselves and in their relations to each other, because there the two exist entirely distinct from each other, whereas almost everywhere else they have become fused together in a mass which, until the fortunate discovery of the separate existence of the two components in Central Australia, had baffled all the tests of our anthropological analysis; in other words, it had commonly been supposed that exogamy was an essential part of totemism. So people who had never met with copper and tin might easily mistake bronze for a single pure metal until they discovered it to be an alloy by finding its two components separately.

In the Australian tribes with which we are at present concerned, wherever exogamy of the totem clans prevails, it

Originally exogamy seems to have been entirely independent of totemism.

[1] See above, pp. 242 *sqq.*

appears, as I have indicated, to be a direct consequence of the subdivision of the tribe into two or more exogamous classes; and we may surmise, though we cannot prove, that the same cause has produced the same effect wherever totem clans are exogamous. In other words, we may conjecture that the totem clans existed before the introduction of exogamy, as they apparently did in Central Australia,[1] and that they only became exogamous through the subdivision of the whole tribe into two or more exogamous classes, between which the totem clans were distributed in such a way that the whole of any one totem clan fell within a single exogamous class. In this way, given the existence of the exogamous classes and the inclusion of the totem clans each in one but not more than one of them, the exogamy of the totem clans would follow as a necessary consequence.[2] Hence we may suspect that wherever we find exogamous totem clans we should find, if we could trace their history far enough back, that they had once been grouped in two or more exogamous classes, and that the exogamy of the totem clans was only an effect of that grouping. In many totemic tribes we cannot do this: the clans indeed remain exogamous, but the grouping of them into classes has disappeared, or at least has not been reported in our imperfect records. Still the bisection of a community into two exogamous classes is sufficiently common to suggest not only that it may once have existed in many places where it now no longer survives, but also that it may have been a widespread, if not universal, stage in the evolution of society, forming, indeed, the first step in the advance from sexual promiscuity to individual marriage.[3]

Thus in a treatise on totemism we seem to be justified in paying attention to exogamy even among tribes like the Arunta, where the exogamous prohibitions do not affect the

It would appear that in Australia, and perhaps elsewhere, totemism existed before exogamy, and that the exogamy of the totem clans, where it prevails, is a direct result of the subdivision of the tribe into two or more exogamous classes.

The reason why the Arunta do not apply

---

[1] See above, p. 162.

[2] This has already been pointed out by Messrs. Spencer and Gillen. See their article "Some Remarks on Totemism as applied to Australian Tribes," *Journal of the Anthropological Institute*, xxviii. (1899) p. 279.

[3] This is the view which, so far as concerns the Australian aborigines, has long been held by Dr. A. W. Howitt. See his article "Notes on the Australian Class Systems," *Journal of the Anthropological Institute*, xii. (1883) pp. 496-504.

totem clans. The reason why the Arunta, though they have adopted a system of exogamy, do not apply it to their totem clans has already been indicated.[1] As their totem clans are not hereditary either in the male or in the female line, it would have been useless to make them exogamous, since to do so would not have prevented those marriages of brothers with sisters and of parents with children which it was apparently the intention of exogamy to put an end to. For instance, suppose that with the Arunta totemic system it had been enacted that no Emu man should marry an Emu woman, an Emu man would still have been at liberty to marry his sister, his mother, or his daughter whenever they were, as they often would be, of other totems than the emu. Similarly, given the strict exogamy of the totem clans, an Arunta man of the kangaroo totem might still marry his mother if she were, say, of the gum-tree totem, his sister if she were of the fish totem, and his daughter if she were of the fire totem. And so on through all the totems. Therefore the application of the exogamous rule to the Arunta totem clans would have been powerless to effect the object of exogamy; hence, so far as we know, the Arunta have never attempted to apply it to them. The totems must be hereditary before the application of exogamy to them can prevent the marriage of near relations who are of the same totem. The Arunta and kindred tribes have adopted exogamy, but with their mode of determining the totem they have been obliged to keep their exogamous organisation quite distinct from their totemic.

{*marginal note:* The rule of exogamy to their totem clans is that in their case the application would not effect the purpose which exogamy was instituted to effect, viz. the prevention of the marriage of brothers with sisters and of parents with children.*}

In the Arunta and all the other tribes between them and the Gulf of Carpentaria the whole community is distributed in eight exogamous sections (subclasses or subphratries), although in some of the tribes only four of the exogamous sections have separate names. The tribes in which the nomenclature is thus defective are the Southern Arunta in the south and the Mara and Anula tribes in the extreme north.[2] In the southern part of the Arunta tribe the four names of the exogamous sections (subclasses or

{*marginal note:* All the tribes from the Arunta northward are divided into eight exogamous subclasses.*}

---

[1] Above, pp. 165 sq.   *Northern Tribes*, pp. 74, 96-98.
[2] *Native Tribes*, pp. 70-72; 116-120.

260 TOTEMISM IN CENTRAL AUSTRALIA CHAP.

Names of the exogamous subclasses in the Southern Arunta, with the rules of marriage and descent.

subphratries) are Panunga, Bulthara, Purula, and Kumara. Of these four subclasses the first two (Panunga and Bulthara) form one exogamous moiety (class or phratry) of the tribe; and the other two (Purula and Kumara) form the other exogamous moiety (class or phratry). In camp, for example, as we have seen, the Panunga and Bulthara always encamp together, and are separated from the Purula and Kumara by some natural feature, such as a creek.[1] The marriage system, in broad outline, is this. A Panunga man marries a Purula woman and their children are Bulthara: a Bulthara man marries a Kumara woman and their children are Panunga: a Purula man marries a Panunga woman and their children are Kumara: a Kumara man marries a Bulthara woman and their children are Purula.[2] To put this in tabular form :—

Husband.	Wife.	Children.
Panunga	Purula	Bulthara
Bulthara	Kumara	Panunga
Purula	Panunga	Kumara
Kumara	Bulthara	Purula

The rule of descent is indirect in the male line, since children belong to their father's class, but not to his subclass.

Hence it appears that a man always marries a woman of a different subclass (subphratry) from his own, and that the children belong to the subclass neither of their father nor of their mother, but to the other subclass of their father's moiety. For example, children of a Panunga man are Bulthara, which is the complementary or twin subclass of their father's subclass, since the two subclasses Panunga and Bulthara together make up one moiety of the tribe. Similarly the children of Purula men are Kumara, which is the complementary or twin subclass of their father's subclass, since the two subclasses Purula and Kumara together make up one moiety of the tribe. Thus we have here what I have called indirect male descent,[3] since the children belong to their father's moiety (class) of the tribe, though not to his subclass (subphratry). It seems evident that such a rule of descent, at once so complex and so regular, cannot be a result of accident, but must have been deliberately devised

[1] *Native Tribes*, p. 70; *Northern Tribes*, p. 96. See above, p. 248.
[2] *Native Tribes*, p. 70.
[3] Above, p. 68.

EXOGAMOUS CLASSES OF THE ARUNTA, ETC.

in order to effect a definite purpose. What that purpose was, I have already indicated.[1] It was to prevent the marriage of parents with children, and that object was attained effectually by arranging that children should always belong to a subclass into which neither their father nor their mother might marry.[2] If that simple rule was observed, the marriage of parents with children was henceforth impossible.

So far it would seem as if the marriage system of the Southern Arunta conformed to that common type of social organisation in Australia, whereby the whole tribe is divided into two exogamous moieties (classes), and each of the two moieties is again subdivided into two exogamous subclasses,[3] so that the total number of subclasses in the tribe is four. But a closer inspection of the system shews that each of the four nominal subclasses of the Southern Arunta really comprises two separate exogamous subclasses, so that the total number of subclasses in that part of the tribe is not four but eight. The two separate subclasses thus comprised under each of the four nominal subclasses Panunga, Bulthara, Purula, and Kumara, have no native names, so that we must indicate them merely by symbols, such as Panunga *a* and Panunga *b*, Bulthara *a* and Bulthara *b*, Purula *a* and Purula *b*, Kumara *a* and Kumara *b*.[4]

Adopting these symbols for the eight actual, though not nominal, subclasses of the Southern Arunta, we may tabulate as follows the rules of marriage and descent in this part of the tribe :—[5]

Though the subclasses of the Southern Arunta are nominally four, they are actually eight in number.

Table shewing the rules of marriage and descent in the Southern Arunta.

---

[1] Above, p. 163.
[2] That the effect and intention of this rule of descent were such as I have said was pointed out long ago by Dr. A. W. Howitt. See his article, "Notes on the Australian Class Systems," *Journal of the Anthropological Institute*, xii. (1883) pp. 498 *sq.*, 504. When I wrote the article, "The Beginnings of Totemism" (reprinted above, see p. 163), this passage in Dr. Howitt's writings had escaped my memory as well as the memory of its writer. See A. W. Howitt, *The Native Tribes of South-East Australia*, pp. 284-286; my note, "The Australian Marriage Laws," *Man*, February 1908, pp. 21 *sq.*; and my article, "Howitt and Fison," *Folk-lore*, xx. (1909) pp. 166 *sq.*
[3] See above, pp. 61 *sq.* Following the example of Dr. Howitt, I now use the terms class and subclass as equivalent and preferable to phratry and subphratry.
[4] *Native Tribes*, p. 71; *Northern Tribes*, p. 97.
[5] Compare *Native Tribes*, p. 71; *Northern Tribes*, pp. 97, 118.

SOUTHERN ARUNTA TRIBE

	Husband.	Wife.	Children.
Class or Moiety A	Panunga *a* Panunga *b*	Purula *a* Purula *b*	Bulthara *b* Bulthara *a*
	Bulthara *a* Bulthara *b*	Kumara *a* Kumara *b*	Panunga *b* Panunga *a*
Class or Moiety B	Purula *a* Purula *b*	Panunga *a* Panunga *b*	Kumara *a* Kumara *b*
	Kumara *a* Kumara *b*	Bulthara *a* Bulthara *b*	Purula *a* Purula *b*

Names of the eight exogamous subclasses in the Northern Arunta.

In the northern part of the Arunta tribe precisely the same rules of marriage and descent prevail, but in practice they are facilitated by the adoption of eight distinct names for the eight subclasses. The following are the names of the eight subclasses, arranged under the two classes or moieties to which they respectively belong. It will be observed that the four original names (Panunga, Bulthara, Purula, Kumara) are retained and four new names (Uknaria, Appungerta, Ungalla, and Umbitchana) have been adopted.[1]

Class or Moiety A	Panunga Uknaria	Class or Moiety B	Purula Ungalla
	Bulthara Appungerta		Kumara Umbitchana

Thus it appears that Panunga *b* of the Southern Arunta is replaced by Uknaria; Bulthara *b* by Appungerta; Purula *b* by Ungalla; and Kumara *b* by Umbitchana.

Rules of marriage and descent in the Northern Arunta.

Substituting these four new names in the table of marriage and descent given above for the Southern Arunta, we get the following as the scheme of marriage and descent in the northern part of the tribe:—

[1] *Native Tribes*, p. 72; *Northern Tribes*, pp. 77, 90.

EXOGAMOUS CLASSES OF THE ARUNTA, ETC.

NORTHERN ARUNTA TRIBE

	Husband.	Wife.	Children.
Class or Moiety A	{ Panunga Uknaria { Bulthara Appungerta	Purula Ungalla Kumara Umbitchana	Appungerta Bulthara Uknaria Panunga
Class or Moiety B	{ Purula Ungalla { Kumara Umbitchana	Panunga Uknaria Bulthara Appungerta	Kumara Umbitchana Purula Ungalla

The same relationships may be tabulated in a more condensed form as follows :—

Parents.		Children.	
1	2	3	4
Panunga Uknaria Bulthara Appungerta	Purula Ungalla Kumara Umbitchana	Appungerta Bulthara Uknaria Panunga	Kumara Umbitchana Purula Ungalla

Here in each vertical column the four subclasses constituting a moiety (class) of the tribe are grouped together. In columns 1 and 2 the intermarrying subclasses are arranged on the same horizontal line; in columns 3 and 4 the subclasses of the children are arranged on the same horizontal line as their parents, column 3 containing the children born of male 1 and female 2, and column 4 containing the children born of male 2 and female 1. Thus to take examples, a Panunga man (column 1) marries a Purula woman (column 2) and the children are Appungerta (column 3). A Purula man (column 2) marries a Panunga woman (column 1) and the children are Kumara (column 4). In the same way an Uknaria man marries an Ungalla woman and the children are Bulthara: an Ungalla man marries an Uknaria woman

Explanation of the table.

and the children are Umbitchana. And similarly with the other subclasses.¹

Four names of the subclasses have been adopted in recent times by the Arunta from the Ilpirra, and the use of them is now spreading southward.

With regard to the four new names (Uknaria, Appungerta, Ungalla, Umbitchana) of the subclasses in the Northern Arunta, it is very important to observe that they have been adopted in recent times by the Arunta from the Ilpirra tribe which adjoins them on the north, and that the use of them is at the present time spreading southwards.² This agrees with the evidence of many other facts,³ all of which tend to shew that, to use a meteorological metaphor, in the tribes we are now considering the centre of social disturbance lies in the north, and that the waves of social change are propagated from there southward and not in the reverse direction. The ultimate source of the disturbance is the sea, which by increasing the rainfall on the coast increases the food supply of the tribes, and thereby facilitates their advance in culture, since every check imposed on the food supply of a community is an impediment to progress.⁴

Thus the natives can work their marriage system without names for the exogamous divisions. We need not therefore suppose that where no names are known for the exogamous divisions, the names must once have existed and been forgotten.

It is very significant that the Southern Arunta should have four exogamous subclasses for which they have as yet no distinctive names, while their brethren in the north have only recently borrowed names for these subclasses from a neighbouring tribe. This seems to shew that the natives are quite able to work their marriage system without names for their exogamous divisions. Now throughout the whole of the Arunta tribe, both north and south, there are no names for the two exogamous moieties (classes) under which the subclasses are grouped. It appears to be commonly supposed that names for the two moieties (classes) must formerly have existed and have afterwards been forgotten, from which again it has been inferred that the marriage system of the Arunta is late and decadent. The analogy of the subclasses points to the opposite conclusion, namely, that the marriage system of the Arunta is developing, not decaying; for if four of the eight subclasses among them are only receiving (not losing) names at the present time and in some places are still nameless, we seem bound in consistency to suppose

---

¹ *Native Tribes*, pp. 72 *sq.*; *Northern Tribes*, p. 77.
² *Native Tribes*, p. 72.
³ See above, pp. 227 *sqq.*
⁴ See above, pp. 167 *sqq.*

EXOGAMOUS CLASSES OF THE ARUNTA, ETC.

that similarly the two classes or moieties have not lost their names, but on the contrary have not yet received them. At least this is more logical than, admitting that the subclasses are gaining their names, to argue that the classes have lost them.

The inference that the two classes or moieties of the Arunta have never yet received names but might one day do so if the natives were left to themselves, is confirmed by the observation that most of the tribes to the north of the Arunta nation who possess complete names for the eight subclasses possess also names for the two classes or moieties. But if the names for the as yet nameless subclasses are at present spreading southward among the Arunta, it is reasonable to suppose that names for their as yet nameless classes or moieties might in time reach them from the same direction.

Immediately to the north of the Arunta nation lies the Warramunga nation, which possesses a complete nomenclature for its two exogamous classes or moieties and its eight subclasses. In the Warramunga, Walpari, and Wulmala tribes of this nation the names for the two classes or moieties are Uluuru and Kingilli; in the Worgaia tribe they are Uluuru and Biingaru; in the Tjingilli they are Willitji and Liaritji; in the Umbaia and Gnanji they are Illitji and Liaritji; in the Bingongina tribe they are Wiliuku and Liaraku.[1] With regard to the names of the subclasses Messrs. Spencer and Gillen observe: "We have been quite unable to discover the meaning of these names in any of the central tribes, or to obtain the slightest clue as to their origin, which must date very far back. They do not appear to be associated in any way with the totemic system."[2]

The following tables exhibit the classes and subclasses in the various tribes of the Warramunga nation together with the rules of marriage and descent. The arrangement is the same as in the table exhibiting concisely the similar subdivisions, marriages, and descents in the Arunta tribe.[3] That is to say, in each vertical column the four subclasses constituting one of the two classes (moieties) of the tribe are grouped together. In columns 1 and 2 the intermarrying

Names of the exogamous classes and subclasses in the Warramunga nation.

Tables exhibiting the rules of marriage and descent in the various tribes of the Warramunga nation.

[1] *Northern Tribes*, p. 102. In *Northern Tribes*, p. 101, the class names of the Bingongina are given, probably by mistake, as Uluuru and Liaritji.

[2] *Ibid.* p. 98.

[3] See above, p. 263.

subclasses are arranged on the same horizontal line; in columns 3 and 4 the subclasses of the children are arranged on the same horizontal line as their parents, column 3 containing the children born of male 1 and female 2, and column 4 containing the children born of male 2 and female 1. Thus to take examples, in the first table a Thapanunga man (column 1) marries a Tjupila woman (column 2) and their children are Thapungarti (column 3). A Tjupila man (column 2) marries a Thapanunga woman (column 1) and their children are Thakomara (column 4). Similarly, a Tjunguri man marries a Thungalla woman and their children are Tjapeltjeri. A Thungalla man marries a Tjunguri woman and their children are Tjambin. And so on with all the other subclasses of all the tribes in the following tables.[1]

WARRAMUNGA, WALPARI, AND WULMALA TRIBES

Parents.		Children.	
1	2	3	4
Uluuru Thapanunga Tjunguri Tjapeltjeri Thapungarti	*Kingilli* Tjupila Thungalla Thakomara Tjambin	*Uluuru* Thapungarti Tjapeltjeri Tjunguri Thapanunga	*Kingilli* Thakomara Tjambin Tjupila Thungalla

TJINGILLI TRIBE

Parents.		Children.	
1	2	3	4
Willitji Thamininja Tjimininja Thalaringinja Thungarininta	*Liaritji* Tjurulinginja Thungallininja Thamaringinja Tjapatjinginja	*Willitji* Thungarininta Thalaringinja Tjimininja Thamininja	*Liaritji* Thamaringinja Tjapatjinginja Tjurulinginja Thungallininja

[1] *Northern Tribes*, pp. 99-101.

EXOGAMOUS CLASSES OF THE ARUNTA, ETC. 267

UMBAIA TRIBE

Parents.		Children.	
1	2	3	4
Illitji Tjinum Tjulum Paliarinji Pungarinji	*Liaritji* Tjurulum Thungallum Tjamerum Yakomari	*Illitji* Pungarinji Paliarinji Tjulum Tjinum	*Liaritji* Tjamerum Yakomari Tjurulum Thungallum

GNANJI TRIBE

Parents.		Children.	
1	2	3	4
Illitji Uanaku Tjulantjuka Paliarinja Pungarinji	*Liaritji* Uralaku Thungallaku Tjamuraku Yakomari	*Illitji* Pungarinji Paliarinja Tjulantjuka Uanaku	*Liaritji* Tjamuraku Yakomari Uralaku Thungallaku

BINGONGINA TRIBE

Parents.		Children.	
1	2	3	4
Wiliuku Thama Tjimita Thalirri Thungari	*Liaraku* Tjurla Thungalla Tjimara Tjambitjina	*Wiliuku* Thungari Thalirri Tjimita Thama	*Liaraku* Tjimara Tjambitjina Tjurla Thungalla

WORGAIA TRIBE

	Parents.		Children.
1	2	3	4
Uluuru Pungarinju Biliarinthu	*Büngaru* Ikamaru Tjamerameru	*Uluuru* Wairgu Blaingu	*Büngaru* Kingelu Warrithu
Blaingu Wairgu	Kingelu Warrithu	Biliarinthu Pungarinju	Ikamaru Tjamerameru

Different names for the men and women of the subclasses.

In all but the last of the tribes whose marriage system is represented in the foregoing tables the women of a subclass bear a different name from the men. For example, in the Warramunga, Walpari, and Wulmala tribes the men of one subclass are called Thapanunga and the women of that subclass are called Napanunga; the men of another subclass are called Thapungarti and the women Napungerta; the men of another subclass are called Thungalla and the women Nungalla; the men of another subclass are called Thakomara and the women Nakomara; the men of another subclass are called Tjambin and the women Nambin. Generally, as in these examples, the feminine names are clearly derivatives from the masculine; but in some cases the two names appear to be distinct. For instance, in the Warramunga, Walpari, and Wulmala tribes the men of one subclass are called Tjupila and the women Naralu.[1] The existence of distinct names for the women of the subclasses adds considerably to the complexity of the nomenclature without modifying the system; hence for the sake of simplicity and clearness I have omitted the feminine names from the tables.

Names of the exogamous subclasses in the Binbinga nation, together with the

To the north of the Warramunga nation lies the Binbinga nation, of which the Binbinga tribe may serve as a type. Its social organisation resembles that of the Arunta and Warramunga nations. Like the Arunta, but unlike the Warramunga, it has no names for its two classes (moieties), whether it has lost them or has never had them. Its sub-

[1] *Northern Tribes*, pp. 100-102.

classes, with the rules of marriage and descent within them, are exhibited in the following table,[1] which is arranged on the same principles as the foregoing tables; that is to say, parents and children are arranged in the same horizontal line, the children of men of column 1 and women of column 2 being contained in column 3, while the children of men of column 2 and women of column 1 are contained in column 4. For example, a Tjuanaku man marries a Tjurulum woman and their children are Pugarinji: a Tjurulum man marries a Tjuanaku woman and their children Tjamerum. And so with the rest.

rules of marriage and descent.

THE BINBINGA TRIBE

Parents.		Children.	
1	2	3	4
Moiety A Tjuanaku Tjulantjuka	*Moiety B* Tjurulum Thungallum	*Moiety A* Pugarinji Paliarinji	*Moiety B* Tjamerum Yakomari
Paliarinji Pungarinji	Tjamerum Yakomari	Tjulantjuka Tjuanaku	Tjurulum Thungallum

In this tribe also the women of each subclass have a name distinct from that of the men. Thus in one subclass the men are called Paliarinji and the women Paliarina; in another the men are Pungarinji and the women Pungarina; in another the men are called Tjurulum and the women Nurulum; in another the men are called Thungallum and the women Nungallum; in another the men are called Tjamerum and the women Niamerum; and in another the men are called Yakomari and the women Yakomarina. In all these six cases the feminine names are clearly derived from, or at any rate akin to, the masculine names. But in the remaining two subclasses the masculine and feminine names appear to be quite distinct. For in one of these two subclasses the men are called Tjuanaku and the women Niriuma; in the other the men are called Tjulantjuka and the women Nurlum.[2]

Different names for the men and women of the subclasses.

[1] *Northern Tribes*, p. 111.   [2] *Ibid.*

Names of the classes and subclasses in the Mara and Anula tribes, together with the rules of marriage and descent.

To the north of the Binbinga nation lie the Mara and Anula tribes on the coast of the Gulf of Carpentaria. At first sight these tribes, like the Southern Arunta, appear to be divided, not like the rest, into eight, but only into four exogamous subclasses, since they have only names for four, not for eight, of these subclasses. But in practice, just as among the Southern Arunta, these four nominal subclasses are split each into two, so that the total number of subclasses is really eight, and the rules of marriage and descent are just the same as in all the tribes from the Arunta northward. In the Mara tribe the four names of the subclasses are Murungun, Mumbali, Purdal, and Kuial, of which the two former compose one class or moiety of the tribe and the two latter compose the other. The names of these two classes or moieties are Urku and Ua, and the subclasses, are arranged under them as follows :—[1]

URKU { Murungun.
        Mumbali.

UA { Purdal.
     Kuial.

In the following table [2] the rules of marriage and descent are exhibited on the principles adopted in the preceding tables, and for the sake of clearness the two actual subclasses into which each nominal subclass falls are distinguished by the letters *a* and *b*. For example, a Murungun *a* man marries a Purdal *a* woman and the children are Murungun *b*; a Purdal *a* man marries a Murungun *a* woman and the children are Purdal *b*.

MARA TRIBE

Parents.		Children.	
1	2	3	4
Urku Murungun *a* Mumbali *a* Mumbali *b* Murungun *b*	*Ua* Purdal *a* Kuial *a* Purdal *b* Kuial *b*	*Urku* Murungun *b* Mumbali *b* Mumbali *a* Murungun *a*	*Ua* Purdal *b* Kuial *b* Purdal *a* Kuial *a*

[1] *Northern Tribes*, pp. 116 *sq.*, 118 *sq.* [2] *Northern Tribes*, pp. 120, 124.

Lastly, in the Anula tribe the four nominal subclasses are Awukaria, Roumburia, Urtalia, and Wialia, of which the two former compose one class or moiety of the tribe and the two latter compose the other. In this tribe no names for the two classes or moieties exist, whether it be that they have not yet been adopted or have been lost. The rules of marriage and descent are exhibited as before in the following table,[1] in which again for the sake of clearness the two actual subclasses into which each nominal subclass is divided are distinguished by the letters *a* and *b*.

THE ANULA TRIBE

Parents.		Children.	
1	2	3	4
Moiety A Awukaria *a* Roumburia *a*	*Moiety B* Urtalia *a* Wialia *a*	*Moiety A* Awukaria *b* Roumburia *b*	*Moiety B* Urtalia *b* Wialia *b*
Roumburia *b* Awukaria *b*	Urtalia *b* Wialia *b*	Roumburia *a* Awukaria *a*	Urtalia *a* Wialia *a*

Neither in the Mara nor in the Anula tribe are there distinct names for the men and women of a subclass.

From the preceding survey it appears that in all the tribes from the Arunta at the centre of Australia to the Mara and Anula on the Gulf of Carpentaria the system of marriage and descent is, under different names, one and the same. Every tribe is divided into two exogamous classes or moieties and into eight actual exogamous subclasses; and in every tribe descent, so far as the rules of marriage are concerned, is in the male line, since a child always belongs to its father's class or moiety, though never to his subclass.

All the tribes from the Arunta northwards have the same social organisation.

§ 5. *On the Exogamous Organisation of Australian Tribes*

We have now briefly surveyed the marriage systems of the Australian tribes which occupy a vast area of territory

[1] *Northern Tribes*, pp. 118-120.

272 TOTEMISM IN CENTRAL AUSTRALIA CHAP.

The marriage system of the Australian tribes in general.

from the Urabunna near Lake Eyre in the south to the Anula and Mara on the Gulf of Carpentaria in the north. We have seen that the systems conform to one or other of two very different types, the Urabunna being divided into two exogamous classes with female descent, while all the other tribes are divided into eight exogamous classes (subclasses) with male descent. Before we proceed further with our survey of Australian totemism and exogamy, it may be well to pause and consider generally these remarkable exogamous divisions in order if possible to form some idea of their origin and meaning. For such an idea, if we can attain to it, will be very useful in clarifying our conceptions of the whole complex system, and so enabling us to fit the many details, which are still to follow, into their proper places.

The great majority of Australian tribes are organised in two, four, or eight exogamous classes.

Leaving out of sight, as we may conveniently do for the present, exceptional or abnormal tribes, the great majority of Australian tribes about whom we possess accurate information are organised for purposes of marriage on one of three patterns, which may be called respectively the two-class system, the four-class system, and the eight-class system; that is, they are divided into two, four, or eight exogamous classes or subclasses, the members of each of which are bound to seek their husbands or wives in a class or subclass different from their own. Thus far in our survey of the central tribes we have met with examples only of the two extremes of this series, namely, with the two-class system and the eight-class system. Some, indeed, of the tribes, as we have seen, simulate the four-class system by having names for only four out of their eight subclasses. But for examples of a true four-class system we must go to other parts of Australia. Thus in Eastern Australia the large group of tribes known as the Kamilaroi is organised in four exogamous subclasses, and so is another group of tribes of which the Kaiabara may be taken as typical; but whereas descent in the Kamilaroi is maternal, descent in the Kaiabara is paternal.[1] Interpolating such four-class systems between the two-class system and the eight-class system we obtain a regular series into which every normally organised Australian tribe

[1] See below, pp. 396 *sqq.*, 442 *sqq.*

will be found to fall. The systems increase in complexity as we pass from one end of the series to the other, beginning with the two-class system, which is the simplest, and ending with the eight-class system, which is the most complex.

In contemplating the series the first thing that strikes us is that the number of exogamous classes in a normal Australian tribe is always either two or a multiple of two; it is never an odd number. This raises a presumption that the organisation throughout is artificial and has been produced by successive and deliberate dichotomies of a previously undivided community, which was first divided into two, then in some cases by a second dichotomy into four, and lastly in other cases by a third dichotomy into eight. For had the origin of these exogamous divisions within a tribe been accidental, it is very unlikely that their number in all normal tribes should be either two or a multiple of two, never an odd number nor an even number indivisible by two. But if for the sake of argument we may assume for a moment that the organisation of Australian tribes in exogamous classes has been purposeful, not fortuitous, we must ask, What was the purpose which these savages had in view when they thus subdivided themselves and thereby imposed, with each successive dichotomy, ever-increasing restrictions on the freedom of marriage? In order to discover the intention of the dichotomies the first step is to ascertain their effect; for if they are artificial, as they appear to be, they must have been devised to produce a certain effect, and if we can find out the effect which they do actually produce we may legitimately argue back from it to the intention of the founders. The argument, though legitimate, is not by itself conclusive, since in human affairs it too often happens that the effects which an institution really brings about are by no means those which it was designed to accomplish. Still in such enquiries the discovery of effects is essential to the ascertainment of motives, and furnishes a valuable, though not infallible, clew to guide us to the object of our search. With this caution let us try to see what are the actual results of dividing a community into two, four, and eight exogamous classes

The regular division of a tribe into two or multiples of two suggests that the division is artificial and intentional. In order to discover its intention, we must ask, What is its effect?

of the Australian pattern with the concomitant rules of descent.

<small>The effect of the successive subdivision into two, four, and eight, with the characteristic rules of descent, is to bar the marriage of brothers with sisters, of parents with children, and of a man's children with his sister's children.</small>

If we may assume that in these successive subdivisions all the children of the same parents are arranged in the same exogamous class, then the effect of dividing a community into two exogamous classes is to prevent brothers from marrying their sisters; the effect of dividing a community into four exogamous classes, with the characteristic rule of descent, is to prevent parents from marrying their children; and the effect of dividing a community into eight exogamous classes, with the characteristic rule of descent, is to prevent a man's children from marrying his sister's children, in other words, it is to prevent the marriage of some, though not all, of those whom we call first cousins. That these are the actual effects of the successive dichotomies will appear from the following explanations and examples.

<small>The division into two classes bars the marriage of brothers with sisters, but not all marriages of parents with children.</small>

Let us begin with the simplest system of the series, that is, with the bisection of the community into two exogamous classes, which we will call A and B. On this system every member of the class A, whether male or female, is forbidden to marry a member of that class and is bound, if he or she marries at all, to marry only a member of the class B. Conversely every member of the class B, whether male or female, is forbidden to marry a member of that class and is bound, if he or she marries at all, to marry only a member of the class A. Further, so far as the organisation in classes is concerned, any member of the class A is free to marry any member of class B, and any member of class B is free to marry any member of class A. Hence if all the children of the same parents are arranged, as we have assumed them to be, in the same exogamous class, it follows that under the two-class system no brother may marry his sister; for if he is an A, his sisters are also As, and therefore forbidden to him; and if he is a B, they are also Bs, and therefore forbidden to him; since according to the fundamental law of the community a married couple must always be composed of an A and a B, never of an A and an A, or of a B and a B. But what happens with regard to the children under this system? If maternal descent is the rule, then the children of a male A and a female B are Bs, and the children of a male B and a female A are As. Conversely if paternal descent prevails, the children of a male A and a female B are As, and the children of a male B and a female A are Bs. Hence if any A may marry any B, it will follow that with maternal descent the two-class system permits a father to marry his daughter, and that with male descent it permits a mother to marry her son. For with maternal descent the daughter of a man A is a B and therefore marriageable to him; and with paternal descent the son of a woman A is a B and therefore marriageable to her. On the other hand it is to be observed that the two-class system with paternal descent prevents a man from marrying his daughter, since she is of his own class; and that the two-class system with maternal descent prevents a woman from marrying her son, since he is of her own class. Thus the two-class system with paternal or maternal descent prevents some, but not all, cases of marriage between a parent and a child.

Let us next examine the four-class system with its characteristic rule of descent. Under this system the two exogamous classes A and B are each subdivided into two exogamous subclasses, which we will call respectively a^1, a^2, and b^1, b^2. Under this system the rule of the two-class system still prevails so far that an A must still marry a B, but instead of being free to marry any B, his or her choice is now restricted to one half of the Bs; and conversely while a B is still bound to marry an A, his or her choice is now restricted to one half of the As. Thus Aa^1 is bound to marry Bb^1, but is forbidden to marry Bb^2; and Aa^2 is bound to marry Bb^2, but is forbidden to marry Bb^1. Hence under the four-class system, just as under the two-class system, a brother cannot marry his sister, since if he, for example, is Aa^1, she will be Aa^1 also and therefore forbidden to him, because his wife must be Bb^1. But what happens with regard to the children? Here we are brought face to face with a most remarkable difference between the two-class system and the four-class system. Whereas under the two-class system, children always belong to the class either of their father or of their mother, under the four-class system

The division into four exogamous classes, with the characteristic rule of descent, bars the marriage both of brothers with sisters and of parents with children.

children never belong to the subclass of their father or of their mother, but always to a subclass which differs both from the subclass of their father and from the subclass of their mother. From this it at once follows that under the four-class system, contrary to what may happen under the two-class system, a father may never marry his daughter and a mother may never marry her son, whether descent be reckoned in the maternal or in the paternal line. For example, if maternal descent is the rule, then the children of a man Aa^1 and a woman Bb^1 are Bb^2, that is, they belong to their mother's class B but not to her subclass b^1; hence the man Aa^1 may not marry his daughter Bb^2, since she is not of the subclass b^1, from which alone he may take a wife. And the woman Bb^1 may not marry her son Bb^2, because he is of her own class B. Conversely, if paternal descent is the rule, then the children of a man Aa^1 and a woman Bb^1 are Aa^2, that is, they belong to their father's class A but not to his subclass a^1; hence the woman Bb^1 may not marry her son Aa^2, since he is not of the subclass a^1, in which alone she may find a husband. And the man Aa^1 may not marry his daughter Aa^2, because she is of his own class A. Thus, whether the rule of descent be maternal or paternal, the four-class system absolutely prevents the marriage of parents with children as well as of brothers with sisters.

But the division into four exogamous classes does not bar the marriage of a man's children with his sister's children.

But let us carry the analysis a step lower down and ask, How does the four-class system affect the third generation? does it prevent the marriage of the children of a brother with the children of his sister? The answer is that it does not. Let us take a man Aa^1 and his sister, who is necessarily also Aa^1, and let us suppose that the rule of descent is maternal. Then the wife of the brother Aa^1 will be a woman Bb^1 and the children will be Bb^2: and the husband of the sister Aa^1 will be Bb^1 and her children will be Aa^2. Hence the children Bb^2 of the brother Aa^1 will be marriageable with the children Aa^2 of his sister Aa^1, because Aa^2 and Bb^2 are intermarrying classes. Conversely, if the rule of descent is paternal, the children of the brother Aa^1 will be Aa^2 and the children of his sister Aa^1 will be Bb^2; hence the children Aa^2 of the brother Aa^1 will be marriageable with the children Bb^2 of his sister Aa^1, for the same reason as before, because Aa^2 and Bb^2 are intermarrying classes. Thus whether the rule of descent be maternal or paternal, the four-class system presents no obstacle to the marriage of the children of a brother with the children of a sister. In other words, under the four-class system first cousins are free to marry each other in the particular case in which they are children of a brother and a sister; but they are not free to marry in the case in which they are children either of two brothers or of two sisters, since the children of two brothers or of two sisters necessarily belong to the same exagamous division and are therefore forbidden to each other.

Lastly, let us consider the eight-class system with its characteristic rule of descent. An examination of it, as exhibited in the preceding tables,[1] will easily satisfy us that it, like the four-class system, prevents the marriage first of brothers with sisters, and, second, of parents with children; and if we trace its effect on the third generation we shall see that it, unlike the four-class system, prevents the marriage of a man's children with the children of his sister, and that too whether descent be reckoned in the maternal or the paternal line.[2] Take, for example, the Warramunga tribe, which has the eight-class system and male descent, and look at the table of marriage and descent, which for the convenience of the reader I will here repeat:— *The division into eight exogamous classes bars the marriage of brothers with sisters, of parents with children, and of a man's children with his sister's children.*

Parents.		Children.	
1	2	3	4
Uluuru Thapanunga Tjunguri	*Kingilli* Tjupila Thungalla	*Uluuru* Thapungarti Tjapeltjeri	*Kingilli* Thakomara Tjambin
Tjapeltjeri Thapungarti	Thakomara Tjambin	Tjunguri Thapanunga	Tjupila Thungalla

[1] See above, pp. 262 *sqq.*
[2] That the eight-class system prevents the marriage of a man's children with his sister's children has already been pointed out by Messrs. Spencer and Gillen. See their *Northern Tribes*, p. 117. The same observation had previously been made by Mr. E. Crawley (*The Mystic Rose*, London, 1902, p. 473).

The first two vertical columns represent the intermarrying subclasses, the second two represent the offspring of these marriages, column 3 containing the children of men 1 and women 2, and column 4 containing the children of men 2 and women 1. For example, a Thapanunga man marries a Tjupila woman and their children are Thapungarti: a Tjupila man marries a Thapanunga woman and their children are Thakomara. And similarly with the rest. Now in the first place it is clear from an inspection of the table that a man may not marry his sister; for if he, for example, is a Thapanunga, his sister must be a Thapanunga too, and therefore forbidden to him, since his wife must be a Tjupila. In the second place it is clear that a man may not marry his daughter; for if he, for example, is a Thapanunga, his daughter will be a Thapungarti, not a Tjupila, whom alone he may marry. Again, it is clear that a woman may not marry her son; for if she is, for example, a Tjupila, her son will be a Thapungarti, and not a Thapanunga, whom alone she may marry. In the third place if by the help of the table we trace the descent to the third generation we shall find that a man's children may not marry his sister's children. Take, for example, a Thapanunga man and his sister, who must of course be a Thapanunga also. Then the wife of this Thapanunga man will be a Tjupila woman, and their children will be Thapungarti. The husband of Thapanunga's sister will be a Tjupila man and their children will be Thakomara. Hence the Thapungarti children of the brother may not marry the Thakomara children of his sister, since the subclasses Thapungarti and Thakomara are not marriageable with each other, Thapungarti marrying only with Tjambin, and Thakomara marrying only with Tjapeltjeri.

The bar is equally effective when the descent is maternal. In the Warramunga tribe, as indeed in all the eight-class tribes known to us, the rule of descent is paternal; but with a rule of maternal descent the bars to marriage, whether of brothers with sisters, or of parents with children, or of the children of a brother with the children of his sister, would under the eight-class system be just the same. With the foregoing explanations and the help of a table the reader could easily trace this out for himself. If, for example, the Warramunga had maternal descent instead of paternal, it would be necessary to transpose columns 3 and 4 in the table; for with maternal descent the children of Uluuru men would be Kingilli instead of Uluuru, and the children of Uluuru women would be Uluuru instead of Kingilli. In that case the children of a Thapanunga man would be Thakomara and the children of his Thapanunga sister would be Thapungarti; therefore the children of this man and of his sister would still be prevented from marrying each other, since they would belong to subclasses (Thakomara and Thapungarti) which do not intermarry.

To sum up. The effect of the two-class system is to bar the marriage of brothers with sisters, but not in all cases the marriage of parents with children, nor the marriage of a man's children with his sister's children. The effect of the four-class system is to bar the marriage of brothers with sisters and of parents with children in every case, but not the marriage of a man's children with his sister's children. The effect of the eight-class system is to bar the marriage of brothers with sisters, of parents with children, and of a man's children with his sister's children. The result of each successive dichotomy is thus to strike out another class of relations from the list of persons with whom marriage may be contracted: it is to add one more to the list of prohibited degrees. *The effect of each successive subdivision is to add another to the list of prohibited degrees.*

But is the effect which these successive segmentations actually produce the effect which they were intended to produce? I think we may safely conclude that it is. For the aborigines of Australia at the present day certainly entertain a deep horror of incest, that is, of just those marriages which the exogamous segmentations of the community are fitted to preclude; and down to recent times they commonly punished all such incestuous intercourse with death.[1] It would therefore be perfectly natural that their ancestors should have taken the most stringent measures to prevent the commission of what they, like their descendants, probably regarded as a crime of the deepest dye and fraught with danger to society. Thus an adequate *The effect which these successive subdivisions actually produce is probably the one which they were intended to produce; for the marriages which these subdivisions prevent are just those which the Australian aborigines abhor.*

[1] The evidence will be given below for the various tribes separately.

motive for the institution of their present marriage laws certainly exists among the Australian aborigines; and as these laws, in their combined complexity and regularity, have all the appearance of being artificial, it is legitimate to infer that they were devised by the natives for the purpose of achieving the very results which they do effectively achieve. Those who are best acquainted at first hand with the Australian savages believe them to be capable both of conceiving and of executing such social reforms as are implied in the institution of their present marriage system.[1] We have no right to reject the deliberate opinion of the most competent authorities on such a point, especially when all the evidence at our disposal goes to confirm it. To dismiss as baseless an opinion so strongly supported is contrary to every sound principle of scientific research. It is to substitute the deductive for the inductive method; for it sets aside the evidence of first-hand observation in favour of our own abstract notions of probability. We civilised men who know savages only at second hand through the reports of others are bound to accept the well-weighed testimony of accurate and trustworthy observers as to the facts of savage life, whether that testimony agrees with our prepossessions or not. If we accept some of their statements and reject others according to an arbitrary standard of our own, there is an end of scientific anthropology. We may then, if we please, erect a towering structure of hypothesis, which will perhaps hang together and look fair outwardly but is rotten inwardly, because the premises on which it rests are false. In the present case the only ground for denying that the elaborate marriage system of the Australian aborigines has been devised by them for the purpose which it actually serves appears to be

[1] A. W. Howitt, "Notes on the Australian Class Systems," *Journal of the Anthropological Institute*, xii. (1883) pp. 499 *sqq.*; *id.*, "Further Notes on the Australian Class Systems," *ibid.* xviii. (1889) pp. 40 *sq.*, 66; *id.*, "Australian Group-Relationships," *ibid.* xxxvii. (1907) pp. 286 *sq.*; *id.*, *Native Tribes of South-East Australia*, pp. 89 *sq.*, 140, 143; Spencer and Gillen, *Native Tribes of Central Australia*, pp. 12-15, 69; *id.*, *Northern Tribes of Central Australia*, pp. 123 *sq.*; *id.*, "Some Remarks on Totemism as applied to the Australian Tribes," *Journal of the Anthropological Institute*, xxviii. (1899) p. 278; Baldwin Spencer, in *Transactions of the Australasian Association for the Advancement of Science*, Dunedin, January 1904, pp. 419 *sq.*

a preconceived idea that these savages are incapable of thinking out and putting in practice a series of checks and counter-checks on marriage so intricate that many civilised persons lack either the patience or the ability to understand them. Yet the institution which puzzles some European minds seems to create little or no difficulty for the intellect of the Australian savage. In his hands the complex and cumbrous machine works regularly and smoothly enough; and this fact of itself should make us hesitate to affirm that he could not have invented an instrument which he uses so skilfully.

The truth is that all attempts to trace the origin and growth of human institutions without the intervention of human intelligence and will are radically vicious and foredoomed to failure. It may seem to some to be scientific to treat savage man as a mere automaton, a shuttlecock of nature, a helpless creature of circumstances, and so to explain the evolution of primitive society, like the evolution of material bodies, by the play of physical forces alone. But a history of man so written is neither science nor history: it is a parody of both. For it ignores the prime factor of the movement, the mainspring of the whole machine, and that is man's conscious life, his thoughts, his aspirations, his endeavours. In every age he has had these, and they, far more than anything else, have moulded his institutions. External nature certainly acts on him, but he reacts on it, and his history is the resultant of that action and reaction. To leave out of account either of these mutually interdependent elements, the external and the internal, is to falsify history by presenting us with an incomplete view of it; but of the two the internal element is, if not the more influential, certainly the more obvious, the more open to our observation, and therefore the more important for the historian, who in his effort to refer the events of the human drama to their sources may more safely ignore the influence of climate and weather, of soil and water, of rivers and mountains, than the thoughts, the passions, the ambitions of the actors. We shall as little understand the growth of savage as of civilised institutions if we persist in shutting our eyes to the deliberate choice

It is futile to attempt to trace the growth of savage institutions without taking into account the factors of intelligence and will; and no savage customs bear the impress of thought and purpose more clearly stamped on them than the marriage system of the Australian aborigines.

which man, whether savage or civilised, has exercised in shaping them. It should always be borne in mind that the savage differs from his civilised brother rather in degree than in kind, rather in the point at which his development has been arrested or retarded than in the direction of the line which it has followed; and if, as we know, the one has used his judgment and discretion in making his laws, we may be sure that the other has done so also. The kings and presidents, the senates and parliaments of civilisation have their parallels in the chiefs and headmen, the councils of elders and the tribal assemblies of savagery; and the laws promulgated by the former have their counterpart in the customs initiated and enforced by the latter. Among savage customs there are few or none that bear the impress of thought and purpose stamped upon them so clearly as the complex yet regular marriage system of the Australian aborigines. We shall do well therefore to acquiesce in the opinion of the best observers, who ascribe the origin of that system to the prolonged reflection and deliberate intention of the natives themselves.

But the system in its more complex forms of four or eight exogamous classes was not struck out at a blow; it was evolved out of the two-class system by a process of bisection, single or repeated.

But while there are strong grounds for thinking that the system of exogamy has been deliberately devised and instituted by the Australian aborigines for the purpose of effecting just what it does effect, it would doubtless be a mistake to suppose that its most complex form, the eight-class system, was struck out at a single blow. All the evidence and probability are in favour of the view that the system originated in a simple bisection of the community into two exogamous classes only; that, when this was found insufficient to bar marriages which the natives regarded as objectionable, each of the two classes was again subdivided into two, making four exogamous classes in all; and finally that, when four exogamous classes still proved inadequate for the purpose, each of them was again subdivided into two, making eight exogamous classes in all. Thus from a simple beginning the Australian aborigines appear to have advanced step by step to the complex system of eight exogamous classes, the process being one of successive bisections or dichotomies. The first bisection barred the marriage of brothers with sisters; the second bisection, combined with the characteristic rule of descent, which places the children in a different class both from the father and from the mother, barred the marriage of parents with children; and the third bisection, combined with a rule of descent like the preceding, barred the marriage of a man's children with his sister's children, in other words, it prevented the marriage of some, but not all, of those whom we call first cousins.

The reformers who devised and introduced these great social changes were probably, as we shall see later on,[1] the council of old men, who in every Australian tribe exercise a preponderating influence over the community and appear to be able to carry through any measure on which they have privately agreed among themselves. When the system had once been adopted by a single local community, it might easily be copied by their neighbours and so might spread by peaceful transmission from tribe to tribe in ever widening circles, until it was embraced by practically the whole aboriginal population of Australia. This supposition is in accord with what we know to be actually taking place at the present day among the Australian tribes. The names for four out of their eight subclasses have been adopted in recent times by the Arunta from their northern neighbours the Ilpirra, and they are gradually spreading southward; in the year 1898 the names had not yet reached the southern part of the Arunta tribe.[2] Similarly dances or ceremonies and their accompanying songs are passed on from tribe to tribe; and when, as often happens, the language of the tribe which has borrowed the ceremony differs from that of the tribe which invented it, the performers may and frequently do chant words which are totally unintelligible both to themselves and to their hearers. Indeed we are told that the ceremonial songs of these savages, like the religious litanies of some more advanced peoples, are generally couched in an unknown tongue.[3] This wide diffusion of customs is greatly facilitated

The system was probably devised and introduced by the council of elders in some one local community, from which it may have gradually spread by peaceful transmission over the whole of Australia.

---

[1] See below, pp. 352 *sqq.*
[2] *Native Tribes,* p. 72; *Northern Tribes,* p. 20.
[3] W. E. Roth, *Ethnological Studies among the North-west-central Queens-* *land Aborigines* (Brisbane and London, 1897), pp. 117 *sq.*; Spencer and Gillen, *Native Tribes of Central Australia,* p. 281 note [1]; *id., Northern Tribes of Central Australia,* p. 20.

by the peaceful and friendly relations which generally prevail between neighbouring Australian tribes. The common assumption that savages live in a state of perpetual warfare with each other does not apply to the aborigines of Australia.¹

The alternative theory that the complex organisation of an Australian tribe was produced by amalgamation rather than subdivision is open to serious objections. For, on that hypothesis, why should the federal communities always be two or multiples of two?

Thus we may accept with some degree of confidence the hypothesis that the remarkable division of the Australian tribes into two, four, or eight exogamous classes, with correspondingly complicated rules of descent, has been brought about by a series of dichotomies purposely instituted for the sake of achieving those very results which in practice they achieve. The only alternative to this hypothesis would seem to be to suppose that these exogamous classes had arisen by accretion rather than by subdivision, or, in other words, by the amalgamation of independent exogamous communities which retained their rule of exogamy after coalescing with each other. On this alternative theory the first observation that occurs is, Why were these federal communities so regularly either two in number or multiples of two? Why not as often three, five, or seven as two, four, or eight? The regular division of the normal Australian tribe into two, four, or eight exogamous classes is perfectly intelligible on the hypothesis that it was produced by dichotomy, single or repeated; on the other hypothesis it remains obscure, if not inexplicable, for it is contrary to all probability that the communities which federated with each other should have regularly, if not invariably, been either two in number or a multiple of two.

Again, on the hypothesis of amalgama-

But even if we grant the possibility that the Australian savage, inspired by a passion for even numbers, or rather for the number two and its multiples, should have resolutely

---

¹ Spencer and Gillen, *Native Tribes of Central Australia*, p. 32; *id.*, *Northern Tribes of Central Australia*, p. 31, "The different local groups within the one tribe and the members of contiguous tribes, where they are in contact, live for the most part in a state of mutual friendship. . . . Of course there are exceptions to this, but, on the whole, it is strikingly true of the Australian savage. To judge from ordinary accounts in popular works, one would imagine that the various tribes were in a state of constant hostility. Nothing could be further from the truth." The authors are careful to remind us that this statement refers only to those central and northern tribes with whom they came personally into contact. But as these tribes have been perhaps less contaminated than any others by European influence, their relations to each other may fairly be taken as typical.

spurned all overtures of union with bodies whose numbers, added up together, did not produce the requisite total, the hypothesis of amalgamation as opposed to subdivision is still open to a very serious objection. For while we may without much difficulty conceive that communities, which in their independent state had been exogamous, should remain exogamous after they had united to form a confederacy, it is far more difficult to understand why in uniting they should have adopted the complicated rules of descent which characterise the four-class and eight-class organisations of the Australian tribes. We can imagine that each community in the confederacy should continue as before to take its wives from another community, but why should the two intermarrying communities now cede their children to a third? Why should the confederacy lay down a new rule that henceforth children should never belong as before to the community either of their father or of their mother, but always to a community different from them both? On the theory of amalgamation what motive can be assigned for this rigid exclusion of all children from the communities of both their parents? That exclusion is perfectly intelligible on the hypothesis that it was devised to prevent the marriage of parents with children, but it is difficult to see how it can be explained on any other.

tion, how are we to explain the rule of descent in the four- and eight-class systems?

On the whole, then, we seem driven to the conclusion that the organisation of the normal Australian tribe in two, four, or eight exogamous classes has been produced by deliberate and, where it has been repeated, successive dichotomy of the tribe for the purpose of preventing those marriages of near kin which the aborigines regard with so much horror.[1] But to this view a European reader may naturally

To the view that the social organisation of an Australian tribe was devised to prevent the marriage of

---

[1] This was the conclusion which that sober and cautious enquirer Dr. A. W. Howitt reached many years ago. In a paper which was read before the Anthropological Institute of Great Britain on 12th December 1882 he thus summed up his views:

"(1) The primary division into two classes was intended to prevent brother and sister marriage in the commune.

"(2) The secondary divisions into subclasses were intended to prevent

the possibility of intermarriage between parents (own and tribal) and children.

"(3) The prohibition of the slightest intercourse between a woman and her daughter's husband was a social enactment intended to forbid connections which the class rules were unable to prevent.

"(4) All these changes have been due to an international reformatory movement in the community itself."

See A. W. Howitt, "Notes on the

object that the institution of these exogamous classes was a clumsy expedient, which, while it certainly fulfilled its purpose of preventing the marriages in question, went far beyond the intention of its authors by prohibiting marriage between large numbers of people who were not related to each other by blood at all. This objection reveals a lack of acquaintance with savage ideas of kinship, which differ very widely from our own. The researches of the American ethnologist L. H. Morgan and others within the last fifty years have proved that like savages in many, if not all, parts of the world the Australian aborigines count kin according to what is called the classificatory system of relationship. The fundamental principle of that system is that kinship is reckoned between groups rather than between individuals; for example, under it a man gives the name of father not to one individual man only but to a group of men, any one of whom might, in accordance with the tribal custom, have been his father; he gives the name of mother not to one individual woman only but to a group of women, any one of whom might, in accordance with the tribal custom, have been his mother; he gives the name of brother and sister, not only to the children of his father and mother, but to a group of men and women who are the offspring of all those women and men whom his father and mother might, in accordance with the tribal custom, have married: he gives the name of wife not only to his actual

near kin it may be objected that it in fact prevents the marriage of many other persons. This objection reveals a lack of acquaintance with the Australian system of relationships, which is based, not on ties of blood between individuals, but on social relations between groups. This system is known as the Classificatory System of Relationship.

Australian Class Systems," *Journal of the Anthropological Institute,* xii. (1883) pp. 499-504. When Dr. Howitt wrote thus, the existence of tribes with an eight-class system was unknown, so necessarily he could not take account of it. The rule that a man must avoid social, as well as sexual, intercourse with his mother-in-law is very widespread among the aborigines of Australia. Examples of it will be found in the sequel. In the passage to which I have referred in this note Dr. Howitt points out that with a two-class system and maternal descent a man's mother-in-law always belongs to the class of women who is marriageable to him, since she belongs to the same class as her daughter, his wife, and Dr. Howitt suggests that the custom of avoidance between a man and his mother-in-law grew up in order to prevent that sexual intercourse between them which the system could not bar. On the other hand, it is to be observed that the marriage of a man with his mother-in-law is barred by the two-class system with paternal descent and by the four-class system both with paternal and maternal descent. See further on this subject the observations of Mr. A. L. P. Cameron, "Notes on some Tribes of New South Wales," *Journal of the Anthropological Institute,* xiv. (1885) p. 353 note [2].

wife but to all the women whom the custom of the tribe would have allowed him to marry; and he gives the name of sons and daughters not only to children whom he has himself begotten but also to all the children of those women whom he might have married but did not. Strange as this system of group relationship seems to us, it is actually prevalent at the present day over a great part, probably the greater part of the world; and it is only explicable, as we shall see presently, on the hypothesis that it sprang from, and accurately represents, a system of group marriage, that is, a system in which a group of men enjoyed marital rights over a group of women, so that any man of the one group might call any woman of the other group his wife and treat her as such; while every child born of such group marriages gave the name of father to every one of the whole group of men to which his actual father belonged, and the name of mother to every one of the whole group of women to which his actual mother belonged. Such titles would not by any means imply a belief that the speaker had been begotten by all the men of his father's group or borne by all the women of his mother's group. It would mean no more than that he stood in a similar social, not physical, relationship to all the men and women of these groups. It would mean that the duties which he owed to them and the rights which he claimed from them were the same in respect of every member of the group, and were neither greater nor less in respect of his physical father and mother than in respect of all the other men and women on whom he bestowed the names of father and mother. In short, under this system paternity and maternity, brotherhood and sisterhood, sonship and daughtership designated social not consanguineous relationships, the tie of blood being either ignored or at all events cast into the background by the greater importance of the tie which bound all the members of the groups together. It was, to all appearance, a period not of individualism but of social communism; and when we remember how feeble each individual man is by comparison with the larger animals, we may be ready to admit that in his early struggles with them for the mastery a system which knit large groups of men and women together by the closest ties was more favourable to progress than one which would have limited the family group to a single pair and their offspring. Then, perhaps even more than now, union was strength : disunion and dispersal would have exposed our ancestors to the risk of being exterminated piecemeal by their ferocious and individually far stronger adversaries, the large carnivorous animals.

Thus the social organisation of an Australian tribe is intended to prevent the intermarriage of certain social groups, and this intention it adequately effects.

Now to revert to the exogamous classes of the Australian tribes. If we assume, as we have every right to do, that the founders of exogamy in Australia recognised the classificatory system of relationship, and the classificatory system of relationship only, we shall at once perceive that what they intended to prevent was not merely the marriage of a man with his sister, his mother, or his daughter in the physical sense in which we use these terms ; their aim was to prevent his marriage with his sister, his mother, and his daughter in the classificatory sense of these terms ; that is, they intended to place bars to marriage not between individuals merely but between the whole groups of persons who designated their group not their individual relationships, their social not their consanguineous ties, by the names of father and mother, brother and sister, son and daughter. And in this intention the founders of exogamy succeeded perfectly. In the completest form of the system, namely, the division of the community into eight exogamous classes, they barred the marriage of group brothers with group sisters, of group fathers with group daughters, of group mothers with group sons, and of the sons of group brothers with the daughters of group sisters. Thus the dichotomy of an Australian tribe in its completest form, namely in the eight-class organisation, was not a clumsy expedient which overshot its mark by separating from each other many persons whom the authors of it had no intention of separating : it was a device admirably adapted to effect just what its inventors intended, neither more nor less. But this will be better understood by the reader on a closer acquaintance with the classificatory system of relationship, with which the exogamy of the Australian tribes is inseparably bound up. To that subject we now turn.

§ 6. The Classificatory System of Relationship in the Central and Northern Tribes

In all the Australian tribes thus far passed in review there prevails what is known as the Classificatory System of Relationship; in other words, the natives count kinship not between individuals merely, as we do, but between classes or groups, and the principle of classification, as we shall see presently, is not blood but marriage. After enumerating the classificatory terms of relationship in use among these tribes, Messrs. Spencer and Gillen observe: "It will at once be seen that the one striking feature, common to the whole series, is that the terms used by the natives apply not to the individual but to the group of which the individual is a member. Whilst we are of course obliged to use our ordinary terms of relationship, such as father, mother, brother, wife, etc., it must always be remembered that this is merely a matter of convenience, and that, for example, the words *oknia*, which we translate by father, or *mia* by mother, *okilia* by brother, and *unawa* by wife, by no means whatever connote the meaning of our English terms. *Oknia*—and the same applies precisely to all the terms—is not applied or regarded by an individual as in the least degree applicable to one man only; it is simply the name of a group of individuals of which he is a member. Strictly speaking, in our sense of the word they have no individual terms of relationship, but every person has certain groups of men and women who stand in a definite relationship to him and he to them. . . . It is absolutely essential in dealing with these people to lay aside all ideas of relationship as counted amongst ourselves. The savage Australian, it may indeed be said with truth, has no idea of relationships as we understand them. He does not, for example, discriminate between his actual father and mother and the men and women who belong to the group, each member of which might have lawfully been either his father or his mother, as the case may be. Any wrong done to his actual father or mother, or to his actual father-in-law or mother-in-law, counts for nothing whatever more than any wrong which he may have

The Classificatory System of relationship in Australia.

done to any man or woman who is a member of a group of individuals, any one of whom might have been his father or mother, his father-in-law or mother-in-law."[1]

The Classificatory System classifies all the members of a community in classes or groups on the principle of marriageability, not of blood: the relations which it recognises are social, not physical: it is a system of marriage, not of consanguinity.

The classificatory system of relationship is not limited to the central and northern tribes of Australia. It is shared by all the aborigines of Australia and, as the great American ethnologist, L. H. Morgan, was the first to prove, by many other races in many other parts of the world.[2] As the system, with differences of detail, is recognised certainly by many and probably by all totemic peoples the world over, and as we shall accordingly meet with it again and again in our survey of totemism, it is desirable to give at the outset some brief general explanations in regard to it, all the more so because the system differs fundamentally from ours, and serious confusion has been created through the failure of some enquirers to perceive the distinction. To put that distinction shortly: whereas our system of relationship is based on consanguinity, on the physical tie of a common blood, the classificatory system of relationship is based on marriage; whereas with us the fundamental relation is that between parent and child, and all other relationships are deduced from it, under the classificatory system the fundamental relation is that between husband and wife, and all other relationships are deduced from it. With us the essential question is, Who is my father? or, Who is my mother? but under the classificatory system the essential question is, Whom may I marry? Accordingly the classificatory system classifies the whole community in classes or groups, the common bond between the members of each class or group being not one of blood but simply the similar relation of marriageability or non-marriageability in which they stand to each other and to the members of every other class or group in the community. Each class or group may, and commonly does, include members who are related to each other by ties of blood; but under the classificatory system such ties are accidental, not essential, they are not

---

[1] Spencer and Gillen, *Northern Tribes of Central Australia*, pp. 95 *sq.*
[2] Lewis H. Morgan, *Systems of Consanguinity and Affinity of the Human Family*, forming vol. xvii. of the *Smithsonian Contributions to Knowledge* (Washington, 1871); *id. Ancient Society* (London, 1877).

the ground on which the persons so related are classed together in the same class or group. If the reader will steadily bear this simple principle in mind, he will escape some of the pitfalls which beset his path in treading the maze of the classificatory system.

The able English anthropologist J. F. McLennan rightly denied that the classificatory terms of relationship which, for want of exact equivalents, we are obliged to translate as "father," "mother," "son," "daughter," "brother," "sister," imply any blood relationship between the persons so designated. With perfect justice he declared that the classificatory term "father" does not mean "the begetting father"; that the classificatory term "mother" does not mean "the bearing mother"; that the classificatory terms "son" and "daughter" do not mean "begotten by" or "born to"; and that the classificatory terms "brother" and "sister" do not imply connexion by descent from the same father and mother. In short McLennan denied that the classificatory system was a system of blood-ties at all;[1] and if we restrict our view to the principles and origin of the system and leave out of account the ideas which have been afterwards imported into it, there can be little doubt that he was perfectly right in his denial. Further, McLennan correctly perceived that the corner-stone on which the whole classificatory system rests is marriage, not consanguinity. He says: "It cannot be doubted that the classificatory system in the Malayan form illustrates a very early social condition of man. We must also believe, from its connecting itself with the family, that it had its origin in some early marriage-law. Indeed, an examination of the leading points of difference presented by the various forms of the classificatory system leaves no doubt that the phenomena presented in all the forms are ultimately referable to the marriage law; and that accordingly its origin must be so also."[2]

Nevertheless, after having gone so far in the right direction as to see clearly what the classificatory system

<small>McLennan rightly saw that the Classificatory System is not a system of consanguinity.</small>

---

[1] J. F. McLennan, *Studies in Ancient History*, New Edition (London, 1886), p. 270.

[2] J. F. McLennan, *Studies in Ancient History*, New Edition (London, 1886), p. 277.

was not (namely a system of consanguinity), and to have had at least a glimpse of what it really is (namely a system of marriage), McLennan abruptly turned aside and declared it to be nothing more than a system of mutual salutations or modes of addressing persons in social intercourse.[1]

{But he erred in thinking that the Classificatory System is a mere system of mutual salutations or modes of address.}

This proposed explanation of the classificatory terms is unhesitatingly rejected by writers who, like L. H. Morgan, and unlike J. F. McLennan, have had the great advantage of living on a footing of intimacy with savages whose whole social structure is built on the classificatory system. Thus, for example, the Rev. Lorimer Fison, who had experience of the classificatory system of relationship in Fiji as well as in Australia, writes as follows:[2] "It has been asserted that the Classificatory System of Relationship is a mere 'system of addresses,' the ground for this assertion being that the members of certain tribes use the terms in addressing one another; but this explanation of the system appears to me to be directly contradicted by the facts. In the first place there are many tribes who never so employ the terms; in the second place, if they are not terms of relationship, the millions of people who use them have no terms of relationship at all, for they have none other than these; and, finally, it is impossible to suppose that the obligations and prohibitions conveyed by the terms could be conveyed by a mere system of addresses. Take for instance the *tabu* between the Fijian *veinganeni*.[3] Any woman whom a Fijian calls his *ngane* is as strictly forbidden to him as our own sisters are to us; her very touch brings pollution upon him, and if he took her to wife he would be regarded with abhorrence by all his tribe. Is it possible to believe that a mere term of address could bring a prohibition such as this? No theories are needed to account for these classificatory terms; they account for themselves, for they are the necessary outcome of the exogamous intermarrying divisions found in Australia and elsewhere; and the fair inference

---

[1] J. F. McLennan, *op. cit.* pp. 273 *sq.*, 277 *sqq.*

[2] L. Fison, "The Classificatory System of Relationship," *Journal of the Anthropological Institute*, xxiv. (1895) pp. 369 *sq.*

[3] "*Ngane* is the term of relation between brother and sister. It means 'one who shuns the other,' and the *veinganeni* are the non-marriageable persons" (L. Fison, *op. cit.* p. 360).

is that, wherever we find the terms, these divisions are, or have been in the past." Speaking of McLennan's attempt to treat the classificatory terms as pure modes of address, Messrs. Spencer and Gillen make the following weighty observations:—" To those who have been amongst and watched the natives day after day, this explanation of the terms is utterly unsatisfactory. When, in various tribes, we find series of terms of relationship all dependent upon classificatory systems such as those now to be described, and referring entirely to a mutual relationship such as would be brought about by their existence, we cannot do otherwise than come to the conclusion that the terms do actually indicate various degrees of relationship based primarily upon the existence of intermarrying groups. When we find, for example, that amongst the Arunta natives a man calls a large number of men belonging to one particular group by the name *oknia* (a term which includes our relationship of father), that he calls all the wives of these men by the common name of *mia* (mother),[1] and that he calls all their sons by the name of *okilia* (elder brother) or *itia* (younger brother), as the case may be, we can come to no other conclusion than that this is expressive of his recognition of what may be termed a group relationship. All the 'fathers' are men who belong to the particular group to which his own actual father belongs; all the 'mothers' belong to the same group as that to which his actual mother belongs, and all the 'brothers' belong to his own group.

"Whatever else they may be, the relationship terms are certainly not terms of address, the object of which is to prevent the native having to employ a personal name. In the Arunta tribe, for example, every man and woman has a personal name by which he or she is freely addressed by others—that is, by any, except a member of the opposite sex who stands in the relationship of *mura* to them, for such may only on very rare occasions speak to one another. When, as has happened time after time to us, a native

The classificatory terms express various degrees of relationship based primarily upon the existence of intermarrying groups.

---

[1] "In using the English term we do not mean to imply that it is the equivalent of the native term, but simply that the latter includes the relationship indicated by the English term."

says, for example, 'That man is Oriaka (a personal name), he is my *okilia*,' and you cannot possibly tell without further inquiry whether he is the speaker's blood or tribal brother —that is, the son of his own father or of some man belonging to the same particular group as his father—then the idea that the term *okilia* is applied as a polite term of address, or in order to avoid the necessity of using a personal name, is at once seen to be untenable.

<small>Wide prevalence in Australia of the classificatory terms of relationship.</small>

"It is, at all events, a remarkable fact that (apart from the organisation of other tribes, in respect of which we are not competent to speak, but for which the same fact is vouched for by other observers) in all the tribes with which we are acquainted, all the terms coincide, without any exception, in the recognition of relationships, all of which are dependent upon the existence of a classificatory system, the fundamental idea of which is that the women of certain groups marry the men of others. Each tribe has one term applied indiscriminately by the man to the woman or women whom he actually marries and to all the women whom he might lawfully marry—that is, who belong to the right group—one term to his actual mother and to all the women whom his father might lawfully have married; one term to his actual brother and to all the sons of his father's brothers, and so on right through the whole system. To this it may be added that, if these be not terms of relationship, then the language of these tribes is absolutely devoid of any such."[1]

I will now illustrate the classificatory terms of relation-

---

[1] Spencer and Gillen, *Native Tribes of Central Australia*, pp. 56-58. The writers add in a note: "To this may be added, still further, the fact that there do exist certain terms applied by men to certain particular individuals which are in the strict sense 'terms of address.' A man, for example, addresses particular men who took part in his initiation ceremonies by such terms as Tapunga, Urinthantima, etc., which express no relationship, and the significance of which is entirely distinct from the true terms of relationship now dealt with." The Todas of Southern India, who have the classificatory system of relationship, employ two well-marked sets of terms expressing bonds of kinship; one set they use in speaking of relatives, the other in speaking to relatives. The terms of address sometimes differ totally from the others. Thus a father is *in*, but he is addressed as *aia*; the son of a father's sister or of a mother's brother is *matchuni*, but he is addressed as *anna*, *egala*, or *enda* according to his age relatively to that of the speaker. See W. H. R. Rivers, *The Todas* (London, 1906), pp. 483 *sqq.*

ship by examples drawn from the languages of the central and northern tribes of Australia. In doing so, for the sake of brevity and clearness, I shall confine myself to the cardinal terms without attempting to follow out the elaborate system into all its ramifications. The cardinal terms, on which the whole system hinges, are those which include, without being equivalent to, our terms father, mother, brother, sister, wife, husband, son, daughter. It will be enough, therefore, for our purpose to give examples of these classificatory terms in the vocabularies of the central and northern tribes.

Examples of the cardinal terms of relationship in the classificatory system.

Thus in the Urabunna tribe[1] a man applies the same term *nia* to his father and to all his father's brothers, whether they are blood or tribal brothers—that is, whether they are brothers of his father in our sense of the term or merely men who belong to the same marriage group as his father. Hence it follows that every man gives the name of father not to one but to many men, any one of whom might, in accordance with the marriage laws of the tribe, have been his father.

Urabunna term for father.

Again, in the Urabunna tribe a man applies the same term *luka* to his mother and to his mother's elder sisters, whether they are blood or tribal sisters—that is, whether they are sisters of his mother in our sense of the term, or merely women who belong to the same marriage group as his mother. Hence it follows that every man gives the name of mother not to one but to many women, any one of whom might, in accordance with the marriage laws of the tribe, have been his mother. But it is to be observed that while the name for mother (*luka*) includes also the elder sisters, whether blood or tribal, of the mother, it does not include her younger sisters, for whom there is a quite different name, viz. *namuma*.[2] This difference of nomenclature suffices to prove that to the Urabunna mind the elder sisters of a mother stand to a man in a totally different relation from his mother's younger sisters, since the names which denote them are absolutely distinct. The distinction suggests that while any of the elder sisters (whether blood

Urabunna term for mother.

---

[1] For the Urabunna terms of relationship, see *Native Tribes*, pp. 66 *sqq.*
[2] *Native Tribes*, p. 66.

or tribal) of his mother might have been his real mother, none of her younger sisters (whether blood or tribal) could have been so; in other words, that among the women of the group into which a man may marry, only those on the senior side are eligible to him, while those on the junior side are forbidden. This agrees with the Urabunna rule that a man may marry only the daughters of his mother's elder brothers or (what comes to the same thing) of his father's elder sisters, not the daughters of his mother's younger brothers or of his father's younger sisters.[1] In both cases we see that preference for seniority in a wife which, as has been suggested,[2] may be based on an old rule that a man might only marry those women who had been initiated before him.

Urabunna terms for elder brother and sister. Again, an Urabunna man applies the same term *nuthie* to his own elder brothers and to the sons of his father's elder brothers, whether blood or tribal, and the same term *kakua* to his own elder sisters and to the daughters of his father's elder brothers, whether blood or tribal.[3] Thus he applies the terms "elder brother" and "elder sister" to many men and women whom we should regard either as cousins or in many cases as no relations at all. The reason for this extension of the terms "brother" and "sister" is found in the Urabunna marriage rule which includes all these persons in the group from which a man may not take a wife; to him, therefore, all these men and women are brothers and sisters. But again, in relation to brothers and sisters, just as in relation to paternal aunts, the distinction of senior and junior is so important that totally different names are assigned to the two; for whereas elder brothers and elder sisters, whether blood or tribal, are called *nuthie*

Urabunna term for younger brother and sister. and *kakua* respectively, younger brothers and younger sisters are called *kupuka*, and this name (*kupuka*) includes not only what we should call younger brothers and sisters, but also the sons and daughters of the father's younger brothers, whether blood or tribal. Thus a man gives the names of "younger brother" and "younger sister" to many men and women whom we should regard either as cousins

---

[1] See above, pp. 177 *sq.*   [2] Above, pp. 179 *sq.*
[3] *Native Tribes*, p. 66.

or in many cases as no relations at all.[1] The reason for this sharp distinction between elder and younger brothers and sisters may be, as Dr. Rivers has suggested,[2] that the relation in which a man stands to those who have been initiated before him differs entirely from that in which he stands to those who have been initiated after him.

Again, an Urabunna man applies the same term *nupa* to his wife and to all the daughters of his father's elder sisters and of his mother's elder brothers,[3] where, as usual, the terms brother and sister are employed in the classificatory sense to include both blood and tribal brotherhood and sisterhood. Thus a man gives the name of "wife" to many women who are not his wives. The reason for this wide extension of the term is to be found in the Urabunna marriage rule which assigns all these women to the particular group from which alone a man may take a wife. *(Urabunna term for wife.)*

Lastly, an Urabunna man applies the same term *biaka* to his own children and to the children of his brothers, whether blood or tribal.[4] Thus he gives the name "my children" to many children who are either his nephews and nieces or in many cases no relations to him at all. The reason for this wide extension of the term is supplied by the Urabunna marriage rule which assigns all brothers to one marriage group and all their wives to another, and treats all the children born of such marriages as if they were one family, the progeny of all the parents in common, without discriminating between the offspring of individual pairs. In short, this classificatory term, like all the preceding, is based on a theory of group marriage. *(Urabunna term for children.)*

When we pass from the Urabunna to the Arunta tribe we find that, though the particular terms of relationship differ, the classificatory principle on which they are based is the same. Thus, in the generation above his own, an Arunta man applies the same term *oknia* to his father and to his father's brothers, whether blood or tribal; and he applies the same term *mia* to his mother and to his mother's sisters, whether blood or tribal. In his own generation he applies the same term *okilia* to his elder *(Classificatory terms of relationship among the Arunta.)*

---

[1] *Native Tribes*, p. 66.
[2] See above, pp. 179 *sq*.
[3] *Native Tribes*, pp. 64, 66.
[4] *Ibid.* p. 66.

brothers and to the sons of his father's elder brothers, whether blood or tribal; the same term *itia* or *witia* to his younger brothers and to the sons of his father's younger brothers, whether blood or tribal; the same term *ungaraitcha* to his elder sisters and to the daughters of his father's elder brothers, whether blood or tribal; the same term *itia* or *quitia* to his younger sisters and to the daughters of his father's younger brothers, whether blood or tribal; and the same term *unawa* to his wife and to the wives of his brothers, whether blood or tribal. In the generation below his own he applies the same term *allira* to his children and to the children of his brothers, whether blood or tribal. But while he applies the same name (*allira*) to his own children and to the children of his brothers, he applies a quite different name (*umba*) to the children of his sisters, whether blood or tribal.[1] The reason for this marked discrimination which a man makes between the children of his brothers and the children of his sisters, all of whom we confound under the common name of nephews and nieces, is as usual to be found in the marriage rules of the tribe; for whereas the children of a man's brothers are the offspring of women whom he might have married, the children of his sisters are the offspring of women whom he is absolutely forbidden to marry. Hence the two sets of children are placed in entirely different categories and distinguished by entirely different names. Lastly, an Arunta woman applies the same term *unawa* to her own husband and to the husbands of her sisters, whether blood or tribal,[2] the reason being that her sisters' husbands all belong to the group from which alone she may receive a husband.

Classificatory terms of relationship among the Luritcha.

With differences of vocabulary and slight variations of detail the classificatory terms of relationship are in use among all the other central and northern tribes of Australia. Thus in the Luritcha tribe, to the west of the Arunta, in the generation above his own a man applies the same term *kartu* to his father and to his father's brothers, blood and tribal; and he applies the same term *yaku* to his mother and to his mother's sisters, blood and tribal. In his own generation he applies the same term *kurta* to his elder

[1] *Native Tribes*, p. 76.   [2] *Ibid.* p. 77.

brothers and to the sons of his father's elder brothers, blood and tribal; the same term *mirlunguna* to his younger brothers and to the sons of his father's younger brothers, blood and tribal; the same term *kangaru* to his elder sisters and to the daughters of his father's elder brothers; and the same term *kuri* to his wife and to his wife's sisters, blood and tribal. In the generation below his own he applies the same term *katha* to his sons and to his brothers' sons, blood and tribal; and he applies the same term *urntali* to his daughters and to his brothers' daughters, blood and tribal. But while a man applies the same term (*katha*) to his own sons and to his brothers' sons, he applies quite a different term (*ukari*) to his sisters' sons. The reason for the difference has already been given: his brothers' children are the offspring of women whom he himself might have married, but his sisters' children are the offspring of women whom he is absolutely forbidden to marry; hence the two sets of children are placed in entirely different categories and distinguished by entirely different names. A wife applies the same term *kuri* to her own husband and to her husband's brothers,[1] the reason being that her husband's brothers all belong to the group from which alone she may receive a husband.

In the Kaitish tribe, which lies further north than the Arunta, in the generation above his own a man applies the same term *akaurli* to his father and to his father's brothers, blood and tribal;[2] and he applies the same term *arungwa* to his mother and to his mother's sisters, blood and tribal. In his own generation he applies the same term *alkiriia* to his elder brothers and to the sons of his father's elder brothers; the same term *achirri* to his younger brothers and to the sons of his father's younger brothers; and the same term *arari* to his elder sisters and to the daughters of his father's elder brothers. In the generation below his own he applies the same term *atumpirri* to his own sons and daughters and to his brothers' sons and daughters. A wife applies the same

Classificatory terms of relationship among the Kaitish.

---

[1] *Native Tribes*, pp. 77 *sq.*

[2] But he distinguishes his father's elder brothers as *akaurli aniaura*, and his father's younger brothers as *ak-aurli maianinga*. Thus a father is discriminated from his brothers. Similar discriminations are made by other tribes further to the north. See below, pp. 302, 303.

term *umbirniia* to her husband and to her husband's brothers, blood and tribal.[1]

Classificatory terms of relationship among the Warramunga.

In the Warramunga tribe, immediately to the north of the Kaitish, in the generation above his own a man applies the same term *gambatja* to his father and to his father's brothers, blood and tribal; and he applies the same term *kurnandi* to his mother and to his mother's sisters, blood and tribal. In his own generation he applies the same term *papati* to his elder brothers and to the sons of his father's elder brothers; the same term *kukaitja* to his younger brothers and to the sons of his father's younger brothers; the same term *kabalu* to his elder sisters and to the daughters of his father's elder brothers; and the same term *katununga* to his wife and to his wife's sisters. In the generation below his own he applies the same term *katakitji* to his children and to the children of his brothers. But while he applies the same term (*katakitji*) to his own children and to his brothers' children, he applies quite a different term (*kulu-kulu*) to his sisters' children. The reason for the difference has already been given. A wife applies the same term *kulla-kulla* to her husband and to her husband's brothers.[2]

Classificatory terms of relationship among the Worgaia.

In the Worgaia tribe, to the east of the Warramunga, in the generation above his own a man applies the same term *wakathua* to his father and to his father's brothers. In his own generation he applies the same term *lalu* to his elder brothers and to the sons of his father's elder brothers; the same term *uranathu* to his younger brothers and to the sons of his father's younger brothers; the same term *lilikia* to his elder sisters and to the daughters of his father's elder brothers; the same term *uranii* to his younger sisters and to the daughters of his father's younger brothers; and the same term *munkara* to his wife and to his wife's sisters. In

---

[1] *Native Tribes*, p. 79. The same term *umbirniia* is applied by a husband to his wife, and on analogy we should expect to find it applied by him also to his wife's sisters, but this is not mentioned by Messrs. Spencer and Gillen. They say that *umbirniia* expresses the relationships of "husband, wife, husband's brothers, blood and tribal, sister's husband, wife's brothers, blood and tribal." Here perhaps "wife's brothers" is a mistake for "wife's sisters."

[2] *Northern Tribes*, pp. 78 *sq.*; *Native Tribes*, p. 80. The lists in these two passages differ slightly. I follow the list in *Northern Tribes* as the later and presumably the more correct.

the generation below his own he applies the same term *ninenta* to his own sons and to his brothers' sons; and the same term *ninianu* to his own daughters and to his brothers' daughters. But while he applies the same terms (*ninenta* and *ninianu*) to his own sons and daughters and to the sons and daughters of his brothers, he applies as usual a different term (*nitharu*) to the children of his sisters. A wife applies the same term *illinathu* to her husband and to her husband's brothers.[1]

In the Umbaia tribe, to the north-east of the Warramunga, in the generation above his own a man applies the same term *ita* to his father and to his father's brothers; and he applies the same term *kutjina* to his mother and to his mother's sisters. In his own generation he applies the same term *pappa* to his elder brothers and to the sons of his father's elder brothers; the same term *kakula* to his younger brothers and to the sons of his father's younger brothers; and the same term *karinnia* to his wife and to his wife's sisters. In the generation below his own he applies the same term *tjatjilla* to his own children and to the children of his brothers. But while he applies the same term (*tjatjilla*) to his own children and to his brothers' children, he applies as usual quite a different term (*kula*) to his sisters' children. A wife applies the same term *kari* to her husband and to her husband's brothers.[2]

Classificatory terms of relationship among the Umbaia.

In the Tjingilli tribe, to the north of the Warramunga, a man applies the same name *kita* to his father and to his father's brothers; the same term *thinkatini* to his mother and to his mother's sisters; the same term *kalini* to his wife and to his wife's sisters; the same term *pappa* to his own children and to his brothers' children; the same term *thaminji* to his own daughters and to his brothers' daughters. A wife applies the same term *nambia* to her husband and to her husband's brothers.[3]

Classificatory terms of relationship among the Tjingilli.

In the Gnanji tribe still further to the north, in the generation above his own a man applies the same term *itipati* to his father and to his father's brothers; and he applies the same term *kutjina* to his mother and to his

Classificatory terms of relationship among the Gnanji.

[1] *Northern Tribes*, pp. 80 *sq.*   [2] *Ibid.* pp. 81 *sq.*
[3] *Ibid.* pp. 83 *sq.*

mother's sisters. In his own generation he applies the same term *pappaii* to his elder brothers and to the sons of his father's elder brothers; the same term *kakula* to his younger brothers and to the sons of his father's younger brothers; the same term *pappana* to his elder sisters and to the daughters of his father's elder brothers; the same term *kakallina* to his younger sisters and to the daughters of his father's younger brothers; the same term *karina* to his wife and to his wife's sisters. A wife applies the same term *kari* to her husband and to her husband's brothers.[1]

Classificatory terms of relationship among the Binbinga.

In the Binbinga tribe, still further north, near the coast of the Gulf of Carpentaria, a man calls his father *kuni*, his father's elder brother *kuni puninjilla*, and his father's younger brother *kuni mopai*. Here, accordingly, we see that a distinction is drawn between the father and his brothers. But in the same tribe a man applies the same term *kutjina* to his mother and to his mother's sisters; the same term *pappa* to his elder brothers and to the sons of his father's elder brothers; the same term *pappaia* to his younger brothers and to the sons of his father's younger brothers; the same term *kakarinnia* to his elder sisters and to the daughters of his father's elder brothers; the same term *tjuluna* to his younger sisters and to the daughters of his father's younger brothers; and the same term *karina* to his wife and to his wife's sisters. A wife applies the same term *kaii-kaii* to her husband and to her husband's brothers.[2]

Classificatory terms of relationship among the Mara.

In the Mara tribe, on the coast of the Gulf of Carpentaria, in the generation above his own a man applies the same term *naluru* to his father and to his father's brothers; and he applies the same term *katjirri* to his mother and to his mother's sisters. In his own generation he applies the same term *guauaii* to his elder brothers and to the sons of his father's elder brothers; the same term *niritja* to his younger brothers and to the sons of his father's younger[3] brothers; the same term *gnarali* to his elder sisters and to the daughters of his father's elder brothers; the

---

[1] *Northern Tribes*, pp. 84 sq.
[2] *Ibid.* pp. 85 sq.
[3] Messrs. Spencer and Gillen say "father's elder brother's son" (*Northern Tribes*, p. 87). But here "elder" is obviously a mistake for "younger."

same term *gnanirritja* to his younger sisters and to the daughters of his father's younger brothers; and the same term *irrimakula* to his wife and to his wife's sisters. In the generation below his own he applies the same term *nitjari* to his sons and to his brothers' sons; and the same term *gnaiiati* to his daughters and to his brothers' daughters. A wife applies the same term *irrimakula* to her husband and to her husband's brothers.¹

Lastly, in the Anula tribe on the Gulf of Carpentaria a man calls his father *winiati*, but his father's elder brother *winiati tjanama*, and his father's younger brother *winiati tjanamaama*. Here again, therefore, as among the Binbinga, the father is discriminated from his brothers. But in this tribe a man applies the same term *parata* to his mother and to his mother's sisters; the same term *tjapapa* to his elder brothers and to the sons of his father's elder brothers; the same term *winaka* to his younger brothers and to the sons of his father's younger brothers; the same term *natjapapa* to his elder sisters and to the daughters of his father's elder sisters; the same term *arunguta* to his wife and to his wife's sisters; and the same term *katja-katja* to his own children and to his brothers' children. But while he applies the same term (*katja-katja*) to his own children and to his brothers' children, he applies as usual quite a different term (*kurnaatinia*) to his sisters' children. A wife applies the same term *arunguta* to her husband and to her husband's brothers.²

Classificatory terms of relationship among the Anula.

This survey of the cardinal terms of relationship in the central and northern tribes of Australia suffices to prove their classificatory nature. They are terms which designate relationships between groups, not between individuals. Each individual is classed as the son or daughter of many fathers and of many mothers: he or she classes as brothers and sisters many men and women who on our system are no relations at all to him or her: every man classes many women as his wives besides the one to whom he is actually married: every woman classes many men as her husbands besides the one to whom she is actually married: every man and every woman class as their children many boys and girls whom they neither begat nor bare. Thus the whole population is

The classificatory terms express group relationships and originated in group marriage.

¹ *Northern Tribes*, pp. 87 *sq.* ² *Ibid.* pp. 88 *sq.*

distributed into groups, and the system of kinship consists of the relations of these groups to each other. The only reasonable and probable explanation of such a system of group relationships is that it originated in a system of group marriage, that is, in a state of society in which groups of men exercised marital rights over groups of women, and the limitation of one wife to one husband was unknown. Such a system of group marriage would explain very simply why every man gives the name of wife to a whole group of women, and every woman gives the name of husband to a whole group of men, with only one or even with none of whom he or she need have marital relations; why every man and every woman apply the names of father and mother to whole groups of men and women of whom it is physically impossible that more than two individuals can be their parents; why every man and every woman apply the names of brother and sister to whole groups of men and women with whom they need not have a drop of blood in common; and why, finally, every man and every woman claim as their sons and daughters whole groups of men and women whom they neither begat nor bare. In short, group marriage explains group relationship, and it is hard to see what else can do so.

<small>The difficulty of understanding how under the classificatory system every man has many "mothers" springs from confusing our word "mother" with the corresponding but not equivalent term in the classificatory system: in short it is based on a verbal fallacy.</small>

Apart from the reluctance which some people feel to admit that a large part or the whole of mankind has passed through a stage of social evolution in which individual marriage was unknown, the only serious obstacle to the acceptance of this simple and adequate explanation of the classificatory system is the difficulty of understanding how a person should ever come to be treated as the child of many mothers. This difficulty only exists so long as we confuse our word "mother" with the corresponding but by no means equivalent terms in the languages of savages who have the classificatory system. We mean by "mother" a woman who has given birth to a child; the Australian savages mean by "mother" a woman who stands in a certain social relation to a group of men and women, whether she has given birth to any one of them or not. She is "mother" to that group even when she is an infant in arms. A grown man has been seen playing with a small girl whom he called quite seriously and, according to his system of relationship, quite rightly his "mother."[1] But he was not such a fool as to imagine that the child had given birth to him. He was merely using the term "mother" in the Australian, not the English, sense; and if we will only clear our minds of the confusion created by the common verbal fallacy of employing the same word in two different senses, the imaginary difficulty about one man and many mothers will cease to block the straight road to the understanding of the classificatory system of relationship. It is not even necessary to suppose that, as Dr. Rivers has suggested,[2] the blood tie between a mother and her offspring may, under a system of group marriage, have been forgotten in later life, so that adults would be as uncertain about their mothers as they were about their fathers. The true relation between mother and child may always have been remembered, but it was an accident which did not in any way affect the mother's place in the classificatory system; for she was classed with a group of "mothers" just as much before as after her child was born. Similarly a man is classed with a group of "fathers" when he is a toddling infant just as much as when he has begotten a large family. The classificatory system is based on the marital, not on the parental, relation. It is founded on the division of the community into two intermarrying groups. From that simple and primary grouping all the other groups and all the group relationships of the system appear to be derived.

The view that the group relationships of the classificatory system originated in group marriage, primarily in the bisection of a community into two exogamous halves, is shared by some of the best authorities on the Australian aborigines.

The view that the group relationships of the classificatory

---

[1] *Native Tribes*, p. 58. The natives of the Gazelle Peninsula in New Britain have the classificatory system of relationship; hence among them "a child gives the name of mother not only to her who bore him, but also to all his maternal aunts. A European not familiar with these relationships is surprised when he hears a native boasting of having three mothers. His confusion is increased when the three alleged mothers stoutly assert: '*Amital qa kava ia*, All three of us bore him.'" See P. A. Kleintitschen, *Die Küstenbewohner der Gazellehalbinsel* (Hiltrup bei Münster, preface dated Christmas 1906), p. 190. Even this claim of triple maternity must be interpreted according to the classificatory ideas of motherhood.

[2] W. H. R. Rivers, "On the Origin of the Classificatory System of Relationships," in *Anthropological Essays presented to Edward Burnett Tylor* (Oxford, 1907), pp. 317 *sq.*

Systems are founded on group marriage is shared by some of the best authorities on the Australian aborigines.

Thus Mr. Lorimer Fison says: "It must, I think, be allowed that the classificatory terms point to group-marriage as well as to group-relationship, to a time when the *veindavolani* groups were, so to speak, married to one another."[1] Again, Dr. Howitt observes that "it is upon the division of the whole community into two exogamous intermarrying classes that the whole social structure is built up; and the various relationships which are brought about by those marriages are defined and described by the classificatory system."[2] "This fundamental law of communal division underlies and runs through all the more developed systems of four or eight subclasses, and even shows traces of its former existence in tribes in which the class system has become decadent, and the local organisation has taken place and assumed control of marriage. The division of the tribal community into two classes is the foundation on which the whole structure of society is built."[3] And to the same effect Messrs. Spencer and Gillen write that "the fundamental feature in the organisation of the Central Australian, as in that of other Australian tribes, is the division of the tribe into two exogamous intermarrying groups. These two divisions may become further broken up, but even when more than two are now present we can still recognise their former existence. In consequence of, and intimately associated with, this division of the tribe, there has been developed a series of terms of relationship indicating the relative status of the various members of the tribe, and, of necessity, as the division becomes more complex so do the terms of relationship."[4] "The conclusion to which we have come is that we do not see how the facts . . . can receive any satisfactory explanation except on the theory of the former existence of group marriage, and further, that this has of necessity given

---

[1] Lorimer Fison, "The Classificatory System of Relationship," *Journal of the Anthropological Institute*, xxiv. (1895) p. 368. The *veindavolani* groups are the persons who in the Fijian system of relationship are marriageable with each other. They consist of such first cousins as are the children of a brother and of a sister respectively. These are the only persons who on the Fijian system should marry each other; other first cousins, namely the children of two brothers or of two sisters, are not marriageable with each other. See L. Fison, *op. cit.* pp. 360 *sq.*

[2] A. W. Howitt, *Native Tribes of South-East Australia*, p. 157.

[3] A. W. Howitt, *op. cit.* p. 174.

[4] *Native Tribes*, p. 55.

rise to the terms of relationship used by the Australian natives."[1] And after completing their second great exploration they wrote: "We are, after a further study of these tribes, more than ever convinced that amongst them group marriage preceded the modified form of individual marriage which is now the rule amongst the majority, though in all of the latter we find customs which can only be satisfactorily explained on the supposition that they are surviving relics of a time when group marriage was universally in vogue amongst all of the tribes."[2]

A similar conclusion is reached by Dr. Rivers, who has investigated the classificatory system in many different communities, none of them Australian. He says: "The classificatory system in one form or another is spread so widely over the world as to make it probable that it has had its origin in some universal, or almost universal, stage of social development, and I have attempted to indicate that the kind of society which most readily accounts for its chief features is one characterized by a form of marriage in which definite groups of men are the husbands of definite groups of women."[3] Further, Dr. Rivers is probably right in holding that "the classificatory system was in its origin expressive entirely of status. The terms would stand for certain relations within the group to which only the vaguest ideas of consanguinity need have been attached."[4] If this view of the classificatory terms of relationship as originally expressive of status rather than of kinship be borne in mind, it is obvious that the imaginary difficulties about the multiplication of fathers and mothers for each individual fall away of themselves. As I have already pointed out,[5] the Australian terms which answer to our "father" and "mother" do not necessarily imply either paternity or maternity in our sense of the terms.

But although it is probable that·in their origin the classificatory terms of relationship denoted status merely and not ties of blood, and although in Australia, for example,

Dr. Rivers on the classificatory system and group marriage.

The classificatory terms probably at first designated status only, not consanguinity.

But though the classificatory terms may

---

[1] *Native Tribes*, p. 59.
[2] *Northern Tribes*, p. 95.
[3] W. H. R. Rivers, "On the Origin of the Classificatory System of Relationship," in *Anthropological Essays presented to Edward Burnett Tylor* (Oxford, 1907), p. 323.
[4] W. H. R. Rivers, *op. cit.* pp. 321 *sq.*
[5] Above, pp. 286 *sq.*, 304 *sq.*

308 TOTEMISM IN CENTRAL AUSTRALIA CHAP.

<small>have originally expressed only status, they are at present certainly used to express also consanguinity and affinity.</small>

at the present day small children may still be spoken of as "fathers" and "mothers" in this sense, it is certain that the classificatory terms are now also used to express ideas of consanguinity and affinity by those who employ them; indeed the people have no other words to convey these ideas. And as time goes on the tendency would seem to be to use these terms more and more to denote consanguinity or affinity and less and less to denote status. At least such a tendency has been remarked by Dr. Rivers in three separate communities which possess the classificatory system. He says: "There is not the slightest doubt that at the present time the system is an expression of consanguinity and affinity to those who use it. I have now investigated the classificatory system in three communities,[1] and in all three it is perfectly clear that distinct ideas of consanguinity and affinity are associated with the terms. The correct use of the terms was over and over again justified by reference to actual blood or marriage ties traceable in the genealogical records preserved by the people, though in other cases in which the terms were used they denoted merely membership of the same social group and could not be justified by distinct ties of blood or marriage relationship. There is in these three peoples definite evidence of the double nature of the classificatory system as an expression of status and of consanguinity, and there are definite indications of a mode of evolution of the systems by which they are coming to express status less and ties of consanguinity and affinity more."[2]

<small>In Australia a form of group marriage persists to this day among some of the central tribes, notably the Urabunna and Dieri.</small>

In Australia we are not left merely to infer the former prevalence of group marriage from the group relationships of the classificatory system, for a form of group marriage persists to the present time in certain of the central tribes, particularly in the Urabunna and in the Dieri, whose social organisation, as we shall see later on, closely resembles that of the Urabunna. In the Urabunna tribe, as in all the tribes with which we are dealing, certain groups of men and

---

[1] "Mabuiag and Murray Islands in Torres Straits, and the Todas in India." Dr. Rivers has since studied the system in other communities.

[2] W. H. R. Rivers, "On the Origin of the Classificatory System of Relationships," in *Anthropological Essays presented to Edward Burnett Tylor* (Oxford, 1907), p. 322.

women are by birth *nupa* or marriageable to each other. On this subject Messrs. Spencer and Gillen write as follows: "Every man has one or more of these *nupa* women who are especially attached to him and live with him in his own camp, but there is no such thing as one man having the exclusive right to one woman; the elder brothers or *nuthi* of the woman, who decide the matter, will give one man a preferential right, but at the same time they will give other men of the same group to which he belongs—that is, men who stand in the same relationship to the woman as he does—a secondary right, and such *nupa* women to whom a man has the legal right of access are spoken of as his *piraungaru*. A woman may be *piraungaru* to a number of men and, as a general rule, men and women who are *piraungaru* to one another are to be found living together in groups. As we have said before, 'individual marriage does not exist either in name or in practice amongst the Urabunna tribe.' In this tribe we have: [sidenote: Group marriage among the Urabunna.]

"(1) A group of men all of whom belong to one moiety of the tribe and are regarded as the *nupas*, or possible husbands, of a group of women who belong to the other moiety of the tribe.

"(2) One or more women specially allotted to one particular man, each standing in the relationship of *nupa* to the other, but no man having exclusive right to any one woman—only a preferential right.

"(3) A group of men who stand in the relationship of *piraungaru* to a group of women, selected from amongst those to whom they are *nupa*. In other words, a group of women of one designation have, normally and actually, marital relations with a group of men of another designation,"[1] or, as the same writers elsewhere put it, "a group of women of a certain designation are actually the wives of a group of men of another designation."[2]

And since in this tribe groups of women are thus common to groups of men, it naturally follows that the children born of such unions are also common to the groups. All the children born of women whom a man might marry, whether [sidenote: The children born of such group marriages are also common to the groups.]

[1] *Northern Tribes*, pp. 72 *sq.* Compare *Native Tribes*, pp. 61-64.
[2] *Native Tribes*, p. 64.

he has marital relations with them or not, call him "father" (*nia*) and he calls them "children" (*biaka*). Whilst naturally there is a closer tie between a man and the children of the women who habitually live in camp with him, still there is no name to distinguish between the children of his own wives and those of women whom he might marry but with whom he has no sexual relations. All children of the men who are at the same level in the generation and belong to the same class and totem are regarded as the common children of these men, and similarly the men are regarded collectively by the children as their fathers.[1]

<small>The group marriage of the Urabunna and Dieri is not an abnormal development.</small>

With respect to this existing custom of group marriage among the Urabunna it is observed by Messrs. Spencer and Gillen that "there is no evidence of any kind to show that the practice in the Dieri and Urabunna tribes is an abnormal development. The organisation of these tribes, amongst whom the two exogamous intermarrying groups still persist —groups which in other tribes of the central area have been split into four or eight—indicates their retention of ancient customs which have become modified in tribes such as the Arunta and Warramunga, though amongst them we find traces of customs pointing back to conditions such as still persist amongst the Urabunna. If they were abnormal developments, then there could not possibly be found the remarkable but very instructive gradation from the system of individual marriage as developed amongst many Australian tribes and the undoubted exercise of group marital relations which is found in the Dieri and the Urabunna.

"In regard to marital relations it may be said that the Central Australian native has certain women, members of a particular group, with whom it is lawful for him and for other men also to have such relations. In the tribes with the simplest and undoubtedly the most primitive organisation these women are many in number. They all belong to a certain group, and, in the Urabunna tribe, for example, a group of men actually does have, continually and as a normal condition, marital relations with a group of women. This state of affairs has nothing whatever to do with polygamy any more than it has with polyandry. It is simply a

[1] *Native Tribes*, pp. 63 *sq.*

question of a group of men and a group of women who may lawfully have what we call marital relations. There is nothing whatever abnormal about it, and in all probability this system of what has been called group marriage, serving as it does to bind more or less closely together groups of individuals who are mutually interested in one another's welfare, has been one of the most powerful agents in the early stages of the upward development of the human race."[1]

<small>Group marriage has probably done much to promote progress.</small>

Even those central and northern tribes of Australia which no longer practise this form of group marriage observe certain customs which seem to be relics or survivals of group marriage, or rather of a sexual communism which must have far transgressed the limits now imposed on the intercourse of the sexes by the existing exogamous divisions, the classes and subclasses. For among all these tribes at marriage before a woman is handed over to one man to be his wife she is obliged to have intercourse not merely with those men of her husband's group who might lawfully be her husbands, but also with men of other groups with whom at other times she is strictly forbidden to cohabit. In most of the tribes even a woman's tribal brothers have access to her on this occasion, though at any other time such a union with tribal brothers would be regarded as incest and punished with death. The extraordinary rights thus regularly accorded to men over every woman just before her marriage cannot be explained as a mere orgy of unbridled lust; for they are not granted to every male without distinction, but only to those who stand to the woman in certain well-defined relationships; and further, the whole proceedings are strictly regulated by custom, for the men have access to the woman in a prescribed order according to the precise position which they occupy towards her in the tribal system, so that the men who at other times would be wholly tabooed to her come first and the men who might lawfully be her husbands come last.[2]

<small>Even in Australian tribes which no longer practise a form of group marriage there are customs which seem to be survivals of group marriage or of still wider sexual communism.</small>

For example, in the Kaitish tribe men of the following relationships have access to a woman just before her

---

[1] *Northern Tribes*, pp. 73 sq.
[2] *Native Tribes*, pp. 92, 96, 102 note [1], 107, 110 sq.; *Northern Tribes*, pp. 133, 136.

Communal rights over a woman before her marriage among the Kaitish.

marriage in the following order: *Ipmunna*, that is, men of the same moiety (class) of the tribe as her own; mothers' brothers' sons; tribal elder and younger brothers; and lastly, men whom she might lawfully marry, but who have no right to her when once she becomes the wife and the property of a member of the group to which they belong. If the woman happens to be, say, of the Panunga subclass, then the men who have access to her on this occasion belong to the four subclasses Ungalla, Uknaria, Purula, and Panunga, but men of the other four subclasses Bulthara, Appungerta, Kumara, and Umbitchana are excluded.[1] Thus two of the subclasses which are granted the privilege, namely, Panunga and Uknaria, belong to the woman's own moiety or class, from which at ordinary times she is strictly debarred by the rule of exogamy. Yet even on this occasion liberty does not degenerate into unregulated licence, since four out of the eight subclasses are excluded from the privilege.

Similar communal rights are exercised among all the central and northern tribes.

In all the other central and northern tribes the customs at marriage are similar, though the men who are accorded the privilege vary from tribe to tribe. "But in all cases the striking feature is that, for the time being, the existence of what can only be described as partial promiscuity can clearly be seen. By this we do not mean that marital rights are allowed to any man, but that for a time such rights are allowed to individuals to whom at other times the woman is *ekirinja*, or forbidden."[2] "In every tribe, without exception, men have intercourse with her who belong to the same group as her husband—that is, are lawfully her husbands, and in various tribes others who stand to her in one or other of the following relationships also have access:—father's sister's sons, mother's brother's sons, mother's brother, mother's mother's brother, elder and younger brothers, but not in blood, father's father, husband's father. To all of these, except on rare occasions, and to some of them always afterwards, she is strictly tabooed. In fact intercourse with any of them, except on such rare occasions, would be immediately followed by punishment, and in the case of certain, such as tribal brothers, by death."[3]

[1] *Native Tribes*, p. 96. [2] *Ibid.* pp. 94 sq., 107.
[3] *Northern Tribes*, p. 136.

I fully agree with Messrs. Spencer and Gillen that these customs are best explained "as lingering relics of a former stage passed through in the development of the present social organisation of the various tribes in which they are found."[1] "They indicate the temporary recognition of certain general rights which existed in the time prior to that of the form of group marriage of which we have such clear traces yet lingering amongst the tribes. We do not mean that they afford direct evidence of the former existence of actual promiscuity, but they do afford evidence leading in that direction, and they certainly point back to a time when there existed wider marital relations than obtain at the present day—wider, in fact, than those which are shown in the form of group marriage from which the present system is derived. On no other hypothesis yet advanced do the customs connected with marriage, which are so consistent in their general nature and leading features from tribe to tribe, appear to us to be capable of satisfactory explanation."[2]

Such communal rights appear to be relics of a former state of sexual communism.

[1] *Native Tribes*, p. 96.   [2] *Ibid.* p. 111.

CHAPTER II

TOTEMISM IN SOUTH-EASTERN AUSTRALIA

§ 1. *Physical Geography of South-Eastern Australia in Relation to Aboriginal Society*

WE have seen that the central and northern tribes of Australia present, first, a practically continuous gradation in their totemic system as we proceed northwards from the centre to the sea, and, second, a nearly complete uniformity in their social organisation, that is, in their exogamous rules, over the whole of the same wide area. It is otherwise with the tribes of South-Eastern Australia, which are, or rather were, as heterogeneous in their totemic and social systems as the others are on the whole homogeneous. The contrast in these respects between the two sets of tribes is probably to be explained in large measure by the different physical configuration of the countries which they occupy. The uniformity of the barren steppes and monotonous plains of Central and Northern Australia presents few obstacles to the intercourse of the tribes, for it is only at rare intervals that the scattered inhabitants of the wilds are parted from each other by a line of rugged mountains, itself cleft by deep gorges which serve as highways between one side and the other of these desolate and stony ranges. The ease of communication between the tribes has naturally facilitated the transmission of customs and ideas from one to the other; hence we can understand the remarkable uniformity of some institutions and the hardly less remarkable gradation of others over the whole of the central and northern region. On the other hand in South-Eastern Australia the dislocation of custom

While the central and northern tribes of Australia are homogeneous in their social organisation, the tribes of South-East Australia are very heterogeneous, and this heterogeneity is probably a consequence of the more varied configuration of the country.

between neighbouring tribes is often a natural consequence of the physical barriers which divide them. For in this part of the continent great rivers, broad lakes, thick forests, and lofty mountains break up the face of nature, and so render communication between the savages in many contiguous districts at once arduous and infrequent. Thus cut off from others by difficult or impassable obstacles, each community has been left free to develop its institutions in its own way, and we need not wonder that as a result of such seclusion the lines of development should have diverged somewhat widely from each other.

But the greater natural diversity of South-Eastern Australia, compared with the dreary monotony of Central and Northern Australia, has fostered the divergence or dislocation of custom in another way than by severing the tribes from their neighbours. The differences of physical features and of geographical situation are inevitably attended by differences of climate, and these again by differences in the supply of water, of game, of fish, of edible plants and fruits, in short, of all the necessities and conveniences of life. From the high Australian Alps of Eastern Victoria and New South Wales, where in winter the tree-ferns lie buried in snow for months together, where traffic at such times is only possible on Norwegian snow shoes,[1] and where, as in the snowfields of Switzerland, the gentian breaks the dazzling veil of white with its blue blossoms,[2] the traveller may pass by almost insensible gradations from one extremity of climate and scenery to another. Through dense forests, where the trees in the ravines are the most gigantic yet seen on earth,[3] he descends to valleys where rivers tumble in graceful cascades or wind between lofty cliffs and hanging woods, rank with creepers, ferns, and vines. In some of these stately forests the flame-tree with its great bunches of red flowers grows in such luxuriance as to wrap the side of a mountain in a crimson pall that may

The differences of climate and of fertility are also much greater in South-Eastern than in Central Australia.

[1] J. W. Gregory, *Australasia*, i. (London, 1907) p. 195 (in *Stanford's Compendium of Geography and Travel*).
[2] A. R. Wallace, *Australasia*, i. (London, 1893) p. 54.
[3] A. R. Wallace, *op. cit.* pp. 49 *sq.*, 274 *sqq.* Many of these trees are over 400 feet in height; one fallen giant has been found to measure 480 feet.

be seen for miles out at sea.¹ With its grand mountains, beautiful waterfalls, numerous lakes, rich soil, luxuriant vegetation, and agreeable climate Victoria is the most favoured part of the continent and well deserves its old name of Australia Felix.²

<small>The Wimmera District of Victoria.</small>

Yet in its north-western portion, the Wimmera District as it is called, the territory of Victoria merges into those boundless flats which characterise the interior of Australia. Here for miles and miles the eye may range over level plains, where the roads run in perfectly straight lines and the paddock fences are arranged with the regularity of a chess-board, where only a few gum-trees dotted here and there along the creeks break the weary monotony of the vast expanse which stretches away till it meets the sky-line on the north or is bounded on the south by the blue peaks of Mount Korong faintly descried in the far distance.³ It is here, too, that our imaginary traveller who has descended from the snowy heights of the Australian Alps will first meet with what is called the mallee scrub, which covers great areas in the interior of Australia. This is a dense shrubbery or thicket of a dwarf species of eucalyptus to which the natives give the name of *mallee*. It resembles a bushy willow or osier; the stems grow to a height of fourteen feet without a branch, and are set as thick in the yellow sandy soil as reeds in a jungle, so that a road cut through the scrub resembles a deep trench enclosed by high banks. The aspect of country covered with such scrub is very gloomy. From any eminence you can perceive nothing on earth but a sea of sombre brown bushes stretching as far as the eye can reach, above which a solitary tree rising at rare intervals seems only to deepen the melancholy of the scene, especially on a dull day when a grey clouded sky broods over the mournful silence of the landscape. Even sunshine hardly cheers the prospect, for if it lightens a little the sad colouring of the endless shrubbery, it at the same time extends the view of it further and

<small>The mallee scrub.</small>

---

¹ A. R. Wallace, *op. cit.* pp. 53, 215, 269, 272. Compare J. W. Gregory, *Australasia*, i. 153.
² A. R. Wallace, *op. cit.* pp. 265, 269 *sq.*, 273. As to the lakes of Victoria, see J. W. Gregory, *Australasia*, i. pp. 407 *sqq.*
³ A. R. Wallace, *Australasia*, i. pp. 267 *sq.*; J. W. Gregory, *Australasia*, i. 394.

further, and so seems to render escape from it still more hopeless.¹

But the mallee scrub is by no means the worst that the traveller has to encounter in these regions. More dreaded still is the mulga scrub, consisting chiefly of dwarf acacias. These grow together in irregular spreading bushes armed with strong spines, and where they are matted and knit together with other shrubs they form a dense mass of vegetation through which nothing but the axe can cleave a way. Fortunately the mulga scrub is far less common than the mallee scrub, or the task of the explorer would be even more laborious and distressing.² But worst of all the products of the Australian wilderness is the spinifex or porcupine grass (*Triodia irritans*), which spreads over sandy plains for hundreds of miles and probably covers a greater extent of surface than any other plant in Australia. It is a hard spiny grass growing in tussocks of sharp yellowish spikes, which, radiating like knitting-needles from a huge pin-cushion, bid defiance even to camels accustomed to munch the thorny vegetation of the desert, while their cruel points so lacerate the legs of horses and goad the beasts into such frenzy that it is often necessary to destroy them. This pest haunts the most arid sandy wastes where no water is to be found either above or below ground. No wonder that it is the dread of the Australian explorer. However, its range is happily limited by about the twenty-eighth parallel of south latitude, so that it only fringes the northern boundary of that part of Australia with which we are at present concerned.³ Indeed with it we reach the true desert country and the heart, the dead heart, of the continent. Here the characteristic feature of the landscape is the long succession of yellow sandhills dying down from time to time into dead flats covered with mulga scrub or, where all vegetation disappears, overlaid with brown and purple stones, which are set so close together as to form as it were a tesselated pavement that stretches away to the horizon. In this dismal and monotonous scenery a

The mulga scrub.

The central deserts of Australia.

---

¹ A. R. Wallace, *Australasia*, i. 46 *sq.*; J. W. Gregory, *Australasia*, i. 395 *sq.*

² A. R. Wallace, *Australasia*, i. 47 *sq.*

³ A. R. Wallace, *Australasia*, i. 48 *sq.* As to the porcupine grass see also Spencer and Gillen, *Native Tribes of Central Australia*, p. 6.

wretched diversity is here and there created by the remains of what once were lakes, but are now nothing but level expanses of white glistering salt hemmed in by low hills overgrown with dreary scrub. Around these waterless basins there is no sign of life, and the most perfect silence reigns.[1]

<small>Great contrasts in rainfall and temperature between the coasts and the interior of Australia.</small>

The extraordinary contrast between these arid wildernesses of the interior and the luxuriant forests and rich park-lands of Victoria, the gulf which divides Australia Deserta from Australia Felix, is an effect of the variation in the rainfall, which diminishes rapidly as we recede inland from the sea and from the lofty mountains of the south-east, and varies from sixty, seventy, eighty, or ninety inches on the coast to five or six inches, or even to less than an inch, in the far interior.[2] And as the rainfall decreases so the heat increases the further we withdraw from the refreshing influence of the sea breezes, laden with moisture and dispensing coolness, fertility, and life. From the chill air of the Australian Alps, where the snowdrifts linger in the gullies even at midsummer, and snow showers may fall at any time throughout the year,[3] the change is great to the torrid heat of the central deserts, where the temperature occasionally rises to such a pitch that were it prolonged at the same height it would inevitably destroy life. The mercury in a thermometer, sheltered both from sun and wind, has been known to rise till it burst the tube, which was graduated to 127° Fahrenheit. Such fervent heat probably does not last for a long time together; yet for three months Captain Sturt found the mean temperature to be over 101° Fahrenheit in the shade; and the drought was such that every screw dropped out of the boxes, combs and horn handles split up into fine flakes, the lead fell out of pencils, the finger-nails of the explorers became as brittle as glass, and the hair of men and the wool of sheep ceased to grow.[4]

---

[1] Spencer and Gillen, *Native Tribes of Central Australia*, pp. 2, 6 *sq.*

[2] J. W. Gregory, *Australasia*, i. 157 *sq.*, 191 *sqq.*; E. Reclus, *Nouvelle Géographie Universelle*, xiv. 757; A. W. Howitt, *Native Tribes of South-East Australia*, pp. 38 *sq.*

[3] A. R. Wallace, *Australasia*, i. 41; J. W. Gregory, *Australasia*, i. 195.

[4] Captain C. Sturt, *Narrative of an Expedition into Central Australia* (London, 1849), i. 305 *sq.*, ii. 90 *sq.* Elsewhere Captain Sturt observes: "I took a straight line for the water-holes, and reached them at half-past 6 P.M., after an exposure, from morning till night, to as great a heat as man ever endured; but if the heat of this day

Even parts of the interior which are drained by great and perennial rivers, such as the basin of the Darling River in New South Wales, nevertheless suffer from long and severe droughts. The Darling River commonly flows between high banks of clay, but occasionally, swollen by the tropical rains in Queensland, it pours over its banks and floods the country for miles. At such a time steamers have been known to sail for hours over the submerged plains without sighting land.[1] Yet even of this country we are told by an early settler, whose account I will quote, that in its natural state it "could not support a large population, being subject to protracted droughts, during which both food and water must have been scarce. During my fifteen years' experience there were three severe droughts, varying in duration from eighteen to twenty-two months. At such times the little rain that fell on the dry and parched ground was insufficient to replenish the water-holes, or soak the ground enough to promote a growth of vegetation. But it appears, from what some of the old natives have told me, that Europeans have not experienced the worst that the country is liable to, for they say that they once saw it in a drier state than it has been since the settlers came, and there has been stock on the country as a drain on the water-supply. On that occasion their only water-supply was at the few springs in the back country and at the rivers. All surface water-holes were dry; some of which would, I know, stand through a two years' drought with stock drinking at them. They camped at the springs or the rivers, existing on the half-starved animals, which were forced to drink from the same supply, and in consequence of their weak condition were killed without much difficulty. In a drought there is neither grass nor herbage in the neighbourhood of water, and the desert-like appearance of the surrounding brick-red sandhills was excessive, that of the succeeding one on which we returned to Joseph was still more so. We reached our destination at 3 P.M., as we started early, and on looking at the thermometer fixed behind a tree about five feet from the ground, I found the mercury standing at 132°; on removing it into the sun it rose to 157°. Only on one occasion, when Mr. Browne and I were returning from the north, had the heat approached to this; nor did I think that either men or animals could have lived under it" (C. Sturt, *op. cit.* i. 288).

[1] J. W. Gregory, *Australasia*, i. 261 *sq.*, 305.

320   TOTEMISM IN SOUTH-EASTERN AUSTRALIA   CHAP.

and grey-coloured clay flats is relieved only by sundry hardy bushes and small trees, which somehow hold up against the extreme dryness and hot winds. These long droughts are generally broken suddenly by a fall of two or three inches of rain, followed by lighter rains, which rapidly improve the appearance of the country; grass and herbage become abundant, and water-fowl return in large numbers to the creeks, and the aborigines gladly avail themselves of the opportunity of moving on to fresh hunting-grounds, which they can only reach when surface water is plentiful." [1]

The larger rainfall and more abundant supply of food have given the natives of the coast an advantage over the natives of the interior.

Similarly Spencer and Gillen have described the marvellous transformation of the face of the country which takes place when, after a long drought, rain has fallen on the arid steppes of Central Australia. At these times what had lately been a sandy desert becomes, as if by magic, a garden teeming with life and gay with the blossoms of endless flowering plants.[2] Such descriptions help us to realise the simple truth that both animals and plants depend directly for their existence on a due supply of water, and where that fails, the inevitable consequence, sooner or later, is sterility and death. Now the coast-lands of Australia are, as we have seen, the best watered parts of the continent;[3] on them, accordingly, the supply of food, both animal and vegetable, is most abundant. Hence the coastal tribes of Australia have, on the whole, enjoyed a great advantage over the inland tribes in the struggle for existence, since they have had to their hand abundance of water, abundance of fish and game, abundance of the fruits of the earth.[4] These favourable conditions have naturally reacted on the life of the natives, who, partially relieved from the need of devoting themselves to the purely animal quest for

---

[1] F. Bonney, "On some Customs of the Aborigines of the River Darling," *Journal of the Anthropological Institute*, xiii. (1884) p. 123.

[2] See above, pp. 170 *sq.*

[3] Above, p. 318.

[4] See A. W. Howitt, *Native Tribes of South-East Australia*, p. 35. The tribes at the head of the Great Australian Bight, in South Australia, form to some extent an exception to this rule, since at this point the desert extends nearly to the sea. Indeed, along the whole extent of the Great Australian Bight, a length of about a thousand miles, not a single stream enters the ocean (A. R. Wallace, *Australasia*, i. 31 *sq.*). Still even here the coastal tribes are better off than the inland tribes, since they can draw a supply of fish and shell-fish from the sea.

food, have had leisure to make some advances on the road to civilisation. For example, whereas the tribes of Central Australia appear not to have conceived the idea of making any kind of clothing as a protection against cold, but huddle naked round their fires on frosty nights, though they might easily clothe themselves in the skins of kangaroos and wallabies,[1] the tribes who inhabit the coast of South Australia make excellent warm rugs out of opossum, kangaroo, wallaby, and other furs. The skins are first dried, then carefully scraped and scored with a sharp stone or shell to make them flexible; afterwards they are cut into squares, which are sewn with the sinews of a kangaroo's tail, the eye-holes being made in the skins with a sharp-pointed bone. In the Port Lincoln tribe the best of these rugs are always worn by the women.[2] Further, the Narrinyeri tribe make thick, durable mats out of the bark of the mallee scrub, which they dry and beat into a fibrous mass. Also they gather seaweed on the shore, wash it in fresh water, dry it, and work it into mats with a shaggy nap, which serve them as beds. Moreover, they take the skins of many animals, peg them out on the ground till they are dry, and then spread them out on the earth whenever they encamp in damp or marshy places.[3] Again, whereas the natives of Central Australia have nothing to protect themselves from the weather but shelters of shrubs placed so as to screen the occupants from the prevailing wind,[4] in South-Western Victoria the aborigines built permanent houses of wood or stone large enough to accommodate a dozen or more persons. Each of these houses was occupied by a family, and when the members of the family were grown up, the house was partitioned off into apartments, each facing the fire, which burned in the centre. When the material employed was wood, the mode of construction was to set up strong limbs of trees in the shape of a dome high enough to allow a tall

Thus whereas the central tribes are naked and houseless, the coastal tribes have made for themselves warm rugs and solid and roomy huts.

---

[1] Spencer and Gillen, *Native Tribes of Central Australia*, pp. 16-19.
[2] G. Taplin and C. W. Schürmann, in *Native Tribes of South Australia*, pp. 43, 210 sq. The Yarra tribe of Victoria make similar rugs out of opossum skins. See R. Brough Smyth, *The Aborigines of Victoria*, i. 271.
[3] G. Taplin, "The Narrinyeri," in *Native Tribes of South Australia*, p. 43.
[4] Spencer and Gillen, *Native Tribes of Central Australia*, p. 18.

man to stand upright under them. The interstices were filled with smaller branches, and the whole was covered with sheets of bark, thatch, sods, and earth till the roof and sides were proof against wind and rain. Where stones were more easily procured than wood and bark, the walls were built of flat stones and roofed with branches and thatch. Where several families lived together, each built its own house facing one central fire. Thus, in what appeared to be one dwelling, fifty or more persons could be accommodated, when, in the words of the natives themselves, they were "like bees in a hive." These comfortable and healthy habitations, as they are called by an early settler in Victoria, whose description of them I have reproduced, were situated on dry spots beside a lake, stream, or salubrious swamp, but never near a malarious morass nor under large trees, which might fall or be struck by lightning.[1] Similarly the tribes of South Australia in the district of Adelaide and the Murray River sometimes built huts of thick, solid logs of wood, which they covered with grass, creepers, and anything else that would make them waterproof. Large, long huts of this sort would contain from five to ten families, each of them with its separate fire.[2] The contrast between these comfortable, well-built houses and the miserable temporary shelters of the Central Australians is immense, and marks a great step upward on the social ladder.

Huts of the coastal tribes of New South Wales. In like manner the early explorers and settlers on the east and west coasts of Australia observed that the natives who dwelt by the sea had larger and better houses than the natives of the interior. Thus Collins, writing of

---

[1] J. Dawson, *Australian Aborigines* (Melbourne, Sydney, and Adelaide, 1881), pp. 10 *sq*. The tribes described by J. Dawson occupied the south-western part of Victoria between Portland, Colac, Ararat, and perhaps Pitfield. See A. W. Howitt, *Native Tribes of South-East Australia*, p. 69. Dr. Howitt tells us that Dawson enjoyed exceptional opportunities of observation from nearly the settlement of the State of Victoria (*op. cit.* p. 307).

[2] E. J. Eyre, *Journals of Expeditions of Discovery into Central Australia* (London, 1845), ii. 302 *sq*. As to the tribes here described, Eyre informs us that his descriptions apply to the natives of South Australia, and particularly to the tribes of the Adelaide district and the Murray River (*op. cit.* ii. 151). He quotes (ii. 301 note) an account of a permanent native village, which consisted of thirteen large huts, warm and well constructed, each hut being built of a strong frame of wood, and covered with thick turf.

the aborigines of New South Wales near the end of the eighteenth century, says: "Their habitations are as rude as imagination can conceive. The hut of the woodman is made of the bark of a single tree, bent in the middle, and placed on its two ends on the ground, affording shelter to only one miserable tenant. These they never carry about with them. On the sea coast the huts were larger, formed of pieces of bark from several trees put together in the form of an oven, with an entrance, and large enough to hold six or eight people."[1] On the opposite side of Australia, when Sir George Grey was exploring the western coast in the neighbourhood of Gantheaume Bay, he came upon a remarkably fertile district, which exhibited tokens of a comparatively dense native population settled in fixed villages. It will be best to allow the explorer to describe his observations and to state his conclusions in his own words. He says:—

Sir George Grey's account of the signs of an advance in material culture among the natives of a fertile region in West Australia.

"We now crossed the dry bed of a stream, and from that emerged upon a tract of light fertile soil, quite overrun with *warran* plants,[2] the root of which is a favourite article of food with the natives. This was the first time we had yet seen this plant on our journey, and now for three and a half consecutive miles we traversed a fertile piece of land, literally perforated with the holes the natives had made to dig this root; indeed we could with difficulty walk across it on that account, whilst this tract extended east and west as far as we could see. It was now evident that we had entered the most thickly-populated district of Australia that I had yet observed, and moreover one which must have been inhabited for a long series of years, for more had here been done to secure a provision from the ground by hard manual labour than I could have believed it in the power of uncivilised man to accomplish."[3] After crossing a low lime-

---

[1] Lieut.-Col. Collins, *Account of the English Colony in New South Wales*, Second Edition (London, 1804), p. 360. The first edition of this work was published at London in 1798. The second edition was posthumous; I quote it because I possess a copy.

[2] "The *warran* is a species of Dioscorea, a sort of yam like the sweet potatoe. It is known by the same name both on the east and west side of the continent."

[3] The manual labour to which Grey here refers is clearly that of digging up the roots. He gives no hint that the natives cultivated them, nor have we any right to assume that they did so, though it is likely enough that they performed magical ceremonies or *intichiuma*, as the Arunta would call them, to make the plants grow. See above, pp. 105 *sqq.*

stone-range, we came down upon another equally fertile *warran* ground, bounded eastward by a high range of rocky limestone hills, luxuriantly grassed, and westward by a low range of similar formation. The native path, about two miles further on, crossed this latter range, and we found ourselves in a grassy valley, about four miles wide, bounded seawards by sandy downs. Along its centre lay a chain of reedy fresh-water swamps, and native paths ran in from all quarters, to one main line of communication leading to the southward. . . .

"Such a heavy dew had fallen during the night, that when I got up in the morning, I found my clothes completely saturated, and everything looked so verdant and flourishing compared to the parched-up country which existed to the north of us, and that which I knew lay to the south, that I tried to find a satisfactory reason, to explain so strange a circumstance—but without success. It seemed certain, however, that we stood in the richest province of South-west Australia, and one which so differs from the other portions of it in its geological characters, in the elevations of its mountains which lie close to the sea coast, in the fertility of its soil, and the density of its native population, that we appeared to be moving upon another continent. As yet however the only means I had of judging of the large number of natives inhabiting this district, had been from their paths and *warran* grounds. . . .

"Being unable to ford the river here, we followed it in a S.E. direction for two miles, and in this distance passed two native villages, or, as the men termed them, towns; the huts of which they were composed differed from those in the southern districts, in being much larger, more strongly built, and very nicely plastered over on the outside with clay, and clods of turf, so that although now uninhabited, they were evidently intended for fixed places of residence. This again shewed a marked difference between the habits of the natives of this part of Australia, and the south-western portions of the continent; for these superior huts, well-marked roads, deeply sunk wells, and extensive *warran* grounds, all spoke of a large and comparatively speaking resident population, and the cause of this undoubtedly must have been, the great facilities for procuring food in so rich a soil." [1]

Thus in material culture, in clothes and habitations, the natives of the better-watered and more fruitful coasts of Australia exhibit a marked superiority over the naked, houseless nomads of the central deserts. It is natural and perhaps inevitable that man's earliest efforts to ameliorate his lot should be directed towards the satisfaction of his physical wants, since the material side of his nature is the indispensable basis on which, in a material world, his intellectual and moral being must rest. But material progress in the arts and comforts of life is at the same time a sure sign of intellectual progress, since every implement, from the rudest club of the lowest savage to the most complex and delicate machine of modern science, is nothing but the physical embodiment of an idea which preceded it in the mind of man.[2] Hence in the evolution of culture, mental improvement is the prime factor, the moving cause; material improvement is secondary, it follows the other as its effect. It would be well if the shallow rhetoricians who rail at the advance of mechanical science in our own age could apprehend this truth. They would then see that in arraigning what they do not understand they are really arraigning that upward movement in the mind of man which, though we know neither its origin nor its goal, is yet the source of all that is best and noblest in human nature.

Material progress in the arts of life is at once a sign and an effect of intellectual progress.

From these considerations it follows that a people's progress in the material arts is not only the most obvious but on the whole the surest measure of its intellectual and social progress. The highest types of human intellect and character are never found among naked, houseless, artless

Advance in the arts is the surest measure of intellectual and social advance.

---

[1] G. Grey, *Journals of two Expeditions of Discovery in North-West and Western Australia* (London, 1841), ii. 12 *sq.*, 15 *sq.*, 19 *sq.*

[2] This dependence of material upon intellectual progress was justly insisted upon by that philosophical student of primitive man, the late General Pitt-Rivers. Thus, for example, speaking of the characteristic Australian weapons, the boomerang and the waddy, he says: "These words and these implements are but the outward signs or symbols of particular ideas in the mind; and the sequence, if any, which we observe to connect them together, is but the outward sign of the succession of ideas in the brain. It is the mind that we study by means of these symbols" (*The Evolution of Culture*, Oxford, 1906, p. 23).

savages; they are only found in countries and in ages which have attained to the highest pitch of material civilisation, which have carried the arts and crafts to their greatest perfection. It is in towns, not in the wilderness, that the fairest flowers of humanity have bloomed. True civilisation begins, as the very name suggests, with the foundation of cities. Where no such ganglia of concentrated energy exist, the population is savage or barbarous.

The coastal tribes of Australia shew signs of political and social, as well as of material, progress by comparison with the central tribes.

Though the aboriginal Australians never advanced so far as to build towns, we have seen that in some parts of the more fertile regions bordering on the sea they established what may fairly be described as permanent villages, both well-built and comfortable. Side by side with this evidence of material progress we find evidence also of political and social progress among the tribes of the coast. For whereas among the aborigines of the central steppes the government of the tribe is in the hands of an oligarchy of old men, who completely control everything without regard to the opinions or wishes of the younger men,[1] the natives of the more fruitful regions near the sea had made, when they were first observed by Europeans, considerable advances towards a monarchical government, which is an essential step in the evolution of civilisation out of savagery.[2]

---

[1] Thus Messrs. Spencer and Gillen tell us that the elder men "form, as it were, an inner council or cabinet and completely control everything. The younger men have absolutely no say whatever in the matter" (*Northern Tribes*, p. 21). Again they write: "Whenever a large number of natives are met together to perform ceremonies, there are always the heads of different local groups present. The elder and more important amongst these seem naturally to associate together as an informal but, at the same time, all-powerful council, whose orders are implicitly obeyed by the other men. The fact that any individual is the headman of his local group gives him, in itself, no claim whatever to attendance upon these councils. If, however, he be at all a distinguished man, whose conduct has shown that he is to be trusted, and that he is deeply interested in tribal matters, then some day he will be honoured by one of the older men inviting him to come and consult over matters, after the advisability of doing so has been agreed upon by the members of the council. He will probably be invited several times, and will then gradually take his place as a recognised member of the inner council of the tribe, his influence increasing as he grows older and older. Not only does this council of elder men determine matters concerned with various ceremonies, but in addition it deals with the punishment of the more serious crimes." This senate or council of elders has the power of life and death, for it sends out avenging parties to punish culprits who have infringed the fundamental laws of the tribe. See *Northern Tribes*, pp. 24 *sq.*

[2] See my *Lectures on the Early History of the Kingship*, pp. 81 *sqq.*

It is true that in the central tribes each local totemic group has its headman or *alatunja*, as the Arunta call him; but his authority is somewhat vague and he has no definite power over the members of his group. His main duties are rather sacred or magical than civil, his principal function being to perform the ceremonies for the multiplication of the totemic animal or plant and to take charge of the secret storehouse in which the most prized possessions of the people, to wit, their *churinga* or sacred sticks and stones, are carefully preserved from the eyes of the profane.[1] The post is within certain limits hereditary, for it passes from father to son, always provided that the son is of the same totem as his father; for example, the headman of a Kangaroo group must be a Kangaroo man, and if he has a son who is also a Kangaroo, he may transmit his office of headman to that son at his death. But since among the true central tribes a man's totem is not determined by that of his father and often differs from it, a son sometimes cannot inherit the post of headman from his father. In that case the father, when he comes to die, nominates his successor, who is always either a brother or a brother's son.[2] As the functions of the local headman in these tribes are to a great extent magical, being concerned with the ceremonies for the multiplication of the totemic animal or plant, so with the gradual diminution of these ceremonies as we proceed from the centre northwards the importance of the office of headman also gradually diminishes until, regarded from the magical or ceremonial point of view, it reaches its lowest point among the coastal tribes. For among these tribes the social aspect of the totemic groups has become more prominent, while their economical and magical aspect is almost obliterated.[3] But while the duties of a totemic headman decrease in importance as we pass from the centre towards the sea, yet the authority of the post becomes concentrated in fewer hands. For whereas among the Arunta there may be, and usually are, several headmen for

Among the central tribes there is no chieftainship.

---

[1] Spencer and Gillen, *Native Tribes*, pp. 9-15, 154, 159-205; *id.*, *Northern Tribes*, pp. 20-27, 285-297, 309 *sq.*, 316.

[2] Spencer and Gillen, *Native Tribes*, pp. 10 *sq.*

[3] Spencer and Gillen, *Northern Tribes of Central Australia*, p. 23.

each totem, among the Warramunga and other northern tribes each totemic clan has only one headman. For example, in these northern tribes all the Kangaroo people recognise the authority of one Kangaroo headman; all the Water people recognise the authority of one Water headman, and so forth. Nay, more than that, the natives recognise in a vague way a headman for each of the two tribal moieties. For example, when Spencer and Gillen visited the Warramunga tribe, an old White Cockatoo man was regarded as the head of one moiety of the tribe, and a man of the mythical water-snake totem (*wollunqua*) was regarded as the head of the other. This honourable position they owed in large measure to their age and learning. When it came to hard knocks, neither of these venerable sages would have put himself in the forefront of the battle. That duty they discreetly left to a veteran of the name of Tjupilla, head of the wind totem, who enjoyed the reputation of being a first-class fighting man.[1] It seems possible that this dual headship of a tribe might in time have developed into a double kingship, if the aborigines had been left free to evolve their institutions on their own lines. As it is, the vague authority attaching to the post of headman in these tribes has never grown even into a chieftainship; for we are told that among these people "there is no such thing as a chief of the tribe, nor indeed is there any individual to whom the term chief can be applied."[2] It is true that in up-country parts a native of appropriate age may sometimes be found decorated with a brass plate whereon is inscribed some such legend as "King Billy, chief of the Gurraburra tribe." But these claims to sovereignty have no foundation in fact.[3]

But on the more fertile coasts the tribes have made some approach to a regular chieftainship. On the other hand, on the more fertile coasts of Australia aboriginal society appears to have made some approach to, if not to have actually evolved, a regular chieftainship. Thus in the days of the first settlement about Botany Bay it was observed by the English colonists that the natives "are

[1] Spencer and Gillen, *Northern Tribes*, pp. 25 sq.
[2] Spencer and Gillen, *Native Tribes*, p. 10. Similarly in their *Northern Tribes* (p. 20) these writers observe:
"There is no one to whom the term 'chief,' or even head of the tribe, can be properly applied."
[3] Spencer and Gillen, *Native Tribes*, p. 103 note[1].

distributed into families, the head or senior of which exacts compliance from the rest. In the early intercourse with them (and indeed at a much later period, on the English meeting with families to whom they were unknown) they were always accosted by the person who appeared to be the eldest of the party; while the women, youths, and children were kept at a distance. The word which in their language signifies father was applied to their old men; and when, after some time, and by close observation, they perceived the authority with which Governor Phillip commanded, and the obedience which he exacted, they bestowed on him the distinguishing appellation of *Be-anna*, or father. This title being conferred solely on him (although they perceived the authority of masters over their servants) places the true sense of the word beyond a doubt, and proves that to those among them who enjoyed that distinction belonged the authority of a chief. When any of these went into the town, they were immediately pointed out by their companions, or those natives who resided in it, in a whisper, and with an eagerness of manner which, while it commanded the attention of those to whom it was directed, impressed them likewise with an idea that they were looking at persons remarkable for some superior quality even among the savages of New Holland."[1]

Again, with regard to the Narrinyeri, who occupied a district on the coast of South Australia, to the south of Adelaide, we are told that "each of the tribes of the Narrinyeri has its chief, whose title is *rupulle* (which means landowner), who is their leader in war, and whose person is carefully guarded in battle by the warriors of his clan. The *rupulle* is the negotiator and spokesman for the tribe in all disagreements with other tribes; and his advice is sought on all occasions of difficulty or perplexity. His authority is supported by the heads of families, and he is expected always to reside on the hunting-grounds of the tribe. The *rupulle* used to possess the right to divide the animals taken in the chase amongst the other heads of families, but this is seldom observed now. The chieftainship is not hereditary, Chieftainship among the Narrinyeri.

[1] Lieut.-Col. Collins, *Account of the English Colony in New South Wales* (London, 1804), pp. 351 *sq.*

but elective. The deceased chief's brother, or second son, is quite as eligible for the dignity as the eldest son, if the heads of families prefer him. . . . But the most real authority exercised by the chief and his supporters is enforced by means of witchcraft. If any young men or women attempt a departure from the customs of their forefathers they are immediately threatened with *ngadhungi*, or *millin*, and this usually restrains them."[1] Of these magical modes of reinforcing the claims of law and morality the one (*ngadhungi*) consists in securing a bone of any animal of which the culprit had partaken and afterwards putting it in the fire. The other (*millin*) consists in the more summary and perhaps more effectual process of knocking him down with a stout cudgel and then operating on him with the same instrument till he is delivered over to the power of a demon called Nalkaru.[2]

Chieftainship in South-Western Victoria.

But it is in the south-western parts of Victoria, the Australia Felix of the older geographers, that the authority of one man over his fellows seems to have been carried furthest. Here, to quote an excellent authority who knew the natives in the early days of the colony, " every tribe has its chief, who is looked upon in the light of a father, and whose authority is supreme. He consults with the best men of the tribe, but when he announces his decision they dare not contradict or disobey him. Great respect is paid to the chiefs and their wives and families. They can command the services of every one belonging to their tribe. As many as six young bachelors are obliged to wait on a chief, and eight young unmarried men on his wife; and, as the children are of superior rank to the common people, they also have a number of attendants to wait on them. No one can address a chief or chiefess without being first spoken to, and then only by their titles as such and not by personal names, or disrespectfully. Food and water, when brought to the camp, must be offered to them first, and reeds provided for each in the family to drink with; while the common people drink in the usual way. Should they fancy any article of dress, opossum rug, or weapon, it must be given

---

[1] Rev. G. Taplin, "The Narrinyeri," *Native Tribes of South Australia*, p. 32.

[2] Rev. G. Taplin, *op. cit.*, pp. 24 *sq.*, 26 *sqq.*

without a murmur. If a chief leaves home for a short time he is always accompanied by a friend, and on his return is met by two men, who conduct him to his *wuurn* [hut]. At his approach every one rises to receive him, and remains silent till he speaks; they then enquire where he has been, and converse with him freely. When a tribe is moving from one part of the country to another, the chief, accompanied by a friend, precedes it, and obtains permission from the next chief to pass, before his followers cross the boundary. When approaching a friendly camp, the chief walks at the head of his tribe. If he is too old and infirm to take the lead, his nearest male relative or best friend does so. On his arrival with his family at the friendly camp, a comfortable *wuurn* is immediately erected, and food, firewood, and attendance are provided during his visit. When he goes out to hunt, he and his friends are accompanied by several men to carry their game and protect them from enemies. A strange chief approaching a camp is met at a short distance by the chief, and invited to come and sit down; a fire is made for him, and then he is asked where he has come from, and what is his business. The succession to the chiefdom is by inheritance. When a chief dies the chiefs of the neighbouring tribes, accompanied by their attendants, assist at the funeral obsequies; and they appoint the best male friend of the deceased to take charge of the tribe until the first great meeting after the expiry of one year, when the succession must be determined by the votes of the assembled chiefs alone. The eldest son is appointed, unless there is some good reason for setting him aside. If there are no sons, the deceased chief's eldest brother is entitled to succeed him, and the inheritance runs in the line of his family. Failing him, the inheritance devolves upon the other brothers and their families in succession."[1]

This incipient tendency to a monarchical rule which manifests itself among the coastal tribes of Australia may be itself the direct consequence of that more regular and plentiful supply of food which the neighbourhood of the sea, with its more abundant rainfall, commonly ensures. For where the means of subsistence are constant and copious,

The incipient tendency to monarchical rule among the coastal tribes of Australia

[1] J. Dawson, *Australian Aborigines*, pp. 5 *sq.*

332 TOTEMISM IN SOUTH-EASTERN AUSTRALIA CHAP.

<small>may be an effect of a more abundant supply of food and more settled habits of life.</small>

the population naturally increases in number and becomes stationary, since the principal motive for a migratory life, namely the exhaustion of the food-supply within the area under occupation, has ceased to operate. And with a larger and more fixed population, concentrated within definite boundaries, the opportunities which a man of superior abilities enjoys for extending his influence over his fellows also increase and multiply, whereas it is difficult for him to assert and enforce his will upon wandering groups thinly scattered over a wide region. Hence it is that the nomadic life does not lend itself readily to monarchy, which, if it is to be stable, must be exercised over a settled, not a migratory people.[1]

<small>The social organisation of the coastal tribes marks a similar advance upon the social organisation of the tribes in the interior.</small>

Thus far we have found that the tribes which occupy the well-watered and fertile coasts of Australia have made some progress in material culture and political constitution by comparison with the tribes which roam over the arid and barren steppes of the interior. A parallel advance in their social organisation and marriage customs was long ago remarked and referred to its true cause by our principal authority on the tribes of South-Eastern Australia, Dr. A. W. Howitt. He wrote: "With the exception of that part of North-Eastern Queensland where the Kamilaroi type touches the coast, the whole of the coast tracts, speaking broadly, between the Great Dividing Range and the sea, both in Queensland and New South Wales, and

---

[1] The view that the migratory life is incompatible with higher progress in civilisation has been rightly maintained by a philosophic historian of America, E. J. Payne. He observes that both agriculture and herdsmanship "have passed through two successive and well-defined stages, which may be called the migratory and the stationary; the former denoting that stage in which food-production is practised over a wide area, portions of which are successively occupied and abandoned, the latter that in which the most favourable spots have been ultimately selected and permanently occupied, and industry, confined within these limited areas, is strenuously directed to the development of their capacities. No pastoral tribe has ever begun to advance until it has thus ceased from habits of wandering and settled within such a limited area. No agricultural tribe which adheres to the method of essartage, by which small separate clearings are made in the forest, where food-plants are temporarily cultivated, and which are afterwards abandoned for others, has ever based any high degree of advancement on this method. The first effective stimulus is invariably given where human effort is confined to narrow physical limits, and where the process of artificial subsistence has consequently assumed a stationary character, which habit has rendered permanent" (E. J. Payne, *History of the New World called America*, i. 330).

between the Murray River and the sea in Victoria and South Australia, were occupied by communities having abnormal types of class system which in most cases count descent through the male line. These coast tracts, taken as a whole, are the best watered and most fertile parts of Australia, and, moreover, the richest in animals and plant food for an aboriginal population. This coincidence of advanced social development with fertility of country is not without some significance. The most backward-standing types of social organisation, having descent through the mother and an archaic communal marriage, exist in the dry and desert country; the more developed Kamilaroi type, having descent through the mother, but a general absence of the *pirauru* marriage practice,[1] is found in the better watered tracts which are the sources of all the great rivers of East Australia; while the most developed types, having individual marriage, and in which, in almost all cases, descent is counted through the father, are found along the coasts where there is the most permanent supply of water and most food. In fact, it is thus suggested that the social advance of the Australian aborigines has been connected with, if not mainly due to, a more plentiful supply of food in better watered districts."[2]

To the same effect Professor Baldwin Spencer observes: "It is a well-marked feature that, if we desire to find a tribe, whether it be one with male or with female descent, which has become specialised or highly modified in regard to its organization, we must search along the coast-line. The most backward and primitive tribes occupy the central area. Now, a very striking feature in the physiography of Australia is the presence of a series of Ranges, of which a very characteristic example are those known as the Great Divide, in the south-east part of the continent, separating a comparatively well-watered coastal fringe from a dry interior, where, over wide areas, conditions of life are more unfavourable. It will be seen that tribes, which will subsequently be shown to be modified, such as the Narrinyeri, of South

---

[1] As to this form of group marriage, see below, pp. 363 *sqq.*
[2] A. W. Howitt, "Further Notes on the Australian Class Systems," *Journal of the Anthropological Institute*, xviii. (1889) pp. 33 *sq.*

Australia, the Victorian tribes generally, the coastal tribes on the east of the continent, and those on the west of the Gulf of Carpentaria, all inhabit areas where conditions of life are relatively favourable."[1]

A better climate and more abundant food seem to have been potent causes in producing the more advanced social condition of the South-East Australian tribes.

Again, in discussing the question whether the magical ceremonies which the Dieri and other tribes of Central Australia about Lake Eyre practise for the purpose of increasing the food-supply are to be considered as a survival of primitive belief and custom, Dr. Howitt observes that "the Dieri tribe in its organisation, and in its customs and beliefs, is one of the most backward-standing tribes I know of, and therefore it would not be surprising if the magical food-producing ceremonies were retained, while the other tribes have departed from them. Assuming that the Dieri do, in fact, continue ceremonies which belonged to the primary functions of the early totemistic groups, it may be worth considering whether there are any apparent reasons why the native tribes in other parts of Australia have abandoned them. I have before pointed out that the tribes can be arranged in a series: first, those with *pirrauru* marriage; then those in which that form of marriage has become a rudimentary custom; and, finally, those which have more or less lost their class organisation, and have developed a form of individual marriage. Now compare such a series of tribes with regard to these magical food-producing ceremonies, and also as to the climatic conditions under which they live. We shall find that the Lake Eyre tribes are under a minimum rainfall, a very high temperature, and a prevailing aridity, with fertile intervals, when there is abundance of animal and vegetable food supplies. At the further end of the series, whether in Queensland, New South Wales, Victoria, or South Australia, the tribes living, say, on the coast lands, are under climatic conditions very different from those of Central Australia, with a good rainfall, a more temperate climate, and a plentiful and constant food supply, both animal and vegetable. This comparison comes out clearly when the tables of rainfall, given in the introductory

[1] Baldwin Spencer, "Totemism in Australia," *Transactions of the Australasian Association for the Advancement of Science*, Dunedin, January 1904, p. 381.

chapter, are inspected. This comparison will fall in line with former conclusions, namely, that the tribes of the Lake Eyre basin have remained in a far more primitive condition socially than those of South-East Australia. If so, it would point to conditions of better climate, and more abundant and regular food supply, as potent causes in the advancement of the social condition of the south-east tribes."[1]

When Dr. Howitt wrote the former of the passages which I have just quoted from his writings he was not aware that to the north of the tribes of Lake Eyre lies another group of central tribes, living under similar climatic conditions, which have a complex marriage system of eight exogamous subclasses with descent of the class and subclass in the male line. That the eight-class system of these central tribes is later and more advanced than the two-class system of the Dieri and other tribes about Lake Eyre is a proposition which, in my opinion, does not admit of dispute, since it seems certain that the eight subclasses have been produced by bisection of four subclasses, and these again by bisection of two primary classes, which two primary classes represent the first dichotomy of an originally undivided commune. Thus we are bound to recognise that, side by side in Central Australia, there are living under similar climatic conditions two sets of tribes, one with the most rudimentary and the other with the most advanced of the normal types of Australian social organisation. The sharp line of cleavage between these two sets of tribes has already been indicated, for it runs between the Urabunna and the Arunta tribes, whose social and totemic systems have been described above.[2] With regard to the question of descent I have pointed out[3] that with a system of group marriage, such as we have strong grounds for believing to have been at one time universal among the Australian aborigines, descent may be traced as easily in the paternal as in the maternal line, since the paternity recognised under such a system is that of a group, not of an individual, and the group of "fathers" is quite as well known as the group of "mothers."

However, among the tribes of the barren interior we find the later eight-class organisation side by side with the earlier two-class organisation.

With group marriage maternal descent is not necessarily more primitive than paternal descent.

[1] A. W. Howitt, *Native Tribes of South-East Australia*, pp. 154 *sq*.
[2] Above, pp. 175 *sqq*.
[3] Above, pp. 167, 249.

Hence there is no need to suppose that paternal descent is necessarily later than maternal descent, and derived from it.[1] Even when group-marriage has been exchanged for individual marriage, the difficulty of tracing descent from the father is hardly greater in savage than in civilised society. In both it is assumed that the man who cohabits with a woman is the father of her child, although, as I have pointed out,[2] fatherhood to a Central Australian savage is a very different thing from fatherhood to a civilised European. To the European father it means that he has begotten a child on a woman; to the Central Australian father it means that a child is the offspring of a woman with whom he has a right to cohabit, whether he has actually had intercourse with her or not. To the European mind the tie between a father and his child is physical; to the Central Australian it is social. If we wish to avoid confusion in discussing the institutions of a race so different from our own, we must

---

[1] Similarly Messrs. Spencer and Gillen observe : " It is, for example, generally assumed that counting descent in the female, is a more primitive method than counting descent in the male line, and that of two tribes, in one of which we have maternal descent and in the other paternal, the former is in this respect in a more primitive condition than the latter; but it may even be doubted whether in all cases the counting of descent in the female line has preceded the counting of it in the male line. The very fact that descent is counted at all, that is, that any given individual when born has some distinguishing name, because he or she is born of some particular woman, indicates the fact that men and women are divided into groups bearing such distinctive names, for it must be remembered that in these savage tribes the name which is transmitted to offspring, and by means of which descent is counted, is always a group name. When once we have any such system, whether it be totemic or otherwise, then we have arrived at a stage in which it is possible to imagine that the men of one particular group have marital relations only with women of another particular group. Supposing we take two of these exogamous groups, which we will designate A and B. Thus men of A have marital relations with women of B, and *vice versa*. When once these groups are established, then, there is, in reality, no difficulty whatever in counting descent in the male just as easily as in the female line. It is quite true that the individual father of any particular child may not be known, but this, so far as counting descent under the given conditions is concerned, is a matter of no importance. The only name which can be transmitted, and by means of which descent can be counted (as indeed it is amongst the Australian tribes of the present day), is the group name, and as women of group B can only have marital relations with men of group A, it follows that the father of any child of a woman of group B must belong to group A, and therefore, though the actual father may not be known, there appears to be no inevitable necessity for the child to pass into group B rather than into group A" (*Native Tribes*, p. 36 note [1]).

[2] Above, p. 167.

clearly distinguish between these two very different conceptions of paternity, the physical and the social, which we confound under the same name.[1]

From these considerations it follows that among the Australian tribes paternal descent is not of itself a proof of social advancement; and thus one of the arguments adduced by Dr. Howitt to prove the advance in culture of the coastal as compared with the inland tribes appears to be invalid. So far as I am aware, there is no evidence that any Australian tribe has exchanged maternal for paternal descent, and until such evidence is forthcoming we are not justified in assuming that those tribes which now trace descent from the father formerly traced it from the mother. *We have no right to assume that tribes which now trace descent through the father formerly traced it through the mother.*

On the other hand the survival of a form of group marriage among the central tribes in the basin of Lake Eyre[2] may fairly, with Dr. Howitt, be regarded as evidence of the more backward state of these tribes in comparison with the tribes of the fertile coasts of Victoria and New South Wales, who practise individual marriage. Yet even this test is not an absolute one, if Dr. Howitt is right in holding that group marriage prevails, or prevailed till lately, among tribes on the southern coast of South Australia.[3] But with regard to the greater part of the territory occupied by the tribes of that coast it is to be remembered that the deserts characteristic of Central Australia here extend nearly to the sea,[4] so that the coastal tribes at this point labour under some of the same natural disadvantages which have retarded progress among the steppe-dwellers of the interior. *The survival of group marriage among the central tribes is evidence of their more primitive state.*

Again, in some districts on the coast the partial or entire breakdown of totemism, or of the exogamous classes, or of both together, appears, as Dr. Howitt has pointed out, to furnish unquestionable evidence of a social advance among the tribes who have thus succeeded in emancipating themselves more or less completely from the thraldom of *The breakdown of totemism and exogamy among the coastal tribes.*

---

[1] The distinction between physical paternity and maternity on the one side and social paternity and maternity on the other side has been clearly pointed out by Mr. A. van Gennep in his *Mythes et Légendes d'Australie* (Paris, 1906), pp. lxiii. *sq.* Much confusion would be avoided if students of primitive marriage would bear this distinction in mind.

[2] See above, pp. 308 *sqq.*, and below, pp. 363 *sqq.*

[3] A. W. Howitt, *Native Tribes of South-East Australia*, p. 191. See below, pp. 369-371.

[4] A. W. Howitt, *op. cit.* p. 35. See also above, p. 320 note[4].

these burdensome superstitions. The evidence of the decay of totemism and exogamy in parts of South-Eastern Australia which border on the sea will come before us in the sequel.

Totemism more primitive in the centre than on the coast.

Further, we have seen reason to believe that the totemic system of the central tribes is more primitive than that of the coastal tribes both in its social and in its religious or magical aspects, namely, in its permission to persons of the same totem to marry each other, in its mode of determining the totem of every individual, in its extensive use of magic for the multiplication of the totemic animals and plants, and in its allowing and even compelling men under certain circumstances to eat their own totems.[1]

Intellectual and religious progress among the tribes of the south-east.

Again, whereas the central tribes are ignorant of, and indeed deny, the part which the father plays in the begetting of offspring,[2] the tribes of South-Eastern Australia on the contrary, affirm that children emanate from the father alone and are merely nurtured by the mother.[3] Lastly, whereas the conception of a supreme supernatural being appears to be wholly lacking among such of the central tribes as have remained unaffected by European influence, the natives of South-Eastern Australia are reported to have believed in a mythical headman somewhere up in the sky, who might in time have developed into a native god of a common pattern, if his career had not been cut short by the arrival of a foreign race with a foreign deity.[4]

Taken altogether the evidence points to the conclusion that the central tribes are on the

Taken altogether the evidence points to the conclusion that such advances as have been made by the Australian aborigines in material culture, tribal government, family life, knowledge of natural processes, and elements of religion, have been made by the tribes of the coast and of those south-eastern portions of the continent where the natural

---

[1] See above, pp. 229 *sqq.*, 242 *sqq.*, 251 *sq.*
[2] See above, pp. 188 *sqq.*
[3] "It is necessary to keep in view the fact that these aborigines, even while counting 'descent'—that is counting the class names—through the mother, never for a moment feel any doubt, according to my experience, that the children originate solely from the male parent, and only owe their infantine nurture to their mother" (A. W. Howitt, "Notes on the Australian Class Systems," *Journal of the Anthropological Institute*, xii. (1883) p. 502). Compare *id.*, *Native Tribes of South-East Australia*, pp. 255, 263; A. L. P. Cameron, "Notes on some Tribes of New South Wales," *Journal of the Anthropological Institute*, xiv. (1885) p. 352.
[4] See above, pp. 145 *sqq.*

conditions in respect of climate, soil, and water have been most favourable to human existence by furnishing the natives with a plentiful supply of food and of other necessaries, and thereby enabling them to multiply and become settled; while on the contrary the more backward and comparatively primitive tribes are those which inhabit the arid wastes of the interior, where the hard conditions of life in the desert have had the effect, which they never fail to produce, of keeping down the numbers and retarding the intellectual and social progress of the poverty-stricken nomads.[1] Yet these steps on the upward road have not been made with a rigid, a mechanical uniformity; for we have seen that side by side with the most primitive form of totemism the central tribes possess the most highly developed type of exogamy, namely, the division of the community into eight exogamous classes. The exception only illustrates the truth, which the whole history of mankind must impress on an attentive student, that in every human society there are marked inequalities of culture; the conditions of progress are too manifold and too complex to allow any single community or group of communities to outstrip its fellows equally in every respect. Amongst the most advanced peoples may be discovered relics of a ruder past; amongst the most backward races may be detected germs and anticipations of a happier future.[2]

whole the most primitive, and the coastal and south-eastern tribes the most advanced.

§ 2. *Tribes with two Classes (Kararu and Matteri) and Female Descent*

For our knowledge of the social and totemic systems of the tribes in the south-eastern regions of Australia

---

[1] In this conclusion I am happy to agree with Messrs. Spencer and Gillen, than whom none has a better right to form and express an opinion as to relative position of the tribes of Central Australia. They say: "Taking every class of evidence into account, it appears to us to be very difficult to avoid the conclusion that the central tribes, which, for long ages, have been shielded by their geographical isolation from external influences, have retained the most primitive form of customs and beliefs" (*Northern Tribes of Central Australia*, p. xii.).

[2] Similarly Dr. Howitt observes: "Yet it may be well to keep in view that no two tribes are practically at the same point of development, as indicated for instance by an advance from group marriage to some form of individual marriage. Thus I see no difficulty in believing that while the Arunta have reached male descent with segmentation into eight subclasses, they may have retained early beliefs as to their totem ancestors" (*Native Tribes of South-East Australia*, p. 155).

340 TOTEMISM IN SOUTH-EASTERN AUSTRALIA CHAP.

Researches of Dr. A. W. Howitt in South-East Australia. we are mainly indebted to the researches of Dr. A. W. Howitt and his colleague the Rev. Lorimer Fison. The results of these researches, which extended over many years, are summed up by Dr. A. W. Howitt in a book which must always remain the standard work on the subject.[1] In the following survey of totemism and exogamy in South-Eastern Australia I shall therefore follow in the main Dr. Howitt's arrangement and presentation of the facts, and shall abstain from using later accounts, because since he collected his information a good many years ago, the process of extinction or decay has gone so far among the tribes of Victoria and New South Wales that little or nothing can now be learned with any certainty from the few survivors as to the ancient customs and beliefs of their forefathers.[2] Dr. Howitt's last message to anthropologists was to urge on them the need of the greatest caution in accepting evidence from the remnants of decaying tribes. I take heed to the warning and shall accordingly treat the tribes of South-East Australia as, for the purposes of this study, practically extinct. In the year 1907 the total number of full-blooded natives in the whole State of Victoria was under two hundred.[3] Hence though, for the sake of convenience, I shall often speak of these tribes in the present tense, the reader is to understand that the customs and beliefs described in the following pages belong for the most part, if not altogether, to the past.

Tribes with two exogamous classes and female descent. We begin our survey with those tribes which have the simplest social organisation, namely, a bisection of the whole community into two exogamous moieties or

---

[1] A. W. Howitt, *The Native Tribes of South-East Australia* (London, 1904). In addition the student should consult the joint work of Messrs. Howitt and Fison, *Kamilaroi and Kurnai* (Melbourne, Sydney, Adelaide, and Brisbane, 1880), and a series of valuable papers contributed partly by Mr. L. Fison, but mainly by Dr. Howitt to the *Journal of the Anthropological Institute of Great Britain and Ireland*, between the years 1880 and 1907. These papers will be referred to from time to time in what follows.

[2] As to the decadence of the aborigines in this part of Australia, see Prof. Baldwin Spencer, "Totemism in Australia," *Transactions of the Australian Association for the Advancement of Science* (Dunedin, January 1904), pp. 403 *sq.*; A. W. Howitt, "The Native Tribes of South-East Australia," *Journal of the Royal Anthropological Institute*, xxxvii. (1907) p. 278; *id.*, "A Message to Anthropologists," *Revue des Études Ethnographiques et Sociologiques*, i. (1908) pp. 481 *sq.*

[3] A. W. Howitt, "A Message to Anthropologists," *op. cit.* p. 481.

classes with descent in the female line. This simple and doubtless ancient type of social organisation is found among the tribes about Lake Eyre, in the interior of South Australia. Properly speaking, this group of tribes should be classed with the central tribes, for though Lake Eyre, about which they cluster, lies a good deal to the south of the true centre of Australia, yet the natural features and climate of the country exhibit all the characteristics of those arid sun-scorched wastes which occupy the greater part of the interior of the continent. The name of Lake Eyre is given to a vast expanse of barren flats and salt swamps, some four thousand square miles in area, which through subsidence of the land now lies nearly forty feet below sea-level, so that the rivers which from time to time pour floods of water into it from the Queensland Hills have no outlet, and the water soon evaporates in the torrid heat of the sun, leaving only a saline crust behind. In summer you may stand on what is called the shore of the lake and sweep the horizon with a powerful glass without seeing a drop of water. The landscape at such times is, to the last degree, desolate and forbidding, indeed one of the most dismal on earth, for the country all round these salt flats is a dreary wilderness of bare sun-baked clay pans, stony deserts, where the pebbles are set so thick that a cart-wheel leaves no rut, or barren sand-dunes which stretch away into the distance with the regularity and monotony of railway embankments. To add to the gloom of the scenery the sky, even in summer, is often overcast for days with banks of heavy clouds which sometimes hang low as if to mock the parched and thirsty wanderer with the sight of water beyond his reach. The prevailing hue of earth and heaven is a dingy monotonous grey; the distance is often blotted by a low dull haze. Not a sound is to be heard, not a living thing is to be seen, the only motion is that of the cloud-rack drifting sullenly across the leaden sky. No wonder that the natives of this forlorn region should be amongst the lowest even of the low Australian savages; no wonder that at times, driven to desperation by the droughts which have blasted their land into a desert, they should, like the prophets of Baal, have slashed themselves with knives and called with

Tribes of Lake Eyre.

The scenery of Lake Eyre.

loud cries on the spirits to send rain from the pitiless heaven.[1] The advent of Europeans has practically exterminated these children of the wilds without enabling their supplanters permanently to occupy the land. Deserted homesteads and wire-fences straggling on the ground now mark the retreat of the white man from these realms of sterility and death.[2]

Though the Australian aborigines are the lowest savages about whom we possess accurate information they are not necessarily degraded.

Before proceeding to give an account of the social and totemic system of the tribes, now much reduced in numbers, which still inhabit these dreary solitudes, I think it well to correct a misapprehension which appears to exist as to the place assigned by modern anthropologists to the Australian race in general and to the tribes of Lake Eyre in particular. It has been assumed [3] that, because we rank the Australian aborigines among the lowest races of mankind, we thereby imply that they are degraded, stupid, lazy, brutal, and so forth. The assumption rests on a confusion of thought. Lowness in the scale of humanity is confounded with degradation, with which it has no necessary connection. Similarly in the animal creation the ant, the bee, the elephant, and the dog are low in the scale by comparison with man, but they are not degraded, and it would be a calumny to describe them as stupid, lazy, brutal, and so on; for many of these creatures display a degree of intelligence and industry, of courage and affection which should put many men to shame. In regard to the Australian aborigines all that modern anthropology maintains is that, on the ground of the comparatively primitive nature of their material culture, superstitious beliefs, and social customs, they rank as the lowest of all the existing races of men about whom we possess accurate information. The pygmies of Central Africa may be, and the extinct Tasmanians almost certainly were, still lower than the Australians in the scale of humanity, but about them we have practically no information of any value. To set the Australians above the Bantu and negro

[1] A. W. Howitt, "The Dieri and other Tribes of Central Australia," *Journal of the Anthropological Institute*, xx. (1891) pp. 91-93.

[2] The extreme desolation of the basin of Lake Eyre is graphically depicted by Professor J. W. Gregory in his book, *The Dead Heart of Australia* (London, 1906), pp. 21, 29 *sq.*, 47, 51 *sq.*, 57, 69, 92 *sq.*, 101, 103 *sqq.*, 109 *sq.*, 112 *sq.*, 120 *sqq.*, 134, 156, etc. See also his *Australasia*, i. 95, 485-487; A. R. Wallace, *Australasia*, i. 23.

[3] By Prof. J. W. Gregory, *The Dead Heart of Australia*, pp. 165 *sqq.*

races of Africa would be absurd ; for the Bantus and negroes have tamed cattle, cultivated the ground, invented or at least practised weaving and pottery, worked the metals, built cities, and founded kingdoms, and the Australians have done none of these things. But though the Australians in their long isolation from the rest of the world have lagged far behind other races in the evolution of culture, they exhibit, so far as I can judge, no symptom at all of physical, mental, or social degradation ; on the contrary they appear to me to display both in their traditions and in their customs unequivocal signs of an advance from a state of savagery much lower than that in which they were found by Europeans. To these marks of progress I have already repeatedly called attention in the course of this work, and I shall have occasion to do so again in the sequel. Indeed I know of no savages who can properly be described as degraded except such as have been corrupted by contact with civilisation, learning the vices without acquiring the virtues of the higher race.

In classing the Australians, on the ground of their material culture, social institutions, and superstitious beliefs, at the bottom of all the existing races of men about whom we are accurately informed, I am happy to agree with an inquirer equally conspicuous for the exactness of his knowledge and the sobriety of his judgment, the late General Pitt-Rivers, who reached the same conclusion from a comparison of the Australian weapons and tools with those of other savages. He observes : "Lowest amongst the existing races of the world of whom we have any accurate knowledge are the Australians. All their weapons assimilate to the forms of nature ; all their wooden weapons are constructed on the grain of the wood, and consequently their curves are the curves of the branches out of which they were constructed. In every instance in which I have attempted to arrange my collection in sequence, so as to trace the higher forms from natural forms, the weapons of the Australians have found their place lowest in the scale, because they assimilate most closely to the natural forms."[1]

Pitt-Rivers on the low place of the Australian aborigines in the human scale.

---

[1] Lieutenant-General A. Lane-Fox Pitt-Rivers, *The Evolution of Culture* (Oxford, 1906), p. 11.

344 TOTEMISM IN SOUTH-EASTERN AUSTRALIA CHAP.

Position and numbers of the Dieri.

The tribes of the Lake Eyre basin occupy, or used to occupy, a territory about three hundred miles long from north to south by three hundred miles broad from east to west. Of these the Dieri tribe, inhabiting the lower course of the Barcoo River on the east and south-east side of Lake Eyre, was the largest and most important, and it may be taken as typical of the rest, all of which appear to have agreed with it in being divided into two exogamous moieties or classes with descent in the female line.¹ At the present day the numbers of the Dieri have dwindled to one hundred and fifty all told, and a mission-station of the German Lutheran Church has been established among them since 1866.² The following account of their totemic and social system is based in large part on the evidence of men who knew the tribe in their purely savage state many years ago.

Exogamous classes and totem clans of the Dieri.

The Dieri are divided into two exogamous intermarrying moieties or classes which bear the names of Kararu and Matteri respectively. Each moiety or class is again subdivided into a number of totem clans. To the exogamous moieties or classes and to the totem clans the Dieri give the name of *murdus* or, more correctly, *madas*.³ The following is a list of the Dieri totem clans, so far as they have been ascertained, but the list is incomplete.⁴ In it the clans are arranged under the classes (moieties or phratries) to which they belong.

---

¹ A. W. Howitt, "The Dieri and other Kindred Tribes of Central Australia," *Journal of the Anthropological Institute*, xx. (1891) pp. 31 *sqq.*; *id.*, *Native Tribes of South-East Australia*, pp. 44 *sq.*

² J. W. Gregory, *The Dead Heart of Australia*, pp. 59 *sq.*, 191.

³ A. W. Howitt, *Native Tribes of South-East Australia*, pp. 90 *sq.*, 779 note ².

⁴ A. W. Howitt, *op. cit.* p. 91. Dr. Howitt's earlier list of the Dieri totems ("The Dieri and other Kindred Tribes of Central Australia," *Journal of the Anthropological Institute*, xx. (1891) p. 38) differs from his later list in several particulars. I have reproduced the later as presumably the more correct. In the earlier list kangaroo (*chukuru*), the mulga tree (*malka*), and the seed of Portulacca oleracea (*kan-aura*) are assigned as totems to the Kararu moiety, and iguana (*kopiri*) and Duboisia Patersoni (*pitcheri*) are assigned as totems to the Matteri moiety. None of these five seems to find a place in the later list. In the Matteri moiety the fish totem (*markara*) of the later list is called a mullet in the earlier, and the *kirhapara* totem, for which no English equivalent is given in the later list, is called "bone fish" in the earlier. The list of Dieri totems given by S. Gason includes kangaroo (*chookooroo*), iguana (*cappirrie*), and the vegetable seed *cannaarra*, as well as rain, mice, emu, rat, grub (*purdie*), fish (*murkara*), dog, and crow. But Gason does not say how the totems are distributed between the moieties or classes. See *Journal of the Anthropological Institute*, xxiv. (1895) pp. 167 *sq.*

DIERI TRIBE

Classes and Totems

Classes.	Totems.
Kararu	Rain, carpet-snake, crow, native companion, red ochre, a small frog, seed of *Claytonia* sp., a rat (*maiaru*), a bat (*tapaiuru*), the pan-beetle (*Helaeus perforatus*), *milketyelparu*, a frog (*kaladiri*), the rabbit-bandicoot, shrew-mouse (*punta*), a small mouse (*karabana*).
Matteri	A caterpillar, (*muluru*, the Witchetty grub of Spencer and Gillen), cormorant, emu, eagle-hawk, a fish, *Acacia* sp., dingo, native cat, *kirhapara* (bone fish ?), small marsupial (*kokula*), kangaroo rat.

The marriage rule is that a man must always marry a woman of the other moiety or class; in other words, Kararu men must marry Matteri women, and conversely Matteri men must marry Kararu women. In regard to totems, a man is free to marry a woman of any totem in the other moiety of the tribe. For example, a Kararu man of the rain totem may marry a Matteri woman of the caterpillar totem, or of the cormorant totem, or of the emu totem, or of the eagle-hawk totem, etc. Both the class (moiety) and the totem clan are hereditary in the female line; in other words, every child takes both of them from his or her mother. Thus, if a Kararu man of the rain totem marries a Matteri woman of the caterpillar totem, then their children, both male and female, will be Matteri-caterpillars; if a Kararu man of the rain totem marries a Matteri woman of the cormorant totem, then their children, both male and female, will be Matteri-cormorants. Or if a Matteri man of the emu totem marries a Kararu woman of the carpet-snake totem, then their children will be Kararu-carpet-snakes; if he marries a Kararu woman of the crow totem, then the children will be Kararu-crows, and so on.[1]

Rules of marriage and descent among the Dieri.

---

[1] A. W. Howitt, *Native Tribes of South-East Australia*, pp. 175 *sq.* The statement of S. Gason that men take their father's totem and women their mother's totem (*Journal of the Anthropological Institute*, xvii. (1888) p. 186) is incorrect. See Dr. A. W. Howitt, in *Journal of the Anthropological Institute*, xx. (1891) pp. 36 *sq.*

Prohibition of marriage between a man's children and his sister's children.

Although a two-class system, like a four-class system, does not of itself prevent the marriage of a man's children with his sister's children,[1] yet the Dieri practically bar such marriages by placing a man's children in the relation of *kami* (which means non-marriageable) to his sister's children; but in the next generation the children of these children are *noa* or marriageable to each other.[2] The effect of this prohibition is, in conjunction with the class system, to bar all marriages between first cousins. For when first cousins are the children of two brothers or of two sisters, their union is barred by the class system;[3] and in the remaining case, when first cousins are the children of a brother and a sister respectively, though their marriage is not barred by the class system, yet it is specially guarded against by this Dieri rule which makes such cousins *kami* or non-marriageable with each other. Thus in regard to such first cousins, the children of a brother and a sister respectively, the Dieri system presents a remarkable contrast to the Urabunna system; for whereas under the Urabunna system a man's proper wife is his first cousin, the daughter of his mother's elder brother or of his father's elder sister,[4] these female first cousins are under the Dieri system prohibited to him by a special rule. We cannot doubt that the Urabunna custom which enjoins a man to marry one of his first cousins is older than the Dieri custom which forbids him to do so. The Dieri prohibition is clearly an innovation on the older system which permitted and even recommended certain consanguineous marriages; it is another step taken by these savages towards the accomplishment of that object at which their whole class system was directly aimed, namely, the prevention of the marriage of near kin. This practical prohibition of a marriage which is not barred by the class system is interesting, because it shews how tribal opinion may condemn and prevent certain unions which yet, so far as the class rules are concerned, might be lawfully contracted. We may reasonably suppose that all the marriages which are now

---

[1] Above, pp. 276 *sq.*
[2] A. W. Howitt, *Native Tribes of South-East Australia*, p. 189.
[3] See above, p. 181.
[4] See above, pp. 177 *sq.*

formally interdicted by the various exogamous class systems, were in like manner informally reprobated by public opinion before the cumbrous machinery of exogamy was put in operation against them. In other words, we may assume that a moral objection to such marriages always preceded, and was the cause of, their legal prohibition.

According to S. Gason,[1] the Dieri do not pay any particular respect to their totems, and will kill and eat them whenever they are edible animals or plants. There is a strong feeling of fellowship between all persons of the same totem. When a visitor arrives in camp, he is entertained by his relatives or, in default of them, by people of his totem. "Those of the same totem keep together, eat and live together, and lend each other their women. Even strangers from a distance of three or four hundred miles are thus hospitably entertained. The first question is, '*Minna Murdu?*' that is to say, 'What is your totem?' The surrounding and distant tribes have some totems different to those of the Dieri, but these can always find out which are the same."[2] *Relations of a man to his totem and to members of his totem clan.*

To account for the origin of their totems the Dieri tell various stories about the *Mura-muras*, the mythical predecessors and prototypes of the tribe, who, like the *alcheringa* ancestors of the Arunta, are said to have wandered about the country instituting the rites and ceremonies which are still, or were till lately, observed by their descendants or successors. These *Mura-muras* were men, women, and children who led the same sort of life as the Dieri, but were far more powerful magicians than even the medicine-men of the present day claim to be. They gave names to the natural features of the country, such as the rocks and the rivers, which they met with in their wanderings; and when their work was done they were themselves turned into rocks or petrified tree-trunks, which the natives still point out as indisputable evidence of the truth of the legends.[3] One of *Dieri legend of the origin of their totems.*

---

[1] In *Journal of the Anthropological Institute*, xvii. (1888) p. 186; *id.*, xxiv. (1895) p. 168.

[2] Rev. H. Vogelsang, of the Lutheran Mission to the Dieri, quoted by A. W. Howitt, "The Dieri and other Kindred Tribes of Central Australia," *Journal of the Anthropological Institute*, xx. (1891) pp. 41 *sq.*

[3] These legends of the *Mura-muras* were collected for Dr. Howitt by the Rev. Otto Siebert, missionary to the

the tales which the Dieri tell to explain the origin of the totems (*murdus, madas*) runs as follows. They say that in the beginning the earth opened in the midst of Perigundi Lake and the totems (*murdus* or *madas*) came trooping out, one after the other. Out came the crow, and the shell parakeet, and the emu, and all the rest. Being as yet imperfectly formed and without members or organs of sense, they laid themselves down on the sandhills which surrounded the lake then just as they do now. It was a bright day, and the totems lay basking in the sunshine, till at last, refreshed and invigorated by it, they stood up as human beings (*kana*) and dispersed in all directions. That is why people of the same totem are now scattered all over the country. You may still see the island in the lake out of which the totems came trooping long ago.[1]

Another Dieri legend of the origin of their totems.

Another Dieri story to explain the origin of the totems, or at least of the totem names, runs thus. Once upon a time there was a *Mura-mura* man and his name was Mandra-mankana. He came to the neighbourhood of Pando, which the white men call Lake Hope. There he saw two girls, who jeered at him, and when he made love to them, they gave him the slip. So he went forth meditating revenge, and as he went he sang songs which made the fruit to grow, some bitter and some sweet. The two girls found these plants and they liked the sweet fruit very much. After a time they came to a *tanyu* bush, laden with its red and yellow fruit. But the sly Mandra-mankana was lurking in the bush, and when the two girls, suspecting nothing, drew near, he killed them both and cut off their breasts. Coming to the camp of the murdered damsels, he decked himself out in paint and feathers, hung the breasts of the girls on his chest, and danced before the people. But two young men recognised the breasts of his victims and knocked him very hard on the head, so that it split open, and then all the

Dieri at Killalpanina on the Cooper River. See A. W. Howitt and Otto Siebert, "Legends of the Dieri and Kindred Tribes of Central Australia," *Journal of the Anthropological Institute,* xxxiv. (1904) pp. 100 *sqq.*; Miss Mary E. B. Howitt, "Some Native Legends from Central Australia," *Folk-lore,* xiii. (1902) pp. 403 *sqq.*; A. W. Howitt, *Native Tribes of South-East Australia,* pp. 90, 475 *sqq.*, 779 *sqq.*

[1] A. W. Howitt, *Native Tribes of South-East Australia,* pp. 476, 779 *sqq.*

people fell upon him; even the little children struck him with their tiny fists. So they buried him and laid wood on his grave, and went away. One day a crow perched on the grave, and pecked thrice at the wood, and said "Caw! caw! caw!" Then the dead man awoke, and came out of the grave, and looked about, but nobody was to be seen. However, he perceived the footprints of the people, and he followed them up to their new camp on Cooper's Creek. When he came up with them, they were wading and splashing in the river, driving the fish before them with bushes and grass. So he hid himself in the water and, opening his mouth very wide, he swallowed them all up, men, fish, grass, water, everything. Some few of the people who were at a distance saw with alarm a monster in the water with his arms round their comrades, hugging them to himself. A remnant escaped by jumping over his arms. As they ran away, the *Mura-mura* man called "Gobbler-up-of-Grass" looked after them and gave to each of them as he ran his totem name. Those who ran to the north were the seed of the *manyura*, the bat, a marsupial rat (*maiaru*), a small marsupial (*palyara*), the shell parakeet, the cormorant, the eagle-hawk, the emu, the crow, a caterpillar (*padi*), called by the whites the witchetty grub, red ochre, the carpet-snake, and the Duboisia Hopwoodii. These, as I said before, all ran away to the north. Those that ran to the south-east were the kangaroo, the dingo, the jew lizard, the lace lizard or iguana, a marsupial rat (*kokula*), a small marsupial (*punta*), another small marsupial (*karabana*), the native companion, the rain, a crane, a water-rat, the native cat (*pira-moku*), a frog (*kaladiri*), another frog (*tidnamara*), the curlew, and the kangaroo rat. Those who ran to the south were a fish (*makara*, the native perch), the native cat (*yikaura*), the box-tree (*Eucalyptus microtheca*), the rabbit-bandicoot or bush wallaby (*Paragale lagotis*), and one more (*kirhapara*), whose English name is uncertain, perhaps the eel. When they were all gone, the *mura-mura* came out of the water and vomited. As he did so, all his teeth fell out, and they are still to be seen at Manatandri. After that he went a little further off, sat down, and died. His body turned into stone, and you may see it looking like a rock on the Cooper Creek to the north of Lake Hope.¹

In this latter legend the list of names helps to supplement the list of totem clans which has already been given,² and it probably throws light on the geographical distribution of the clans; for we can hardly doubt that the majority of each totem clan was found in that quarter to which its mythical ancestor was said to have run in order to escape the maw of the *mura-mura* man in the river.

<small>Dieri legend of the origin of exogamy.</small> The Dieri have also a legend of the origin of exogamy. As reported by S. Gason the legend runs thus: "*Murdoo* (subdivision of tribe into families). *Murdoo* means taste, but in its primary and larger signification implies family, founded on the following tradition. After the creation, as previously related, fathers, mothers, sisters, brothers, and others of the closest kin intermarried promiscuously, until the evil effects of these alliances becoming manifest, a council of the chiefs was assembled to consider in what way they might be averted, the result of their deliberations being a petition to the Mooramoora, in answer to which he ordered that the tribe should be divided into branches, and distinguished one from the other by different names, after objects animate and inanimate, such as dogs, mice, emu, rain, iguana, and so forth, the members of any such branch not to intermarry, but with permission for one branch to mingle with another. Thus the son of a dog might not marry the daughter of a dog, but either might form an alliance with a mouse, an emu, a rat, or other family. This custom is still observed, and the first question asked of a stranger is, 'What *murdoo*?' namely, Of what family are you?"³

<small>Another version of the legend.</small> In this version of the legend the Mooramoora, whom Gason regarded as a Good Spirit or deity,⁴ is clearly one of the *Mura-muras*, the mythical predecessors or ancestors of the Dieri.⁵ The version of the same legend which the Rev. Otto Siebert, a missionary to the Dieri, obtained for Dr. A. W. Howitt, is as follows: "The several families

---

¹ A. W. Howitt, *Native Tribes of South-East Australia*, pp. 476, 781-783.
² Above, pp. 344 sq.
³ S. Gason, "The Dieyerie Tribe," in *Native Tribes of South Australia*, pp. 260 sq.
⁴ S. Gason, *op. cit.* p. 260.
⁵ See above, pp. 148 sq.

of *Murdus* married in themselves without shame. This occasioned great confusion, and sexual disorder became predominant. The *Pinnarus* (elders) observing this, came together to consider how these evils might be avoided. They agreed that the families should be divided, and that no member of a segment should marry within it. In accordance with this it was ordered that ' *Yidni padi madu (murdu) wapanai kaualka kuraterila, yidni kaualka wapanai warugatti kuraterila*, etc.' That is, ' Thou grub totem, go to produce crow; thou crow totem, go to produce emu, etc.,' and so on for the other totems."[1]

Both these versions of the legend agree in alleging that there was a time when the present restrictions on marriage were unknown, and when consequently near kinsfolk married among themselves without shame; both agree in alleging that the exogamous rules were deliberately introduced for the purpose of regulating the intercourse of the sexes and putting an end to a state of sexual promiscuity which had come to be regarded as a great evil. These traditions, therefore, accord perfectly with the conclusion, which we have reached independently from the consideration of other evidence, that the exogamous prohibitions were deliberately devised and enforced for the sake of preventing the union in marriage of persons whom the natives regarded as too near of kin.[2] But, as Dr. Howitt has pointed out, there is a discrepancy between the two versions of the Dieri legend as to the introduction of exogamy. For whereas in Gason's version the totem clans were introduced simultaneously with, and as a means of carrying out, the exogamous rules, in Mr. Siebert's version the totem clans existed before the introduction of exogamy and had been till then endogamous, that is, people of the same totem clan had been free to marry each other. Thus Siebert's version agrees with the traditions of the other Central Australian tribes which represent endogamy as habitually practised by the totem clans before the introduction of the exogamous classes.[3]

The tradition that the exogamous rules were deliberately introduced for the purpose of regulating marriage accords with other evidence.

---

[1] A. W. Howitt, *Native Tribes of South-East Australia*, p. 481; A. W. Howitt and Otto Siebert, "Legends of the Dieri and Kindred Tribes of Central Australia," *Journal of the Anthropological Institute*, xxxiv. (1904) p. 129.
[2] See above, pp. 273 *sqq.*
[3] See above, pp. 251 *sq.*

352 TOTEMISM IN SOUTH-EASTERN AUSTRALIA CHAP.

Kulin legend of the origin of exogamy.

This agreement is a strong argument in favour of the truth of the tradition. The Kulin tribe of Victoria had a similar legend that their ancestors used to marry without any regard to kinship, until two medicine-men went up to Bunjil, the great mythical headman of the tribe in the sky, and requested that the people should divide themselves into two exogamous classes. Bunjil granted their request and ordained that one of these classes should be called *Bunjil* (eagle-hawk) and the other *Waang* (crow).[1]

The tradition that exogamy was introduced by the older men or by medicine-men is confirmed by the practice of the present day.

With regard to the agency by which these great changes of tribal custom were introduced, it is to be observed that in Gason's version of the Dieri legend the innovation is ascribed to the mythical predecessors or ancestors of the people (the *Mura-muras*), that in Mr. Siebert's version it is attributed to the tribal elders, and that in the Kulin legend it is set down to two medicine-men, who had previously obtained the sanction of Bunjil, the mythical headman of the tribe. In so far as these stories refer the introduction of social reform to the authority of the older men, and especially of the medicine-men, they are confirmed by what appears to be the practice of the present day; for the best modern observers of the Australian aborigines are of opinion that if the elders, who practically rule the tribe, agree on the advisability of introducing even an important change of custom, they have it in their power to persuade the people to adopt it.

Dr. Howitt's view of the way in which social changes may be introduced in Australian tribes.

Thus Dr. Howitt says: "From what I know of the Australian savage I can see very clearly how such a social change might be brought about. They universally believe that their deceased ancestors and kindred visit them during sleep, and counsel or warn them against dangers, or communicate to them song-charms against magic. I have known many such cases, and I also know that the medicine-men see visions that are to them realities. Such a man if of great repute in his tribe might readily bring about a social change, by announcing to his fellow medicine-men a command received from some supernatural being such as Kutchi of the Dieri, Bunjil of the Wurunjerri, or Daramulun of the Coast Murring. If they received it favourably, the next step might be to announce it to the assembled head-

[1] A. W. Howitt, *Native Tribes of South-East Australia*, pp. 126, 491.

men at one of the ceremonial gatherings as a supernatural command, and this would be accepted as true without question by the tribes-people."[1] As to the particular reform with which we are here concerned, Dr. Howitt writes: "I cannot see any reason to doubt that the first division of Australian communities into two exogamous intermarrying communes was an intentional act arising from within the commune prior to its division. The evidence which I have before me, drawn from the existing customs and beliefs of the aborigines, not only leads me to that conclusion, but also to the further conclusion that the movement itself probably arose within the council of elders, in which the tribal wizard, the professed communicant with ancestral spirits, holds no mean place. The change, whenever it was effected, must, I think, have been announced as having been directed by the spirits of the deceased ancestors (*e.g.* Mura Mura of the Dieri), or by the Headman of Spiritland himself (*e.g.* Bŭnjil of the Kūlin, or Daramūlūn of the Mŭrring)."[2]

A similar view as to the agency by which changes of tribal custom are effected among the Australian aborigines is held by Messrs. Spencer and Gillen, who have had excellent opportunities of forming an opinion on the subject. Speaking of the headmen of the central tribes they observe: "It is undoubtedly by means of the meetings and consultations of leading men such as these that changes in regard to customs can be introduced. The savage is essentially a conservative. What was considered by his father and, more important still, by his grandfather and great-grandfather, to be the right and proper thing to do, is the only right and proper thing for him. But yet at the same time, despite this very strong feeling, changes are introduced. It is these old men, the heads of the totemic groups, who are most interested in all matters concerned with tribal government and custom. If we are safe in regarding the traditions of the different tribes as affording evidence of any value, it is interesting to find that not a few

_{Spencer and Gillen's view of the way in which social changes may originate with influential men and gradually spread from group to group and from tribe to tribe.}

---

[1] A. W. Howitt, *Native Tribes of South-East Australia*, pp. 89 *sq.*
[2] A. W. Howitt, "Notes on the Australian Class Systems," *Journal of the Anthropological Institute*, xii. (1883) pp. 500 *sq.*

of them refer to changes introduced by special individuals of note. Almost every tribe has a tradition of special men or women who first introduced the stone knife for use at initiation, in place of the fire-stick, which previously had caused the deaths of many of the young men. So again every tribe ascribes the introduction of the present marriage system to special eminent *alcheringa* ancestors. In some cases, further, we find that some special ancestor proposed a change, and was supported in this by some other individual. Probably this really explains what has taken place in the past and is still going on in the present. Every now and again there arises a man of superior ability to his fellows; indeed in every tribe there are always one or two individuals who are regarded as more learned than the others, and to whom special respect is paid. During the performance of important ceremonies, when large numbers of the tribe and even members of other tribes are gathered together, the informal council of the leading men is constantly meeting. Matters of tribal interest are discussed day after day. In fact, unless one has been present at these tribal gatherings, which often extend over two or three months, it is difficult to realise the extent to which the thoughts of the natives are occupied with matters of this kind. A change may perhaps have been locally introduced by some strong man acting in conjunction with the older men of his own group. This is discussed amongst the various leading men when they meet together, and then, if the innovation gains the support of other leaders, it will be adopted and will gradually come to be recognised as the right thing."[1]

Another statement of their view of the means by which social reforms may be carried out in the tribes.

And elsewhere Spencer and Gillen tell us that "after carefully watching the natives during the performance of their ceremonies and endeavouring as best we could to enter into their feelings, to think as they did, and to become for the time being one of themselves, we came to the conclusion that if one or two of the most powerful men settled upon the advisability of introducing some change, even an important one, it would be quite possible for this to be agreed upon and carried out. That changes have been introduced, in fact, are still

[1] Spencer and Gillen, *Northern Tribes of Central Australia*, pp. 26 sq.

being introduced, is a matter of certainty; the difficulty to be explained is, how in face of the rigid conservatism of the native, which may be said to be one of his leading features, such changes can possibly even be mooted. The only possible chance is by means of the old men, and, in the case of the Arunta, amongst whom the local feeling is very strong, they have opportunities of a special nature. Without belonging to the same group, men who inhabit localities close to one another are more closely associated than men living at a distance from one another, and, as a matter of fact, this local bond is strongly marked—indeed so marked was it during the performance of their sacred ceremonies that we constantly found it necessary to use the term 'local relationship.' Groups which are contiguous locally are constantly meeting to perform ceremonies; and among the *alatunjas* [headmen] who thus come together and direct proceedings there is perfectly sure, every now and again, to be one who stands pre-eminent by reason of superior ability, and to him, especially on an occasion such as this, great respect is always paid. It would be by no means impossible for him to propose to the other older men the introduction of a change, which, after discussing it, the *alatunjas* of the local groups gathered together might come to the conclusion was a good one, and, if they did so, then it would be adopted in that district. After a time a still larger meeting of the tribe, with head men from a still wider area . . . might be held. At this the change locally introduced would, without fail, be discussed. The man who first started it would certainly have the support of his local friends, provided they had in the first instance agreed upon the advisability of its introduction, and not only this, but the chances are that he would have the support of the head men of other local groups of the same designation as his own. Everything would, in fact, depend upon the status of the original proposer of the change; but, granted the existence of a man with sufficient ability to think out the details of any change, then, owing partly to the strong development of the local feeling, and partly to the feeling of kinship between groups of the same designation, wherever their local habitation may be, it seems quite possible that the markedly

356 TOTEMISM IN SOUTH-EASTERN AUSTRALIA CHAP.

conservative tendency of the natives in regard to customs handed down to them from their ancestors may every now and then be overcome, and some change, even a radical one, be introduced. The traditions of the tribe indicate, it may be noticed, their recognition of the fact that customs have varied from time to time. They have, for example, traditions dealing with supposed ancestors, some of whom introduced, and others of whom changed, the method of initiation. Tradition also indicates ancestors belonging to particular local groups who changed an older into the present marriage system, and these traditions all deal with special powerful individuals by whom the changes were introduced."[1] Among the qualities which confer this commanding influence on certain men a knowledge of ancient lore and skill in magic are particularly mentioned.[2]

Codes of laws have often been fathered on divine beings.

Hence if the best authorities on the subject are right, the elaborate class system of the Australian aborigines may have originated with a single man of keener mind and stronger character than his fellows, who persuaded them to accept his invention either on its own merits or as a revelation directly imparted to him by the higher powers. Thus it would seem that among these rude savages we may detect the germ of that policy which, among more civilised peoples, has led so many legislators to father their codes on gods or heroes of the remote past. For example, the most famous body of ancient Hindoo law is said to have been revealed to human sages by the divine or heroic Manu, who figures in legends as the father of mankind, the founder of social and moral order, the author of legal maxims, and especially as the inventor of sacrificial rites—in short, as what the Central Australians would call an *alcheringa* ancestor or a *mura-mura*.[3] The sacred laws of the ancient Persians, embodied in the Avesta, are said to have been revealed by the supreme deity Ahura Mazda to the prophet Zoroaster,[4] just as the sacred laws of the Hebrews were

---

[1] Spencer and Gillen, *Native Tribes of Central Australia*, pp. 12, 14 *sq.*
[2] *Ibid.* p. 12.
[3] *The Laws of Manu*, translated by G. Bühler, pp. xii. lvii. *sqq.*, 1 *sqq.* (*Sacred Books of the East*, vol. xxv.).
[4] *The Zend-Avesta*, translated by J. Darmesteter, part i. pp. 4 *sqq.* (*Sacred Books of the East*, vol. iv.); A. V. Williams Jackson, *Zoroaster, the Prophet of Iran* (New York, 1901), pp. 36 *sqq.*

revealed by Jehovah to Moses. The Babylonian King Hammurabi apparently claimed to have received his famous code direct from the Sun-god,[1] and Lycurgus was popularly supposed to have received the Spartan laws from the inspired lips of the Delphic priestess.[2] So too the Greeks thought that King Minos obtained the Cretan laws from the mouth of Zeus himself in the sacred Dictæan cave,[3] and the Romans imagined that King Numa instituted their sacrificial rites and ceremonies through the inspiration of the nymph Egeria, with whom he consorted in her holy grove.[4] It is thus that in many lands and many ages religion or superstition is invoked to enforce the dictates of human wisdom or folly upon the more credulous portion of mankind.

Like the central and northern tribes described by Spencer and Gillen, the Dieri perform magical ceremonies for the multiplication of their totemic animals, no doubt with the intention of thereby increasing the food-supply of the tribe. For example, the carpet-snake (*woma*) and the lace-lizard or iguana (*kaperi* or *kapiri*) are two of their totems,[5] and in order to produce a plentiful crop of these reptiles, members of the Dieri, Yaurorka, Yantruwunta, Marula, Yelyuyendi, Karanguru, and Ngameni tribes assemble periodically at Kudna-ngauana on the Cooper River. Here there is a certain sandhill, under which a *mura-mura* named Minkani is supposed to live in a cave. To judge from the description of him, he seems to be one of those fossil beasts or reptiles which are found in the deltas of rivers flowing into Lake Eyre. Such fossil bones are called *kadimarkara* by the Dieri. When the

Magical ceremony performed by the Dieri for the multiplication of carpet-snakes and lace-lizards, which are two of their totems.

---

[1] This is not directly alleged in the code itself, but at the head of the now celebrated monument on which the code is inscribed there is carved a figure of the king in an attitude of adoration before the sun-god, and if H. Winckler is right, the scene represents the monarch receiving his laws from the deity. See H. Winckler, *Die Gesetze Hammurabis*[2] (Leipsic, 1903), p. 3.

[2] Herodotus, i. 65; Polybius, x. 2; Strabo, xvi. 2. 38 *sq.*, pp. 761 *sq.*; Xenophon, *Reipubl. Lacedaem.* 8; Plutarch, *Lycurgus*, 5; Dionysius Halicarnasensis, *Antiquit. Roman.* ii. 61.

[3] Plato, *Minos*, 13 *sq.*, pp. 319 *sq.*; Strabo, xvi. 2. 38, p. 762; Dionysius Halicarnasensis, *Antiquit. Roman.* ii. 61.

[4] Livy, i. 19. 5; Ovid, *Fasti*, iii. 154, 259 *sqq.*; Ovid, *Metam.* xv. 479 *sqq.*; Plutarch, *Numa*, 4; Dionysius Halicarnasensis, *Antiquit. Roman.* ii. 60 *sq.*

[5] A. W. Howitt, *Native Tribes of South-East Australia*, p. 783; A. W. Howitt and O. Siebert, in *Journal of the Anthropological Institute*, xxxiv. (1904) p. 105.

time has come for performing the ceremony, the men leave the women behind in the camp and go alone to the sandhill, where the *mura-mura* resides. On reaching the spot they dig down until they come to damp earth and what they call the excrement of the *mura-mura*. The digging then proceeds very carefully until, as they say, the elbow of the *mura-mura* is uncovered. Then two men stand over him, and, a vein in the arm of each having been opened, they allow the blood to fall on his remains. The Minkani song is now sung, and the men, roused to a frenzy of excitement, strike at each other with weapons till they reach the camp, distant about a mile from the sandhill. The women come out to meet them, and, rushing forward with loud cries, hold shields over their husbands to protect them and stop the fighting. The *tidnamadukas*, that is, the men who claim the land as theirs in right of their mothers,[1] thereupon collect the blood dripping from the wounds, and scatter it, mixed with the supposed excrement from the Minkani's cave, over the sandhills in order that they may bring forth the young carpet-snakes and iguanas which are hidden in them. This ceremony, as Dr. Howitt observes, is clearly similar to the *intichiuma* ceremonies which the Arunta and other central tribes perform for the multiplication of their totems, and the intention is the same, namely, to produce a supply of the totemic animal in order that it may be eaten by the tribe. On the analogy of these Arunta rites the men who perform the ceremony ought to have for their totem the particular animal or plant which they seek to propagate by their magic. Hence, in the Minkani ceremony the performers should be men of the carpet-snake and iguana totems; but Dr. Howitt has not been able to ascertain that this is so.[2]

[1] The word *tidnamaduka* is compounded of *tidna*, "foot," and *maduka*, "mother," "grandmother," or "ancestress." "A *tidnamaduka* is a man who claims a certain tract of country as his, and whose mother and her brothers claim it for him. *Tidnamaduka*, or, shortly, *maduka*, is the complement of *pintara*. *Maduka* includes everything belonging to the maternal line, as *pintara* includes everything belonging to the paternal line. For instance, a father's *muramura*, together with his 'fatherland,' is his *pintara*, while the mother's brother, speaking of his mother's *muramura* and his 'motherland,' calls it his *maduka*" (A. W. Howitt, *Native Tribes of South-East Australia*, p. 785, note [2]).

[2] A. W. Howitt, "Legends of the Dieri and Kindred Tribes of Central

Another ceremony observed by the tribes of Lake Eyre for the multiplication of iguanas, which are one of their principal articles of food, has been described by S. Gason. He tells us that the Dieri do not themselves perform it, but that they are invariably invited, and attend the ceremony. When iguanas are scarce, a day is appointed for the rite, and the men assemble and sit down in a circle. The old men thereupon take leg-bones of emus, sharpened at both ends, and pierce their own ears with them several times, while, regardless of the pain, they sing the following song: "With a boomerang we gather all the iguanas from the flats and plains, and drive them to the sandhills, then surround them, that all the male and female iguanas may come together and increase." Should there be a few more iguanas after the ceremony than there were before, the natives boast of having produced them; but if the creature is as scarce as ever, they fall back on their customary excuse that some other tribe took away their power.[1] *Magical ceremony for the multiplication of iguanas.*

Again, the Dieri perform a strange ceremony for the purpose of making the wild fowl lay their eggs. This they do after heavy rains, when the smaller lakes, lagoons, and swamps are generally full of fresh water and flocks of wild fowl congregate about them. On a fine day, after the rains, all the able-bodied men sit in a circle, each with the sharpened leg-bone of a kangaroo; the old men sing an obscene song, and while they do so the others pierce their scrotum with the sharp bone. The pain must be great, but they show no sense of it, though they are generally laid up for two or three weeks afterwards, unable to walk. While they are thus torturing themselves, the women are crying.[2] They also perform a ceremony for the multiplication of wild dogs, which are one of their totems, and another ceremony *Dieri ceremony to make wild fowls lay their eggs.*

Australia," *Journal of the Anthropological Institute*, xxxiv. (1904) pp. 124 *sq.*; A. W. Howitt, *Native Tribes of South-East Australia*, pp. 797 *sq.* In the latter passage the words "the young *Woma* and *Kapiri* (carpet-snake) lizard" seem to be a mistake for "the young *Woma* (carpet-snake) and *Kapiri* (lizard)." Compare p. 783 of the same work and *Journal of the Anthropological Institute*, xxxiv. (1904) p. 105, where *woma* is defined as "carpet-snake," and *kaperi* (not *kapiri*) is defined as "lace lizard, commonly called iguana."

[1] S. Gason, "The Dieyerie Tribe," in *Native Tribes of South Australia*, p. 279.

[2] S. Gason, *op. cit.* pp. 278 *sq.*

for the multiplication of snakes; but both of these are reported to be so obscene that they are indescribable.¹ We may conjecture that these ceremonies are performed by men of the wild dog and snake totems respectively. The Dieri also perform ceremonies, based on the principle of imitative magic, for the making of rain. In these ceremonies the wished-for rain is simulated by blood drawn from the arms of two medicine-men, and clouds are represented partly by down floating in the air, partly by two large stones, which are afterwards placed as high as possible in the branches of the tallest trees, as if to cause the clouds to mount in the sky. Also they make a hut of logs and branches and then knock it down with their heads. "The piercing of the hut with their heads symbolizes the piercing of the clouds; the fall of the hut, the fall of the rain." On the analogy of the practice of the central and northern tribes described by Spencer and Gillen, we should expect to find that among the Dieri this rain-making ceremony was performed by men of the rain or water totem. However, Dr. Howitt tells us that the whole tribe joins in the ceremony under the direction of the medicine-man.²

Dieri ceremony for making rain.

In the Dieri tribe, as in all the other tribes akin to it, the oldest man of a totem clan is its *pinnaru* or head. Further, each horde or local division of the tribe has also its *pinnaru* or head, who may happen also to be the head of a totem clan. But the head of a totem clan or of a local division need not have much or any authority

Headmen of the totem clans and other divisions among the Dieri.

---

¹ S. Gason, *op. cit.* p. 280.

² S. Gason, "The Dieyerie Tribe," *Native Tribes of South Australia*, pp. 276-278; A. W. Howitt, in *Journal of the Anthropological Institute*, xx. (1891) pp. 90-93; *id.*, *Native Tribes of South-East Australia*, pp. 394-397. The two stones used in the rain-making ceremony are heart-shaped and represent two young men named Dara-ulu, who are believed to be the senders of rain. When rain is wanted, the Dieri smear the two stones with fat and sing a long song. At other times the stones are kept carefully wrapt up in feathers and fat; for the Dieri think that were the stones to be scratched, the whole people would suffer perpetual hunger and could never be satisfied, however much they might eat. And if the stones were broken, the sky would redden, the dust of some dried witchetty grubs, which they tell of in one of their legends, would spread from the westward over the whole earth, and at the sight of it men would die of terror. See A. W. Howitt and O. Siebert, "Legends of the Dieri and Kindred Tribes of Central Australia," *Journal of the Anthropological Institute*, xxxiv. (1904) pp. 125 *sq.*; A. W. Howitt, *Native Tribes of South-East Australia*, pp. 799 *sq.*

outside of his clan or division. For example, Dr. Howitt knew a man who was head of the Eagle-hawk clan in virtue of his great age, but who otherwise had little influence, because he was neither a warrior, a medicine-man, nor an orator. The *pinnarus* collectively are the headmen of the tribe, and of them some one is superior to the rest. In 1862-63, when Dr. Howitt knew the Dieri, the principal headman was a certain Jalina-piramurana, who was head of a seed totem, and was also recognised as the head of the whole tribe. The seed which this man had for his totem is called *kunaura* by the Dieri; it is the seed of the *Claytonia* sp., and forms at times the principal vegetable food of the tribes about Lake Eyre, being ground into a porridge and eaten raw or baked into a cake in hot ashes. The headman of this totem used to boast of being the "tree of life" or the "stay of life," and sometimes he was spoken of as the plant itself (*manyura*, that is, *Claytonia* sp.) of which the seed is the totem. In the Dieri tribe the heads of the totem clans and local divisions, together with eminent warriors, orators, and, generally speaking, old men of standing and importance, compose what may be called the inner council or senate of the tribe, which discusses and decides on all matters of importance at secret sittings held in some place away from the camp. Admission to this inner council is a jealously guarded privilege, and to divulge its secrets is a crime punished with death. The principal headman presides, and among the business transacted at it are the arrangements for hunting game, for festive or ceremonial gatherings, and the punishment of offences, such as the procuring of death by magic, murder, breach of the marriage laws, and the revelation of the secrets of the initiation ceremonies to uninitiated persons or to women. The heads of the totem clans and of the local divisions and other distinguished men wear, or used to wear, circlets of red feathers on their heads as a sign of rank. The Dieri is the only Australian tribe in which Dr. Howitt remembers to have seen this red badge of honour.[1]

The headman of a seed totem.

---

[1] A. W. Howitt, "The Dieri and other Kindred Tribes of Central Australia," *Journal of the Anthropological Institute*, xx. (1891) pp. 64-71; *id.*, *Native Tribes of South-East Australia*, pp. 297-300, 320-323. In

362 TOTEMISM IN SOUTH-EASTERN AUSTRALIA CHAP.

Classificatory terms of relationship in use among the Dieri.

Like all other Australian tribes about whom we have exact information, the Dieri have the classificatory system of relationship. For example, in the generation above his own a man applies the same term *ngaperi* (*appiri*) to his father and to his father's brothers; and he applies the same term *ngandri* (*andri*) to his mother and to his mother's sisters. In his own generation he applies the same term *negi* (*niehie, neyi*) to his elder brothers, to the sons of his father's brothers, and to the sons of his mother's sisters; and he applies the same term *kaku* to his elder sisters, to the daughters of his father's brothers, and to the daughters of his mother's sisters. He applies the same term *noa* to his wife, to his wife's sisters, and to his brothers' wives; and on her side a woman applies the same term *noa* to her husband, to her husband's brothers, and to her sisters' husbands. In the generation below his own a man applies the same term *ngata mura* (*athamoora*) to his own sons, to the sons of his brothers, and to the sons of his wife's sisters.[1] Thus a Dieri man may have many "fathers" who never begot him, many "mothers" who never bore him, many "brothers" and "sisters" who are the children of neither of his parents, and many "sons" whom he never begot. In the mouth of the Dieri these terms of relationship, while they include the relationships which we designate by them, also include many more: they mark the relationship of the individual not to individuals merely but to groups. It has already been pointed out that such classificatory terms, descriptive of group relationships, are only explicable on the hypothesis that they are directly derived from group-marriage.[2] That inference has long been rightly drawn by Dr. A. W. Howitt, our principal authority on the Dieri and other tribes of South-Eastern Australia.[3]

the former passage Dr. Howitt identifies the *manyura* plant (of which the seed is the *kunaura* totem) as *Portulacca oleracea*; in the latter he identifies it as *Claytonia* sp.

[1] A. W. Howitt, "The Dieri and other Kindred Tribes of Central Australia," *Journal of the Anthropological Institute*, xx. (1891) pp. 43-50; id., *Native Tribes of South-East Australia*, p. 160; id., "Australian Group-Relationships," *Journal of the Royal Anthropological Institute*, xxxvii. (1907) pp. 287 sq.

[2] See above, pp. 303 sqq.

[3] A. W. Howitt, "The Dieri and other Kindred Tribes of Central Australia," *Journal of the Anthropological Institute*, xx. (1891) pp. 99, 102; id., in *Folk-lore*, xvii. (1906) pp. 185, 189.

TRIBES WITH TWO CLASSES

Nor in dealing with the Dieri are we left merely to infer the former existence of group-marriage from the present use of terms descriptive of group relationship; for a form of group-marriage still survives among the Dieri, as among the Urabunna,[1] side by side with a more specialised, though not strictly individual, marriage. In order to explain these two forms of marriage we must begin by premising that in the Dieri tribe, as in other Australian tribes, certain groups of men and women in the intermarrying classes are by birth marriageable to each other, in other words, they are potential spouses. The Arunta call these potential spouses *unawa*;[2] the Urabunna call them *nupa*;[3] the Dieri call them *noa*. In the Dieri tribe this *noa* relationship of marriageability or potential spouseship is specialised by the betrothal to each other of a boy and a girl who are *noa* one to the other, and have been born about the same time. The betrothal is arranged by the mothers of the two children with the concurrence of the brothers of the girl's mother. The fathers have no part in the arrangement. In every such case a sister, whether own or tribal, of the betrothed boy must be promised as a wife to a brother, whether own or tribal, of the betrothed girl. The new relation thus created between the betrothed is called *tippa-malku*, and as a sign of betrothal the navel strings of the two children are tied up with emu feathers and different coloured strings.[4] "By the practice of betrothal two *noa* individuals of opposite sexes become, if I may use the term, specialised to each other as *tippa-malku* for the time being, to the exclusion of any other man in that relation. In other words, no woman can be *tippa-malku* to two or more men at the same time. It seems to me that out of this system of specialisation the individual marriage of some tribes has been developed. The germ of individual marriage may be seen in the Dieri practice, for, as I shall show later on, a woman becomes a *tippa-malku* wife before she becomes a *pirrauru* or group-wife. But

Group-marriage among the Dieri.

Marriageable groups among the Dieri and other Australian tribes.

Tippa-malku marriage among the Dieri.

---

[1] See above, pp. 308 *sqq.*

[2] Spencer and Gillen, *Native Tribes of Central Australia*, pp. 71, 74.

[3] Spencer and Gillen, *op. cit.* pp. 61 *sq.* See above, pp. 308 *sq.*

[4] A. W. Howitt, *Native Tribes of South-East Africa*, p. 177. Compare *id.*, "The Dieri and other Kindred Tribes of South-East Australia," *Journal of the Anthropological Institute*, xx. (1891) pp. 53 *sqq.*

at the same time it must be remembered that every woman is potentially a group-wife, and unless she dies after she becomes a *tippa-malku* wife, she becomes actually a group-wife. The woman is one of a group, over whom in advance a man is given special rights by being made *tippa-malku* to her, but at the same time with the fullest knowledge that she is not to be his individual wife as we understand the term. These explanations are necessary to guard against the misconception from using the words 'individual wife.'"[1]

Pirrauru marriage among the Dieri.

This form of marriage secures that a woman is specialised, though not exclusively appropriated, to one particular man. She may therefore be called his primary wife. But in addition to his primary wife (*tippa-malku*) every Dieri man may have one or more secondary wives called *pirraurus*, who at the same time may be, and commonly are, the primary wives of other men. These secondary wives are formally and ceremoniously allotted to him by the headmen or tribal council in presence of the tribe, so that the relationship thus formed is public and lawful. When the proposal to contract these secondary marriages has been mooted and agreed upon, the persons concerned assemble with their friends at some place in the camp about noon. If the men who are to be married are of the same totem, the head of their totemic clan attends with his ceremonial or magical staff called *kandri*, which is made out of the root of a certain tree. He and his fellow headmen, if there are more totemic clans than one concerned, make ridges of sand with their staves, one for each of the persons who is about to contract the *pirrauru* or secondary marriage. Then each pair of ridges is brought together to form a single ridge higher and broader than either of the two singly, thus symbolising the joining together of the married couple. Finally, one of the men, usually he who is given as a secondary husband (*pirrauru*), takes sand from the ridge and sprinkles it over the upper part of his thighs, and, as the Dieri express it, buries the

Ceremony of pirrauru marriage.

---

[1] A. W. Howitt, *Native Tribes of South-East Australia*, p. 179. The statement in this passage that "a woman becomes a *tippa-malku* wife before she becomes a *pirrauru* or group-wife" was afterwards corrected by Dr. Howitt. See below, p. 366 note[1].

pirrauru in the sand. In the case of two men who exchange their primary wives to be secondary wives (*pirraurus*) the same procedure is observed, and the ceremonies are completed in the evening. When the marriage ceremony takes place at noon, it is, so to say, a private affair; but when it is celebrated in the evening all the people in the camp attend. When that is so, the headmen of the two totemic clans concerned take their stand opposite to each other, about fifty yards apart, each of them holding two pieces of burning wood. The two pairs of secondary spouses (*pirraurus*) are loudly announced by name, the whole assembly repeats the names in a loud voice, and the two pieces of wood are struck together. But commonly it is not merely two pairs of secondary spouses (*pirraurus*) who are thus allotted to each other. The whole of the marriageable or married people are usually either allotted or re-allotted to each other by this ceremony, which is performed for batches of them at the same time.[1]

We are told that a secondary wife (*pirrauru*) is always a "wife's sister" or a "brother's wife," and that the relation arises through the exchange of wives by brothers;[2] but probably brother and sister are here to be understood in their wide classificatory sense, which, besides brother and sisters in our sense of the terms, includes many persons whom we should call cousins, and many more whom we should not regard as relations at all.[3] If two brothers are married to two sisters, they commonly live together in a group-marriage of four. When a man becomes a widower, he has the use of his brother's wife as his secondary wife (*pirrauru*), for which he makes presents to his brother. A guest is offered his host's primary wife as a temporary *pirrauru*, provided the woman is marriageable (*noa*) to him, that is, provided that she belongs to the class into which he may marry. A man may always exercise marital rights over his secondary wife (*pirrauru*) when they meet in the absence of her primary husband (*tippa-malku*);[4] but he

Relationship of the pirrauru or secondary spouses to each other.

---

[1] A. W. Howitt, *Native Tribes of South-East Australia*, pp. 181 sq.
[2] *Ibid.* p. 181.
[3] See above, p. 362.
[4] The terms *tippa-malku* and *pir-rauru* are both reciprocal. A man calls his primary wife *tippa-malku*, and she calls him *tippa-malku*. A man calls his secondary wife *pirrauru*, and she calls him *pirrauru*.

366 TOTEMISM IN SOUTH-EASTERN AUSTRALIA CHAP.

cannot take her from him without his consent except at certain ceremonial times, when a general sexual licence prevails between the intermarrying classes, as for instance at the initiation ceremonies, or at one of the marriages arranged between a man and a woman of two different tribes. When the primary husband (*tippa-malku*) is absent, his wife is taken and protected by one of her secondary husbands (*pirraurus*), for every woman may have several secondary husbands, just as every man may have several secondary wives. It is an advantage to a man to have many secondary wives, for in the absence of their primary husbands they supply him with a share of the food which they procure. A man may also obtain great influence in the tribe by lending his secondary wives to other men and receiving presents in return; and the property which he thus amasses he may employ to extend his power still further by distributing it among the headmen and other persons of consequence. Hence the leading men of the tribe generally have more primary wives and more secondary wives than other men. A primary wife takes precedence of a secondary wife; for example, if they are both with their husband in camp, the man will sleep next to the fire with his primary wife beside him and his secondary wife beyond her. When a primary wife dies, a secondary wife will take charge of her children, and tend them affectionately. A man may have a secondary wife (*pirrauru*) before he has a primary one (*tippa-malku*), and similarly a woman may have a secondary husband before she has a primary one. In other words, a man or woman may enter into the *pirrauru* relationship before he or she is married in what we should regard as the regular way.[1] A man calls the children of his secondary wife his sons and daughters; and on their side they call him father, and give the name of mother to his primary wife as well as to their real mother. But if a man

Relation of a primary wife (*tippa-malku*) to a secondary wife (*pirrauru*).

---

[1] In his *Native Tribes of South-East Australia*, pp. 179 and 181, Dr. Howitt stated that every woman became a primary wife (*tippa-malku*) before she became a secondary or group-wife (*pirrauru*). But this statement he afterwards corrected. See *Folk-lore*, xviii. (1907) pp. 166 *sq*., where Dr. Howitt says: "A girl becomes marriageable after she has been initiated to womanhood at the Wilpadrina ceremony, and may then be allotted as a *pirrauru*, whether she be in the relation of *tippa-malku* or not." Compare *id.*, in *Journal of the R. Anthropological Institute*, xxxvii. (1907) p. 268.

were more narrowly questioned, he would qualify his statement by saying that the primary husband of his mother is his "real father," and that the secondary husband (*pirrauru*) of his mother is his "little father." In like manner he would more precisely define his father's secondary wife (*pirrauru*) as his "little mother," to distinguish her from his "real mother." Often the women do not know whether their primary or their secondary husband is the father of a particular child; indeed they sometimes refuse to admit that there is only one father. Thus the child is indeed regarded as the offspring of the group-father and not of the individual-father.[1]

The *pirrauru* relationship in the Dieri tribe, like the *piraungaru* in the Urabunna,[2] is clearly a form of group-marriage, for under it a group of men and a group of women are publicly allotted to each other as husbands and wives by the highest tribal authority, and exercise marital rights accordingly over each other.[3] And it appears that this form of group-marriage was not confined to these tribes, but was shared by many others. Thus in 1861-62 Dr. Howitt found an equivalent of the *pirrauru* system among the Yantruwanta tribe, who live higher up than the Dieri on Cooper's Creek or the Barcoo River,[4] and some hundred and twenty miles further up the same river, within the Queensland boundary, the Kurnandaburi tribe practised *pirrauru* marriage under the name of *dilpa-malli*. The Kurnandaburi tribe is, like the Dieri, divided into two intermarrying moieties or classes, which bear the names of Matara and Yungo; and in addition to a system of primary marriage (*nubaia*) corresponding to the *tippa-malku* marriage of the Dieri, they have a system of secondary or group-marriage corresponding to the *pirrauru* marriage of the Dieri. These secondary spouses bear the name of *dilpa-malli*, and consist of a group of own or tribal brothers on

The pirrauru relationship is a form of group-marriage.

Group-marriage among the Yantruwanta and Kurnandaburi.

---

[1] For the original authorities on which the above account of *pirrauru* marriage is based, see A. W. Howitt, "The Dieri and other Kindred Tribes of Central Australia," *Journal of the Anthropological Institute*, xx. (1891) pp. 53-59; *id.*, *Native Tribes of South-East Australia*, pp. 181-187; *id.*, in *Folk-lore*, xvii. (1906) pp. 174 *sqq.*, xviii. (1907) pp. 166 *sqq.*

[2] Above, p. 309.

[3] A. W. Howitt, *Native Tribes of South-East Australia*, p. 187.

[4] A. W. Howitt, in *Folk-lore*, xviii. (1907) pp. 183 *sq.*

the one side, and a group of own or tribal sisters on the other side; and these two groups cohabit whenever the tribe assembles, or at any time when the two groups meet. But these secondary or group-marriages, like the primary or individual marriages (*nubaia*), are subject to the law of exogamy, which forbids a man to marry a woman of the same class and totem as himself; hence in these group-marriages it is necessary that all the husbands should be of one exogamous class (whether Matara or Yungo), and that all the wives should be of the other. Provided she does not transgress the class laws, every woman may have as many of these secondary husbands (*dilpa-mallis*) as she likes, and they are constantly changing them. Besides the marital relations which openly exist between groups of *dilpa-malli* men and women, similar relations exist secretly between men and their brothers' wives and between women and their sisters' husbands. Ostensibly these persons are tabooed to each other, and may not sit in the same camp or converse freely; but, nevertheless, they have sexual intercourse with each other in private. This is clearly, as Dr. Howitt observes, an equivalent of the *pirrauru* relation of the Dieri, and it may very well illustrate a transition from group-marriage to the more specialised form of marriage which the Dieri call *tippa-malku*. That more specialised form of marriage is recognised and practised by the Kurnandaburi tribe under the name of *nubaia*, and in this tribe, as among the Dieri, the mode in which the specialisation has been brought about appears to be betrothal. A female child is betrothed by her parents to some boy or man, who becomes her *abaija*. When the two are married, their relation is called *nubaia*; and, just as among the Dieri, an exchange of sisters is a regular accompaniment of a *nubaia* marriage, that is, the boy who gets a wife must give a sister in exchange to his wife's brother.[1]

Group-marriage among the Yandairunga.

Again, we find a system of group-marriage in the Yandairunga or Yendakarangu tribe, which occupied the country extending from the western shores of Lake Eyre

[1] A. W. Howitt, "The Dieri and other Kindred Tribes of Central Australia," *Journal of the Anthropological Institute*, xx. (1891) pp. 60-62; *id.*, *Native Tribes of South-East Australia*, pp. 192 *sq.*

westward for about a hundred and forty miles, and north and south for the same distance south of the Peak. This tribe is a southern division of the Urabunna, and their system of group-marriage, which they call *pira*, corresponds to the *piraungaru* of the northern Urabunna on the one side,[1] and to the *pirrauru* of the Dieri on the other side; while their other form of marriage (*nupa*) corresponds to the *nupa* of the northern Urabunna and the *tippa-malku* of the Dieri. Under the latter and more specialised form of marriage (*nupa*) a young girl is betrothed by her relations, such as her brothers or her mother's brothers, to a man who must be of the proper class. Under the system of group-marriage (*pira*) men claim certain women as their wives (*piras*) by birthright.[2] Again, a system of group-marriage appears to have existed in the Parnkalla tribe, whose social organisation in two exogamous classes, with maternal descent, agrees with that of the Lake Eyre tribes, though their territory lies far to the south of Lake Eyre, terminating at Port Lincoln on the sea. The marriage customs of the tribe are thus described by the missionary, Mr. C. W. Schürmann: "The aborigines of this portion of the province are divided into two distinct classes, viz. the Mattiri and Karraru people. This division seems to have remained among them from time immemorial, and has for its object the regulation of marriages; none being allowed within either of these classes, but only between the two; so that if a husband be Mattiri, his wife must be Karraru, and *vice versa*. The distinction is kept up by the children taking invariably the appellation of that class to which their mother belongs. There is not an instance of two Mattiri or Karraru being married, although they do not seem to consider less virtuous connections between parties of the same class incestuous. There are of course other limitations to marriage between nearly related people besides this general dis-

<small>Group-marriage in the Parnkalla tribe at Port Lincoln.</small>

---

[1] Above, pp. 308 *sqq*.

[2] A. W. Howitt, "The Dieri and other Kindred Tribes of Central Australia," *Journal of the Anthropological Institute*, xx. (1891) p. 60; as to the territory of this tribe, see *ib.* pp. 33 *sq*. In *Native Tribes of South-East Australia* (pp. 93, 187 *sq*.) Dr. Howitt calls the tribe Yendakarangu, which is presumably the more correct form of the name. As to the classes and totems of the tribe, see below, pp. 374 *sq*.

tinction; but it is very difficult to ascertain them, on account of the innumerable grades of consanguinity that arise from polygamy, and from frequent interchanging and repudiating of wives. Besides, friendship among the natives assumes always the forms and names of relationship, which renders it almost impossible to find out the difference between real or nearly adopted relatives. . . . The loose practices of the aborigines, with regard to the sanctity of matrimony, form the worst trait in their character; although the men are capable of fierce jealousy, if their wives transgress unknown to them, yet they frequently send them out to other parties, or exchange with a friend for a night; and, as for near relatives, such as brothers, it may almost be said that they have their wives in common. While the sending out of the women for a night seems to be regarded as an impropriety by the natives themselves, the latter practice is a recognised custom, about which not the least shame is felt. A peculiar nomenclature has arisen from these singular connections; a woman honours the brothers of the man to whom she is married with the indiscriminate name of husbands; but the men make a distinction, calling their own individual spouses *yungaras*, and those to whom they have a secondary claim, by right of brotherhood, *kartetis*."[1] In this account of the marriage customs of the Parnkalla tribe at Port Lincoln the exogamous classes Mattiri and Karraru are clearly identical in name and substance with the Matteri and Kararu classes of the Dieri, while it is highly probable, as Dr. Howitt has pointed out,[2] that the *yungara* spouses correspond to the primary or specialised spouses (*tippa-malku*), and the *karteti* spouses to the secondary or group spouses (*pirrauru*) of the Dieri; and in this tribe, as in the Dieri, the Kurnandaburi, and the Yendakarangu tribes, the specialisation of women to men seems to have been effected by betrothal of them in their youth or infancy; for we are told that among the Port Lincoln natives "the mode of marrying is the most unceremonious in the world. Long before a young girl

---

[1] C. W. Schürmann, "The Aboriginal Tribes of Port Lincoln," *Native Tribes of South Australia*, pp. 222, 223.

[2] A. W. Howitt, *Native Tribes of South-East Australia*, p. 191.

arrives at maturity, she is affianced by her parents to some friend of theirs, no matter whether young or old, married or single, and as soon as she shows symptoms of puberty, she is bid to follow him without any further ceremony, and without consulting her own inclinations."[1]

Altogether Dr. Howitt reckons that the tribes which practised a form of group-marriage like the *pirrauru* of the Dieri must have occupied an area of some 500,000 square miles, extending for a distance of 850 miles from Oodnadatta, the northern boundary of the Urabunna, to the eastern frontier of the Dieri or of the Mardala tribe between the Flinders Range and the Barrier Range.[2] In this great area the old system of group-marriage appears to have survived till to-day, or at all events till within living memory, though side by side with this relic of sexual communism there now exists in these same tribes a more specialised form of marital union which approximates, without attaining, to the exclusive appropriation of a woman or of women to one man. This existing system of group-marriage (*pirrauru, piraungaru*) clearly supplies the key to the classificatory system of relationship, since it shows us in actual operation those very group relationships which the classificatory system of relationship expresses in words. As Dr. Howitt has well put it: "The *pirauru* practice is clearly a form of group-marriage, in which a number of men of one exogamous division cohabit with a number of women of the other division. The children of this group necessarily also constitute a group in which the members are brothers and sisters, and between them marriage is prohibited. Here we find the idea which underlies the prohibition of marriage within the class division. All in it, in any given level of the generation, are brothers and sisters. The preceding level in the generation is the group-progenitor of the fraternal group, and this latter in its turn produces a group of children which stands in the filial relation to it. Here we have the actual fact as it exists in the *pirauru* group, and this pictures to us the

Extent of country occupied by tribes which have group-marriage.

This existing system of group-marriage supplies the key to the classificatory system of relationship.

---

[1] C. W. Schürmann, in *Native Tribes of South Australia*, pp. 222 sq.

[2] A. W. Howitt, in *Folk-lore*, xviii. (1907) p. 184. The southern boundary, which Dr. Howitt here omits to mention, was in his opinion the sea, from Port Lincoln on the east to Eucla on the west. See A. W. Howitt, *Native Tribes of South-East Australia*, p. 191.

former condition of the class divisions, which condition has been fossilized, so to say, in the relationship terms used. The classificatory system of relationships, to use the term employed by the late Dr. Morgan, has been a great stumbling-block in the path of many anthropologists, who in following their lines of enquiry have been guided by ideas in which they have grown up from infancy, as to the nature of the relations which exist between individuals. It has probably not suggested itself to them that since our system of counting relationships arises out of and is fitted to the conditions of our society, it might be that savages whose social conditions are so different may require some terms to define their relationships quite different in their character to those which we have. This error has probably arisen from considering a savage as a human being who in a rude exterior thinks much as does a civilized man. Such an idea cannot have a sound foundation. We see its results perhaps in the most marked form in the writings of Rousseau, but even later writers are not free from it."[1]

A powerful instrument in restricting the old system of group-marriage appears to have been the practice of betrothal.

If we ask how it is that in these tribes a more specialised, though not yet individual, form of marriage (*tippa-malku*) has arisen side by side with the system of group-marriage, one answer suggested by Dr. Howitt is that a powerful instrument in thus restricting the old group rights appears to have been the practice of betrothal, in other words "the rise and establishment of the right to give away a girl in marriage to some particular individual of the group which intermarries with the group to which she belongs. This is a very common custom in Australian tribes, and must have been a powerful agent in producing a feeling of ownership in the husband. The further rise of individual possession would also bring about a sense of individual paternity as regards the wife's children which could not exist under group-marriage."[2] In fact, when a man came to regard his wife as his individual property, he would naturally come to regard her children as also belonging exclusively to him, and thus, as I have already pointed out,[3] he might well look

---

[1] A. W. Howitt, "The Dieri and other Kindred Tribes of Central Australia," *Journal of the Anthropological Institute*, xx. (1891) p. 99.
[2] *Ibid.* p. 102.
[3] Above, p. 167.

upon his children as his property long before he knew that they were his offspring; and on their side the children might recognise him as their master long before they were aware that he was their begetter. The recognition of social paternity by no means carries with it the recognition of physical paternity; for whereas social paternity is a fact patent to the eyes of the whole community, physical paternity in the strict sense is a physiological process which no human eye has seen, and of which the true nature can hardly be understood by a savage.

Another agency which, as Dr. Howitt has indicated,[1] may well have contributed to the restriction of group rights and to the rise of individual marriage is the dispersal of the people in small groups or even in single couples over the country in their search for food. For the separation which such a dispersal entails could hardly fail to weaken the ties which bound each of these scattered groups to the rest of the tribe, while the prolonged and intimate association between individuals, which their isolation favoured, would naturally often endear them to each other and render them unwilling to resign the objects of their affection to the embraces of others who, although they were members of the same tribe, had through long absence become almost strangers. *The dispersal of the people in small groups or single couples may also have helped to restrict the old communal rights over women.*

However the change has been brought about, we shall hardly err in regarding the specialised form of marriage (*tippa-malku*) in these tribes as an encroachment on the old communal rights of the tribe and as a step towards that system of purely individual marriage which is found among other Australian tribes, particularly among tribes which inhabit more fertile regions than the burning and arid wastes of Lake Eyre; though even in these more advanced communities an unwonted and startling event, such as the sudden illumination of the nightly sky by the Southern Streamers, sufficed to produce a temporary reversion to the older practice of partial promiscuity, as if thereby they sought to expiate the habitual neglect of their ancestral customs.[2] *Specialised marriage of the tippa-malku type is probably an encroachment on the old communal rights.*

[1] A. W. Howitt, in *Journal of the Anthropological Institute*, xx. (1891) p. 103.

[2] A. W. Howitt, "The Dieri and other Kindred Tribes of Central Australia," *Journal of the Anthropological Institute*, xx. (1891) p. 101. Compare *id.*, *Native Tribes of South-East Australia*, pp. 276 *sq.*

Thus far we have dealt with the totemic and social system of the Dieri. Concerning the other tribes of the Lake Eyre basin, which possess a similar system, our information is far less abundant, and accordingly we shall despatch them more summarily. Thus, to begin with the Yendakarangu or Yandairunga tribe, which is a southern branch of the Urabunna, inhabiting the country to the west of Lake Eyre, the Yendakarangu are divided, just like the Dieri, into two exogamous intermarrying classes or moieties called respectively Kararu and Matteri, with descent in the female line, and, just as with the Dieri, each exogamous class includes a number of totem clans. But in one important respect the marriage rules of the Yendakarangu tribe differ from those of the Dieri and agree with those of the Urabunna. For whereas with the Dieri a man is free to marry a woman of any totem in the other exogamous class, in the Yendakarangu he is not so free, but is restricted in his choice of a wife to one or more definitely assigned totems. The following table exhibits a list of Yendakarangu totems with the marriages appropriate to each.[1]

Marginal note: The Yendakarangu or Yandairunga tribe, its classes, totems, and rules of marriage.

YENDAKARANGU (YANDAIRUNGA) TOTEMS

Classes.	Totems.	Marries with
Kararu	Cloud	Wadnamura.
	Crow	Wadnamura and Eagle-hawk.
	Red ochre	Cormorant and *Eagle-hawk*.
	Rat	Cormorant and Bull-frog.
	Wallaby	Iguana and *Lizard*.
	Emu	Eagle-hawk and *Bull-frog*.
	Musk duck	Eagle-hawk and *Dog*.
	Snake	Wadnamura.
Matteri	Eagle-hawk	Red ochre, Musk duck, and *Crow*.
	Cormorant	Rat and Red ochre.
	Iguana	Wallaby.
	Dog	Musk duck.
	Wadnamura	Snake, Cloud, Crow.
	Mulga tree	Emu.
	Bull-frog	Rat.
	Lizard	Wallaby.

[1] A. W. Howitt, *Native Tribes of South-East Australia*, pp. 187 *sq.* Compare *id.*, "The Dieri and other Kindred Tribes of Central Australia," *Journal of the Anthropological Institute*, xx. (1891) pp. 39, 41.

On this list Dr. Howitt observes: "This table is evidently imperfect. According to the almost universal rule, which obtains also with the Yendakarangu, that sisters are exchanged as wives, there should be reciprocity between the totems in their marriages. In the list this is the case as to some of each class, and therefore one is fairly justified in believing that it is so with the others. On this view I have added those totems which have been omitted, but which appear to be reciprocal, and which are in italics to distinguish them."[1]

As children in the Yendakarangu tribe take their class and totem from their mother, not from their father, it follows that if, for example, a Kararu man of the red ochre totem marries a Matteri woman of the cormorant totem, their children will be Matteri and Cormorants; if a Matteri man of the bull-frog totem marries a Kararu woman of the rat totem, then their children will be Kararu and Rats; and similarly with the rest. In this tribe there is the like feeling of fellowship between persons of the same totem which prevails among the Dieri. When a stranger arrives at a camp, he is entertained by men of the same totem as himself.[2] And like other Australian tribes the Yendakarangu have the classificatory system of relationship. For example, in the generation above his own a man applies the same term *kuyia* to his father and to his father's brothers. In his own generation he applies the same term *nuthi* to his elder brothers, to the sons of his father's brothers, and to the sons of his mother's sisters; he applies the same term *kaku* to his elder sisters, to the daughters of his father's brothers, and to the daughters of his mother's sisters; and he applies the same term *nupa* to his wife and to his wife's sisters (whom, however, he may also call *bilya*, the term which he applies to the daughters of his father's sisters and to the daughters of his mother's brothers). In the generation below his own he applies the same term *wardu* to his own sons and to his brothers' sons. On her side a woman applies the same term *nupa* to her husband and to her husband's

Rules of descent among the Yendakarangu.

Classificatory terms of relationship among the Yendakarangu.

---

[1] A. W. Howitt, *Native Tribes of South-East Australia*, p. 188.
[2] A. W. Howitt, "The Dieri and other Kindred Tribes of Central Australia," *Journal of the Anthropological Institute*, xx. (1891) p. 42.

brothers.¹ As usual, these terms express the relationship of the individual not to individuals merely but to groups. Every man has many wives, and every woman has many husbands; every child has many fathers and many mothers, and so forth. And as usual these terms expressive of group relationships doubtless originated in group-marriage, one form of which actually exists, or existed till lately, in this particular tribe.²

The Wonkamala tribe, its classes and totems.

To the north-west of Lake Eyre there is a tribe called the Wonkamala whose social organisation resembles that of the Dieri; for it is divided into the same two exogamous moieties or classes, Kararu and Matteri, with totem clans in each class and descent in the female line. The totems of the Kararu class are rain, carpet-snake, crow, and red ochre. The totems of the Matteri class are a caterpillar (*padi*),³ cormorant, emu, a pouched mouse (*kokula*), *Duboisia Hopwoodii* (of which the native name is *pitcheri*), and *wolkutyi*, of which the English equivalent seems to be unknown.⁴ The Wonkamala, like the Dieri, apply the same name *murdu* to their exogamous classes and to their totems.⁵

The Ngameni tribe, its classes and totems.

To the north of Lake Eyre is the Ngameni tribe, with a similar social organisation and rule of descent. The two exogamous classes are the same (Kararu and Matteri), and the totem clans included under each are exhibited in the following table.⁶

¹ A. W. Howitt, "The Dieri and other Kindred Tribes of Central Australia," *Journal of the Anthropological Institute*, xx. (1891) pp. 50 *sq*.

² See above, pp. 368 *sq*. It is to be remembered that the Yendakarangu are a southern branch of the Urabunna. As to group-marriage among the Urabunna, see above, pp. 308 *sqq*.

³ This caterpillar (*padi*), which is a totem also of the Dieri is said to be the witchetty grub, which is an important totem and article of food of the Arunta.

See A. W. Howitt, "The Dieri and other Kindred Tribes of Central Australia," *Journal of the Anthropological Institute*, xx. (1891) p. 38; *id.*, *Native Tribes of South-East Australia*, p. 783, who, however, elsewhere (*Native Tribes of South-East Australia*, pp. 91, 799) gives *muluru* as the Dieri name for the witchetty grub.

⁴ A. W. Howitt, *Native Tribes of South-East Australia*, p. 95.
⁵ *Ibid.* p. 91.
⁶ *Ibid.* p. 94.

[TABLE.

NGAMENI TOTEMS

Classes.	Totems.
Kararu	Rain, carpet-snake, crow, native companion, a small frog (*tidnamara*), seed of *Claytonia* sp., a bat (*tapairu*), the pan-beetle, *milkityerpara* (?), a frog, the rabbit-bandicoot, slow-worm, a small pouched mouse (*balyara*), kangaroo.
Matteri	A caterpillar (*muruwali*), cormorant, emu, eagle-hawk, a fish (*markara*), a variety of acacia, dingo, native cat, *kirrhapara* (?), a small marsupial (*kokula*), kangaroo rat, *Duboisia Hopwoodii* (*pitcheri*), expedition for red ochre, a lizard (*wompirka*), iguana-lizard, curlew, shell-parakeet, a crane (black with white on the wings).

The Ngameni, like the Dieri, apply the same name *murdu* to their exogamous classes and to their totems.[1]

To the south of the Ngameni, in the desert country between Cooper's Creek on the south and the Diamantina River on the north, is or used to be the Wonkanguru tribe with a similar organisation and rule of descent. Its totems, arranged under the same two exogamous classes, Kararu and Matteri, are exhibited in the following table.[2]

The Wonkanguru tribe, its classes and totems.

WONKANGURU TOTEMS

Classes.	Totems.
Kararu	Rain, carpet-snake, crow, red ochre, small frog (*tidnamara*), seed of *Claytonia* sp., a rat (*maiaru*), a bat (*tapairu*), the rabbit-bandicoot.
Matteri	A caterpillar (*wonamara*), cormorant, emu, eagle-hawk, dingo, a small marsupial (*kokula*), *Duboisia Hopwoodii* (*pitcheri*).

[1] A. W. Howitt, *op. cit.* p. 91.
[2] A. W. Howitt, *Native Tribes of South-East Australia*, p. 92.

378 TOTEMISM IN SOUTH-EASTERN AUSTRALIA CHAP.

The Wonkanguru, like the Dieri, apply the same name *murdu* to their exogamous classes and to their totems.[1]

The Yaurorka tribe, its classes and totems.
Another tribe in the country between Cooper's Creek and the Diamantina, but to the east of the Wonkanguru and higher up the basins of the rivers, is the Yaurorka tribe. It has the same two exogamous classes, Kararu and Matteri, with totem clans and descent in the female line. Its totems are exhibited in the following table.[2]

YAURORKA TOTEMS

Classes.	Totems.
Kararu	Rain, carpet-snake, native companion, red ochre, seed of *Claytonia* sp., pan-beetle, a frog (*kuyarku*), the rabbit-bandicoot, slow-worm, a small pouched mouse (*baliyara*), box eucalyptus, water-rat, shrew-mouse, mesembrianthemum.
Matteri	A caterpillar (*muluru*), cormorant, emu, eagle-hawk, a fish (*ngampuru*), dingo, native cat, *widla*, kangaroo rat, *Duboisia Hopwoodii* (*pitcheri*), *karingara* (?), iguana-lizard, curlew, *tillngaru* (?), a crane (black with white on wing), a large grey hawk.

The Yaurorka, like the Dieri, apply the same name *murdu* to their exogamous classes and to their totems.[3]

The Yantruwunta tribe, its classes and totems.
Still further to the east, higher up the course of Cooper's Creek, is the Yantruwunta tribe. It also has a similar social organisation with two exogamous classes, totem clans, and descent in the female line. But the names of the two classes are different, being Kulpuru and Tiniwa, instead of Kararu and Matteri. Its totems are exhibited in the following table.[4]

[1] A. W. Howitt, *op. cit.* p. 91.

[2] A. W. Howitt, *Native Tribes of South-East Australia*, p. 95.

[3] A. W. Howitt, *op. cit.* p. 91.

[4] A. W. Howitt, *Native Tribes of South-East Australia*, p. 92. In the class Tiniwa it will be observed that the dingo occurs twice. This may be a mistake.

YANTRUWUNTA TOTEMS

Classes.	Totems.
Kulpuru	Rain, carpet-snake, a rat (*kunamari*), *kanunga*, the pan-beetle, a frog (*kutyarku*), the rabbit-bandicoot, shrew-mouse.
Tiniwa	A caterpillar (*padingura-padi*), a caterpillar (*ngampuru*), dingo, *widla* (?), a pouch-mouse (*padi-padi*), *Duboisia Hopwoodii* (*pitcheri*), a lizard (*mungalli*), iguana-lizard, curlew, shell-parakeet, a crane (black with white on wings), bream, dingo.

The Yantruwunta apply the same name *kamiri* to their exogamous classes and to their totems.[1]

Still further up the course of Cooper's Creek or the Barcoo River, within the territory of Queensland, is the Kurnandaburi tribe. Its social organisation is similar to that of the foregoing tribes, for it is divided into two exogamous classes with totem clans and descent in the female line. But the names of the two exogamous classes differ from those of the preceding tribes, being Yungo and Matara, of which Matara, however, is probably equivalent to the Matteri of the Dieri and other Lake Eyre tribes. The totems of the Kurnandaburi are exhibited in the following table.[2]

The Kurnandaburi tribe, its classes and totems.

KURNANDABURI TOTEMS

Classes.	Totems.
Yungo	Kangaroo, native companion, iguana, large black cormorant, small black cormorant, blue crane, dingo, carpet-snake, crow, small crow, small grubs found in trees (*paringoro*), a frog (*orekomatu*), a rat (*parina*), teal-duck.
Matara	Brown snake, emu, frilled lizard, kangaroo rat, speckled brown snake, opossum, small bandicoot, small burrowing rat (*korinya*).

[1] A. W. Howitt, *op. cit.* p. 91.

[2] A. W. Howitt, *Native Tribes of South-East Australia*, p. 97. Compare *id.*, "The Dieri and other Kindred Tribes of Central Australia," *Journal of the Anthropological Institute*, xx. (1891) pp. 31, 39.

The Kurnandaburi apply the same name *gaura* to their exogamous classes and their totems. Dr. Howitt could not ascertain whether a man may marry a woman of any totem in the other class, or whether he is restricted to the women of one particular totem.[1] We have seen that a system of group-marriage obtains, or used to obtain, in this tribe.[2]

<small>Classificatory terms of relationship among the Kurnandaburi.</small> The Kurnandaburi have the classificatory system of relationship. Thus in the generation above his own a man applies the same term *kamundi* to his mother, to his mother's sisters, and to the wives of his father's brothers. In his own generation he applies the same term *kokundi* to his brothers, and to the sons of his father's brothers. He applies the same term *abaija* to his wife, to his wife's sisters, and to his brothers' wives. A woman applies the same term *abaija* to her husband, to her husband's brothers, and to her sisters' husbands. In the generation below her own a woman applies the same term *worua* to her sons and to her sisters' sons.[3]

§ 3. *Tribes with two Classes (Mukwara and Kilpara) and Female Descent*

<small>Eastern group of tribes with two exogamous classes, Mukwara and Kilpara, and female descent.</small> To the eastward of the Dieri the boundaries of tribes with the two exogamous classes Kararu and Matteri are marked roughly by the Grey and Barrier Ranges. Beyond these mountains to the east is another group of tribes, which are also divided each into two exogamous classes with totem clans in both classes and with descent both of the class and of the totem in the female line; but whereas among the tribes to the west of the mountains the two exogamous classes are named Kararu and Matteri, among the tribes to the east of the mountains they are named Mukwara and Kilpara. This eastern group of tribes with the classes Mukwara and Kilpara is of great extent and appears to comprise at least three nations, namely the Itchumundi, the

---

[1] A. W. Howitt, *Native Tribes of South-East Australia*, pp. 96, 192.

[2] See above, pp. 367 sq.

[3] A. W. Howitt, "Australian Group-Relationships," *Journal of the Royal Anthropological Institute*, xxxvii. (1907) pp. 287 sq.

Karamundi, and the Barkinji. Almost all the territory of these nations seemingly lies within the boundaries of New South Wales, and together they occupy practically the whole course of the Darling River from the Barwon River to the junction of the Darling with the Murray, and for some fifty miles back from the Darling towards the Bogan and Lachlan Rivers.[1] Other tribes having the same two exogamous classes (Mukwara and Kilpara) also extended for some distance up the Murray River from its junction with the Darling River. Among these were the Wiimbaio, the Ta-tathi, and the Keramin.[2]

In this group of tribes, according to Mr. A. L. P. Cameron, "the class divisions are always strictly exogamous (Mukwara marrying Kilpara, and Kilpara marrying Mukwara), yet this general rule is restricted by nearness of blood, so that, apart from the class regulations, there are special laws prohibiting consanguineous marriages. The strictness with which the class laws are always carried out is surprising. Even at the present day, when the decrease of their numbers has made it very difficult to obey all their ancient customs, any infringement of the marriage law, if persisted in, is punished by death. . . . Even in casual amours, which are not of infrequent occurrence, the class laws are invariably observed. Instances might be found in each of the tribes I am concerned with, but one from the Ta-ta-thi will perhaps suffice to show the general resemblance of custom. In this tribe there is at times a good deal of promiscuous intercourse between the sexes, but this is always within the class limits, any infringement of which always brings down upon the offenders the swift wrath of the tribe. My Ta-ta-thi informants tell me that members of this tribe were rarely ever known to break the law, but that if a man and a woman of forbidden classes did marry, the man would be put to death and the woman be beaten or speared, or both, till she was nearly dead; the reason given for not meting out to her the same punishment

In this group of tribes the rule of exogamy is very strictly enforced.

---

[1] A. W. Howitt, *Native Tribes of South-East Australia*, pp. 49 *sq.*, 97, 194; A. L. P. Cameron, "Notes on some Tribes of New South Wales," *Journal of the Anthropological Institute*, xiv. (1885) pp. 344 *sqq.*
[2] A. L. P. Cameron, *op. cit.* pp. 346, 349; A. W. Howitt, *Native Tribes of South-East Australia*, pp. 51 *sq.*, 100 *sq.*

as to the man being that she was in a manner probably coerced."[1] Similarly Dr. Howitt tells us that when the question was put to several men of one of these tribes, "What would be done if a Mukwara took a Mukwara for his wife?" the reply was an emphatic, "No good—suppose that, then we kill him."[2]

Practice of betrothal in childhood.

In this group of tribes, as in the tribes of Lake Eyre, an advance towards individual marriage has been made by a custom of betrothing girls in childhood. When a betrothed girl becomes marriageable she is taken to her future husband's camp by her mother or mother's brother. "The father has nothing to do with the disposal of his daughter. The reason given is that the daughter belongs to the class of her mother's brother, not to that of her father. Notwithstanding this, they believe that the daughter emanates from her father solely, being only nurtured by her mother."[3] In this view of fatherhood the Darling River tribes differ widely from the Arunta and other tribes of Central Australia, while, on the other hand, they agree with the opinion which Aeschylus puts in the mouth of Apollo,[4] and which the sapient James Boswell inclined to accept, "that our species is transmitted through males only, the female being all along no more than a *nidus*, or nurse, as Mother Earth is to plants of every sort; which notion seems to be confirmed by that text of scripture, 'He was yet *in the loins*

Belief that a child emanates from the father alone.

---

[1] A. L. P. Cameron, "Notes on some Tribes of New South Wales," *Journal of the Anthropological Institute*, xiv. (1885) pp. 351 *sq.*

[2] A. W. Howitt, *Native Tribes of South-East Australia*, p. 194. However, according to another observer of the Darling River tribes, offences against the law of the exogamous classes were not visited so severely. He says: "These tribes are divided into two classes called Muckwarra and Keelparra; the relationship between the two is called *Kengoojah*. A Muckwarra must marry a Keelparra, and *vice versa*. Children belong to the same class as their mother, and when quite young are often betrothed by their parents. It is considered a very serious offence for two persons of the same class to marry, and one that cannot be forgiven. The offenders are spoken of by all as bad, and are generally despised. The loss to them of the love and respect of their friends is a very heavy punishment; illegal marriages are therefore rare." See F. Bonney, "On some Customs of the Aborigines of the River Darling, New South Wales," *Journal of the Anthropological Institute*, xiii. (1884) pp. 128 *sq.*

[3] A. L. P. Cameron, *op. cit.* p. 352. The custom of betrothal in these tribes is mentioned also by F. Bonney (*op. cit.*, p. 129), who says: "Children belong to the same class as their mother, and when quite young are often betrothed by their parents."

[4] Aeschylus, *Eumenides*, 657 (627), *sqq.*

of his FATHER when Melchisedeck met him;' (Heb. vii. 10) and consequently, that a man's grandson by a daughter, instead of being his *surest* descendant, as is vulgarly said, has, in reality, no connexion whatever with his blood."[1]

But although in the Darling River tribes, with which we are here concerned, girls are very often betrothed in childhood, and wives are bound to be faithful to their husbands,[2] nevertheless among them "a custom, which seems to indicate a time when marriage was in the group, is that of exchanging wives, either at some grand assembly of the tribe, or in order to avert some threatened calamity. This custom is, I think, rare at present. It is also an occasional custom, that two tribal brothers having quarrelled, and wishing for a reconciliation, the one sends his wife to the other's camp, and a temporary change is effected. These facts seem to show, when taken in consideration with other tribal customs, that in New South Wales there was a time in the past when group marriage was in force, for even now one class is theoretically husband or wife to another class."[3] For instance, in the Barkinji nation every Mukwara man speaks of every Kilpara woman as "wife," while every Kilpara woman speaks of every Mukwara man as "husband."[4]

Traces of group-marriage in the Darling River tribes.

All these tribes appear to possess the classificatory system of relationship. At all events, Mr. A. L. P. Cameron, who has given us a valuable account of some of them, tells us that the system is found in all the tribes described by him, and he records in detail the classificatory terms of relationship in use among the Wathi-Wathi, a tribe which seems to have the same social organisation as the rest, though its territory lies further east on the Murray River.[5] With regard to the relationships expressed by the classificatory terms Mr. Cameron says: "They are as real to them as are our own to us, and any man who married a woman who was, according to this system, his sister, that is to say, the daughter of his father's brother, or of his mother's

Classificatory terms of relationship in these tribes, particularly in the Wathi-Wathi.

---

[1] James Boswell, *Life of Samuel Johnson*, Ninth Edition (London, 1822), ii. 399 note 2.
[2] A. L. P. Cameron, "Notes on some Tribes of New South Wales," *Journal of the Anthropological Institute*, xiv. (1885) p. 352.
[3] A. L. P. Cameron, *op. cit.* p. 353.
[4] A. L. P. Cameron, *op. cit.* p. 352.
[5] A. L. P. Cameron, *op. cit.* p. 346; A. W. Howitt, *Native Tribes of South-East Australia*, pp. 50, 52.

sister, would be deemed guilty of incest, and would incur the penalty of death. The same system of relationships is found in all the tribes I deal with in these notes, and in them all a man regards his mother's sister's child, or his father's brother's child, in precisely the same light as he regards his mother's child or his father's child."[1] Thus, to take the terms used by the Wathi-Wathi, in the generation above his own a man applies the same term *mamui* to his father and to his father's brothers. In his own generation he calls his elder brother *wawi* and his younger brother *mamui*, and he applies the same terms to the sons of his father's brothers and to the sons of his mother's sisters, calling them either *wawi* or *mamui* according as they are older or younger than himself. Similarly, he calls his elder sister *tatui* and his younger sister *minukui*, and he applies the same terms to the daughters of his father's brothers and to the daughters of his mother's sisters, calling them *tatui* or *minukui* according as they are older or younger than himself. A husband applies the same term *nopui* to his wife, to his wife's sisters, and to his brothers' wives; and a wife applies the same term *nopui* to her husband and to her husband's brothers. In the generation below his own a man applies the same term *wa-ipui* to his own sons, to the sons of his brothers, and to the sons of his wife's sisters.[2] As usual, these classificatory terms express group relationships, and are probably derived from a system of group-marriage, of which, as we have seen,[3] there are traces in these tribes of the Darling River.

Traditions of the Bookoomuri, a wonder-working race of men who occupied

Like the tribes of Central Australia, the natives of the Darling River have traditions of a wonder-working race of men who occupied the country long ago, excelled in the magical arts, transformed themselves into animals, and gave rise to some of the natural features of the landscape. On this subject Mr. A. L. P. Cameron says: "There is a tradition very

---

[1] A. L. P. Cameron, *op. cit.* p. 354.
[2] A. L. P. Cameron, *op. cit.* pp. 354 *sq.* It is singular that the same term *mamui* should be applied to the father and to the younger brother. In his list of the Watu-Watu (Wathi-Wathi?) terms of relationship Dr. Howitt gives only one term *wawi* as the equivalent of "brother." See A. W. Howitt, "Australian Group-Relationships," *Journal of the Royal Anthropological Institute*, xxxvii. (1907) p. 288.
[3] Above, p. 383.

widespread among the tribes I am concerned with, that the country long ago, the earth was originally peopled by a race much more like the powerful, especially in the arts magic, than that which now *mura-mura* of inhabits it. This first race is in different localities known the Dieri by different names, but as the legends regarding them are and the *alcheringa* much the same, those of one tribe will serve for illustra- ancestors tion. The Wathi-wathi call them *Bookoomuri*, and say they of the Arunta. were famous for fighting, hunting, etc., and were eventually changed into animals by Tha-tha-puli, who then created the present race. Others say that the *Bookoomuri* effected the transformation themselves, and that as animals they felt an interest in the new race that succeeded them, and imparted to it much valuable knowledge. A belief exists that the magical powers of the doctors, disease-makers, and rain-makers has been handed down to them from the *Bookoomuri*."[1] In these marvellous *Bookoomuri* it is easy to see the equivalent of the *mura-mura* of the Dieri and the *alcheringa* ancestors of the Arunta. The writer who reports them further observes: "There are many traditions of the wonderful feats performed by the *Bookoomuri*, and I think that most, if not all, the tribes of New South Wales, and perhaps of Australia, believe that the country was formerly inhabited by a different race from that which occupies it at the present day." And he acutely asks: "Is it possible that the totemic divisions of a tribe are connected with this belief in a race of men who afterwards became animals? It might be, for instance, that the class which has for its totems Eagle-hawk, Kangaroo, Bandicoot, believes that the *Bookoomuri* who were transformed into those animals were the ancestors of that class. But I have no direct evidence of such a belief."[2] The conjecture thus cautiously put forward by Mr. Cameron many years ago has been to a large extent confirmed by the fuller knowledge which we have since acquired of the native Australian legends, though in these legends the founders of the totem clans appear oftener to have been animals or semi-animals who afterwards became men than men who were subsequently transformed into animals.

[1] A. L. P. Cameron, "Notes on some Tribes of New South Wales," *Journal of the Anthropological Institute*, xiv. (1885) p. 368.
[2] A. L. P. Cameron, *op. cit.* p. 369.

386 TOTEMISM IN SOUTH-EASTERN AUSTRALIA CHAP.

Wathi-wathi tradition of the origin of fire.

As an example of the stories which the Darling River natives tell about the wonderful *Bookoomuri* we may take the legend of the origin of fire. The Wathi-wathi say that once upon a time there were two *Bookoomuri*, of whom one was a water-rat and the other a codfish. They alone were in possession of fire, and they jealously guarded it in a clearing among the great thickets of reeds on the banks of the Murray River. The other *Bookoomuri* as well as the present race of men made many efforts to get a spark of the fire, but all in vain. At last one day a hawk, who of course had been a *Bookoomuri*, discovered the water-rat and the codfish in the act of cooking mussels, which they had procured from the river. Up he flew to a great height and caused a strong wind to blow sparks from the fire among the dry reed-beds. The conflagration which ensued was, however, extinguished by the efforts of the water-rat and the codfish. Then the hawk sent a wind from the opposite direction, and after that a whirlwind. Sweeping the sparks before it, the storm set the whole of the reed-beds in a blaze, and soon the roaring conflagration spread to the forests and laid waste vast tracts of country, so that a tree has never grown there since. That is why there are now immense treeless plains where once there were greenwoods. But the natives thus obtained fire and learned to make it by friction.[1] In this Australian legend the hawk plays the same beneficent part that is played in Greek legend by the fire-bringer Prometheus, who has himself been identified by an eminent scholar with the eagle which preyed on his vitals.[2]

---

[1] A. L. P. Cameron, *op. cit.* p. 368. A very similar legend is told by the Ta-ta-thi (*ib.* pp. 368 *sq.*). These stories have all the appearance of being native and genuine. But in the pit of fire in which, according to some of these people, bad men are roasted after death, we may perhaps detect a ray of Gospel truth illuminating with a somewhat lurid light the darkness of heathendom. See A. L. P. Cameron, *op. cit.* pp. 364 *sq.*

[2] Salomon Reinach, *Prométhée* (Paris, 1907), pp. 24 *sqq.*; *id.*, *Cultes, Mythes et Religions*, iii. (Paris, 1908) pp. 68 *sqq.* As to the discovery or theft of fire the Kurnai tell how the brown hawk recovered fire for them after it had been stolen by some thieves, who were making off with it and climbing up a cord into the sky, when the hawk swooped on them and dashed the fire with its wings from their hands. The fire fell to the ground, and the robin blew it into a flame and smeared it on his breast, where you may see the red mark of it to this day. See A. W. Howitt, "Further Notes on the Australian Class Systems," *Journal of the Anthropological Institute*, xviii. (1889) p. 54. The Wurunjerri relate how the crow (*waang*) stole fire from some

TRIBES WITH TWO CLASSES

We have seen that the Darling River tribes may be divided into three nations, the Itchumundi, the Karamundi, and the Barkinji.[1] Of these the Itchumundi nation occupies the country which lies back from the Darling River and is bounded on the west by the Grey and Barrier Ranges. It includes the Wilya, Kongait, Bulali, and Tongaranka tribes. Of these the Wilya occupied the country about the Grey Ranges, with its headquarters about Endeavour Lake.[2] Its totems, divided between the two exogamous classes Mukwara and Kilpara, are shown in the following table.[3]

The Itchumundi nation.

The Wilya tribe, its classes and totems.

WILYA TOTEMS

Classes.	Totems.
Mukwara	Eagle-hawk, kangaroo, bandicoot, duck, frilled lizard, opossum, dingo.
Kilpara	Emu, carpet-snake, bone-fish, padi-melon, wallaby.

In this nation the two classes, Mukwara and Kilpara, were as usual strictly exogamous; that is, Mukwara might only marry Kilpara, and *vice versa*. But there was a further limitation of marriage in regard to the totems, for a man of one class was not always free to marry a woman of any totem of the other class. For example, a Mukwara of the eagle-hawk totem married a Kilpara of the bone-fish totem: a Mukwara of the kangaroo totem married a Kilpara of the emu totem; a Mukwara of the dog totem married a Kilpara of the padi-melon totem; and so on. As a child took its class and totem from its mother, it follows that if a Mukwara man of the eagle-hawk totem married a Kilpara woman of the bone-fish totem, the children would be Kilpara and Bone-fish: if a Mukwara man of the kangaroo totem married a Kilpara woman of the emu totem, the children would be Kilpara and Emus; and so on.[4]

Wilya rules of marriage and descent.

---

young women who are identified with the Pleiades. See A. W. Howitt, *Native Tribes of South-East Australia*, p. 430.

[1] Above, pp. 380 *sq*.

[2] A. W. Howitt, *Native Tribes of South-East Australia*, pp. 49, 98.

[3] A. W. Howitt, *op. cit.* p. 98.

[4] A. W. Howitt, *op. cit.* p. 194.

388 TOTEMISM IN SOUTH-EASTERN AUSTRALIA CHAP.

The Karamundi nation. The Karamundi nation occupied the basin of the Darling River from the junction of the Culgoa with it downwards to Wilcannia and beyond. It included the Milpulko, Naualko, Guerno, and Barrumbinya. Of these the territory of the Milpulko bordered on the Darling River from Wilcannia downwards.[1] Its totems, divided between the two exogamous classes Mukwara and Kilpara, are shown in the following table.[2]

The Milpulko tribe, its classes and totems.

MILPULKO TOTEMS

Classes.	Totems.
Mukwara	Eagle-hawk, kangaroo, bandicoot, duck, frilled lizard.
Kilpara	Emu, carpet-snake, bone-fish, iguana, padi-melon, opossum, wallaby.

In this tribe, again, a child takes its class and totem from its mother. For example, if a Mukwara man of the kangaroo totem marries a Kilpara woman of the emu totem, the children will be Kilpara and Emus. The tribes of the Karamundi nation, to which the Milpulko belong, have a rule like that of the Itchumundi nation, according to which a member of either class may marry only in one totem clan of the other class. For example, a Mukwara man of the kangaroo totem may marry a Kilpara woman of the emu totem and of no other.[3]

There is reason to believe that the Karamundi nation also includes tribes on the Paroo and Warrego Rivers, to the north of the Darling. Among them is the Paruinji tribe, which occupies the course of the Paroo River from Hungerford, at the Queensland boundary, southward to Bootha-bootha.[4] It has the same two exogamous classes (Mukwara and Kilpara) as the preceding tribes, with totem clans and descent both of the classes and of the totems in the female line. Its totems, arranged under

The Paruinji tribe, its classes and totems.

---

[1] A. W. Howitt, *Native Tribes of South-East Australia*, pp. 49 sq., 98.
[2] A. W. Howitt, op. cit. p. 98.
[3] A. W. Howitt, op. cit. p. 189.
[4] A. W. Howitt, op. cit. pp. 50, 99.

TRIBES WITH TWO CLASSES

the two exogamous classes, are exhibited in the following table.[1]

Paruinji Totems

Classes.	Totems.
Mukwara	Eagle-hawk, kangaroo, bandicoot, opossum, lizard.
Kilpara	Emu, bream, carpet-snake, iguana.

The Barinji, another tribe on the Paroo River, has the following totems distributed between the same two exogamous classes, Mukwara and Kilpara.[2]

The Barinji tribe, its classes and totems.

Barinji Totems

Classes.	Totems.
Mukwara	Eagle-hawk, kangaroo, *bilbae* (a rabbit-like burrowing animal), turkey, whistling duck, bandicoot.
Kilpara	Emu, snake, lizard, wallaby, iguana, native companion.

The last of the three nations which occupied the lower basin of the Darling River was the Barkinji. This was a large nation, whose territory, averaging some fifty miles in breadth, skirted the Darling River on its south-eastern side from the junction of the Bogan River with it down to a point about half-way between Menindie and Pooncarrie. According to Mr. A. L. P. Cameron, tribes belonging to this nation occupied the country west as well as east of the Darling River for a mean breadth of eighty miles.[3] This

The Barkinji nation, its classes and totems.

---

[1] A. W. Howitt, *Native Tribes of South-East Australia*, p. 99.

[2] A. L. P. Cameron, "Notes on some Tribes of New South Wales," *Journal of the Anthropological Institute*, xiv. (1885) p. 348, where the Barinji totems are given on the authority of Mr. J. D. Scott. Dr. A. W. Howitt has, apparently in error, assigned these totems to the Barkinji (*Native Tribes of South-East Australia*, p. 99). But Mr. Cameron, to whom he refers, distinguishes the Barkinji from the Barinji and says that he cannot give the list of Barkinji totems.

[3] A. L. P. Cameron, "Notes on some Tribes of New South Wales," *Journal of the Anthropological Institute*, xiv. (1885) p. 346; A. W. Howitt, *Native Tribes of South-East Australia*, p. 50.

390 TOTEMISM IN SOUTH-EASTERN AUSTRALIA CHAP.

nation also had the two exogamous classes Mukwara and Kilpara, but all that we know of its totems is that Mukwara included emu and whistling duck, while Kilpara included lizard and kangaroo.[1]

The Wiimbaio tribe, its classes and totems. The Wiimbaio tribe occupied the country at the junction of the Darling and Murray Rivers for a distance of about thirty miles up and down the Murray River on its south bank. Their territory did not go back southward from the river for more than a day's journey, or about twenty miles. They had the two exogamous classes Mukwara and Kilpara; and with regard to totems Mukwara included eagle-hawk, lizard, and others, while Kilpara included crow, bone-fish, and others. Children took their class and totem from their mother. Girls were betrothed in infancy. The Wiimbaio intermarried with the adjoining tribes both on the Murray and the Darling Rivers.[2]

The Ta-tathi tribe, its classes and totems. On the northern bank of the Murray River, from its junction with the Darling River upwards to Euston, lived the Ta-tathi, a strong tribe, which had the same two exogamous classes Mukwara and Kilpara with the following totems distributed between them.[3]

TA-TATHI TOTEMS

Classes.	Totems.
Mukwara	Light brown eagle-hawk, teal-duck, jew lizard.
Kilpara	Crow, iguana, brown-coloured eagle-hawk.

Sex totems of the Ta-tathi. In the Ta-tathi group of tribes, besides the regular totems, the bat was very much reverenced by the men, and was never killed by them. If a woman killed a bat, there used to be a great disturbance, in which the women were

---

[1] A. L. P. Cameron, "Notes on some Tribes of New South Wales," *Journal of the Anthropological Institute*, xiv. (1885) p. 348, note 2.

[2] A. W. Howitt, *Native Tribes of South-East Australia*, pp. 51 sq., 100, 194.

[3] A. W. Howitt, *op. cit.* pp. 52, 100; A. L. P. Cameron, "Notes on some Tribes of New South Wales," *Journal of the Anthropological Institute*, xiv. (1885) p. 349. Dr. Howitt tells us that he is unable to assign the totems of this tribe to their respective class; but Mr. A. L. P. Cameron, to whom he refers, assigns them as in the text without any remark to indicate that he was in doubt.

sometimes wounded. Similarly the women reverenced a species of small owl, and attacked the men if they tried to kill one of the birds. They called the bat *rakur* and the small owl *dhrail*. The Wathi-wathi called the bat *benalongi* and the small owl *yeraliri*. Thus the bat and the little owl were the sex totems of the men and women respectively. " In this group of tribes a man never kills his totem, but he does not object to eat it when killed by another. Everything in the universe is divided among the different members of the tribe; some claim the trees, others the plains, others the sky, stars, wind, rain, and so forth." [1]

Adjoining the Ta-tathi on the Murray River were the Keramin, a tribe which had the same two class divisions Mukwara and Kilpara, with the following totem clans distributed between them.[2]

<small>The Keramin tribe, its classes and totems.</small>

KERAMIN TOTEMS

Classes.	Totems.
Mukwara	Dark-coloured eagle-hawk, red kangaroo, teal-duck, spoonbill, bandicoot, lizard.
Kilpara	Silverfish, emu, crow, padi-melon, whip-snake.

With regard to the totems in these tribes we are informed that in the Barkinji, Ta-tathi, and Keramin tribes any totem of Mukwara may marry any totem of Kilpara, and *vice versa*.[3]

Tribes with the same two exogamous classes (Mukwara and Kilpara) extended up the Murray River as far as the junction of the Loddon, a tributary which flows into the Murray from the south; but the totems of these tribes are unknown.[4] Moreover, another large tribe or nation called

---

[1] A. L. P. Cameron, "Notes on some Tribes of New South Wales," *Journal of the Anthropological Institute*, xiv. (1885) p. 350. As to sex totems see above, pp. 47 *sq.*

[2] A. L. P. Cameron, *op. cit.* pp. 346, 349.

[3] A. L. P. Cameron, "Notes on some Tribes of New South Wales," *Journal of the Anthropological Institute*, xiv. (1885) p. 351; A. W. Howitt, *Native Tribes of South-East Australia*, p. 195.

[4] A. W. Howitt, *Native Tribes of South-East Australia*, pp. 100 *sq.*, 195 *sq.*

392 TOTEMISM IN SOUTH-EASTERN AUSTRALIA CHAP.

The Berriait nation.

the Berriait, which occupied a great extent of country between the Darling, Murray, and Lachlan Rivers, was also divided into two exogamous classes bearing the names of Mukwara and Kilpara, but the names of their totems have not been recorded. The wide region over which the Berriait roamed is almost waterless, and the natives were driven to wring a substitute for water from the roots of trees, particularly from the mallee (a species of eucalyptus) and from a species of Hakea locally known as the "needle bush." These roots they cut and allowed to drip an unpalatable but welcome fluid into vessels placed to receive it. When even this precarious supply failed, there was nothing left for them but to fight their way through hostile tribes to the rivers or perish miserably of thirst.[1]

§ 4. *Tribes with two Classes (Eagle-hawk and Crow) and Female Descent*

Tribes of the Alpine tablelands.

Beyond the sources of the Yarra and the Goulbourn Rivers the lofty Dividing Range of South-Eastern Australia widens out into great Alpine tablelands, where grassy downs alternate with mountain summits. In winter these uplands are buried deep under snow, in summer they are carpeted with Alpine flowers. The lower slopes and tablelands are habitable throughout the year. These high plateaux, extending from about Woodspoint in Victoria to New South Wales, where they culminate in Mount Kosciusko, were inhabited by several tribes, among whom were the Ya-itma-thang, the Ngarigo, and the Wolgal.[2] Of these the Ya-itma-thang, commonly called the Omeo tribe, inhabited the mountainous country in which the rivers Mitta-Mitta and Tambo take their rise. Unfortunately for them gold was discovered in their country in 1852, a great rush of miners set in, the natives went down before them, and when ten years had passed only four or five members of the once numerous tribe remained alive. Very little has been recorded of this hapless folk, but among their totems were

The Ya-itma-thang tribe.

[1] A. L. P. Cameron, "Notes on some Tribes of New South Wales," *Journal of the Anthropological Institute*, xiv. (1885) pp. 346 *sq.*, 349; A. W. Howitt, *Native Tribes of South-East Australia*, p. 51.

[2] A. W. Howitt, *Native Tribes of South-East Australia*, p. 77.

the rabbit-rat and the bat. The same totems are found in the neighbouring Ngarigo tribe, with which the Theddora branch of the Ya-itma-thang intermarried. The rule of marriage was that of the two-class tribes with female descent, but it is not known whether a man was free to marry a woman of any totem in the other class, or whether he was restricted to certain totems. In this tribe, as in the Urabunna, a man's proper wife was the daughter, own or tribal, of his mother's brother. In the Theddora branch of the Ya-itma-thang a girl was betrothed by her father, usually at or after her birth, and was given to her husband when she had grown up. A man to whom a girl had been promised endeavoured to obtain a lock of her hair, and if she afterwards jilted him, he would wrap the hair in an eagle-hawk's feather and put it in a water-hole. As the hair rotted, the jilt would sicken and die. Dr. Howitt tells us that he knew a woman of this tribe named Old Jenny, who had broken the tribal law by marrying a man to whom she stood in the classificatory relation of mother. Years afterwards her sin, or at all events her kinsfolk, found her out at the Black Mountain station on the Snowy River. They essayed to correct their erring sister with the persuasive argument of clubs, but the stout old lady gave such an exceedingly good account of herself with a digging-stick that they were fain to desist.[1]

The Ngarigo and Wolgal tribes were divided each into two exogamous classes which bore the names of Eagle-hawk and Crow respectively. Each class included a number of totem clans; and the men of either class were free to marry women of any totem in the other class. Children took both their class and their totem from their mother.[2] The Ngarigo tribe occupied the Manero tableland, between the Wolgal on the north, the Ya-itma-thang on the north-west, the Kurnai on the west and south-west, and the Yuin or Coast Murring on the south-east.[3] Their totems were distributed between the two exogamous classes Eagle-hawk and Crow as follows:—[4]

Eagle-hawk and Crow classes.

The Ngarigo tribe, its classes and totems.

[1] A. W. Howitt, *Native Tribes of South-East Australia*, pp. 77, 101, 196, 197.
[2] A. W. Howitt, *op. cit.* pp. 101 sq., 197.
[3] A. W. Howitt, *op. cit.* p. 78.
[4] A. W. Howitt, *op. cit.* pp. 101 sq.

NGARIGO TOTEMS

Classes.	Totems.
Eagle-hawk (*Merung*)	Lyre-bird, bat, flying squirrel (*bulemba*), tuan, black snake, a fish (*mulan* or *munja*), the mopoke, black opossum, red wallaby.
Crow (*Yukembruk*)	A small hawk, rabbit-rat, flying squirrel (*baua*), kangaroo, emu, lace-lizard, native companion, spiny ant-eater, sleeping lizard.

Betrothal among the Ngarigo. The practice of betrothing girls in childhood prevailed among the Ngarigo, the rule being that a man married the daughter of his mother's brother. When a betrothed girl was marriageable her father took her to her husband's camp and handed her over to him. The widow of a Ngarigo man did not go to his brother who was of the same mother, but to the son of his father's elder brother, that is, to the man who, under their system of relationship, was the elder brother of the deceased.[1]

The Wolgal tribe, its classes and totems. The Wolgal tribe inhabited the tablelands of the highest Australian Alps and their northern slopes, their boundaries beginning at Kauwambat, near Pilot Mountain, and running along the Indi River to Walleregang.[2] By 1870 the tribe was nearly extinct, but among the few survivors was the bard or singer of the tribe, with whom Dr. Howitt was acquainted. The Wolgal totems were distributed between the two exogamous classes Eagle-hawk and Crow as follows :—[3]

WOLGAL TOTEMS

Classes.	Totems.
Eagle-hawk (*Malian*)	Kangaroo, emu, hawk, dingo, flying squirrel, lyre-bird, bat.
Crow (*Umbe*)	Wombat, brown snake, a star (? Venus), bandicoot, spiny ant-eater, rabbit-rat.

[1] A. W. Howitt, *Native Tribes of South-East Australia*, pp. 196, 198 *sq.*
[2] A. W. Howitt, *op. cit.* p. 78.
[3] A. W. Howitt, *op. cit.* p. 102.

In these tribes a man was free to marry a woman of any totem in the other class; but his proper wife was the daughter, own or tribal, of his mother's brother. In the Wolgal tribe it was usual to betroth a girl in her childhood to a full-grown or even old man of the proper class. When she was old enough to be married, her father, accompanied by his brother, took her to her future husband's camp and left her there. A Wolgal man, speaking to Dr. Howitt, said that a father could do what he liked with his daughter, because the child is his, and "he only gives it to his wife to take care of for him." Contrasted with the practice of the Dieri, among whom the mother alone disposes of her infant daughter, this Wolgal custom marks an advance towards paternal descent.[1]

Wolgal rules of marriage and betrothal.

Among all these tribes the rule that a man must avoid his wife's mother was strictly observed. For example, in the Ngarigo tribe a woman might not see her son-in-law nor even hear his name pronounced. If any one chanced to mention his name in her hearing, she would put her fingers in her ears and say, "Be quiet."[2]

Avoidance of mother-in-law.

In the dense forests, jungles, and swamps which intervene between the high Australian Alps and the coast of Gippsland, in South-Eastern Victoria, there lived a tribe of broken men called the Biduelli. They appear to have been a medley composed of refugees who had fled from the neighbouring tribes. Both their language and their totems were mixed. They dwelt dispersed in small open glades of the thick jungle which covers their dreary inhospitable country. Their classes and totems descended in the female line. Among them Dr. Howitt found one family with the class-name Crow (*yukembruk*) and the totem rabbit-rat, which accords with the Ngarigo system. The Biduelli also had the two sex totems of the Kurnai, namely, emu-wren (*yürung*) and superb warbler (*djütgun*).[3]

The Biduelli tribe.

§ 5. *Tribes with four Subclasses and Female Descent*

From tribes which are organised in the simplest fashion, namely, in two exogamous moieties or classes, with descent

---

[1] A. W. Howitt, *Native Tribes of South-East Australia*, pp. 197 sq.
[2] A. W. Howitt, *op. cit.* p. 199.
[3] A. W. Howitt, *op. cit.* pp. 79-81, 102 sq.

Tribes with four subclasses and female descent.

Tribes in the female line, we now pass to the consideration of tribes which possess a more complex social organisation, the two primary exogamous classes being among them subdivided into four exogamous subclasses with descent in the female line.

The Kamilaroi nation of New South Wales.

We may begin with the Kamilaroi, a large nation of North-Eastern New South Wales, consisting of many tribes under the same designation, which is derived from the negative *kamil* or *kumil*. The territory of the Kamilaroi included nearly the whole of the pastoral district of Liverpool Plains; it stretched north to the Queensland border, and westward down the Darling River from Walgett to Bourke.[1] With regard to the extent and physical nature of the country occupied by tribes which possessed the Kamilaroi type of social organisation, Dr. Howitt writes as follows: "To the eastward of the boundary which I have marked for the Barkinji type,[2] the country is better watered and has far greater food-supply for an aboriginal population, until at the eastern coast the food-supply reaches its maximum. I am now speaking generally, and not with reference to isolated spots, which might be picked out where the coast is barren. Over this better watered and provisioned country extends the Kamilaroi type of system, with a range also along the northern watershed to the boundary of South Australia, and probably beyond it to the westward. It appears to touch the eastern coast line, and to follow it to about Rockhampton, where it leaves the coast and, striking southwards along the coast range, follows its general direction until at about the Hunter River, in New South Wales, it reaches its most southerly limit. Thence the boundary of the Kamilaroi type strikes, westward to the junction of the Murrumbidgee and Murray Rivers, where it joins the south-eastern boundary of the Barkinji type. Thus the true Kamilaroi organisation, with small variations, mainly in dialectic forms of the class names, spreads over an area in Eastern Australia at the very least 1000 miles north and south by 500 miles east and west. This area comprises some of the best watered and

Extent and nature of their country.

---

[1] A. W. Howitt, *Native Tribes of South-East Australia*, p. 57.

[2] As to the Barkinji type of social organisation, with its two exogamous classes Mukwara and Kilpara, see above, pp. 389 *sq*.

most fertile tracts, exclusive of the rich lands of the coast line."[1]

In the Kamilaroi type of social organisation the two primary exogamous moieties or classes, which bear the names of Kupathin and Dilbi, are subdivided each into two subclasses, which bear the names of Ipai, Kumbo, Muri, and Kubi. Included under the classes (moieties) and subclasses there are, as usual in Australian tribes, a number of totem clans. The following table exhibits the classes (moieties), subclasses, and totem clans of the Kamilaroi type as they existed on the Gwydir River, a tributary of the Darling River in the north-east of New South Wales.[2]

Kamilaroi classes, subclasses, and totems.

KAMILAROI SYSTEM

Classes (Moieties).	Subclasses.	Totems.
Kupathin	Ipai Kumbo	Emu, carpet-snake, black snake, red kangaroo, honey, walleroo, frog, codfish.
Dilbi	Muri Kubi	Kangaroo, opossum, bandicoot, padimelon, iguana, black duck, eaglehawk, scrub turkey, yellow-fish, honey-fish, bream.

[1] A. W. Howitt, "Further Notes on the Australian Class Systems," *Journal of the Anthropological Institute*, xviii. (1889) pp. 32 *sq.*

[2] A. W. Howitt, "Notes on the Australian Class Systems," *Journal of the Anthropological Institute*, xii. (1883) p. 500; *id.*, *Native Tribes of South-East Australia*, p. 104. In the latter passage Dr. Howitt has transposed, apparently by accident, the totems of Kupathin and Dilbi, and omitted the iguana from the list of Dilbi totems. Compare the Kamilaroi totems mentioned by the Rev. W. Ridley, in *Journal of the Anthropological Institute*, ii. (1873) p. 264, and quoted by Dr. A. W. Howitt, *Native Tribes of South-East Australia*, pp. 202, 204. Miss Mary E. B. Howitt has kindly consulted her father's manuscripts for me and has confirmed the names and the distribution of the totems which I have given in the text. The table which stands on p. 104 of *Native Tribes of South-East Australia* should therefore be corrected accordingly. Miss Howitt's letter to me is dated April 27th, 1908. In the Kamilaroi tribe corresponding to the masculine names of the subclasses (Ipai, Kumbo, Muri, and Kubi) there are feminine names (Ipatha, Butha, Matha, and Kubitha). See Fison and Howitt, *Kamilaroi and Kurnai*, pp. 36, 37 note; and above, p. 62. Here, again, in the text I omit the feminine forms for the sake of simplicity. In his *Native Tribes of*

On this system Dr. Howitt observes: "Kupathin and Dilbi divide the tribal community into two moieties, just as Matteri and Kararu or any other of the pairs of class names do. Omitting for a moment the four subclasses, there remain only the two classes, each with its group of totems, and the analogy to the two-class system is at once apparent. It is clear that the difference consists in the interpolation between the totems and the two classes of four subclasses; or perhaps the more correct statement would be that each primary class has been divided into two moieties, and that the totems either remain with the primary, and are common to both, as in some tribes, or, as in others, have been divided between the subclasses. When this occurs it is evidently a further stage in the process of subdivision."[1]

The rules of marriage and descent in the Kamilaroi system have been already explained,[2] but it may be well to repeat them. The marriage system in outline is this. An Ipai man marries a Kubi woman and their children are Muri. A Kumbo man marries a Muri woman and their children are Kubi. A Muri man marries a Kumbo woman and their children are Ipai. A Kubi man marries an Ipai woman and their children are Kumbo. To put this in tabular form:—

Husband.		Wife.	Children.
Kupathin	{ Ipai { Kumbo	Kubi Muri	Muri Kubi
Dilbi	{ Muri { Kubi	Kumbo Ipai	Ipai Kumbo

South-East Australia, pp. 200 *sqq.*, Dr. Howitt has used the feminine forms without explanation.

[1] A. W. Howitt, *Native Tribes of South-East Australia*, p. 104 *sq.* But it is doubtful whether in these tribes the totems are really subdivided between the subclasses. See below, pp. 408 *sq.*, 419, 433 *sq.*

[2] Above, pp. 62, 68 *sq.* See W. Ridley, "Report on Australian Languages and Traditions," *Journal of the Anthropological Institute*, ii. (1873) pp. 263 *sqq.*; *id.*, *Kámilarói and other Australian Languages*, Second Edition (Sydney, 1875), pp. 161 *sq.*; Fison and Howitt, *Kamilaroi and Kurnai*, pp. 36 *sq.*; A. W. Howitt, *Native Tribes of South-East Australia*, pp. 200 *sq.*

Hence it appears that a man always marries a woman belonging to one of the two subclasses which make up the other moiety of the tribe, and that the children belong to the subclass neither of their father nor of their mother, but to the other subclass of their mother's moiety. For example, the children of an Ipai man and a Kubi woman are Muri, which is the complementary subclass of their mother's subclass, since Muri and Kubi together make up one moiety or class (namely, Dilbi) of the tribe. Similarly, the children of a Muri man and a Kumbo woman are Ipai, which is the complementary subclass of their mother's subclass. Thus we have here what I have called indirect female descent,[1] since the children belong to their mother's moiety (class) of the tribe, but not to her subclass. The rules of marriage and descent are precisely analogous to those which prevail among the Southern Arunta, except that in the Southern Arunta there is indirect male descent instead of indirect female descent, since the child belongs to its father's class and to his complementary subclass,[2] instead of, as among the Kamilaroi, to its mother's class and to her complementary subclass. As I have already observed, it seems evident that rules of marriage and descent at once so complex and so regular cannot be the result of a train of accidents, but must have been deliberately devised in order to effect a definite purpose. That purpose appears to have been to prevent the marriage of parents with children, and it was effectually attained by arranging that children should always belong to a subclass into which neither their father nor their mother might marry. If that simple rule was observed, the marriage of parents with children was thenceforth impossible. Only we must remember that in speaking of fathers, mothers, and children in this connection we employ these terms of relationship not in our narrow sense of the words, but in the much wider classificatory sense which the Australian aborigines give to them, and in accordance with which every person has a whole group of "fathers" and a whole group of "mothers." Hence, when we say that the complex rules of the four subclasses were deliberately devised to prevent the marriage of mothers with sons and of fathers with daughters,

The rule of indirect descent, which is characteristic of the four-class system, seems to have been devised to prevent the marriage of parents with their children. At least it effects this by always placing parents and children in different subclasses.

[1] Above, p. 68.   [2] See above, p. 260.

we do not mean that they were intended merely to hinder a son from marrying the mother who bore him and a daughter from marrying the father who begat her, but that they were also intended to hinder a man from marrying any one of his group-mothers and a woman from marrying any one of her group-fathers.[1]

<small>The aversion to marriages between parents and their children was probably felt before legal expression was given to it by the four-class system.</small>

In the light of this explanation we can understand the object of that great restriction on freedom of marriage which the four-class system imposes on the tribes which have adopted it. Under the simple two-class system a man is theoretically free to marry any woman in the other moiety of the tribe, though practically at the present day he is debarred from a number of these women by customs which operate independently of the class system. For example, if the two-class system is combined with female descent, a man's daughter will belong to his wife's class, and will therefore be marriageable to him. Or, again, if the two-class system be combined with male descent, a woman's son will belong to her husband's class, and will therefore be marriageable to her. But such marriages, though theoretically possible under the two-class system, are practically forbidden even in those Australian tribes which have only the two-class system. This proves that the aversion to such marriages may and does exist before it finds, so to say, legal expression in a tribal ordinance forbidding them. The subdivision of the two original exogamous classes into four exogamous subclasses, with the rule that a child is born into the subclass neither of its father nor of its mother, appears to be nothing more than a successful attempt to give legal expression to what had previously been only a moral or instinctive feeling. The council of elders, it would seem, in certain tribes came to the conclusion that it was not enough to trust to this purely instinctive feeling, and that it was advisable to incorporate it in the formal law of

---

[1] That this, and not the mere prohibition of marriage between actual parents and their children, was the aim of the subdivision of the tribe into four subclasses was long ago perceived by Dr. Howitt, who observes: "The secondary divisions into subclasses were intended to prevent the possibility of intermarriage between parents (own and tribal) and children." See A. W. Howitt, "Notes on the Australian Class Systems," *Journal of the Anthropological Institute*, xii. (1883) p. 504. See further above, pp. 285 *sqq.*

the tribe. This they did by an ingenious extension of the existing class system, dividing the two old classes into four subclasses, and ordaining that children should never belong to the subclass of either parent, so that marriage between parent and child would be henceforth impossible. The new rule, in all probability, only gave formal sanction to what had long been the informal custom of the tribe.[1] Hence it is that, whereas under the two-class system a man is theoretically, though at the present day not practically, free to marry any woman of the other class, under the four-subclass system he is not so free either in theory or in practice. Instead of having, as under the two-class system, one half of the women of the tribe open to him as wives, he has now, roughly speaking, only one quarter of them so open. The new rule excludes him from one quarter of the women who previously were marriageable with him. If descent is in the female line, as among the Kamilaroi, then in the quarter from which under the new rule he is excluded are comprised all the women who under the classificatory system are reckoned his daughters. If descent is in the male line, then in the quarter from which under the new rule he is excluded are comprised all the women who under the classificatory system are reckoned his mothers. With female descent a man is already prevented by the two-class system from marrying his mother, because she belongs to his own class. With male descent a man is already prevented by the two-class system from marrying his daughter, because she belongs to his own class. Hence the innovation which the introduction of the four-class system effected was to bar the marriage of a man either with his daughter or with his mother, according as descent was reckoned in the female or in the male line.

If this view of the development of the four-subclass system out of an original two-class system be correct, it raises a presumption that the two-class system itself had a *If the four-class system was devised to*

[1] This also has been clearly recognised by Dr. Howitt, who observed long ago: "I think that the subdivision of the classes was intended to render impossible those unions which were perhaps even then forbidden by public opinion; for, while these subdivisions have only a local range, the social prohibition which forbids the intermarriage of parents and children, or brother and sisters, is universal throughout Australia." See A. W. Howitt, "Notes on the Australian Class Systems," *Journal of the Anthropological Institute*, xii. (1883) p. 502.

402 TOTEMISM IN SOUTH-EASTERN AUSTRALIA CHAP.

<small>prevent the marriage of parents with their children, it is probable that the two-class system was devised to prevent the marriage of brothers with their sisters.</small>

similar origin ; in other words, that just as the community seems to have split itself into four in order to render marriage between parents and children impossible, so it may previously have split itself into two in order to render marriage between brothers and sisters impossible. Both segmentations of the community, on this theory, were reformatory in the sense that they were deliberately instituted in order to give legal and formal sanction to what had hitherto been an informal custom of the tribe. The agents who brought about the reforms were not single despots or legislators, of whom there is no evidence in aboriginal Australian society, but the council of elders, who in the opinion of the most competent observers possess both the sagacity to conceive and the power to initiate such changes of tribal custom.[1] At least this view of the evolution of the apparently complex marriage laws of the Australian aborigines has the merit of simplicity and consistency. We can thus explain by a few clear principles the otherwise bewildering complexity of a social system which some have attempted to account for by theories as complicated and cumbrous as the cycles and epicycles which a misplaced ingenuity invented to explain the solar system, till Copernicus swept these cobwebs away for ever by the convincing simplicity of truth.

<small>Kamilaroi descent of the totem.</small>

In the Kamilaroi tribes, with their system of female descent, children take their totems as well as their primary class (moiety) from their mother. Thus if a Kupathin man of the emu totem marries a Dilbi woman of the kangaroo totem, the children will be Dilbi Kangaroos. If a Kupathin man of the emu totem marries a Dilbi woman of the opossum totem, the children will be Dilbi Opossums. If a Dilbi man of the iguana totem marries a Kupathin woman of the black snake totem, the children will be Kupathin Black Snakes. And so on.[2] From this it appears that, so far as the primary classes (moieties) and totems are concerned, descent is precisely the same in the four-class system with female descent as in the two-class system with female

---

[1] See above, pp. 352 sqq.
[2] W. Ridley, "Report on Australian Languages and Traditions," *Journal of the Anthropological Institute*, ii. (1873) pp. 264 sq.; Fison and Howitt, *Kamilaroi and Kurnai*, p. 43; A. W. Howitt, *Native Tribes of South-East Australia*, p. 202.

descent; in both of them descent is direct in the maternal line, since children take their primary class (moiety) and their totem from their mother. In neither the primary class nor the totem is descent at all affected by the interpolation between the two of the four subclasses.

In one of the Kamilaroi tribes a remarkable exception to the exogamy of the subclasses has been recorded. A man of any subclass was allowed to marry any woman of his own subclass provided her totem was different from his. Thus, for example, an Ipai man of the emu totem might marry an Ipai woman of the black snake totem but not of the emu totem. A Kubi man of the kangaroo totem might marry a Kubi woman of the iguana totem, but not of the kangaroo totem. And so with the rest. Curiously enough this violation of the exogamy of the subclasses did not affect the children, for they took the same subclass and totem which they would have taken if their mother had married a man of the proper subclass instead of a man of her own subclass; that is to say, the children took their mother's totem and the subclass which was complementary to her subclass. For example, the children of an Ipai man and an Ipai woman were Kumbo, which is the complementary subclass of their mother's subclass Ipai, and if her totem was black snake, their totem was black snake too. The children of a Kubi man and a Kubi woman were Muri, which was the complementary subclass of their mother's subclass Kubi, and if her totem was iguana, so was theirs. This exception to the exogamy of the subclasses seems to be unique, but it is well attested. It shows that in the tribe which admitted of it, the exogamy of the totem was more firmly established than the exogamy of the subclass, since the exogamy of the totem was strictly maintained, while that of the subclass was relaxed.[1]

Among the Kamilaroi "a female captive would be the property of her captor, if she were of the proper class-name; but in any case he must be a noted fighting-man to be

Exception to the exogamy of the subclasses in one of the Kamilaroi tribes.

Rule as to female captives.

---

[1] Fison and Howitt, *Kamilaroi and Kurnai*, pp. 45-48, 63 sq.; A. W. Howitt, *Native Tribes of South-East Australia*, pp. 203 sq. The authorities for this remarkable exception to the exogamy of the subclasses are Mr. T. E. Lance and the Rev. W. Ridley, both experienced and trustworthy observers.

allowed to have more than one wife. If the woman did not belong to the proper class, he had to give her back to her relations. If a man among the Kamilaroi took a woman to wife contrary to the tribal laws, her kindred would complain to the local division to which he belonged, and they were bound to take the matter up. If they did not do this, a fight would be sure to arise between members of the two subclasses concerned. In some cases, however, if a man persisted in keeping a woman as his wife who was of one of the subclasses with which his subclass could not marry, he was driven out of the company of his friends. If that did not induce him to leave the woman, his male kindred followed him and killed him. The female kindred of the woman also killed her."[1]

Punishment for breach of marriage laws among the Kamilaroi.

Avoidance of mother-in-law.

In the Kamilaroi nation, as in many if not all Australian tribes, a woman might neither speak with nor look at her daughter's husband. The rule was rigidly observed. If a man met his mother-in-law by chance, they instantly turned round, back to back, and remained at a distance. If one of them desired to communicate with the other, the message had to be sent through a third party. They seemed to think that it would be extremely indelicate for a mother-in-law and a son-in-law to speak together. So far did they carry this custom of mutual avoidance that from the hour that an infant girl was betrothed by the promise of her parents, the man to whom she was betrothed had strictly to avoid the sight of his future mother-in-law.[2] Among the Kamilaroi of the Gwydir River the custom was enforced with the most rigorous severity, for we learn that these people inflicted the penalty of death on any man who spoke or held any communication with his wife's mother.[3] It is worth while observing that with a custom of female descent, such as prevails among the Kamilaroi, a woman and her

---

[1] Cyrus E. Doyle, quoted by Dr. A. W. Howitt, *Native Tribes of South-East Australia*, p. 208. Similarly the Rev. W. Ridley, speaking of the Kamilaroi marriage customs, says: "Any breach of these laws incurs sentence of death, or of exposure to an ordeal that may end in death" ("Report on Australian Languages and Traditions," *Journal of the Anthropological Institute*, ii. (1873) p. 267). The ordeal consists in standing exposed to a shower of spears, which the culprit is allowed to parry or avoid.

[2] W. Ridley, *Kámilarói*,[2] pp. 157 sq.

[3] A. W. Howitt, *Native Tribes of South-East Australia*, p. 208, referring to Cyrus E. Doyle as his authority.

daughter's husband necessarily belong to different primary classes and are therefore so far marriageable to each other, though their union is actually barred by the subdivision into four subclasses. This suggests that the institution of four subclasses may have been designed to prevent the marriage of a man with his wife's mother as well as with his daughter.

If a man killed another maliciously and unfairly, an obligation rested on the men of the same subclass and totem as the victim to avenge his death by slaying a man of the same subclass and totem as the murderer. For example, if an Ippai man of the emu totem murdered a Kubi man of the padi-melon totem, then the other Kubi Padi-melons would kill an Ippai Emu, thus satisfying the demands of justice, as justice is conceived by the Kamilaroi.[1] *Rule of blood feud.*

The Kamilaroi had the classificatory system of relationship, though the terms appear not to have been fully recorded. In the generation above his own a man applied the same term *umbathi* to his mother, to his mother's sisters, and to the wives of his father's brothers. In his own generation he applied the same term *ungina* to his wife, to his wife's sisters, and to his brothers' wives; and a wife applied the same term *golid* to her husband, to her husband's brothers, and to her sisters' husbands.[2] *Classificatory system of relationship among the Kamilaroi.*

To the west and south-west of the Kamilaroi lay the Wiradjuri, a very large and powerful tribe or nation of tribes occupying a vast extent of country in Central New South Wales, and distinguished by a common language which was spoken in various dialects. To the westward this tribe or nation bordered on those tribes of New South Wales who have the two-class Mukwara and Kilpara system, which has been already described.[3] The territory of the Wiradjuri extended from Mudgee to Hay and for a long way down the Lachlan River. The name Wiradjuri is derived from *wirai*, a word which in the tribal language means "no."[4] *The Wiradjuri nation.*

[1] W. Ridley, "Report on Australian Languages and Traditions," *Journal of the Anthropological Institute*, ii. (1873) p. 268; compare *id.*, *Kámilarói*,[2] p. 159.
[2] A. W. Howitt, "Australian Group-Relationships," *Journal of the Royal Anthropological Institute*, xxxvii. (1907) pp. 287 *sq.*
[3] See above, pp. 380 *sqq.*
[4] A. L. P. Cameron, "Notes on some Tribes of New South Wales,"

406 TOTEMISM IN SOUTH-EASTERN AUSTRALIA CHAP.

Classes, subclasses, and totems of the Wiradjuri.

Like the Kamilaroi the Wiradjuri are divided into two primary classes and four subclasses, all exogamous, with descent in the female line; and the names of the subclasses are the same, or nearly the same, as those of the Kamilaroi subclasses. Included under the classes and subclasses there are, as usual, a number of totem clans. The social system of that tribe of the Wiradjuri nation which occupied the greater part of Riverina is shown in the subjoined table.[1]

WIRADJURI SYSTEM, RIVERINA DISTRICT

Classes.	Subclasses.	Totems.
Moiety A	Yibai	eagle-hawk, mallee-hen, opossum, fly, English bee, kangaroo-rat, native bee
	Wumbi	bloodsucker-lizard, padi-melon, crow
Moiety B	Murri	red kangaroo, a small lizard, young emu
	Kubbi	flying squirrel, bush-rat, chicken-hawk, bandicoot

Wiradjuri rules of marriage and descent.

The names of the primary classes or moieties in this tribe have not been ascertained. The rules of marriage and descent, so far as the classes and subclasses are concerned,

Journal of the Anthropological Institute, xiv. (1885) p. 345; A. W. Howitt, *Native Tribes of South-East Australia,* pp. 55 *sq.*, 105.

[1] A. W. Howitt, *Native Tribes of South-East Australia,* pp. 105 *sq.*

The name of one of the subclasses is given variously as Wumba, Wumbi, and Wumbo. For the sake of uniformity I have adopted the form Wumbi, which is used repeatedly by Dr. Howitt (*op. cit.* p. 209).

are the same as in the Kamilaroi system. An Yibai man marries a Kubbi woman and the children are Murri: a Wumbi man marries a Murri woman and the children are Kubbi: a Murri man marries a Wumbi woman and the children are Yibai: a Kubbi man marries an Yibai woman and the children are Wumbi.[1] To put this in tabular form:—

Husband.	Wife.	Children.
{ Yibai { Wumbi	Kubbi Murri	Murri Kubbi
{ Murri { Kubbi	Wumbi Yibai	Yibai Wumbi

But in respect of the totems the marriage rules of the Wiradjuri differ from those of the Kamilaroi. For whereas among the Kamilaroi a man is apparently free to marry a woman of any totem in the other class or moiety of the tribe, among the Wiradjuri, at least in the southern branch of the tribe, each totem is restricted to marriage with certain totems of the other class. The following table exhibits the intermarriage and descent of the totems in the southern branch of the Wiradjuri tribe, so far as Dr. Howitt could ascertain them, but with regard to some of the totems he was not able to obtain the necessary information.[2]

Marriage and descent of the totems in the Wiradjuri tribe.

---

[1] A. W. Howitt, *Native Tribes of South-East Australia*, pp. 106, 209. In this tribe, as in the Kamilaroi, there are feminine as well as masculine forms of the names of the subclasses. The feminine forms are Yibatha, Butha, (corresponding to the masculine Wumbi), Matha (corresponding to Murri), and Kubbitha. For the sake of simplicity I use only the masculine forms in the text.

[2] A. W. Howitt, *Native Tribes of South-East Australia*, pp. 208 *sq.* I again omit the feminine forms of the names (Yibatha, Butha, Matha, and Kubbitha) for the sake of simplicity.

[TABLE.

WIRADJURI TRIBE, SOUTHERN BRANCH

Marriage and Descent

	Husband.		Wife.		Children.	
A {	Yibai	eagle-hawk	Kubbi	bush-rat	Murri	bush-rat
	Yibai	mallee-hen	Kubbi	flying-squirrel	Murri	flying-squirrel
	Yibai	opossum	Kubbi	bush-rat	Murri	bush-rat
	Yibai	opossum	Kubbi	flying-squirrel	Murri	flying-squirrel
	Wumbi	bloodsucker-lizard	Murri	young emu	Kubbi	young emu
B {	Murri	young emu	Wumbi	bloodsucker-lizard	Yibai	bloodsucker-lizard
	Kubbi	bush-rat	Yibai	eagle-hawk	Wumbi	eagle-hawk
	Kubbi	flying-squirrel	Yibai	mallee-hen	Wumbi	mallee-hen
	Kubbi	bush-rat	Yibai	opossum	Wumbi	opossum
	Kubbi	bandicoot	Yibai	opossum	Wumbi	opossum

In the four-class system the totems of each class alternate between the sub-classes of that class in alternate generations.

From this table it may be observed that while the totems remain constantly within the same class (moiety) from generation to generation, they alternate from one subclass to its complementary subclass with each generation reckoned from a mother to her children. For example, in the one moiety the eagle-hawk totem belongs to a woman of the Yibai subclass in one generation and to her children of the Wumbi subclass in the next: in the other moiety the totem bush-rat belongs to a woman of the Kubbi subclass in the one generation and to her children of the Murri subclass in the next. This alternation of the totems between the subclasses is not peculiar to the Wiradjuri; it necessarily occurs wherever hereditary totemism exists with the four-class system. For since under these conditions a child always takes its totem from one of its parents, while its subclass always differs from theirs, the totem shifts like a shuttle backwards and forwards with each generation between the complementary subclasses of its mother's class or between the complementary subclasses of its father's class, according as descent is in the maternal or in the paternal line. In the Wiradjuri tribe descent is in the maternal line, and accordingly the totem shifts in alternate generations between the complementary subclasses of the mother's class. For example, the daughter of a Kubbi bush-rat woman is a Murri bush-rat woman, and the daughter of this Murri bush-rat woman is a Kubbi bush-rat woman, just as was her maternal grandmother. Thus the bush-rat totem swings backwards and forwards like a pendulum between the complementary subclasses Kubbi and Murri. And the same rule holds of all the other totems.[1] This shews, as I shall point out again later on, that though the clan totems may be and commonly are permanently divided between the primary classes or moieties, they cannot be so divided between the two complementary subclasses which compose each of the two primary classes, since they are constantly fluctuating with each generation between these two complementary subclasses. Hence tables which represent the clan totems as divided between the two subclasses of a primary class must, it would seem, be so far erroneous.

In the Southern Wiradjuri children were betrothed to each other in very early youth. When the boy is old enough to marry, that is, when his beard has grown after he has passed through the initiation ceremony, and the consent of the kindred on both sides has been given, he fetches his betrothed to be his wife. Commonly a brother of the bride accompanies his sister to her new home in order to receive a sister of the bridegroom to wife in exchange. This custom of exchanging sisters had a special name, *gun-gun-mur*.[2] With regard to the initiation ceremonies of the Wiradjuri, which they call *burbung*, it is a rule that the members of a class, subclass, or totem cannot initiate their own boys, but must invite the members of the intermarrying class, subclass, and totem to assist in the ceremonies.[3] {margin: Betrothal among the Wiradjuri.}

In the Wiradjuri tribes of the Lachlan River the names of the two primary classes or moieties are Mukula and Budthurung, and the totems are arranged under them as follows :—[4] {margin: Wiradjuri tribes of the Lachlan River, their classes, subclasses, and totems.}

[1] A. W. Howitt, *Native Tribes of South-East Australia*, p. 210.
[2] A. W. Howitt, *op. cit.* pp. 210 sq.
[3] A. W. Howitt, *op. cit.* p. 584.
[4] A. W. Howitt, *op. cit.* p. 107.

WIRADJURI SYSTEM, LACHLAN RIVER

Classes.	Subclasses.	Totems.
Mukula	Ipai	mallee-hen, padi-melon, opossum
Mukula	Kumbo	mallee-hen, emu, opossum
Budthurung	Murri	red kangaroo (*murri*), bandicoot, black duck, snake, lace-lizard
Budthurung	Kubbi	red kangaroo, black duck (*budthurung*)[1], lace-lizard, bandicoot

Marriage and descent in the Wiradjuri tribes of the Lachlan River.

In the marriage system of these Lachlan River tribes there is an anomalous feature: in his choice of a wife a man is not restricted to one of the two subclasses of the other moiety; he is free to marry into either of them. This, it is obvious, is so far to abandon the four-subclass system and revert to the original two-class system, under which a man is theoretically at liberty to marry any woman of the other moiety. The reversion may, as Dr. Howitt suggests,[2] have been caused by a diminution of numbers, which perhaps rendered the restrictions imposed by the four-subclass system incompatible with the continued existence of the tribe. The following table exhibits the rules of marriage and descent in the Wiradjuri tribes of the Lachlan Rivers, as they were ascertained by Mr. A. L. P. Cameron.[3] In the table the anomalous marriages are indicated by italics.

[1] It will be observed that *budthurung* (black duck) is the name of the primary class as well as of the totem. Of this fact Dr. Howitt has found no explanation. Similarly *murri* (red kangaroo) is the name of a subclass as well as of a totem.
[2] A. W. Howitt, *Native Tribes of South-East Australia*, p. 212.
[3] A. W. Howitt, *op. cit.* pp. 211 *sq*.

WIRADJURI TRIBE, LACHLAN RIVER
Marriage and Descent

	Husband.		Wife.		Children.
Mukula	Ipai	mallee-hen or	Kubbi	black duck	
	Ipai	padi-melon	Kubbi	red kangaroo	
			Kubbi	lace-lizard	
			Murri	*bandicoot*	
	Ipai	opossum	Kubbi	bandicoot	
			Murri	*black duck*	
			Murri	*red kangaroo*	
			Murri	*snake*	
	Kumbo	mallee-hen or	Murri	red kangaroo	The children are always of their mother's class and totem, and of the subclass which is complementary to her subclass. Thus if she is Ipai, they are Kumbo; if she is Kumbo, they are Ipai. If she is Murri, they are Kubbi; if she is Kubbi, they are Murri.
	Kumbo	emu	Murri	black duck	
			Murri	snake	
			Kubbi	*bandicoot*	
	Kumbo	opossum	Murri	bandicoot	
			Kubbi	*black duck*	
			Kubbi	*red kangaroo*	
			Kubbi	*lace-lizard*	
Budthurung	Murri	red kangaroo	Kumbo	mallee-hen	
	Murri	black duck	Kumbo	emu	
	Murri	snake	*Ipai*	*opossum*	
	Murri	bandicoot	Kumbo	opossum	
			Ipai	*mallee-hen*	
			Ipai	*padi-melon*	
	Kubbi	red kangaroo	Ipai	padi-melon	
	Kubbi	black duck	Ipai	mallee-hen	
	Kubbi	lace-lizard	*Kumbo*	*opossum*	
	Kubbi	bandicoot	Ipai	opossum	
			Kumbo	*mallee-hen*	
			Kumbo	*emu*	

Some confusion seems to have crept into Dr. Howitt's table. I have endeavoured to correct it, but cannot feel sure that I have succeeded. For the sake of simplicity I have again omitted the feminine forms (Ipatha, Butha, Matha, and Kubbitha) which Dr. Howitt uses without explanation.

Personal totems of medicine-men among the Wiradjuri.

In the Wiradjuri, as in other tribes of South-East Australia, the medicine-men had what Dr. Howitt calls their secret personal totems in addition to their clan totems. For example, we hear of a Wiradjuri medicine-man whose clan totem was kangaroo, but whose secret personal totem was tiger-snake. The account which he gave to Dr. Howitt of the way in which he received his personal totem (*budjan*) and became a medicine-man is instructive.[1] He said : "When I was about ten years old I was taken to the initiation ceremony (*burbung*) and saw what the old men could bring out of themselves ; and when my tooth was out[2] the old men chased me with the quartz-crystals (*wallungs*) in their mouths, shouting '*Ngai, Ngai*,' and moving their hands towards me. I went into the bush for a time, and while there my old father came out to me. He said, 'Come here to me'; and he then showed me a piece of quartz-crystal in his hand, and when I looked at it he went down into the ground and I saw him come up all covered with red dust. It made me very frightened. He then said, 'Come to me,' and I went to him, and he said, ' Try and bring up a quartz-crystal (*wallung*).' I did try, and brought one up. He then said, 'Come with me to this place.' I saw him standing by a hole in the ground, leading to a grave. I went inside and saw a dead man, who rubbed me all over to make me clever, and who gave me some quartz-crystals. When we came out my father pointed to a tiger-snake (*gunr*) saying, 'That is your *budjan* (secret personal totem) ; it is mine also.' There was a string tied to the tail of the snake and extending to us. It was one of those strings which the doctors bring up out of themselves, rolled up together. He took hold of it saying, 'Let us follow him.' The tiger-snake went through several tree-trunks, and let us through. Then

---

[1] A. W. Howitt, "On Australian Medicine Men," *Journal of the Anthropological Institute*, xvi. (1887) p. 50; *id., Native Tribes of South-East Australia*, pp. 406 *sq.* There are small verbal differences in the account as reported in these two passages. I have used my discretion as to which to follow in the text, and I have occasionally inserted the equivalent English word instead of, or in addition to, the native Australian term.

[2] In many tribes of South-East Australia one or sometimes two teeth are knocked out of the mouth of each novice at initiation. See A. W. Howitt, *Native Tribes of South-East Australia*, pp. 538 *sqq.*, 563, 564, 565, 566, 569, 571, 576, 586 *sq.*, 588, 589, 592, 613, 616, 641, 655 *sq.*, 675 *sq.*

we went to a great Currajong tree,¹ and went through it, and after that to a tree with a great mound or swelling round its roots. It is in such places that Daramulun² lives. Here the tiger-snake went down into the ground, and we followed him, and came up inside the tree, which was hollow. There I saw a lot of little Daramuluns, the sons of Baiame.³ After we came out again the tiger-snake took us into a great hole in the ground in which were a number of tiger-snakes, which rubbed themselves against me, but did not hurt me, being my *budjan* (personal totem). They did this to make me a clever man and a doctor or wizard (*wulla mullung*)." The name *budjan*, which the Wiradjuri apply to their personal totems, is applied by the Murring or Yuin tribe to their totems, both personal and hereditary.⁴

To the north of the Wiradjuri of the Lachlan River is

---

¹ *Brachychiton populneum.*

² The mound or swelling in which the mythical Daramulun is said to live is the circular mound on which in the Wiradjuri tribe boys were placed at the rites of initiation. On these occasions a figure of Daramulun was moulded or cut in the ground, representing him as a one-legged being with a sharp-pointed bone instead of a second leg. See A. W. Howitt, *Native Tribes of South-East Australia*, pp. 584 *sq.*; *id.*, "On some Australian Ceremonies of Initiation," *Journal of the Anthropological Institute*, xiii. (1884) p. 452 *sq.* The medicine-man's narrative, quoted in the text, shews that there were supposed to be many Daramuluns, some of them small, and that they lived in the ground. The belief in a mythical being called Daramulun is shared by other tribes than the Wiradjuri. The Yuin say that Daramulun used to live on earth and taught them what to eat and how to celebrate the initiation ceremonies. When he died and was put in the ground, his ghost went up to the sky. Others say that he ascended up to heaven in the flesh, just as the medicine-men still do. See A. W. Howitt, *Native Tribes of South-East Australia*, pp. 494 *sq.* The Theddora, according to an old woman of the tribe, called Daramulun "father" (*papang*), and thought that he came down with a noise like thunder to make the boys into men. See A. W. Howitt, *op. cit.* p. 493. The thundrous noise with which Daramulun came down for this purpose was the booming sound of the bull-roarers which were swung at the initiation ceremonies; their roar was supposed to represent thunder, which was the voice of Daramulun. See A. W. Howitt, *op. cit.* p. 538; *id.*, in *Journal of the Anthropological Institute*, xiii. (1884) p. 446.

³ Baiame is a mythical being in whom the Kamilaroi believed. Some missionaries have regarded him as an aboriginal god, the maker and preserver of all things. Dr. Howitt explained him as the native ideal of a headman. See W. Ridley, *Kámiláròi*,² pp. 135 *sq.*; A. W. Howitt, *Native Tribes of South-East Australia*, pp. 494, 499 *sqq.*, 506 *sq.*

⁴ See below, pp. 489 *sq.* As to personal or, as I have called them, individual totems, see above, pp. 49 *sqq.* The subject will be more fully discussed when we come to deal with totemism in America, where such personal totems or guardian spirits, as perhaps they should rather be called, are much commoner than in Australia.

the country of the Wonghibon tribe, which may be roughly defined by the townships of Mossgiel, Ivanhoe, Cobar, Nymagee, and Nyngan. The only permanent water in this district is at its north-eastern extremity, where it skirts the Bogan River for some way. Hence the natives of the southern parts must have either gone to the Lachlan or Darling in time of drought, or else lived on the water extracted from the mallee and other roots. The Wonghibon appear to be an offshoot or branch of the Wiradjuri nation, with whom they live on friendly terms.[1] Their system of classes, subclasses, and totems, as reported by Dr. A. W. Howitt, is as follows :—[2]

WONGHIBON SYSTEM

Classes.	Subclasses.	Totems.
Ngielbumurra	Ipai Kumbo	mallee-hen emu opossum
Mukumurra	Murri Kubbi	black duck bandicoot red kangaroo

From this it appears that the Wonghibon totems are similar to those of the Wiradjuri, and that their subclasses are the same as those of the Kamilaroi. We are told that the same names for the subclasses "are also used by tribes

[1] A. W. Howitt, *Native Tribes of South-East Australia*, pp. 56, 107 *sq.*
[2] A. W. Howitt, *op. cit.* pp. 108, 214. Mr. A. L. P. Cameron gives the Wonghibon totems differently as follows :—

Subclasses.	Totems.
Ipai Kumbu	crow kangaroo
Murri Kubbi	iguana bandicoot opossum

See A. L. P. Cameron, "Notes on some Tribes of New South Wales," *Journal of the Anthropological Institute*, xiv. (1885) p. 348. Probably both lists are incomplete.

II TRIBES WITH FOUR SUBCLASSES 415

which are wholly unacquainted with the Kamilaroi language, but among whom the organisation of society is the same as in the Kamilaroi tribes."[1]

In regard to marriage and descent the Wonghibon tribe presents the same anomalous feature as the Wiradjuri of the Lachlan River; that is to say, a man is free to marry a woman of either subclass of the other moiety, provided that her totem differs from his. The following table exhibits the rules of marriage and descent in the Wonghibon tribe, so far as they have been ascertained by Mr. A. L. P. Cameron and revised by Dr. Howitt.[2] In the table the anomalous marriages are indicated by italics.

Marriage and Descent in the Wonghibon tribe.

WONGHIBON TRIBE

Marriage and Descent

	Husband.		Wife.		Children.
Ngielbumurra	Ipai	mallee-hen	Kubbi *Murri* *Murri*	black duck *kangaroo* *bandicoot*	The children are always of their mother's class and totem, and of the subclass which is complementary to her subclass. Thus if she is Ipai, they are Kumbo; if she is Kumbo, they are Ipai. If she is Murri, they are Kubbi; if she is Kubbi, they are Murri.
	Ipai	emu	Kubbi Kubbi *Murri*	black duck bandicoot *kangaroo*	
	Ipai	opossum	Kubbi *Murri* *Murri*	kangaroo *black duck* *bandicoot*	
	Kumbo	mallee-hen	Murri *Kubbi* *Kubbi*	black duck *bandicoot* *kangaroo*	
	Kumbo	emu	Murri Murri *Kubbi*	black duck bandicoot *kangaroo*	
	Kumbo	opossum	Murri *Kubbi* *Kubbi*	kangaroo *black duck* *bandicoot*	

[1] A. L. P. Cameron, *op. cit.* pp. 347 sq.
[2] A. W. Howitt, *Native Tribes of South-East Australia*, pp. 213-215. In the table I have omitted the feminine forms (Ipatha, Butha, Matha, and Kubbitha) of the subclass names for the sake of simplicity.

WONGHIBON TRIBE (*continued*)
Marriage and Descent

Husband.		Wife.		Children.
Murri	kangaroo	Kumbo	opossum	
		Ipai	*mallee-hen*	
		Ipai	*emu*	
Murri	bandicoot	Kumbo	emu	The children are always of their mother's class and totem, and of the subclass which is complementary to her subclass. Thus if she is Ipai, they are Kumbo; if she is Kumbo, they are Ipai. If she is Murri, they are Kubbi; if she is Kubbi, they are Murri.
		Ipai	*mallee-hen*	
		Ipai	*opossum*	
Murri	black duck	Kumbo	mallee-hen	
		Kumbo	emu	
		Ipai	*opossum*	
Kubbi	wild duck	Ipai	mallee-hen	
		Ipai	emu	
		Kumbo	*opossum*	
Kubbi	bandicoot	Ipai	emu	
		Kumbo	*opossum*	
		Kumbo	*mallee-hen*	
Kubbi	kangaroo	Ipai	opossum	
		Kumbo	*mallee-hen*	
		Kumbo	*emu*	

(Left brace spanning all rows: Mukumurra.)

Practical reversion to two-class system. Just as with the Wiradjuri of the Lachlan River, so with the Wonghibon the permission to marry a woman of either subclass of the other moiety is, in so far as it removes the subclass restrictions on marriage, practically a reversion to the old two-class system, which in theory allows a man to marry any woman of the other moiety.

Avoidance of mother-in-law. In the foregoing tribes we again meet with the custom that mother-in-law and son-in-law mutually avoid each other. The custom, says Mr. A. L. P. Cameron, "is of universal occurrence so far as I know throughout the whole of Australia, certainly in every tribe of aborigines I have ever come in contact with in New South Wales and Queensland. A man never speaks to his wife's mother if he can possibly avoid it, and she is equally careful in shunning all communication with him."[1]

A similar system of two classes and four subclasses, with totem clans and descent in the female line, is found among the Kuinmurbura, a tribe which claimed the peninsula between Broad Sound and Shoalwater Bay on the coast of Queensland, to the north of Rockhampton. But while the Kuinmurbura system resembles that of the Kamilaroi, the Wiradjuri, and the Wonghibon, the names both of the classes and of the subclasses are quite different, as may be seen from the following table:—[2]

The Kuinmurbura tribe, its classes, subclasses, and totems.

KUINMURBURA SYSTEM

Classes.	Subclasses.		Totems.
Yungeru	Kurpal	the barrimundi	black eagle-hawk
	Kuialla	a hawk	laughing-jackass
Witteru	Karilbura	good water	curlew
	Munal	iguana	clear water (*kauara*)
			scrub wallaby
			a hawk (*kolpobora*)

The Kuinmurbura is one of the few tribes in which the names for the classes or subclasses are those of animals or other natural objects. Other tribes in which the classes or subclasses or both are so named are the Wolgal and Ngarigo in New South Wales,[3] the Kulin tribes of Victoria,[4] and the Annan River tribe of Queensland.[5]

In the Kuinmurbura tribe the rules of marriage and

[1] A. L. P. Cameron, "Notes on some Tribes of New South Wales," *Journal of the Anthropological Institute*, xiv. (1885) p. 353.

[2] A. W. Howitt, *Native Tribes of South-East Australia*, pp. 60, 111. Feminine forms of the subclass names are formed by post-fixing *an* to them, as masculine *Kurpal*, feminine *Kurpalan*.

[3] See above, pp. 393 *sq.*   [4] See below, p. 435.

[5] The system of the Annan River tribe near Cooktown is this:

Classes.	Subclasses.	
Walar, a bee	Wandi,	eagle-hawk
	Walar,	a bee
Murla, a bee	Jorro,	a bee
	Kutchal,	salt-water eagle-hawk

Descent is in the male line. See A. W. Howitt, *Native Tribes of South-East Australia*, p. 118.

Marriage and descent in the Kuinmurbura tribe. descent are as follows :—A Kurpal man marries a Karilbura woman and the children are Munal. A Kuialla man marries a Munal woman and the children are Karilbura. A Karilbura man marries a Kurpal woman and the children are Kuialla. A Munal man marries a Kuialla woman and the children are Kurpal. This is the ordinary rule of marriage and descent in a four-subclass system with female descent; a man of any particular subclass always marries a woman of a particular subclass in the other moiety of the tribe, and the children belong to the subclass which is complementary to their mother's subclass. And as regularly happens under such a system, children take their totem as well as their primary class (moiety) from their mother. The following table exhibits the rules of marriage and descent in the tribe,[1] from which it would seem that men were not free to marry women of any totem in the subclass with which they intermarried, but that they might only marry the women of one particular totem. But the rules appear to be incomplete, for nothing is said of the marriage of women of the water and wallaby totems.

KUINMURBURA TRIBE
Marriage and Descent

	Husband.		Wife.		Children.	
Yungeru	Kurpal	eagle-hawk	Karilbura	hawk	Munal	hawk
	Kurpal	laughing-jackass	Karilbura	curlew	Munal	curlew
	Kuialla	eagle-hawk	Munal	hawk	Karilbura	hawk
	Kuialla	laughing-jackass	Munal	curlew	Karilbura	curlew
Witteru	Karilbura	curlew	Kurpal	laughing-jackass	Kuialla	laughing-jackass
	Karilbura	water	Kurpal	eagle-hawk	Kuialla	eagle-hawk
	Karilbura	wallaby	Kurpal	laughing-jackass	Kuialla	laughing-jackass
	Karilbura	hawk	Kurpal	eagle-hawk	Kuialla	eagle-hawk
	Munal	curlew	Kuialla	laughing-jackass	Kurpal	laughing-jackass
	Munal	water	Kuialla	laughing-jackass	Kurpal	laughing-jackass
	Munal	hawk	Kuialla	eagle-hawk	Kurpal	eagle-hawk

[1] A. W. Howitt, *Native Tribes of South-East Australia*, p. 218. Here again I omit the feminine forms of the subclass names (Kurpalan, Kuiallan, Karilburan, and Munalan) for the sake of simplicity.

From this table it may be seen that, as regularly happens in the normal four-subclass system, the totems oscillate between the two subclasses of a moiety in alternate generations. Thus if the mother is a Hawk of the Karilbura subclass, her children are Hawks of the Munal subclass, and her daughters' children are Hawks of the Karilbura subclass, just like their maternal grandmother; so that in three generations the pendulum (represented by the hawk totem) has swung from Karilbura through Munal and back to Karilbura. And the other totems perform similar oscillations.

Alternation of the totems between the two subclasses of each class.

In the Kuinmurbura tribe, and the neighbouring tribes which had the same social system, marriage was commonly preceded by betrothal of the girl in her infancy. The ceremony of betrothal was performed by the girl's male cousin, that is, either by her mother's brother's son or by her father's sister's son. When the girl was mature, all the unmarried men of the same class and totem as her future husband had access to her as a matter of right before she was handed over to him. This custom is probably a rudimentary survival of group-marriage; the men who, in virtue of their class and totem, belong to the group which is marriageable with the girl's group, exercise the old group right over the woman for the last time before resigning her to her husband. The relation in which they stand to her bears the name of *durki*, which seems to answer to the *noa* relationship of the Dieri, the *nupa* of the Urabunna, and the *unawa* of the Arunta.¹ In the Kuinmurbura tribe a widow went to the elder brother (*murang*) or to the younger brother (*woern*) of her deceased husband. A female captive was the property of her captor, if she was of the proper class and totem.²

Betrothal among the Kuinmurbura.

Survival of group-marriage among the Kuinmurbura.

The Kuinmurbura had the classificatory system of relationship. Thus in the generation above his own a man applied the same term *bena* to his father, to his father's brothers, and to the husbands of his mother's sisters; and he applied the same term *aia* to his mother, to his mother's sisters, and to the wives of his father's brothers. In his own generation he applied the same term *murang* to his

Classificatory system of relationship among the Kuinmurbura.

---

¹ A. W. Howitt, *Native Tribes of South-East Australia*, pp. 219 *sq.* As to *noa*, *nupa*, and *unawa*, see above, pp. 178, 297, 298, 362, 363.

² A. W. Howitt, *op. cit.* p. 220.

brothers, to the sons of his father's brothers, and to the sons of his mother's sisters. He applied the same term *gingil* to his wife, to his wife's sisters, and to his brothers' wives; and a wife applied the same term *nupa* to her husband, to her husband's brothers, and to her sisters' husbands. In the generation below his own a man applied the same term *manbon* to his sons, to his brothers' sons, and to the sons of his wife's sisters; and similarly a woman applied the same term *nugin* to her sons and to her sisters' sons.[1]

<small>The Kongulu tribe, its classes, subclasses, and totems.</small>

To the south-west of the Kuinmurbura, between the Mackenzie River and the Lower Dawson, there lived down to 1895 a tribe called the Kongulu which had a similar social organisation, consisting of two primary classes (moieties), four subclasses, and totem clans with descent in the female line. The names of the two primary classes, Yunguru and Wutthuru, are clearly equivalent to the Yungeru and Witteru of the Kuinmurbura. These classes were each divided into two subclasses as follows:—[2]

KONGULU SYSTEM

Class.	Subclasses.	Class.	Subclasses.
Yunguru	Bunya / Tarbain	Wutthuru	Kaiyara / Bunjur

<small>Marriage and descent in the Kongulu tribe.</small>

The rules of marriage are normal. A Bunya man marries a Kaiyara woman and the children are Bunjur. A Tarbain man marries a Bunjur woman and the children are Kaiyara. A Kaiyara man marries a Bunya woman and the children are Tarbain. A Bunjur man marries a Tarbain woman and the children are Bunya. To put this in tabular form:—[3]

[1] A. W. Howitt, "Australian Group-Relationships," *Journal of the Royal Anthropological Institute*, xxxvii. (1907) pp. 287 sq.

[2] A. W. Howitt, *Native Tribes of South-East Australia*, pp. 111, 220. In the former passage the names Tarbain and Kaiyara appear as Jarbain and Kairawa.

[3] A. W. Howitt, *op. cit.* p. 220. The feminine forms of the subclass names are formed by adding *gun* to the masculine forms, thus Bunyagun, Tarbaingun, Kaiyaragun, and Bunjurgun. For the sake of simplicity I omit these feminine forms.

KONGULU TRIBE

Marriage and Descent

Husband.	Wife.	Children.
Yunguru {Bunya / Tarbain}	Kaiyara / Bunjur	Bunjur / Kaiyara
Wutthuru {Kaiyara / Bunjur}	Bunya / Tarbain	Tarbain / Bunya

In the Kongulu tribe the totems were called *baikain*, and were transmitted from mother to child. They were usually animals, but sometimes trees. The totem names appear to have been grouped under certain collective names, such as Mirunjul, the effect of which has not been explained. The following list gives the totems and collective names, so far as they have been ascertained :—[1]

{Grouping of the totems in the Kongulu tribe.}

Collective Names.	Totems.
Mirunjul . . .	black or brush wallaby black iguana eagle-hawk sandal-wood
Jiimi . . .	great owl frilled iguana brigalow
Kulpuwura . .	crow scrub wallaby

West of the Great Dividing Range, and separated by it from those Queensland tribes whose social system has just been described, there were many tribes with the four sub-

{Four-class tribes in Queensland to the}

[1] A. W. Howitt, *Native Tribes of South-East Australia*, p. 112.

422 TOTEMISM IN SOUTH-EASTERN AUSTRALIA CHAP.

west of the Great Dividing Range. class system on the waters of the Belyando, Barcoo, Thomson, and Flinders Rivers. Strictly speaking, these Queensland tribes belong rather to North-Eastern Australia than to South-Eastern Australia, with which we are here concerned; but since they have been dealt with by Dr. A. W. Howitt they may find a place in this chapter. Of these tribes the Wakelbura on the Belyando River, above its junction with the Suttor River, may serve as an example. The name of the tribe is derived from *wakel* "eels" and the possessive postfix *bura*. Formerly their name was Kerbulbura, derived from *kerbul*, the edible root of a water-lily which grows in the swamps and watercourses.[1]

The Wakelbura tribe, its classes, subclasses, and totems. The Wakelbura tribe is divided into two primary exogamous classes (moieties) called Mallera and Wuthera, and four subclasses called Kurgilla, Banbe, Wungo, and Obu. Thus the names both of the classes and of the subclasses are entirely different from those of the Kamilaroi; but on the other hand one of the class names (Wuthera) seems clearly to be equivalent to Witteru and Wutthuru in the Kuinmurbura and Kongulu tribes.[2] The two class names Mallera and Wuthera extend as far as Charters Towers, where the Akulbura tribe speaks a different dialect and has different names for the classes and subclasses. At about Muttabura, on the Thomson River, and near Clermont, these class names cease with the Bathalibura tribe, which has the same names for its four subclasses as the Wakelbura, but calls its two primary classes Yungaru and Wutheru.[3] The classes, subclasses, and totems of the Wakelbura tribe are shown in the following table:—[4]

[1] A. W. Howitt, *Native Tribes of South-East Australia*, pp. 62, 112.
[2] See above, pp. 417, 420.
[3] A. W. Howitt, *Native Tribes of South-East Australia*, pp. 112 *sq.*
[4] A. W. Howitt, *op. cit.* p. 112, on the authority of Mr. J. C. Muirhead, who elsewhere (*Journal of the Anthropological Institute*, xili. (1884) p. 191, note [1]) repeatedly spells the name of one of the primary classes Mallera, not Malera, as Dr. Howitt here gives it. For the classes and subclasses of the Wakelbura, see also Mr. J. [C.] Muirhead, cited by E. M. Curr, *The Australian Race*, iii. 26 *sq.*

[TABLE.

WAKELBURA SYSTEM

Classes.	Subclasses.	Totems.
Mallera	Kurgilla	opossum, spiny ant-eater, eagle-hawk, turkey, iguana, black bee, kangaroo
	Banbe	forest kangaroo, ringtail opossum, iguana
Wuthera	Wungo	emu, carpet-snake, gidya-tree, wallaby
	Obu	black duck, carpet-snake, large bee, emu, walleroo, gidya-tree, wallaby

"In the Wakelbura tribe the totem animal is spoken of as 'father.' For example, a man of the *Binnung-urra* (Frilled-lizard totem) holds that reptile as sacred, and he would not only not kill it, but would protect it by preventing another person doing so in his presence. Similarly a man of the Screech-owl totem would call it 'father,' and likewise hold it sacred and protect it. So far does the feeling go, that when a man could not get satisfaction for an injurious action by another, he has been known to kill that beast, bird, or reptile which that man called 'father,' and thus obtain revenge, and perhaps cause the other to do the same, if he knew of it. A man who was lax as to his totem was not thought well of, and was never allowed to take any important part in the ceremonies."[1]

Respect shewn by the Wakelbura for their totems.

The rules of marriage and descent of the classes in the Wakelbura tribe are such as usually prevail in tribes with the four-subclass system and female descent. Thus a Kurgilla man marries an Obu woman and the children are Wungo. A Banbe man marries a Wungo woman and the children are Obu. A Wungo man marries a Banbe woman and the children are Kurgilla. An Obu man marries a Kurgilla woman and the children are Banbe. Thus the children as usual belong to their mother's class (moiety)

Marriage and descent in the Wakelbura tribe.

---

[1] A. W. Howitt, *Native Tribes of South-East Australia*, pp. 147 *sq.*, on the authority of Mr. J. C. Muirhead. The frilled-lizard and screech-owl totems here mentioned do not appear in Dr. Howitt's list of Wakelbura totems given above.

and to the subclass which is complementary to her subclass. To put this in tabular form :—

Husband.		Wife.	Children.
Mallera	{ Kurgilla { Banbe	Obu Wungo	Wungo Obu
Wuthera	{ Wungo { Obu	Banbe Kurgilla	Kurgilla Banbe

Peculiar assignment of the totems in the Wakelbura tribe.

But in the Wakelbura tribe the descent, or perhaps rather the determination, of the totems is abnormal, for the children take their totems neither from their mother nor from their father. No reason has been ascertained for this peculiarity, and the tribe is now extinct. The following table was compiled from data furnished by the marriages and descents in four generations in one case, five in another, and two in a third.[1]

WAKELBURA TRIBE

Marriage and Descent

	Husband.		Wife.		Children.	
Mallera	Kurgilla	opossum	Obu	emu	Wungo	carpet-snake
	Kurgilla	plains-turkey	Obu	carpet-snake	?	
	Kurgilla	plains-turkey	Obu	hill kangaroo	?	
	Kurgilla	small honey-bee	Obu	carpet-snake	?	
	Banbe	iguana	Wungo	carpet-snake	Obu	emu
Wuthera	Wungo	carpet-snake	Banbe	iguana	Kurgilla	opossum
	Obu	emu	Kurgilla	opossum	Banbe	emu

In the Wakelbura tribe a wife was obtained only by betrothal, except in the rarer cases of elopement and capture.

[1] A. W. Howitt, *Native Tribes of South-East Australia*, p. 221. I omit the feminine forms of the subclass names, which are formed by the postfix *an* attached to the masculine forms, thus, Kurgillan, Banbean, Wungoan, Obuan.

It was the mother who chose a husband for her daughter as soon as the child was born, and when the girl was marriageable her betrothed husband took her away with him. If she eloped, her betrothed husband fought her paramour, and the victor kept her. If after she had consented to marry the man to whom she had been betrothed in infancy she eloped with some other man, even of the proper class and totem, she would be almost cut to pieces by her own brothers and her father's brothers, and also by the men of her betrothed husband's totem. Her brothers might even almost kill her, because by her elopement they would lose the woman by whose exchange they might have obtained a wife for one of them.[1]

The tribal law among the Wakelbura was extremely strict as to irregular connections or elopements between persons too nearly related to each other. "Such persons would be, for instance, those whom we call cousins, both on the father's and the mother's side, or who are of the class, subclasses, or totems which do not intermarry. For instance, if a Kurgilla-*tunara* man ran off with an Obuan-*wallaroo* (hill kangaroo) woman, who ought properly in due course to have married a Kurgilla-*burkum* (plains-turkey) man, his own and tribal brothers would be against him, as well as the brothers, own and tribal, of the woman, and those also of the promised husband. In short, he would have to fight with all of them." In such fights, when the missiles were exhausted, the combatants closed on each other with knives, a dense ring of blacks forming round them to see fair play. The knives were formerly of stone, but in later times of iron, sometimes made out of a sheep-shears blade, ground to a sharp edge. The fight was sometimes to the death. The offender always came off worst, there were so many against him. In any case the woman was terribly gashed with the knives. Her own mother would cut and sometimes kill her. If she survived, she was compelled to go with her betrothed or to return to her husband, if she were already married.[2]

At festive meetings of the Wakelbura tribe men of the

---

[1] A. W. Howitt, *Native Tribes of South-East Australia*, pp. 221 *sq*.
[2] A. W. Howitt, *op. cit.* pp. 222-224. It does not appear what is the English equivalent of the totem name *tunara*.

Exchange of wives, etc., among the Wakelbura. same totem exchanged wives for two or three days, and they also lent women to friendly visitors, provided these were of the proper class, subclass, and totem. A widow went to the brother of her deceased husband, or, if there were none, to his best friend of the same totem. The brother must be of the same mother, but might be of a different father. If children of an unlawful amour or unlawful marriage were allowed to live, they were called "mongrels" (*kongara*), and belonged to their mother's subclass; for instance, if she were Wungo, her illegitimate child would be Wungo also, but it would have no totem.[1]

Group-marriage in the Wakelbura tribe. "In this tribe, as will be seen from the following example, there was group-marriage. Say that there are seven men, all Mallera-kurgilla-small-bee, and who are, some own, and some tribal brothers. One of these men is married, his wife being Wutheran-obukan-carpet-snake. None of the other six men is married. They and the woman married to their brother call each other husband and wife, and the six men have and exercise marital rights as to her. Her child calls each of these six men father, as well as the seventh man, who is the actual husband of its mother, and the six men have to protect the child. This clearly is a form of the *pirrauru* marriage of the Lake Eyre tribes. The importance of this occurrence in a tribe, so distant from those of Lake Eyre, is that the Wakelbura is one of a large group of tribes who have the same organisation."[2]

Capture of wives from other tribes. In the group of tribes to which the Wakelbura belonged women were sometimes captured by the tribes who came to attend an initiation or other ceremony. This was done when the ceremonies were over, and the people were going homewards. But it was the visitors who captured women from their hosts, not the hosts who captured them from their guests. However, an opportunity for such a rape did not always present itself, for the practice was well known and the women were closely guarded. Yet at times a woman would wait till the visitors were gone two or three days on their homeward journey, and then steal after the man who had won her heart, and who lingered behind the rest for her.

[1] A. W. Howitt, *Native Tribes of South-East Australia*, p. 224.
[2] A. W. Howitt, *op. cit.* p. 224.

A captured woman belonged to her captor, if she were of the class and totem with which he might marry. But he did not keep her if she had been severely mauled with knives. The issue of such a union was called *ungkara* or *unguru*, which also means "mongrel."[1]

The initiation ceremonies of the Wakelbura tribe are called *Umba*. They can only be held by men of the primary class Mallera or of the primary class Wuthera, not by both combined. Men of one primary class initiate the boys of the other primary class. Thus men of the primary class Wuthera initiate boys of the Kurgilla and Banbe subclasses, which together compose the other primary class Mallera. This is in accordance with the usual rule of Australian tribes that men of one moiety initiate the youths of the other moiety. The reason for the rule, as Dr. Howitt has pointed out, "seems to be that it is only when the youth has been admitted to the rights and privileges of manhood in the tribe that he can obtain a wife. As his wife comes to him from the other moiety, it is the men of that moiety who must be satisfied that he is, in fact, able to take his place as the provider for, and the protector of, the woman, their sister, who is to be his wife. In this connection one can therefore see why it is that the future wife's brother, who is also his sister's husband, is the guardian of the youth in the ceremonies."[2]

In the Wakelbura and kindred tribes everything in the world, both animate and inanimate, is arranged under the two classes Mallera and Wuthera, and belongs in a manner to the members of one or other of these classes.[3] From

---

[1] A. W. Howitt, *Native Tribes of South-East Australia*, pp. 224 *sq*.

[2] A. W. Howitt, *Native Tribes of South-East Australia*, pp. 607 *sq*. In this passage Dr. Howitt says that the Wakelbura practice is an exception to the rule that men of one moiety initiate the youths of the other moiety. But the example which he gives (the initiation of Kurgilla-Banbe boys by Wuthera men), if it is correctly reported, refutes his statement, since Wuthera is the other moiety from Kurgilla-Banbe. He says: "The ceremonies are called *Umba*, and can only be held by Malera or Wuthera men, not by both combined. Thus if there are Kurgilla and Banbe boys to be made men, it would be Wuthera men who would hold the *Umba*, that is to say, the men of the one subclass Kurgilla initiate the boys of the other subclass Banbe, or *vice versa*." There seems to be some confusion in this statement.

[3] J. C. Muirhead, cited by Dr. A. W. Howitt, in *Journal of the Anthropological Institute*, xiii. (1884) p. 438 note [2]; *id.*, xviii. (1889) p. 61 note [3].

this curious classification of the universe are derived various practical rules, which confer certain privileges and impose certain restrictions on members of the classes and subclasses. Thus in regard to diet all the game and other food is divided into two sorts called Mallera and Wuthera respectively, and the Mallera primary class eats Mallera food, while the Wuthera primary class eats Wuthera food. Moreover, each subclass has its special sorts of food allotted to it, of which alone it is permitted to partake. The Banbe subclass is restricted to opossum, kangaroo, dog, honey of small bee, etc. The Wungo subclass has for its food emu, bandicoot, black duck, black snake, brown snake, etc. The Obu subclass eats carpet-snakes, honey of the stinging bee, etc. And the Kurgilla subclass lives on porcupine, plain-turkey, etc. To the Kurgilla also belong apparently water, rain, fire, and thunder, and they enjoy the reputation of being able to make rain at pleasure. If a Wungo man, camped out by himself, were to dream that he had killed a porcupine, he would believe that next day he would see a Kurgilla man, since the porcupine is one of the animals on which Kurgilla men live.[1] On this subject we read further that "certain animals are the especial game of each class. Obu, for instance, claims as his game emu and wallaby, and if he wishes to invite his fellows of the same subclass, in a neighbouring tribe, to hunt the common game, he must do this by means of a message-stick, made from the wood of a tree which is, like themselves, of the Obu subclass."[2] "If a young man or young woman of the Wakelbura tribe eats forbidden game, such as emu, black-headed snake, porcupine, they will become sick, and probably pine away and die, uttering the sounds peculiar to the creature in question. It is believed that the spirit of the creature enters into them

Among the Wakelbura each class and subclass has its own special kinds of food.

---

[1] E. M. Curr, *The Australian Race*, iii. 27, on the authority of Mr. James [C.] Muirhead, where the names of the subclasses are given as Kargilla, Banbey, Wongoo, Oboo.

[2] A. W. Howitt, *Native Tribes of South-East Australia*, p. 113. "I learn from Mr. J. C. Muirhead that the practice of sending a message through a totem [*i.e.* by a messenger of the same totem as the sender of the message] occurs in Northern Queensland, and further, that even the message-stick which is carried by the messenger must be made of some tree which belongs to the same class division as both the sender and the bearer of the message. In the tribes referred to, the whole universe is, so to say, arranged under the two primary class" (A. W. Howitt, in *Journal of the Anthropological Institute*, xiii. (1884) p. 438 note [2].)

and kills them."[1] A similar belief, as we have seen, used to prevail in Samoa as to the effect of eating the flesh of a tabooed or sacred animal.[2]

Further, when a Wakelbura man desires to perform a magical rite, he must use for the purpose only things which are of the same class as himself, and when he dies he is laid on a stage made of the branches and covered with the leafy boughs of a tree of his class.[3] For example, if the deceased was of the Banbe subclass, boughs of the broad-leaved box-tree would be used to cover him, because that tree is of the Banbe subclass. Men of the primary class Mallera would lay the boughs on the corpse, since the Mallera class includes the two subclasses Banbe and Kurgilla. Further, after placing the body on the stage, they carefully work the ground underneath with their feet into dust, and smooth it so that the slightest mark or print on it can be observed. Then they make a large fire near the spot and retire to their camp. But before they leave the place they mark the trees in such a way that this "blazed line" leads back to the frame with the corpse. This they do to prevent the dead man from following them. Next morning the relations of the deceased inspect the ground under the corpse. If the track or mark of a beast, bird, or reptile is visible in the dust, they infer from it the totem of the person who caused the death of their kinsman by witchcraft. For example, if a black or brown snake has been there, the culprit must be a Wungo man; if a carpet-snake has crawled over the dust, the guilty man must be an Obu, because carpet-snakes are Obu; if a native dog has left the print of his feet, the murderer must be a Banbe man, since dogs are of the Banbe subclass; and so on. But if no animal had left its tracks on the prepared ground, the friends of the deceased would try to frighten the ghost out of his bark shroud. Failing in the attempt, they would again smooth down the dust and return morning and evening to the spot, till they caught the ghost and learned from him

Subtotems of the Wakelbura in magical and funeral rites.

---

[1] A. W. Howitt, *Native Tribes of South-East Australia*, p. 769.
[2] Above, pp. 17 *sq.*
[3] A. W. Howitt, *Native Tribes of South-East Australia*, p. 113, and in *Journal of the Anthropological Institute*, xviii. (1889) p. 61 note [3], citing Mr. J. C. Muirhead as his authority.

who had been the cause of his death. When they had ascertained this to their satisfaction, they would bury the body temporarily for two months, then dig it up, chop it in pieces, and making as small a parcel of it as possible give it to the mother or sister of the deceased to carry to all the meetings of the tribe, till the death was avenged. Sometimes a man's remains would be carried about thus for two years. When the woman tired of her burden, she would drop it down the stem of a hollow tree and strip a ring from the bark of the trunk to mark the spot.[1]

Subtotems in other tribes. This remarkable distribution of all the objects of nature under the exogamous classes and subclasses of the tribe is not peculiar to the Wakelbura. Examples of similar classifications in other Australian tribes have already been noticed.[2] The various objects which, without being a man's totem, are yet reckoned to his class and subclass have been called by Dr. Howitt subtotems.[3] The precise relation in which a man's subtotems stand to his totem is not clear to us, and probably the ideas of the natives themselves on the subject are vague; but we are told that "among all the natural objects of his class, there is some one which is nearer to him than any other. He bears its name, and it is his totem."[4]

The Port Mackay tribe in Queensland, its classes and subclasses. The class system of the Wakelbura was found also, with some variation of nomenclature, in the tribe which inhabited the district of Port Mackay on the eastern coast of Queensland, to the north of Broad Sound. In this tribe the names of the two primary classes were Yungaru and Wutaru, of which the latter clearly corresponds to the Wuthera of the Wakelbura. The names of the subclasses were Gurgela, Bunbai, Wungo, and Kubaru, which answer to the Kurgilla, Banbe, Wungo, and Obu of the Wakelbura. And the rules of marriage and descent were the same. Thus a Gurgela man married a Kubaru woman and the children

---

[1] J. C. Muirhead, quoted by Dr. A. Howitt, in *Journal of the Anthropological Institute*, xiii. (1884) p. 191 note [1]; E. M. Curr, *The Australian Race*, iii. 28 *sq.*

[2] Above, pp. 78-80, 133-136. See also below, pp. 431 *sq.*, 451 *sqq.*, 462 *sq.*, 470 *sqq.*

[3] A. W. Howitt, "Australian Group Relations," *Annual Report of the Smithsonian Institution for 1883*, p. 818.

[4] A. W. Howitt, *Native Tribes of South-East Australia*, p. 113.

were Wungo. A Bunbai man married a Wungo woman and the children were Kubaru. A Wungo man married a Bunbai woman and the children were Gurgela. A Kubaru man married a Gurgela woman and the children were Bunbai. To put it in tabular form :—[1]

PORT MACKAY TRIBE

Marriage and Descent

Husband.		Wife.	Children.
Yungaru	{ Gurgela { Bunbai	Kubaru Wungo	Wungo Kubaru
Wutaru	{ Wungo { Kubaru	Bunbai Gurgela	Gurgela Bunbai

In this tribe it was deemed shameful and unnatural if a man cohabited with a woman of a wrong class. Every Gurgela man called every other Gurgela his brother, every Kubaru woman his wife, and every Wungo his son, unless the Wungo man belonged to the preceding generation, in which case the Gurgela man called him father.[2] Hence it appears that the Port Mackay tribe employed the classificatory system of relationship.

Like the Wakelbura, the Port Mackay tribe appeared to imagine that the system of their exogamous classes was a universal law of nature, so they divided everything between them. They said that wind belongs to one class, and the rain to the other; that alligators are Yungaru and kangaroos

Classificatory system of relationship in the Port Mackay tribe.

Subtotems of the Port Mackay tribe.

[1] Mr. G. F. Bridgman, cited by E. M. Curr, *The Australian Race*, iii. 45 *sq.*, and by R. Brough Smyth, *The Aborigines of Victoria*, i. 91. In the latter passage the name of one of the subclasses is given as Bembia instead of Bunbai. Compare Fison and Howitt, *Kamilaroi and Kurnai*, p. 34. As with the Wakelbura, the feminine forms of the subclass names are formed by postfixing *an* to the masculine. As usual I have omitted these feminine forms for the sake of simplicity.

[2] E. M. Curr, *The Australian Race*, iii. 47. Compare Mr. G. F. Bridgman, quoted by R. Brough Smyth, *The Aborigines of Victoria*, i. 91 : "On the system just described hinges [*sic*] all their ideas of relationship. Their terms for father, mother, brother, sister, uncle, aunt, etc., etc., are by no means synonymous with ours, but convey different ideas," etc.

Wutaru; that the sun is Yungaru and the moon Wutaru; and so on with the constellations, with the trees, and with the plants. If you pointed out a star to them, they would tell you to which class it belonged.[1]

The Buntamurra tribe of Queensland, its subclasses and totems. Another tribe whose subclass system conforms to that of the Wakelbura is the Buntamurra in South-Western Queensland. The territory of the tribe reaches from about Thargominda in the south to Kaiabara Creek on the north-west, to the Paroo River on the east, and a good way up the Bulloo River northwards. The tribe is distant about four hundred miles in a straight line from the Wakelbura, and marks the extreme southern limit of this particular type of the four-subclass system. On the other side, towards the south, it borders on the two-class system of the Darling River tribes.[2] The names of the two primary classes of the Buntamurra have not been ascertained, but the names of the four subclasses are Gurgela, Banbari, Wongo, and Guberu, which correspond to the Kurgilla, Banbe, Wungo, and Obu of the Wakelbura. The following is a list of the totem clans arranged under the subclasses:—[3]

BUNTAMURRA TRIBE

Subclasses.	Totems.
Gurgela	Kangaroo, padi-melon, wallaby, eagle-hawk.
Banbari	Crow, mountain snake, porcupine (*Echidna sp.*).
Wongo	Wild goose, wild turkey, white duck, swan, opossum, diving duck.
Guberu	Bandicoot, iguana, smallest iguana.

As in the Kongulu tribe, the feminine forms of the subclass

[1] G. F. Bridgman, quoted by R. Brough Smyth, *The Aborigines of Victoria*, i. 91, and by Fison and Howitt, *Kamilaroi and Kurnai*, pp. 167 *sq.*; E. M. Curr, *The Australian Race*, iii. 45.

[2] A. W. Howitt, *Native Tribes of South-East Australia*, p. 64.

[3] A. W. Howitt, *op. cit.* pp. 113 *sq.*, 226. In the former passage Gurgela, Banbari, and Guberu are spelled Gurgilla, Banburi, and Gubero.

names were formed by postfixing *gun* to the masculine form, as masculine Guberu, feminine Guberugun.[1]

The rules of marriage and descent of the classes and subclasses in the Buntamurra are normal; that is, a Gurgela man marries a Guberu woman and the children are Wongo. A Banbari man marries a Wongo woman and the children are Guberu. A Wongo man marries a Banbari woman and the children are Gurgela. A Guberu man marries a Gurgela woman and the children are Banbari. To put this in tabular form :—[2]

Marriage and descent in the Buntamurra.

THE BUNTAMURRA TRIBE

Marriage and Descent

Husband.	Wife.	Children.
{ Gurgela { Banbari	Guberu Wongo	Wongo Guberu
{ Wongo { Guberu	Banbari Gurgela	Gurgela Banbari

As usually happens under this system, children take their totem from their mother, while their subclass is the complementary subclass of hers. For example, if a Wongo-opossum man married a Banbari-crow woman, the son and daughter of the marriage would be Gurgela-crows; and if this Gurgela-crow woman married a Guberu-bandicoot man, the son and daughter would be Banbari-crows, just like their maternal grandmother. Thus in the direct female line the totem (in this case crow) would never change, but it would alternate between the two subclasses (in this case Banbari and Gurgela) of a moiety in alternate generations. Yet the native informant in this as in other tribes with the four-subclass system asserted that each subclass had its own totems, and in accordance with this statement the totems of the Buntamurra are arranged

Alternation of the totems between the two subclasses of a moiety.

---

[1] A. W. Howitt, *Native Tribes of South-East Australia*, p. 114. As to the feminine subclass names of the Kongulu, see above, p. 420 note [3].

[2] A. W. Howitt, *op. cit.* p. 226.

under the various subclasses in the table above. It is difficult to understand why certain totems should be thought to belong to a particular subclass, when the regular rule of descent in the four-subclass system necessitates the alternation of the totem between the two subclasses of a moiety in alternate generations; from which it seems to follow that though the totems are certainly divided between the two moieties or classes, they are not subdivided between the two subclasses which compose a moiety or class. The only explanation of the native statements that each subclass has its own totems would seem to be the one suggested by Dr. Howitt, namely, that the native who has been questioned on the subject has had in his mind his own subclass and the subclasses of some of his acquaintances, and that he has accordingly assigned to these subclasses the particular totems which he himself and they happened to possess, forgetting that these totems would in every case pass into another subclass in the next generation.[1]

§ 6. *Tribes with two Classes and Male Descent*

Tribes with two classes and male descent.

We have now concluded our survey of tribes with a normal class system and female descent in South-Eastern Australia. The tribes which combine the regular class system with male descent appear to be far less numerous, and we shall therefore be able to dismiss them more rapidly. Just as in dealing with tribes which have female descent, we shall begin with the simpler social organisation in two primary classes before we take up the more complex organisation in two primary classes and four subclasses.

The Kulin nation, its territory.

The Kulin nation, which was organised in two classes with male descent, occupied a large area of Central and Southern Victoria, ranging from Colac and Murchison on the west to Mount Baw Baw and Wangaratta on the east, and touching the sea at Port Phillip and Western Port on the south.[2] Thus their country comprised a great part of

[1] A. W. Howitt, *Native Tribes of South-East Australia*, pp. 210, 221, 226 sq.
[2] A. W. Howitt, *op. cit.* p. 70.

the high Victorian mountains with their woods and waters. The lofty and extensive uplands from which Mount Baw Baw rises are still covered with dense forests of gum-trees, traversed by paths and roads leading to the camps of the miners.[1] Here the great spurs sent out by the central mountains enclose valleys through which rivers flow northward to join the Murray or southward into Bass Strait. Tribes of the Kulin nation claimed these rivers to their sources in the Alpine heights, where they hunted in summer as soon as the inhospitable snows of winter had melted.[2]

Unfortunately very little has been recorded of the class organisation of the Kulin people. However, Dr. Howitt obtained some scanty information from a few survivors of Wurunjerri, Thagunworung, and Galgalbaluk tribes, which are now practically extinct. As to the other tribes of the nation all he could learn was that they had the names of the two primary classes Bunjil (Eagle-hawk) and Waang (Crow). These two class names, Eagle-hawk and Crow, appear to have extended, with slight variations, over Victoria north and south for a distance of a hundred and seventy miles, from Echuca to Port Phillip Heads, and east and west for a distance of two hundred miles from St. Arnaud to Buffalo.[3] In the Jajaurung tribe the class name Bunjil (Eagle-hawk) was replaced by Wrepil, which also meant Eagle-hawk. As to the totems of the Kulin nothing definite is known, except that in the Wurunjerri tribe there was a totem the swamp-hawk (*thara*) in the Eagle-hawk class.[4] However, traces of totemism may perhaps be detected in the legends told of certain mythical animals, which are called the sons or the boys of Bunjil, and are said to have been carried up with him when he went aloft in a whirlwind, being wafted to the upper regions by a blast which the Musk-crow at his order let out of a skin-bag. Among the sons of Bunjil are the green parroquet, the blue mountain parrot, the

The Kulin were divided into two classes, Eaglehawk and Crow.

Traces of totemism among the Kulin.

---

[1] J. W. Gregory, *Australasia*, i. 388.
[2] A. W. Howitt, *Native Tribes of South-East Australia*, pp. 36 sq., 72.
[3] A. W. Howitt, *op. cit.* p. 126.
[4] A. W. Howitt, *op. cit.* pp. 126, 252. However, elsewhere Dr. Howitt, writing of this group of tribes, observes that "the two intermarrying divisions were Eaglehawk (Bunjil) and Crow (Waa), and there was one totem attached to the Crow division" (*Journal of the Anthropological Institute*, xviii. (1889) p. 47).

swamp-hawk, the nankeen kestrel, the flying mouse, and the brush-tailed Phascologale; and all of them, with the possible exception of the flying mouse, may be seen to this day shining as stars in the sky. Bunjil himself, according to the Wurunjerri, is the star Altair; the brush-tailed Phascologale is Achernar; the swamp-hawk and the nankeen kestrel glitter in the constellation of the Centaur; while the green parroquet and the blue mountain parrot add fresh lustre to the nocturnal glories of the Southern Cross.[1]

Rules of marriage and descent among the Kulin.

In respect of marriage the Kulin nation observed the usual law of the classes; for an Eagle-hawk (Bunjil) man must marry a Crow (Waang) woman, and a Crow man must marry an Eagle-hawk woman. But contrary to the custom of the tribes of South-Eastern Australia which we have hitherto been considering, children took their class from their father and not from their mother; hence the children of an Eagle-hawk man and a Crow woman were Eagle-hawks, and the children of a Crow man and an Eagle-hawk woman were Crows.[2] A curious rule of etiquette was observed by Eagle-hawk and Crow men of the Wurunjerri tribe. When they were encamped at the same fire, each man had his own stick to stir it with and to cook his food. If he touched the stick of a man of the other class he thought that his fingers would swell, and that he would have to go to the medicine-man in order to have the wood drawn out from his hand.[3]

The institution of the exogamous classes was ascribed by the Kulin to Bunjil, a celestial headman.

The institution of the marriage laws was attributed by the Kulin to the sagacity of Bunjil. In spite of his name, which means Eagle-hawk, Bunjil appears in the legends as a kindly old man, the head of his tribe, who lived up in the sky with his two Black Swan wives, and his son the Rainbow. He made earth, trees, and mankind, fashioning men out of clay and then causing them to live, while his brother the Bat (Vallina) brought women up out of the water to be the wives of these Australian Adams. The interest of Eagle-

---

[1] A. W. Howitt, *Native Tribes of South-East Australia*, p. 128. For the ascension of Bunjil to heaven, see *id.*, pp. 491 *sq.*

[2] A. W. Howitt, *op. cit.* p. 252; *id.*, "Further Notes on the Australian Class Systems," *Journal of the Anthropological Institute*, xviii. (1889) pp. 47 *sq.*

[3] A. W. Howitt, *Native Tribes of South-East Australia*, p. 401.

hawk or Bunjil in the human race did not cease with his creation of them out of clay. He taught them the arts of life, and when they married without any regard to kinship he showed them a better way. It is said that a deputation consisting of two medicine-men, waited upon him in his mansion aloft, and received from him the sage advice that Eagle-hawk should be on this side and Crow on that, and that Eagle-hawk should always marry Crow, and Crow marry Eagle-hawk. Which accordingly they did ever afterwards. In their simple speech the name of Bunjil or Eagle-hawk, the creator and benefactor of mankind, was a synonym for wisdom or knowledge, and they called him "Our Father."[1] We need not suppose that the Kulin learned these childish fancies from the whites.

While in the northern tribes of the Kulin nation, for example in the Bangerang tribe, Eagle-hawks and Crows were intermixed and scattered over the tribal country, in the southern tribes of the nation, for example, in the Wurunjerri and Bunurong, the members of these two exogamous classes Eagle-hawk and Crow were segregated from each other and dwelt in separate districts, so that the rule of class exogamy was combined with a rule of local exogamy; that is, a man had to marry a woman not only of the other class but also of another district.[2] This is the first instance we have hitherto met with of that custom of local exogamy which we shall find in the sequel practised by several coastal tribes of South-Eastern Australia. Amongst the exogamous districts of these Southern Kulin tribes were the following.[3] The watershed of the Yarra River, which flows through Melbourne from the eastern highlands, was occupied by the Warunjerri-baluk, who were all Crows. The western slopes of Mount Macedon, the summit of which looks down from the north on the spreading bay of Port Phillip, and westward over the beautiful and fertile lands of Australia Felix,[4] were inhabited by another Crow people, the Gunung-willam-

In the Southern Kulin tribes exogamy of the classes was combined with local exogamy: a man had to marry a woman of another district as well as of another class.

[1] A. W. Howitt, *Native Tribes of South-East Australia*, pp. 484, 491 sq. Compare id., "On some Australian Beliefs," *Journal of the Anthropological Institute*, xiii. (1884) pp. 192, 193, 194.

[2] A. W. Howitt, *Native Tribes of South-East Australia*, pp. 126 sq.

[3] A. W. Howitt, op. cit. p. 127.

[4] J. W. Gregory, *Australasia*, i. 63.

baluk. Some forty miles to the east of Melbourne yet another Crow people, the Ngaruk-willam, had their home on the southern side of that vast pile of igneous rocks known as the Dandenong Ranges, where in the ravines the gum-trees soar to a height of over four hundred feet.[1] And the Bunurong people, who were all Eagle-hawks, inhabited the sea coast from the Werribee River to Anderson's Inlet, and inland till they touched the southern boundaries of the Crows.

Intermarriage of the tribes near Melbourne.

With regard to the intermarriage of these clans or tribes of Eagle-hawks and Crows, each occupying its separate territory, Protector Thomas, quoted by Dr. Howitt, has said that "between the five nearest tribes to Melbourne there is a kind of confederacy or relationship. Thus the Yarra, Western Port, Geelong, Goulburn, and Devil's River tribes, though continually quarrelling, nevertheless are in a degree united. A Yarra black must get himself a wife, not out of his own tribe, but either of the other tribes. In like manner a Goulburn man must get his lubra[2] from the Yarra, Devil's River, Western Port, or Geelong tribe. Thus a kind of social compact is formed against any distant tribe who might intrude upon their country, when all united to expel the intruder."[3]

Girls given in marriage

In the Kulin nation it was the father of a girl who disposed of her in marriage "through and by his elder brother," but before doing so he talked the matter over with his wife. However, the actual exchange of girls in marriage took place only by the authority of the respective fathers, when the assembled old men had decided that the damsels were old enough to be married. Each girl would then be sent away under the care of her elder brother, who brought back his brother's future wife.[4] In these tribes all

---

[1] A. R. Wallace, *Australasia*, i. 49 sq.; J. W. Gregory, *Australasia*, i. 388.

[2] That is, wife.

[3] A. W. Howitt, *Native Tribes of South-East Australia*, pp. 252 sq. Mr. Thomas's evidence was given before a committee of the Legislative Council of Victoria in 1858.

[4] A. W. Howitt, *op. cit.* p. 253. However, on p. 255 Dr. Howitt writes: "The actual ceremony of marriage was by the girl's father and some of the old men taking the girl to the camp of her promised husband, and there saying to her, 'That is your husband; if you run away from him, you will be punished.'"

marriages between first cousins, without exception, whether the children of two brothers, or of two sisters, or of a brother and a sister respectively, were absolutely forbidden, it being held that the children of brothers and sisters were too near to each other to marry.[1] Hence it would seem that by a simple prohibition the Kulin attained the same object which the Arunta and other central tribes secured by the more complicated machinery of the eight-class system; that is, they prevented a man's children from marrying his sister's children, for the other marriages between first cousins (viz. the marriage between the children of two brothers and the marriage between the children of two sisters) were already barred by the two-class system as well as by the four-class system, whether with male or female descent.[2] Indeed the Kulin went even further and forbade the marriage not only of a man's children with his sister's children, but also of the descendants of these children on both sides as far as the relationship could be traced; for such descendants were still held to be "too near" and only a little removed from "brother and sister."[3] This extended prohibition marks an advance on the system of the Urabunna, which not only allows but enjoins the marriage of a man's children with his sister's children, though the brother and sister whose children marry each other need be brother and sister only in the classificatory sense of the terms.[4] The adoption of male descent by the Kulin may also, though it need not necessarily,[5] be another stage on the upward road of these savages towards civilisation. Certainly their unhesitating recognition of physical paternity is a clear gain to knowledge which distinguishes them from the Arunta and other central tribes. They told Dr. Howitt that "the child comes from the man, and the woman only takes care of it." On this subject one of Dr. Howitt's native informants said, "I remember what old Boberi, the brother of Billibilleri, said at Dandenong, when

<small>All marriages between cousins forbidden.</small>

<small>Recognition of physical paternity.</small>

---

[1] A. W. Howitt, *Native Tribes of South-East Australia*, p. 254.
[2] See above, pp. 180 *sq.*
[3] A. W. Howitt, *op. cit.* p. 257. This statement seems to apply particularly to the Bangerang tribe, which lived at the junction of the Goulburn and Murray Rivers. It was one of the northern tribes of the Kulin (A. W. Howitt, *op. cit.* p. 126).
[4] See above, pp. 177 *sq.*
[5] See above, pp. 167, 248 *sq.*, 335 *sq.*

some of the boys were grumbling and would not mind him. The old man got vexed, and said to his son, 'Listen to me! I am here, and there you stand with my body!'"[1]

<small>Punishment of unlawful marriages.</small>

If a girl eloped with a man who was within the forbidden degrees, all the young men gave chase, and if they overtook the culprits they mauled or even killed them. Sometimes a man of one local tribe would carry off a woman from another local tribe. When that happened, the headman of the injured tribe sent a challenge to the offender to come and fight. The people on both sides then mustered and fought, the men attacking the men with boomerangs, spears, and shields, while the women belaboured each other with digging sticks. A widow went to the brother of her deceased husband. If there were no brother, her father or her brother disposed of her.[2]

<small>Mutual avoidance of mother-in-law and son-in-law, etc.</small>

In the Kulin nation, as in Australian tribes generally, a man might hold no communication with his wife's mother and her sister, nor might a woman look at or speak to her daughter's husband and his brother. If she did so, it was thought that her hair would turn white. Hence when a man sent a present of game to his father-in-law, the mother-in-law would rub charcoal over her face, and especially over her mouth, before she would venture to partake of the meat; after that she might eat of it safely without her hair blanching.[3]

<small>Blood-revenge among the Wurunjerri.</small>

In the Wurunjerri tribe, when a man of one class, say an Eagle-hawk, was called on to appear and answer for having killed a man of the other class, say a Crow, all his fellow Eagle-hawk men would stand on one side under their headman, and all the Crow men, the kindred of his victim, would stand on the other side also under their headman. Then the avengers would throw spears at the culprit till he was either killed or so hurt that he could no longer defend himself, or until his headman called out "Enough."[4] The Wurunjerri, like so many Australian tribes, were governed by the old men, among whom individuals distinguished for

---

[1] A. W. Howitt, *Native Tribes of South-East Australia*, p. 255.

[2] A. W. Howitt, *op. cit.* pp. 255-257.

[3] A. W. Howitt, *op. cit.* pp. 256 *sq.*

[4] A. W. Howitt, *op. cit.* p. 336.

their sagacity and good character were especially listened to and obeyed. Each local group had its headman, and of these headmen one was recognised as the head of all. Some of these men were great warriors, others great orators, and greatest of all, at the time when Melbourne was founded, was a celebrated bard.[1]

The Wurunjerri tribe had the classificatory system of relationship. Thus in the generation above his own a man applied the same term *mamen* to his father, to his father's brothers, and to the husbands of his mother's sisters; and he applied the same term *babun* to his mother, to his mother's sisters, and to the wives of his father's brothers. In his own generation he applied the same term *bangan* to his brothers, to the sons of his father's brothers, and to the sons of his mother's sisters. He applied the same term *bimbang* to his wife, to his wife's sisters, and to his brothers' wives; and a wife applied the same term *nangurung* to her husband, to her husband's brothers, and to her sisters' husbands. In the generation below his own a man applied the same term *mumum* to his sons, to his brothers' sons, and to the sons of his wife's sisters. Similarly a woman applied the same term *wurungin* to her sons and to her sisters' sons.[2]

Classificatory system of relationship among the Wurunjerri.

§ 7. *Tribes with four Subclasses and Male Descent*

In South-Eastern Queensland, round about Maryborough, there was a group of tribes with four subclasses and male descent. Their territory stretched along the coast as far south as Brisbane and northward somewhat beyond latitude 25°. Inland it extended for a distance of about two hundred miles.[3] The country occupied by these tribes belongs in respect of climate and fertility to the most

Queensland tribes with four subclasses and male descent.

---

[1] A. W. Howitt, *Native Tribes of South-East Australia*, pp. 307, 308.
[2] A. W. Howitt, "Australian Group-Relationships," *Journal of the Royal Anthropological Institute*, xxxvii. (1907) pp. 287 sq.
[3] A. W. Howitt, *Native Tribes of South-East Australia*, pp. 58-60, 115, with the map facing p. 90. Dr. Howitt observes (pp. 117 sq.): "I am not able to define the northern limits of this class system, but it must be south of Rockhampton, for a new set of names comes in there with female descent, of which the Kuinmurbura tribe, which occupied the peninsula between Broad Sound and Shoalwater Bay, is the example." As to the system of the Kuinmurbura tribe, see above, pp. 417 *sqq.*

442 TOTEMISM IN SOUTH-EASTERN AUSTRALIA CHAP.

Natural fertility of their country.

favoured regions of Australia. Compared with the rest of Queensland this eastern or coastal district "is the most varied, the most fertile, and in every way the most important. It has the best climate, the richest soil, the highest mountains, and the most beautiful scenery, and it comprises the larger portion of the settled country. Its abundant rains and high temperature make it suited to the growth of almost all tropical and sub-tropical products, while sheep and cattle also thrive in it. It is almost wholly covered with wood, either scrub or forest, and has much fine woodland scenery and a very luxuriant vegetation. The coast is thickly strewn with islands, which often form fine harbours; and within the tropics the great Barrier coral-reef extends itself at some miles from the coast, producing a calm sea, in which are numerous islands of various sizes, and offering scenes of great beauty."[1] As a great part of Queensland lies within the tropics, its climate is more uniformly hot than that of the southern portions of the continent. Yet it may be doubted whether the heat is so oppressive here as further south, for Queensland suffers neither from the scorching winds nor from the sudden and extreme changes of temperature which are such trying features in the climate of other parts of Australia. Though the rainfall in all the coast districts is heavy, yet during much of the year the weather is fine, the sky cloudless, the atmosphere dry and exhilarating. At Brisbane the winter is a delightful season, with cool mornings and evenings, bright and warm days, the sky always blue, and the air wonderfully transparent.[2]

Great diminution of these tribes.

About the year 1859 the blacks who inhabited this happy land might be counted by thousands, and they strictly observed their native customs; but by the year 1888 the whole of the Maryborough tribes, with which we are here concerned, could not muster a hundred and fifty individuals all told.[3] Surrounding them on the inland side were tribes with the system of four subclasses and female descent,[4] which has already been dealt with.[5] Of the tribes with four subclasses

---

[1] A. R. Wallace, *Australasia*, i. 349. The Barrier Reef does not skirt the territory of the tribes we are here concerned with; it begins further north.

[2] A. R. Wallace, *op. cit.*, i. 352, 353.

[3] A. W. Howitt, *Native Tribes of South-East Australia*, p. 60.

[4] A. W. Howitt, *op. cit.* p. 115.

[5] Above, pp. 395 *sqq.*

and male descent the Kaiabara may be taken as a type. They inhabited the Bunya-Bunya mountains about sixty miles inland from Maryborough. The triennial harvest of the *bunya-bunya* tree, which grows in their country, was the occasion of great gatherings and festivities, to which other tribes were summoned from a distance by messengers.¹ The tree (*Pinus Bidwelliana*) is the principal constituent of a vast, scrubby, almost impassable forest which extends, or used to extend, between Wide Bay and the head of the River Boyne. Rising to a height sometimes of seventy feet, with a stem as straight as a mast, the *bunya-bunya* branches out at the top into a mass of cone-shaped foliage, and every three years it is laden with a magnificent crop of fruit, which was greedily eaten by the natives. The fruit grows in the shape of a pine-apple cheese, consisting of some fifty or more little triangular nuts, which adhere together in a bunch till they are quite ripe, when a sharp blow easily severs them. For six months, from November to May, all the blacks within a hundred miles used to eat these fruits and nothing else. It was their great jubilee, a season of gladness and festivity.² The Kaiabara were divided into two primary classes called Kubatine and Dilebi, four subclasses called Bulkoin, Bunda, Baring, and Turowain, and totem clans. The names of the two primary classes (moieties) Kubatine and Dilebi are clearly identical with the Kupathin and Dilbi of the Kamilaroi system. The Kaiabara system may be exhibited in tabular form as follows:—³

The Kaiabara tribe, its classes, subclasses, and totems.

KAIABARA SYSTEM

Classes.	Subclasses.	Totems.
Kubatine {	Bulkoin Bunda	Carpet-snake, flood water, native cat, white eagle-hawk.
Dilebi {	Baring Turowain	Turtle, lightning, rock carpet-snake, bat, black eagle-hawk.

[1] A. W. Howitt, *Native Tribes of South-East Australia*, pp. 60, 595, 768.
[2] C. P. Hodgson, *Reminiscences of Australia* (London, 1846), pp. 147 *sq.*
[3] A. W. Howitt, *Native Tribes of South-East Australia*, pp. 115 *sq.*;

444 TOTEMISM IN SOUTH-EASTERN AUSTRALIA CHAP.

Marriage and descent among the Kaiabara.

The rules of marriage and descent of the subclasses in the tribe are as follows. A Bulkoin man marries a Turowain woman and the children are Bunda. A Bunda man marries a Baring woman and the children are Bulkoin. A Baring man marries a Bunda woman and the children are Turowain. A Turowain man marries a Bulkoin woman and the children are Baring. To put this in tabular form :—[1]

KAIABARA TRIBE

Marriage and Descent

Husband.		Wife.	Children.
Kubatine	{ Bulkoin { Bunda	Turowain Baring	Bunda Bulkoin
Dilebi	{ Baring { Turowain	Bunda Bulkoin	Turowain Baring

The four-class system, whether with male or female descent, was apparently devised to prevent the marriage of parents with children.

Thus a man must always marry a woman from one of the two subclasses in the other moiety of the tribe, and the children belong to the subclass neither of their father nor of their mother, but to the subclass which is complementary to their father's subclass. Hence the children always belong to their father's class (moiety), though never to his subclass. For example, if the father is Kubatine-Bulkoin, the children will be Kubatine-Bunda; if the father is Dilebi-Baring, the children will be Dilebi-Turowain. From this we see that the classes descend directly and the subclasses indirectly in the male line; in other words, every child belongs to its

Journal of the Anthropological Institute, xiii. (1884) p. 336. In the latter passage Dr. Howitt interprets the class names Dilebi and Cubatine as meaning "flood-water" and "lightning" respectively, while Baring is interpreted as "turtle," Turowain as "bat," Bulkoin as "carpet-snake," and Bunda as "native cat." But these interpretations are not repeated by Dr. Howitt in his book. Perhaps in his earlier statement (*Journal of the Anthropological In-* *stitute*, *l.c.*) the names of the classes and subclasses were confused with those of the totems, of which none were given.

[1] A. W. Howitt, *Native Tribes of South-East Australia*, pp. 228 *sq.* The Kaiabara had a mode of recording the four subclasses and their marriages in a diagrammatic form on a stick, the markings being made in such a manner as to represent a man with his arms crossed. See A. W. Howitt, *op. cit.* pp. 230 *sq.*

father's class and to the subclass which is complementary to his. The general principle is the same as in the system of four subclasses with female descent; for in both systems a man is restricted in his choice of a wife to, roughly speaking, one fourth of the women of the tribe, and in both systems the children belong neither to the subclass of their father nor to that of their mother. The only difference is that in the one system the children belong to their father's complementary subclass and in the other system to their mother's complementary subclass; in the former accordingly there is male descent, in the latter there is female descent. In both systems the subclasses with their peculiar rule of descent appear to have been instituted for the purpose of preventing marriages between parents and children, and this purpose was effected very simply by the arrangement that children should always belong to a section of the community into which neither their father nor their mother was allowed to marry. To speak more exactly, the two-class system with female descent prevents a man from marrying his mother (because she is of the same class with him), but not from marrying his daughter (because she is of the other class). Conversely, the two-class system with male descent prevents a man from marrying his daughter (because she is of the same class with him), but not from marrying his mother (because she is of the other class). Hence where female descent prevailed, the introduction of the four subclasses was intended to prevent the marriage of a man with his daughter; where male descent prevailed, the introduction of the four subclasses was intended to prevent the marriage of a man with his mother. Marriages between brothers and sisters had already been prevented by the simpler division of the tribe into two exogamous classes; for under that system brothers and sisters always belonged to the same exogamous class, and therefore could not marry each other. That older two-class system was retained when the new four-class system was introduced, so that every man in the tribe had his class as well as his subclass, and was thus effectually debarred from marrying his sister, his mother, or his daughter. Only in speaking of brothers and sisters, and parents and children, we must remember that these terms are used in their wide classificatory

More exact statement of the effects of the two-class and four-class systems respectively.

sense so as to include many persons whom we should not designate by them. The intention first of the two-class and afterwards of the four-class system was to debar from each other whole groups of men and women between many of whom we should recognise no blood relationship whatever.[1]

Peculiar rule as to the descent of the totems in the Kaiabara tribe.

But while the rules of marriage and descent in the Kaiabara tribe are normal so far as the classes and subclasses are concerned, they are abnormal with respect to the totems. For whereas the rule of male descent, direct or indirect, prevails as to the classes and subclasses, the rule of female descent, with a certain peculiarity, prevails as to the totems, as may be seen by the following table :—[2]

KAIABARA TRIBE

Marriage and Descent of Totems

	Husband.		Wife.		Children.	
Kubatine.	Bulkoin	carpet-snake	Turowain	black eagle-hawk	Bunda	white eagle-hawk
	Bunda	native cat	Baring	rock carpet-snake	Bulkoin	scrub carpet-snake
Dilebi.	Baring	turtle	Bunda	white eagle-hawk	Turowain	black eagle-hawk
	Turowain	bat	Bulkoin	female carpet-snake	Baring	scrub carpet-snake

Hence it appears that though the child takes his father's class and the subclass which is complementary to his father's subclass, he takes a totem which is neither that of his father nor that of his mother, but which is more akin to that of his mother, since it is a beast or bird of the same species as hers but of a different colour or sex. For example, if a Carpet-snake man marries a Black Eagle-hawk woman, the children are White Eagle-hawks ; if a Turtle man marries a White Eagle-hawk woman, the children are Black Eagle-hawks. And so with the rest. The custom seems to be an attempt to extend to the totems the rule of alternation

---

[1] See also above, pp. 271 *sqq.*
[2] A. W. Howitt, *Native Tribes of South-East Australia*, pp. 229 *sq.*

in alternate generations which prevails with the subclasses, so that just as the child takes a subclass which is neither that of his father nor that of his mother, but which is akin to one of them, so he should take a totem which is neither that of his father nor that of his mother, but which is akin to one of them. Only it is curious that, with male descent of the class and subclass, the totem of the child should be akin to that of its mother instead of to that of its father.

The Kaiabara had the classificatory system of relationship. Thus in the generation above his own a man applied the same term *baboin* to his father, to his father's brothers, and to the husbands of his mother's sisters; and he applied the same term *avang* to his mother, to his mother's sisters, and to the wives of his father's brothers. In his own generation he applied the same term *nuni* to his brothers and to the sons of his father's brothers. He applied the same term *malemungan* to his wife, to his wife's sisters, and to his brothers' wives; and a woman applied the same term *malaume* to her husband, to her husband's brothers, and to her sisters' husbands. In the generation below his own a man applied the same term *nogoin* to his sons and to his brothers' sons. Similarly a woman applied the same term *nogoin* to her sons and to her sisters' sons.[1]

In the tribes between the Kaiabara and the sea the names of the subclasses, though substantially the same as those of the Kaiabara, varied slightly in form; but the rules of marriage and descent, so far as concerns the classes and subclasses, appear to have been in some of the tribes identical. This may be seen by the following table:—[2]

Classificatory system of relationship among the Kaiabara.

The tribes about Maryborough in Queensland, their classes and subclasses.

---

[1] A. W. Howitt, "Australian Group-Relationships," *Journal of the Royal Anthropological Institute*, xxxvii. (1907) pp. 287 *sq*.
[2] A. W. Howitt, *Native Tribes of South - East Australia*, pp. 116 *sq*., 231. However, in regard to the tables of marriage and descent which were collected for him by Mr. H. E. Aldridge among these tribes and in Great Sandy Island, Dr. Howitt observes that they "differed considerably amongst themselves in the arrangement of the subclasses and in the marriages and descents. So much so that the correctness of some of them seemed doubtful."

[TABLE

TRIBES ABOUT MARYBOROUGH

Marriage and Descent

Husband.		Wife.	Children.
Kupathin	Balgoin Bunda	Theirwain Parang	Bunda Balgoin
Tilbi	Parang Theirwain	Bunda Balgoin	Theirwain Parang

Direct descent of the class and indirect descent of the subclass.

From this it will be seen that, just as among the Kaiabara, children belong to their father's class and to his complementary subclass. For example, if he is Kupathin-Balgoin and his wife Tilbi-Theirwain, the children will be Kupathin-Bunda; that is, they will be of their father's class Kupathin and of the subclass Bunda, which is complementary to his subclass Balgoin. Thus descent both of the class and of the subclass is in the male line; but whereas the descent of the class is direct (since the children belong to their father's class), descent of the subclass is indirect (since the children belong not to their father's subclass but to the one which is complementary to it).

Personal totems (*pincha*) among the Maryborough tribes.

A remarkable feature in the totemism of these tribes is reported by Dr. Howitt. He says: "In the tribes within fifty miles of Maryborough (Queensland), each boy has a totem called *Pincha*, which is given to him by his father, and which he calls *Noru*, that is, 'brother.' For instance, say that a man's *Pincha* is Fish-eagle (*kunka*), he gives to each of his sons a *Pincha*; for instance, to one a kangaroo (*guruman*), to another a large white grub (*pu-yung*) which is found in gum-trees, and so on. A man does not kill or eat his *Pincha*. Moreover, he is supposed to have some particular affinity to his father's *Pincha*, and is not permitted to eat it."[1] From this account it would seem that in these tribes every man had a personal totem which was assigned to him by his father, though on what principle the

[1] A. W. Howitt, *Native Tribes of South-East Australia*, p. 147, on the authority of Mr. Harry E. Aldridge.

assignation was made does not appear, and the personal totems of brothers differed from each other as well as from that of their father. Parallel to the personal totems (*pincha*) of these Maryborough tribes are the *budjan* or *jimbir* of the Wiradjuri and the Yuin and the *thundung* or "elder brothers" of the Kurnai.[1]

In the Muruburra tribe, living at White Cliffs on Great Sandy Island, the names of the four subclasses were practically the same as in the Kaiabara and Maryborough tribes, and descent was in the male line both for the subclass and the totem; but the names of the two primary classes have not been ascertained. The following list of subclasses and totems was obtained by Dr. Howitt from a member of the Muruburra tribe, who was of the Theirwain class and the fire totem :—[2]

The Muruburra tribe, its subclasses and totems.

MURUBURRA TRIBE

Class System

Classes.	Subclasses.	Totems.
{	Balgoin	water-snake, carpet-snake, red kangaroo, emu, turtle, iguana.
	Bunda	black dingo, black duck, thunder, yellow dingo.
{	Baring	fish-hawk, bream.
	Theirwain	fire, opossum.

In this Queensland group of tribes with four subclasses and male descent, just as in the Kulin nation of Victoria with two classes and male descent,[3] the marriage of all cousins was forbidden; that is, not only were the children of two sisters and the children of two brothers forbidden to marry, as they necessarily are in all Australian tribes with a two- or four-class system, but the children of a brother and a sister were equally forbidden to marry, and for the

Marriage between cousins prohibited.

---

[1] See above, pp. 412 *sq.*, and below, p. 495.
[2] A. W. Howitt, *Native Tribes of*
[3] See above, pp. 438 *sq.*

South-East Australia, pp. 117, 230.

450 TOTEMISM IN SOUTH-EASTERN AUSTRALIA CHAP.

same reason, namely, that they were too near of kin. It sometimes, however, happened that cousins fell in love with each other and made a runaway match of it, but if they were caught they were severely punished and sometimes killed.[1]

<small>Betrothal of girls and capture of women.</small>

In these tribes wives were obtained in various ways. Sometimes girls were betrothed in their infancy to suitable men. A woman captured from a hostile tribe belonged to her captor, if she were of the proper class. Nearly all their fights resulted from the capture of women; indeed these people made forays for the purpose of carrying off wives.[2] Also there was a curious practice of capturing women after two tribes had met at the *Dora* or initiation ceremonies of young men. On the last evening, when the last dance was over, and the assembly was dispersing in the darkness, spreading out like a fan from the ceremonial ground, the young men of both sides of the community used to lie in wait for the women, then rush out and carry them off as they returned to their camps. This had to be done quietly, or the girls' friends would hear and rescue them. If the ravishers were confident in their numbers, they defended their captives; if not, they let them go and fled for their lives, sometimes receiving very ugly wounds from their pursuers. The women thus taken might be either married or single, but a preference was always shown for single women. A young man would learn beforehand which was the right girl for him, and when he seized her he would ask her of what class she was; for if she was not of the class into which he might marry he would at once let her go. His object was to get a wife of the right class. At such gatherings there was always some one who could tell everybody's class, subclass, and totem.[3]

<small>Custom of the levirate.</small>

When a man died, his surviving brother, whether elder or younger, might marry the widow; but he must be either

---

[1] A. W. Howitt, *Native Tribes of South-East Australia*, p. 232. Yet Dr. Howitt tells us (*op. cit.* p. 230) that in the Muruburra tribe a man's proper wife was the daughter of his mother's brother. Perhaps the Muruburra were exceptional in permitting, or rather recommending, this case of cousin-marriage.

[2] A. W. Howitt, *op. cit.* pp. 232, 235 *sq.*

[3] A. W. Howitt, *op. cit.* pp. 233 *sq.* As to the *Dora* or initiation ceremonies of these tribes, see *id.* pp. 599-606.

a full or a half-brother in our sense of the word, and not merely a tribal brother.¹

The tribes about Maryborough observed the usual rule of avoidance between son-in-law and mother-in-law. The two would never look at or towards each other. A man would hide himself anywhere or anyhow, if his wife's mother were near. The relation between them was called *mulong*.² {Mutual avoidance of mother-in-law and son-in-law.}

§ 8. *Tribes with Anomalous Class Systems and Female Descent*

We have now completed our survey of the tribes with normal class systems, whether of the two-class or of the four-class type, in South-Eastern Australia. It remains to notice some tribes whose class systems present certain anomalous features. We begin with those which trace descent in the female line. Among these the first to be considered will be the Wotjobaluk, whose tribal name is derived from *wotjo*, " man," and *baluk*, " people." ³ {Tribes with anomalous marriage systems.}

The Wotjobaluk occupied a considerable area of what is known as the Wimmera district of North-Western Victoria. Their country extended from the Wimmera to the Richardson River and northward to the salt lakes in which these streams lose themselves before they reach the Murray.⁴ The whole of this district, as we have seen, consists of vast sandy plains, sparsely covered with grass and intersected with belts of scrub and forests of Casuarina, Banksia, and eucalyptus. The climate is very dry, the rainfall very low, and the drought sometimes severe.⁵ {The Wotjobaluk of Victoria.}

The Wotjobaluk were divided into two exogamous classes (moieties) called Krokitch and Gamutch respectively, and each of these classes included a number of totem clans, the members of which claimed to own various natural species and natural phenomena. The things which the {The Wotjobaluk, their classes and totems.}

---

¹ A. W. Howitt, *Native Tribes of South-East Australia*, p. 236.
² A. W. Howitt, *op. cit.* p. 236. Similarly among the tribes about Brisbane a man and his mother-in-law never looked at or spoke to each other (A. W. Howitt, *op. cit.* p. 237).
³ A. W. Howitt, *op. cit.* p. 54.
⁴ A. W. Howitt, *op. cit.* p. 54.
⁵ A. R. Wallace, *Australasia*, i. 267 *sq.*, 273. See above, pp. 316 *sq.*

members of a totem clan thus claimed as belonging to them may be called their subtotems. Examples of similar subtotems have met us before.[1] "The whole universe," says Dr. Howitt, "including mankind, was apparently divided between the classes. Therefore the list of subtotems might be extended indefinitely. It appears that a man speaks of some as being 'nearer to him' than others. I am unable to ascertain the precise meaning of this expression. When pressed upon this question, a black would say, 'Oh, that is what our fathers told us.'"[2] The social system of the Wotjobaluk tribe with its classes, totems, and subtotems is set forth in the following table :—[3]

WOTJOBALUK SYSTEM

Classes.	Totems.	Subtotems.
Krokitch	the sun	the star Fomalhaut (*Bunjil*), plains turkey, opossum, a grub (*gur*), a tuber (*garuka*), grey kangaroo, red kangaroo.
	galah (or white) cockatoo	native companion, bandicoot, emu, mussel, musk duck, mountain duck, magpie goose.
	a cave	subtotems not known.
	pelican	,, ,,
	carpet-snake	,, ,,
	the hot wind	a venomous snake, a small snake, Pennant's lorikeet, a small bird (*wurip*), the moon.
	a tuber (*munya*)	subtotems not known.

[1] See above, pp. 78-80, 133-136, 430, 431 sq.
[2] A. W. Howitt, *Native Tribes of South-East Australia*, pp. 454 sq.
[3] A. W. Howitt, *op. cit.* p. 121. Compare, *id.*, "Australian Group Relations," *Annual Report of the Smithsonian Institution for 1883*, pp. 818 sq.; *id.*, "Further Notes on the Australian Class Systems," *Journal of the Anthropological Institute*, xviii. (1889) pp. 60-64.

WOTJOBALUK SYSTEM (*continued*)

Classes.	Totems.	Subtotems.
Gamutch	deaf adder	native cat, black swan, tiger-snake, sulphur-crested cockatoo, crow, dingo.
	the sea	subtotems not known.
	pelican	thunder, magpie, native cat, fire, white gull, white-bellied cormorant, small black cormorant, large cormorant, bull oak (*Casuarina glauca*), a wader, grey heron, chough.
	black cockatoo	a small iguana, lace-lizard, black duck, a small snake, teal duck, a bird (*jering*).

In this tribe the classes, totems, and subtotems are all called *mir*.[1] On the Wotjobaluk system Dr. Howitt observes that it appears to be a peculiar development of the two-class system of the Darling River tribes with totem clans but no subclasses.[2] But in the case of the Wotjobaluk, he says, "some of the totems have advanced almost to the grade of subclasses, and they have a markedly independent existence. The new features are the numerous groups of subtotems attached to the classes Gamutch and Krokitch respectively It seems as if some of the totems of a two-class system had grown in importance, leaving the remaining totems behind in obscurity; and probably this has arisen through this tribe dividing the whole universe between the two classes, as, for instance, the Wiradjuri do."[3]

Peculiar features of Wotjobaluk totems.

As to the respect which a Wotjobaluk entertained for his totem animal, we are told that he "would not harm his totem if he could avoid it, but at a pinch he would eat it in default of other food. In order to injure

Intimate connection between a man and his totem.

[1] A. W. Howitt, *Native Tribes of South-East Australia*, p. 122.
[2] See above, pp. 380 *sqq*.
[3] A. W. Howitt, *Native Tribes of South-East Australia*, p. 122.

another person he would, however, kill that person's totem. To dream about his own totem means that some one has done something to it for the purpose of harming the sleeper or one of his totemites. But if he dreams it again, it means himself, and if he thereupon falls ill, he will certainly see the wraith of the person who is trying to 'catch' him. The same beliefs are held by the other tribes of this nation."[1] Such beliefs illustrate the intimate connection which is supposed to subsist between a man and his totem; the totem animal appears to be to some extent identified with the man, since any injury done to it will be felt by him.

Relation of certain totems with each other.

Further, several of the totems are thought to be specially related to each other. Thus the sun totem (*ngaui*) is in some way associated with the white cockatoo (*garchuka*) totem. For a man of the sun totem has been known to claim the white cockatoo as a second name of his totem (*mir*); he maintained that both Sun and White Cockatoo were his names, but that Sun was specially his name and White Cockatoo "came a little behind it." On the other hand, another man who claimed to be both Sun and White Cockatoo, said that he was especially White Cockatoo, and that Sun "came a little behind his White Cockatoo name." The exact relation of the two Dr. Howitt was not able to ascertain. He inclines to regard the two as "very slightly divergent branches of the same totem," or as "slightly divergent appendages of the class Krokitch, under new names."[2]

Totemic burial customs among the Wotjobaluk.

Some light is thrown on the relation of the totems to each other by the mechanical method which the Wotjobaluk employed to preserve and explain a record of their classes and totems. It was their custom to bury the dead with their heads pointing in different directions according to their class and totem, and the various directions were all fixed with reference to the rising sun. Two of Dr. Howitt's informants, who were old men, spent about two hours in laying out the mortuary directions on the ground with sticks, and Dr. Howitt took their bearings with a compass. The

---

[1] A. W. Howitt, *Native Tribes of South-East Australia*, pp. 145 sq.

[2] A. W. Howitt, *op. cit.* p. 122;

id., in *Journal of the Anthropological Institute*, xviii. (1889) p. 61.

TRIBES WITH ANOMALOUS CLASS SYSTEMS

diagram which he thus constructed, he tells us, may not be altogether correct because the list of totems is probably incomplete. It is as follows :—[1]

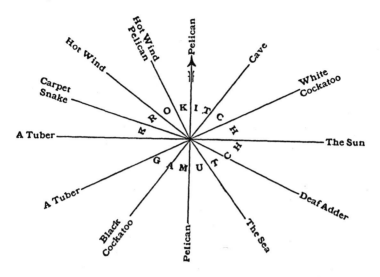

Thus it will be observed that men of the Sun totem are laid in the grave with their heads to the east; men of the White Cockatoo totem are buried with their heads to the north-east; men of the Hot Wind totem are buried with their heads to the north-west, which was appropriate, since in the country of the Wotjobaluk the hot wind blows from that quarter. And similarly with the other totems. It will be noticed that the pelican totem is found in both the two primary classes Krokitch and Gamutch. No explanation of this repetition is given by Dr. Howitt. He tells us that the Sun was the principal totem, and that from it all the other totems are counted.[2] When a man died, he was no longer called by his old totem name, but received a new name, which varied with the particular totem. These new names are called by Dr. Howitt "mortuary totems." Thus when a man of the sun totem died, he would no longer be

Mortuary totems of the Wotjobaluk.

---

[1] A. W. Howitt, *Native Tribes of South-East Australia*, pp. 453 *sq.*; id. "Further Notes on the Australian Class Systems," *Journal of the Anthropological Institute*, xviii. (1889) pp. 62 *sq.*

[2] A. W. Howitt, in *Journal of the Anthropological Institute*, xviii. (1889) p. 63.

spoken of as Sun (*ngaui*) but as "Behind the sun" (*wurtingaui*), that is, as a shadow cast behind the speaker by the sun. When a man of the Krokitch class and the pelican totem died, he would no longer be called Pelican (*batchangal, batya-ngal*) but "Bark of the mallee" (*mitbagragr*); and so on with the other totems. The custom probably originated in the extreme dislike of the aborigines to name the dead.[1]

<small>Relation of men to their subtotems.</small> The relation in which people stand to their subtotems as distinguished from their totems is, as usual, somewhat vague and indefinite. A man claims to own his subtotem, but he does not identify himself with it or name himself after it, as he names himself after his totem. For example, a man of the Sun totem claims kangaroos as his property because they are his subtotems, but he is not called Kangaroo; he is called Sun after his totem the sun. Similarly a man of the sun totem claims the star Fomalhault (*Bunjil*) as his, but he is not named after the star. Again, a man of the hot wind totem claims two sorts of snakes, two sorts of birds, and the moon as his, but he is not called after any of them; he is called Hot Wind. "The true totem," says Dr. Howitt, "owns him, but he owns the subtotem."[2]

<small>Sex totems among the Wotjobaluk: the bat is the "brother" of the men, the owlet-nightjar is the "sister" of the women.</small> The totemic system of the Wotjobaluk is still further complicated by the possession of what I have called sex-totems.[3] Among them the sex-totem or, as they called it, the "brother" of the men was the bat, and the sex-totem or "sister" of the women was the owlet-nightjar, which was also called the "wife" of the men. These sex-totems of the Wotjobaluk, says Dr. Howitt, "were real totems, although of a peculiar kind. They were called *yaur* or flesh, or *ngirabul* or *mir*, just as were the totems proper." The only difference was that, whereas the bat was the brother of all the men and the owlet-nightjar the sister of all the women, an ordinary totem was the brother or sister only of the men

---

[1] A. W. Howitt, in *Journal of the Anthropological Institute*, xviii. (1889) p. 64; *id., Native Tribes of South-East Australia*, p. 123.

[2] A. W. Howitt, *Native Tribes of South-East Australia*, p. 123; *id.*, in *Annual Report of the Smithsonian Institution for 1883*, pp. 818 *sq.*; *id.*, "Further Notes on the Australian Class Systems," *Journal of the Anthropological Institute*, xviii. (1889) pp. 61 *sq.*

[3] See above, pp. 47 *sq.*

and women who bore its name. In regard to their sex-totems the Wotjobaluk said that "the life of the bat is the life of a man, and the life of the owlet-nightjar is the life of a woman," and that when either of these creatures is killed the life of some man or of some woman is shortened. In such a case every man or every woman in the camp feared that he or she might be the victim, and from this cause great fights arose in the tribe between the men on one side and the women on the other. For example, some men might kill an owlet-nightjar and then boast of their exploit in camp. The women would then in their turn kill a bat and carry it to the camp on the point of a stick, and with a piece of wood in its mouth to keep it open. This was held aloft in triumph, the oldest woman walking at the head of the procession and the younger women following, while they all shouted *Yeip Yeip* (hurrah)! The men then turned out, armed with clubs, boomerangs, and even spears, and engaged the women, who fought with their digging-sticks, belabouring the men with them and cleverly parrying or breaking the spears that were thrown at them. Sometimes, however, the spears went home and the women were wounded or killed. But at other times they got the better of their male adversaries, who had to retire discomfited with broken heads and sore bones. These curious fights between men and women over their sex-totems seem to have occurred in all the tribes of South-Eastern Australia among whom sex-totems have been found.[1] The true character of the sex-totem, as Dr. Howitt justly observes, appears to be shown by the statement of the Wotjobaluk that "the life of a bat is the life of a man," and that "the life of an owlet-nightjar is the life of a woman"; for such a belief fully explains the rage of either sex when one of their sex-totems has been killed.[2] Thus

The life of men and women is thought to be bound up with the life of their sex-totem.

---

[1] A. W. Howitt, "Further Notes on the Australian Class Systems," *Journal of the Anthropological Institute*, xviii. (1889) pp. 57 *sq.*; *id.*, *Native Tribes of South-East Australia*, pp. 148, 150, 151. In the first of these passages we read: "The Wotjo said that the Bat was the man's 'brother' and that the Nightjar was his 'wife.'" From this it is not quite clear whether the Nightjar was deemed the wife of the man or of the Bat.

[2] A. W. Howitt, *The Native Tribes of South-East Australia*, p. 148: "The true character of the sex totem is shown by the Wotjobaluk expression, 'The life of a bat is the life of a man,' meaning that to injure a bat is to injure some man, while to kill one is to cause some man to die. The same saying applies to the Owlet-nightjar with respect to women."

among the Wotjobaluk the conception of a sex-totem, as well as of an ordinary totem,[1] seems to involve a more or less complete identification of a man or woman with his or her totem animal. His or her life is apparently thought to be so bound up with that of the animal that an injury done to the animal injures correspondingly the man or woman, while its destruction entails his or her death. On these and similar facts I formerly based a theory that a totem may have been supposed to contain the external soul of the person who claimed it.[2]

<small>Marriage and descent among the Wotjobaluk.</small>

The rule of marriage in the Wotjobaluk tribe was that a man of one class (Krokitch or Gamutch) must marry a woman of the other class (Gamutch or Krokitch), but that he was free to marry a woman of any totem in that class. The children took their class and totem from their mother. For example, if a Krokitch man of the sun totem married a Gamutch woman of the black swan totem, the children would be Gamutch Black Swans. If a Gamutch man of the tiger-snake totem married a Krokitch woman of the bandicoot totem, the children would be Krokitch Bandicoots, and so on.[3] In all negotiations with a view to marriage the first question was, "What is the *yauerin* ('flesh') of the two persons?" For *yauerin* meant class and totem as well as flesh, and no marriage could take place between persons of the wrong class or totem. But besides this class restriction on marriage there was in the Wotjobaluk tribe a local restriction also, since a man was forbidden to marry a woman of the same place as his mother: they thought his flesh (*yauerin*) was too near to the flesh of the women who lived there. Hence he had to go for a wife to some place where there was no flesh (*yauerin*) near to his. The same rule applied to the woman.[4] Thus we find that in the Wotjobaluk, as in the southern tribes of the Kulin nation,[5] class exogamy is combined with local exogamy. This is

<small>Local exogamy among the Wotjobaluk.</small>

---

[1] See above, pp. 453 *sq.*

[2] *The Golden Bough*,[2] iii. 413 *sqq.*

[3] A. W. Howitt, "Australian Group Relations," *Annual Report of the Smithsonian Institution for 1883*, p. 819; *id.*, in *Journal of the Anthropological Institute*, xviii. (1889) pp. 60 *sq.*; *id.*, *Native Tribes of South-East Australia*, pp. 241 *sq.* In the last of these passages Dr. Howitt omits to state the rule of marriage with respect to the totems.

[4] A. W. Howitt, *Native Tribes of South-East Australia*, p. 241.

[5] See above, pp. 437 *sq.*

the anomalous feature in the class system of the Wotjobaluk, which in other respects appears to be normal.

Besides the restrictions imposed by the class and the maternal district, the Wotjobaluk, like all other Australian tribes, prohibited marriage between persons who stood in certain degrees of kinship to each other. In particular they laid great stress on forbidding the marriage of a *marrup* with a *marrup-gurk*; that is, a man might not marry the daughter of his mother's brother nor of his father's sister. Two such persons might not mix their flesh, their *yauerin* being too near. Nay more than that, their descendants were prohibited from marrying each other so long as the relationship between them could be traced. However, the native informants added " that they remembered that one or two cases had occurred in which such a marriage had been permitted, but in them the parties were from places far distant from each other, for instance, the Wimmera and Murray Rivers, and that in those cases their respective parents were distant tribal brothers and sisters."[1] This Wotjobaluk prohibition to marry the daughter of a mother's brother or of a father's sister is, as Dr. Howitt observes,[2] a great remove from the custom of the Urabunna, among whom, on the contrary, a man's proper wife is precisely the daughter of his mother's (elder) brother or of his father's (elder) sister.[3] The same view as to the propriety of marriage with the daughter of a mother's brother or of a father's sister was held also by the Jupagalk, a tribe which bordered on the Wotjo nation, but they said that the woman should be obtained from a distant place so as not to be too near him in flesh.[4] We have seen that the Kulin, like the Wotjobaluk, also prohibited not only the marriage of first cousins, the children of a brother and a sister, but also the marriage of the descendants of such cousins, so far as the relationship could be traced.[5]

In the Wotjobaluk tribe, when it had been ascertained that there were no impediments of any kind to the marriage of two persons, whether a girl and a boy, or a girl and a

Wotjobaluk prohibition of marriage between cousins, the children of a brother and a sister.

Betrothal and marriage among the Wotjobaluk.

---

[1] A. W. Howitt, *Native Tribes of South-East Australia*, pp. 241-243.
[2] A. W. Howitt, *op. cit.* p. 243.
[3] See above, pp. 177 *sq.*
[4] A. W. Howitt, *op. cit.* p. 243.
[5] See above, pp. 438 *sq.*

man, they were betrothed by their respective fathers, whose consent was essential. Yet it was the elder brothers of the pair who made the arrangements. Such engagements might be made at any time, but they were most commonly arranged at the great gatherings when the intermarrying tribes met together to feast or perform ceremonies. In anticipation of these meetings the young men used to ascertain what unmarried girls had not been betrothed, which of them were of the class with which theirs might marry, and what were the places from which they might take a wife. Having ascertained these particulars two young men would meet at one of these assemblies and agree to give their sisters in exchange to be the wives of their respective younger brothers.[1] The ceremony of marriage was simple. The bride was taken to the bridegroom's camp by her father, accompanied by the father, father's brothers, brothers, and male paternal cousins of the bridegroom. At the camp the father's sister of the bride said to her, "That is your husband. He will give you food. You must stop with him." No one but the bridegroom had access to the bride at marriage in this tribe. Men too were very strict in requiring fidelity from their wives, and would not lend them to friends or visitors from a distance.[2]

Punishment of elopement and of unlawful marriages among the Wotjobaluk.

It happened not uncommonly that a girl who had been betrothed to a man in her infancy liked some one else better and eloped with him. All her male kindred pursued the runaway couple, and if they caught them, the lover had to fight them or rather to parry the spears which they threw at him. The girl's father and brothers were the first to cast their spears at him, and the others followed. If he passed through the ordeal successfully, he was allowed to keep the girl, provided always that he was of the right class and not within the prohibited degrees of relationship. But he had to find a sister to give in exchange for her.[3] Very different was the case if the man who ran away with a girl was of

---

[1] A. W. Howitt, *Native Tribes of South-East Australia*, pp. 241 sq.

[2] A. W. Howitt, *op. cit.* p. 245. However, in the Mukjarawaint tribe, which was the southern branch of the Wotjo nation, men of the same totem as the bridegroom had access to the bride at marriage. See A. W. Howitt, *op. cit.* pp. 243, 245 sq.

[3] A. W. Howitt, *op. cit.* p. 245 sq.

the wrong class or within the prohibited degrees of relationship. Such an offence against the tribal morality was punished with great severity. All the men of both the intermarrying classes gave chase, and if they caught the culprit they would kill and bury him. "My Wotjobaluk informants said that this was always done in the old times before white men came; but that they did not do as their western neighbours did, namely, eat him. It was the duty of the woman's father and brothers, in such a case, to kill her. This was confirmed to me by a Mukjarawaint man, who said that if a man took a woman who was of the same *yauerin* as himself, the pursuers, if they caught him, killed him, and with the exception of the flesh of the thighs and upper arms, which were roasted and eaten, they chopped the body into small pieces, and left them lying on a log. The flesh was eaten by his totemites, including even his brothers. This he said was also the custom of the Jupagalk."[1]

It was not customary in the Wotjobaluk tribe for a widow to be taken by her deceased husband's brother. They had a feeling against the practice. An old man explained to Dr. Howitt that it was unpleasant to lie in the place of a dead brother, and so to be always reminded of him.[2] Similarly some of the Queensland tribes near Brisbane considered it monstrous that a man should marry his brother's widow, and such marriages never took place among them; but the brother of the deceased had a voice in giving the widow to another.[3]

Widow not married by her late husband's brother.

The Wotjobaluk had the classificatory system of relationship. Thus in the generation above his own a man applied the same term *maam* to his father, to his father's brothers, and to the husbands of his mother's sisters; and he applied the same term *bap* to his mother, to his mother's sisters, and to the wives of his father's brothers. In his own generation he applied the same term *wau* to his brothers, to the sons of his father's brothers, and to the sons of his mother's sisters. He applied the same term *matjun* to his wife, to his wife's sisters, and to his brothers' wives. A woman applied the same term *nanitch* to her husband, to her husband's brothers,

Classificatory system of relationship among the Wotjobaluk.

[1] A. W. Howitt, *Native Tribes of South-East Australia*, pp. 246 sq.
[2] A. W. Howitt, *op. cit.* p. 248.
[3] A. W. Howitt, *op. cit.* p. 237.

462 TOTEMISM IN SOUTH-EASTERN AUSTRALIA CHAP.

and to her sisters' husbands. In the generation below his own a man applied the same term *ngaluk* to his sons, to his brothers' sons, and to the sons of his wife's sisters. Similarly a woman applied the same term *nunungyep* to her sons, to her sisters' sons, and to the sons of her husband's brothers.[1]

The Mukjarawaint.

In the south-western part of Victoria, to the south of the Wotjobaluk, there was a tribe or subtribe who were reckoned to the Wotjobaluk, but who called themselves Mukjarawaint. They lived in the northern parts of the picturesque Grampian Mountains and at the sources of the Wimmera River.[2] Their system of classes and totems has not been recorded; but we hear of a black cockatoo totem and a white cockatoo totem among them, and learn incidentally that a White Cockatoo man might marry a Black Cockatoo woman.[3]

The Mara nation.

From the southern limits of the Mukjarawaint to the sea on the south, and from Mount Gambier on the west to Eumerella Creek on the east, there was a nation who called themselves Mara, a name which in their language signified "man" or "men."[4] A small tribe of this nation bore the name of Gournditch-mara, and had its headquarters at Gournditch or Lake Condah.[5] This tribe was divided into two exogamous classes, Krokitch and Kaputch, the names of which are clearly identical with the Krokitch and Gamutch of the Wotjobaluk. Two totems are recorded, namely, White Cockatoo and Black Cockatoo, each of which claimed a number of subtotems. The system may be exhibited in tabular form as follows:—[6]

The Gournditch-mara tribe, their classes and totems.

[1] A. W. Howitt, "Australian Group-Relationships," *Journal of the Royal Anthropological Institute*, xxxvii. (1907) pp. 287 *sq.*

[2] A. W. Howitt, *Native Tribes of South-East Australia*, pp. 54 *sq.*, 243. As to the Grampian Mountains compare A. R. Wallace, *Australasia*, i. 267, 269.

[3] A. W. Howitt, *op. cit.* pp. 245 *sq.*

[4] A. W. Howitt, *op. cit.* pp. 69, 124.

[5] A. W. Howitt, *op. cit.* p. 69. See the account of this tribe by the Rev. J. H. Stähle, of the Church Mission, Lake Condah, reported by Fison and Howitt, *Kamilaroi and Kurnai*, pp. 274-278.

[6] A. W. Howitt, *op. cit.* p. 124, on the authority of the Rev. J. H. Stähle.

GOURNDITCH-MARA TRIBE

Classes and Totems

Classes.	Totems.	Subtotems.
Krokitch	white cockatoo	pelican, laughing-jackass, parrot, owl, mopoke, large kangaroo, native companion.
Kaputch	black cockatoo	emu, whip-snake, opossum, brush kangaroo, native bear, swan, eagle-hawk, sparrow-hawk.

In this tribe the child took its class and totem from its mother, but belonged to the local division of its father and spoke his language. Wives were obtained from distant places, because such women were thought not to be so "close in flesh" as those who lived in the same or neighbouring districts. Here, accordingly, as in the Wotjobaluk and the southern tribes of the Kulin nation, a rule of local exogamy was superadded to the rule of class exogamy. Children were betrothed by their parents, sister being exchanged for sister in the usual way. "There was no sexual licence allowed at any time in this tribe, although occasionally a man lent his wife to others, but this was always the occasion of fight between him and the better-thinking of the tribes-people."[1]

Marriage and descent among the Gournditch-mara.

The Gournditch-mara belonged to a large group of tribes in South-Western Victoria, which have been well described by Mr. James Dawson.[2] He tells us that the aborigines are divided into tribes, each of which has its own country distinguished by the name or language of the tribe.[3] "Every person is considered to belong to his father's tribe, and cannot marry into it. Besides this division, there is another which is made solely for the purpose of preventing marriages with *maternal* relatives. The aborigines are

Tribes of South-Western Victoria, their exogamous classes or clans.

---

[1] A. W. Howitt, *Native Tribes of South-East Australia*, pp. 69, 249.
[2] James Dawson, *Australian Aborigines* (Melbourne, Sydney, and Adelaide, 1881).
[3] J. Dawson, *op. cit.* p. 1.

everywhere divided into classes; and every one is considered to belong to his mother's class, and cannot marry into it in any tribe, as all of the same class are considered brothers and sisters. There are five classes in all the tribes of the Western District, and these take their names from certain animals—the long-billed cockatoo (*kuurokeetch*), the pelican (*kartpoerapp*), the banksian cockatoo (*kappatch*), the boa snake (*kirtuuk*), and the quail (*kuunamit*)." Of these five classes the first two, namely, Long-billed Cockatoo and Pelican, were looked upon as sister classes and no marriage between them was permitted. The same was true of the third and fourth classes, namely Banksian Cockatoo and Boa Snake; they were sister classes and no marriage between them was allowed. The fifth class, namely Quail, was not so related to another class, and might therefore marry into any class but its own. The first two classes (Long-billed Cockatoo and Pelican) were allowed to marry into any of the remaining three classes, and so were the third and fourth classes (Banksian Cockatoo and Boa Snake).[1] To put this in tabular form:—

TRIBES OF SOUTH-WESTERN VICTORIA

Classes or Totems

{ Long-billed Cockatoo (*kuurokeetch*)
{ Pelican (*kartpoerapp*)

{ Banksian Cockatoo (*kappatch*)
{ Boa Snake (*kirtuuk*)

Quail (*kuunamit*)

It is doubtful whether these divisions were exogamous classes or totem clans.

It might be doubted at first sight whether these divisions, which Mr. Dawson calls classes, are what we call classes or subclasses or totem clans. Their uneven number is against the view that they are what we now call classes or subclasses, since such classes are regularly found in groups of two and subclasses in groups of four or eight. Probably Dr. Howitt is right in treating Mr. Dawson's classes as totem clans. He points out that the first four of the animals which give their

---

[1] J. Dawson, *Australian Aborigines*, pp. 26 *sq.* The feminine forms of these class names are formed by adding *heear* to the masculine form; for example, masculine *kartpoerapp*, "pelican," feminine *kartpoerapp heear*.

names to these classes are totems of the Wotjobaluk, and that the third is one of the totems of the Gournditch-mara. On the whole Dr. Howitt inclines to believe that classes or sub-classes, in the sense in which we employ these terms, did not exist among the tribes of South-Western Victoria at the time when they were described by Mr. James Dawson, for otherwise that experienced observer could hardly have overlooked them.[1]

Inquiries made by Mr. A. L. P. Cameron among the natives near Mortlake, which is within the area of the tribes described by Mr. Dawson, elicited the following list of totems :—[2]

Black and White Cockatoo totems.

{ *Krokage*, white cockatoo, red crest.
{ *Karperap*, pelican.

{ *Kubitch*, black cockatoo.
{ *Kartuk*, whip snake.

Of these totems Pelican was supplementary to White Cockatoo, and Whip Snake was supplementary to Black Cockatoo. Thus it appears that with these people, just as with the Gournditch-mara, the two principal totems were White Cockatoo and Black Cockatoo, and their native names Krokage and Kubitch are clearly equivalent to the class-names of the Gournditch-mara, namely Krokitch and Kaputch, which in their turn are identical with the class-names of the Wotjobaluk, namely Krokitch and Gamutch. The names which Mr. Dawson assigns to the two cockatoo "classes," namely Kauurokeetch and Kappatch, are also, it would seem, merely slightly different forms of the same two class-names Krokitch and Gamutch.[3]

The aborigines of South-Western Victoria, described by Mr. Dawson, had a tradition that the first progenitor of their tribes was a Long-billed Cockatoo, who had for his wife a Banksian Cockatoo. These two were the great-great-grandfather and great-great-grandmother of the people. They had sons and daughters who belonged to their mother's class, and were therefore Banksian Cockatoos. As the laws

Tradition as to the origin of the classes or clans.

---

[1] A. W. Howitt, *Native Tribes of South-East Australia*, pp. 124 sq., 250.

[2] A. W. Howitt, *op. cit.* p. 125.

[3] A. W. Howitt, *op. cit.* pp. 125, 250.

of consanguinity forbade marriages between them, it was necessary to introduce "fresh flesh" (*wambepan tuuram*), which could only be obtained by marriage with strangers. The sons got wives from a distance, and their sons, again, had to do the same. That is how the Pelican, Snake, and Quail classes were introduced, which, together with those of their first parents, the Long-billed Cockatoo and the Banksian Cockatoo, form the five maternal classes or totem clans which exist, or rather used to exist, all through the Western District of Victoria.[1]

<small>The tribes of South-Western Victoria combined local exogamy with class or totem exogamy.</small>

In these tribes of South-Western Victoria, as in other tribes inhabiting the better-watered and more fertile regions on or near the coast, strict rules of local exogamy were superadded to the rule of class exogamy. For every man was forbidden to marry into his father's tribe, into his mother's tribe, into his grandmother's tribe, into an adjoining tribe, and even into any tribe that spoke his own dialect.[2] These complex marriage laws appear to have been strictly enforced. On this subject Mr. James Dawson, who knew the people well, writes as follows: "No marriage or betrothal is permitted without the approval of the chiefs of each party, who first ascertain that no 'flesh' relationship exists, and even then their permission must be rewarded by presents.

<small>Strictness with which their marriage laws were enforced.</small>

So strictly are the laws of marriage carried out, that, should any signs of affection and courtship be observed between those of 'one flesh,' the brothers or male relatives of the woman beat her severely; the man is brought before the chief, and accused of an intention to fall into the same flesh, and is severely reprimanded by the tribe. If he persists, and runs away with the object of his affections, they beat and 'cut his head all over'; and if the woman was a consenting party she is half-killed. If she dies in consequence of her punishment, her death is avenged by the man's receiving an additional beating from her relatives. No other vengeance is taken, as her punishment is legal. A child born under such conditions is taken from the parents, and handed over to the care of its grandmother, who is compelled to rear it, as no one else will adopt it.

---

[1] J. Dawson, *Australian Aborigines*, p. 27.
[2] J. Dawson, *op. cit.* pp. 26, 27.

It says much for the morality of the aborigines and their laws that illegitimacy is rare, and is looked upon with such abhorrence that the mother is always severely beaten by her relatives, and sometimes put to death and burned. Her child is occasionally killed and burned with her. The father of the child is also punished with the greatest severity, and occasionally killed. Should he survive the chastisement inflicted upon him, he is always shunned by the woman's relatives, and any efforts to conciliate them with gifts are spurned, and his presents are put in the fire and burned. Since the advent of Europeans among them, the aborigines have occasionally disregarded their admirable marriage laws, and to this disregard they attribute the greater weakness and unhealthiness of their children."[1]

Among these people children were betrothed to each other in marriage as soon as they could walk. The proposal was made by the girl's father. A youth was not allowed to marry until he had been formally initiated into manhood. No person related to him by blood might interfere or assist in the rites of initiation. Should the boy have brothers-in-law, they came and took him away to their own country to be initiated, and there he had to stay for twelve moons. If he had no brothers-in-law, strangers from a distant tribe came and took him away to their country. During his residence in this far country he was not allowed to speak the language of the tribe, but he learned to understand it when spoken. At the end of the time all the hairs of his beard were plucked out, and he was made to drink water mixed with mud. That completed his initiation into manhood. The upper front teeth of the novice were not knocked out in the Western District of Victoria, as they were in many other Australian tribes. He was then introduced to the young woman who was to be his wife. They might look at each other, but were not allowed to converse.[2] *Betrothal and initiation among the tribes of South-Western Victoria.*

When the young man's beard was grown again and the young woman had attained a marriageable age, she was sent away from her tribe and placed under the care of the young man's mother, or his nearest female relative, who *Marriage customs: husband and wife always spoke different languages.*

[1] J. Dawson, *Australian Aborigines*, p. 28.
[2] J. Dawson, *op. cit.* pp. 28, 30.

kept her till the two were married, but not in the same hut with her future husband. She was constantly attended by one of his female relatives, but was not allowed to speak the tribal language. She was expected, however, to learn it sufficiently to understand it. On the marriage day bride and bridegroom were adorned on their brows with bunches of red feathers from the neck of the long-billed cockatoo, while the bridegroom had besides the white feather of a swan's wing, the web of which was torn so as to flutter in the wind. Feasting and dancing celebrated the happy day, and the young pair were conducted to a new hut, which was to be their home. But for two moons the two were not allowed to look at or speak to each other. During all that time they were attended day and night by a bridemaid and a brideman, and had to sleep on opposite sides of the fire, the bride beside the bridemaid and the bridegroom beside the brideman. In order that she might not see her husband during this time, the bride kept her head and face covered with her opossum rug while he was present, and he kept his face turned away from her. This mutual avoidance of the newly-wedded couple used to afford much amusement to the young people of the tribe, who would peep into the hut and laugh at them. If the pair needed to communicate with each other they had to speak through their friends.[1] Even after these temporary barriers between husband and wife were removed, they had always to speak to each other in different languages, he using the speech of his tribe, and she using the speech of hers. On this subject Mr. Dawson writes: "Every person speaks the tribal language of the father, and must never mix it with any other. The mother of a child is the only exception to this law, for, in talking to it, she must use its father's language as far as she can, and not her own. At the same time, she speaks to her husband in her own tribal language, and he speaks to her in his; so that all conversation is carried on between husband and wife in the same way as between an Englishman and a Frenchwoman, each speaking his or her own language. This very remarkable law explains the preservation of so many distinct dialects within so limited a space, even where

Marginal note: Mutual avoidance of husband and wife for some time after marriage.

[1] J. Dawson, *Australian Aborigines*, pp. 30-32.

there are no physical barriers to ready and frequent communication between the tribes."[1]

These customs illustrate the stringency with which the rule of local exogamy was enforced by the natives of South-Western Victoria. The same people also rigidly observed the usage which in many Australian tribes obliges a man and his mother-in-law to keep aloof from each other. Indeed, among the natives of South-Western Victoria this mutual avoidance began with the betrothal of the infants. The girl's mother and her aunts might not look at the future son-in-law, nor speak to him from the time of his betrothal till his death. Should he come to the camp where they were living, he must lodge at a friend's hut, as he was not allowed to go within fifty yards of their abode; and if he met them on a path, they at once left it, clapped their hands, covered up their heads with rugs, walked in a stooping posture, and spoke in whispers till he had passed. When they spoke in each other's presence they had to use a special lingo called "turn tongue," but not for the sake of concealing their meaning, for everybody understood it. The future son-in-law never at any time mentioned the name of his future mother-in-law. Similar rules of avoidance were observed after the marriage had taken place. They might not look upon each other even when one of them was dying. After death, however, the living looked upon the dead. "The aborigines," says Mr. Dawson, "who show great willingness to give explanations of their laws and habits to those persons they respect, cannot give any reason for this very extraordinary custom, which is said to be observed all over Australia, and in several island groups in the Pacific Ocean."[2]

<small>Mutual avoidance of mother-in-law and son-in-law.</small>

In these tribes, when a married man died, his brother was allowed to marry the widow, and if she had a family he was bound to marry her, for it was his duty to protect her and rear his brother's children. If there was no brother, the chief sent the widow to her own tribe, with whom she must remain till her period of mourning was ended. Those of her children who were under age were

<small>Relation of a man to his brother's widow.</small>

[1] J. Dawson, *Australian Aborigines*, p. 40.
[2] J. Dawson, *op. cit.* pp. 29, 32 *sq.*

sent with her, and remained with their mother's tribe till they came of age, when they returned to their father's tribe, to which they belonged.[1]

Sex-totems, the bat and the fern-owl or goatsucker.

Among the tribes of South-Western Victoria the common bat was the sex-totem of the men, and the fern-owl or large goatsucker was the sex-totem of the women. For Mr. Dawson tells us that "the common bat belongs to the men, who protect it against injury, even to the half-killing of their wives for its sake. The fern owl, or large goatsucker, belongs to the women, and, although a bird of evil omen, creating terror at night by its cry, it is jealously protected by them. If a man kills one, they are as much enraged as if it was one of their children, and will strike him with their long poles."[2]

The Buandik tribe, its classes, totems, and subtotems.

Immediately to the west of the tribes which we have just been considering there was the Buandik tribe about Mount Gambier in the extreme south-eastern corner of South Australia. Its territory extended along the coast from the Glenelg River on the east to Rivoli Bay on the west.[3] The tribe was divided into two exogamous classes, with totem clans and subtotems, like the Wotjobaluk; and the names of its two classes, Kroki and Kumite, are probably only altered forms of the two Wotjobaluk class names Krokitch and Gamutch. The following is the system of the classes, totems, and subtotems in tabular form :—[4]

---

[1] J. Dawson, *Australian Aborigines*, p. 27.
[2] J. Dawson, *op. cit.* p. 52.
[3] A. W. Howitt, *Native Tribes of South-East Australia*, pp. 68 sq., 251.
[4] A. W. Howitt, *op. cit.* p. 123; Fison and Howitt, *Kamilaroi and Kurnai*, p. 168, on the authority of Mr. D. S. Stewart.

[TABLE

BUANDIK TRIBE

Classes and Totems

Classes.	Totems.	Subtotems.
Kroki	tea-tree (*werio*)	duck, wallaby, owl, crayfish, etc.
	an owl (*wirmal*)	?
	an edible root (*murna*)	bustard, quail, dolvich (a small kangaroo), etc.
	white crestless cockatoo (*karaal*)	kangaroo, she-oak, summer, sun, autumn, wind, etc.
Kumite	fish-hawk	smoke, honeysuckle tree (Banksia), etc.
	pelican	dog, blackwood tree (*Acacia melanoxylon*), fire, frost, etc.
	crow (*waa*)	lightning, thunder, rain, clouds, hail, winter, etc.
	black cockatoo (*wila*)	moon, stars, etc.
	a harmless snake (*karato*)	fish, eels, seals, stringbark tree, etc.

The usual law of exogamy prevailed as to the classes; that is, Kroki might only marry Kumite and *vice versa*. Descent of the class was in the female line.[1]

With regard to the Buandik classification of nature under the subtotems, and the relation in which a man stood to them and to his totem, Mr. D. S. Stewart says: "All this appears very arbitrary. I have tried in vain to find some reason for the arrangement. I asked, 'To what division does a bullock belong?' After a pause, came the answer, 'It eats grass: it is Boortwerio.'[2] I then said, 'A crayfish does not eat grass: why is it Boortwerio?' Then came the standing reason for all puzzling questions: 'That is what our fathers said it was.' A man does not kill, or use

Subtotems of the Buandik.

---

[1] A. W. Howitt, *Native Tribes of South-East Australia*, p. 251.

[2] Each totem name had the prefix *boort* meaning "dry," which in the table has been omitted for the sake of simplicity (A. W. Howitt, *Native Tribes of South-East Australia*, p. 124). *Werio* means tea-tree. Hence *Boortwerio* means "of the tea-tree totem." Similarly *Boortwa* means "of the crow totem."

as food, any of the animals of the same subdivision with himself, excepting when hunger compels ; and then they express sorrow for having to eat their *wingong* (friends) or *tumanang* (their flesh). When using the last word they touch their breasts, to indicate the close relationship, meaning almost a part of themselves. To illustrate :—One day one of the black fellows killed a crow. Three or four days afterwards a Boortwa (crow), named Larry, died. He had been ailing for some days, but the killing of his *wingong* hastened his death. A Kumite may kill and eat any *tuman* of the Kroki, and a Kroki may likewise use any *tuman* of the Kumite. In the blood revenge arrangement, these subdivisions bear a prominent part. Also, in cases of uncertain death, the *tuman* of the slayer will appear at the inquest."[1] This account of the relation in which a man stands to his *wingong* (friend) or *tuman* (flesh) clearly shows how closely he identifies himself with his totem animal, since the death of the animal hastens his own.

§ 9. *Tribes with Anomalous Class Systems and Male Descent*

Tribes with anomalous class systems and male descent. The Yerkla-mining.

We now pass to the consideration of tribes with anomalous class systems and male descent. The first to be noticed is the Yerkla-mining, a tribe situated on the coast of the Great Australian Bight at the boundary between South Australia and West Australia. From Eucla the territory of the tribe stretches westward for about forty miles and eastward for about a hundred. Inland the tribesmen range as far as they dare go, but the barren nature of the country in this direction has set limits to their wanderings ; and their imagination has peopled the great Nullarbor Plains, the southern edge of which is about twenty-five miles from the sea, with a gigantic and very dreadful snake, which devours every living thing and spares not even the stones and trees. The tribe calls itself Yerkla-mining, which means " men of the Morning Star."[2] They are reported to have the following totems :—

[1] D. S. Stewart, quoted by Fison and Howitt, *Kamilaroi and Kurnai*, p. 169.

[2] A. W. Howitt, *Native Tribes of South-East Australia*, pp. 65, 129 ; *id.*, "Notes on the Australian Class

Yerkla-mining Tribe

Totems

Budera	root
Budu	digger (one who digs)
Kura	dingo
Wenung	wombat

These totem clans appear to be localised; for the Budera and Budu are said to live inland in the cliff country, while the Kura and Wenung inhabit the coast.[1] Girls are betrothed in their childhood, and may be claimed by their husband at any time. It is the father who betrothes his daughter, but he may be overruled by his elder brother, especially if his brother has the support of the chief medicine-man of the local group. If a girl elopes with another man, the old men give chase and punish her severely when they catch her. Her lover has to fight her promised husband, if the latter desires it. The number of spears thrown at the culprit is determined by the medicine-men. A wife is bound to be faithful to her husband, and is rarely lent to a visitor. For repeated infidelities she may be killed. When a man dies, his widow goes to his brother.[2] *Marriage customs of the Yerkla-mining.*

In Yorke Peninsula of South Australia, between Spencer Gulf and the Gulf of St. Vincent, lives a tribe called the Narrang-ga. The tribe is divided into four classes, which bear the names of Emu, Red Kangaroo, Eagle-hawk, and Shark; and the tribal country is divided into four parts, each of which is inhabited by the people of one class only. The Emu people live in the north, the Red Kangaroo people in the east, the Eagle-hawk people in the west, and the Shark people in the south of the peninsula. Thus the class *The Narrang-ga tribe, its classes, totems, and local divisions.*

Systems," *Journal of the Anthropological Institute*, xii. (1883) p. 508. *Yerkla* is "the morning star," and *mining* is "man" or "men."

[1] A. W. Howitt, *Native Tribes of South-East Australia*, p. 129.

[2] A. W. Howitt, *op. cit.* pp. 257 *sq.* For the reported marriage rules of the totem clans in this tribe, see A. W. Howitt, "Notes on the Australian Class Systems," *Journal of the Anthropological Institute*, xii. (1883) pp. 508-510; also above, p. 70. Dr. Howitt's authority for the rules was Mr. Elphinstone Roe, formerly telegraph operator at Eucla. As Dr. Howitt did not repeat these rules in his volume *Native Tribes of South-East Australia*, he seems to have entertained well-founded doubts as to their correctness. I now follow him in omitting them.

organisation has become completely localised: the class divisions coincide with the local divisions.[1] Each class includes, or used to include, a number of totems, which are shown in the following table:—

NARRANG-GA TRIBE

Classes, Totems, and Local Divisions

Classes.	Totems.	Local Divisions.
Emu (*Kari*)	swallow, mullet, wild turkey, magpie, mopoke, lark, dingo	Kurnara—the northern part of the peninsula south of Wallaroo, Kadina, and Clinton.
Red Kangaroo (*Waui*)	all totems together with the class name are extinct	Windera—the eastern part of the peninsula.
Eagle-hawk (*Wiltu*)	wombat, wallaby, kangaroo (*nantu*), seal (*multa*), crow (*gua*)	Wari—the western part of the peninsula.
Shark (*Wilthuthu*)	wild goose, pelican, butter-fish, sting-ray, whiting	Dilpa—the extreme (southern) part of the peninsula.

Marriage and descent among the Narrang-ga. It will be observed that the four classes all bear the names of animals; hence it might, as Dr. Howitt suggests,[2] be better to call them primary totems than classes. With regard to the rules of marriage and descent in the Narrang-ga tribe Dr. Howitt says: "The restrictions which affect marriage are neither class, totem, nor locality, but relationship. The class and totem names pass from father to child, the totems having, as in some other cases of male descent, become attached to localities instead of being scattered over the tribal country. In tabulating the marriages and descents in this tribe from the data given by the old men, I found that descent is in the male line, and that a man might *Marriage of cousins forbidden.* marry a woman even of his own totem. As in all tribes, sister-marriage was strictly forbidden. This rule, of course,

[1] A. W. Howitt, *Native Tribes of South-East Australia*, pp. 67, 129 sq. The tribe was formerly called Turra by Dr. Howitt. See Fison and Howitt, *Kamilaroi and Kurnai*, pp. 284 sq.

[2] A. W. Howitt, *Native Tribes of South-East Australia*, p. 259.

included the father's brother's daughter and the mother's sister's daughter, but a prohibition also attached to the daughter of the mother's brother and of the father's sister."[1] In other words, the Narrang-ga, like the Kulin, the Wotjobaluk, and some Queensland tribes,[2] forbade all marriages between first cousins, whether the cousins were the children of two brothers, or of two sisters, or of a brother and a sister. According to old men whose memory went back to the time before Yorke Peninsula was occupied by the whites, the Narrang-ga used to wage wars with other tribes and capture women. "Men were allowed to keep women whom they captured, because there was no law which restricted a man to any particular class or totem."[3]

Such is the account of the marriage rules and totemic system of the Narrang-ga which Dr. Howitt gives in his great work, *Native Tribes of South-East Australia*. If the account is correct, as we may assume it to be, the social system of the Narrang-ga is very anomalous, for the classes, if they are indeed classes and not totem clans, have become completely localised, and neither class nor totem has any influence on marriage. But in an earlier work Dr. Howitt gave a somewhat different account of the social system of the Narrang-ga or Turra tribe (as he then called it), referring to the Rev. W. Julius Kühn, of the Boorkooyanna Mission, as his authority.[4] As that earlier account, where it differs from the later, has not, so far as I know, been withdrawn by Dr. Howitt, I think it well to repeat it here for comparison with the other. It is possible that Mr. Kühn's statements refer to a state of things which has since passed away. According to him, the Turra (that is the Narrang-ga) tribe was divided into two exogamous classes, Eagle-hawk and Seal, with totem clans arranged as follows :—[5]

Different account of the class system of the Narrang-ga or Turra tribe given by Mr. W. J. Kühn.

---

[1] A. W. Howitt, *Native Tribes of South-East Australia*, pp. 258 *sq.*
[2] See above, pp. 438 *sq.*, 449 *sq.*, 459.
[3] A. W. Howitt, *op. cit.* p. 260.
[4] See Fison and Howitt, *Kamilaroi and Kurnai* (Melbourne, etc., 1880), pp. 284-287. Dr. Howitt's later inquiries seem to have been made by or for him in 1887 and 1899. In the latter year (1899) Mr. F. J. Gillen resided for some time at Moonta and had opportunities of investigation. Another of Dr. Howitt's informants was Mr. Sutton, manager of the aboriginal station in Yorke Peninsula. See A. W. Howitt, *Native Tribes of South-East Australia*, pp. 67 note [1], 259.
[5] Fison and Howitt, *Kamilaroi and Kurnai*, pp. 284 *sq.*

Classes.	Totems.
Eagle-hawk (*Wiltu*)	wombat, wallaby, kangaroo, iguana, wombat-snake, bandicoot, black bandicoot, crow, rock wallaby, emu.
Seal (*Multa*)	wildgoose, butter-fish, mullet, schnapper, shark, salmon.

"The classes are exogamous, but any totem of one class may intermarry with any totem of the other class; the children take the father's class and totem.

<small>Marriage customs of the Narrang-ga or Turra tribe.</small> "Girls are given in marriage by their parents, whose consent is essential; wives are also obtained by exchange of female relatives. If the parents refused their consent, it might be that a young man would run off with a girl. The parents would search for him for the purpose of killing him, and the penalty as to the girl, if caught, was death, which was inflicted by the parents or nearest relatives. The man was generally protected by his class division. When opinion was divided as to this, a fight might take place to decide his right to keep the girl. For instance, if a Wiltu-wortu [Eagle-hawk-wombat] man were to elope with a Multa-worrimbru [Seal-butter-fish] woman, he would be protected by the Wiltu-wortu men. But a Wiltu-wortu man would not be permitted to keep a Wiltu-wortu woman as his wife. Even if he were to capture one she would be taken from him, and if she persisted in following him she would be killed. When a female was captured in war, she was the property of her captor;[1] but the section of the tribe to which she belonged would fight for her recovery. Failing to do that, they would endeavour to capture a woman from the other section of the tribe, and keep her.

"Women were bound to be faithful to their husbands, also the husbands to their wives. Whoever was guilty of unfaithfulness was liable to be punished by death at the hands of the class of the offender.

---

[1] "It follows from the preceding statement that it would only be the case if she were of some class from which he might legally take a wife."

"When the two subtribes Wiltu [Eagle-hawk] and Multa [Seal] met for a grand corrobboree, the old men took any of the young wives of the other class for the time, and the young men of the Wiltu exchanged wives with those of the Multa, and *vice versa*, but only for a time, and in this the men were not confined to any particular totem. Yet at other times men did not lend their wives to brothers or friends."[1]

According to this account, the social system of the Turra or Narrang-ga tribe was a normal one, consisting of two exogamous classes with totem clans and descent of the class and of the totem in the paternal line. Nothing is said as to the localisation of the classes in separate districts. And the list of totems differs in several particulars from that given by Dr. Howitt in his later work. It will be observed that Seal (*Multa*), which, according to Mr. Kühn, was one of the two exogamous classes, was a totem of the Eagle-hawk class according to Dr. Howitt's later account, and further that Emu and Shark, which were classes according to Dr. Howitt, were totems according to Mr. Kühn. How these discrepancies are to be explained, I cannot say; but I have thought it right to call attention to them.

Discrepancies between Dr. Howitt and Mr. Kühn in their accounts of the Narrang-ga or Turra tribe.

On the opposite side of St. Vincent Gulf from the Narrang-ga lived the Narrinyeri, a tribe of which a valuable account has been given by the Rev. George Taplin.[2] Their country extended along the south-eastern coast of South Australia from Cape Jervis to Lacepede Bay, and inland to a point about thirty miles above the place where the Murray River flows into Lake Alexandrina.[3] The tribal territory was divided into eighteen districts, of which fourteen were inhabited each by the members of a single totemic clan. Three of the districts were inhabited by three clans each, and one district was inhabited by two. Thus the process of localising each totem clan in a single district was nearly, though not quite, complete.[4] According to Mr. Taplin, each

The Narrinyeri, their totem clans and local districts.

---

[1] Fison and Howitt, *Kamilaroi and Kurnai*, pp. 285 *sq.*
[2] Rev. George Taplin, "The Narrinyeri," in *Native Tribes of South Australia* (Adelaide, 1879), pp. 1-156. See also Mr. Taplin's account of the tribe in E. M. Curr's *The Australian Race*, ii. 242-267.
[3] *Native Tribes of South Australia*, p. 1; A. W. Howitt, *Native Tribes of South-East Australia*, p. 68.
[4] A. W. Howitt, *op. cit.* p. 130.

of these eighteen local clans or, as he calls them, tribes "is regarded by them as a family, every member of which is a blood relation, and therefore between individuals of the same tribe no marriage can take place. Every tribe has its *ngaitye* or tutelary genius or tribal symbol in the shape of some bird, beast, fish, reptile, insect, or substance."[1] But while marriage with a woman of the same district was prohibited wherever the district was inhabited by a single totemic clan or (as Mr. Taplin calls it) tribe, the custom was different where three such clans, or perhaps rather subclans, dwelt in one district. In this last case the three clans or subclans were allowed to intermarry with each other just as if they inhabited separate districts. But this relaxation of the rule of local exogamy was not extended to the case where two clans or subclans dwelt together in one district; both these clans or subclans were for purposes of marriage treated as one, and all marriages between them were prohibited.[2] Children belonged to the local clan of their father, not of their mother, and a man's sons always inherited their father's property.[3]

The following is the list which Dr. Howitt gives of the clans and totems of the Narrinyeri :—[4]

[1] G. Taplin, "The Narrinyeri," *Native Tribes of South Australia*, p. 1. Elsewhere the same writer says, "The Narrinyeri are exogamous, and never marry in their own tribe" (p. 12).

[2] A. W. Howitt, *Native Tribes of South-East Australia*, p. 260. In Dr. Howitt's statement, here referred to, the words "or more" appear to introduce confusion and contradiction. I have accordingly omitted them.

[3] G. Taplin, "The Narrinyeri," in *Native Tribes of South Australia*, p. 12; A. W. Howitt, *Native Tribes of South-East Australia*, p. 68.

[4] A. W. Howitt, *Native Tribes of South-East Australia*, p. 131. Compare G. Taplin, "The Narrinyeri," in *Native Tribes of South Australia*, p. 2; *id.*, in E. M. Curr's *The Australian Race*, ii. 244. In addition to Mr. George Taplin's published account of the tribe Dr. Howitt had at his disposal some facts and explanations furnished to him both by Mr. George Taplin and by the late Mr. T. W. Taplin (*Native Tribes of South-East Australia*, p. 68).

[TABLE

NARRINYERI TRIBE

Clans and Totems

Name of Clan.[1]	English of the Name.	Totem.	
Raminyeri[2]	*rumaii*, the west	*wirulde* or *tangari*	wattle gum
Tanganarin	where shall we go?	*mangurit-puri* or *nori*	pelican
Kandarl-inyeri	whales	*kandarli*	whales
Lungundararn	seaside men	*tyellityelli*	fern
Turarorn	coot men	*turi* or *tettituri*	coot
Park-inyeri	deep water	*kunguldi*	butter-fish
Kanmeraorn	mullet men	*kanmeri*	mullet
Kaikalab-inyeri	watching	(1) *ngulgar-inyeri* (2) *pingi*	bull-ant a water-weed
Mungul-inyeri	thick or muddy water	*wanyi*	chocolate sheldrake (mountain duck)
Rangul-inyeri	howling dog	*turiit-pani*	dark-coloured dingo
Karat-inyeri	signal smoke	*turiit-pani*	light-coloured dingo
Pilt-inyeri	ants	(1) *maninki* (2) *pomeri* (3) *kallkalli*	leech cat-fish a lace-lizard
Talk-inyeri	fulness	(1) ? (2) ? (3) *tiyawi*	leech cat-fish a lace-lizard
Wulloke	Artemus sp. the wood-sparrow	(1) ? (2) ? (3) ?	leech cat-fish a lace-lizard
Karowalli	gone over there	*waiyi*	whip-snake
Punguratpula	place of bulrushes	*peldi*	musk duck
Wel-inyeri	belonging to itself or by itself	(1) *nakare* (2) *ngumundi*	black duck black snake with red belly
Luth-inyeri	belonging to the sun-rising	(1) *kungari* (2) *ngeraki* (3) *kikinummi*	black swan seal black snake with grey belly
Wunyakulde	corruption of *walkande*, the north	*nakkare*	black duck
Ngrangatari or Gurrangwari	at the south-west or at the south-east	*waukawiye*	kangaroo rat

On this list Dr. Howitt observes: "The names of the clans are such as might have been at one time totems. For

---

[1] The postfix *yeri* or *inyeri*, "belonging to," is omitted from some of the names.

[2] In his table Dr. Howitt gives the name of this clan as Bamir-inyeri. But elsewhere (p. 132) he gives the name as Raminyeri, and as this form is supported by Mr. G. Taplin (*Native Tribes of South Australia*, p. 2; E. M. Curr, *The Australian Race*, ii. 244), I conclude it to be the more correct.

Names of the Narrinyeri clans explained.

instance, Piltinyeri, which means 'belonging to ants,' has three subtotems—leech, cat-fish, and lace-lizard. This is analogous to the system of the neighbouring Buandik, and to the totems and subtotems of the Wotjobaluk. In others the name is strictly local, and resembles the local designations of the Narrang-ga and of the Kurnai."[1] Further explanations of the origin and meaning of these clan names are given by Dr. Howitt as follows: "The Raminyeri are the most westerly clan of the Narrinyeri. The Tanganarin occupy the country at the bend of the Murray mouth. Tradition says that the tribe was nonplussed when they came down the river and found that it went into the sea, and said one to another, 'Where shall we go?' The Kandarl-inyeri inhabit a tract of country near the Murray mouth. Whales were frequently stranded on their coast, being possibly flurried by getting into the volume of fresh water of the Murray River. The Park-inyeri owned the deepest part of the Coorong. The Kaikalab-inyeri occupied a promontory running partly across the Coorong, and were in a good position to watch all that went to and fro. The Rangul-inyeri and the Karat-inyeri had a country infested by wild dogs. The Karat-inyeri possess a bold bluff on the shores of Lake Alexandrina, which was a good position for making and observing signals, and at this spot a lighthouse has since been built. The Pilt-inyeri is the name by which this clan is usually known, Talk-inyeri and Wulloke being in some sort subclans. Their arrangement of totem[s] is singular, there being three kinds of leeches, cat-fish, and lace-lizards, and each one of these has a distinct name. *Maninki* is a large dark-coloured leech; *pomeri* is the largest kind of cat-fish, and also is the name of cat-fish generally. *Kallkalli* is the dark-coloured lace-lizard. These are the totems belonging to the Pilt-inyeri. The *tiyawi*, belonging to the Talk-inyeri, is a spotted lace-lizard. The *warrangumbi* belonging to the Wulloke is a very large species of lace-lizard. The Luth-inyeri call themselves by this name, but their neighbours call them Kalatin-yeri. *Kalatin* means shining, this clan having grassy slopes that are visible at a long distance when the sun shines on them."[2]

[1] A. W. Howitt, *Native Tribes of South-East Australia*, pp. 130 *sq.*
[2] A. W. Howitt, *op. cit.* p. 132.

Among the Narrinyeri the totem as well as the local clan passed by inheritance from father to child, who, when it was an animal, might not kill or eat it, although another person might do so.[1] On this subject the Rev. George Taplin wrote as follows: "There is another superstition believed in by the Narrinyeri. Every tribe has its *ngaitye*; that is, some animal which they regard as a sort of good genius, who takes an interest in their welfare—something like the North American Indian totem. Some will have a snake, some a wild dog, some a bird, and some an insect. No man or woman will kill her *ngaitye*, except it happens to be an animal which is good for food, when they have no objection to eating them. Nevertheless, they will be very careful to destroy all the remains, lest an enemy might get hold of them, and by his sorcery cause the *ngaitye* to grow in the inside of the eater, and cause his death. I know several persons whose *ngaityar* are different kinds of snakes, consequently they do not like to kill them; but when they meet with them they catch them, pull out their teeth, or else sew up their mouths, and keep them in a basket as pets. Once I knew of a man catching his *ngaitye* in the person of a large female tiger snake, and, after pulling out the teeth, he put it in a basket, and hung it up in his wurley [hut]. The next morning they found that she had brought forth sixteen young ones. This increase of family was too much for those blacks to whom she did not stand in the relation of *ngaitye*, so they killed them all. . . . One day a couple of wild dogs came on a predatory expedition into my neighbourhood, so I shot one of them; and immediately after was reproached very much for hurting the *ngaitye* of two or three blacks residing here. People are sometimes named from their *ngaitye*; as, for instance, Taowinyeri, the person whose *ngaitye* is Taow; the native name of the guana."[2] Again, speaking of the same subject, Mr. Taplin says: "I then found in the course of my reading and observation that there are superstitions and customs amongst the Narrinyeri identical even in name with the Samoans and the Tanese.

<small>Narrinyeri totems (*ngaitye*).</small>

<small>Similarity of the Narrinyeri beliefs to those of the Samoans.</small>

---

[1] A. W. Howitt, *Native Tribes of South-East Australia*, p. 147, referring to Mr. F. W. Taplin as his authority.

[2] G. Taplin, "The Narrinyeri," in *Native Tribes of South Australia*, pp. 63 *sq.*

For instance, every Samoan has, or had, according to Dr. George Turner, his *aitu*. This consisted in some fish, or bird, or insect, which was the totem of his family, and he supposed that if he ate the *aitu* it would form in his inside and kill him. Well, the Narrinyeri believe that every tribe has its *ngaitye* (observe the similarity of the word to *aitu*), and this *ngaitye* is the totem of the tribe, and they suppose that if they eat a portion of the *ngaitye*, and an enemy of the tribe gets hold of the remainder, he can make it the means of powerful sorcery, and cause it to grow in the inside of the eater of it. Therefore when a man eats of his tribe's *ngaitye*, he is careful either to eat it all or else to conceal and destroy the remains. I remember an old man killing a large mygale spider, which was the *ngaitye* of his tribe, and, to prevent mischief, he immediately swallowed it."[1] This belief that the totem animal may grow up inside of the person who eats it has already met us in South-East Australia.[2] Such beliefs may have a bearing on the origin of totemism, if I am right in thinking that totemism was at first a theory devised to explain the origin of conception.[3] The Narrinyeri word for a totem (*ngaitye*) means literally "friend." All the members of a totemic clan were regarded as blood relations.[4]

Personal totems of Narrinyeri medicine-men.

In the Narrinyeri tribe, at least in that part of the tribe which lived about Encounter Bay, every medicine-man had a personal totem (*ngaitye*) or guardian spirit in the shape of an animal or vegetable which he regarded as his friend or protector. These totems differed with the individuals. One man would have a snake, another an ant, another seaweed, and so on. The totem was his only remedy for every disease. When a patient came to him the doctor would suck the part affected and then spit out his totem or some part of it. For example, if his totem was seaweed, he would spit out seaweed. One doctor in this tribe used to cure large boils, which the natives were very subject to, by sucking out the

---

[1] Rev. George Taplin, "Further Notes on the Mixed Races of Australia," *Journal of the Anthropological Institute*, iv. (1875) p. 53. As to the Samoan belief see above, pp. 17 *sq*. The resemblance between the words *aitu* and *ngaitye* is probably accidental.
[2] Above, pp. 428 *sq*.
[3] See above, pp. 157-159.
[4] Rev. George Taplin, in E. M. Curr's *The Australian Race*, ii. 244.

matter and swallowing it, alleging that it was his friend or protector (*ngaitye*).¹ Thus it appears that the Narrinyeri applied the same name *ngaitye* " friend " to their clan totems and to their personal totems or guardian spirits, which shows how closely the two different sorts of totems were associated in their minds.

In the Narrinyeri tribe a girl was given in marriage, usually at a very early age, sometimes by her father, but generally by her brother. "The ceremony," we are told, "is very simple, and with great propriety may be considered an exchange, for no man can obtain a wife unless he can promise to give his sister or other relative in exchange. The marriages are always between persons of different tribes, and never in the same tribe. Should the father be living he may give his daughter away, but generally she is the gift of the brother."² "It is considered disgraceful for a woman to take a husband who has given no other woman for her. But yet the right to give a woman away is often purchased from her nearest male relative by those who have no sisters. Of course this amounts to the same thing. In most instances a brother or a first cousin gives a girl away in exchange for a wife for himself."³ The first inquiry with regard to a proposed marriage was, whether there existed any tie of kinship between the parties, for any such tie was a bar to their union. The Narrinyeri were very strict on this point. They had a very great aversion to the marriage even of second cousins.⁴ "Marriage by elopement occurred, but the woman was looked on with disfavour, because there had been no exchange of a sister

Marriage customs of the Narrinyeri.

Aversion to marriages of cousins.

Elopement.

---

¹ H. E. A. Meyer, "Manners and Customs of the Aborigines of the Encounter Bay Tribe," in *Native Tribes of South Australia*, pp. 197 *sq*.

² Rev. H. E. A. Meyer, quoted by G. Taplin, "The Narrinyeri," *Native Tribes of South Australia*, p. 10; A. W. Howitt, *Native Tribes of South-East Australia*, p. 260. By "tribe" Mr. Meyer no doubt means a local division, which, among the Narrinyeri, as we have seen (p. 477), generally coincides with a totem clan.

³ Rev. G. Taplin, in E. M. Curr's *The Australian Race*, ii. 245.

⁴ G. Taplin, "The Narrinyeri," in *Native Tribes of South Australia*, p. 12. Elsewhere Mr. Taplin writes: "The Narrinyeri never marry one who belongs to the same *ngaitye* or totem—that is, of the same clan; neither do they allow near relations to marry, although of different clans. This is always regarded as of the first importance. Cousins never marry" (in E. M. Curr's *The Australian Race*, ii. 245).

for her. In the cases of elopement the young man might call in the aid of his comrades, who then had the right of access to the girl, and his male relatives would only defend him from the girl's kindred on the condition of access to her. In regard to this, I may point out here that the initiated youth, during the time he was *narumbe*, had complete licence as to the younger women, and could even approach those of his own class and totem. This shows a survival of older customs, and at the same time marks the distinction between the mere inter-sexual intercourse and the proprietary right of marriage."[1]

The condition of *narumbe* or noviciate, to which Dr. Howitt refers, lasted in the Narrinyeri tribe until the young men's beards had been thrice plucked out and had thrice grown again to a length of two inches. During all this time they were forbidden to eat any food which belonged to women, and twenty different kinds of game besides were tabooed to them. It was thought that if they ate any of these forbidden foods, they would grow ugly and break out in sores, and that their hair would turn prematurely grey. Only the animals most difficult to procure were assigned for their subsistence. Everything which the novices possessed or obtained became itself *narumbe* or sacred from the touch of women. Even the bird hit by their waddy, or the kangaroo speared by their spear, or the fish taken by their hook was forbidden to all females, and that, too, even when the weapons had been wielded by the hands of others. Yet in spite of this, and although they were not permitted to take a wife until the time of their noviciate had expired, the novices were allowed the privilege of promiscuous intercourse with the younger portion of the other sex. A single clan could not initiate its youths without the aid of other clans. The Narrinyeri practised neither circumcision nor the knocking out of teeth at initiation.[2]

Among the Narrinyeri there is a family which performs, or used to perform, a magical ceremony to ensure a supply

---

[1] A. W. Howitt, *Native Tribes of South-East Australia*, p. 261.

[2] G. Taplin, "The Narrinyeri," *Native Tribes of South Australia*, pp. 15-18; *id.*, in E. M. Curr's *The Australian Race*, ii. 253-255; A. W. Howitt, *op. cit.* pp. 673-675.

of water and fish. At a certain point of Lake Victoria, in the country of the tribe, when the water at long intervals sinks very low, the stump of a tree emerges from its surface. Whenever this happens, it is the duty of a man of a certain family to anoint the stump with grease and red ochre; for otherwise they think that the lake would dry up and the supply of fish be cut off. The duty passes by inheritance from father to son.[1] This custom reminds us of the magical ceremonies (*intichiuma*) performed for the multiplication of plants, the procuring of rain, and so forth, by totem clans in Central Australia.

Magical ceremonies performed by the Narrinyeri in connection with water and fish.

Another ceremony observed by the Narrinyeri to ensure success in the chase has been described by Mr. George Taplin. He says: "The remains of a kind of sacrifice is found amongst them. When they go on a great kangaroo hunt they knock over the first wallaby which comes near enough to the hunters. A fire is then kindled and the wallaby placed on it, and as the smoke ascends a kind of chant is sung by the men, while they stamp on the ground and lift up their weapons towards heaven. This is done to secure success in hunting, but the reason of the custom they know not."[2] The Narrinyeri also practised some curious rites at the cutting up of an emu; and though these rites like the preceding ceremonies may not be directly connected with their totems, yet a description of them may find a place here, since they illustrate the mental attitude of the natives towards animals, and so indirectly throw light on the origin of totemism. "Among the Narrinyeri, when an emu is killed, it is first plucked, then partly roasted, and the skin taken off. The oldest men of the clan, accompanied by the young men and boys, then carry it to a retired spot away from the camp, all women and children being warned not to come near them. One of the old men undertakes the dissection of the bird, and squats near it, with the rest standing round. He first cuts a slice off the front of one of the legs, and another piece off the back of the leg or thigh; the carcase is turned over, and similar pieces cut off the other leg. The piece off the front of the legs is called

Ceremonies observed by the Narrinyeri to ensure success in the chase and at cutting up of an emu.

---

[1] A. W. Howitt, *Native Tribes of South-East Australia*, pp. 399 sq.

[2] G. Taplin, in E. M. Curr's *The Australian Race*, ii. 252.

ngemperumi; that off the back of the leg or thigh, *pundarauk*. The bird is then opened and a morsel of fat taken from the inside and laid with the sacred or *narumbe* portions already cut off on some grass. The general cutting up of the whole body is then commenced, and whenever the operator is about to break a bone, he calls the attention of the bystanders, who, when the bone snaps, leap and shout and run about, returning in a few minutes only to go through the same performance when another bone is broken. When the carcase has been cut up into convenient pieces for distribution, it is carried by all to the camp, and may then be eaten by men, women, and children, but the men must first blacken their faces and sides with charcoal. The sacred pieces *ngemperumi* and *pundarauk* can only be eaten by the very old men, and on no account even touched by women or young men. If the men did not leap and yell when a bone is broken, they think their bones would rot in them; and the same if any but the deputed person should break a bone. This ceremony was practised by all the clans of the Narrinyeri."[1] These curious rites seem to imply a belief in a sympathetic connection between the bones of men and the bones of the game which they kill and eat. Many savages superstitiously abstain from breaking the bones of the animals which they eat, and some will not suffer dogs to gnaw them.[2] Perhaps the key, or at least one key, to such superstitions is furnished by the Narrinyeri practice, the motive for which seems to be a belief that the breaking of the animal's bones will sympathetically break the bones of the person who eats its flesh, unless he proves his bodily frame to be quite intact by skipping and leaping at the critical moment.

Classificatory terms of relationship among the Narrinyeri.

The Narrinyeri had the classificatory system of relationship. Thus in the generation above his own a man applied the same term *nanghai* to his father, to his father's brothers, and to the husbands of his mother's sisters; and he applies the same term *nainkana* to his mother, to his mother's sisters, and to the wives of his father's brothers. In his own

---

[1] A. W. Howitt, *Native Tribes of South-East Australia*, p. 763, referring to Mr. F. W. Taplin as his authority.

[2] *The Golden Bough*, Second Edition, ii. 416 *sq*.

generation he applied the same term *gelanaui* to his brothers, to the sons of his father's brothers, and to the sons of his mother's sisters. In the generation below his own he applied the same term *porlean* to his sons, to his brothers' sons, and to the sons of his wife's sisters. A woman applied the same term *porlean* to her sons, to her sisters' sons, and to the sons of her husband's brothers.¹ As commonly happens under the classificatory system of relationship, the Narrinyeri had quite different terms for elder and younger brothers and sisters. Thus a man said, *gelanowe*, "my elder brother," but *tarte*, "my younger brother": he said, *maranowi*, "my elder sister," but *tarte*, "my younger sister."² This shews that the Narrinyeri, like many other tribes with the classificatory system of relationship, carefully distinguish between elder brothers and elder sisters, but confound younger brothers and younger sisters under the same name.

The general account which the Rev. George Taplin gives of the classificatory system of relationship among the Narrinyeri applies, *mutatis mutandis*, to most other peoples who live under the same system. As a clear statement of the relationships which flow from the system in so many peoples it deserves to be quoted. Mr. Taplin writes thus:—³

"The following is the system of relationship amongst the Narrinyeri:—

"1. I being male, the children of my brothers are my sons and daughters, the same as my own children are; while the children of my sisters are my nephews and nieces. The grandchildren of my brothers are called *maiyarare* [which is also the term applied by me to my own grandchildren]; while the grandchildren of my sisters are called *mutthari*.

"2. I being female, the children of my sisters are my sons and daughters, the same as my own sons and daughters are; while the children of my brothers are my nephews and

---

¹ A. W. Howitt, "Australian Group-Relationships," *Journal of the Royal Anthropological Institute*, xxxvii. (1907) pp. 287 *sq.* Compare Rev. George Taplin, "The Narrinyeri," *Native Tribes of South Australia*, pp. 48-53.

² Rev. George Taplin, "The Narrinyeri," *Native Tribes of South Australia*, p. 52.

³ Rev. G. Taplin, *op. cit.* pp. 49 *sq.* The words printed in square brackets in the first numbered paragraph have been interpolated by me. See Rev. G. Taplin, *op. cit.* p. 52.

nieces; consequently it is common to hear a native address as *nanghy*, or my father, the man who is his father's brother, as well as his own father; and as *nainkowa*, or my mother, the woman who is his mother's sister, as well as his own mother.

"3. All my father's brothers are my fathers, but all my father's sisters are my aunts. But my father's elder brothers have the distinguishing title of *ngoppano*, and his younger have the title of *wyatte*. These terms would be used in the presence of my own father. The name for aunt is *barno*.

"4. All my mother's sisters are my mothers, but all my mother's brothers are my uncles. *Wanowe* is the word for uncle.

"5. The children of my father's brothers are my brothers and sisters, and so are the children of my mother's sisters; but the children of my father's sisters, and those of my mother's brothers, are my cousins. The word for cousin is *nguyanowe*.

"6. I being male, the children of my male and female cousins are called by the same name as the grandchildren of my sisters, *mutthari*.

"7. The brothers of my grandfathers, and those of my grandmothers, and also their sisters, are my grandfathers and grandmothers. Whatever title my father's father has, his brothers have, and so of the sisters of my mother's mother.

"8. My elder brother is called *galanowe*, and my younger brother is called *tarte*. My elder sister is called *maranowe*, and my younger sister is called *tarte*. There is no collective term by which I can designate all my brothers and sisters, whether older or younger than myself."

The Murring, particularly the Yuin tribes.

The last group of tribes with an anomalous class system and male descent which we shall notice are the Murring and more especially the Yuin tribes. Their country is far away from that of the Narrinyeri whom we have just been considering; for while the Narrinyeri inhabit the coast of South Australia, the Murring inhabit the coast of New South Wales from its extreme south point at Cape Howe northwards to the Shoalhaven River. Inland their territory extended from the sea to the slopes of the mountains which run parallel to the coast.¹

Among the Yuin the class system is in a decadent condition; indeed they are said to have neither class names nor even traces of them. But there are many totems scattered over the country, and their names are inherited from the father, not from the mother. "The totem name was called *budjan*, and it was said to be more like *joïa*, or magic, than a name; and it was in one sense a secret name, for with it an enemy might cause injury to its bearer by magic. Thus very few people knew the totem names of others, the name being told to a youth by his father at his initiation." In many cases Dr. Howitt found that men had two totem names (*budjan*), one hereditary and the other bestowed by a medicine-man at the initiation rites.²

Totems (*budjan*) of the Yuin, both hereditary and personal.

For example, Dr. Howitt knew a man whose clan totem, inherited from his father, was kangaroo, but whose personal totem was wombat. This personal totem had been assigned to him at initiation by the medicine-man, who warned him not to eat it. Another Yuin man, whose hereditary clan totem was kangaroo, believed that the animal gave him warnings of danger by hopping towards him, and he said that it would not be right for a man of the kangaroo (*kaualgar*) totem to kill a kangaroo. Similarly, another man of the black duck totem thought that black ducks warned him against enemies and other perils, therefore he would not eat the birds. This Black Duck man told Dr. Howitt that once while he was asleep a man of the lace-lizard totem sent a lace-lizard to him, and that the reptile went down his throat and almost ate his totem, the black duck, which was in his breast, so that he nearly died. This narrative is very instructive because it shews, as Dr. Howitt points out, that the totem is conceived as forming part of the man, residing in his body. We need not wonder therefore that among the Yuin it was a rule that a man should neither kill nor eat his totem (*budjan* or *jimbir*).³ Hence too we

Belief that a man's totemic animal resides in his body.

¹ A. W. Howitt, *Native Tribes of South-East Australia*, pp. 81 *sq.*
² A. W. Howitt, *op. cit.* p. 133.
³ A. W. Howitt, *op. cit.* p. 147.

490 TOTEMISM IN SOUTH-EASTERN AUSTRALIA CHAP.

List of Yuin totems

can understand why it was that at one of the dances in the initiation ceremonies, when the totem name "Brown Snake" was shouted, a medicine-man produced from his mouth a small live brown snake, which his tribesmen believed to be his familiar.[1] The following is the list of totems which Dr. Howitt obtained from Yuin old men :—[2]

YUIN TRIBE

Totems

kangaroo	bream
emu	black snake
bush-rat	black duck
kangaroo-rat	a small owl (*jaruat*)
dingo	a small owl (*tiska*)
eagle-hawk	fat
crow	Echidna histrix (?) (*janan-gabatch*)
pelican	grey magpie
white-breasted cormorant	bandicoot
lace-lizard	water-hen
brown snake	*gunimbil* (?)

Sex-totems. Like various other tribes of South-East Australia the Yuin had sex-totems. With them the bat and the emu-wren were the "brothers" of all the men, and the tree-creeper (*Climacteris scandens*) was the "sister" of all the women.[3]

Local exogamy among the Yuin. Although the clan totems of the Yuin were decadent, they still regulated marriage, for no person might marry a person of the same totem as himself. But in addition to exogamy of the totem clan the Yuin, like the tribes of Western Victoria and coastal tribes such as the Narrinyeri and the Kurnai, observed a rule of local exogamy; for no man might marry a woman who inhabited the same district as himself. The principles of marriage were thus laid down for his son's

---

[1] A. W. Howitt, "On Australian Medicine Men," *Journal of the Anthropological Institute*, xvi. (1887) pp. 43 *sq.*

[2] A. W. Howitt, *Native Tribes of South-East Australia*, p. 133.

[3] A. W. Howitt, "On the Migrations of the Kurnai Ancestors," *Journal of the Anthropological Institute*, xv. (1886) p. 416; *id.*, *Native Tribes of South-East Australia*, p. 150.

guidance by an old Braidwood man : "No one should marry so as to mix the same blood, but he must take a woman of a different name (*mura*, totem) than his own; and besides this, he must go for a wife to a place as far as possible from his own place." This man, being of Braidwood, went for a wife to Moruya, and he had to give a sister in exchange to his wife's brother. The people who got their living by climbing trees for game in the forests of the interior had to go down to the sea-coast and obtain wives from the people who maintained themselves by fishing; and similarly the fisher-folk married the sisters of the tree-climbers or waddymen, as they were called. The limits within which wives were thus procured by the exchange of sisters is indicated by the round which a boy's tooth, knocked out at the initiation ceremonies of the tribe, used to make, being passed on from one headman to another. In old times the limits were Bem Lake, Delegate, Tumut, Braidwood, and so on to Shoalhaven, and thence following the sea-coast to Bem Lake. As Bem Lake was within the territory of the Kurnai tribe, its inclusion seems to show that the Yuin intermarried with the Kurnai.[1] Among the Yuin the father's sister's child was free to marry the mother's brother's child: in other words, marriage was permitted between first cousins, provided that the two were the children of a brother and a sister respectively and that they belonged to the proper intermarrying districts.[2]

Cousin marriages among the Yuin.

In the Yuin tribe marriages were arranged solely by the father. They said that the child belongs to the father, because his wife merely takes care of his children for him, and that therefore he can do what he likes with his daughter. Often a father would betroth his daughter in her infancy; in that case, when she was grown up, her future husband claimed her and gave a sister in exchange to his wife's brother. Sometimes the fathers would arrange matches between their children at the end of the initiation ceremonies, when the whole intermarrying community met.[3] If a man ran away with a woman whom he might not lawfully marry,

Betrothal among the Yuin.

Punishment of unlawful marriages.

[1] A. W. Howitt, *Native Tribes of South-East Australia*, pp. 133, 261, 262.
[2] A. W. Howitt, *op. cit.* p. 262.
[3] A. W. Howitt, *op. cit.* pp. 262, 263.

all the other men would pursue him, and if they caught him and he refused to give the woman up, the medicine-man of the place would probably say, "This man has done very wrong, you must kill him." Then some one would thrust a spear into him, his kinsmen not daring to interfere, lest they should meet the same fate.¹ A widow went to her husband's brother, if he had one. If not, her male kindred gave her to a man of their choice. In these tribes men did not lend their wives to their brothers. And among them the common rule of aboriginal Australian society which forbade a man to hold any direct communication with his wife's mother was very strictly observed. He might not look at her nor even in her direction. If so much as his shadow fell on his mother-in-law, he would have to leave his wife, and she would have to return to her parents. This law of avoidance was strongly impressed on the novices at the initiation ceremonies.² In the Hunter River tribe, further to the north, a man was formerly forbidden to speak to his mother-in-law under pain of death; but in later times the death penalty was commuted into a severe reprimand and banishment from the camp for a time.³

The Yuin had the classificatory system of relationship. Thus in the generation above his own a man applied the same term *mamung* to his mother, to his mother's sisters, and to the wives of his father's brothers. But on the other hand he applied different terms to his father (*banga*), to his father's brothers (*nadjung*), and to the husbands of his mother's sisters (*kaung*). Thus the Yuin discriminated between a father and his brothers, but not between a mother and her sisters. In his own generation a Yuin man applied the same term *dadung* to his brothers, to the sons of his father's brothers, and to the sons of his mother's sisters. He applied the same term *nadjanduri* to his wife, to his wife's sisters, and to his brothers' wives; and a wife applied the same term *tarrama* to her husband, to her husband's brothers, and to her sisters' husbands. In the generation below his own a man applied the same term

---

¹ A. W. Howitt, *Native Tribes of South-East Australia*, pp. 264, 266.
² A. W. Howitt, *op. cit.* p. 266.
³ A. W. Howitt, *op. cit.* p. 267, on the authority of C. F. Holmes.

wurum to his sons, to his brothers' sons, and to the sons of his wife's sisters. A woman applied the same term *wurum* to her sons, to her sisters' sons, and to the sons of her husband's brothers.[1]

§ 10. *Tribes with neither Exogamous Classes nor Totem Clans*

In a few tribes of South-East Australia the organisation of society in exogamous classes and totem clans has not been found, whether it be that such an organisation never existed among them or, as is more probable, that it has perished. Of these tribes the best known is the Kurnai of Gippsland, who have had the good fortune to be examined and described by Dr. A. W. Howitt.[2] Their territory occupied almost the whole of Gippsland, stretching along the coast for about two hundred miles and extending inland for about seventy miles to the Dividing Range.[3] It is a land of giant mountains, great forests, fine streams, and fertile plains, with a climate and a soil well fitted to the growth of the orange. Much of the rugged region to the north and east is still unexplored, and indeed almost inaccessible, so broken is it by precipices and ravines.[4] To the native inhabitants before the advent of the whites, this rich and beautiful country teemed with the means of subsistence. The grassy forests and savannahs were stocked with kangaroos and other sorts of herbivorous marsupials: the forest trees harboured opossums, the native bear, and the iguana: the rivers and lakes swarmed with varieties of fish and eels: plants, bushes, and trees of different kinds afforded edible substances in roots, berries, or seeds; and both on land and water birds were many and various. Food was therefore abundant and varied, including almost everything from the grubs of insects to the great kangaroo. In such a country, lying between the ocean and the high snowy

---

[1] A. W. Howitt, "Australian Group-Relationships," *Journal of the Royal Anthropological Institute*, xxxvii. (1907) pp. 287 *sq.*

[2] They were first described by him in the work which he published jointly with the late Rev. Lorimer Fison, *Kamilaroi and Kurnai* (Melbourne, 1880), pp. 177 *sqq.*

[3] A. W. Howitt, *Native Tribes of South-East Australia*, p. 73.

[4] A. R. Wallace, *Australasia*, i. 285-287.

ranges of the Australian Alps, droughts such as periodically desolate the interior of the continent are rare, if not unknown.[1] Great indeed is the difference between this happy, fruitful, temperate land and the arid, sun-scorched wilderness of Lake Eyre; and accordingly great is the difference between the social system of the natives in these two sharply contrasted regions.[2]

Local exogamy of the Kurnai.

While the Kurnai were divided neither into exogamous classes nor into totem clans, they recognised the principle of exogamy, for among them marriages could only properly take place reciprocally between members of certain districts.

Traces of a class-system among them.

However, judging from similarities of language, from tradition, and from common customs, Dr. Howitt concludes that the Kurnai were probably an offshoot of the Kulin nation and may at one time have been organised like the Kulin in two exogamous classes, Eagle-hawk (Bunjil) and Crow.[3] For while among the Western Port tribes to the west of the Kurnai the name Bunjil signified "eagle-hawk," and was applied to a supernatural old man who lived at the sources of the Yarra River, among the Kurnai the title Bunjil was regularly bestowed on every old man, being compounded with another word significative of some quality or peculiarity. For example, one man was called Bunjil-tambun from his skill in catching perch (*tambun*). Another was named Bunjil-barlajan from his skill in spearing platypus (*barlajan*). Another was called Bunjil-daua-ngun from *daua-ngun*, "to turn up," because he was noted for making bark canoes, much turned up at the bow.[4] Another was called Bunjil-bataluk, because he was attended by a tame lace-lizard (*bataluk*).[5] This usage of the title Bunjil may possibly be connected with the former existence of an exogamous class named Bunjil or Eagle-hawk. Again, the reverence which the Kurnai showed for the crow (*ngarugal*) may perhaps have been derived from a time when the crow gave its

[1] Fison and Howitt, *Kamilaroi and Kurnai*, p. 208.
[2] As to Lake Eyre and its tribes see above, pp. 340 *sqq.*
[3] A. W. Howitt, *Native Tribes of South-East Australia*, p. 134. As to the Kulin class system, see above, pp. 434 *sqq.*
[4] Fison and Howitt, *Kamilaroi and Kurnai*, pp. 323 *sq.*; A. W. Howitt, *Native Tribes of South-East Australia*, pp. 738 *sq.*
[5] A. W. Howitt, *op. cit.* p. 277.

name to a second exogamous class and was revered by its members. The crow was said to be the friend of the Kurnai, and it was deemed wrong to kill a crow. To do so, they thought, would bring on stormy weather.[1]

Further, every Kurnai received the name of some marsupial, bird, reptile, or fish from his father, when he was about ten years old or at initiation. A man would say, pointing to the creature in question, "That is your elder brother (*thundung*); do not hurt it." Dr. Howitt knew of two cases in which the father said to his son, "It will be yours when I am dead." While each man protected his animal "elder brother" (*thundung*), the animal was in its turn believed to protect his human "younger brother" by warning him in dreams of approaching danger or by coming towards him in bodily shape. Sometimes, too, it was appealed to in song-charms to relieve him in sickness. And apparently people claimed to exercise power over their "elder brothers"; for Dr. Howitt knew a man whose "elder brother" was shark (*yalmerai*), and who would not hurt a shark; but if there were too many sharks about, the man would "sing" them, and then they were supposed to go away. The animal "elder brothers" (*thundung*) of the Kurnai included the wombat, kangaroo, platypus, water-hen, a small bird (*blitburing*), eagle-hawk (*gwanomurrung*), tiger-snake, sea-salmon, small conger-eel, and large conger-eel. Dr. Howitt justly observes that these "elder brothers" are clearly the equivalents of the totems of other tribes; but if, as he supposes, the Kurnai were formerly divided into two exogamous moieties Eagle-hawk and Crow, he is unable to say to which of the moieties the various totems belonged.[2] Close parallels to the "elder brothers" of the Kurnai are furnished by the personal totems of the Yuin and of the tribes about Maryborough. Like the Kurnai, the tribes about Maryborough called their personal totems their "brothers."[3]

Kurnai "elder brothers" the equivalents of totems.

---

[1] A. W. Howitt, *Native Tribes of South-East Australia*, pp. 134 *sq.*

[2] A. W. Howitt, *op. cit.* p. 135. The interesting information as to the man who had a shark for his "elder brother" and used to "sing" sharks was communicated to me by Dr. Howitt in a letter dated Clovelly, Metung, 12th March 1904. Dr. Howitt seems not to have embodied it in his book. In this letter, which announced the discovery of the animal "elder brothers" of the Kurnai, Dr. Howitt also mentions that a woman would call her personal totem *bauung*, that is, "elder sister."

[3] See above, pp. 448 *sq.*, 489 *sq.*

Sex-totems among the Kurnai, the emu-wren and the superb warbler, the "brother" and "sister" of the men and women respectively.

But not only had every Kurnai his own animal "elder brother" or personal totem, as we may call it; all the Kurnai men united in reverencing the emu-wren (*Stipiturus Malachurus*) as their "elder brother," and all the women similarly united in reverencing the superb warbler (*Malurus Cyaneus*) as their "elder sister." In short, the emu-wren, which they called *yeerung*, and the superb warbler, which they called *djeetgun*, were the sex-totems of the men and women respectively. Sometimes, if the men and women quarrelled, the women would go out and kill an emu-wren in order to spite the men by the death of their "brother." When they returned to the camp with the dead bird, the men would attack them with their clubs, and the women would defend themselves with their digging-sticks. Or the men might be the aggressors by killing a superb warbler, and the women would then avenge the death of their "sister" by attacking the men. Curiously enough, these fights over the two birds, the men's "brother" and the women's "sister," were sometimes deliberately provoked by the women as a means of inducing the young unmarried men to offer marriage to the young unmarried women. When bachelors were shy and backward, the elder women would go out into the forest, kill some emu-wrens, and bring them back to the camp. Then they would show the dead birds to the men, who flew into a rage at the murder of their "brothers." Young men and young women now attacked each other with sticks, heads were broken, and blood flowed. Even married men and women joined in this free fight. Next day some of the young men would go out and kill some of the superb warblers, the women's "sisters"; so there would be another fight, perhaps worse than the first, when they came back. By and by, it might be in a week or two, when the wounds and bruises were healed, a young man might meet a young woman and say, "Superb Warbler! What does the Superb Warbler eat?" She would answer, "She eats kangaroo, opossum," and so forth. This constituted a formal offer of marriage and an acceptance, and the couple thereafter eloped with each other in the customary fashion of the tribe. While fights of this sort between the sexes on account of the killing of their sex-totems seem to have been common among the tribes which practised this curious form of totemism, the Kurnai are the only tribe who are known to have used such combats as a means of promoting marriage.¹ With regard to sex-totems in general, which have as yet been found nowhere but among the tribes of South-East Australia, Dr. Howitt observes : " I am quite unable to offer any suggestion as to the origin of the sex totems. I am not aware of any case in which they have been eaten. They are thought to be friendly to the sex they are akin to, and are protected by it." ²

Moreover, Kurnai medicine-men were sometimes believed to possess what we may call a personal totem of their own which they had obtained by dreaming about the animal. For example, a Kurnai man dreamed several times that he had become a lace-lizard and, as such, had assisted at a corrobboree of these reptiles. Hence it was believed that he had acquired power over them, and he had actually a tame lace-lizard, about four feet long, in his camp, while his wife and children lived in another camp close by. As he put it, his lace-lizard (*bataluk*) and himself were like the same person, as he was a lace-lizard (*bataluk*) also. The lizard accompanied him wherever he went, sitting on his shoulders or partly on his head, and people thought that it informed him of danger, helped him in tracking his enemies or young couples who had eloped, and in fact was his friend and protector. It was also believed that he could send his familiar lizard at night to injure people in their camps while they slept. In consequence of this comradeship with lace-lizards, and probably because he was in some manner one of them, he received the name of Bunjil-lace-lizard.³ Another Kurnai medicine-man had a tame brown snake which he fed on frogs. People were very much afraid of him, because they supposed that he sent the snake out at night to injure them.⁴ One of the best remembered of the Kurnai seers or

Personal totems of Kurnai medicine-men.

---

¹ Fison and Howitt, *Kamilaroi and Kurnai*, pp. 201 *sq.*; A. W. Howitt, " Further Notes on the Australian Class Systems," *Journal of the Anthropological Institute*, xviii. (1889) pp. 56 *sq.*; *id.*, *Native Tribes of South-East Australia*, pp. 148 *sq.*, 273 *sq.*

² A. W. Howitt, *Native Tribes of South-East Australia*, p. 151.

³ A. W. Howitt, " On Australian Medicine Men," *Journal of the Anthropological Institute*, xvi. (1887) p. 34 ; *id.*, *Native Tribes of South-East Australia*, p. 387.

⁴ A. W. Howitt, *Native Tribes of South-East Australia*, pp. 387 *sq.*

498   TOTEMISM IN SOUTH-EASTERN AUSTRALIA   CHAP.

wizards was a man named Mundauin. It is related of him that he became a seer (*birraark*) by dreaming thrice that he was a kangaroo, and as such participated in a corrobboree of these animals. In consequence of this kinship with kangaroos he might not eat any part of a kangaroo on which there was blood, nor might he even carry home one which had blood on it. Others carried and cooked the bleeding animal for him, and then gave him cooked pieces of the flesh which he was allowed to eat. He said that if he were to eat any kangaroo flesh with blood on it, or touch the fresh blood of a kangaroo, the spirits or ghosts (*mrarts*) would no longer take him up aloft. For after he had dreamed of kangaroos, he began to hear the ghosts drumming and singing up on high, and at last one night they came and carried him away. And afterwards, when the ghosts wished to communicate with him they used to catch him up by night, and people could hear him and the spirits up in the air or among the tree-tops whistling and shouting, till at last, as the night grew late, a hollow muffled voice said, "We must now go home, or the west wind may blow us out to sea."[1] These accounts shew that in Australia personal totems or guardian spirits were sometimes acquired in dreams, just as they commonly were in North America.[2] If personal totems so obtained came to be afterwards transmitted by inheritance, as they might be, it seems clear that they would be indistinguishable from clan totems of the ordinary type.

Relation of the personal totems (*thundungs*) to the intermarrying localities.

While marriage among the Kurnai was regulated by locality and not by the *thundungs* or personal totems of the parties, it nevertheless happened that under the rule of male descent the personal totems (*thundungs*) were segregated into the intermarrying districts, and so indirectly affected or seemed to affect marriage. For since a man regularly brought his wife to his own district, and she did not transmit her personal totem (*thundung* or rather *bauung*[3]) to the children, while he transmitted his to them, it follows that in the same district the same totem was inherited without change

[1] A. W. Howitt, "On Australian Medicine Men," *Journal of the Anthropological Institute*, xvi. (1887) p. 45; *id.*, *Native Tribes of South-East Australia*, pp. 390 *sq.*

[2] See above, p. 50.

[3] See above, p. 495, note [2].

from generation to generation. Thus, under the influence of paternal descent these personal totems became localised in certain areas; and as marriage was regulated by these areas, it might appear that the totemic area, in so far as it coincided with the exogamous local area, also regulated marriage.[1] Marriage among the Kurnai was individual, not communal. It is true that in the common case of elopement the men who had been initiated at the same time as the bridegroom had a right of access to the bride. But after marriage no sexual licence was allowed, except when, terrified by the glare of the Southern Streamers in the nightly sky, the old men ordered the people to exchange wives for the day, and swung the dried hand of a dead man to and fro with cries of "Send it away!"[2] *Sexual license in certain occasions.*

The custom of local exogamy, combined with the numerous prohibited degrees of relationship, had the effect of placing so many impediments in the way of marriage among the Kurnai that the propagation of the tribe would almost have ceased if the young people had not often taken matters into their own hands, and set all the rules at defiance by running away with each other. Indeed, elopement was commonly the only way out of the deadlock, and it became in fact the ordinary mode of marriage in the tribe, being tacitly connived at, though publicly denounced and severely punished, by the professedly indignant parents of the runaways.[3] The exaggerated scrupulosity of the Australian savage as to the marriage of near kin had at last landed him in a grave dilemma; he had to choose between law-breaking and extinction, and he naturally chose to break the law. *Elopement the customary form of marriage among the Kurnai.*

---

[1] A. W. Howitt, *Native Tribes of South-East Australia*, p. 269. A table of the intermarrying localities is given by Dr. Howitt (*op. cit.* p. 272).

[2] A. W. Howitt, *op. cit.* pp. 276 *sq.*

[3] Fison and Howitt, *Kamilaroi and Kurnai*, pp. 200-202; A. W. Howitt, *Native Tribes of South-East Australia*, pp. 273-279. One of Dr. Howitt's informants was a certain woman Nanny, the oldest of the Gippsland aboriginals then living, for she had been a widow with grey hair when Angus M'Millan discovered the country. "She stated positively that the rule was that all young women ran off with their husbands; and she could only recollect three cases where girls had been given away." See Fison and Howitt, *op. cit.* p. 200 note *. "Among the Kurnai elopement was the recognised and most frequent form of marriage, yet here both parties, if caught, were severely —the woman savagely—punished" (A. W. Howitt and L. Fison, "From Mother-right to Father-right," *Journal of the Anthropological Institute*, xii. (1883) p. 39).

500 TOTEMISM IN SOUTH-EASTERN AUSTRALIA CHAP.

Classificatory terms of relationship among the Kurnai.

Yet in the classificatory terms of relationship the Kurnai preserved a record of a time when their ancestors had been as loose as their descendants were strict in sexual relations. Thus in the generation above his own a man applied the same term *mungan* to his father, to his father's brothers, and to the husbands of his mother's sisters; and he applied the same term *yukan* to his mother, to his mother's sisters, and to the wives of his father's brothers. Further, as commonly happens under the classificatory system, the Kurnai had quite different terms for elder and younger brother, and again for elder and younger sister. Thus a man called his elder brother *thundung*, but his younger brother *bramung*; he called his elder sister *bauung*, but his younger sister *lunduk*; and he applied these same words for brother and sister to his first cousins, the sons and daughters of his father's brothers and sisters, and the same words to his other first cousins, the sons and daughters of his mother's sisters and brothers. He applied the same term *maian* to his wife, to his wife's sisters, and to his brothers' wives; and a woman applied the same term *bra* to her husband, to her husband's brothers, and to her sisters' husbands. In the generation below his own a man applied the same term *lit* to his children, to his brothers' children, and to the children of his wife's sisters; and a woman applied the same term *lit* to her children, to her sisters' children, and to the children of her husband's brothers.[1] Terms thus expressive of group relationship are best explicable, as I have already pointed out,[2] on the hypothesis that they are derived from a system of group-marriage.

Custom of the Levirate among the Kurnai.

Among the Kurnai on the death of a married man his wife went by right to his surviving brother, and if he had several wives they went to his brothers in order of seniority. The reason alleged for this custom was that a brother is the proper person to support his brother's widow and his brother's children. The widow might, however, refuse to marry her husband's brother and might choose another

---

[1] A. W. Howitt, *Native Tribes of South-East Australia*, p. 169; id., "Australian Group-Relationships," *Journal of the Royal Anthropological Institute*, xxxvii. (1907) pp. 287 sq. Compare Fison and Howitt, *Kamilaroi and Kurnai*, pp. 236 sqq.

[2] Above, pp. 303 sqq.

man whom she liked better.¹ This custom of succession to a deceased brother's widow is known as the Levirate.² It occurs in many, though not in all, Australian tribes,³ and it has been practised by many other peoples in many other parts of the world. The custom is probably to be explained with Dr. Howitt,⁴ at least for Australia, as a relic of group-marriage: the brothers, who under that system would have shared their wives in their lifetime, afterwards inherited them successively, each stepping one after the other into the shoes of his deceased predecessor. The eminent anthropologist, J. F. McLennan, indeed, proposed to explain the Levirate as a relic of polyandry, not of group-marriage.⁵ But against this view it is to be said that group-marriage is found in Australia, whereas polyandry is not; so that the cause presupposed by Howitt actually exists in the region where the custom is practised, while the cause presupposed by McLennan does not. Further, it should be borne in mind, that whereas both the Levirate and the classificatory system of relationship, with its plain testimony to group-marriage, occur very widely over the world, the custom of polyandry appears to have been comparatively rare and exceptional, and the reason for its rarity is simply that the only basis on which polyandry could permanently exist, to wit, a great numerical preponderance of men over women, appears never to have been a normal condition with any race of men of whom we have knowledge. In Africa, for example, as in Australia, the custom of the Levirate is very common and the classificatory system of relationship seems to be widely spread, but the custom of polyandry is apparently unknown.⁶ It is more reasonable, therefore, to look for the origin of the widely diffused custom of the Levirate in a custom like group-marriage, which we have good reason for

The Levirate is probably a relic of group-marriage, not of polyandry.

---

¹ Fison and Howitt, *Kamilaroi and Kurnai*, p. 204.
² The name is derived from the Latin *levir*, "husband's brother." As to the custom, see A. H. Post, *Grundriss der ethnologischen Jurisprudenz*, i. 186 *sqq.*; *id.*, *Afrikanische Jurisprudenz*, i. 419 *sqq.* The evidence might easily be multiplied.
³ For some exceptions, see above, p. 461.
⁴ A. W. Howitt, *Native Tribes of South-East Australia*, p. 281.
⁵ J. F. McLennan, *Studies in Ancient History* (London, 1886), pp. 108 *sqq.*; J. F. McLennan and D. McLennan, *The Patriarchal Theory* (London, 1885), pp. 156 *sqq.*, 266 *sqq.*
⁶ A. H. Post, *Afrikanische Jurisprudenz*, i. 419 note ⁵.

believing to have been at one time very widely diffused, rather than in a custom like polyandry for which no such evidence is forthcoming.

With changed surroundings the custom of the Levirate has assumed a different character among different peoples.

But when the Levirate survived, as it often did, among peoples who had left group-marriage far behind them, it would naturally assume a different character with its changed surroundings. Thus wherever the rights of property and the practice of purchasing wives had become firmly established, the tendency was to regard the widow as part of the inheritance which passed to the heir, whether he was a brother, a son, or any other relation of the deceased husband. This, for example, appears to be the current view of the Levirate in Africa, where the custom is commonly observed.[1] Again, wherever it came to be supposed that a man's eternal welfare in the other world depends on his leaving children behind him, who will perform the rites necessary for his soul's salvation, it naturally became the pious duty of the survivors to remedy as far as they could the parlous state of a kinsman who had died childless, and on none would that duty appear to be more incumbent than on the brother of the deceased. In such circumstances the old custom of the Levirate might be continued, or perhaps revived, with the limitation which we find in Hebrew and Hindoo law, namely that a brother must marry his brother's widow only in the case where the deceased died childless, and only for the purpose of begetting on the widow a son or sons for him who had left none of his own. Thus what had once been regarded as a right of succession to be enjoyed by the heir might afterwards come to be viewed as a burdensome and even repulsive obligation imposed upon a surviving brother or other kinsman, who submitted to it reluctantly out of a sense of duty to the dead. This is the light in which the Levirate has been considered by Hindoo lawgivers.[2]

But neither of these explanations can apply to the Levirate as practised by the aborigines of Australia, for

---

[1] A. H. Post, *Afrikanische Jurisprudenz*, i. 419-425.
[2] J. Jolly, *Recht und Sitte*, pp. 70 sq. (in G. Bühler's *Grundriss der Indo-Arischen Philologie und Altertumskunde*, vol. ii.); J. F. McLennan and D. McLennan, *The Patriarchal Theory*, pp. 156 sqq., 266 sqq.

these savages neither buy their wives and transmit them like chattels to their heirs, nor do they believe in a heaven from which the childless and friendless are excluded. Accordingly we must look for another explanation of their custom of handing over a widow to her deceased husband's brother, and such an explanation lies to our hand in the old custom of group-marriage, which still survives among the more backward of the tribes.

But to return to the Kurnai. "The curious custom," says Dr. Howitt, "in accordance with which the man was prohibited from speaking to, or having any communication or dealings with, his wife's mother, is one of extraordinary strength, and seems to be rooted deep down in their very nature. So far as I know it is of widespread occurrence throughout Australia." Dr. Howitt mentions a Kurnai man of his acquaintance, who was a member of the Church of England, but who nevertheless positively refused to speak to his mother-in-law and reproached Dr. Howitt for expecting him to commit so gross a breach of good manners.[1] The most probable explanation of this singular rule of avoidance appears to be the one which Dr. Howitt has suggested, namely that it is intended to prevent the possibility of that marriage with a mother-in-law which, while it was repugnant to the feelings of the native, was yet not barred by the old two-class system with maternal descent.[2] This view is not indeed free from difficulties, some of which have been already pointed out;[3] but on the whole it seems open to fewer objections than any other explanation that has yet been put forward. *Avoidance of a wife's mother among the Kurnai. This avoidance is probably intended to prevent improper relations between the two.*

Professor E. B. Tylor has suggested that the ceremonial avoidance in question springs from a practice of the husband's residing after marriage with his wife's family, who regard him as an intruder and therefore pretend to ignore him.[4] But this explanation can hardly apply to Australia, where the wife regularly goes to live with her husband's people. Yet nowhere apparently is the custom of avoidance more widely *Professor Tylor's explanation of the custom seems inapplicable to Australia.*

---

[1] Fison and Howitt, *Kamilaroi and Kurnai*, p. 203. Compare A. W. Howitt, *Native Tribes of South-East Australia*, p. 279.
[2] See above, note on pp. 285 *sq*.
[3] Above, p. 286 note.
[4] E. B. Tylor, "On a Method of investigating the Development of Institutions," *Journal of the Anthropological Institute*, xviii. (1889) pp. 246-248.

However, although in Australia a man does not take up his abode with his wife's parents, he is often bound to provide them with food, which may perhaps be a relic of a closer tie between him and them.

spread and more deeply rooted than in Australia. However, while Messrs. Spencer and Gillen know of no Australian tribe in which it is the custom for a man to take up his abode with his wife's family and to work for them, they point to certain observances which may possibly be relics of such a practice. Thus in the Arunta, Unmatjera, and Kaitish tribes a man is bound to provide his father-in-law (*ikuntera*), whether actual or tribal, with food even before he partakes of it himself; and on the other hand he is strictly forbidden to eat the flesh of any animal which his father-in-law, actual or tribal, has killed or even only seen. More than that, he must be careful not to let men who stand to him in the relation of father-in-law see him eating any food, lest they should spoil it by "projecting their smell into it." It is believed that were he to eat the flesh of game which has been killed or seen by his father-in-law, the food would disagree with him and he would sicken and suffer severely.[1] Similarly among some of the tribes of South-East Australia a man was bound to provide his wife's parents and sometimes other members of her family with food according to certain fixed and definite rules. Thus amongst the Kurnai if a man killed five opossums, he had to give two of them to his wife's parents and two of them to her brothers. If a Kurnai killed a wombat, the whole of the carcass went to his wife's parents; for this animal was reckoned the best of food. If a man killed a native sloth bear, he gave it to his wife's parents; if he killed two, he gave one to his wife's parents and one to his own parents; if he killed three, he gave two to his wife's parents and one to his own parents; and so on. He might probably keep the liver of the sloth bear for himself and his wife. If he killed several swans, he kept one or more for his family and sent the remainder to his wife's parents; but if he had killed a large number of the birds, he sent most of them to his wife's parents and a smaller number to his own parents. If a man killed a conger-eel, it went to his wife's father. This custom of providing a wife's parents with food was called by the Kurnai *neborak*; and we are told that "in all cases the

---

[1] Spencer and Gillen, *Native Tribes of Central Australia*, pp. 469 *sq.*; *id.*, *Northern Tribes of Central Australia*, pp. 609 *sq.*

largest supply and the best of the food is sent to the wife's parents." Apparently, though we are not expressly told so, the food thus given to the parents of a man's wife was sent through his wife, not given by him directly to them. And next morning his parents-in-law sent him some food in return through their daughter, his wife, "on the assumption that their son-in-law provided for his family on the preceding day, but may want some food before going out to hunt afresh."[1] Similarly among the Manero natives the custom of providing a wife's parents with food was strictly observed; a man had to supply his father-in-law and mother-in-law with the best parts of the game, and if possible with wombat flesh, that being considered the best of all. The food was always carried by the wife to her parents.[2] Again, among the Mukjarawaint, if a married man killed a kangaroo, he sent some of it to his parents-in-law through his wife, because he might not go near her mother, or her father might come himself to fetch it.[3] Such customs may possibly, as Messrs. Spencer and Gillen observe, be derived from a time when a man owed allegiance to his wife's group.[4] But it is also possible that the customs have an entirely different origin.

Another tribe which appears to have lost both its exogamous classes and its totems was the Chepara. They occupied the extreme south-east corner of Queensland, between Brisbane and the New South Wales boundary. Their territory skirted the sea, but also extended inland. Among them marriage was regulated by locality, and names descended in the male line.[5] If an unmarried girl was captured on a raid, she belonged to her captor, and his

The Chepara tribe, its marriage customs and traces of totems.

---

[1] Fison and Howitt, *Kamilaroi and Kurnai*, pp. 261-263; A. W. Howitt, *Native Tribes of South-East Australia*, pp. 756-758.

[2] A. W. Howitt, *Native Tribes of South-East Australia*, p. 760.

[3] A. W. Howitt, *op. cit.* p. 764.

[4] Spencer and Gillen, *Native Tribes of Central Australia*, p. 470.

[5] A. W. Howitt, *Native Tribes of South-East Australia*, pp. 86, 135 *sq.*, 280. Yet Dr. Howitt says (p. 280) that in this tribe "a wife was obtained from any clan, even that of the husband." As Dr. Howitt regularly employs the term clan in the sense of a local division of a tribe with male descent (*op. cit.* p. 43), it would seem from the statement which I have just quoted that in the Chepara tribe the districts were not exogamous. It is therefore difficult to see how they can have regulated marriage.

comrades had no right of access to her. Wives were not exchanged under any circumstances, nor were they lent to friendly visitors.¹ At the initiation ceremonies of this tribe men used to give pantomimic representations of flying foxes on branches, of bees flying about, of curlews, and of many other creatures. Perhaps, as Dr. Howitt suggests, these representations may be relics of totems which have disappeared.²

Among the Chepara a woman was not allowed to see her daughter's husband in camp or elsewhere. When he was present she kept her head covered by an opossum rug. The camp of the mother-in-law faced in a different direction to that of her son-in-law. A screen of high bushes was erected between both huts, so that nobody could see over from either, and husband and wife conversed in a tone which her mother could not overhear. When the mother-in-law went for firewood, she crouched down, as she went in or out, with her head covered. If the son-in-law climbed a tree to take a hive of native bees, his wife might sit at the foot of it, but her mother had to stay a long way off with her head muffled up. When the man had got the hive, descended the tree, and gone off, the mother-in-law might come and help her daughter to cut up the comb and carry it away.³

The Chepara possessed the classificatory system of relationship. Thus in the generation above his own a man applied the same term *bing* to his father and to his father's brothers; and he applied the same term *buyung* to his mother and to his mother's sisters. In his own generation he applied the same term *nabong* to his brothers, to the sons of his father's brothers, and to the sons of his mother's sisters. He applied the same term *nubunpingun* to his wife and to his wife's sisters; and a woman applied the same term *nubunping* to her husband and to her husband's brothers. In the generation below his own a man applied the same term *naring* to his sons, to his brothers' sons, and to the sons of his wife's sisters. Similarly a woman applied the

---

¹ A. W. Howitt, *Native Tribes of South-East Australia*, p. 280.
² A. W. Howitt, *op. cit.* pp. 581 sq.
³ A. W. Howitt, *op. cit.* pp. 280 sq.

same term *naring* to her sons, to her sisters' sons, and to the sons of her husband's brothers.[1]

§ 11. *Equivalence of the Exogamous Classes*

From the foregoing survey of totemism and exogamy in South-Eastern Australia it may be seen how diversified are the social systems which have been based on these two principles. In some tribes we find the simple two-class system, in others the more complex four-class system, while in others, again, the system of exogamous classes has vanished or left only faint traces behind. In some tribes there is male descent; in others there is female descent. In some tribes the totem clans are well developed and clearly defined; in others they are decadent or almost, if not wholly, obliterated. On the whole, the extinction of the class system is most marked among the tribes of the coast, who, retaining the principle of exogamy, have applied it to local districts instead of to kinship groups, or rather perhaps have identified the local groups with the kinship groups. The chief factor in this conversion of kinship exogamy into local exogamy has been the adoption of paternal in preference to maternal descent; for where the men remain in the same district, and transmit their family names unchanged from generation to generation, while the names of the wives whom they import from other districts die out with their owners, the result is to make the kinship group, indicated by the possession of a common hereditary name, coincide more or less exactly with the local group, and thus the principle of class or kinship exogamy tends to pass gradually and almost insensibly into the principle of local exogamy.[2]

Diversity of marriage systems in South-East Australia.

The different types of social organisation, being distributed over the continent, are necessarily in contact with each other at many points. A tribe, for example, with the two-class system may border on a tribe with the four-class system: and a tribe with female descent may have for its neighbour another

Where tribes with different marriage systems meet and intermarry, they have

---

[1] A. W. Howitt, "Australian Group-Relationships," *Journal of the Royal Anthropological Institute*, xxxvii. (1907) pp. 287 *sq.*

[2] See also above, pp. 81, 83.

to adjust their systems so as to fit into each other.

with male descent; and so on. No great difficulty would be created by this contact of discordant systems if the relations between the tribes were uniformly hostile, for then each tribe would go its own way, indifferent as to the modes in which their enemies across the border married and reared their children. But, on the whole, the relations between neighbouring tribes in Australia have been peaceful and friendly, and intermarriage between them has been the rule rather than the exception. Accordingly, wherever two intermarrying tribes possessed different types of social organisation, it has been necessary for them to come to an understanding with each other on the subject of marriage, to dovetail, so to say, the matrimonial system of the one into the matrimonial system of the other, so that every person in the one tribe may know whom in the other tribe he or she, in accordance with the rigorous principles of savage exogamy, is at liberty to marry. This nice and sometimes complex adjustment of the divergent marriage laws of neighbouring tribes has been carried out, on the whole, by the Australian aborigines with a skill which does credit to their intelligence. "Wherever two systems touch each other," says Dr. Howitt, "the members of the adjacent tribes invariably know which of the neighbouring classes corresponds to their own, and therefore the individual knows well with which class or subclass of the other tribe his own intermarries; and he knows also, though perhaps not quite so well, the marriage relations of the other class or subclass, as the case may be."[1]

Equivalence of the various class systems.

With regard to the equivalence of the various marriage systems to each other, I will quote the observations of Dr. Howitt. He says: "The equivalence of class or subclasses long ago attracted my attention when I was studying the organisation of the Kamilaroi tribes. I found on comparing the class divisions of any large group of allied tribes such as the Kamilaroi, that the several tribes have more or less marked differences in their classes and subclasses, either in the names themselves or, in extreme cases, in their arrangement. These differences are often merely dialectic variations of name; but in other cases they amount to

[1] A. W. Howitt, *Native Tribes of South-East Australia*, pp. 141 *sq.*

differences in the structure of the system itself. When a still larger group of tribes is examined, the variations become wider and the differences greater. Nevertheless, the general identity of structure and of the fundamental laws of the classes over wide areas proves, beyond doubt, that these varied forms are substantially equivalent. I may note here that the boundaries of a class system are usually wider than those of a tribe, and that the boundaries of any one type of system have a still wider range, and include those aggregates of tribes which I have termed nations. All such aggregates are bound together by a community of class organisation which indicates a community of descent."[1]

Examples will show how this equivalence of the exogamous classes is carried out in practice. In the Wotjobaluk tribe the two class names are Krokitch and Gamutch. To the north the Wotjobaluk bordered on the Wiimbaio, whose class names are Mukwara and Kilpara. A Wotjobaluk man, who was Krokitch, told Dr. Howitt that when he went to the Wiimbaio tribe he was Kilpara, and that the people there told him that the Gamutch of the Wotjobaluk was the same as the Mukwara of the Wiimbaio. A similar statement was made to Dr. Howitt by a man of the tribe which is next to the Wiimbaio up the Murray River. He said that he was Kilpara, but that when he went south he was Krokitch; and his wife added that, being Mukwara at home, she was Gamutch in the south.[2] *Examples of the equivalence of the class systems.*

From a survivor of the Gal-gal-baluk clan of the Jajaurung tribe, who lived on the Avoca River, Dr. Howitt learned that two sets of class names met there, Bunjil and Waang of the Jajaurung tribe, and Krokitch and Gamutch of the tribe living to the west of the river. In the south-west of Victoria the same sets of class names meet between Geelong and Colac, where Kroki is equivalent to Bunjil and Kumitch to Waang.[3]

On the Maranoa River in Southern Queensland two types of the four-class system meet, the equivalents of the Kamilaroi names on the one side, and the equivalents of the Northern Queensland names on the other. There, as it was put to Dr. Howitt, "a Hippai man is also Kurgilla," *More examples of the equivalence of the class systems.*

[1] A. W. Howitt, *Native Tribes of South-East Australia*, p. 137.
[2] A. W. Howitt, *op. cit.* pp. 137 *sq.*
[3] A. W. Howitt, *op. cit.* p. 138.

and so on with the other names of the subclasses. To the north-east of the Marona tribe three types of the four-class system meet. There is a tribe called the Bigambul with four subclasses, called, in Kamilaroi fashion, Hipai, Kombo, Murri, and Kobi. There is a tribe called the Emon with four subclasses called Taran, Bondan, Barah, and Bondurr. And there is a tribe called the Ungorri with four subclasses called Urgilla, Anbeir, Wungo, and Ubur. The equivalence of all these three sets of subclasses is recognised by the tribes in the manner indicated in the subjoined table :—[1]

BIGAMBUL.	EMON.	UNGORRI.
Hipai	Taran	Urgilla
Kombo	Bondan	Anbeir
Murri	Barah	Wungo
Kobi	Bondurr	Ubur

A similar equivalence between the exogamous classes of different tribes has been recorded of the tribes of North-Western Queensland towards the Gulf of Carpentaria.[2]

More examples of the equivalence of the class systems.

West of the Wiradjuri nation is a vast area occupied by tribes with the two-class system. Here the two class names Kilpara and Mukwara extend north-west to the Grey Range, where they adjoin the two class names Kulpuru and Tiniwa of such tribes as the Yantruwunta. Here it seems that Kulpuru is the equivalent of Kilpara, and that Tiniwa is the equivalent of Mukwara. The Yantruwunta

---

[1] A. W. Howitt, *Native Tribes of South-East Australia*, pp. 109, 138. The recorded totems of the Emon tribe are emu, water, carpet-snake, and scrub turkey. Those of the Ungorri tribe are kangaroo, bandicoot, opossum, flying fox, brown snake, and lizard. Probably both lists are incomplete. Neither in the Emon nor in the Ungorri tribe could Dr. Howitt ascertain the names of the two exogamous moieties or classes. See A. W. Howitt, *op. cit.* pp. 109 *sq.*

[2] E. Palmer, "Notes on some Australian Tribes," *Journal of the Anthropological Institute*, xiii. (1884) p. 300. See Mr. Palmer's evidence, quoted below, pp. 521 *sq.* "The Maikolon [Mycoolon] names on the Cloncurry River are the equivalents of those of the Kugobathi on the Mitchell River, on the east side of the Gulf of Carpentaria" (A. W. Howitt, *Native Tribes of South-East Australia*, p. 138, on the authority of Mr. Edward Palmer).

names in their turn have their equivalents to the west in the names of the Dieri classes, Kararu and Matteri, for Tiniwa is the same as Kararu, and Kulpuru is the same as Matteri. This identification of the class names would therefore carry us southward through a number of tribes to Port Lincoln, where the Dieri class names occur.[1]

To the westward of Lake Eyre are the Urabunna with the same class names of the Dieri in the forms of Kirarawa and Matthurie.[2] On the north the Urabunna with their two-class system and female descent border on the southern Arunta with their system of four nominal though eight real subclasses and male descent.[3] The arrangement of marriages between persons of two tribes with such very different social organisations is necessarily a matter of some nicety, which cannot be carried out without the exercise of a good deal of thought and sagacity. Yet this feat, which might puzzle a civilised lawyer, has been successfully accomplished by the Australian savages. As to the mode in which the adjustment is made it will be best to quote the statement of our informants, Messrs. Spencer and Gillen. They say: "It sometimes happens, in fact not infrequently, that a man from the neighbouring Arunta tribe comes to live amongst the Urabunna. In the former where it adjoins the latter there are four subclasses, viz. Bulthara and Panunga, Kumara and Purula, and in addition descent is counted in the male line. Accordingly the men of the Bulthara and Purula classes are regarded as the equivalents of the Matthurie moiety of the Urabunna tribe, and those of the Panunga and Kumara classes as the equivalents of the Kirarawa. In just the same way a Matthurie man going into the Arunta tribe becomes either a Bulthara or Purula, and a Kirarawa man becomes either a Panunga or a Kumara man. Which of the two a Matthurie man belongs to is decided by the old men of the group into which he goes. Sometimes a man will take up his abode permanently, or for a long time, amongst the strange

Mutual adjustment of the two-class system of the Urabunna with female descent to the four-class system of the Arunta with male descent.

---

[1] A. W. Howitt, *Native Tribes of South-East Australia*, p. 138. For the class names (Karraru and Mattiri) of the Port Lincoln tribe see C. W. Schürmann, in *Native Tribes of South Australia*, p. 222; above, p. 369.
[2] See above, pp. 176 *sqq.*
[3] See above, pp. 259 *sqq.*

tribe, in which case, if it be decided, for example, that he is a Bulthara, then his children will be born Panunga, that is, they belong to his own adopted moiety. He has, of course, to marry a Kumara woman, or if he be already provided with a wife, then she is regarded as a Kumara, and if he goes back into his own tribe then his wife is regarded as a Kirarawa, and the children also take the same name. This deliberate change in the grouping of the classes and subclasses so as to make them fit in with the maternal line of descent or with the paternal, as the case may be, will be more easily understood from the accompanying table:—

Arunta.	Urabunna arrangement of the Arunta subclasses.
Bulthara ⎫ moiety A. Panunga ⎭	Bulthara ⎫ moiety A (Matthurie). Purula ⎭
Kumara ⎫ moiety B. Purula ⎭	Panunga ⎫ moiety B (Kirarawa). Kumara ⎭

"The working out of this with the result that the children belong to the right moiety of the tribe into which the man has gone may be rendered clear by taking one or two particular examples.

"Suppose that a Matthurie man goes into the Arunta tribe, then he is told by the old men of the group into which he has gone that he is, say, a Bulthara. Accordingly he marries a Kumara woman (or if, which is not very likely, he has brought a woman with him, then she is regarded as a Kumara) and his children will be Panunga, or, in other words, pass into the father's moiety as the subclasses are arranged in the Arunta, but not into that of the mother as they are arranged amongst the Urabunna.

"Again, suppose a Purula man from the Arunta tribe takes up his abode amongst the Urabunna. He becomes a Matthurie, and as such must marry a Kirarawa (or if married his wife is regarded as such). His children are Kirarawa, which includes the subclass Kumara into which they would have passed in the Arunta tribe, and to which they will belong if ever they go into the latter.

"These are not merely hypothetical cases, but are, in the district where the two tribes come in contact with one

II EQUIVALENCE OF THE EXOGAMOUS CLASSES 513

another, of by no means infrequent occurrence; and, without laying undue stress upon the matter, this deliberate changing of the method of grouping the subclasses so as to allow of the descent being counted in either the male or female line, according to the necessity of the case, is of interest as indicating the fact that the natives are quite capable of thinking such things out for themselves. It is indeed not perhaps without a certain suggestiveness in regard to the difficult question of how a change in the line of descent might possibly be brought about."[1]

The effect of that rearrangement of the Arunta subclasses, which Messrs. Spencer and Gillen have thus explained, is that so long as an Urabunna man lives in the Arunta tribe his children belong to his own moiety of the tribe, in accordance with the Arunta rule of paternal descent; but that whenever he goes back to the Urabunna, his children belong to their mother's moiety of the tribe, in accordance with the Urabunna rule of maternal descent. Conversely, when an Arunta man lives in the Urabunna tribe, his children belong to their mother's moiety of the tribe in accordance with the Urabunna rule of maternal descent; but whenever he goes back to the Arunta tribe, his children belong to his own moiety of the tribe, in accordance with the Arunta rule of paternal descent. This result is attained simply enough by arranging the four Arunta subclasses in different pairs so as to suit the different systems of the two tribes. *Effect of the rearrangement of the Arunta subclasses.*

This and more evidence of the same sort[2] confirms the view, which Messrs. Howitt and Fison long ago advanced, that the changes made in the social organisation of the tribes, including the classificatory system of relationships, were matters of deliberate intention and not the result of chance.[3] Reviewing the whole series of intermediary steps which we have surveyed in this chapter, from the two-class system of the Dieri with group marriage and female descent to the classless system of the Kurnai with local exogamy, individual marriage, and male descent, the experienced *The social organisation of the Australian tribes appears to have been a matter of deliberate intention, not a result of chance.*

---

[1] Spencer and Gillen, *Native Tribes of Central Australia*, pp. 68 sq.
[2] See Spencer and Gillen, *Northern Tribes of Central Australia*, pp. 120-124.
[3] A. W. Howitt, *Native Tribes of South-East Australia*, p. 140. Compare Fison and Howitt, *Kamilaroi and Kurnai*, pp. 160 sq.

and cautious Dr. Howitt concludes as follows: "The two exogamous class divisions begin the series of changes which I have described, and it may now be asked how they themselves originated. My opinion is that it was by the same process as that by which the four arose from the two, namely by the division of an original whole, which I have referred to as the Undivided Commune. The two classes have been intentionally divided into four and eight subclasses, so that it does not seem to me unreasonable to conclude also that the segmentation of the hypothetical Commune was made intentionally by the ancestors of the Australian aborigines."[1] With this conclusion of the veteran anthropologist I cordially agree.

[1] A. W. Howitt, *Native Tribes of South-East Australia*, p. 143. Elsewhere Dr. Howitt had written as follows: "I cannot see any reason to doubt that the first division of Australian communities into two exogamous intermarrying communes was an intentional act arising from within the commune prior to its division. The evidence which I have before me, drawn from the existing customs and beliefs of the aborigines, not only leads me to that conclusion, but also to the further conclusion that the movement itself probably arose within the council of elders, in which the tribal wizard, the professed communicant with ancestral spirits, holds no mean place. The change, whenever it was effected, must, I think, have been announced as having been directed by the spirits of the deceased ancestors (*e.g.* Mura Mura of the Dieri), or by the Headman of Spiritland himself (*e.g.* Bunjil of the Kulin, or Daramulun of the Murring)." See A. W. Howitt, "Notes on the Australian Class Systems," *Journal of the Anthropological Institute*, xii. (1883) pp. 500 *sq.* Compare *id.*, *Native Tribes of South-East Australia*, pp. 89 *sq.*

CHAPTER III

TOTEMISM IN NORTH-EAST AUSTRALIA

NORTH-EAST Australia coincides with the Colony of Queensland. Some of the tribes of that colony have been dealt with in the preceding chapter, because they fell within the scope of Dr. Howitt's researches, who is our principal authority for the tribes of South-East Australia. In the present chapter I shall describe the exogamous and totemic systems of the remaining tribes of Queensland, so far as these have been reported by competent witnesses. Our chief authority for the natives of this region is Mr. W. E. Roth, who has given us valuable accounts of the tribes of North-West Central Queensland.[1] The area covered by his researches includes the districts of Upper Flinders, Cloncurry, Leichhardt-Selwyn, Upper Georgina, and Boulia.[2] In what follows I shall rely mainly on the information supplied by Mr. Roth.

Tribes of North-West Central Queensland.

Throughout North-West Central Queensland the type of social organisation is the four-class system with maternal

---

[1] W. E. Roth, *Ethnological Studies among the North-West-Central Queensland Aborigines* (Brisbane and London, 1897). The information given in these *Studies* has since been supplemented by Mr. Roth in a series of *Bulletins* published by the Government of Queensland (Numbers 1-12, Brisbane and Sydney, 1901-1909). An excellent, though brief, account of some Queensland tribes has been given by Mr. Edward Palmer ("Notes on some Australian tribes," *Journal of the Anthropological Institute* xiii. (1884) pp. 276-334).

The region covered by Mr. Palmer's observations partly coincides with that described by Mr. W. E. Roth; for it comprises the valleys of the Saxby, Flinders, Cloncurry, Leichhardt, and Gregory Rivers, but it also extends further to the north-east so as to include part of the valley of the Mitchell River as far down as its junction with the Lynd.

[2] See the map of North-West Central Queensland forming Plate I. of W. E. Roth's *Ethnological Studies*.

Throughout these tribes the type of social organisation is the four-class system with female descent.

descent. To be more precise, the native tribes are regularly subdivided into two exogamous classes or moieties and four exogamous subclasses with descent in the female line. The names of the classes are Ootaroo and Pakoota or local varieties of these names (Woodaroo, Urtaroo, Pakŭtta, Burgŭtta); the names of the subclasses are in general Koopooroo, Woongko, Koorkilla, and Bunburi. Of these four subclasses, Koopooroo and Woongko together make up the class or moiety Ootaroo; while Koorkilla and Bunburi make up the other class or moiety Pakoota. The children belong to the class of their mother, but to the other subclass, according to the usual rule of descent in Australian tribes with four or more subdivisions. Thus if the mother belongs to the Ootaroo class and the Koopooroo subclass, the children will belong to the Ootaroo class, but to the Woongko subclass. And similarly with the rest. Further, the men of any particular subclass may only marry the women of one other subclass, and *vice versa*. Thus, a Koopooroo man may only marry a Koorkilla woman, and their children are Bunburi: a Woongko man may only marry a Bunburi woman, and their children are Koorkilla: a Koorkilla man may only marry a Koopooroo woman, and their children are Woongko: a Bunburi man may only marry a Woongko woman, and their children are Koopooroo. This may be put in tabular form as follows:—[1]

Classes.	Husbands.	Wives.	Children.
Ootaroo	Koopooroo Woongko	Koorkilla Bunburi	Bunburi Koorkilla
Pakoota	Koorkilla Bunburi	Koopooroo Woongko	Woongko Koopooroo

Thus the subclasses fall as usual into pairs which may, for convenience of reference, be called complementary or twin

---

[1] W. E. Roth, *Ethnological Studies among the North-West-Central Queensland Aborigines* (Brisbane and London, 1897), pp. 56-58. I have substituted the terms class and subclass for Mr. Roth's *gamo-matro-nym* and *paedo-matro-nym*, to which they are clearly equivalent.

subclasses, each pair being subdivisions of one of the two primary classes. Koopooroo and Woongko are complementary or twin subclasses of the primary class Ootaroo, while Koorkilla and Bunburi are complementary or twin subclasses of the primary class Pakoota. The social system is identical with that of the Kamilaroi,[1] though the names of the classes and subclasses are different. Descent of the primary classes (Ootaroo and Pakoota) is direct in the female line, since children belong to their mother's primary class; but descent of the subclasses is indirect in the female line, since children belong, not to their mother's subclass, but to its complementary or twin subclass. *Complementary or twin subclasses. Direct and indirect descent in the female line.*

The names of the four subclasses Koopooroo, Woongko, Koorkilla, and Bunburi are those which are in use among the Pitta-Pitta tribe at Boulia. But the same subclasses with the same names exist universally throughout the Boulia District among the dozens of different tribes occupying it. Also outside that district exactly the same terms are applied to the subclasses at Roxburgh on the Georgina River, among the Miorli and Goa people of the Middle and Upper Diamantina River, and among the natives of the Cloncurry and Flinders Districts. Nay more than that they occur along the eastern coast of Queensland for a long way, certainly as far as from Cooktown on the north to Broadsound on the south.[2] They are also found in the Yerrunthully tribe near Hughenden, at the headwaters of the Flinders River in Central Queensland;[3] and the same subclasses occur too in the Ringa-Ringa tribe on the Burke River in Queensland.[4] *Subclasses in the Pitta-Pitta, Miorli, Goa, etc. tribes.*

In three other tribes of North-West Central Queensland, namely the Kalkadoon, Miubbi, and Workoboongo, equivalent subclasses are found, but their names are different; and in *Subclasses in the Kalkadoon,*

---

[1] See above, pp. 396 sqq.
[2] W. E. Roth, *Ethnological Studies*, etc., p. 57; *id.*, *Notes on Social and Individual Nomenclature among certain North Queensland Aboriginals*, p. 3 (paper read before the Royal Society of Queensland, November 13, 1897, separate reprint).
[3] E. Palmer, "Notes on some Australian Tribes," *Journal of the Anthropological Institute*, xiii. (1884) pp. 301 sq. Mr. Palmer writes the names of the subclasses, Coobaroo, Woonco, Koorgielah, and Bunbury, which are clearly the same as Mr. Roth's Kooparoo, Woongko, Kurkilla, and Bunburi. The names of the primary classes of the Yerrunthully are not given by Mr. Palmer.
[4] Mr. Jno. Lett, cited by Dr. A. W. Howitt, *Journal of the Anthropological Institute*, xiii. (1884) p. 337, where the names are given as Coobooroo, Wonko, Goorkela, and Bunbury.

Miubbi, and Workoboongo tribes.

the Kalkadoon tribe the name of one of the moieties or primary classes is Mullara instead of Pakoota. The names of the subclasses in these three tribes are as follows:—[1]

Pitta-Pitta, etc.	Kalkadoon.	Miubbi.	Workoboongo.
Koopooroo = Woongko =	Patingo Kunggilungo	Badingo Jimmilingo	Patingo Jimmilingo
Koorkilla = Bunburi =	Marinungo Toonbeungo	Youingo Maringo	Kapoodungo Maringo

Marriage and descent in the Kalkadoon tribe.

The rules of marriage and descent in the Kalkadoon tribe may be tabulated as follows:—[2]

Classes.	Husband.	Wife.	Children.
Ootaroo {	Patingo Kunggilungo	Marinungo Toonbeungo	Toonbeungo Marinungo
Mullara {	Marinungo Toonbeungo	Patingo Kunggilungo	Kunggilungo Patingo

Marriage and descent in the Miubbi tribe.

The rules of marriage and descent in the Miubbi tribe may be tabulated as follows:—[3]

---

[1] W. E. Roth, *Ethnological Studies among the North-West Central Queensland Aborigines*, pp. 56, 57. The names of the Kalkadoon primary classes (Ootaroo and Mullara) are clearly identical with Wuthera and Mallera, the names of the primary classes of the Wakelbura tribe, at Elgin Downs, on the Belyando River, Queensland. It is worthy of note that in the Wakelbura tribe the names of two of the subclasses, viz. Kurgilla and Wungo, agree with the names (Koorkilla and Woongko) of two of the subclasses of the Queensland tribes mentioned above, though not with those of the Kalkadoon. See *Journal of the Anthropological Institute*, xiii. (1884) pp. 337, 342; A. W. Howitt, *Native Tribes of South-East Australia*, pp. 112, 221; above, pp. 422 *sq.* Further, the class name Ootaroo is found also, in slightly disguised forms (Witteru, Wutthuru, or Wutaru), in the Kuinmurbura, Kongulu, and Mackay tribes of Queensland. See L. Fison and A. W. Howitt, *Kamilaroi and Kurnai*, p. 34; *Journal of the Anthropological Institute*, xiii. (1884) p. 336; A. W. Howitt, *Native Tribes of South-East Australia*, p. 111; above, pp. 417, 420, 431.

[2] W. E. Roth, *Ethnological Studies*, etc., p. 58.

[3] W. E. Roth, *Ethnological Studies*, p. 59. As to the names (Woodaroo and Pakutta) of the primary classes among the Miubbi, see *ibid.* p. 56.

Classes.	Husband.	Wife.	Children.
Woodaroo	Badingo Jimmilingo	Youingo Maringo	Maringo Youingo
Pakutta	Youingo Maringo	Badingo Jimmilingo	Jimmilingo Badingo

The Mycoolon tribe of North-West Queensland, on the Flinders River, about a hundred miles south of Normanton, has the same subclasses and rules of descent as the Miubbi, but like many other Australian tribes it has two sets of names for the subclasses, one set for the men and the other set for the women. These names are as follows:— *Marriage and descent in the Mycoolon tribe.*

Male.	Female.
Bathingo Jimalingo Yowingo Marringo	Munjingo Goothamungo Carburungo Ngarran-ngungo

The rules of marriage and descent are these:—[1]

Husband.	Wife.	Children.
Bathingo	Carburungo	Marringo (*male*) and Ngarran-ngungo (*female*)
Jimalingo	Ngarran-ngungo	Yowingo (*m.*) and Carburungo (*f.*)
Yowingo Marringo	Munjingo Goothamungo	Jimalingo (*m.*) and Goothamungo (*f.*) Bathingo (*m.*) and Munjingo (*f.*)

[1] E. Palmer, "Notes on some Australian Tribes," *Journal of the Anthropological Institute*, xiii. (1884) pp. 302 *sq.* I have changed Mr. Palmer's order of the names for the sake of easier comparison with Mr. Roth's. The names of the classes of the Mycoolon are not given by Mr. Palmer. Other Australian tribes have, like the Mycoolon, two sets of names for the subclasses, one for the men and the other for the women; but the female names are sometimes merely variants of the male names. See above, pp. 268, 269, 397 note [2], 407 note [1], 415 note [2], 417 note [2], 418 note [1], 420 note [3], 424 note [1], 431 note [1], 463 note [2].

Or if, for the sake of simplicity, the feminine forms of the subclass names be omitted, the table will stand thus :—

Classes.	Husband.	Wife.	Children.
A {	Bathingo	Yowingo	Marringo
	Jimalingo	Marringo	Yowingo
B {	Yowingo	Bathingo	Jimalingo
	Marringo	Jimalingo	Bathingo

Thus it will be seen that the Mycoolon system, like that of the other Queensland tribes just described, agrees essentially with the Kamilaroi system of New South Wales. It consists of two exogamous classes or moieties and four subclasses with descent in the female line, children belonging to their mother's class and to her complementary or twin subclass; so that we have direct female descent of the classes and indirect female descent of the subclasses.

<small>Equivalent subclasses in other Queensland tribes.</small> Equivalent subclasses under different names are found also among other Queensland tribes. Thus the Woolangama at Normanton (who came originally from between Spear Creek and Croydon) call the subdivisions Rara, Ranya, Awunga, and Loora, these being equivalent respectively to the Koopooroo, Woongko, Koorkilla, and Bunburi of the Pitta-Pitta. The Koreng-Koreng of the Miriam Vale, south of Gladstone, name them Deroin, Balgoyn, Bunda, and Barung ; while a number of tribes, such as the Taroombul at Rockhampton, the Duppil at Gladstone, the Karoonbara at Rosewood and Yaamba, the Rakivira at Yeppoon, the Bouwiwara at Marlborough, and the Koomabara at Torilla, all agree in naming the subclasses Koorpul, Koodala, Karalbara, and Munnul for the males, and Koorpulan, Koodalan, Karalbaran, and Munnulan for the females. These equivalent names for the subclasses may be tabulated as follows :—[1]

---

[1] W. E. Roth, *Notes on Social and Individual Nomenclature among certain North Queensland Aborigines*, p. 3 (paper read before the Royal Society of Queensland, November 13th, 1897, separate reprint).

Pitta-Pitta, etc.	Woolangama.	Koreng-Koreng.	Toorambul, Duppil, etc.
⎰ Koopooroo ⎱ Woongko ⎰ Koorkilla ⎱ Bunburi	Rara Ranya Awunga Loora	Deroin Balgoyn Bunda Barung	Koorpul Koodala Karalbara Munnul

Although the names of the subclasses vary in some of these Queensland tribes, yet under different names these exogamous divisions are treated by the natives themselves as equivalent to each other even in tribes that live far apart. On this subject Mr. Palmer says: "There is no well-authenticated instance with which I am acquainted of any Australian blacks who were without one form or another of divisions into classes; where such divisions have been believed to be absent it has been from the want of their being discovered by the observer, and not from their non-existence. The blacks are born into these divisions, and are reared up with the idea instilled into them that it is necessary for them to observe as sacred the class rules; indeed, to many it would be like sacrilege to marry contrary to these established rules. They do not give any traditions as to when these rules were first introduced, the fact being that they have carried the idea of the divisions with them through all their wanderings since they first settled in Australia. It seems strange, but is perhaps not unaccountable, that the classes and their divisions found in all the tribes correspond with each other, although differing in name or in totem, over localities separated from each other by hundreds of miles.

"Like all other Australian tribes, those of the Gulf of Carpentaria are divided into separate divisions. Taking the Mycoolon tribes as an instance, adjoining tribes have the same class names, and have totems having the same meaning. Tribes at a greater distance have a different set of divisions, with distinguishing totems for each class. In cases of distant tribes it can be shown that the class divisions correspond with each other, as, for instance, in the class divisions of the Flinders River and Mitchell

Equivalence of the class divisions in different tribes.

River tribes; and these tribes are separated by four hundred miles of country, and by many intervening tribes. But for all that, class corresponds to class in fact, and in meaning, and in privileges, although the name may be quite different, and the totems of each dissimilar. Some tribes have males and females of the same name, while others have separate class names for males and females. It is well known now that from Moreton Bay to the shores of the Gulf of Carpentaria, a distance of over fifteen hundred miles in length, and for seven hundred miles inland, or even to a much greater distance, the blacks are divided into divisions for the purpose of preventing too close connections in marriage, and that all these divisions correspond with each other. Thus a blackfellow from one of the most southern tribes could easily tell from what division he could obtain a wife if he were to visit a tribe in the far north, if such a visit could be effected, and he were received by them."[1]

Meaning of the names of the classes and subclasses.

The meaning of the names of the subclasses in these Queensland tribes has not been reported either by Mr. W. E. Roth or by Mr. E. Palmer, our chief authorities on the subject. Indeed Mr. Roth tells us that he could not ascertain it.[2] But on the other hand he points out that the names of the two moieties or primary classes (Ootaroo and Pakoota) bear a resemblance to the Pitta-Pitta numerals for "one" and "two," namely *oorooroo* and *pakoola*.[3] If this etymology should prove to be correct, it would favour the view that the moieties or primary classes are not totemic, but that they originated in a simple bisection of the tribe which was devised and carried out for the purpose of regulating marriage.[4] Further research into the nomenclature of the classes and subclasses of Australian tribes might perhaps lead to the discovery of other names borrowed from simple numerals.

Mr. Roth does not find totemism in Queensland.

The preceding account of the exogamous divisions among the tribes of North-West-Central Queensland proves that they are organised on the regular four-class system

---

[1] E. Palmer, "Notes on some Australian Tribes," *Journal of the Anthropological Institute*, xiii. (1884) pp. 299 *sq*.

[2] W. E. Roth, *Ethnological Studies*, p. 57.

[3] *Op. cit.* pp. 26, 56.

[4] See above, pp. 282 *sqq*.

with descent in the maternal line. But whereas the ordinary Australian tribe is further subdivided into clans, each with its totem or totems, no such totemic clans have been found by Mr. W. E. Roth to exist among the tribes of North-West-Central Queensland.[1] It is possible, however, that they exist but have escaped his attention. For totem clans of the ordinary type, with hereditary totems and a rule of exogamy, apparently occur in some of the Queensland tribes,[2] and wherever the organisation in exogamous classes exists in Australia we expect to find the totemic organisation underlying it.

Moreover, another careful observer, Mr. Edward Palmer, has reported totemism as existing among some of the Queensland tribes which possess the very same exogamous subclasses that are recorded by Mr. Roth. His evidence will be adduced presently. Meantime it is important to note that Mr. Roth himself has discovered and described among the Queensland tribes an elaborate system of food taboos, which, while they resemble the food taboos observed by totemic clans, yet differ from them in two remarkable respects. For in the first place the social groups which observe them are not totemic clans but the four exogamous subclasses; and in the second place each group (in this case, each subclass) has not, like an ordinary totemic clan, only one forbidden food, whether animal or vegetable, on the contrary it has regularly several or even many tabooed articles of diet, from all of which every member of the subclass is expected rigorously to abstain under severe penalties. These taboos are imposed on men and women as soon as

Elaborate system of food taboos strictly observed by the exogamous subclasses in Queensland.

---

[1] Mr. Roth says: "So far, I have met with no examples of totemism in Northern or North - West - Central Queensland" (*Notes on Social and Individual Nomenclature among certain North Queensland Aboriginals*, pp. 11 *sq.*). In his latest published work Mr. Roth modifies this statement as follows: "By totemism I understand a certain connection between an animal or plant, or group of animals or plants, and an individual or group of individuals respectively, and judged by this standard, the only totemism discoverable throughout North Queensland is that met with in the animals, etc., forbidden to the different exogamous groups, and to a far less degree to women and children generally, and to the novices temporarily at the initiation ceremonies." See W. E. Roth, "On certain Initiation Ceremonies," *North Queensland Ethnography, Bulletin No.* 12 (Sydney, 1909), p. 168. In this passage by "exogamous groups" Mr. Roth means what I call the subclasses.

[2] For example, in the Kuinmurbura, Kongulu, and Wakelbura tribes. See above, pp. 417, 421, 422 *sq.*

they have passed through the first initiation ceremony. The forbidden foods are nearly all animals ; indeed Mr. Roth at first reported that after very careful search he could find no plants, trees, fruits, shrubs, and grasses laid under an interdict. However, in a later publication, as we shall see, he mentions the stinging-tree among the things associated with, and therefore probably tabooed to, one of the exogamous subclasses. While the members of each subclass are strictly forbidden to eat certain species of animals, they are not necessarily prohibited from killing them. The list of tabooed foods is constant for each subclass throughout a tribe, but it varies for corresponding subclasses in different tribes, and these variations appear to be well known to the more intelligent natives. For example, a man of the Koopooroo subclass in the Pitta-Pitta tribe has not the same restrictions on his diet as a man of the same Koopooroo subclass in the neighbouring Mitakoodi tribe at Cloncurry.[1] These taboos are rigorously observed and enforced. "Upon this point," says Mr. Roth, "these aboriginals appear to be extremely particular, and should one of them wilfully partake of that which is 'tabooed,' he is firmly convinced that sickness, probably of a fatal character, will overtake him, and that certainly it would never satisfy his hunger. Should such a delinquent be caught red-handed by his fellow-men, he would in all probability be put to death."[2]

Foods forbidden to the subclasses. Lists of animals which are forbidden as food to the various subclasses have been recorded by Mr. Roth. They may be tabulated as follows :—[3]

---

[1] W. E. Roth, *Notes on Social and Individual Nomenclature among certain North Queensland Aboriginals*, pp. 3 sq. (paper read before the Royal Society of Queensland, November 13, 1897, separate reprint); *id.*, *Ethnological Studies*, p. 57.

[2] W. E. Roth, *Ethnological Studies*, p. 57.

[3] W. E. Roth, *Ethnological Studies*, pp. 57 sq.

TOTEMISM IN NORTH-EAST AUSTRALIA

Pitta-Pitta Tribe (Boulia District)

Subclasses.	Tabooed Animals (Totems?).
Koopooroo	iguana, whistler-duck, black-duck, "blue-fellow" crane, yellow dingo, and small yellow fish "with-one-bone-in-him."
Woongko	scrub-turkey, eagle-hawk, bandicoot or "bilbi," brown snake, black dingo, and "white altogether" duck.
Koorkilla	kangaroo, carpet-snake, teal, white-bellied brown-headed duck, various kinds of "diver" birds, "trumpeter" fish, and a kind of black bream.
Bunburi	emu, yellow snake, golah parrot, and a certain species of hawk.

Kalkadoon Tribe (Leichhardt-Selwyn Ranges)

Subclasses.	Tabooed Animals (Totems?).
Patingo (= Koopooroo)	emu, carpet-snake, brown-snake, mountain-snake, etc., porcupine, wallaby, rat, opossum, and "mountain" kangaroo.
Kunggilungo (= Woongko)	emu, carpet-snake, brown-snake, "mountain" snake, porcupine, "mountain" kangaroo, wallaby, opossum, "sugar-bag" (i.e. honey), and various fish.
Marinungo (= Koorkilla)	pelican, whistler-duck, black duck, turkey, "plain" kangaroo (i.e. living on the plains), and certain kinds of fish.
Toonbeungo (= Bunburi)	whistler-duck, wood-duck, "native companion," "plain" kangaroo, rat, bandicoot, and carpet-snake.

Mitakoodi Tribe (Cloncurry District)

Subclasses.	Tabooed Animals (Totems?).
Koopooroo	principally iguana, whistler-duck, and carpet-snake.
Woongko	„ porcupine, emu, and kangaroo.
Koorkilla	„ water-snake, corella, eagle-hawk, black-duck, and turkey.
Bunburi	principally carpet-snake and dingo.

Woonamurra Tribe (Flinders District)

Subclasses.	Tabooed Animals (Totems?).
{ Koopooroo . . { Woongko . .	principally carpet-snake and emu. ?
{ Koorkilla . . { Bunburi . .	,, eagle-hawk, black-snake, and brown-snake. principally black-duck and turkey.

Goa Tribe (Upper Diamantina)

Subclass.	Tabooed Animals (Totems?).
Koopooroo . .	emu and kāngaroo.

Animals, plants, etc., associated with the subclasses on the Proserpine River.

Among the natives of the Proserpine River the four subclasses bear the names Kupuru, Wungko, Kurchilla, and Banbari, which are practically identical with the Koopooroo, Woongko, Koorkilla, and Bunburi of the Pitta-Pitta; and associated with each subclass are certain animals, plants, or other objects, which, so far as they are edible, are probably tabooed to the members of the respective subclass. The list of these associated or tabooed objects is this:—[1]

Subclasses.	Associated Objects (Totems?).
{ Kupuru . . { Wungko . .	stinging-tree, emu, eel, turtle. wind, rain, brown-snake, carpet-snake.
{ Kurchilla . . { Banbari . .	rainbow, opossum, ground-iguana, frilled lizard. honey, sting-ray, bandicoot, eagle-hawk.

An inspection of the foregoing tables may suffice to convince us that the restrictions in respect of food which

[1] W. E. Roth, *North Queensland Ethnography, Bulletin No.* 5, *Superstition, Magic, and Medicine* (Brisbane, 1903), p. 21.

such a system of taboos lays on every member of a subclass must be much more burdensome than those which are imposed on members of an ordinary totemic clan; for whereas the members of a totemic clan have as a rule to abstain only from one sort of animal or plant, members of these subclasses have each to abstain from several or even many sorts of animals under pain of death. The question naturally arises, How is this multiplex, abnormal totemism, as we may call it, of the subclasses, related to the simple, normal totemism of the clans? Has it been developed out of that system by the absorption of the totemic clans in the subclasses? or does it on the contrary represent an earlier stage in the evolution of totemism, a stage out of which in process of time the normal totemism of the clans might have been evolved by a segmentation of the exogamous subclasses? In short, is the totemism of the subclasses totemism in decadence or totemism in germ? If one of these solutions is true, it appears to me that the probabilities are all in favour of the former, that is, of the view that the totemism of the subclasses is decadent, and that it has been produced by the absorption of the old totem clans in the newer exogamous classes. For we have seen grounds for believing that the original organisation of the Australian tribes was in totemic clans, and that the exogamous classes were introduced later for the purpose of regulating marriage by barring the union of persons too near of kin.[1] If that is so, it would be contrary to all analogy to suppose that the subclasses of these Queensland tribes represent a stage of social evolution prior to the development of the totemic clans, that they are, so to say, the hive from which totemic clans in time might have swarmed, if the process of evolution had not been rudely interrupted by the coming of the white race. Far more likely is it that the weight of the newer social organisation in exogamous classes has crushed the old totem clans out of existence, while at the same time it has inherited from them the system of totemic taboos, which, no longer distributed among a number of small separate groups (the clans) so as to sit lightly on all, are now heaped together and press heavily on every member of the newer

The food taboos of the exogamous subclasses in Queensland seem to be totemism in decay: the subclasses have apparently superseded the totemic clans and inherited their taboos.

[1] See above, pp. 162 *sq.*, 251 *sq.*, 257 *sq.*

and larger group (the subclass) which has superseded and obliterated its predecessors. In point of fact we have already detected among the northern tribes of Central Australia, whose totemism is more advanced than that of the true central tribes, clear traces of a gradual supersession of the totemic clans by the exogamous classes.[1] It is, therefore, natural enough to find the same process of development carried a stage further among the neighbouring tribes of North-Western Queensland.

Mr. Palmer's evidence as to the existence of totemism in Queensland.

But I have said that the existence of totemism of the normal sort in these Queensland tribes appears to be vouched for by an excellent observer, Mr. Edward Palmer. Let us now look at his evidence closely and see whether it really conflicts with that of Mr. Roth, who finds no instances of normal totemism, that is, of totemic clans, in this region.

That totemism exists among the tribes of North-Western Queensland certainly appears to be attested by Mr. E. Palmer, who says: "They have a great reverence for the particular animal symbolising their respective classes, and if any one were to kill say, a bird belonging to such a division in the sight of the bearer of its family name, he might be heard to say, 'What for you kill that fellow? that my father!' or 'That brother belonging to me you have killed; why did you do it?'"[2]

Again, we have seen that the subclasses of the Yerrunthully and Ringa-Ringa tribes of Queensland bear the same names as the subclasses of the Pitta-Pitta and other tribes described by Mr. Roth.[3] Now, according to Mr. Palmer, the subclasses of the Yerrunthully tribe on the Flinders River "are represented by totems," which are reported as follows:—[4]

---

[1] See above, pp. 225, 227 *sq.*, 235 *sq.*

[2] E. Palmer, "Notes on some Australian Tribes," *Journal of the Anthropological Institute*, xiii. (1884) p. 300.

[3] Above, p. 517.

[4] E. Palmer, "Notes on some Australian Tribes," *Journal of the Anthropological Institute*, xiii. (1884) p. 302.

Subclasses.		Totems.	
Bunbury		Carpet-snake	Tharoona
Coobaroo	}	Brown snake	Warrineyah
		Emu	Goolburry
Koorgielah	}	Plain turkey	Bergamo
		Native dog	Cubburah
Woonco		Whistling-duck	Chewelah

The totems of the Ringa-Ringa tribe on the Burke River, according to Mr. J. Lett, are said to be these :—[1]

Subclasses.	Totem Names.
Goorkela } Bunbury }	Turkey, emu, iguana.
Wonko } Coobooroo }	Carpet-snake, death adder, native cat, kangaroo, rat.

Again, we have seen that the subclasses of the Mycoolon tribe of Queensland bear the same names as the subclasses of the Miubbi tribe described by Mr. Roth.[2] In regard to the Mycoolon we learn from Mr. Palmer that "each class name has a symbol or totem in this tribe, or animal representing that class. Each young lad is strictly forbidden to eat of that animal or bird which belongs to his respective class, for it is his brother. The classes are represented as follows :—

Marringo	Black duck		Karrabah
Yowingo	{ Plain turkey		Thoorna
	{ Eagle-hawk		Cooreythilla
Bathingo	{ Carpet-snake		Koorema
	{ Iguana		Yangolah
Jimalingo	Whistling-duck		Wallatho

[1] Mr. Jno. Lett, Burke River, Queensland, reported by Dr. A. W. Howitt in *Journal of the Anthropological Institute*, xiii. (1884) p. 337.

[2] Above, pp. 518, 519.

"On the Leichhardt River, Jimalingo is represented by Wootharoo, whose totem is catfish."¹

On the whole it seems that in North-West Queensland the old totemism of the clans has been superseded by totemism of the exogamous subclasses.

The question now arises, Does the foregoing evidence of Messrs. Palmer and Lett as to the totems of the Yerrunthully, Ringa-Ringa, and Mycoolon tribes suffice to establish for these tribes the existence of totemic clans of the ordinary pattern? It appears to me that it does not. In every case the totemic animal is associated with an exogamous subclass, precisely as in Mr. Roth's fuller account of the system. There is nothing to shew that, as in other Australian tribes, the totems are inherited by every person directly from his father or mother, so as to remain constant from generation to generation, while the twin subclasses alternate in alternate generations.² To say this is simply to say that there is no proof of the existence of true totemic clans in these particular tribes. Therefore we have no reason to assume that the evidence of Messrs. Palmer and Lett conflicts with that of Mr. Roth on this subject; and as Mr. Roth has investigated the question fully, and appears moreover to be a careful and accurate observer, it is difficult to suppose that totemic clans of the ordinary sort could have escaped his observation if they really existed. The conclusion of the whole matter is that among the tribes of North-West Queensland the old totemism of the clans has apparently been superseded by a new and more burdensome totemism of the exogamous subclasses.

The same thing may perhaps have happened in other Australian tribes.

In the light of the foregoing discussion it seems possible that as to some tribes of South-East Australia Dr. Howitt's native informants may after all have been right in affirming that the totems were permanently attached to the subclasses and did not alternate between them in alternate generations, as Dr. Howitt thought they must do.³ For in these tribes, as apparently in the Queensland tribes which we are considering, the totemic clans may have been absorbed in the exogamous subclasses, bequeathing to them their totemic

---

¹ E. Palmer, "Notes on some Australian Tribes," *Journal of the Anthropological Institute*, xiii. (1884) p. 303. Wootharoo as the name of a subclass is probably identical with Ootaroo (Woodaroo), the name of a class in some Queensland tribes. See above, pp. 516, 518 note ¹.

² As to this alternation or oscillation of the totems between the subclasses in alternate generations, see above, pp. 408 *sq.*, 419, 433 *sq.*

³ See above, pp. 433 *sq.*

taboos, so that the totems, instead of oscillating between two subclasses in alternate generations, would come to rest finally in one of them. For with totemism of the subclasses instead of the clans these oscillations or alternations necessarily cease; the totems become permanently attached each to its particular subclass.

A point of great interest in these totemic taboos of the subclasses is that they only come into force when the boy or girl has passed through the first ceremony of initiation,[1] in other words, has attained to puberty and been allowed to rank with the men or women of the tribe. Strange as it may seem, observers have in general failed to record whether the ordinary taboo as to eating the totemic animal or plant applies to every member of a totem clan from birth or only from puberty. We know indeed that many kinds of food are tabooed to a youth before or at initiation;[2] but so far as I remember we are not told whether among the foods so tabooed is his totemic animal or plant. The point may be of great importance for an understanding of totemism. For if it should appear that the prohibition to eat the totem only begins to be observed by men and women when they become marriageable, this would be a strong argument in favour of the intimate relation between what I have called the religious and the social side of totemism; since in the life of the individual the two characteristic commands of normal totemism, "Thou shalt not eat thy totem," and "Thou shalt not marry a woman of thy totem," would then come into operation simultaneously and might therefore reasonably be thought to be mutually interdependent. Whereas, if the prohibition to eat the totem begins to be observed in infancy, this would favour the view, to which the Australian evidence seems to point, that the prohibition was originally independent of the prohibition to marry a woman of the same totem. It is to be hoped that information on this subject may yet be forthcoming before it is too late.

The totemic taboos of the subclasses only come into force when the boy or girl has passed through the first ceremony of initiation.

[1] This is expressly stated by Mr. W. E. Roth in his *Notes on Social and Individual Nomenclature among certain North Queensland Aboriginals*, p. 3. Elsewhere (*Ethnological Studies*, p. 57) he merely says that the taboos come into force for every individual "as soon as he or she arrives at the necessary age," by which, however, he probably means puberty.

[2] See above, pp. 40-42.

532 TOTEMISM IN NORTH-EAST AUSTRALIA CHAP.

Benefits conferred by the totems.

In some of these Queensland tribes thunder, rain, wind, rainbow, stinging-tree, and honey are included among the totems, if we may call them so, of the subclasses; and the totems, whether animals or things, are supposed to benefit the men and women in various ways, provided they be duly called upon at the proper times. The practice of thus invoking the totems is described by Mr. Roth as follows:—

Custom of calling upon name-sake animals, etc., in order to ensure success in the chase or to obtain warning of danger.

"*Calling upon name-sakes, etc., before going to sleep, etc.*— On the Tully River, also, whenever a man (or woman) lies down and stretches himself for a spell, or on going to sleep, or on arising of a morning, he mentions in more or less of an undertone, the name of the animal, etc., after which he is called, or belonging to his group-division, prefixing it with *wintcha? wintcha?* (= where? where?). If there is any particular noise, cry, or call connected with such name, he may mimic it. The objects aimed at in carrying out this practice, which is taught by the elders to the youngsters as soon as they are considered old enough to learn such things, are that they may be lucky and skilful in hunting, and be given full warning as to any danger which might otherwise befall them from the animal, etc., after which they are named. If a man, named after a fish, thus regularly calls upon it, he will be successful in catching plenty on some future occasion, should he be hungry. If an individual neglects to call the thunder, rain, etc., provided of course they are his name-sakes, he will lose the power of making them. Snakes, alligators, etc., will never interfere with their name-sakes, provided they are thus always called upon, without giving a warning — a 'something' which the aboriginal feels in his belly, a tingling in his thighs or legs, etc. If the individual neglects to do so, it is his own fault that he is bitten or caught. This calling upon name-sakes is not supposed to benefit the women very much. If people were to call upon others than their name-sakes, under the circumstances above mentioned, it would bear no results either for good or harm.

"A similar practice prevails on the Proserpine River, where the native, before going to sleep, calls upon one or other of the names of the animals, plants, or other objects connected with his particular primary group-division, thus:—

"Kurchilla: rain-bow, opossum, ground-iguana, frilled lizard.
"Kupuru: stinging-tree, emu, eel, turtle.
"Banbari: honey, sting-ray, bandicoot, eagle-hawk.
"Wungko: wind, rain, brown-snake, carpet-snake.

"In reply to inquiries, the reason given me is that when called upon they warn the people, who have summoned them, of the advent of other animals, etc., during sleep."[1]

From this account it appears that by observing certain rules a man, whose name-sake or totem, if we may call it so, is thunder or rain, can make thunder or rain; that a man whose totem is a fish can catch plenty of that sort of fish; that a man whose totem is a snake or an alligator will not be bitten by a snake or an alligator, and so forth. In other words, the man is apparently credited with possessing a magical control over his totem species, whether the totem be an animal or a thing, so that if the animal be edible he can catch plenty of the species; if it be a dangerous creature, it will not harm him; and if it be an inanimate object like thunder or rain, he can produce it at pleasure. Similarly, as we have seen, in the Arunta and other tribes of Central Australia the men of the various totem clans perform magical ceremonies (*intichiuma*) for the multiplication of their totem animals and plants in order that these may serve as food for their fellow-tribesmen; while the men of the totem themselves abstain, as a rule, from eating of their totem animal or plant.[2]

Thus men seem to have power over their totems, like the Arunta and other central tribes.

But here a difficulty arises. For Mr. Roth has told us that the Queensland natives strictly abstain, under pain of death, from eating the edible animals associated with their particular subclasses or paedo-matronymic groups, as he calls them. Yet in the passage just quoted he seems to affirm that men may kill and eat such animals, indeed that they possess a special power of catching them. How is the apparent discrepancy to be explained? The work from which the latter passage (about the killing of the animals) is extracted was published some six years later than the work from which the former passage (about the forbidden foods)

Difficulty in reconciling Mr. Roth's statements.

[1] W. E. Roth, *North Queensland Ethnography, Bulletin No. 5, Superstition, Magic, and Medicine* (Brisbane, 1903), pp. 20 *sq.*
[2] See above, pp. 104 *sqq.*, 183 *sqq.*, 214 *sqq.*

was extracted; and in the interval Mr. Roth may very well have ascertained that the rule against eating the totem (if we may call it so) was not so absolute as he had at first supposed; he may possibly have discovered that, just as among the Central Australian tribes, there are circumstances in which the clansmen are permitted or even required to eat their clan totem. In that case, the analogy between the magical aspect of the totems in Queensland and in Central Australia would be fairly complete.

The namesakes which are invoked may be personal or individual totems rather than clan totems. But the solution of the difficulty may perhaps lie in a different direction. It will be observed that while Mr. Roth speaks of the animal or thing in question as "belonging to his group-division," he also speaks of it as the man's namesake. Thus it is possible that the animal or thing which the man calls upon and which benefits him in various ways, may not be the totem of his subclass, but merely an object specially associated with him as an individual; in fact that it may be his individual or personal totem or guardian spirit. That there are such personal totems or guardian spirits in Queensland, as in other parts of Australia,[1] appears from Mr. Roth's account of the individual names

Mode of bestowing names on children at birth. bestowed on boys and girls at birth. He says: "At Princess Charlotte Bay, Cape Bedford, on the Proserpine River, etc., the choice of an infant's pet name depends upon augury. The mother's mother, or other old female, takes a small portion of the navel-string, with after-birth attached, and keeps shaking it pretty violently while the other old women sitting around call out proposed names one after the other: the moment the string breaks, the name which was then called is chosen. From the fact, however, at the Cape, of the same names occurring in the same family, there is every reason for believing that there is some collusion when the navel-string becomes finally torn. On the Bloomfield, certain of the women will come round the child soon after its birth, talk to it somewhat as follows :—'Your name is the same as mine, isn't it, dear?' and accept the kicking of a leg, the turning of the head, a gurgling in the throat—in fact, anything on the part of the infant as a sign or token of affirmation. The name thus given to a child is either that of an

---

[1] See above, pp. 448 sq., 489 sq., 495.

animal, plant, locality, or that of some relative (a name already known, but the meaning of which, in many cases, has been lost). Tully River girls are never named after snakes, fish, or crocodiles. There is no necessarily connecting dependence — though I am prepared to admit the possibility of its having once existed—between the child and its name-sake animal, or plant, which in different districts may or may not be destroyed and eaten by it."[1] These animals and plants, which in some districts the human namesakes may not destroy or eat, are not far removed from personal totems, and in so far as the same names occur, as we are told that they do, in the same family, they approximate also to clan totems. In districts where a man is permitted to destroy and eat his namesake animal, we could understand why he should call upon the creature in order that he may be successful in catching and killing members of the species.

Something like a personal totem seems also to be in use among the Yaraikanna tribe of Cape York, the extreme northern point of Queensland. They call it an *ari*. A man has one or more *ari*, which may be acquired in several ways. The *ari* of a lad is determined at the ceremony of initiation into manhood. The youth lies down on his back and a man loosens one of his front teeth with a kangaroo bone. When the tooth is loosened, the operator taps it smartly, mentioning at each tap one of the "countries" owned by the lad's mother, or by her father, or by another of her relatives. These names are recited in a regular order, and the country whose name is mentioned when the tooth breaks away is the land to which the lad will belong. The lad is then given some water with which to rinse his mouth, and he gently lets the gory spittle fall into a water-basket made of leaves. The old men carefully inspect the clot of blood and spittle and trace in it some likeness to a natural object, an animal, plant, stone, or whatever it may be. The natural object thus chosen will be the *ari* of the newly made man. Again, a person may get an *ari* through a dream. It appears that if an old man dreams of anything at night, that thing is the *ari* of the first person he sees

Personal totems (ari) in the Yaraikanna tribe of Cape York. A lad receives his personal totem (ari) when his tooth is knocked out at puberty.

[1] W. E. Roth, *North Queensland Ethnography, Bulletin No. 5, Superstition, Magic, and Medicine* (Brisbane, 1903), p. 19.

next morning, "the idea being that the animal, or whatever appears in the dream, is the spirit of the first person met with on awakening." Thus a native of the Yaraikanna tribe, Tomari by name, has three *ari*: (1) *aru*, a crab, which he got through blood divination at initiation; (2) *untara*, diamond fish; (3) *alungi*, crayfish. The two latter were given to him as the result of dreams. The *ari* of Tomari's father is a carpet snake, that of his mother an oyster, and that of his wife a kind of fruit. This shows that the *ari* is not hereditary. Women obtain their *ari* in the same way as men. "The *ari* is thus a purely individual affair and is not transmissible, nor has it anything to do with the regulation of marriages."[1] In these respects, therefore, the *ari* resembles the totem of the Central Australians, which in like manner is not transmitted either from the father or from the mother and has nothing to do with the regulation of marriage.

<small>Belief of the Pennefather blacks that babies are made of mud and put into women by a being called Anjea.</small>

The resemblance thus traceable between what we may call the personal totems (*ari*) of the extreme northerly point of Australia and the totems of the central tribes is strengthened by the customs and beliefs of the natives of the Pennefather River in Queensland; for these customs and beliefs seem to form an intermediate link between the one set of totems and the other. The Pennefather blacks think that a being called Anjea, who was originally made by Thunder, fashions babies out of swamp-mud and inserts them in the wombs of women. He is never seen, but can be heard laughing in the depths of the bush, amongst the rocks, down in the lagoons, and along the mangrove swamps;

---

[1] A. C. Haddon, *Head-hunters, Black, White, and Brown* (London, 1901), pp. 193 *sq.*; *Reports of the Cambridge Anthropological Expedition to Torres Straits*, v. pp. 193, 221. In regard to marriage, however, Dr. Haddon says: "If it was true, as I was told, that men and women may not marry into the same *ari* in their own place, but may do so when away from home, its sanctity is local rather than personal. A wife must be taken from another 'country,' as all belonging to the same place are brothers and sisters; which indicates that there is a territorial idea in kinship and in the consequent marriage restrictions" (*Head-hunters*, p. 194). But this statement is not repeated, so far as I have observed, in the *Reports of the Cambridge Anthropological Expedition to Torres Straits*. The similarity of the *ari* to the personal totem (the *manitoo* or *okki* of some North American tribes) has been already indicated by Dr. Haddon (*Head-hunters*, p. 194). As to the totems of the Central Australians, see above, pp. 187 *sqq.*

and when they hear him, the blacks say, "Anjea he laugh; he got him piccaninny." Women do not know when the infants are put inside them, because they may be placed in position by day or by night or in a dream; only when they are placed, the women feel them. Now when Anjea makes the mud-baby, he animates it with a piece of its father's spirit (*choi*), if it is a boy, but with a piece of the spirit of its father's sister, if it is a girl; and when he makes the next little brother or sister, he puts another piece of the spirit of the father or of the father's sister in the mud-baby, and so on. You must not, however, suppose that these portions of spirit are abstracted from the living father or the living father's sister. That is not so. What happens is this. When a child is born into the world, a portion of its spirit stays in its after-birth. Hence the grandmother takes the after-birth away and buries it in the sand, and she marks the place by thrusting sticks in a circle into the ground and tying their tops together into a sort of cone. So when Anjea comes along and sees the circle of sticks, he knows what is there and he takes out the spirit and carries it away to one of his haunts, and there it may remain for years, in a cleft of the rock, in a tree, or in a lagoon. Near Mapoon there are three or four such places where Anjea keeps the spirits of babies ready for use. One of them is among the sand-stone rocks at Tullanaringa, which white people call Cullen Point; another is on the beach of Baru; another is among the rocks of Tronkanguno, at the meeting of the waters of the Batavia and Ducie Rivers; another is in the woods among the mangrove swamps of Lalla; and a fourth is in the fresh-water lagoons. There the spirits live till Anjea takes them and puts them into mud-babies, and then they are born again. So when a new baby is born, the father and mother know quite well whose spirit is in it; for if it is a boy, his father's spirit is in it, and if it is a girl, its father's sister's spirit is in it. But what they do not know is where Anjea has been keeping the spirit all these years. And the way they find that out is this. While the grandmother cuts the navel-string, they call out the haunts of Anjea, whether they be on the beach, or in the lagoons, or in the woods among the mangrove swamps, or in the

Every child contains a portion of the spirit of its father or of its father's sister.

A portion of the child's spirit stays in its after-birth.

Places where the spirits of babies stay till they are reincarnated.

rocks at the meeting of the waters, or wherever they may be; and the place which is mentioned when the string breaks is the place where the spirit lived all that long time. That place is the child's own country, its true home, where in future it will have the right to roam and to hunt, though it may be far away from the place where it was born. Hence a baby is sometimes spoken of as an infant got from a tree, a rock, a stone, or fresh water.¹

<small>Comparison of the beliefs of the Pennefather natives with those of the Yaraikanna tribe of Cape York and the tribes of Central Australia.</small>

Thus the mode of determining the country to which a person belongs or which belongs to him is very similar among the Yaraikanna tribe of Cape York and the natives of the Pennefather River; only in the one case the determination takes place at puberty, in the other case at birth, and accordingly in the one case the decisive moment is the breaking of the tooth, in the other the breaking of the navel-string. From the similarity of the two customs we may fairly infer that the country assigned to a man of the Yaraikanna tribe at the extraction of his tooth is the one in which his spirit was supposed to tarry since its last incarnation; and further, though this is more doubtful, we may conjecture that his *ari* or personal totem, which is determined at the same time, is the animal, plant, or what not, in which his spirit resided since its last embodiment in human form, or perhaps in which a part of his spirit may be thought to lodge during life. In favour of this last conjecture it may be pointed out that according to the Pennefather blacks a portion of a man's spirit resides permanently in his after-birth and is thus in a sense the man's external

---

¹ W. E. Roth, *North Queensland Ethnography, Bulletin No. 5, Superstition, Magic, and Medicine*, pp. 18, 23. An almost identical belief obtains among the natives of the Proserpine River, on the eastern coast of Queensland (W. E. Roth, *op. cit.* p. 18). With the expression an infant "got from a tree or a rock" we may compare the Greek phrase οὐ γὰρ ἀπὸ δρυός ἐσσι παλαιφάτου οὐδ' ἀπὸ πέτρης (Homer, *Odyssey*, xix. 163), as to which see A. B. Cook, "Oak and Rock," *The Classical Review*, xv. (1901) pp. 322 *sqq.* As to the rights of families or of individuals over special districts, Dr. J. D. Lang observes: "The territory of each tribe is subdivided, moreover, among the different families of which it consists, and the proprietor of any particular subdivision has the exclusive right to direct when it shall be hunted over, or the grass burned, and the wild animals destroyed; for although there is always a general assembly of the tribe, and sometimes of neighbouring tribes, on such occasions, the entertainment is supposed to be provided exclusively by the proprietor of the land, who is accordingly master of the ceremonies" (J. D. Lang, *Queensland* (London, 1861), p. 336).

soul. However that may be, the beliefs of the Pennefather natives in the reincarnation of ancestral spirits seem clearly to be akin to those of the Central Australian tribes; and the trees, rocks, or water in which Anjea keeps the spirits of the dead till it is time for them to be born again are very like the *nanja* trees, rocks, or water where, according to the Arunta and other Central tribes, the souls of the dead dwell in the intervals between their incarnations.[1] Further, the magical power which the Queensland natives are thought to wield over their namesake animals, plants, or things so as to be able to produce them at pleasure or to catch and kill them,[2] bear a striking resemblance to the magical powers which the Central Australians exert over their totems for precisely the same purposes.[3] Finally, the *ari* of the Yaraikanna and the namesakes of the other Queensland tribes resemble the Central Australian totems in this that they appear to have nothing to do with the regulation of marriage.[4]

The mode of determining a man's personal totem by the knocking out of his tooth at puberty may perhaps help us to understand the motive of the similar ceremony which is so commonly observed among the tribes of South-East Australia.[5] Can it be that the practice of knocking out a tooth at initiation was everywhere associated with the assignment of a personal totem to the novice? and if this was true of the custom of tooth-extraction as an initiatory rite, may it not be true also of the customs of circumcision and subincision? I have elsewhere conjectured that all such rites, the essence of which seems to consist in removing from the novice a vital part of his person, may have been intended to ensure the rebirth of his spirit at a future time.[6]

Rites of initiation perhaps connected with totemism and the doctrine of reincarnation.

---

[1] Spencer and Gillen, *Native Tribes of Central Australia*, pp. 123 *sqq.*; *id.*, *Northern Tribes of Central Australia*, pp. 145 *sqq.*, 341, 396; above, pp. 188 *sqq.* Can the name *Anjea* be connected with the word *nanja*?
[2] See above, p. 532.
[3] See above, pp. 104 *sqq.*, 183 *sqq.*, 214 *sqq.*
[4] See, however, the note on p. 536.
[5] See above, p. 412 note [2].
[6] J. G. Frazer, "The Origin of Circumcision," *The Independent Review*, November 1904, pp. 204-218. In the Queensland tribes described by Mr. E. Palmer "The custom of knocking out the two front teeth is connected with the entry into their heaven. If they have the two front teeth out they will have bright clear water to drink, and if not they will have only dirty or muddy water" (E. Palmer, "Notes on some Australian Tribes," *Journal of the Anthropological Institute*, xiii. (1884) p. 291).

If there is any truth in these conjectures, it would seem to follow that rites of initiation are intimately connected with totemism and the theory of the reincarnation of the dead. But the precise nature of the connection, if indeed it exists at all, remains still obscure.

<small>Subtotems in Queensland.</small>

The tribes of North-Western Queensland described by Mr. E. Palmer appear to have had subtotems; that is, they apparently distributed all the objects of nature between their exogamous classes, just as some tribes of South-Eastern Australia are known to have done.[1] On this subject Mr. Palmer writes: "All nature is also divided into class names, and said to be male and female. The sun and moon and stars are said to be men and women, and to belong to classes just as the blacks themselves."[2]

<small>Breaches of the class-laws punished with death.</small>

Among these tribes any breach of the class-laws in respect of marriage was punished by the death of the guilty pair, the blood-relations on both sides consenting to the execution.[3] It was the council of elders which condemned the culprits and despatched its ministers to execute the sentence. Once, on the Bloomfield River, when the criminal escaped the agents of justice, an effigy of him was made of soft wood and buried,[4] no doubt for the purpose of killing him magically thereby.

<small>Modes of obtaining wives.</small>

Wives were obtained in various ways. Sometimes a man would exchange his blood-sister for the blood-sister of another man, provided the women were of the proper classes and subclasses; but the camp-council had to give its consent unanimously to this arrangement. At other times the camp-council assigned a wife to a man without consulting his wishes. If the council refused to allow a man to marry the woman whom he loved, though she was of the right class and subclass, the two would sometimes elope with each other, and afterwards return as man and wife to the camp. On their return they had to run the gauntlet, the people hacking them with knives and belabouring them with sticks and boomerangs.

---

[1] See above, pp. 427 *sqq.*, 431 *sq.*, 451 *sqq.*, 470 *sqq.*

[2] E. Palmer, "Notes on some Australian Tribes," *Journal of the Anthropological Institute*, xiii. (1884) p. 300.

[3] W. E. Roth, *Ethnological Studies*, p. 181.

[4] W. E. Roth, *North Queensland Ethnography, Bulletin No. 8, Notes on Government, Morals, and Crime* (Brisbane, 1906), p. 5.

But when they had passed through this ordeal, they were allowed to live together.¹ Boys and girls were sometimes betrothed to each other. If a woman was captured or taken in war, she might be kept by her captor, provided she was of the class and subclass into which he was allowed to marry. The tribes made raids into each other's territories to steal women, sometimes going long distances to get them.² Men inherited the widows of their deceased brothers in accordance with the custom of the Levirate.³

The Levirate.

A man never looked at, spoke to, or approached his mother-in-law, "but the father-in-law did not come under the same restriction."⁴ However, the custom in this respect appears to vary in different tribes of Queensland, as we learn from the following account, in which the term step-parents is seemingly used in the sense of parents-in-law. "Certain of an individual's relatives are strictly tabu from him, in so much that he may neither approach, converse with, accept from, nor give them anything. This especially refers to the father-in-law and mother-in-law. These and other relationship restrictions are, however, far from constant. Thus, on the Pennefather a man must not look at either of his step-parents, though it is permissible for him to converse with them with face averted; a woman may talk with both in a natural manner, the business of the mother-in-law here being to attend her in her confinements. At Miriam Vale, south of Rockhampton, and at Boggy Creek, Upper Normanby River, as well as elsewhere, a man may, under certain circumstances, address his step-parents from a distance in a comparative whisper. On the Tully, both male and female talk to the father-in-law either by his individual name, whatever it may be, or by the generic one of *ni-ubi*; but their teeth would rot out were they to converse with the mother-in-law, though they may speak of her by the generic term of *wai-min*, but never by her individual name. With the sole exception, perhaps, of those cases where the mother-in-law acts as midwife, the practice of

Custom of avoidance between relations by marriage.

---

¹ W. E. Roth, *Ethnological Studies*, p. 181.

² E. Palmer, "Notes on some Australian Tribes," *Journal of the Anthropological Institute*, xiii. (1884) p. 301. As to betrothal, compare W. E. Roth, *Ethnological Studies*, p. 181.

³ E. Palmer, *op. cit.* pp. 282, 298.

⁴ E. Palmer, *op. cit.* p. 301; W. E. Roth, *Ethnological Studies*, p. 182.

both males and females refusing to touch any food prepared by their step-parents is universal. In some districts it is usual for the wife not even to converse with her husband's blood-brothers, but on the Tully she may lawfully have marital relations with them; the converse of husband and wife's blood-sisters, with its corresponding inconstancy, also holds true. It is the usual practice for a man never to talk to his blood-sister, or sometimes not even mention her name, after she has once reached womanhood."[1] This custom of mutual avoidance between blood brothers and sisters from puberty onwards will meet us again in Melanesia and other places. That it is intended as a precaution against incest appears highly probable.

<small>Custom of avoidance between brothers and sisters.</small>

<small>The tribes are governed by the older men in council.</small>

With regard to the government of these tribes we are told that "there is no hereditary chieftainship, or any one possessing authority among the northern tribes, so far as can be made out; one man being as good as another. To old men, however, great respect is shown, and whatever authority is acknowledged among them is centred in the aged, on account of their years and grey hairs. All matters connected with their social affairs are settled in open council at night, when each man speaks from his camp in turn, and is listened to without interruption. No young men or lads join in the talk."[2] Similarly Mr. Roth says that "the general government of the community is carried on by an assembly of elders, a camp council, as it were, of the elder males: not that this council has any fixed constitution or definite name applied to it, but by common consent it is accepted that all the older males take part in its deliberations, which, after all, are more or less informal. . . . Matters with which such a camp council concerns itself are those connected with the welfare and interests of the tribe collectively, and mainly relate to its external affairs, though events may take place in the home-life which call for interference. The question of peace or war would fall within its province, as well as the conditions for any proposed covenant. Covenants for the extermination of a common

---

[1] W. E. Roth, *North Queensland Ethnography*, Bulletin No. 11, p. 78 (extract from *Records of the Australian Museum*, vol. vii. No. 2, 1908).

[2] E. Palmer, *op. cit.* p. 282.

enemy may be made by two tribes on the basis of settling existing differences between themselves, without having recourse to mutual bloodshed."[1]

As apparently always happens in aboriginal Australian society, the marriage system of these Queensland tribes is combined with the classificatory system of relationship. On this subject I will again quote Mr. Edward Palmer. After speaking of the exogamous classes he proceeds: "The relationships of the natives are founded on these laws: they call their father's brother the same as father, and mother's sister the same as mother. Our ideas of kinship are so different to theirs that calling them uncles or aunts or cousins or sisters or brothers does not convey any such meaning to them as it does to us, for they regard as brothers all those who belong to the same class or division as themselves; and among all blacks they discover some degree of affinity. They have a clear enough idea of their relationships; the fault seems to lie with us who do not comprehend theirs. Being founded on such a totally different system to ours, the individual relationship is, I believe, ignored for the sake of the class system. They recognise its relationships; hundreds of times a black boy has said, 'Such and such a one is my brother,' when I knew that he was not a brother, as we call such a relationship, and the same with father and mother. A blackfellow will say, and will be correct in saying, 'So many are my fathers,' or 'So many mothers I have'; he should call them uncles or aunts; but brought up under the influence of their class system of relationships, it is as difficult for them to understand our system as it is for us to get at the secret of theirs. But there can be little doubt but that all their relationships are founded on the class systems or divisions, and they recognise such relationships, and call each other by them. From their earliest youth they comprehend such relationships and know no other."[2]

Hence in these tribes persons belonging to the same subclass call each other "brothers" and "sisters," whether they

<small>Classificatory system of relationship among the Queensland tribes.</small>

---

[1] W. E. Roth, *North Queensland Ethnography, Bulletin No. 8, Notes on Government, Morals, and Crime* (Brisbane, 1906), p. 5.

[2] E. Palmer, "Notes on some Australian Tribes," *Journal of the Anthropological Institute*, xiii. (1884) pp. 300 *sq.*

544 TOTEMISM IN NORTH-EAST AUSTRALIA CHAP.

The classificatory terms imply group relationships and probably originated in group marriage.

are related to them by blood or not: they call the members of their complementary or twin subclass their "mother's brothers" and "mothers," whether they are related to them by blood or not: they call the members of the subclass into which alone they may marry "brothers-in-law" and "sisters-in-law," whether they are married or not: and they call the members of the remaining subclass (the complementary or twin subclass of the preceding) their "fathers" and "father's sisters," whether they are related to them by blood or not. For example, if we take a man of the Koopooroo subclass, he will call members of his own subclass (Koopooroo) his brothers and sisters, because his brothers and sisters are included in it. He will call members of his complementary or twin subclass (Woongko) his mother's brothers and his mothers, because his mother and her brothers are included in it. He will call members of the subclass into which alone he may marry (Koorkilla) his brothers-in-law and sisters-in-law, because his wife, present or future, and her brothers and sisters, are included in it. And he will call members of the remaining subclass (Bunburi, the complementary or twin subclass of his wife's subclass) according to their generation either his fathers and father's sisters, or his sons and daughters, because his father and father's sisters, and his own sons and daughters, are included in it. Thus throughout North-West-Central Queensland every person, male or female, young or old, is related to every other person in one or other of the following capacities: "brother," "sister," "brother-in-law," "sister-in-law," "mother's brother," "mother," "father," "father's sister," "son," "daughter," and that, too, even when, according to our notions, they are in no way related to each other either by blood or marriage. Hence every person may have, and generally has, many "fathers" and "mothers," as well as "brothers" and "sisters"; and he or she may be, and commonly is, "son-in-law" or "daughter-in-law" and "father" or "mother" to many men and women, even when he or she is not only unmarried but an infant.[1] Thus as

---

[1] W. E. Roth, *Ethnological Studies among the North-West-Central Queensland Aborigines*, pp. 56, 59 *sq.*, 63 *sq.* Compare *id., Notes on Social and Individual Nomenclature among certain North Queensland Aboriginals*, p. 2: "These terms, mother, father, brother, sister, in addition to their generally

usual in the classificatory system relationships are conceived as existing between groups rather than between individuals, and these group relationships are in all probability derived from a system of group-marriage. In some of the Queensland tribes which we are considering a relic of group-marriage, if not of promiscuity, still survives in the rule which obliges every girl at puberty to have intercourse with all the men in the camp, except with her own father and with those who belong to her own subclass; indeed, even men of her own subclass are allowed access to her, if they belong to another tribe.[1]

Relic of group-marriage.

As examples of the classificatory terms of relationship which are used by the Queensland aborigines we may take those of the Pitta-Pitta tribe in the Boulia district. In the generation above his own a Pitta-Pitta man applies the same term *upperi* to his father and his father's brothers, both blood and tribal; and he applies the same term *umma* to his mother and to his mother's sisters, both blood and tribal. In his own generation he applies the same terms *titi* and *kako* to his brothers and sisters and to his first cousins, the sons and daughters of his father's brothers and of his mother's sisters respectively. In the generation below his own he applies the same term *uttapeukka* to his own children and to the children of his brothers, both blood and tribal.[2]

Classificatory terms of relationship in the Pitta-Pitta tribe.

---

accepted meaning of relationship by blood, express a class or group-connection quite independent of it. Mother is the one and the same name used by an aboriginal to express not only the woman that gave him birth, but also the sisters (matron or virgin) connected with her by blood, as well as the dozens of women connected with her by class or group. . . . Similarly with the terms brother, father, sister."

[1] W. E. Roth, *Ethnological Studies among the North-West-Central Queensland Aborigines*, pp. 69, 174. The custom is observed in the Pitta-Pitta and neighbouring tribes of the Boulia, Leichhardt-Selwyn, and Upper Georgina Districts.

[2] W. E. Roth, *Ethnological Studies*, p. 64.

CHAPTER IV

TOTEMISM IN WEST AUSTRALIA

OUR information with regard to the natives of West Australia is unfortunately very scanty, but it suffices to shew that in its general lines their social organisation resembles that of most other Australian tribes; for here as elsewhere the tribes appear to be regularly divided into exogamous classes, and perhaps, though that is not so clear, into totem clans.

§ 1. *Totemism in South-West Australia*

Exogamous classes among the natives at King George's Sound.

The first place apparently at which the exogamous classes so characteristic of the Australian aborigines were observed and described was King George's Sound at the extreme south-west point of Australia. Here, we are told, "the whole body of the natives are divided into two classes, *Erniung* and *Tem* or *Tāāman*; and the chief regulation is, that these classes must intermarry, that is, an *Erniung* with a *Tāāman*. Those who infringe this rule are called *Yuredangers*, and are subject to very severe punishment. The children always follow the denomination of the mother. Thus, a man who is *Erniung* will have all his children *Tāāman*; but his sister's children will be *Erniungs*. This practice is common to all the tribes in the neighbourhood, with the exception of the *Murram*."[1] "With respect to

[1] "Description of the Natives of King George's Sound (Swan River Colony) and Adjoining Country, written by Mr. Scott Nind, and communicated by R. Brown, Esq., F.R.S.," *Journal of the Royal Geographical Society*, i. (1832) pp. 37 *sq*. Mr. Nind resided as medical officer at King George's Sound from 1827 to 1829.

the divisions and subdivisions of tribes, there exists so much intricacy, that it will be long before it can be understood. The classes *Erniung* and *Tem* are universal near the Sound; but the distinctions are general, not tribal. Another division, almost as general, is into *Moncalon* and *Torndirrup*; yet there are a few who are neither. These can scarcely be distinguished as tribes, and are very much intermingled. The *Moncalon*, however, is more prevalent to the eastward of our establishment, and the *Torndirrup* to the westward. They intermarry, and have each again their subdivisional distinctions, some of which are peculiar, and some general; of these are *Opperheip*, *Cambien*, *Mahnur*, etc.

"What I, however, consider more correctly as tribes, are those which have a general name and a general district, although they may consist of *Torndirrup* or *Moncalon*, separate or commingled. These are, I believe, in some measure named by the kind of game or food found most abundant in the district. The inhabitants of the Sound and its immediate vicinity are called *Meananger*, probably derived from *mearn*, the red root above mentioned and *anger*, to eat. It is in this district that the *mearn* is the most abundantly found; but distant tribes will not eat the *mearn*, and complain much of the brushy nature of the country—that it scratches their legs. Kangaroos of the larger sort are scarce here, but the small brush kangaroo is plentiful, and grass-trees and Banksia are abundant, as is also, in the proper season, fish. The natives residing on the right, and extending to the coast about North-West Cape, are called *Murram*. This country, or district, is said to be more fertile, and produces different kinds of edible roots. It affords also more ponds of water, more wild fowl, and more emus.

"These tribes are also not universally divided into *Erniung* and *Tem*, and frequently infringe the rule. Adjoining them inland is the *Yobberore*. This country appears more hilly and better wooded; but we have had very little intercourse with the natives who belong to it. Next to them is the *Will* or *Weil* district, which is a very favourite country, and may probably be named from *Weil* or *Weit* (ants' eggs).... Next to the *Weil* district is that

_{The divisions named from the game or other food most abounding in the several districts.}

of *Warrangle* or *Warranger*, from *warre* (kangaroo), and seems to be of the same character as the *Weil*, which is chiefly open forest land, with a little short grass, and abounding in kangaroos, opossums, and other animals, as well as many birds, which are not found near the coast. The *Corine* district—the name of which may be derived from *qūur* (which I believe to be the bush kangaroo)—is said to be very open and nearly free from wood. . . .

<small>Descent of the exogamous classes.</small>

"Although every individual would immediately announce to us his tribal name and country, yet we have not been enabled to trace any regular order of descent. The son follows his mother as *Erniung* or *Tem*, and his father as *Torndirrup* or *Moncalon*. Beyond this we have not been able to penetrate, for *half* brothers are not unfrequently different. This would probably be caused by cross marriages. From the same cause also their divisions of relationship are very numerous. *Eicher*, mother; *cuinkur*, father; *mourert*, brother or sister; *konk* or *conk*, uncle, etc., etc.

<small>Wives procured from a distance.</small>

"In their marriage, they have no restriction as to tribe; but it is considered best to procure a wife from the greatest distance possible. The sons will have a right to hunt in the country from whence the mother is brought. They are very jealous as to encroachments on their property, and the land is divided into districts, which is the property of families or individuals."[1]

<small>General inferences as to exogamy among the tribes of King George's Sound.</small>

From the foregoing account we may infer that some of the tribes of South-West Australia in the neighbourhood of King George's Sound were divided into two exogamous classes called *Erniung* and *Tem* respectively, with descent in the maternal line; while other tribes appear to have been divided into two exogamous classes named *Torndirrup* and *Moncalon* respectively with descent in the paternal line. Further, it would seem that the tribes with the two primary classes *Torndirrup* and *Moncalon* were subdivided into sub-classes, which bore the names of *Opperheip, Cambien, Mahnur*, etc. Further, the practice of taking wives from as great a distance as possible seems to shew that among these

---

[1] Scott Nind, in *Journal of the Royal Geographical Society*, i. (1832) pp. 42-44.

tribes, as among some of the coast tribes of South-East Australia, a custom of local exogamy was superadded to the custom of class exogamy; in other words, that a man was bound to marry a woman of another district as well as of another class. However, the information which I have quoted is both vague and meagre, and the only conclusions we can deduce with certainty from it are that exogamous subdivisions existed among the tribes near King George's Sound, and that in some of them these divisions were hereditary in the maternal line.

Among these tribes polygamy was in vogue, and one man might have many wives. Girls were seemingly at the disposal of their fathers and were generally betrothed in their infancy or even before birth. The men to whom they were betrothed were often middle-aged or old; indeed the majority of the men remained single until past thirty years of age, and some of them continued bachelors much longer. The old men, on the other hand, had several wives of all ages. "This state of things is in some measure compensated by what is called *tarramanaccarack*; it is, in fact, courting a wife whilst her husband is living, upon the understanding with both parties that she is to be the wife of the lover after the death of the husband. The presents in this case are made to the husband, as well as to the woman; but what she receives she generally divides with him. This practice is done openly, and permitted; but it must be carried on in so decorous a manner as not to occasion scandal to the parties, or jealousy to the husband."[1] Widows were not uncommonly inherited by the nearest relations of their deceased husband. When twins were born, one of them was killed; if the children were of different sexes, they killed the boy and preserved the girl. The reasons which they gave for destroying a twin were "that a woman has not sufficient milk for two children, and cannot carry them and seek her food."[2] In these tribes the men who possessed most influence were the doctors or medicine-men (*mulgarradocks*); they were

Marriage customs among the tribes of King George's Sound.

The Levirate.
Twins.

Medicine-men.

[1] Scott Nind, in *Journal of the Royal Geographical Society*, i. (1832) p. 39.
[2] Scott Nind, *l.c.*

thought to be able to cause or cure disease, to bring down lightning, and to drive away wind or rain."[1]

Sir George Grey's account of totemism and exogamy in West Australia.

Much fuller and more precise information as to exogamy and totemism in South-Western Australia is furnished by Sir George Grey, formerly Governor of South Australia, whose account was published in 1841. As his account is both lucid and important, I will reproduce it entire for the convenience of my readers. Sir George Grey was the first to point out the resemblance between the totemic systems of Australia and North America. He writes as follows:—[2]

The families, clans, or classes of the natives of West Australia.

"*Traditional Laws of Relationship and Marriage.*—One of the most remarkable facts connected with the natives, is that they are divided into certain great families, all the members of which bear the same names, as a family, or second name: the principal branches of these families, so far as I have been able to ascertain, are the

Ballaroke
Tdondarup
Ngotak
Nagarnook
Nogonyuk
Mongalung
Narrangur.

"But in different districts the members of these families give a local name to the one to which they belong, which is understood in that district, to indicate some particular branch of the principal family. The most common local names are,

Didaroke
Gwerrinjoke
Maleoke
Waddaroke
Djekoke
Kotejumeno
Namyungo
Yungaree.

"These family names are common over a great portion of the continent; for instance, on the Western coast, in a

[1] Scott Nind, *op. cit.* pp. 41 *sq.*
[2] George Grey, *Journals of two Expeditions of Discovery in North-West and Western Australia during the years 1837, 38, and 39* (London, 1841), ii. 225-231.

tract of country extending between four and five hundred miles in latitude, members of all these families are found. In South Australia, I met a man who said that he belonged to one of them, and Captain Flinders mentions Yungaree, as the name of a native in the Gulf of Carpentaria. *Wide prevalence of these family names.*

"These family names are perpetuated, and spread through the country, by the operation of two remarkable laws:—

"1st. That children of either sex, always take the family name of their mother.

"2nd. That a man cannot marry a woman of his own family name.

"But not the least singular circumstance connected with these institutions, is their coincidence with those of the North American Indians. . . .

"The origin of these family names is attributed by the natives to different causes, but I think that enough is not yet known on the subject, to enable us to form an accurate opinion on this point—one origin frequently assigned by the natives is, that they were derived from some vegetable or animal being very common in the district which the family inhabited, and that hence the name of this animal or vegetable became applied to the family. I have in my published vocabulary of the native language, under each family name, given its derivations, as far as I could collect them from the statements of the natives.[1] *The names are often derived from some animal or plant common in the district.*

"But as each family adopts some animal or vegetable, as their crest or sign, or *Kobong* as they call it, I imagine it more likely, that these have been named after the families, than that the families have been named after them.

"A certain mysterious connection exists between a family and its *kobong*, so that a member of the family will never kill an animal of the species, to which his *kobong* belongs, should he find it asleep; indeed he always kills it reluctantly, and never without affording it a chance to escape. This arises from the family belief, that some one individual of the species is their nearest friend, to kill whom would be a great crime, and to be carefully avoided. Similarly, a native who has a vegetable for his *kobong*, may not gather *Mysterious connection between a family and its kobong or totem.*

[1] See below, pp. 555 *sq.*

it under certain circumstances, and at a particular period of the year. The North American Indians have this same custom of taking some animal as their sign. Thus it is stated in the *Archæologia Americana*,[1] 'Each tribe has the name of some animal. Among the Hurons, the first tribe is that of the bear; the two others of the wolf and turtle. The Iroquois nation has the same divisions, only the turtle family is divided into two, the great and the little.' And again, in speaking of the Sioux tribes[2]:—'Each of these' derives its name from some animal, part of an animal, or other substance, which is considered as the peculiar sacred object or *medicine*, as the Canadians call it, of each band respectively.' To this we may add the testimony of John Long, who says,[3] 'one part of the religious superstition of the savages consists in each of them having his own *totam*, or favourite spirit, which he believes watches over him. This *totam* they conceive assumes the shape of some beast or other, and therefore they never kill, hunt, or eat the animal whose form they think the *totam* bears.'

"Civilized nations, in their heraldic bearings, preserve traces of the same custom.

Marriage customs.

"Female children are always betrothed, within a few days after their birth; and from the moment they are betrothed, the parents cease to have any control over the future settlement of their child. Should the first husband die, before the girl has attained the years of puberty, she then belongs to his heir.

"A girl lives with her husband at any age she pleases, no control whatever is in this way placed upon her inclinations.

The Levirate.

"When a native dies, his brother inherits his wives and children, but his brother must be of the same family name as himself. The widow goes to her second husband's hut, three days after the death of her first.

Old men monopolise the women.

"The old men manage to keep the females a good deal amongst themselves, giving their daughters to one another, and the more female children they have, the greater chance

---

[1] "Vol. 2, p. 109, quoting from Charlevoix, vol. 3, p. 266."

[2] "*Ibid.* p. 110, quoting from Major Long's *Exp.* vol. i. ch. 15."

[3] "*Voyages and Travels*, p. 86."

have they of getting another wife, by this sort of exchange; but the women have generally some favourite amongst the young men, always looking forward to be his wife at the death of her husband.

"But a most remarkable law is that which obliges families connected by blood upon the female side, to join for the purpose of defence and avenging crimes; and as the father marries several wives, and very often all of different families, his children are repeatedly all divided amongst themselves; no common bond of union exists between them, and this custom alone would be sufficient to prevent this people ever emerging from the savage state. *[Law of the blood feud.]*

"As their laws are principally made up of sets of obligations due from members of the same great family towards one another,—which obligations of family names are much stronger than those of blood,—it is evident that a vast influence upon the manners and state of this people must be brought about by this arrangement into classes. I therefore devoted a great portion of my attention to this point, but the mass of materials I have collected is so large, that it would occupy much more time to arrange it, than I have been able to spare, so as to do full justice to the subject; but in order to give an accurate idea of the nature of the enquiries I pursued, I have given in the Appendix (A)[1] a short genealogical list, which will show the manner in which a native gives birth to a progeny of a totally different family name to himself; so that a district of country never remains for two successive generations in the same family. These observations, as well as others made with regard to the natives, can be only considered to apply, as yet, to that portion of Western Australia lying between the 30th and 35th parallels of S. lat. unless the contrary is expressly stated; though I think there is strong reason to suppose that they will, in general, be found to obtain throughout the continent." *[Rules of marriage and descent among the classes.]*

The genealogies which Sir George Grey gives in an Appendix[2] are summarised in the following table, where the names given are those of what the writer calls the *[Genealogies.]*

[1] See below, pp. 553 *sq.* [2] *Op. cit.* ii. 391-394.

principal branches of the great families into which the natives are divided :—

Husband.	Wife.	Children.
Ballar-oke	Ngotak	Ngotak
„	No-go-nyuk	No-go-nyuk
Tdon-dar-up	Ballar-oke	Ballar-oke
Ngotak	Ballar-oke	Ballar-oke
„	Na-gar-nook	Na-gar-nook
No-go-nyuk	Ngotak	Ngotak
„	Tdondarup	Tdondarup
Ngotak	Na-gar-nook	Na-gar-nook
„	No-go-nyuk	No-go-nyuk
„	Ballar-oke	Ballar-oke

<small>Horror of incest.</small> Amongst these tribes, as amongst most Australian tribes, the rules of exogamy seem to have been rigidly enforced. At least Grey tells us that "the crime of adultery is punished severely—often with death. Anything approaching the crime of incest, in which they include marriages out of the right line, they hold in the greatest abhorrence, closely assimilating in this last point with the North American <small>Similar horror of incest among the North American Indians.</small> Indians, of whom it is said in the *Archæologia Americana*: 'They profess to consider it highly criminal for a man to marry a woman whose *totem* (family name) is the same as his own, and they relate instances when young men, for a violation of this rule, have been put to death by their own nearest relatives.'[1]

"And again : 'According to their own account, the Indian nations were divided into tribes for no other purpose than that no one might ever, either through temptation or mistake, marry a near relation, which at present is scarcely possible, for whoever intends to marry must take a person of a different tribe.'[2]

"The same feeling was remarked by Dobrizhoffer in South America; for, speaking of an interview with a native tribe, to whom he was preaching, he says :—'The

---

[1] "Vol. 2, p. 110, quoting from Tanner's *Narrative*, p. 313."
[2] "*Ibid.*"

old man, when he heard from me that marriage with relations was forbidden, exclaimed, "Thou sayest well, father, such marriages are abominable; but that we know already." From which I discovered that incestuous connexions are more execrable to these savages than murder or robbery.'[1]

"Any other crime may be compounded for, by the criminal appearing and submitting himself to the ordeal of having spears thrown at him by all such persons as conceive themselves to have been aggrieved, or by permitting spears to be thrust through certain parts of his body; such as through the thigh, or the calf of the leg, or under the arm. The part which is to be pierced by a spear, is fixed for all common crimes, and a native who has incurred this penalty, sometimes quietly holds out his leg for the injured party to thrust his spear through."[2]

Elsewhere Grey gives briefly some of the native stories as to the origin of the families or clans. Thus the Ballaroke family is said to derive its name from having in former times subsisted mainly on a very small species of opossum, to which the natives give the name of *ballard*.[3] They say, too, that the Ballarokes were a species of swan called *kuljak* before they were transformed into men.[4] The Nagarnook family is said to take its name from a species of small fish called *nagkarn*, on which in former times they chiefly fed.[5] The Tdondarup or Dtondarup family is related to have been a species of water-fowl called *koolama* before they were changed into men.[6] The Ngotak family is reported to have

Legends of the origin of the various families.

---

[1] "*Account of the Abipones*, vol. i. p. 69." Dobrizhoffer here tells us that "the Abipones, warned by nature alone and by the example of their forefathers, shun marriage with any relations whatever and shrink from it more than from a serpent" (*Historia de Abiponibus*, Vienna, 1784, ii. 222).

[2] G. Grey, *Journals of two Expeditions of Discovery in North-West and Western Australia*, ii. 242 sq.

[3] G. Grey, *Vocabulary of the Dialects of South-Western Australia*, 2nd edition (London, 1840), p. 4. The *Descriptive Vocabulary of the Languages in common use amongst the Aborigines of Western Australia*, by G. F. Moore (appended to the same writer's *Diary of Ten Years eventful Life of an early settler in Western Australia*, London 1884), is avowedly based on Grey's *Vocabulary*, and contains little or nothing new of importance with reference to the exogamous divisions. The writer says (*s.v.* "Ballarok") that there are four principal families, namely, Ballarok, Dtondarup, Ngotak, and Naganok.

[4] G. Grey, *Vocabulary*, p. 71.

[5] G. Grey, *Vocabulary*, p. 95.

[6] G. Grey, *Vocabulary*, p. 66.

been either widgeons (*eroto*) or a species of duck (*djin-be-nong-era*) before they were transformed into human beings.[1] So too the Nogonyuk family are believed to have been a species of water-fowl, the mountain-duck (*karbunga*), before their metamorphosis into men.[2] And a like tale was told of "the Didaroke family, a branch of the Ngotaks": they also had been a sort of water-fowl (*kij-jin-broon*) before they exchanged their bird-shape for human form.[3]

<small>Summary of Grey's information as to the West Australian tribes.</small>

Thus from Grey's account we gather that the tribes of South-Western Australia, from the thirtieth parallel of south latitude southward were divided into at least seven exogamous totem clans with descent in the female line. Two of the names of these clans, namely Tdondarup and Mongalung, seem to be clearly identical with Torndirrup and Moncalon which we met with as names of exogamous divisions, whether classes or totem clans, among the tribes near King George's Sound.[4] Further, it appears from Grey's account that the members of one of these clans or families, as he calls them, were not limited in their choice of wives or husbands to the members of one other clan or family only; for in his genealogies he records several cases in which a man of one clan married wives of two different clans, and one case in which a man married wives of three different clans. Some of the legends related to account for the origin of the families or clans shew that here as in other parts of Australia the natives believed themselves to be descended from animals of their totem species; while two of the legends seem to preserve a reminiscence of a time when men habitually ate their totems, as if that had been the right and proper thing for them to do. These latter traditions agree with and are confirmed by the similar traditions current among the central tribes.[5]

<small>Sir John Forrest's account of the exogamous classes among the aborigines of West Australia.</small>

It is possible that some of the exogamous divisions which Grey seems to have regarded as totem clans were not totem clans but classes or subclasses (phratries or sub-phratries). At least Sir John Forrest's account of what he calls the two "great tribes" Tordnerup and Ballarook, which

---

[1] G. Grey, *Vocabulary*, pp. 29, 37.
[2] G. Grey, *Vocabulary*, p. 61.
[3] G. Grey, *Vocabulary*, p. 63.
[4] See above, p. 547.
[5] See above, pp. 238 *sqq.*

are clearly the same as Grey's Tdondarup and Ballaroke, seems to shew that these are exogamous classes or subclasses rather than totem clans. He writes as follows: "The natives of Western Australia are divided into tribes, which bear certain names; there are several, but they all merge into two great tribes called the Tornderup and the Ballarook. Wherever a native goes, so long as he does not go beyond the limit of these tribes, he will always be protected by his own tribe, although he may be a perfect stranger to them; in fact they look upon him as a brother. The marriage laws are also very strict. A Tornderup must not marry a Tornderup, although she may be quite a stranger; if he wants a wife he must take a Ballarook. Sometimes they break through this rule, and generally get speared or killed for their pains. They are constantly quarrelling about their wives, and running away with one another's wives is very common. The poor women generally get the worst of it, being often speared, and even sometimes killed. Still, even this severe punishment does not deter them, and it is just as common now as it was forty years ago. Betrothal is very general. A child a year old will sometimes be betrothed to an old man, and it will be his duty to protect and feed her, and (unless she is stolen by some one else) when she is old enough she becomes his wife. In the case of a husband's death his wife belongs to the oldest man of his family, who either takes her himself or gives her to some one else. There is no marriage ceremony, merely handing over the woman to the man. Children always take after the mother's tribe. If a mother is Tornderup, the child is Tornderup, and so on."[1]

The suspicion that Grey may have mistaken exogamous classes or subclasses for totem clans is confirmed by the account which Bishop Salvado of the Catholic Mission at New Norcia, in South-Western Australia, has given of the marriage laws observed by the aborigines of that district, which is situated some fifty miles inland on the low Darling Range, about the thirty-first parallel of south latitude. The Bishop has set forth the exogamous classes and rules

Bishop Salvado's account of the exogamous classes at New Norcia.

[1] John Forrest, "On the Natives of Central and Western Australia," *Journal of the Anthropological Institute*, v. (1876) p. 317.

of marriage of the tribe in an elaborate genealogical tree;[1] and the information thus supplied has been digested by Mr. Lorimer Fison into tables, which, with his explanations and comments, I will here reprint. They give a clear statement of the system, which in certain of its features is anomalous, that is, it differs from the regular patterns of Australian tribal organisation in two, four, or eight exogamous classes. Mr. Fison's statement is as follows:—[2]

Mr. Fison's statement of the marriage customs recorded by Bishop Salvado.

"The New Norcia tribe is divided into six classes, its system therein differing from that found among the West Australian natives in the neighbourhood of the N.W. Cape, which is of the four-class Kamilaroi type, with the usual arrangements as to marriage and descent.

"The six classes are called respectively, Palarop, Nokongok, Jirajiok, Mondorop, Tondorop, and Tirarop. Their marriage prohibitions are exhibited in the following table:—

Class	May not marry
Palarop	Jirajiok, Palarop.
Nokongok	Jirajiok, Nokongok.
Jirajiok	Jirajiok, Palarop, Nokongok.
Mondorop	Tirarop, Mondorop.
Tondorop	Tirarop, Tondorop.
Tirarop	Tirarop, Tondorop, Mondorop.

"A glance at this table shows that the six classes range themselves into two sets of three each, and the prohibitions reveal an exogamous law, which is strictly binding upon every class, and partially binding upon each set. A clear distinction between the two sets is thus arrived at; in fact, each set represents a primary class, like Dilbi or Kupathin of the Kamilaroi, but with three subclasses belonging to it, instead of two, as in the Kamilaroi system. Distinguishing these primary classes as A and B, we have:—

---

[1] See E. M. Curr, *The Australian Race*, i. 320 *sq.*
[2] Lorimer Fison, "The New Norcia Marriage Laws," *Journal of the Anthropological Institute*, xviii. (1889) pp. 68-70. I have tacitly corrected a few misprints in the names of the classes.

A = Palarop, Nokongok, Jirajiok.
B = Mondorop, Tondorop, Tirarop.

"In the following table the marriages are shown, those which offend against the usual exogamous law of the primary classes being distinguished thus * :—

Table shewing the regular and the anomalous marriages in these classes.

Primary Class A	Marries	Primary Class B	Marries
Palarop	Mondorop B Tondorop B Tirarop B Nokongok A*	Mondorop	Palarop A Nokongok A Jirajiok A Tondorop B*
Nokongok	Mondorop B Tondorop B Tirarop B Palarop A*	Tondorop	Palarop A Nokongok A Jirajiok A Mondorop B*
Jirajiok	Mondorop B Tondorop B Tirarop B	Tirarop	Palarop A Nokongok A Jirajiok A

"From the foregoing we get the social organisation of the tribe which is as follows :—

"(1) Two primary classes.

"(2) Each primary class has three exogamous subclasses, any one of which may marry into any subclass of the other primary division.

"(3) In each primary class two of the subclasses intermarry with one another as well as with all those of the other primary division.

"It will be observed that one subclass in each primary division (Jirajiok A, Tirarop B) marries only into the other division. That is to say, these two subclasses observe the usual exogamous rule of the primary classes, and the question is, why the other subclasses do not observe it? One or two conjectural solutions of this problem might be offered; but our experience in these researches has made us shy of such solutions how plausible soever they may appear. If we knew the regulations as to descent and the totemic divisions of the subclasses (supposing them to exist here as elsewhere) we should probably find in them much to help us. Unfortunately Dr. Salvado not only does not give these particulars, but he turns a deaf ear to our appeals for information concerning them, and all our efforts to obtain the information from other sources have been equally unsuccessful."

Maternal descent of the classes.

The classes or subclasses in this New Norcia tribe were hereditary in the female line, the children taking them from their mother, not from their father.[1] Two of the class-names, namely Tondorop and Nokongok, appear to be identical with two of the family names given by Grey, namely Tdondarup and Nogonyuk, which confirms, as I have said, the suspicion that Grey may have mistaken some of the names of exogamous classes or subclasses for the names of totem clans.

Mrs. Bates's account of the exogamous classes of the West Australian aborigines.

The suspicion is further strengthened by the evidence of Mrs. Daisy M. Bates, who has personally investigated the exogamous divisions of the natives of South-West Australia. She reports as follows :—[2]

"From my personal investigations amongst those of the old southern natives with whom I have lived for over four months, I find that the whole of the southern peoples occupying the line of coast from about Jurien Bay to Esperance (or thereabouts) have two primary divisions which intermarry, but which are strictly forbidden to marry within themselves. These divisions are called respectively Wor-dung-mat and Manytchmat. . . . These two primary divisions have been subdivided into four, viz. :—

>Bal-lar-ruk
>Na-gar-nook
>Ton-da-rup
>Did-ar-ruk.

"Of these four, Bal-lar-ruk and Na-gar-nook represent the Wordungmat division and Tondarup and Didarruk the Manytchmat division.

---

[1] E. M. Curr, *The Australian Race,* i. 320.

[2] Mrs. Daisy M. Bates, M.R.G.S.A., "The Marriage Laws and some Customs of the West Australian Aborigines," *Victorian Geographical Journal,* xxiii.-xxiv. (1905-1906) pp. 42-44.

"The four classes have been further segmented as under :—

Ballarruk, Nagarnook, Waijuk, Kootijcum, Gwalook, Gooanuk, Noganyuk, and Eedalyuk, all included in the primary Wordungmat division.
Tondarup, Didarruk, Kayganook, Jeedalyuk, Melamurnong, included in the Manytchmat division.

"These numerous subdivisions may be only local; they certainly obtain amongst the people living on the south coast between Mandurah and Cape Leeuwin, but the four principal class names are to be found along the whole coast line between Jurien Bay and Esperance. I have met a Jurien Bay Tondarup and an Esperance Bay Ballarruk and Didarruk. . . .

"The marriage laws and forms of descent of the two primary classes are as under :— *Marriage and descent in the classes.*

Man.   Woman.   Children.

Wordungmat marries Manytchmat, their children are Manytchmat.
Manytchmat marries Wordungmat, their children are Wordungmat.

"Of the four subdivisions, the marriages are as follows :—

Ballarruk marries Tondarup or Didarruk, children Tondarup or Didarruk.
Nagarnook marries Tondarup or Didarruk, children Tondarup or Didarruk.
Tondarup marries Ballarruk or Nagarnook, children Ballarruk or Nagarnook.
Didarruk marries Ballarruk or Nagarnook, children Ballarruk or Nagarnook.

"Ballarruk and Nagarnook cannot marry, either between themselves or with any of their subdivisions, but they can marry any of the other classes; also Tondarup and Didarruk cannot marry each other nor their subdivisions, but they can marry Ballarruk, Nagarnook, and their subdivisions."

From the foregoing account it appears that the natives of the southern coast of West Australia between Jurien Bay and Esperance are divided into two exogamous classes and four subclasses as follows :— *Tables shewing the classes, marriages, and descent*

	Class.	Subclasses.	Class.	Subclasses.
among the natives of the southern coast of West Australia.	Wordungmat	Ballarruk Nagarnook	Manytchmat	Tondarup Didarruk

The rules of marriage and descent may be tabulated as follows:—

Husband.	Wife.	Children.

Wordungmat. { Ballarruk
    ,,
Nagarnook
    ,,
	Tondarup
	Didarruk
	Tondarup
	Didarruk } Manytchmat.
		Tondarup
		Didarruk
		Tondarup
		Didarruk } Manytchmat.

Manytchmat. { Tondarup
    ,,
Didarruk
    ,,
	Ballarruk
	Nagarnook
	Ballarruk
	Nagarnook } Wordungmat.
		Ballarruk
		Nagarnook
		Ballarruk
		Nagarnook } Wordungmat.

Anomalous marriages. If these rules are correctly reported, it appears that descent both of the class and the subclass is maternal in the direct line: in other words, children belong to their mother's subclass as well as to her class. This is a departure from the normal type of an Australian tribe with four sub-classes, since, as we have seen, in tribes thus organised the children regularly belong to a different subclass both from their mother and from their father, whether descent be traced in the maternal or in the paternal line.[1] Further, it is to be observed that in these tribes each subclass is free to marry into either of the two subclasses of the other primary class, which is equivalent to abandoning the exogamy of the subclasses, while retaining the exogamy of the primary classes. These facts appear to be symptoms of decay in the exogamous system of the people.

Three of the four names of subclasses recorded by Mrs. Bates, namely, Ballarruk, Nagarnook, and Tondarup, are

[1] See above, pp. 395 *sqq.*, 443 *sqq.*

clearly identical with three of the names of families or clans (namely, Ballaroke, Nagarnook, and Tdondarup) recorded by Grey.

The names of the classes, according to Mrs. Bates, "appear to have totemic meanings. Wordungmat are crows. Manytchmat are cockatoos. Ballarruk are *Bootallung*, pelicans. Nagarnooks are *Weja*, emus. Tondarups are *Dondurn*, fishhawks. Didarruk are *Didara* (or *Wadarn*), the sea. The Walja, or eaglehawk, is supposed to be the *Mamangur* or father, of all; Wordung and Manytch are his nephews. I obtained some information recently with reference to the Walja. I had made close and continuous inquiries as to whether there was a tribe named after the Walja, and I discovered that there has been a small tribe of Waljuks in the neighbourhood of Beverley and York. I learn, however, that the tribe, as such, appears to have died out."[1] " The eaglehawk was sometimes called *Mamangurra*, and was supposed by the southern coastal natives to have made all living things into *noyyung* or *ngunning*.[2] He was himself both *noyyung* and *ngunning*. He had a wife in the squeaker crow. Many of their legends have the eaglehawk as the central figure, but animals, birds, and reptiles figure in all native legendary lore."[3] Totemic meanings of the class names.

If Mrs. Bates's derivations are right, it would seem that the names of the classes or moieties of these West Australian tribes, like those of some tribes of South-East Australia, are totemic. The totems of the classes and subclasses on her shewing are these:— Classes, subclasses, and totems of South-West Australian tribes.

Classes.	Totems.	Subclasses.	Totems.
Wordungmat	crow {	Ballarruk Nagarnook	pelican emu
Manytchmat	cockatoo {	Tondarup Didarruk	fishhawk the sea

---

[1] Mrs. Daisy M. Bates, "The Marriage Laws and some Customs of the West Australian Aborigines," *Victorian Geographical Journal*, xxiii.-xxiv. (1905-1906) p. 47.

[2] These are the two terms of relationship applied to the two primary classes. See below, p. 566.

[3] Mrs. Daisy M. Bates, *op. cit.* p. 58.

<small>Mrs. Bates's account of West Australian totems.</small>

The following is the account which Mrs. Bates gives of totems in West Australia. "Every native has a totem of some animal, bird, or fish. ... The word for 'totem' in the Vasse district is *oobarree*, at Perth it is *oobar*, on the Gascoyne and Ashburton it is *walaree*, and on the De Grey River it is *wooraroo*, in York and Beverley it is *boorongur*.

"Marriages are independent of personal totems, and a man whose *oobarree* is a kangaroo may marry a woman who is of his proper marrying class and who may have the same totem, a different totem being bestowed upon the children. Totems in the south appear to be always given from some circumstance attendant on the birth of the children. I will give you a few instances of this.

"*Beyoo* means swollen. Beyooran, a female, was so called from the fact of her father missing the whereabouts of a kangaroo he had killed, and finding it in the afternoon all swollen from the sun's heat. The girl's *oobaree* or totem was a kangaroo. Put-bee-yan, a female, was named after a tame opossum which used to make a noise like *put-put* when coming for its food. Put-bee-yan's totem was an opossum. Baaburgurt's name was given him from his father observing a sea mullet leaping out of the water and making a noise like Brrr-Baaburr. The *kalda* or sea mullet is Baabur's totem. Baabur's father and his father's brothers also had the *kalda* as their totem, but his grandfathers had different totems. Nyilgee was named after a swamp wallaby (called *woorark*) which her father was about to kill, but in the act of raising his spear the little wallaby escaped. '*Yalgy yookan*,' the father said, 'if he had only stood a moment longer, I should have got him,' and he called his daughter Nyilgeean; her totem is the *woorark*."[1]

<small>These totems appear to be totems of individuals, not of clans.</small>

From this account it appears that the totems of West Australia here described are personal or individual totems, not totems shared by whole clans, and that they are bestowed on children at birth, being often determined by the appearance of some animal, which henceforth becomes the child's totem. It is possible that clan totems may have disappeared, as they have done in some tribes of South-East Australia.[2] A trace of clan or perhaps subclass totems seems to survive

---

[1] Mrs. Daisy M. Bates, *op. cit.* p. 49.   [2] See above, pp. 493 *sqq.*

in the belief of the southern natives that their ancestors were once animals or birds. "For instance, the Nagarnooks are called Wejuk (emus), and are even supposed at the present time to be able to transform themselves from men to emus at will."[1] Among the names for a totem Mrs. Bates does not mention *kobong*, the word for it given by Grey.

The rule that a man must avoid his mother-in-law seems to prevail, under various names (*too-ah, doo-ah, ngan-yerri, nganya, kenjir, dar-ar-buk*), throughout West Australia. He may not speak to her nor look at her, nor enter her hut, nor eat the food she has prepared; and she must avoid him in like manner. The men believe that they will become bald if they look at their mothers-in-law, and the women think that their hair will turn grey if they speak to their sons-in-law.[2] Sometimes a bull-roarer is swung to warn the mother-in-law to keep away from her son-in-law.[3]

Avoidance of mother-in-law.

Further, amongst some at least of the tribes of West Australia brothers and sisters mutually avoid each other; indeed, from the time that a lad has attained to puberty, he may never speak to or even look at his sisters again. The practice is thus reported by Mrs. Bates:—

Rule of avoidance between brothers and sisters.

"I am informed that amongst the native tribes near the head of the Grenough River, when a boy is taken away from [for?] the ceremony of initiation, which includes circumcision and subincision, he takes a ceremonious farewell of his sister or sisters, as on his return from the initiation ground, he must never look at or speak to them again. A. L. P. Cameron, writing in *Science of Man*, July 1904, states that the Cooper Creek tribe had a similar custom. It is, however, the general rule throughout the State for 'own' sisters and brothers to keep apart from each other. Paljeri[4] boys cannot play with or speak to Paljeri girls, nor can Tondarup boys and girls play together. Paljeri boys and Kymera girls (or *vice versa*) when very young can play together, and Tondarup boys and Nagarnook or Ballarruk girls can also play with each other, as also with other

[1] Mrs. Daisy M. Bates, *op. cit.* p. 58.
[2] Mrs. Daisy M. Bates, *op. cit.* p. 50.
[3] This I learned in conversation from the Bishop of West Australia at Liverpool, 29th May 1908.
[4] As to the Paljeri and other sub-classes here mentioned, see below, pp. 569 *sqq.*

classes."[1] We have met with this custom of avoidance between brothers and sisters in Queensland,[2] and we shall meet with it again among totemic tribes in other parts of the world.

System of relationship among the West Australian aborigines. "With regard to the relationship existing amongst the West Australian aborigines; taking the two primary divisions of the southern people Wordungmat and Manytchmat, there are two terms always applied to these, *noy-yung* and *ngunning*. These terms are interchangeable according to the division that is speaking.

"For instance, I have been adopted into the Tondarup class [of the primary division Manytchmat],[3] therefore all Tondarups, Didarruks, and their subdivisions are 'my own' family, they are *ngunning* to me. Into whatever district I go I sit by a *ngunning* fire. Now the various relationship terms which I use amongst the Tondarup and Didarruks are *demma-mat* and *murranmat* (grandparent's stock), *ngangarmat* (mother stock), *ngoondanmat* (brother stock), and *jookamat* (sister stock). I will find representatives of some of these amongst all the tribes which I may visit.

"*Noy-yung* is the word I (as a Tondarup) would use in speaking to the Wordungmat division. *Noy-yung* are my relations-in-law, so to speak, and the terms of relationship are *demma-mat* and *murranmat* (these words are applied to maternal or paternal grandparents), *kor-da-mat* (husband stock), *ngooljarmat* or *deenamat* (brother-in-law or sister-in law stock), *mungartmat* (aunt stock), *konganmat* (uncle stock). My father (*mamman*) is *noy-yung*.

"These are some of the *noy-yung* relationships (I give the English equivalents of the terms merely for the sake of clearness). As regards nearer relationships, all my father's brothers are my fathers (*mamanmat*), yet my father's sisters are *mungart* (aunt stock), and I can marry my *mungart's* (aunt's stock) sons, who are my *kordamat* (husband stock).

"All my mother's sisters are my mothers (*ngangamat*), but my mother's brothers are *konganmat* (uncle stock), and I can marry their sons who are also my *kordamat* (husband stock).

"The children of my fathers and mothers are my

---

[1] Mrs. Daisy M. Bates, *op. cit.* p. 51.
[2] See above, p. 542.
[3] See above, pp. 561 *sqq.*

brothers and sisters, they are *ngunning*, 'my own,' but the children of my father's sisters and my mother's brothers are *kordamat* (husband stock) and are *noy-yung*."[1]

From this account it appears that the natives of South-West Australia employ the classificatory system of relationship, and that a man's proper wife is the daughter of his mother's brother or (what comes to the same thing) the daughter of his father's sister. {Classificatory system of relationship.}

Further, these tribes, like some tribes of South-East Australia and of Queensland,[2] extend their class system so as to include the whole of nature under it. Thus we are told that "the terms *noy-yung* and *ngunning* are also used to denote the relationship that every tree, shrub, root, etc., bears to the person who is speaking. For instance, the Red Gum is a male, and belongs to the Manytchmat division; it is *ngunning* to me. The White Gum is a female, and belongs to the Wordungmat division; it is *noy-yung* to me, and so on." "In fact the primary classes, Wordungmat and Manytchmat divide all natural objects between them, and every living thing and every tree, root, and fruit is *noy-yung* or *ngunning*."[3] {Subtotems.}

§ 2. *Totemism in North-West Australia*

The natives of the north-western region of West Australia are less decadent than those of the south-western parts, because they have been far less demoralised by contact with whites.[4] Like the tribes of the South-West, they are divided into exogamous classes, but the names of the classes are different. They differ also from the tribes of the South-West in practising circumcision, and some of them practise subincision as well. On this subject Sir John Forrest, speaking of the natives of West Australia, observes: "The rite of circumcision is also universal with all I have met, except those belonging to the south-west corner of Australia; it is a sort of religious ceremony with them. They gather {Tribes of North-West Australia less decadent than those of the South-West.} {Rites of circumcision and subincision.}

---

[1] Mrs. Daisy M. Bates, *op. cit.* pp. 47 *sq.*

[2] See above, pp. 427 *sqq.*, 431 *sqq.*, 451 *sqq.*, 470 *sqq.*, 540.

[3] Mrs. Daisy M. Bates, *op. cit.* pp. 48, 49.

[4] This I learned in conversation from the Bishop of West Australia at Liverpool, 29th May 1908.

568   TOTEMISM IN WEST AUSTRALIA   CHAP.

together in large numbers, and the men and women part for a fortnight or more, and are not expected to see one another; if they accidentally meet they run for their lives."[1] As to the line of demarcation between the circumcised and the uncircumcised tribes in West Australia Mrs. Daisy M. Bates writes as follows: "Here in this State there seem to be two great divisions, a northern and southern, or perhaps they might be defined more particularly by classifying them as a circumcised and uncircumcised people. Both these divisions bear distinct class names, and both have peculiar customs and laws handed down by oral tradition from father to son for countless generations. The great northern division covers, as far as I have at present ascertained, the portion of country lying between East Kimberley and a point somewhere in the neighbourhood of Jurien Bay, about lat. 30° South, but at what exact point I cannot find out until I make a personal investigation. The same customs, habits, marriage laws, and laws of descent obtain amongst the northern division, a slight difference in nomenclature being the only variation. This division from Kimberley [in the North-East] down to a little below the De Grey River practises circumcision or subincision, the former compulsory, the latter not generally so. Just below the Grey River, from the coast inland to about forty miles or so, the coastal natives have given up the practice, and all along the coast down to Point Malcolm (or thereabouts) the natives have substituted nose piercing for circumcision. The circumcised tribes touch the coast at the De Grey and Point Malcolm. The nearest

Marginal note: Boundary between the circumcised and the uncircumcised tribes.

[1] J. Forrest, "On the Natives of Central and Western Australia, *Journal of the Anthropological Institute*, v. (1876) pp. 317 *sq.* "All the tribes of N.W. Australia practise circumcision" (E. Clement, "Ethnographical Notes on the Western Australian Aborigines," *Internationales Archiv für Ethnographie*, xvi. (1904) p. 9). "Circumcision, or splitting the prepuce as a rite, is universal, and is usually performed early in the morning, at 4 or 5 A.M., the whole tribe being gathered together" (P. W. Bassett-Smith, "The Aborigines of North-West Australia," *Journal of the Anthropological Institute*, xxiii. (1894) p. 327). In the district of North-West Australia which is roughly comprised between lat. 21° and 23° S. and long. 117° and 120° E. all the males are circumcised at puberty, and "to prevent the too rapid increase of children the *mika* operation is performed on a number of young men. It consists of splitting the urethra for about 5 centimetres with a sharp flint-stone" (E. Clement, "Ethnographical Notes on the Western Australian Aborigines," *Internationales Archiv für Ethnographie*, xvi. (1904) p. 13).

point at which they touch the coast between these two places is at Geraldton, where they encroach within twenty miles of that port, the reason for this being that the uncircumcised are being constantly adopted into the circumcised tribes. A circumcised man does not enter into and reside amongst the uncircumcised people, but an uncircumcised man may be adopted into the circumcised tribes. . . . There is traditional evidence that the custom of circumcision has only comparatively recently died out in many parts of the Nor'-West below the De Grey. At Roebourne it has been replaced by the tying at initiation of a ligature so tightly round the upper part of the arm that if worn for a lengthy period it sometimes causes that member to wither and become useless, but this is a rare occurrence."[1] "The inland tribes in the neighbourhood of the De Grey River are all circumcised, but not the tribe [namely, the Ngurla] about which I am writing. However, they frequently intermarry, the class system of marriage, as I understand, obtaining in all. But few of them pierce the septum of the nose. On the arrival of the males at the age of puberty, or shortly after, the Ngurla and other tribes in the neighbourhood amongst whom circumcision is not practised subject them to the painful ordeal of having their arms tied tightly round above the elbow, when the hands and arms swell and become powerless, in which state they are kept for some weeks, being hand-fed by their friends during the time. A similar custom prevails in the Umbertana tribe."[2]

The tying of a tight ligature round the upper arm has been substituted for circumcision in some tribes.

The natives of North-West Australia are divided into four exogamous classes or subclasses, which are reported to bear substantially the same names over the great extent of country from Derby in the north-east to the Murchison River in the south-west. They have certainly been recorded in the territory between the Fortescue and De Grey Rivers, including Nickol Bay. The names of these classes are Boorong, Banaka, Kymera, and Paljeri, and the rules of

Exogamous classes among the natives of North-West Australia.

---

[1] Mrs. Daisy M. Bates, "The Marriage Laws and some Customs of the West Australian Aborigines," *Victorian Geographical Journal*, xxiii.-xxiv. (1905-1906) pp. 40 *sq.* That the natives of West Australia practise subincision was mentioned to me in conversation by the Bishop of West Australia.

[2] Ch. Harper, in E. M. Curr's *The Australian Race*, i. 291.

marriage and descent among them are indicated in the following table :—[1]

Table of marriage and descent.

Husband.	Wife.	Children.
Boorong	Banaka	Kymera
Banaka	Boorong	Paljeri
Kymera	Paljeri	Boorong
Paljeri	Kymera	Banaka

[1] Mrs. Daisy M. Bates, "The Marriage Laws and some Customs of the West Australian Aborigines," *Victorian Geographical Journal*, xxiii.-xxiv. (1905-1906) p. 41. The names of the four classes or subclasses are variously spelled by our authorities, the differences probably representing local differences of pronunciation. These variations are indicated, with the names of the respective authorities for them, in the following table :—

Mrs. Bates.	Sir J. Forrest.	L. H. Gould.	A. K. Richardson.	E. Clement.	E. Clement.
Boorong	Boorunggnoo	Poronga	Booroongoo	Burong	Burong
Banaka	Banigher	Banaka	Panaka	Baniker	Banaka
Kymera	Kimera	Kimera	Kymurra	Caiemurra	Kymerra
Paljeri	Paljarie	Paliali	Palyeery	Ballieri	Paljarri

See J. Forrest, quoted by L. Fison, "Australian Marriage Laws," *Journal of the Anthropological Institute*, ix. (1880) p. 356 ; L. H. Gould, in Fison and Howitt's *Kamilaroi and Kurnai*, p. 36; A. K. Richardson, in E. M. Curr's *The Australian Race*, i. 298 ; E. Clement, "Ethnographical Notes on the Western Australian Aborigines," *Internationales Archiv für Ethnographie*, xvi. (1904) p. 12. The statements of Sir John Forrest and Mr. A. K. Richardson refer to the natives at Nickol Bay ; the statements of Mr. E. Clement refer to the Gnalluma and Gnamo tribes respectively, of which the Gnalluma tribe inhabits the district between the Nickol and Yule Rivers, while the Gnamo tribe inhabits the Nullagine district between the Oakover and Turner Rivers. The Ngurla tribe at the mouth of the De Grey River has the same four class-names in slightly different forms (Poorungnoo, Banakoo, Kiamoona, Parrijari), but the rules of marriage and descent are reported to be different, as appears from the following table :—

Husband.	Wife.	Children.
Poorungnoo	Parrijari	Kiamoona
Banakoo	Kiamoona	Parrijari
Kiamoona	Banakoo	Poorungnoo
Parrijari	Poorungnoo	Banakoo

See Ch. Harper, in E. M. Curr's *The Australian Race*, i. 290. However, we are told that Mr. Harper was not quite certain as to the details of the system, and it is possible that he may have made a mistake as to the rules of marriage. All the other authorities cited above are unanimous as to the rules of marriage and descent in the classes.

It is probable that these four classes are in reality subclasses which are grouped in pairs under two primary classes; but the existence of such primary classes is not recorded, and without a knowledge of the primary classes and of the grouping of the subclasses under them, we cannot say whether descent in these tribes is traced in the maternal or in the paternal line. For, as usually happens with a four-class system, the children belong to a subclass which differs both from the subclass of the mother and from the subclass of the father, and unless we know whether the subclass to which the children belong is the complementary subclass of their mother's or of their father's subclass, we cannot say whether descent is maternal or paternal. However, a trace of two primary classes may perhaps be detected in the statement that the Kymera and Paljeri (Kimera and Paljarie) are the parent stock.[1]

It is not clear whether descent in these tribes is maternal or paternal.

It would seem that the names of three out of the four subclasses in these tribes agree with the names of three subclasses in the Arunta tribe, as these are recorded by Messrs. Spencer and Gillen, Banaka answering to Panunga, Kymera to Kumara, and Paljeri perhaps to Bulthara.[2] If these three identifications are right, it will follow that the West Australian subclass Boorong answers to the Arunta class Purula. Accepting these equivalences provisionally, we may arrange the West Australian subclasses on the Arunta model as follows:—

Similarity of the names of the subclasses to those of the Arunta.

Conjectural arrangement of the North-West Australian subclasses on the Arunta pattern.

	Husband.	Wife.	Children.
Class A	{ Banaka { Paljeri	Boorong Kymera	Paljeri Banaka
Class B	{ Boorong { Kymera	Banaka Paljeri	Kymera Boorong

In this table it will be observed that the rules of marriage and descent are those which are given independently by five authorities on the West Australian

[1] Sir J. Forrest, cited by L. Fison, "Australian Marriage Laws," *Journal of the Anthropological Institute*, ix. (1880) p. 357. [2] See above, pp. 259 *sqq.*

572   TOTEMISM IN WEST AUSTRALIA   CHAP.

tribes. All that I have done is, accepting these rules and provisionally identifying the West Australian subclasses with the Arunta subclasses which they resemble in name, to arrange the four West Australian subclasses in pairs corresponding to the Arunta pairs. The result is to yield a normal four-class system with descent in the paternal line, which accordingly corresponds closely to the system of the Southern Arunta, among whom there are only four names for the subclasses.

Rules of marriage. Persons bearing the same class-name may not marry each other. Any such marriage is regarded as incest and rigorously punished. For instance, "the union of Boorong and Boorong is to the natives the union of brother and sister, although there may be no real blood relationship between the pair, and a union of that kind is looked upon with horror, and the perpetrators very severely punished and separated, and if the crime is repeated they are both killed."[1]

Cousin marriages. A man may marry two or more sisters. The children of a brother are marriageable (*nuba*) with the children of his sister; but as usual the children of two brothers may not marry each other nor may the children of two sisters.[2] The permission granted to first cousins, the children of a brother and of a sister respectively, to marry each other, suffices of itself to prove that these tribes have not got the eight-class system, since that system, as we have seen,[3] bars all such marriages.

Betrothal. Avoidance of wife's mother. The Levirate. Girls are betrothed to men at birth or in their infancy. After betrothal a man may not see his future mother-in-law. Should it be absolutely necessary for him to speak to her, the two must turn their backs to each other. When a man dies before or after marriage, his surviving brother takes the betrothed girl or widow to be his wife. But if he already has as many wives as he wants, he will cede her to his younger brother or to any man who is her tribal husband (*nuba*). Old men generally have the most and the youngest wives. Men often exchange

---

[1] Mrs. Daisy M. Bates, in *Victorian Geographical Journal*, xxiii.-xxiv. (1905-1906) p. 42. The statement quoted in the text was made by a settler who had lived in the Tableland district, inland from Roebourne, for twenty years.

[2] E. Clement, "Ethnographical Notes on the Western Australian Aborigines," *Internationales Archiv für Ethnographie*, xvi. (1904) p. 12.

[3] See above, pp. 277 *sqq*.

their wives for one or two nights, especially at corrobborees.[1] Yet adultery, we are told, is generally punished with death.[2]

The natives of North-West Australia, between the Fortescue and Turner Rivers, perform magical ceremonies for the multiplication of edible animals and plants, whenever these become scarce. So far as appears, the performers at any one of these ceremonies must be drawn exclusively from one of the four exogamous classes; but the different classes officiate in different ceremonies. The rites, which seem to be partly based on the principle of imitative magic, regularly take place at a large heap of stones called a *tarlow* or more rarely at a single stone. Different cairns (*tarlows*) are set apart for the multiplication of different animals or plants, and each of them is under the charge of one of the four exogamous classes. For example, if kangaroos grow scarce in a season of drought, the headman of the class (say the Ballieri) which has charge of the kangaroo cairn (*tarlow*) will go with as many members of the same Ballieri (Paljeri) class as he can muster to the cairn, which may perhaps be thirty or forty miles distant. There they perform their rites, such as hopping round and round the cairn in imitation of kangaroos, drinking kangaroo-fashion from troughs placed on the ground, and beating the cairn with spears, stones, and fighting clubs. In the evening a corrobboree is held, at which the men and women are grotesquely painted with red or yellow ochre or charcoal, and everything connected with the hunting and killing of kangaroos is freely displayed. Monotonous chants are sung, boomerangs are rattled together, and a kangaroo bone is moved rapidly up and down in the lateral incisions of a throwing-stick.[3]

Magical ceremonies for the multiplication of edible animals and plants.

Again, if seeds which are used as food grow scarce, another cairn (*tarlow*) set apart for the multiplication of these seeds is visited by the headman of the class (say the

Ceremonies for the growth of seeds

---

[1] E. Clement, *op. cit.* p. 13. The writer met with a single case of polyandry. "A mother-in-law must not speak to her prospective son-in-law" (P. W. Bassett-Smith, in *Journal of the Anthropological Institute*, xxiii. (1894) p. 327).

[2] P. W. Bassett-Smith, "The Aborigines of North-West Australia," *Journal of the Anthropological Institute*, xxiii. (1894) p. 327.

[3] E. Clement, "Ethnographical Notes on the Western Australian Aborigines," *Internationales Archiv für Ethnographie*, xvi. (1904) pp. 6 *sq.*

and the multiplication of fish, emus, etc.

Caiemurra) together with as many people, both men and women, of the Caiemurra (Kymera) class as he can get together. In the ceremony at the cairn the wooden bowls used for winnowing grass-seeds and the stone mills used in grinding them play a prominent part. The ground about the cairn is beaten flat with stones and sprinkled with water, and the women go through the performance of winnowing and grinding, while songs are sung and dances danced. Again, when it is desired to multiply fish, the particular cairn set apart for that purpose is visited by people of the Ballieri (Paljeri) class, if it should be under their care for the time being; and in the ceremony fishing-nets and a poisonous plant (*kurraru*) which they throw into the pools to stupefy the fish, are much displayed. In like manner there are cairns for the multiplication of bustards, hawks, iguanas, cockatoos and nearly every animal, as well as for the multiplication of seeds which are used as foods. At the cairn for the increase of emus the walk and run of that bird are closely imitated, and ornaments made of emu feathers are worn.[1]

Inheritance of the sacred cairns at which the magical ceremonies are performed.

When a headman who has charge of a particular cairn dies, the care of the sacred stones descends to his son or daughter; and as the children always belong to a class different from that of their parents, it follows that the custody of the cairns passes from one exogamous class to another with each generation. For example, when a headman of the Caiemurra (Kymera) class dies, the cairn of which he had charge will be inherited by his son, who is of the Burong (Boorong) class, and so the keepers of the cairn will be the Burongs instead of the Caiemurras. For a similar reason, when a Ballieri (Paljeri) headman dies, his cairn passes to the Baniker (Banaka) class, because that is the class to which his son belongs. Both men and women may inherit the control of a cairn, and one exogamous class may have the charge of several cairns at the same time. But no members of other classes may be present at the magical ceremonies for the multiplication of animals or plants; for it is believed that their presence would break

[1] E. Clement, "Ethnographical Notes on the Western Australian Aborigines," *Internationales Archiv für Ethnographie*, xvi. (1904) p. 7.

the spell, and that the rite would have to be deferred till the next new moon, the proper time for weaving the magic spells being when the moon is about three days old.[1]

Both in their aim and in their methods these ceremonies for the multiplication of animals and plants clearly correspond to the *intichiuma* ceremonies which the Arunta and other Central Australian tribes perform for the increase of their totems; only whereas among the central tribes these rites are observed by members of the respective totem clans, among the western tribes they are performed by members of the exogamous classes. This seems to shew that here as elsewhere among tribes dwelling on or near the coast the old organisation in totem clans has been or is being ousted by the newer organisation in exogamous classes.[2] *Resemblance of these ceremonies to the intichiuma ceremonies of the Central Australians.*

It is not clear why these savages regularly perform their ceremonies for the increase of animals and plants either at heaps of stones or sometimes at single stones. Perhaps, like some of the Central Australians, they believe that the disembodied spirits of animals and plants congregate in the stones, from which they can be driven out by magic in order to be reborn as real animals and plants, and so in due time to be killed or gathered and eaten. This may be why they beat the kangaroo cairn with spears, clubs, and stones. *Perhaps the disembodied spirits of animals and plants are thought to be in the cairns.*

The foregoing information, scanty as it is, appears to indicate a close similarity in customs between the north-western and the central tribes of Australia, as the latter have been described by Messrs. Spencer and Gillen. In both sets of tribes we see circumcision[3] and subincision *Resemblances between the central and the north-western tribes.*

---

[1] E. Clement, *l.c.*

[2] See above, pp. 225, 227 *sq.*, 235 *sq.*, 526-530.

[3] Amongst the north-western tribes the rite of circumcision is called *buckli*, and bull-roarers (*boonan-gharries*) are swung at it in order to keep the evil spirit (*djuno*) away. The operation is performed with a stone knife named *borulla* or *cundemarra*; whilst it is proceeding the women set up a frightful howling in their camp, which they are not allowed to leave. The severed foreskin of each novice is tied to his hair and left there till the wound is perfectly healed. After that in some tribes it is pounded up with kangaroo meat and given to the novice to eat; in others it is taken by the kinsfolk to a large tree and inserted beneath the bark. While their wounds are healing, the novices swing bull-roarers to warn off young women. See E. Clement, "Ethnographical Notes on the Western Australian Aborigines," *Internationales Archiv für Ethnographie*, xvi. (1904) pp. 10 *sq.* In these respects the rites present some analogies to those of the central tribes. Thus, for example, among the

practised as initiatory rites, marriage regulated by classes, the names of some of which are clearly the same in both regions, and magical ceremonies performed for the multiplication of edible animals and plants. Further, amongst the northern tribes about Port Darwin and the Daly River, particularly the Larrekiya and Wogait, "conception is not regarded as a direct result of cohabitation." The old men of the Wogait say that there is an evil spirit who takes babies from a big fire and places them in the wombs of women, who must then give birth to them. When in the ordinary course of events a man is out hunting and kills game or gathers vegetable food, he gives it to his wife, who must eat it, believing that the food will cause her to conceive and bring forth a child. When the child is born, it may on no account partake of the particular food which produced conception until it has got its first teeth.[1] This theory of child-birth resembles those which are current among the tribes of Central Australia and Queensland in so far as conception is regarded as not resulting directly from cohabitation; and it confirms to some extent the suggestion which I have made, that a person's totem may have been most commonly determined by the particular food which a woman had partaken of immediately before she first felt the child in her womb.[2] To judge by these indications, the view is shared by all the tribes of Central

The northern tribes disbelieve in the cohabitation of the sexes as the direct cause of conception.

Unmatjera the severed foreskin is preserved for some time after the operation and is then, under cover of night, deposited by the lad in a hollow tree; he tells no one but a cousin (his father's sister's son) where he has put it. Again, among the Warramunga the severed foreskin is placed in a hole made by a witchetty grub in a tree, and it is supposed to cause a plentiful supply of the grub. See Baldwin Spencer and F. J. Gillen, *Northern Tribes of Central Australia*, pp. 341, 353 *sq.*

[1] Herbert Basedow, *Anthropological Notes on the Western Coastal Tribes of the Northern Territory of South Australia*, pp. 4 *sq.* (separate reprint from the *Transactions of the Royal Society of South Australia*, vol. xxxi. 1907). The tribes described by Mr. Basedow are not in West Australia, but in the extreme north of the Northern Territory of South Australia. Mr. Basedow gives no information as to the social organisation of these tribes. The Wogait tribe practises circumcision, but the Larrekiya tribe does not. Among the Wogait the severed foreskin is shewn by the novice to his mother and then to his future wife. Afterwards it is worn in a bag round the neck of the operator till the wound which he has made in the novice is healed, when it is thrown into the fire. The operation is performed with a flint knife. See H. Basedow, *op. cit.* p. 12.

[2] See above, p. 159.

and Northern Australia. In point of fact I am informed by the Bishop of North Queensland (Dr. Frodsham) that the opinion is held by all the tribes with which he is acquainted both in North Queensland and in Central Australia, including the Arunta; not only are the natives in their savage state ignorant of the true cause of conception, but they do not readily believe it even after their admission into mission stations, and their incredulity has to be reckoned with in the efforts of the clergy to introduce a higher standard of sexual morality among them.[1] Among the tribes around the Cairns district in North Queensland " the acceptance of food from a man by a woman was not merely regarded as a marriage ceremony but as the actual cause of conception."[2] Such a belief confirms the suggestion I have made that a child's totem may often have been determined by the last food which a mother ate before she felt her womb quickened;[3] for when the true cause of conception was unknown a woman might very naturally attribute the strange stirring within her to the last food she had partaken of; she might fancy that the animal or the plant, of which she had certainly received a

The acceptance of food from a man by a woman is regarded by some tribes as the cause of conception.

---

[1] This information was given to me in conversation by the Bishop of North Queensland (Dr. Frodsham) at Liverpool, 18th May 1908. His lordship told me that amongst the tribes with whom he is personally acquainted are the Arunta. He also referred to a form of communal or group marriage, which he believes to be practised among aboriginal tribes whom he has visited on the western side of the Gulf of Carpentaria; but unfortunately I had not time to obtain particulars from him on the subject. I urged on him the importance of publishing his information, and he assented to my proposal that he should do so; but he has not yet found leisure to carry out his intention. Meantime he has kindly authorised me by letter (dated Bishop's Lodge, Townsville, Queensland, 9th July 1909) to publish this statement. The information was voluntarily given, not elicited by questions, at the close of a public lecture of mine, which his lordship did me the honour of attending.

In his letter to me the Bishop speaks of "the belief, practically universal among the Northern tribes, that copulation is not the cause of conception." See *Folk-lore*, xx. (1909) pp. 350-352; *Man*, ix. (1909) pp. 145-147.

[2] Extract from a letter of the Bishop of Queensland (Dr. Frodsham) to me, dated 9th July 1909. See the preceding note. The Bishop's authority for the statement in the text is the Rev. C. W. Morrison, M.A., of Emmanuel College, Cambridge, Acting Head of the Yarrubah Mission. Mr. Morrison further told the Bishop that "monogamy was the custom in these tribes, except in the case of sisters"; and the Bishop writes to me that this latter statement agrees with his own observation, for he knows an aboriginal who married four sisters. The custom of marrying several sisters at once or successively is widespread. Many instances of it will meet us in the sequel. It was particularly common among the North American Indians.

[3] See above, pp. 158 *sqq.*

portion into her body, was growing up within her, and that the child, when it came forth from her womb, was nothing but that animal or that plant in a slightly disguised form. Further, with the Australian evidence before us, we may surmise that a common marriage ceremony, which consists in husband and wife eating together,[1] may originally have had a deeper meaning than that of a mere covenant; it may have been supposed actually to impregnate the woman.

<small>Reported endogamous classes at Raffles Bay and Port Essington.</small> Lastly, to complete our survey of the exogamous systems of Australia, it may be mentioned that at Raffles Bay and Port Essington at the extreme north of the continent the natives are said to be "divided into three distinct classes, who do not intermarry. The first and highest is named *Mandro-gillie*, the second, *Manbur-ge*, and the third *Mandrowillie*. The first class assumes a superiority over the others, which is submitted to without reluctance; and those who believe in real difference of blood amongst civilized nations, might find here some apparent ground for such opinion, as the *Mandro-gillies* were observed to be more polite, and unaffectedly easy in their manners, than the others, who, it was supposed, were neither so shrewd nor so refined: this, however, might be only imaginary."[2] Similary Commander J. L. Stokes of the *Beagle* reports that the natives of this district were "divided in three distinct classes, which do not intermarry. The first is known as Maudrojilly [*sic*], the second as Mamburgy, the third as Mandrouilly. They are very particular about the distinction of classes, but we could never discover which was the superior and which the inferior class, though it is supposed by most of those who have inquired into the subject, that Madrojilly [*sic*], or first class, head the others in war, and govern the affairs of the tribe."[3]

<small>The report may be mistaken.</small> These accounts clearly imply that the natives were divided into three endogamous classes or castes, the members of each of which married among themselves and refused

[1] For examples of the ceremony, see E. S. Hartland, *The Legend of Perseus*, ii. (London, 1895) pp. 343 *sqq*. See below, pp. 262 *sq*.

[2] T. B. Wilson, *Narrative of a Voyage round the World* (London, 1835), p. 163.

[3] J. Lort Stokes, *Discoveries in Australia* (London, 1846), i. 393.

to marry members of another class or caste. But endogamous divisions of this sort are so contrary to all we know of the marriage systems of the Australian aborigines that we cannot but suspect that the writers misunderstood their informants, and that the classes which they describe were exogamous rather than endogamous. The mistake might the more easily arise if one of the three exogamous classes, as might well happen, married into only one of the other two classes and refused to marry into the third. But with such meagre information it is impossible to reach any definite conclusion on the subject.

END OF VOL. I

Printed by R. & R. CLARK, LIMITED, *Edinburgh.*

COSIMO is a specialty publisher of books and publications that inspire, inform, and engage readers. Our mission is to offer unique books to niche audiences around the world.

COSIMO BOOKS publishes books and publications for innovative authors, nonprofit organizations, and businesses. **COSIMO BOOKS** specializes in bringing books back into print, publishing new books quickly and effectively, and making these publications available to readers around the world.

COSIMO CLASSICS offers a collection of distinctive titles by the great authors and thinkers throughout the ages. At **COSIMO CLASSICS** timeless works find new life as affordable books, covering a variety of subjects including: Business, Economics, History, Personal Development, Philosophy, Religion & Spirituality, and much more!

COSIMO REPORTS publishes public reports that affect your world, from global trends to the economy, and from health to geopolitics.

FOR MORE INFORMATION CONTACT US AT
INFO@COSIMOBOOKS.COM

- if you are a book lover interested in our current catalog of books

- if you represent a bookstore, book club, or anyone else interested in special discounts for bulk purchases

- if you are an author who wants to get published

- if you represent an organization or business seeking to publish books and other publications for your members, donors, or customers.

COSIMO BOOKS ARE ALWAYS AVAILABLE AT ONLINE BOOKSTORES

VISIT COSIMOBOOKS.COM
BE INSPIRED, BE INFORMED